ADAM SMITH ACROSS NATIONS

ADAM SMITH ACROSS NATIONS

Translations and Receptions of *The Wealth of Nations*

Edited by
Cheng-chung Lai

OXFORD
UNIVERSITY PRESS

OXFORD
UNIVERSITY PRESS

Great Clarendon Street, Oxford OX2 6DP
Oxford University Press is a department of the University of Oxford.
It furthers the University's objective of excellence in research, scholarship,
and education by publishing worldwide in

Oxford New York

Athens Auckland Bangkok Bogotá Buenos Aires Calcutta
Cape Town Chennai Dar es Salaam Delhi Florence Hong Kong Istanbul
Karachi Kuala Lumpur Madrid Melbourne Mexico City Mumbai
Nairobi Paris São Paulo Singapore Taipei Tokyo Toronto Warsaw

and associated companies in Berlin Ibadan

Oxford is a registered trade mark of Oxford University Press
in the UK and certain other countries

Published in the United States
by Oxford University Press Inc., New York

Editorial arrangement and apparatus © Cheng-chung Lai 2000

British Library Cataloguing in Publication Data

Data availble

Library of Congress Cataloging in Publication Data
Adam Smith Across Nations: Translations and Receptions of The Wealth of Nations/
edited by Cheng-chung Lai.
p.   cm.
A collection of 29 papers about the translation and reception of Smith's book in
10 non-English speaking countries, 3 commissioned for this volume and 26 previously
published in English or in English translation from various languages.
Includes bibliographical references and index.
1. Smith, Adam, 1723–1790. Inquiry into the nature and causes of the wealth of nations.
I. Lai, Cheng-chung.
HB161. S6623   1999   330.12'2–dc21   99–17607

ISBN 0–19–823339–6 (hardcover)

1 3 5 7 9 10 8 6 4 2

Typeset by J&L Composition Ltd, Filey, North Yorkshire
Printed in Great Britain
on acid-free paper by
Biddles Ltd
Guildford & Kings Lynn

BR Title: *Preface* ed.

The materials collected in this volume are about the translation and reception of Adam Smith's *An Inquiry into the Nature and Causes of the Wealth of
Nations* (WN) in ten non-English-speaking countries. Some texts focus on the
translation aspect and some on reception, but most texts treat both themes
simultaneously.

In a paper on "Adam Smith and Yen Fu", I asked two questions. First, how
was WN translated into Chinese in 1902, when the language lacked both
vocabulary and concepts to introduce this unknown discipline from a very
different cultural system? Second, given that Yen Fu, the translator, regarded
WN as a prescription for China's wealth and power, was WN, which advocates
laissez-faire and free trade, helpful to China's peripheral economic situation?

That paper was completed in May 1987, and I was curious about the cases of
other non-English-speaking countries; but since relevant documents are quite
scarce in Taiwan, I moved on to something else. My curiosity was rekindled in
June 1989, during the annual conference of the History of Economics Society
held at the University of Richmond. I asked historians of economic thought
from different countries their views on the feasibility of this project, and I
started to collect references and documents.

The research was slow and discouraging, but then I learned of the Vanderblue
Memorial Collection of Smithiana at the Kress Library, within the Baker
Library of Harvard Business School. I dreamed of visiting this collection and
the famous Kress Library, where Schumpeter prepared his *History of Economic
Analysis*. In February 1992 I obtained a visiting faculty scholarship offered by
Harvard–Yenching Institute, and in early July 1992 I arrived at Harvard, staying
there until early June 1993 to work on this project.

The Vanderblue Collection and the Widener Library provided a wealth of
documents—many of which I had not been aware of. After a few months of
searching, the concept and scope of this project were modified radically: an
impressive example of learning-by-doing.

I consider the twenty-nine papers in this volume as the hors-d'oeuvre of a
rich banquet: the cases of France, Germany, Italy, Japan, and Russia are so rich

that each deserves an independent volume for fuller analysis. And other countries warrant inclusion: I was unable to locate suitable texts for Greece, India, Korea, and the Netherlands, in particular, and would be grateful for suggestions of significant texts, either in English or in their original languages, to be included in the next edition.

I have always been passionate about the international transmission of ideas, and in that sense I regard this volume as a source book to formulate further propositions, a stimulus for further investigation. For historians of economic thought, there is a similar book edited by Peter Hall on the reception of Keynesian economic policies in seven countries from the 1930s to the 1980s (*The Political Economy of Economic Ideas: Keynesianism Across Nations*, Princeton University Press, 1989). And I would urge historians of economic thought, historians of demography, and general economic historians to study "Malthus across Nations", for the population problem is relevant to most countries in most time periods.

There are many people and institutions to thank. In 1986 my university financed my "Adam Smith and Yen Fu" paper, which encouraged me to think of extending the Chinese case to other countries; further financial support from my university in 1996 is also gratefully acknowledged. The scholarship and research facilities provided by Harvard–Yenching Institute were crucial. The assistance that I received from the Kress Library, especially from Albert Bartovics, research archivist in the Historical Collections Department at Baker Library, was invaluable. Equally important is that Smith scholars in different countries helped me by answering my questions, sent me documents, and translated texts to be included in this volume, giving me both technical and moral support. To name a few: Glen Alexandrin (Villanova University, Pennsylvania), Kenneth Carpenter (Widener Library, Harvard University), Aiko Ikeo (Kokugakuin University, Tokyo), Hiroshi Mizuta (Nagoya, Japan), and Torbjörn Vallinder (Lund University, Sweden).

I also learned a lot from the rich Harvard–MIT economics (including economic history) seminars. It is a special feeling when one has no teaching load and can devote most of one's energy to an adventurous project. Our 1992–3 sojourn in Cambridge and Boston was also a memorable time for my wife and my son.

Lai

lai@mx.nthu.edu.tw

ω A

Acknowledgements

Among the 29 texts collected in this volume, three texts (chapters 6.3, 9.3, 10.1) are commissioned; I am grateful to their authors. Nine texts (chapters 1.3, 1.4, 2.2, 2.3, 3.1, 5.1, 5.2, 6.1, 6.2) are translated from various languages; I am grateful to their translators and original publishers for the permissions. The remaining 17 texts are reprinted from English texts with permissions from their original publishers. Since the authors, translators and sources of each text are listed in the Table of Contents, I shall not name them individually excepted for the following four cases whose permissions are not yet granted:

1. Paris: *Journal des savants* for chapter 3.1. The text appeared in 1777 and the publisher is no longer in existence.
2. London: George G. Harrap & Co. for chapter 3.4 (several contacts were attempted but unsuccessful).
3. London: Longmans, Green & Co. for chapter 4.2 (several contacts were attempted but unsuccessful).
4. Florence: Editore Quattrini for chapter 5.2 (a text appeared in 1876).

Although every effort has been made to trace and contact copyright holders prior to publication, however, in some instances this has proved impossible. If notified, the editor and publisher will be pleased to rectify any omissions at the earliest opportunity.

Contents

Part 1. China

Part 2. Denmark

Part 3. France

Part 4. Germany

Part 5. Italy

Part 6. Japan

Part 7. Portugal

Part 8. Russia

Contents

Part 9. Spain

Part 10. Sweden

Reader's Guide

1. Texts by Category

	Previously published English texts	Translations from previously published non-English texts	Previously unpublished texts
Part 1. China	2	2	
Part 2. Denmark	1	2	
Part 3. France	3	1	
Part 4. Germany	3		
Part 5. Italy		2	
Part 6. Japan		2	1
Part 7. Portugal	1		
Part 8. Russia	5		
Part 9. Spain	2		1
Part 10. Sweden			1
Total	17	9	3

Note: The editor would appreciate copies of printed texts and manuscripts related to this book for the next revised edition. These should be mailed to Cheng-chung Lai, Department of Economics, National Tsing Hua University, Sinchu 30043, Taiwan (e-mail: lai@econ.nthu.edu.tw).

2. *General references*. Since the literature on Adam Smith is abundant, some CD-ROM databases are useful: Social Sciences Citation Index (SSCI), EconLit (economics literature), BIP+ (Books in Print), and Historical Abstracts on Disc. It is now easy to check the references related to Adam Smith in these sources. However, most of these databases contain references from the 1970s or 1980s on, and hence are not always sufficient. Below are some closely related bibliographical references.

BLAUG, MARK (ed.) (1991), *Adam Smith, 1723–1790*, 2 vols., London: Edward Elgar.

FRANKLIN, B. and CORDASCO, F. (1950), *Adam Smith: A Bibliographical Checklist*, New York: Burt Franklin [an international record of critical writings and scholarship relating to Smith and Smithian theory, 1876–1950]

LIGHTWOOD, M. B. (ed.) (1984), *A Selected Bibliography of Significant Works about Adam Smith*, London: Macmillan.

RECKTENWALD, HORST (1978), "An Adam Smith Renaissance *anno* 1976? The Bicentenary Output—A Reappraisal of his Scholarship", *Journal of Economic Literature*, 16(1): 56–83.

SCOTT, W. R. (1940), "Studies Relating to Adam Smith during the Last Fifty Years", *Proceedings of the British Academy*, 26: 249–74.

Vanderblue Memorial Collection of Smithiana (1939), publication no. 2 of the Kress Library of Business and Economics, Baker Library, Harvard Graduate School of Business Administration [although published almost sixty years ago, this catalogue is still an important source for the study of Adam Smith across nations and across disciplines. It is still in print, available from the Special Collections of the Baker Library].

WOOD, JOHN C. (ed.) (1984), *Adam Smith: Critical Assessments*, 4 vols., London: Croom Helm [reprints 150 journal papers].

3. *Some similar papers not included in this volume.* Six papers closely related to the topic of this volume are collected in H. Mizuta and C. Sugiyama (eds.) (1993), *Adam Smith: International Perspectives*, London: Macmillan. This book was published when the first draft of the present volume was almost completed. Since Mizuta and Sugiyama (1993) is easily accessible, it is not necessary to reprint these six papers here. Instead, they are listed below and recommended as complementary reading. Among them, Gioli (Italy) and Diatkine (France) are the most original papers. An important difference between the Mizuta–Sugiyama book and the present volume is that their book is based on a 1990 conference, basically from the point of view of 1990 (a cross-sectional perspective), whereas the texts collected in this volume span 1776 to 1993 (a long-run perspective).

1. Waszek, Norbert, "Adam Smith in Germany, 1776–1832", pp. 163–80.
2. Diatkine, Daniel, "A French Reading of the *Wealth of Nations* in 1790", pp. 213–23.
3. Gioli, Gabriella, "The Diffusion of the Economic Thought of Adam Smith in Italy, 1776–1876", pp. 225–49.
4. Anikin, Andrei, "Adam Smith in Russia", pp. 251–60.
5. Zhu, Shaowen, "Adam Smith in China", pp. 279–91.
6. Sugiyama, C., Omori, I., and Takemoto, H., "Adam Smith in Japan", pp. 293–313.

4. *The Spread of* WN *in Europe in general.* The following references are on the translation and spread of *WN* in continental Europe, mainly France, Germany, and Italy. The problem is that they treat several countries simultaneously, so that it is difficult to break them down according to the Parts of this book. In his descriptive text Rae (1895) reports the process of publishing *WN* and its immediate reception at home and abroad, based on Smith's correspondence and contemporary publications. The time-span is quite short (1776–84) and the information is very detailed, but I think it is still useful to read it a century later

to see people's reactions to *WN* when it was just published. The paper by Kenneth Carpenter (1977), written by a bibliographer, is a general but informative account of the translations and the reception of *WN* in Denmark, France, The Netherlands, Germany, Italy, Spain, and Sweden. It serves well as an overview of the spread of *WN* on the Continent. Kaufmann (1887) was written ten years after the first centenary of *WN* and is perhaps the first analytical account of the reception of *WN* in Britain, France, and Germany. Kaufmann was a defender of Smith's theories, almost unreservedly. It is amusing to read such a paper on *WN* and its critics a century later. Palyi (1928) is a long and very rich paper. It has been quoted time and again during the past half century. Some textbooks on the history of economic thought also discuss the spread of Smithian economics in European countries, but none of them focuses on *WN* in particular. However, three deserve to be mentioned: Cossa (1893), Haney (1949), and Pribram (1983). Among them, Pribram (1983) treats the spread of Smithian (i.e. post-Smith) economics in France, Italy, and Germany, rather than the spread of *WN per se*. Schumpeter (1954) also discusses this issue, but not in great detail, for the cases of France (pp. 490–1) and Germany (pp. 501–5).

Cossa, Luigi (1893), "Adam Smith and His Immediate Successors", *An Introduction to the Study of Political Economy*, ch. 8, London: Macmillan.

Carpenter, Kenneth (1977), "Adam Smith's *Wealth of Nations* on the Continent of Europe", draft, Harvard University Widener Library.

Haney, Lewis (1949), "The Expositors of the English Classical Political Economy outside of England", *History of Economic Thought*, ch. 17, New York: Macmillan.

Kaufmann, M. (1887), "Adam Smith and his Foreign Critics", *The Scottish Review*, 10: 378–411.

Palyi, Melchior (1928), "The Introduction of Adam Smith on the Continent", in J. M. Clark *et al.* (eds.), *Adam Smith, 1776–1926*, pp. 190–233, University of Chicago Press (reprinted 1966, New York: Augustus Kelley).

Pribram, Karl (1983), "The Spread of Smithian Economics", *A History of Economic Reasoning*, ch. 13, Johns Hopkins University Press.

Rae, John (1895), "*The Wealth of Nations*" and "*The Wealth of Nations* Abroad and at Home", *Life of Adam Smith*, chs. 18 and 24, New York: Macmillan.

Schumpeter, J. (1954), *History of Economic Analysis*, Oxford University Press.

Translations of The Wealth of Nations

> So the study of economic processes must include the study of economists, or of the origin, flow, and development of their ideas—for one can hardly separate the study of the origin of ideas from that of the change and flow of ideas. Such a study includes as well as all the processes of changes in ideas, and how ideas originate, also the processes by which they succeed, catch on, and dominate their time; it includes also the lags and impediments in the flow of ideas, both across and within national and linguistic frontiers.
>
> T. W. Hutchison

1. Introduction

The Wealth of Nations (WN) is an ideal subject for studying the international transmission of economic ideas because it is generally regarded as the foundation of modern political economy; it has been read (or at least mentioned) for more than two centuries, and it is still being read around the world, in many different ways, regardless of ideological background. It is also reasonable to say that it is the most translated, although not necessarily the most read, economics book in history.

Translation is a neglected part of the study of the international transmission of economic ideas; the problems of misunderstanding and distortion are important but unexploited territory. It is not enough to study only the act of translation or the economic context alone. Translations of WN must be seen within the dynamic framework of broader intellectual movements. For example, the first Italian translation of WN (Naples, 1790) may be regarded as evidence of the intense participation of Italian scholarship in the general European movement towards cultural renewal or, more broadly, the Enlightenment movement (Gioli, 1993: 227).

2. Speed and Number of Translations

The speed with which WN was translated into the major European languages may have owed much to Smith's previous famous book, The Theory of Moral Sentiments (TMS), which was published in 1759 and well received by the

European intellectual community. Recall that political economy was not an important discipline in the eighteenth century, whereas moral philosophy was.

Table 1 shows the spread of *TMS* and *WN* in five countries: in each case the time lag between the English edition and the translation was much shorter for *WN* than for *TMS* (compare columns 3 and 5). However, there are two patterns: (1) in France and Germany, *TMS* was well known and well received, and this paved the way for the rapid translation of *WN* (time lags of 2 and 0 years, respectively); (2) in Russia, Spain, and Japan, where *WN* was better known (perhaps earlier than *TMS*), *TMS* was translated much later than *WN* (time lags of 66, 149, and 78 years, respectively). I am inclined to conjecture that France and Germany translated *WN* just as they did *TMS*, from an intellectual perspective; whereas Russia, Spain, and Japan (then developing countries) were primarily interested in learning something useful of "the nature and causes of the wealth of nations", and then realized that *TMS*, as its philosophical foundation, was an important source for a better understanding of *WN*.

Table 2 is derived from the Appendix to this volume, which provides details of editions of *WN* in eighteen languages. Some remarks are appropriate. First, these eighteen languages are but a fraction of the number of modern living languages (although between them they offer *WN* an enormous readership). Among the Asian languages, there are no translations in Thai or Malay, among others; and the same is true of many Indo-European languages.

Second, the translation movement continues. I am informed that new Danish, Korean, and Spanish translations are to be completed in the near future.

Table 1. *The Theory of Moral Sentiments* (1759) and *The Wealth of Nations* (1776): first translation and time lag from first publication in English

Language	First translation of *TMS* published	Time lag (years)	First translation of *WN* published	Time lag (years)	*TMS* earlier than *WN* (years)	*TMS* later than *WN* (years)
(1)	(2)	(3)	(4)	(5)	(6)	(7)
French	1764	5	1778	2	14	
German	1770	11	1776	0	6	
Russian	1868	109	1802	26		66
Spanish	1941	182	1792	16		149
Japanese	1948–9	189	1870	94		78

Source: For *The Theory of Moral Sentiments* (*TMS*), see the Introduction to the 1976 Oxford University Press edition, pp. 32–3; it seems that *TMS* has been translated into only these five languages. For *WN*, see the Appendix.

Table 2. Translations of *WN* in 18 languages

(a) First translation (regardless of whether full or abridged)		(b) Number of full and partial translations in each country	
Year	Language	Time(s)	Country
1776	German	14	Japan
1778	French	10	Germany
1779	Danish	6	Italy
1790	Italian	6	Russia
1792	Spanish	6	Spain
1796	Dutch	5	France
1800	Swedish	5	Sweden
1802	Russian	3	China
1811	Portuguese	3	Korea
1870	Japanese	2	Denmark
1901	Chinese	2	Poland
1927	Polish	2	Portugal
1928	Czech	2	Romania
1933	Finnish	1	Czechoslovakia
1934	Romanian	1	Egypt
1948	Turkish	1	Finland
1957	Korean	1	Holland
1959	Arabic	1	Turkey

Third, countries with fewer than five or six editions seem to be the norm. Why, then, did Germany and Japan show so much interest in the book, translating it time after time, often owing to dissatisfaction with previous translations? In Japan, which probably has the highest proportion of economists involved in Smith studies in the world, there are fourteen translations derived from various English editions, with or without Cannan's copious notes (Ch. 6.1; see Sugiyama *et al.*, 1993: 293–300).

In those countries with more than three translations, we may discern distinct patterns in the timing of their publication. In China the translation movement occurred between the turn of the twentieth century and the 1930s; in Korea, between the 1950s and the 1970s; in France, between the 1770s and the 1820s; in Sweden, in the 1800s; in Italy between the 1790s and the 1850s and from 1945 to 1976; in Russia between the beginning of the nineteenth century and the 1930s (quite evenly). Germany, Japan, and Spain all show a continuous interest in *WN*.

By contrast, where there is only one translation it is generally a selective or abridged one. Why have these countries been so cool about *WN*? An easy

xvii

explanation is that most intellectuals can read either English or other major-language translations. This may explain why there is no complete Swedish translation, for example, and why Japan has so many translations (much of the general public is interested in this classic work but most do not read English easily); but it cannot explain the case of Germany, where a high percentage of intellectuals can read English-language publications.

Here we may mention an interesting anecdote concerning the speed of translation. In the *Mémoires de l'Abbé Morellet* (1823: 243), Morellet states that he spent the autumn of 1776 in Champagne assiduously translating the just-published *WN*. At the same time, l'Abbé Blavet, a former Benedictine who translated *TMS* in 1774, translated *WN* in weekly instalments for the *Journal de l'agriculture, du commerce, des arts et des finances*, where it was published between January 1779 and December 1780 (Table A7, 1.1–2.1). In 1781 Blavet's translation, which was endorsed by Smith (see Ch. 3.2), was reprinted in six volumes in Yverdon (Switzerland) and in Paris. Morellet complained that this "proved an obstacle to the publication of mine. I offered it for a hundred louis, and then for nothing, but the competition caused its rejection". He was rejected once more by the Archbishop of Sens, and complained that "poor Smith was traduced rather than translated . . . My translation was carefully made. Everything of an abstract character in Smith's theory becomes unintelligible in Blavet's translation, but in mine may be read with profit."

3. Some Problems of Translation

FALSE EDITIONS

In the first Italian edition (1790), the translator claimed that his translation was based on the English edition, when in fact it was based on Blavet's 1779–80 French edition. Another example of a false edition is the first Spanish translation (1792). According to R. S. Smith (see Ch. 9.2), this edition was an expurgated translation of Condorcet's synopsis of *WN*, which appeared in French in the *Bibliothèque de l'homme public*, published in Paris (1790). The translator "not only suppressed or garbled parts of Condorcet's work but failed to identify the original as the work of Smith".

AN UNIDENTIFIED EDITION

The first French translation was published in 1778–9 in The Hague with the translator's name given as "M***". In another French edition, published in Paris in 1781, the translator's name was not given, but it is generally acknowledged that he was l'Abbé Blavet. Many people considered both editions to be by the same translator but printed in different places and different formats (see table A7, 1.1 and 2.1). By comparing the two translations, Murray (see Ch. 3.3) concluded that "The Hague translation was thus a year earlier in date, and was evidently by a different hand", but this still does not identify the translator of the 1778–9 The Hague edition.

CENSORSHIP

The Spanish Inquisition banned the original (French) version of *WN* on 3 March 1792, but Sir John Macpherson told Edward Gibbon that the Spanish government had permitted an extract of *WN* to be published in Spanish in 1792 (see Ch. 9.2). This extract, by Carlos Martínez de Irujo (Oficial de la Primera Secretaría de Estado), was translated from Condorcet's synopsis of *WN*. The translator gave assurances "that he had deleted everything which could induce error or relaxation on religious and moral matters" (Smith 1968: 308).

This censorship carried over to the first (virtually) complete Spanish translation of *WN* (1794), by José Alonso Ortíz, a lawyer attached to the royal councils and chancery in Valladolid and a professor of canon law and sacred theology. On 15 February 1793, Ortíz appeared before the Inquisition, explaining that he had translated *WN* some time ago, "purging it of various impious proposals . . . and eliminating entirely an article . . . in which the author favours tolerance on points of religion, so that it stands cleansed of anything that could lead to error or relaxation in moral and religious matters". Only after some delays and some minor revisions by Ortíz was the work published in 1794 with government permission (see Chs. 9.1 and 9.2 for a detailed account).

TRADOTTORE TRADITORE

Examples of rewriting rather than faithful translation are abundant. For the Chinese edition (1902), Yen Fu did as much rewriting as translating (see Ch. 1.2), not to mention his heavy abridgement (only about 54 per cent of Smith's text was "translated"). Even within the parts which were translated, there are many digressions in Smith's text (e.g. the history of wheat prices in London) which the translator judged to be of little interest to his readers, given the different cultural environment.

The Chinese language lacked sufficient vocabulary for many of Smith's terms and concepts. Moreover, the analytical tools, methods of reasoning, and historical background of *WN* were completely alien to the Chinese cultural system. For a very common term like "bank", Yen Fu could find no equivalent in Chinese, and so picked two random Chinese characters which sound like "banke" as the translation. What is worse for readers is that he did not explain what "bank" means and did not include the English term in parentheses so that some readers could look up its meaning for themselves. He translated "labour" into something like "ability" and could make no distinction between "productive" and "unproductive" labour. He translated the name "F. Quesnay" with three Chinese characters which sound like "genisi", so that no reader can possibly imagine that this refers to Quesnay. Moreover, I doubt that Chinese readers can grasp Quesnay's significance in the history of economic analysis from Yen Fu's translation.

More difficult still for Yen Fu were new concepts, such as "induction" and "stock". His solutions included finding similar terms from classic Chinese books, straightforward omission, invention, and borrowing from Japanese. Despite these difficulties, he essentially transmitted Smith's main ideas to Chinese readers—conveying concrete economic policies more successfully than the more theoretical parts.

In Japan, Kenji Takeuchi, one of the most famous and serious translators of *WN* (see Table A10, 5.1–5.3), published a book whose title translates as "Mistranslation" (1963), in which he discussed the problems of misunderstanding in translating *WN* and Ricardo's *Principles*. He criticized mistranslations by Japanese professors, commented on their "errors" and "ignorance" and the inconsistencies between different translations, and professed himself ashamed of such "ugly translations". Reading this piece of self-criticism, one can easily understand why there are fourteen translations in Japan. If Japanese Smith scholars are so obsessed with perfection—their attention to detail is incomparable—they may have another fourteen in the next two centuries.

References

GIOLI, GABRIELLA (1993), "The Diffusion of the Economic Thought of Adam Smith in Italy, 1776–1876", in H. Mizuta and C. Sugiyama (eds.), *Adam Smith: International Perspectives*, pp. 225–49, London: Macmillan.

SMITH, R. S. (1968), "English Economic Thought in Spain, 1776–1848", *South Atlantic Quarterly*, 67(2): 306–37.

SUGIYAMA, C. *et al.* (1993), "Adam Smith in Japan" in H. Mizuta and C. Sugiyama (eds.), *Adam Smith: International Perspectives*, pp. 293–313, London: Macmillan,

TAKEUCHI, KENJI (1963), *Goyaku: daigaku kyoju no atama no hodo* (Mistranslation), Tokyo: Yuki Shobo.

Receptions of The Wealth of Nations

When a given body of information passes the national frontiers it acquires a new complexion, a new national, cultural physiognomy.

Thorstein Veblen

1. Method of Analysis and Difficulties

This essay is a survey of the receptions of, and objections to, *The Wealth of Nations* (*WN*) in ten non-English-speaking countries. The purpose is to present a picture of the international transmission of economic ideas, taking *WN* as an example. The language barrier is obvious but of secondary importance, for the real difficulty lies in having a good knowledge of the economic situations and the currents of economic thought in these countries.

Let us take Germany as an example. *WN* was translated into German in 1776, the year the first English edition came out; the most recent German edition was published in 1974. The contents of *WN* have changed little between various editions, but the economic situation and economic thought (mentality) in Germany have changed radically. Because of this dynamic change, it would be a challenging task for any single person to write a monograph on the receptions of *WN* in Germany during the past two centuries—let alone handle ten countries simultaneously in one essay.

This kind of cross-country comparative study is necessarily factual, fragmentary, and "superficial", but a first step must be taken. What I am offering is a general (and mosaic) picture of the issue, based on the literature I have been able to collect, and focusing more on the early (eighteenth- and nineteenth-century) receptions than on the recent period.

Another characteristic of this study is that I can only concern myself with the "external" aspects: the "economic affairs" issue in *WN* and the reception and debate of these economic policies. The "internal" aspects—Smith's theory of value, the invisible hand, self-interest, and market efficiency, etc.—also elicited much discussion in the ten countries and influenced many important thinkers, including Marx; but these internal aspects are much more delicate and virtually impossible to tackle in a cross-country comparison.

In his now classic text on the introduction of Smith on the Continent (mainly focused on France, Germany, and Italy), Palyi (1928: 180) begins by stating three analytical difficulties. First, who could say exactly how much of Smith's apparent influence on the Continental free trade movement was in reality due to other liberal thinkers? Second, it is difficult to separate the practical influences from the scientific ones; economic thought affects both science and practice. Third, it is even more difficult to distinguish in what proportion Smith's influence on the Continent was due to his ideas, and to what degree it was due to his style, and the charming personality it expressed.

Palyi's is the first (perhaps still the only) "comparative" study of this kind. In fact, the case of Italy was handled marginally in his paper, and his study was not strictly comparative because he treated Germany and France in different sections. By contrast, my comparative approach in this essay does not take an individual country as its unit of analysis; rather it deals with individual topics to see what general patterns emerge.

As one can see from Palyi's footnotes, he used many documents, including brochures, pamphlets, textbooks, and encyclopaedia published at different times, to support his arguments. I do not possess such rich documentation for all the countries analysed here, and even if I did and if I could read all the languages, my background knowledge would still be insufficient to understand the whole issue to the extent of being able to present a synthesis of Palyi's depth (he was particularly good in the case of Germany).

I rely heavily on secondary studies. The availability of these secondary studies in each country varies greatly. Countries such as Germany and Russia have more documentation in English than do France, Italy, Japan, and Spain— although these countries have rich literature in their own languages. China, Denmark, Portugal, and Sweden have only very limited documentation in English of use to us. Therefore, more emphasis is unavoidably put on document-rich countries. The analysis falls into five topics: (1) motives for translating (introducing) *WN*; (2) methods of introducing *WN*; (3) receptions of *WN* (our main issue); (4) objections to *WN*; and (5) a retrospective review on the impact of *WN* in the ten countries analysed.

Limited by space I can only select one or two examples to illustrate each topic. Some secondary issues, such as receptions by general readers, are excluded here; a fuller version is available upon request. Rather than use quotations extensively, I have chosen to paraphrase different authors in order to keep this survey concise and the style consistent. This method seems somewhat mechanical but nevertheless efficient, and it certainly makes the survey easier to follow. Another point is that in this kind of survey it is difficult to have a hypothesis or thesis to verify. In terms of style, then, I wish to follow the motto of Dunoyer: "Je n'impose rien, je ne propose rien, j'expose" (I impose nothing, I propose nothing, I [only] expose; see Kaufmann 1887: 404).

2. Motives for Introducing *WN*

I have identified three different motives for translating *WN*. The first is wanting to learn from England's experience as a powerful empire—as described by the title of Schwartz's classic book (1964) *In Search of Wealth and Power: Yen Fu and the West*. I have argued (see Ch. 1.2) that Yen Fu's main reason for translating Smith's 1776 book at the turn of this century may have been that the title *The Wealth of Nations* was strikingly attractive for Yen Fu, who was keen for China to be wealthy and powerful. Whereas Chinese intellectuals came to hear of *WN* as late as 1902, Russia's intellectuals and decision-makers already knew the main ideas of *WN* before its publication in England in 1776. In Russia's eyes England was a symbol of superlative naval power, technology, and engineering; its nascent manufacturing industry was watched with envy. The fact that *WN* was written in that country and by a sensible, personable University of Glasgow professor—a friend of Hume—added legitimacy to the thoughts expressed in *WN*.

The second motive is a strong inclination towards free trade. Thus, a few Portuguese texts written between 1792 and 1802 contain scattered references to *WN*, nearly always concerning the division of labour and freedom of production and trade. The increasing audience for *laissez-faire* arguments was a strong incentive for a wider diffusion of the book. In the short introduction to the first Portuguese edition of *WN* (1811), Lisboa explains the importance of the translation for understanding the profound changes taking place in Brazil (where he lived). The acknowledged reason for the significance of *WN* was the doctrinal instrumentalization of the principles of *laissez-faire* it contained (see Ch. 7.1).

The third type of motive is more intellectual than practical. The Danish translator Frants Dræbye was tutor to the sons of the Norwegian merchant James Collett. He took a European trip with Collett's sons which brought them to England in 1776, when Smith's book had just been published and was much discussed. This prompted a desire in Dræbye to acquaint Danish and Norwegian readers with such a significant work (see Ch. 2.2). Similarly, French readers were interested in *WN* mainly for intellectual reasons, but the level of understanding of economic analysis was higher in France: the free trade policy and *laissez-faire* principle, which Smith so emphasized, had originated from French physiocrats.

The case of Japan combines all three motives. *WN* was translated at one time owing to the practical need for free trade policy and at another time from a purely scholarly point of view. Especially after the First World War, great importance was attached to *WN* as the source of social and economic ideas; furthermore it was evaluated, and translated, from the viewpoint of socialist thought. It is not that *WN* was translated in various ways according to different social backgrounds and social needs, but it may be that the attempt to read *WN* from those points of view naturally led people to recast their Japanese versions (see Ch. 6.1).

3. Methods of Transmission

Alexandrin (Ch. 8.5) offers an interesting framework for the analysis of methods of transmission. In his overlooked paper on *WN* in early Russia, he distinguishes five agents of transmission: source, admirer, medium, transmitter, and receptor. He then lists policies suggested by Smith (Table 1) and policy interests of Russia (Table 2) to investigate the real effect of *WN*. Unfortunately, I do not have sufficient information to apply this framework to other countries, but I can present three different ways in which *WN* was introduced.

The first, and most usual, way is direct translation. This was the route taken by translators who knew Smith personally (in the case of Denmark, Frants Dræbye), or had corresponded with him and had obtained his authorization (l'Abbé Blavet in France), or had studied in England (Yen Fu in China).

Russia shows us a more complex mode of transmission, through different channels in the same period. There were two Russians students who had gone to Glasgow University, studied with Smith, and brought his ideas to Russia. Amongst the followers of Smith were Desnitsky, Tretyakov, Countess Catherine Dashkov (*née* Vorontsov), and her very young son Paul; Count Mordinov, who was also sent to London to "specialize"; and Count Vorontsov, who was the Russian ambassador to the court of St. James (Ch. 8.5).

The third type of transmission is assimilation of *WN* into one's own system of economic discourse. France, a country with strong national self-consciousness and with aspirations towards the political or at least cultural domination of the world, could not easily accept the leadership of a foreigner, except when assimilated through the work of a native writer. Gide and Rist (Ch. 3.4) make the following observation:

a complete triumph, so far as the Continent at least was concerned, had to be the work of an interpreter. Such an interpreter must fuse all these ideas into a coherent body of doctrines, leaving useless digressions aside. This was the task that fell into the hands of J. B. Say. Among his merits (and it is not the only one) there is that of popularizing the ideas of the great Scots economist on the Continent, and of giving to these ideas a somewhat classical appearance. The task of discrediting the first French school of economists and of facilitating the expansion of English political economy fell, curiously enough, to the hands of a Frenchman.

The case of Germany, where Sartorius produced the first "Smithian" text-book in 1796, is even more telling. Sartorius précised the theses advanced in *WN*, although the later sections show some sign of accommodation between Smith and the more traditional German treatment of *Staatwirtschaft*. This textbook, which was used at Göttingen University and translated into Swedish in 1800, marked the beginning of a more positive reception of *WN* (Ch. 4.3). In his preface, Sartorius says: "The author of the following summary has lectured for five years on the principles given here, and he is able to say that he has also been so fortunate as to make them comprehensible to beginners. The author is convinced that Smith has discovered the truth and he considers it his duty to contribute his share towards its dissemination" (Ch. 4.1).

Also in Germany, K. H. Rau's three-volume economics textbook (published between 1826 and 1837, with numerous later editions) incorporated Smithian doctrines and principles into an older structure. It remained the most widely used textbook of economics, and many eminent German economists (e.g. Roscher, Wagner, and C. Menger) were raised on it. Although the book cannot claim analytical novelty (see Schumpeter's harsh criticism), it smoothed the way for the reception of *WN* in Germany by incorporating its main ideas into what seemed to be traditional Cameralistic discourse (Waszek 1993: 169).

4. Receptions

I select five topics to illustrate this complicated issue: (1) difficulties of reception; (2) *WN*'s impact on decision-makers; (3) the free trade and *laissez-faire* doctrine as the most received message; (4) the lack of interest in Smith's theoretical investigation; (5) receptions of *WN* by Marxist readers.

DIFFICULTIES OF RECEPTION

There were two types of difficulty in the reception of *WN*. First, the general intellectual and economic environment in most receiving countries was not yet mature enough to receive Smith's theories and economic policies. In mercantilist 1780s Italy, *WN* perhaps did not seem to display any more common sense than the writings of the leading Italian authors. It even appeared rather dogmatic and doctrinaire on purely theoretical matters such as the value problem, and it was often less clear and less profound than the best Italian writings. Consequently, even the few contemporary free-traders hardly mentioned the book. The most influential of them, the Neapolitan Gaetano

Filangieri, in his rather able eclectic synthesis of physiocratic principles and mercantilist practices (1780) does not mention either Turgot or Smith. Even a comparatively pronounced free-trader like the Count d'Arco of Mantova (1739–91) does not seem to have known him. The Neapolitan Giuseppe Palmieri, presenting in 1790 a cautious treatment of commercial policy, does not reveal any Smithian influence; to him universal free trade and moderate protection were debatable alternatives (Palyi, 1928: 189).

The second type of difficulty is resistance to Smithianism by the dominant current of economic thought, which is illustrated by Cameralism in Germany. It was not surprising that the Cameralist professors, whose textbooks were brought out in new editions even as late as the 1820s, often preferred to disregard the liberalism of *WN*. Sonnenfels' remained the official textbook of Cameralism in the whole Austrian Empire until the revolution of 1848. Not until 1846 did his pupil von Kudler (1786–1853), a professor in Vienna, have the courage to pour Smithian spirit into the old writings of his master. The opposition later found its most characteristic literary expression in the writings of men like Buesch and Rehberg (1754–1836), both under the influence of James Steuart and both opposed to *WN*, though conceding some of its merits (Palyi, 1928: 194–6).

IMPACT ON DECISION-MAKERS

I am somewhat struck to find that Smith's impact on decision-makers was so limited. In France, Napoleon's policy—he had read *WN* as well as Filangieri and Necker in the military school in Paris—of sound money and a stable interest rate, his severe economy in public expenditure, his distaste for public debts except in an emergency, and especially his decisive stance against every kind of direct state participation in trade may have been suggested, partly at least, by Smith and his French followers (Palyi 1928: 209). Yet this is far from proven.

The case of Russia is more concrete. Desnitsky, another Russian student who studied at Glasgow University, is regarded as one of the most outstanding Russian social and political thinkers of the second half of the eighteenth century, the father of Russian jurisprudence. In 1767–8 Desnitsky wrote a remarkable work, *Predstavlenie*, in response to the setting-up of Catherine II's Legislative Commission. The appendix which Desnitsky devoted to state finance was incorporated by Catherine into the Second Supplement to her *Nakaz*, completed on 8 April 1768. Since there are clear traces of Smith's influence in this appendix, it is evident that not only Desnitsky but also (indirectly) Smith exercised influence over Catherine's *Nakaz*, published eight years before *WN*. No fewer than twenty-six articles of the *Nakaz* (articles

575–600) bear a definite relationship to Desnitsky's formulation. In his financial proposals, in particular, Desnitsky transmits a number of Smith's ideas (Ch. 8.3). But the real influence was a different matter. Smith wrote about (improving) the functioning of free, independent, established, and *operable* economic units. Catherine II, on the other hand, was concerned with building the political, social, and administrative infrastructure of her continent-sized kingdom. Although Catherine and her successor stated an intent to facilitate the creation of manufacturing and to aid the rise of the bourgeoisie, they continued to enslave their people, monopolize land (land for "well-born persons" only), and vent their reactionary views. Smith's doctrine of free external trade and freedom in social and economic relations at home and abroad seems never to have been very influential in Russia (Ch. 8.5).

Finally, by 1807 (the disastrous collapse of Prussia) Smithian principles (with important modifications) were fairly accepted in Germany, and were making themselves felt in the activities of such statesmen as Stein, Hardenberg, and von Schön. The direction taken by the reforms coincided in large measure with the direction indicated by Smith; for any revival of the Prussian state could only proceed by liberalization, loosening the fetters of the Frederician system. But such reforms did not always result from Smith's teaching, nor did they go to the lengths indicated as best by him or by his ardent followers in Germany (Ch. 4.1).

FREE TRADE AND *LAISSEZ-FAIRE*

The free trade and *laissez-faire* principle was the best received part of *WN*, at least at the level of ideas, not necessarily in practice. Every country received this message differently based on their own particular features.

In Italy, through Mengotti's work, Smith's ideological message of the freedom of commerce was broadly accepted in its more or less radical guise. Around the 1840s, the acceptance of Smith took root in the Italian political and cultural terrain. The principles of liberalism and free trade had become the means of uniting the most lively forces in the country. These joined together to form the Piedmontese free-market movement, represented by an enthusiastic supporter of Smith's doctrines, the statistician Camillo Cavour (Gioli 1993: 227–8, 231, 234).

A few Portuguese texts written between 1792 and 1802 contain scattered references to *WN*, nearly always concerning the division of labour and freedom in production and trade. Lisboa, writing in Portugal's chief colony, Brazil, embraced Smith's clear-cut support of economic freedom. Praise for *WN* appears frequently in a group of pamphlets Lisboa published in Rio de Janeiro from 1808 to 1810, which expressed the ideas of a Brazilian intelligentsia looking towards autonomous economic development. The motives which made Lisboa such a wholehearted follower of Smith's doctrine of free trade thus become increasingly understandable: his role as a Brazilian author impelled him to it and justified the insistence with which he used Smith to explain the advantages of making Brazil part of the international division of labour (Ch. 7.1).

The same was true in early nineteenth-century Russia, where writers in *The St Petersburg Journal*, the official organ of the government, referred to Smith as "a great man, who had seized an important truth". According to them the duty of the government should be simply to refrain from interfering. It should only encourage the natural freedom of industry. In his report for 1803, Kochubey, the Minister of the Interior, apparently impressed with the physiocratic side of Smith's doctrines, speaks of the advisability of leaving private industry free, but of obtaining full information about its progress and furnishing it with aid when necessary. Between 1815 and 1820 the free-traders of the Imperial Free Economic Society had an organ, *The Spirit of the Journals*, in which they energetically campaigned for the abolition of protection, translating extracts from the writings of J. B. Say, Bentham, Sismondi, and other Western European writers. The free-traders were not, however, thoroughgoing disciples of Smith, but belated physiocrats, at least in terms of their enthusiasm for agriculture as the sole source of national wealth (Mavor 1914: 556–8).

In Spain, liberal economics seeped into the Spanish colonies through several channels. Possibly, as González Alberdi suggests, *WN* encouraged some colonialists to press for even greater freedom in their colonial dependence, but few, it would seem, were persuaded to accept all the principles defended by Smith and Say.

Much of the credit for making Smith known in Spain is conventionally attributed to Say, whom some Spaniards called "the French Smith" (Smith 1968: 309). However, Perdices Blas (Ch. 9.3) argues that, if liberal teachers preferred Say for his clarity and simplicity, more radical liberals preferred the less theoretical Bastiat. Smith was a symbol for free trade supporters and "the father of economics" for teachers, but the book read was Bastiat's *Economic sophisms*. Mirabeau, too, was more successful among Spanish economists. Perdices Blas's arguments are instructive; it is perhaps time to rethink the assumption that Smith was the master of free trade and *laissez-faire* for other countries.

LACK OF INTEREST IN SMITHIAN THEORY OF ECONOMIC ANALYSIS

Most studies on the international reception of *WN* focus mainly on the free trade principle, which reflects contemporary concerns. The other important issues raised in *WN*, such as education, public debt, capital accumulation, and division of labor (for Smith these are the major "causes of the wealth of nations"), received little attention. Thus, in the early stage of the spread of *WN*, it seems that, except for France, most of the countries under discussion were interested in the practical aspects, especially in the issue of free trade (Ch. 5.1). The theoretical aspects were largely neglected, or considered irrelevant. Generally speaking, *WN* was known only in fragmentary form, and writers lacked the ability to capture a sense of the overall content.

The case of Portugal shows this clearly. Portuguese authors of 1790–1810 did not grasp the theoretical and analytical structures of mainstream European economic thought of the second half of the eighteenth century. The principles of *laissez-faire* were used as an argument against the excessive role of the state in the economy and as a banner for a programme of gradual reform of *ancien régime* institutions. Insofar as the original messages were filtered for non-scientific purposes, the doctrinaire nature of the assimilation inhibited a clear-cut distinction between the Portuguese authors and the sources which inspired them. Thus, Portuguese scholars cannot be called disciples of these foreign masters; they were popularizers of a doctrinal message partly accepted as an instrument for desired reform (Ch. 7.1).

RECEPTION BY MARXIST READERS

With the founding of the Chinese Communist Party in 1921, Marxist economic thought began to find its way into China and was well received by Chinese intellectuals. They started to criticize classical economic thought, including that of Smith, in the light of Marxist viewpoints, and their criticism gradually gained momentum and continued into the 1930s. *WN* once again attracted academic attention in the late 1920s, but because Yen Fu's classical Chinese translation (1902) was difficult to read, Guo and Wang (two Marxists) decided to retranslate *WN*. It is interesting to note that translating *WN* was part of their preparation for translating and disseminating Marx's *Capital* in China, so they would be able to understand the *Capital* better. (Chinese versions of both *WN* and the *Capital* were published in 1931.) Neither Guo nor Wang did any research on Smith's economic thought, nor did they comment on it. It is clear that left-wing readers in China during the 1930s and 1940s simply criticized Smith's economic views and principles without evaluating his social philosophy and economic thought as a whole from a historical viewpoint. From the 1950s on, Chinese economists were heavily influenced by the Soviet Union, and *WN* was dismissed as bourgeois and outdated. However, since classical economics was one of the three sources of Marxism, Guo and Wang's Chinese edition of *WN* was reissued in 1972 (Zhu 1993: 286–9).

A similar phenomenon existed in Japan, where there was and is a strong

Marxist tradition of economics in general and of the history of economic thought in particular (Ch. 6.3). Smith tended to be studied in relation to Marx because Marxism had greatly influenced Japanese social scientists and social thinkers since around 1910, and even more so in the post-war period, when the study of Marx was enthusiastically resumed. In fact, these Marxist studies boosted the study of Smith in Japan (Ch. 6.2).

The Smith–Marx connection in Russia was understandably even more evident. Lenin studied and cited Smith in its original version and in Russian. In many cases he employed the analysis of Smith's ideas found in Marx's *Capital*. Lenin characterized Smith as a "great ideologue of the leading bourgeoisie", and his evaluation provides the foundation for the determination of a correct Marxist position in relation to bourgeois and petty-bourgeois ideologies. Somewhat paradoxically, Russian Marxists had to defend Smith and the classical school against Populist and nationalist critics. In the heated discussions of the 1890s, late Russian Populists tried to revive some of Sismondi's teachings, whereas Marxists tried to prove that Smith's and Ricardo's ideas developed by Marx were basically applicable to Russia. In the course of these ideological confrontations, Lenin coined the basic attitude of Russian Marxists towards Smith, calling Smith's and Ricardo's political economy the sources of Marxism (Anikin 1993: 256–7).

5. Objections

The objection to the general suitability of Smith's free trade and *laissez-faire* principle was very clear in Russia. Although Catherine II considered Smith's economic ideas in her *Nakaz* (via Desnitsky's *Predstavlenie*), it appears that her policy needs were of a social and political nature, and very much in line with the traditional Russian Imperial policy. The economic, social, and "humanitarian" objectives of Smith and those of the Russian government of the time were widely disparate on the whole. Even if Catherine had been anxious to improve the conditions of the peasantry, for example, she was blocked by the fact that the whole administrative machinery was in the hands of the class who had power over the peasantry (Ch. 8.5). Common among Populist writers was the idea that Smith's theory might well have been good for Britain and other Western countries but that it was totally inapplicable to Russia with its traditions of collectivism and communal spirit. The introduction of the concept of objective economic laws was one of Smith's great achievements, but this concept ran counter to the Populists' view of the laws and consequences of socio-economic development as changeable by the activities of individuals (Anikin 1993: 255).

In Germany, harsh objections were voiced by Friedrich List in 1916 (Ch. 4.2). Here are some representative parts of his criticisms:

Adam Smith's doctrine is, in respect to national and international conditions, merely a continuation of the physiocratic system. Like the latter, it ignores the very nature of nationalities, seeks almost entirely to exclude politics and the power of the State . . . Adam Smith fell into these fundamental errors in exactly the same way as the physiocrats had done before him, namely, by regarding absolute freedom in international trade as an axiom . . . and by not investigating to the bottom how far history supports this idea . . . The mistake has been simply, that this system at bottom is nothing else than a system of the *private economy of all the individual persons in a country, or of the individuals of the whole human race, as that economy would develop and shape itself, under a state of things in which there were no distinct nations, nationalities, or national interests— no distinctive political constitutions or degree of civilizations—no wars or national animosities*; that it is nothing more than a theory of values; a mere shopkeeper's or individual merchant's theory—not a scientific doctrine, showing how the productive powers of an entire nation can be called into existence, increased, maintained, and preserved—for the special benefit of its civilization, welfare, might, continuance, and independence . . . if an opinion was needed as to the entire character of a man or of a book, one could not be sufficiently astonished at the narrowness and obliquity of his views. [emphasis in original]

In China, Liang Ch'i-ch'ao (1873–1929), an important reformist and intellectual of the time, favoured protectionism and mercantilism: "The ideas of Adam Smith were a good prescription for Europe at that time, but are by no means good for modern China" (Ch. 1.2). The most influential critic of *WN* in Spain was the Catalan jurist Ramón Lázaro de Dou y de Bassols (1742–1832). He acknowledged the profundity of *WN* but refused to accept Smith's views on commercial policy, criticizing those who, in the spirit of novelty and scepticism, opposed tariffs and taxes on the import and export of produce and manufactures and portrayed Smith as the Achilles of their opinion. England had never adopted free trade and Dou believed that "the further a nation is from equalling or surpassing other nations in industries, the further it must be from adopting Smith's system". Without examining the logic of the case for free trade, Dou eagerly espoused a vigorous programme for the industrialization of Catalonia behind tariff walls (Ch. 9.1).

As a final example, in Sweden in 1820-1, Carl Adolph Agardh, professor of botany and practical economy in Lund (Sweden), who attended the lectures of J. B. Say in Paris, raised several objections against Smith's theories in *WN*. Generally Agardh took a somewhat more positive view of the activities of the government than did Smith; he also took a more negative view of the division of labour than Smith (Ch. 10.1).

6. Smith's Impact in Retrospect

As mentioned above, the evidence does not support the idea that Smith's impact has been significant in these countries during the past two centuries. To give some further examples, in France, the Italian-born Rossi, Say's successor to the chair of the Collège de France, remarked in the 1840s that Smith's doctrine of economic freedom was enthusiastically accepted by the French bourgeoisie *until* they became the rulers of the state, but that from then on they seemed to be interested only in protection and in state interference. After the Revolution, Smith had, on the whole, great scientific success but little direct influence on economic policies (Palyi 128: 217–18).

Some Spanish economic writers are regarded as having been largely influenced by Smith, and yet other important authors show no sign of Smith's influence, as was the case with Bernardo Joaquín Danvila y Villarrasa and Lozano Normante y Carcavilla, the first two economists to hold economics classes in Spain. Both were influenced by Cantillon's *Essai sur la nature du commerce en général*. Spanish economists had advanced in their knowledge of economics before reading *WN*. The ideas of free domestic trade and free trade with the colonies, the importance of the institutional framework and tax reform, preceded Smith (Ch. 9.3).

Although Smith was recognized as the father of free trade and free economy, the cases of France, Italy, and Spain provide evidence that their first ideas of free trade did not come from Smith. The language of culture on the Continent until the end of the nineteenth century was French rather than English, and the idea of free trade spread through the works of the physiocrats rather than through *WN*. In other, non-European countries, such as China and Japan, it was certainly through *WN* that the ideas of free trade and *laissez-faire* were transmitted. However, Smith's impact on economic policy was limited both across countries and across centuries; his contribution was more at the level of ideas than of real policy. Seventy years later, my conclusion bears similarity to the observation of Palyi (1928: 180): "the influence of Adam Smith's own idea may have been limited".

References

ANIKIN, ANDREI (1976), "Adam Smith i russkaja ekonomiceskaja mysl" [Adam Smith and Russian economic thought], *Voprosky Economiki*, 3: 112–22 (translated by Glen Alexandrin).

—— (1993), "Adam Smith in Russia", in H. Mizuta and C. Sugiyama (eds.), *Adam Smith: International Perspectives*, pp. 251–60, London: Macmillan.

GIOLI, GABRIELLA (1993), "The Diffusion of the Economic Thought of Adam Smith in

Italy, 1776–1876", in H. Mizuta and C. Sugiyama (eds.), *Adam Smith: International Perspectives*, pp. 225–49, London: Macmillan.

KAUFMANN, M. (1877), "Adam Smith and His Foreign Critics", *The Scottish Review*, 10: 378–411.

MAVOR, JAMES (1914), *An Economic History of Russia*, New York: E.P. Dutton & Co.

PALYI, MELCHIOR (1928), "The Introduction of Adam Smith on the Continent", in J. M. Clark *et al.* (eds.), *Adam Smith, 1776–1926*, pp. 190–233, University of Chicago Press (reprinted New York: Augustus Kelley, 1966).

SMITH, R. S. (1968), "English Economic Thought in Spain, 1776–1848", *South Atlantic Quarterly*, 67(2): 306–37.

WASZEK, NOBERT (1993), "Adam Smith in Germany, 1776–1832", in H. Mizuta and C. Sugiyama (eds.), *Adam Smith: International Perspectives*, pp. 163–80, London: Macmillan.

ZHU, SHAOWEN (1993), "Adam Smith in China", in H. Mizuta and C. Sugiyama (eds.), *Adam Smith: International Perspectives*, pp. 279–91, London: Macmillan.

Part 1. China

For readers who are not familiar with the case of China, Zhu (1993) is a useful background text. It offers a detailed and accessible history of the responses to WN from 1900 until the 1970s. For the reasons given in the "Reader's Guide", Zhu's text is not included in this volume, but it can be consulted easily.

In terms of what is included in this Part, Schwartz (1964) is taken from Chapter 5 of his classic study on Yen Fu. A paragraph from the jacket of the book describes his contribution: "This is a powerful account of the effect Western political philosophy had on the Chinese intelligentsia of the late nineteenth century, as symbolized by the translator Yen Fu—the first Chinese literatus to relate himself seriously, and in a sustained fashion, to modern Western thought. Underlying Yen Fu's years of laborious translation of the works of Spencer, Huxley, Adam Smith, Mill, and Montesquieu was his deep concern to discover the secret of the West's success in achieving wealth and power. Although he held a minor official position in China, his main contribution to his country was the propagation of Western ideas—ideas that were to a large extent the antithesis of traditional Chinese thought." As an intellectual historian and sinologist, Schwartz offers a "macro" perspective on the meaning of translating WN and on Smith's ideas for China. He did not examine the Chinese version of WN in detail to investigate the economic impact of Smith's doctrines.

My own paper on Yen Fu (Lai, 1989) was inspired by Schwartz's piece. I thought something might be said from the point of view of a historian of economic thought, and I focused on the problems of translation and on the applicability of Smith's ideas in China between the 1900s and the 1920s. The English version reprinted here is condensed from a much longer Chinese paper.

As supplementary readings, I have translated the Preface and Foreword of the first Chinese edition of WN (1902), written by the translator Yen Fu (1853–1921) and Wu Rulun (1840–1903), his stylistic mentor. In the translator's foreword, Yen Fu begins with the question "What is economics?". He gives a brief etymological explanation of its meaning in the West and its parallel meaning for Chinese readers. He explains what Adam Smith tried to do in *WN*, and compares that with what certain famous Chinese administrators had done in the past in attempting to increase the wealth of the nation. Yen Fu then provides a short history of Western political economy (economics), its progress from the classical school (Smith, Ricardo, etc.) to the current school (J. Mill, J. S. Mill, Jevons, and Marshall), and the analytical tools used (deduction, calculus, geometric presentation). He then explains why a book published in 1776 still merits translation in the twentieth century, in preference to a more modern work such as Marshall's *Principles of Economics* (1890).

In the Preface to this first Chinese edition, Wu Rulun explains the importance of *WN* in the West, why and in what ways the Chinese economy was so vulnerable, and why *WN* would be useful given late Imperial China's economic situation. This preface largely reflects the general attitude of reformist Chinese intellectuals towards the nation's economic problems and the usefulness of "Western truth". These two texts were written in elegant classical Chinese style and in some respects need to be taken with a pinch of salt: Western readers may feel that they say things that are truisms today, and that Wu's text is rambling, repetitious, and unclear. Nevertheless, despite these drawbacks, they reflect something of the economic mentality of Chinese intellectuals reading *WN* during the 1900s.

Taken together, these five texts complement each other quite well: one on the general history of Smithian economics in China; one from the point of view of intellectual history; one with a modern focus; and the final two from the translator and his mentor.

Further Reading

Texts with a * are printed is this Part

*LAI, C. (1989), "Adam Smith and Yen Fu: Western Economics in Chinese Perspective", *Journal of European Economic History*, 18(2): 371–82.

*SCHWARTZ, B. (1964), "The Wealth of Nations", *In Search of Wealth and Power: Yen Fu and the West*, ch. 5, pp. 113–29, Harvard University Press.

*WU RULUN (1902), "Preface" to the first Chinese edition of *The Wealth of Nations*. Taipei: The Commercial Press, 1977, pp. 1–4.

*YEN FU (1902), "Foreword" to the first Chinese edition of *The Wealth of Nations*. Taipei: The Commercial Press, 1977, pp. 1–8.

ZHU SHAOWEN (1993), "Adam Smith in China", in H. Mizuta and C. Sugiyama (eds.), *Adam Smith: International Perspectives*, pp. 279–91, London: Macmillan.

NA except

1.1. Benjamin Schwartz, 1964.
The Wealth of Nations

Yen Fu had been aware from the very outset of the crucial importance of economics. The concern with wealth and power which he had carried with him to England naturally drew his attention most forcefully to England's machinery for creating wealth. Implicit in the phrase itself is the assumption that wealth is the fuel of power. Economics is also central, of course, to the whole Spencerian synthesis. The emergence of the "industrial stage" of human development marks the highest stage of human evolution, and Spencer's views of the evolution of the industrial stage manage to incorporate all the assumptions of the classical economists. The "egoistic" energies which are celebrated in Spencer's writings are, above all, the energies of the industrial entrepreneur. This was the constructive egoism which Yen Fu was now prepared to defend against the highest values of Confucianism. Here again, it is not merely the doctrine of Spencer but the concrete fact of Great Britain's unprecedented economic power which leads him back to the man who was widely acclaimed as the intellectual fountainhead of this phenomenal development—Adam Smith. His first reference to Smith, as already noted, can be found in his "On Strength." "When we of the East contemplate the enormous wealth of the West, its countless techniques for increasing livelihood and regulating finances, we find it difficult to account for this state of affairs."[1] In the West itself, Yen Fu informs us, it is commonly held among those in a position to know that the credit for this is to be ascribed to the "book of Adam Smith." Again, in a commentary on a passage of the *Evolution and Ethics* in which Huxley makes a somewhat lukewarm concession to the positive role of self-interest in men's lives,[2] Yen Fu ardently defends the positive role of self-interest. He states: "The wealth and power of modern Europe are attributed by experts to the science of economics. Economics began with Adam Smith, who

3

developed the great principle . . . that in serving the greater interest (*ta li*) the interests of both sides must be served."[3]

Here again, we note what may be considered an excessive weight placed on the role of ideas or of "sages" in shaping the course of human events. This attribution of England's economic process to the doctrine of one man seems to be in conflict with Yen Fu's own new-found faith in the vast impersonal forces of evolution. Here again, however, we may refer back to discussion of the relationship between "destiny" and "the sages" in Chapter III. The fact that England produced a sage who was able to articulate the dynamic principles of economic growth while China produced no such sage is a fact which Yen Fu cannot overlook. The sages may be only "a factor in destiny," but they seem to be an indispensable factor nevertheless.

The motives for undertaking a translation of the *Wealth of Nations* thus emerge quite clearly. Yen Fu began this enormous undertaking in 1897 and had completed half the book by the end of 1898. The entire translation was completed by the end of 1900 and was again favoured with a foreword (as in the case of *T'ien-yen lun—Evolution and Ethics*) by his stylistic mentor, Wu Ju-lun. The translation is somewhat more literal, less paraphrastic, than the *Evolution and Ethics* translation and is copiously interlaced with commentaries.

It must further be noted that while Yen Fu regards Adam Smith as the source of economic wisdom, he is by no means unconscious of all that has happened in economics since Smith. The evolutionary-historic sense which he derives from Spencer has not deserted him. In his translator's introduction, he mentions Jevons and Marshall, in particular, as economists who had developed economics into a deductive science, while Smith, in his view, had derived most of his views inductively. This, of course, is entirely in keeping with Mill's views on the natural evolution of the sciences. "Economics has made great advances in the last two hundred years. If one wished to have a total picture of economic science in addition to Smith's *Wealth of Nations* one would have to translate Mill, Walker, and Marshall."[4] He has chosen Smith's work because it is the fountainhead rather than the last word. Throughout his many commentaries he points to the vast economic changes which have occurred since Smith, some of which have rendered certain views of the master obsolete. While he is on the whole convinced that most of these changes have simply confirmed Smith's perspicacity, occasionally he points to revisions and improvements introduced by later economists such as Ricardo, Mill, and Rogers. At one point he presents a long and difficult exposition of Ricardo's theory of rent,[5] and elsewhere he takes some issue with the labour theory of value.[6] The translation, together with the commentaries, provides a good elementary course in the tenets of classical economics in its whole development, at least through Marshall.

Throughout the book we remain constantly aware of the familiar preoccupation with the wealth and power of the state. How, then, is this concern reconciled with Smith's economic individualism? Is not Smith known in the textbooks as the deadly enemy of mercantilism, and is not economic growth for state power almost the heart of mercantilism? Eli Heckscher in his classical work on mercantilism defines mercantilism at one point as that system which "would have had all economic activity subservient to the state's interest in power,"[7] and he also says that "mercantilism as a system of power was thus primarily a system for forcing economic policy into the service of power as an end in itself."[8] Here we have a definition of the fundamental nature of mercantilism which draws it very close to Yen Fu's own preoccupation with wealth and power. How can Smith be used for mercantilist purposes?

First of all, we must note that Adam Smith, like the utilitarians in general, is no Max Stirner. He does not pit the Ego in irreconcilable conflict against society and the universe. To him the complement of the enlightened self-interest of the individual is the general interest of the community. Like Bentham, he is ultimately concerned with the greatest good of the greatest number. The whole notion of the "invisible hand" is that of a pre-established harmony between the enlightened self-interest of individuals and the interests of society as a whole. He constantly uses terms such as "the general interest" or "public happiness,"[9] or simply the word "society" itself (as in the statement that "the study of his own [the individual's] advantage naturally, or rather necessarily, leads him to prefer that employment which is most advantageous to society")[10] to designate the ultimate beneficiary of all economic activity.

Of course, the word "society," is to be understood in Smith (with an extremely important reservation which we shall note below) as designating the sum total of individuals who compose a society. In this sense the ultimate beneficiaries are individuals. On the other hand, when he refers to "a society" he generally refers to the nation-state societies with which he is most familiar, so that the words "society," "nation," and "country" are interchangeable, as is clearly indicated by the title of the whole work, *An Inquiry into the Nature and Causes of the Wealth of Nations*, or when he entitles one of his chapters, "How the Commerce of the Towns Contributed to the Improvement of the Country." We can thus immediately see how all language in Smith which refers to the "general interest" or "the nation" or "society" easily becomes transmuted in Yen Fu's translation into language which refers to the state interest.

Again, one need not assume that Yen Fu is completely uninterested in the greatest happiness of the greatest number as an ultimate goal, but words such as *ch'ün* (the "social organism") and *kuo* ("nation-state") are already heavily freighted with the connotation of state power as an end in itself. If to Smith the "wealth of nations" refers in the first instance to the wealth of the sum total of individuals who compose the nation-society, to Yen Fu the wealth of the *kuo* refers in the first instance to the wealth and hence to the power of the nation-state as a collective entity struggling for existence in a world of similar collective entities. We thus emerge from the study of Yen Fu's *Wealth of Nations* with one overriding conclusion—that the system of economic liberalism developed in the book of Smith and demonstrated in the living example of Victorian England is a system admirably designed to achieve the wealth and power of the state. Here again we come back to the theme we have met before—that the wealth and power of the state can only be achieved by a release of energies and capacities (in this case specifically economic) of the individual.

Again and again in his commentaries Yen Fu takes up this theme. Thus in the very last chapter of *The Wealth of Nations*—"Of Public Debts"—we come across a passage in which Smith deplores the practice of increasing the national debt by funding. He points out that this kind of large-scale borrowing from subjects and mortgaging of revenues is possible only in a state of society where commerce and manufacture have achieved a high state of development. He also points out that war has, on the whole, been the main cause of large-scale fundings of this type. However, while he regards "perpetual funding" as a "ruinous expedient,"[11] he concedes that Great Britain has so far not suffered from "the weakness and desolation" which the practice of funding has caused in other states. In England "the frugality and good conduct of individuals seem to have been able, by saving and accumulation, to repair all the breaches which the waste and extravagance of government has made in the general capital of the society. At the conclusion of the late war, the most expensive that Great Britain ever waged, her agriculture was as flourishing, her manufactures as numerous as they had ever been before. Great Britain seems capable of supporting a burden which half a century ago nobody believed her capable of supporting."[12] In spite of this admission, however, the whole tenor of Smith's discussion is negative. In the end, excessive funding must ruin even England.

Yen Fu, however, is profoundly struck by one fact above all else—the fact that Great Britain has been able to maintain and increase its wealth even while increasing its national debt. What perspicacity and what a depth of patriotism are revealed in Smith's explanation of this paradox! "Even though the [national] debt of England is heavy, the state continues to gain in wealth and power! . . . There is always a reason for things . . . The policies which account for

England's growth in wealth and power since Smith are innumerable . . . The growth of scientific knowledge, the effectiveness of her steam and electric powered engines, the enlightenment and knowledge of her sovereign and ministers and the daily innovations which are introduced by them. However, the most relevant factor was the adoption of the principles advocated in this book . . . They have eliminated the fetters of mercantilism (*hu shang*) and have adopted a policy of free unrestricted commerce." In Great Britain, where everything has been done to encourage and release the economic energies of the people, the state has been able to tap this inexhaustible source of wealth for its own purposes. If this was true in Smith's own day when mercantilism (in the narrower sense of "protecting commerce') prevailed, how much more has this been the case since Smith's death, when his principles have been applied and the fetters on economic activity which still existed in his day have been eliminated!

What a contrast with China! Ever since the Sino-Japanese war and the Boxer Rebellion, China has become more and more indebted to foreign powers. It cannot tap the economic energies of its own people, which remain woefully undeveloped and fettered, and the increase in national debt can lead only to an ever greater and more abysmal poverty. Throughout Chinese history, as a matter of fact, any increase in national debt or in taxation could result only in an abstraction from the wealth of the society as a whole, since the economy was static both in conception and in fact. Where the people are oriented toward production, the state can assume more and more burdens without fear of impoverishment.[13]

So impressed is Yen Fu with this insight that it is brought up again and again and is even mentioned in his short introductory biography of Adam Smith, where he states, "The English have not been free of national debt for a day. Although their financial burdens are heavy, their treasure is abundant. Is not the fact that instead of growing poor and weak they have become wealthy and powerful due to the fact that they have broken the locks, opened wide the doors, and allowed the people to exercise their freedom?"[14] When Smith soberly warns, "Let us not, however, upon this account rashly conclude that she [Great Britain] is capable of supporting any burden nor even be too confident that she could support without great distress a burden a little greater than what has already been laid upon her,"[15] and when he further advises that England "accommodate her future views and designs to the real mediocrity of her circumstances,"[16] Yen Fu is able to point out from his vantage ground in time that Great Britain has not followed Smith's advice and that its "views and designs" have expanded enormously since Smith's day. It is precisely because Great Britain has realized Smith's principles that it has been able to ignore his advice and increase its national debt astronomically. Smith simply failed to realize the nuclear potentialities, as it were, of the economic liberation which he was proposing.

When Smith points out the necessity of opulence, given the expense of modern (eighteenth-century) military technology,[7] Yen Fu is again able to refer to the undreamt-of expansion of the state's burdens in this area. "Comparing the military expenses of European states in Smith's day to those of our own, they seem like child's play . . . As a result of the extension of popular rights in Europe ever since the Ch'ien-lung, Chia-ching period [the end of the eighteenth and beginning of the nineteenth century] and of the spectacular advance of various industries, it is no exaggeration to say that more has been accomplished in a hundred years than in the previous millennium. As the states have become daily richer, their defences have become ever more formidable . . . The power or weakness of a state depends on various sources of wealth, and if one wishes to enrich the state, one must expand the people's knowledge and improve its economic system (lit., "system of finances')."[18] The lesson for China is clear. If it is ever to overcome its debility, the Chinese state must enormously increase its financial burdens, and this can only be done, as Smith has shown, by orienting the people toward economic activities and releasing their economic energies.

Here again, to the extent that Adam Smith's aims are purely economic, to the extent that his ultimate goal is the welfare of individuals, Yen Fu's argument that economic freedom is to be justified precisely because it makes possible an enlargement of the state's "designs" might appear to be a monstrous and unexpected inversion of Smith's own doctrine.

The fact is, however, that Smith is more complex than the school which claims him as a father. While much of his polemic is directed against mercantilism in the narrow sense of that term, what he rejects fundamentally is the mercantilists' conception of means. He does not totally reject their end—the enhancement of the wealth and power of the state. Living in the world of monarchic eighteenth-century states, he accepts as a matter of course this world of contending states and the considerations of *Staatsräson* so charactistic of the age. He is not, to be sure, a nineteenth-century nationalist, but neither is he a doctrinaire nineteenth-century cosmopolitan like some of his own orthodox followers (or Herbert Spencer), who believe that the nation-state is about to be dissolved by the inexorable march of free trade and a liberal economy. He certainly has no notion that the "militant stage" of human history is about to disappear. Hence, alongside his general social aims he also accepts the aims of the state qua state as a legitimate concern. In his very definition of political economy he asserts that it has two distinct objects. "It proposes to enrich both the people and the sovereign."[19] In defining the duties of the sovereign he states, "The first duty of the sovereign—that of protecting society from the violence and invasion of other independent societies—can be performed only by military force."[20] Elsewhere in his defense of the Navigation Act he goes so far as to maintain that "defense is of much more importance than opulence,"[21] and in the chapter on the "Employment of Capitals" he states that "the great object of political economy is to increase the riches and power of that country"[22]—language which translates itself without the slightest distortion into the language of Yen Fu's concerns.

Thus we find that, if Yen Fu distorts, the distortion is mainly one of emphasis. In the total context of the *Wealth of Nations* the concern with "public happiness" in terms of the economic welfare of the sum total of individuals certainly overshadows the concern with state-power goals. In Yen Fu's commentaries the concern with welfare (*min sheng*, "people's livelihood') is by no means absent, but it is overshadowed by the more immediate concern with state power. To both Smith and Yen Fu, liberal economic principles admirably serve both ends. However, while Yen Fu finds little difficulty in relating Smith's economic principles to his own "mercantilist" purposes, his real problem lies elsewhere. He must confront head-on the contradiction between the exaltation of enlightened self-interest and the Confucian detestation of material gain as a conscious object of pursuit. From the Confucian point of view, Adam Smith's economics are infinitely more subversive than Herbert Spencer's metaphysics.

There is, to be sure, a kind of *laissez faire* in the orthodox line of Confucian political economic theory. The state is constantly admonished not to engage in activities which are properly those of merchants, and a good state, as we have seen, is one which refrains from interfering overmuch with the livelihood of the people.[23] It is a *laissez faire*, however, which has nothing whatsoever to do with any exaltation of economic pursuits. There is an extremely modest conception of what merchants are to be "allowed to do" and the whole anti-economic morality is simply assumed.

As we have seen, by the nineties a considerable number of the literati had tacitly revised their Confucian views on the pursuit of wealth by the state as a collective entity. Li Hung-chang, Chang Chih-tung, and others had certainly embraced the aims of wealth and power, but the resistance to an acceptance of the morality of enlightened self-interest as applied to individuals was still profound. The prejudice against any revaluation of the merchant and his presumed ethos was still bone-deep and grounded solidly on both the class interest and the deepest convictions of the literati.

It is interesting to note that Yen Fu's friend and mentor, Wu Ju-lun, in his introduction to the translation, also finds the crux of the matter in this area.

"Unless we make every effort to change our mental habit of shunning all talk of interest (*li*), unless we resolutely break our attitude of emphasizing agriculture and suppressing commerce, our wealth will remain undeveloped . . . If interest is taboo (*hui*) there can be no science of economics."[24]

Yen Fu does not shrink from confronting the issue, but, as we have already noted elsewhere, he does attempt to mitigate it. Adam Smith himself, like Herbert Spencer, comes to his aid. Yen Fu is well aware of the fact that the same Adam Smith who had written *The Wealth of Nations* had also written *The Theory of Moral Sentiments*.[25] Smith by no means reduces the whole man to the model of economic man. Here we see the advantage enjoyed by Yen Fu in knowing Smith, Spencer, and his other heroes from the source rather than from textbook simplifications. In areas other than the economic, Smith differs from the philosophers of his time who trace the origins of social morality to self-interest alone. In his *Theory of Moral Sentiments*, he claims that "morality arises out of the feeling of sympathy in the human heart.'

It is interesting to note that Spencer and Huxley had both been influenced by Smith's moral theory; Huxley specifically refers to it in *Evolution and Ethics*.[26] Yen Fu himself is inclined to accept Spencer's view of egoism as the ultimate source of social solidarity and sympathy as derivative, but from all these sources (as well as John Stuart Mill) Yen Fu is able to derive the view that both self-interest and sympathy or "reciprocity" (*shu*) may subsist side by side. Unlike the puristic Bentham, who had fanatically insisted on explaining everything in terms of the single principle of self-interest, Smith had not taught that righteousness (*i*) must completely give way to self-interest (*li*) but that both are, in some sense, complementary. "There may be those who maintain that Smith's book is concerned purely with utility (*kung-li*). They say that according to the economists human morality is a matter of calculating gains and losses and that if mortality is to be nothing more than a matter of self-interest and the pursuit of profit, the principles of heaven will be lost. Such is their harsh judgment! What they do not understand is that science concerns itself with questions of truth and falsehood and not with whether its findings coincide with benevolence and righteousness. What [the economists] discuss is economics. They decidedly do not discuss that which lies outside the realm of economics. But they do not assert that human morality is nothing but a matter of economics. If one were to condemn them, how would this be different from reading books on military strategy and censuring them for dealing with matters of violence (lit., 'subjecting other countries'), or from reading treatises on acupuncture and moxibustion and blaming them for advocating the infliction of pain!"[27]

The argument here is most shrewd. Military technology and medicine had long been a respectable part of the Chinese canon of studies in spite of the pacifistic bent of Confucianism. The tradition had reconciled itself to the role of violence in societies as they actually are. Many scholars had busied themselves with *Sun-tzu* and other treatises on war. It had long been recognized that the achievement of the aims of military defense and medicine required a scientific techne—certain rational methods, in the Weberian sense, which enjoyed a degree of independence from the general moral code. Economics is an autonomous sphere in the same sense, and the achievement of economic ends depends on the use of rational economic means. The means can only be discovered "scientifically." With the growing acceptance of the aims of wealth and power, the prestige of the practitioner of violence—the new soldier—was rapidly rising, even among conservative literati. How could the literati object to a similar revaluation of the techne for creating wealth and of the ethos which necessarily accompanies that techne? One cannot blame the entrepreneur for thinking in terms of material gain any more than one can blame the soldier for thinking in terms of violence. On the contrary, within his area of competence it is his duty to think in terms of gain.[28]

Elsewhere Yen Fu points out that, in passing from a morality of negation to a morality which affirms the positive role of enlightened self-interest, China will by no means be unique. The true cleavage here is not so much between China and the West as between the modern world and the past. "The cleavage between "righteousness" and "interest" (*i li*) has been most detrimental to the advance of civilization. Mencius states, "All one needs is righteousness and humanity. Why speak of interest?" Tung Chung-shu asserts, "Act righteously and do not scheme to advance your interests. Make manifest the Way and do not calculate advantage." The ancient teachings of both East and West all draw a sharp line between righteousness and interest. The intention was most sublime, but the effect in terms of bringing men to the Way has been negligible in all cases."[29] Yen Fu is aware of the fact that the morality of enlightened self-interest has won only a recent victory in the West, and he is able to point to this fact to assuage the cultural pride of his fellow literati. In transvaluating its own values China will simply be following a universal path of human evolution which has begun in the West. China has not been alone in regarding self-interest as demonic and in basing its morality on a negation of men's constructive energies.

Between enlightened interest and "righteousness" there is no cleavage. "Ever since the emergence of the theory of evolution it has become as clear as a burning flame that without righteousness there can be no utility and without the Way no profit, and it was the economists who anticipated this insight. Smith always maintained that, while the world is full of shallow men and ignorant men, there are no genuine 'mean men' (*hsiao jen*). The 'mean man' presumably sees only his own interest. However, if we assume that he discerns his long-term, real interests, how does he differ in his behavior from the virtuous man? . . . The process of evolution does not treat the self-interest of the short-sighted and ignorant as true self-interest and does not treat narrowly abnegating self-righteousness or extravagant and excessive 'righteousness' as true 'righteousness.'"[30] Here we almost have a description of Weber's "Protestant Ethic." Not only do Adam Smith and Herbert Spencer allow for a self-restraining morality in realms other than the economic; they advocate a conception of self-interest which demands the presence of sober virtues. A self-interest which is channeled into constructive entrepreneurial endeavours and leads to wealth and power is divided by a yawning abyss from the degraded selfishness of the corrupt officialdom in China, which is simply a blind consumer hedonism feeding on the substance of society and giving nothing in return. In the West, man's self-regarding and other-regarding tendencies are harnessed to constructive national goals. In China both the negative "righteousness" and the hedonist selfishness of the literati lead to the society's growing debility.

There is, of course, an assumption throughout that the British path of economic growth is the only path and that Great Britain has achieved its wealth by adhering to the principles of Adam Smith. There is the further assumption that economic liberalism, political liberalism, the rule of law, and the march to democracy are all parts of one inseparable organic whole. At the end of the nineteenth century Yen Fu can as yet discern little that disturbs this image, although the somewhat divergent economic models of Imperial Germany, Tsarist Russia, and Meiji Japan are already on the scene. He does mention Imperial Germany at one point and even remarks on the spectacular advance of Germany during the last fifty years. The context is provided by Smith's discussion on the state's role in creating "institutions for the Education of the Youth." "There is no country in the modern world which has paid more attention to the education of its people than Germany, and the results can be seen. In times of peace the results are visible in industry, commerce, and agriculture. In times of war the results can be seen in their military arts . . . Thus Germany has within the space of fifty years been able to pass from weakness to power, from poverty to wealth."[31] All of this praise is, of course, directed to public education—an issue on which Adam Smith himself takes a most positive view, uninfluenced by Herbert Spencer's social Darwinist prejudices. To the extent that Germany has diverged from the British path of economic development, however, Yen Fu does not seem to be acutely aware of this divergence.

Meiji Japan's economy[32] is not mentioned; if he had turned his attention in that direction, he would have found most of the economic thinkers and industrialists of Meiji Japan, such as Taguchi and others, accepting the very assumptions which underlie his own image—the assumptions that Great Britain was the model par excellence of wealth and power, and the assumption that this wealth and power had been achieved by adhering to the principles of economic liberalism. As for Russia, Yen Fu by no means shares Smith's high opinion of Peter the Great's reforms, which "almost all resolve themselves into the establishment of a well-regulated standing army."[33] The fact that Russia had simply adopted a standing army (truly free states, in Yen Fu's view, can rely on the infinitely more effective weapon of a loyal conscript army), without adopting any of the political, economic, or legal roots from which national strength draws sustenance, means that Russia was a hollow giant: "Outwardly it appears strong, but one cannot expect it to remain stable for long. It has used Peter's system to rise and as a result of Peter's system it will fall."[34] In the same passage he notes that Germany and Austria still leave much to be desired in the realm of people's rights, but they have, at least, a mixed constitution. Nothing that he observes in the world of his time is sufficient to shake his faith in Smith's economic principles.

Yen Fu's translation of the *Wealth of Nations* was widely read, according to all accounts. In retrospect, however, it would not appear that Yen Fu's effort to spread the gospel of economic individualism as an operating value was notably successful in twentieth-century China. There was, to be sure, at the turn of the century a new orientation on the part of gentry elements to such matters as railroad investments. Yet whatever may have been the actual motives of such new interests, they were probably seldom justified in terms of enlightened self-interest.[35]

However, beneath the specific doctrines of economic liberalism, there is in Adam Smith a much broader message. Smith is not only the father of the classical school, he is the great theorist of economic orientation in general. He was by no means the originator of this orientation, but he certainly was its earliest great systematizer. Dugald Stuart in a memoir[36] on the works of Adam Smith points to the "striking contrast between the spirit of ancient and modern policy in respect to the *Wealth of Nations*. The great object of the former was to counteract the love of money and a taste for luxury by positive institutions and to maintain in the great body of the people habits of frugality and a severity of manners. The decline of states is uniformly ascribed by the philosophers and historians both of Greece and Rome to the influence of riches on national character . . . How opposite to this is the doctrine of modern politicians! Far from considering poverty as an advantage to a state their aim is to open new

13

sources of national opulence and to animate the activity of all classes of the people by a taste for the comforts and the accommodations of life."[37] He then goes on to point out that Smith was a great theoretician of this transvaluation of values: "The great and leading object of his speculation is to illustrate the provisions made by nature in the principles of the human mind and in the circumstances of man's external situation for a gradual and progressive augmentation in the means of national wealth."[38] In other words, Smith is one of the great initiators of the orientation to what is now called economic development. It is thus entirely conceivable that the main message which Yen Fu's readers derived from this work was not so much the specific message of economic individualism as the gospel of economic development in general. From Smith and from Yen Fu's commentaries on Smith one could gain a vivid comprehension of the "contrast between ancient and modern policy" mentioned by Dugald Stuart. Smith had demonstrated that a purposeful systematic application of human energies to the increase of national wealth could yield undreamt-of results whatever the ends to which this wealth was applied. With the emergence in the twentieth century of anti-capitalistic schools of economic development, the gospel of economic individualism no longer seemed to be the inevitable means to the achievement of these ends.

NOTES

1. "Yüan-ch'iang," pp. 55–56.
2. "Self-restraint, the essence of the ethical process, which is no less an essential condition of the existence of the polity, may by excess become ruinous to it" (*Evolution and Ethics*, p. 31).
3. *T'ien-yen lun*, Pt. I, p. 34.
4. "Ssu-shih chi-hsüeh li-yen" (An Introduction to Smith's economics), *Yen Chi-tao shih-wen ch'ao*, IV, 9.
5. Yen Fu, *Yüan-fu* (The wealth of nations), *Yen i ming-chu ts'ung'k'an*, Vol. 2, "I-shih li-yen" (Translator's introduction), p. 2.
6. *Yüan-Fu*, p. 26.
7. Eli Heckscher, *Mercantilism* (London, 1935), II, 15.
8. *Ibid.*, 17.
9. Smith, *Wealth of Nations*, p. 329.
10. *Ibid.*, p. 352.
11. *Ibid.*, p. 737.
12. *Ibid.*, p. 744.
13. See *Yüan-fu*, p. 959.
14. "Ssu-mi Ya-tan chuan" (Biography of Adam Smith), *Yüan-fu*, p. 2.
15. Smith, *Wealth of Nations*, p. 744.
16. *Ibid.*, p. 760. This is the last sentence in the book.

17. *Ibid.*, p. 560.

18. *Yüan-fu*, p. 707.

19. Smith, *Wealth of Nations*, p. 333.

20. *Ibid.*, p. 546.

21. *Ibid.*, p. 361.

22. *Ibid.*, p. 297. At one point (p. 560) Smith even seems to employ Yen Fu's own line of reasoning: "In modern war the great expense of firearms gives an evident advantage to the nation which can best afford that expense and consequently to an opulent and civilized over a poor and barbarous nation."

23. E.g., see the argument of the Confucian party in Huan K'uan.

24. *Yüan-fu*, Introduction, p. 2.

25. See "Ssu-mi Ya-tan chuan," *Yüan-fu*, pp. 1, 3.

26. Huxley, *Evolution and Ethics*, p. 30.

27. "I-shih li-yen," *Yüan-fu*, p. 6.

28. In the end, however, the traditional morality is more resistant to the re-evaluation of the merchant than to the re-evaluation of the soldier. The warrior ethos is, after all, still hedged about with the aura of self-sacrifice and public service.

29. *Yüan-fu*, p. 91.

30. *Ibid.*

31. *Ibid.*, p. 790.

32. There is, however, a reference to Japan's success in procuring the abolition of legal extraterritoriality as a result of its legal reforms (*Yüan-fu*, p. 721).

33. Smith, *Wealth of Nations*, p. 558.

34. *Yüan-fu*, p. 703.

35. Smith, *Wealth of Nations*, p. 7.

36. See the abridgment of Dugald Stuart's "Life and Work of Adam Smith," in *ibid.*, p. 7.

37. *Ibid.*

38. *Ibid.*, p. 8.

1.2. Cheng-chung Lai, 1989

Adam Smith and Yen Fu: Western Economics in Chinese Perspective

1. Introduction

The purpose of this paper is two-fold. First, we shall examine how *The Wealth of Nations* (hereafter *WN*) was introduced into China at the turn of this century (1902). The translation was not easy because the Chinese language at that time had insufficient vocabulary to introduce this unknown discipline from a completely different cultural system.[1] Second, Yen Fu (1853–1921), the translator of *WN*, saw the text as a prescription for China's "Wealth and Power". The central question is: was *WN*, a book which advocates laissez-faire and free trade, helpful for China's peripheral economic situation?

The paper is organized as follows. The background and career of Yen Fu is briefly described in Section 2. Section 3 compares the contents of *WN* in its Chinese and English versions; explains why and how Yen Fu translated *WN* with 310 translators' notes and how these notes can be classified and interpreted. A question is posed in Section 4: were Chinese readers and policy makers influenced by Smith's doctrines through Yen Fu? Apparently not. The concluding remarks are contained in Section 5.

2. Life and Times of Yen Fu

Yen Fu (1853–1921) was born in the Province of Fukien, in South-eastern China, in a modest family. His father died when he was fourteen, and consequently his family could not afford his study in a traditional private school. By that time the Chinese government was suffering so much from the invasion of Western countries that they realized that a direct and efficient way to "Wealth and Power" was to import Western technology immediately.[2] One of the measures taken was the founding of a Navy School in 1886 in Fukien. Yen Fu passed the exams as the first top student. He was awarded full tuition and a scholarship.

As a result he moved from a traditional local education to Western poly-technic training. After some unexpected political disorders, he was finally sent by the government to study in England, from March 1877 to August 1879. During his study in Portsmouth and then in the Royal Naval College, his attention was also focused on social, economic and political aspects of England. In short, he was an alert foreign student in many respects.

After returning to China in 1879, he served as a professor in the Navy School in Fukien, from which he had graduated three years previously. The next year he was promoted to be Dean of the Naval School near Peking/Beijin, the capital. In 1890 he became the president of that School until 1900 when the school was dissolved as a result of the Boxer Rebellion. So ended his period as a teacher.

During this period, he tried to pass the State Functionary Exams four times, but failed each time (1885, 1888, 1889, 1893). In a depressed state he started to translate Western works in the hope that he could thereby awaken his ignorant compatriots. His period as a translator had begun, but to avoid unnecessary complication for Western readers, we shall omit his entanglement in politics and go directly to his translation of Western works in general, and then to Adam Smith's *WN* in particular.

Yen Fu translated ten works between 1894 and 1914.[3] Among the ten translations, there is no doubt that T. H. Huxley's *Evolution and Ethics* was the most influential. The reason is straightforward: the Chinese public was deeply depressed by the foreign invasions since the Opium wars of the 1840s. The ideas of social Darwinism which were revealed in Huxley's book (such as "Survival of the fittest", and "Natural selection") had a strong impact on Chinese people, who were eager to take any necessary counter-action against foreign dominance. The influence of this book and the reputation of Yen Fu was thereafter established.

3. Interpretation Through Translation

We shall first compare Smith's *WN* with Yen Fu's translation, to see how Yen Fu condensed and added materials to the Chinese version.[4] Table 1 compares Adam Smith's *WN* and Yen Fu's translation. In my pocket-sized edition, a page in Chinese contains approximately 60% of the contents of the page in the

Table 1. A comparison of *The Wealth of Nations* and Yen Fu's translation

		Contents	Original pages	Yen Fu's pages	No. of translator's notes
Book I		Factor productivities and factor income distribution	258	276	116
	Chapter	1–3 Division of labour	21	18	4
		4 Origin and use of money	8	5	3
		5–7 Prices of commodities, etc.	34	41	17
		8 Wages of labour	23	40	16
		9 Profit of stock	12	18	8
		10 Wages of profits in labour and stock	45	54	24
		11 Rent of land	115	110	44
Book II		The nature, accumulation, employment of stock	98	98	39
	Chapter	1 Division of stock	8	9	3
		2 Money as instrument of circulation	46	42	12
		3 Accumulation of capital	20	22	11
		4 Stock lent at interest	9	9	3
		5 Different employment of capitals	15	16	10
Book III		Different progress of opulence in different nations	42	34	12
	Chapter	1 Nature and progress of opulence	6	5	1
		2 Discourgement of agriculture in Europe	12	14	5
		3 Rise and progress of cities and towns	11	10	2
		4 Contributions of towns commerce to the country	13	16	4
Book IV		System of political economy	256	267	64
	Chapter	1 Mercantile system	23	27	6
		2–6 Free trade	103	100	31
		7 Colonies	84	95	20
		8 Conclusions of the mercantile system	20	20	3
		9 Physiocratic system	26	25	3
Book V		Revenue of the nation	248	293	79
	Chapter	1 National expenditure	116	149	42
		2 National revenue	90	97	30
		3 Public debts	42	47	7

Note: One page of Yen Fu's translation corresponds approximately to the half page of Smith's original version

Source: The Cannan edition of *The Wealth of Nations* (1902), Modern Library version; and from Yen Fu's 1902 translation, Taipei: The Commercial Press, 3 volumes.

English version. In addition, the 310 translator's notes account for about 14% of the total space in the Chinese version. This means that Yen Fu translated about 46% of *WN*. If one says that Yen Fu's elegant classical style used less words than modern Chinese, it is still fair to say that he translated only about 50–60% of the whole material.

He declared explicitly in his translator's preface that he had translated every chapter of the whole book, except two passages.[5] He says that these two subjects are irrelevant to Chinese concerns. He did translate every chapter and every section, but very often rewrote the text in a condensed form. The version on which he based his translation was the third version of *WN* (1784) commented and annotated by Professor Thorold Rogers (1823–1900). He frequently mentioned Roger's opinion in his translator's notes (see Table 2).

With this background in mind, we can then examine the following questions. 1. Why did Yen Fu choose an old economics book (1776) to translate? 2. What kinds of error did Yen Fu commit in his translation? 3. How can his 310 translator's notes be classified and explained?

3.1. Why Yen Fu Translated *The Wealth of Nations*

If Yen Fu's primary concern was the wealth and power of China, why did he translate a book of 1776 rather than a more recent one? In his translator's preface, Yen Fu answered this question in four points. First, one can learn something new from the old master's book. Second, Adam Smith's criticism of British economic policies seemed relevant for China. Third, past European systems could serve as a reference for reform in China, Four, Smith's book is clearly written and supported with historical facts. The four reasons are rather superficial. The question can be restated as follows. How could Yen Fu expect a book like *WN*, which advocates "minimum government" and "laissez-faire" to be useful in a country like China in which the public sector was inefficient and the private sector in disorder at the turn of the century?

Schwartz (1964: 114–117) tried to explain this in different ways, at both philosophical and practical levels. Philosophically, he explained that Smith's individual freedom does not necessarily conflict with the interests of the state. At a practical level, Schwartz provided a good reason: *WN* was written in an epoch in which Great Britian dominated the world, so the "Wealth and Power" of Britain was a living example for China to imitate.

Our explanations are as follows. When Yen Fu was translating *WN* (1897), western economics was entering the neoclassical phase. In his translator's preface, Yen Fu mentioned the names of Stanley Jevons, Alfred Marshall, etc., and he was also informed that their method of analysis was to use calculus as a new tool with induction and deduction as methods of reasoning. In other words, western economics at the end of the last century was concerned with what is now termed microeconomics: "consumer's surplus", "marginal utility analysis", "theory of the firm". All these were not directly useful for China's wealth and power. What was useful for China was the political economy analysed by the Classical economists such as Adam Smith and Thomas Malthus, in other words: macroeconomic policy analysis. How can one expect the mathematical analysis contained in Walras' general equilibrium system, which represents neoclassical economics, to help China? With China's situation in mind, Yen Fu had absolutely no reason to translate any economic work of the neoclassical school. What was more important, we suppose, was the title of Adam Smith's book, which attracted Yen Fu passionately: The Wealth of Nations!

Yen Fu faced another problem: The dominant mentality that prevailed among Chinese intellectuals was pro-agricultural and anti-commercial. How could he convince the readers that Smith's ideas were useful for China? The traditional mentality looked down on affairs related to commerce: the long-run immobility of the agricultural economy made them deep-rooted physiocrats. One of Smith's main concerns in *WN* was "Anti-mercantilism", so if the Chinese readers looked only at his term, without knowing the motives of Smith's doctrines, then Smith's anti-mercantilism corresponded perfectly with the traditional Chinese mentality. However, since one of Yen Fu's purposes was to attack this mentality, how could he solve this paradox?

In a preface to the Chinese version of *WN*, Yen Fu's teacher Wu Julun strongly criticized Chinese intellectuals, saying that they "always avoid talking about profits and interests, they are also used to being physiocrats and despising commerce". He then painfully explained the social reason why the study of economics was not developed in China, and blamed the mandarins for doing nothing when economic crises occurred: "When the dangerous situation appeared, they could not find useful solutions, but faced the problem helplessly". Then he entered the defence of Smith's book by saying: "The book of Adam Smith is a book on interests and profits. He criticized the commercial activities of the epoch, but this does not imply that the translation of this book is to support our anti-commerce tradition. The readers should have this point in mind".

Naturally, this kind of argument could not convince the traditional intellectuals. Yen Fu's defence of *WN* is much clearer and more convincing in the following ways. He explained that the reason for Smith's anti-mercantilism was that the international commercial activities of England were corrupted.[6] Like his teacher, he hoped that Chinese readers would not use Smith's anti-mercantilism as a support for the traditional Chinese anti-commerce mentality. In short, Yen Fu and his teacher Wu Julun tried to explain that Smith's anti-mercantilism should not prevent China from learning the method of "Wealth and Power" from that book. We doubt if the readers were convinced. On the contrary, as will be seen in Section 4, some important intellectuals disagreed with Yen Fu.

Yen Fu provided another argument to convince people to accept Smith's book: at the turn of this century, the whole of China was impressed by Western technology and opened its arms to welcome everything that was "scientific"; Yen Fu took advantage of this attitude by presenting Smith's book as a "scientific analysis". We have no information to determine if these arguments convinced people.

3.2. Misunderstanding and Distortion

In his translator's preface to J. S. Mill's *On Liberty* in 1903, Yen Fu claimed that: "Readers find my translations hard to follow. They do not realize that the original versions are much more difficult than my translations.The difficulty lies in the logic and argument, and has nothing to do with the language that I used". This claim reveals at least two things. First, readers generally found his translations difficult to understand. Second, Yen Fu did not (necessarily) grasp the spirit and the inner logic of WN which contained so many diversified subjects. Also, since Yen Fu's formal education was in a polytechnic, one would doubt his qualification for translating works such as WN.

We examine first the terminology which appeared in Yen Fu's version of WN. The three-volume version has 978 pages, and following the last page there are 80 more pages of "Terminology of WN" (about 8% of the total pages) to help the readers understand the text. The 80 pages were added by the publisher afterwards, but they are only of limited help to modern readers. The most important oversight of Yen Fu was that he never put the original names and terminology (in English) in parentheses so that the readers can trace the real meaning or explore more from other references like encyclopaedias and dictionaries. Perhaps he was right in thinking at the turn of the century that most Chinese readers were unable to use Western references.

From the point of view of readers (past and present) his translation of WN is difficult to understand for at least the following reasons. First, it used terminology and names that were unfamiliar to the Chinese reader. For instance, in terms of new terminology, how can the Western concepts of "bank deposit", "free trade", "point of maximum return" be translated into classical Chinese? Yen Fu did it by using several Chinese characters which sound like "bank" in English as the approximate "translation" of "bank", without further explanation. Readers have to guess the meaning from the text. Perhaps some advanced readers can understand this kind of "translation". But how can one understand who F. Quesnay (1694–1774) is, when Yen Fu pronounced this French econo-mist's name in an English way and used three Chinese characters to show this pronunciation, without explaining who he was. There are countless examples like this. Serious readers are obliged to put down the book after every paragraph to think carefully what it means. Usually, modern readers get lost.

One might argue that despite the inexact translation, Adam Smith's main ideas were still successfully conveyed to the Chinese readers. We doubt this. Yen Fu had no formal training in economics and he stayed less than three years in England, so one can doubt his ability to understand the complicated mercantilism debates during the XVII–XVIII centuries. This partly explains why he translated only about 50% of *WN*.

3.3. The 310 Translator's Notes

In translating *WN* Yen Fu added 310 translator's notes, which we have classified into seven categories in Table 2. In terms of the five books of *WN*, Books I, IV and V take up a very large part of his notes (116, 64 and 79 respectively). Taken by categories, most of the notes fall into Categories 2 and 3 (95 and 89 respectively). Yen Fu was very probably not conscious of the distribution of his 310 notes.

Some of his notes can be singled out as independent economic propositions. For instance, on pages 339–340 of his translation, irrelevant to Smith's text, he raises the question of whether China should at that time advocate saving (in order to accumulate investible capital) or advocate consumption (Keynesian type of increasing effective demand), as some of Yen Fu's contemporaries did. Yen Fu used nearly two pages to attack the "consumption school". This debate, though independent of Smith's text, provides an interesting view of different schools of economic thought in China at the turn of the century.

Some of his notes are not classifiable in the seven categories of Table 2. Example: his conception of religion (p. 827). Smith mentioned religion in Chapter 1 of Book V, then in his notes Yen Fu started to compare the religions of China and the West. This is completely irrelevant to the main text. Yen Fu was sometimes arbitrary in writing his notes in order to express his own special ideas. Another example is as follows: "When I read the text, in some places it is so moving that I cannot keep from crying. Alas! how touching Smith's sen-tences are!" What we can say is that in the notes he expressed on many occasions his personal feelings, sentiments, unsystematic and impromptu ideas.

Looking over his 310 notes, one obtains an impression that the method he used to write translator's notes are the following. First, his knowledge of economic theory was limited to the basic "supply and demand" paradigm. Second, with this tool in hand he made some supplements to Smith's text (Categories 2 and 3). He possessed a great deal of general knowledge about

Table 2. Yen Fu's 310 Translator's Notes by Categories

	Book I	Book II	Book III	Book IV	Book V	Total
1. Explain that the situation has changed since *WN* was published (1776)	22	5	1	4	1	33
2. Add new information to supplement the text	34	12	5	25	19	95
3. Comment on Smith's text	33	17	2	24	13	89
4. Compare Chinese ways of thinking with Smith's text	7	0	3	1	5	16
5. Compare Chinese economy with European economy	2	2	1	2	1	8
6. Use European examples to show the weakness of China	14	1	0	6	17	38
7. Present Thorold Rogers' comments on Smith's text	4	2	0	2	23	31
Total	116	39	12	64	79	310

Notes: 1. The contents of the five books of *WN* can be found in Table 1.

2. Some notes are hard to classify, some belonging to two or more categories. In these cases (which were not few), I have chosen one category in which to classify it.

China and Europe, hence Categories 4 and 5. Third, his main concern was the unfavourable situation of China facing penetration by Western countries and Japan. So he used European examples to show the weakness of China (Category 6). In the notes of this Category 6, he frequently added his opinions about state affairs (such as Chinese military training).

Objectively speaking, political economy was not his main concern; *WN* was only one of ten books he translated. He did not possess a sufficient foundation in the science of economics. He used general knowledge of XIXth century neoclassical economics to comment on or to criticize Smith's text. His notes revealed his unsystematic knowledge in this field. If one reads them retrospectively, with the knowledge of post-Keynesian economics in mind, then Yen Fu's notes appeared somewhat elementary. Naturally, it is neither fair nor necessary to blame his translation of *WN*.

4. An Inappropriate Prescription for Wealth and Power

If a main motivation for Yen Fu in translating *WN* was to find a means by which China could attain wealth and power, then this section tries to deal with three directly related questions. 1. Were Smith's ideas as revealed in *WN*, an appropriate prescription to cure China's unfavourable economic situation? 2. Why did the intellectual and political milieu react passively to Smith's ideas? 3. What were the opinions held by other intellectuals concerning Chinese political economy?

After the Opium war of 1840, the Chinese economy was invaded by Western industrial products and her international payments were in serious deficit. The situation was somewhat similar to that of Germany and Japan in the early XIXth century. What China should have learned from these two living examples was to adopt the (tariff) protection policy in order to develop light industry (termed as "import substitution" in modern development economics). The policy advocated by the German national economy School (such as Friedrich List, 1789–1846) should be a good economic doctrine.

What Yen Fu introduced to the Chinese public was an economic policy of "laissez-faire" and "free trade". It is logically inappropriate to introduce such an economic doctrine from a "core" economy (England) to a peripheral economy (China). It is quite possible that he was not informed about the doctrine of the German national economy School. In addition, England at that time was in the mainstream of intellectual activity, and Yen Fu was familiar with the English language and general situation. It is possible that he simply translated a famous book without investigating the inner operational meaning of *WN*.

In response to the second question, it seems that the intellectuals and political milieu did not react warmly to his translation of *WN*. Socially speaking, for those "new" intellectuals, Yen Fu's text was too hard to understand, and the contents of *WN* were just too remote for them; those traditional and conservative intellectuals simply disliked and rejected books concerning "interests and profits", such as *WN*. Politically speaking, the mandarins of the Imperial Court were more realistic than Yen Fu. They had already taken some important measures such as establishing steel factories, shipping companies, industrial manufactories etc. in order to compete with foreign firms and imported products.[7] Restricted by an old inert imperial administrative system and the inability of mandarins to be effective entrepreneurs, the actions unfortunately failed. The ideas from *WN* were not directly useful for them.

The third question is: what other opinions were held by intellectuals regarding Chinese economic policy? It is sufficient to cite the case of an important intellectual, Liang Ch'i-ch'ao (1873–1929), who wrote: "The ideas of Adam Smith were a good prescription for Europe at that time, but are by no means good for modern China, . . . mercantilism hindered the economic growth of Europe after the XVIth century, but if we transplant it into China today, then it is the only way to save the Chinese economy. A big country like

China has all necessary industrial materials and abundant labour. Foreign products invaded China simply because they had the advantage of advanced machinery. If we can have Western technology and tariff protection, then we can compete with foreign products. . . . A man requires at least ten years of protection so that he can be brought up as an adult. Similarly, the industry and commerce of a nation also need protection and subsidies".[8] Clearly, Liang is pro-mercantilism, and disagreed with Adam Smith's "free trade" and "laissez-faire". In short, the prescription that Yen Fu introduced from Smith was not well received by the intellectuals and policy makers. Moreover, readers did not obtain a clearer and more systematic knowledge of western economics through Yen Fu's translation.

5. Concluding Remarks

"Adam Smith and Yen Fu" is a multi-dimensional subject. It belongs to the fields of intellectual history, economic history and history of economic thought. In dealing with this complex issue, this paper has presented only two points. 1. That Yen Fu translated *WN*, with his 310 notes in a particular style. 2. The economic doctrines contained in *WN* seem inappropriate for China's peripheral situation.

There are many important related elements that have not been presented, and they require further investigation. For instance, it is not easy for non-Chinese readers to conceive clearly how Yen Fu translated *WN* in elegant classical Chinese and how he distorted it in doing so. This distortion is almost impossible to present in a short paper in European languages. Also, this paper has not treated (1) an overview of the Chinese economy of Yen Fu's time, nor shown (2) how the mandarins and intellectuals thought about economic policies. A book-length work would be required to treat the whole subject.

NOTES

The research grant from National Tsing Hua University (Nov. 1986–Aug. 1987) is gratefully acknowledged. The usual disclaimer applies. An earlier version of this paper has been presented at the 15th conference of the History of Economics Society, June 19–21 1988, University of Toronto, Canada. This English text is condensed from a much longer Chinese language version which will appear in *Chinese Studies*, vol. 7 (2), December 1989, published by the National Central Library, Taiwan. Reprints are available upon request.

1. The first Western economics book translated into Chinese was Henry Fawcett (1863): *Manual of Political Economy*. It was orally explained by a professor of the Institute of Foreign Languages (Tongwenguan), W. A. P. Martin, written in Chinese

by Wang Fengjao, and published in 1880 as *Policy of National Wealth* in three volumes.

2. See Chapter 18 of Hsu (1983) "Late Ch'ing Intellectual, Social, and Economic Changes, with Special Reference to 1895–1911" for an interesting and concise review.

3. See *Yen Fu and His Translations*, edited and published by the Commercial Press, Peking, 1982. Eight papers of different authors are collected with many photos of the books that Yen Fu translated. Much useful information is provided including the works by and on Yen Fu.

4. There are three translations of *WN* in Chinese, fourteen in Japanese and one (to the best of our knowledge) in Korean. The first Chinese version was translated by Yen Fu during 1897–1900 and published in 1902 (now republished in Taiwan and China in different editions). The second and third versions were by Kuo and Wang (1931), and by Chou and Chang (1964). Both were full versions. The story of the Japanese translations is quite complicated. There is a full account by Professor Okochi, as an appendix to the most recent three-volume Japanese translation (see Okochi 1976). According to him, the first Japanese version was published in 1870, in a condensed form.

5. One is immediately after Part III, Chapter XI of Book I: Digression concerning the variations in the value of silver during the course of the last four centuries; and Digression concerning banks of deposit, particularly concerning that of Amsterdam (Chapter III of Book IV).

6. It is quite unlikely that Yen Fu understood European economic history enough to explain to his readers why Smith advocated "laissez-faire" and anti-mercantilism.

7. Chapters of 1 and 18 of *The Cambridge History of China* vol. 11 (Part. 2), 1800–1911 provide good information in this regard.

8. Cited briefly from Hou Chia-chu (1982: 406).

References

The Cambridge History of China, vol. 11 (Part 2), "Late Ch'ing 1800–1911", Cambridge University Press (1980).

Hou, C. C. (1982): *History of Chinese Economic Thought*, Taipei (in Chinese).

Hsu, I. C. Y. (1983): *The Rise of Modern China*, Oxford University Press.

Okochi, Kazuo (1976): "The Translations of the Wealth of Nations in Japan", in Ohgawa *et al.* translated *The Wealth of Nations*, Tokyo, 3 vols.

Smith, Adam (1776): *An Inquiry into the Nature and Causes of the Wealth of Nations*, ed. and noted by E. Cannan (1902).

Schwartz, B. (1964): *In Search of Wealth and Power: Yen Fu and the West*, Harvard University Press.

Yen Fu and His Translations, Papers collected and published by the Commercial Press, Beijin (1982), in Chinese.

1.3. Yen Fu, [1902]

Foreword to the First Chinese Edition
of *The Wealth of Nations*

Translated by Cheng-chung Lai

What is now called "economics" in the West corresponds to what we call *Jixue* ("learning of calculation") in Chinese. Etymologically "economy" comes from the Greek "oikonomia", with the meanings of "management" and "calculation", derived from "the management of the household". It stems from the meaning of thrift in consumption and calculation in the process of production. Its meaning has since expanded into the planning and management of national production and expenditure.

Translated into Japanese, the term "economics" is *Jinji* ("managing the nation and supplying the people"). This broad term is used to indicate the wide range of this discipline. In Chinese we translate it as *Licai* ("management of finance"). Precisely speaking, *Jinji* is too broad, and *Licai* is too narrow, so I use the term *Jixue* to denote economics. What I mean by *Jixue* ("learning of calculation") is not limited to the narrow sense of "calculation"; it refers also to the broad sense of calculation in land production, supply of and demand for food, natural resources, national accounting, etc.; it also refers to national planning, which corresponds well to the original meaning of "economy" in Greek. That is why I consider *WN* to be a book on economics.

Then, why do I use not *Jixue* but *Origins of Wealth* (OW) as the Chinese title for *WN*? Well, the title used by Smith in fact emphasizes the nature and causes of national wealth; it thus seems appropriate that I use *OW* for the Chinese edition. Moreover, the contents and style of *WN* also differ from what is now called "economics" in two ways: first, *WN* is more a practice-oriented book

27

than an economic-theory-oriented book; second, Smith put more emphasis on the correction of the "economic errors" of his time than on the discipline of economics itself. For instance, chapters 2–3 of Book III and chapter 5 of Book V are digressions on practical questions only indirectly related to economics, and we cannot consider these parts as a scientific discourse. As the title of *WN* indicates, the book was intended as an inquiry into the nature of profits and finance, the causes of wealth and poverty, and the sources of national revenue. That is why I maintain that *WN* is a book of *Jixue* ("learning of calculation") rather than a book on scientific (orthodox) economics.

It is flattery to consider Smith the founding father of economics. Discussions on finance and tax are widespread in many books in China and the West and do not originate in Western political economy. In Chinese economic history, one can easily find famous administrators in different dynasties who wrote treatises about market supply and demand, about eminent entrepreneurs, on particular economic events, on the monopoly of iron and salt, and so forth. Although there was no such systematic development of economic discourse as in the West, one cannot deny that there are some insightful observations in the history of Chinese economic activities. In the West, there were economic experts in ancient Greece and Rome. Smith's doctrines were influenced by his teachers and friends, such as Cantillon, Turgot, Hume, Hutchison, Locke, Montesquieu, Petty, and others, whose arguments about political economy we see in this book (*WN*). The main emphasis of this book is on the doctrines of the physiocrats, which are indebted to the French intellectuals. What is particular in Smith is that he was able to pick up the essences of different authors and spell them out in a precise way, side by side with concrete examples. He used a practical style of analysis, and his rhetoric was so skilful that readers of various levels of intelligence can understand it. It is due to this book that people came to acknowledge that political economy can be regarded as an independent discipline. That is why Smith is regarded as the prime economist and the father of this new teaching.

In terms of science, economics is a science of induction. Induction means that one observes the changes, understands the rules of change, then spells out economic laws. Works by people such as Smith, Ricardo, and Mill (father and son) all belong to this category. Recent works by scholars such as Jevons and Marshall gradually shifted to the method of deduction, using tools such as calculus and geometric presentation to infer the logic of economic phenomena. The reasoning of the discipline therefore became much more precise. Over two centuries, this is significant progress in political economy. If readers want to understand economics in a more comprehensive sense, the works by Mill, Walker, and Marshall must also be translated. Only after mastering these works is one safe from ignorance. Although I understand the importance of this task, it is beyond my ability. Our younger generation must have someone fulfil this need.

Since modern economics is much more precise and more deeply analytical, why do I choose an old book by Smith (1776)? First, because we need to know what happened before, and reading history is helpful for understanding our contemporary situation. Second, what blame Smith attributed to the administrators of his time in this book (*WN*) corresponds quite well to the mistakes committed by our economic decision-makers. *WN* is, therefore, a "mirror book" to reflect our errors. Third, as this book was written when Europe and Asia started to have contacts, it contains much information concerning British and French laws and institutions, which can be useful to us. Fourth, Smith's style is easily accessible, for he offers evidence for every principle which he advocates; some other political economy books, while clear in style and full of theoretical reasoning, are elegant but not easy for beginners.

Obvious "truths" are not always easy to understand if the timing is not right; sages and wise men are not always aware of simple realities. For example, nowadays we consider gold (and precious metals) as the wealth of a nation; this was also so in Europe two centuries ago. From Adam Smith on, people became aware that gold is nothing but a commodity. It is a means (source) of investment, a source which all the people can use and share, the monopoly of none. From today's point of view, this is common sense and not hard to understand. However, had we been born at that time, it is not certain that we would have held such a view; we might have been in agreement with the ideas of the time. A living example in China is commercial policy: free domestic trade policy (liberalizing commercial activities) was strongly debated among decision-makers twenty years ago, but now is a matter of national consensus. After a certain concept reaches consensus, it is easy to put it into practice. But before that day comes, there are long nights when incorrect concepts prevail; and during that time one needs unusual insights to unveil the truth. This process is not confined to economic affairs.

When people considered gold as the wealth of a nation, the strategy was to maximize the balance of trade, to export as much as possible and to minimize imports. The tactics used were replete with commercial barriers and even the protection of trade by military force. People did not realize that this is not a key factor for the wealth or poverty of a nation. The whole of Asia is still obsessed with the idea of gold as wealth; it is a valuable thing that Smith unveiled this illusion two centuries ago.

Our current endeavour is to maximize trade surplus, protecting our merchant class, encouraging domestic trade, and discouraging the competition of foreign commodities. England was an outstanding example of these kinds of policy: exports were subsidized, there were rebates for export taxes, there was a Navigation Act to protect trade gains, and so on. All of these were designed to increase British gold-wealth. However, why did England ultimately get no richer and lose its territories in America? It was due to Smith's book that people started to understand that under the name of "protection policy", the real effect was to create barriers to trade. Perhaps some traders benefited at certain times, but in the long run such protective measures were hurting the wealth of the nation. Reactions and protests naturally arose, conflicts were widespread between rulers and merchants. Truth is not generated only by debates, it must also be evident from facts. Copernicus' doctrine is now fully accepted and no one can reject it; his theory is true when we project millions of years backwards, and it will still be true millions of years hence. We should not doubt the principles contained in Smith's book; we will benefit if we follow his principles, and will be damaged if we do not.

Policies on protecting trade through the granting of monopolies in China are not impartial. Moreover, these policies can in fact damage the development of commercial activities. All people concerned with economic affairs are critical of these policies. I think it is fair to criticize the policies; but since they are already in place, caution should be used when trying to replace them with alternative measures. For when people become irritated and emotional, policy-makers and the beneficiaries of these policies must be cautious about unpredictable incidents.

At the time of reform, decision-makers should proceed with particular caution, for people who have invested in business before could lose their assets, and long-established customs cannot be changed radically within a short time. So however bad the old laws are and however good the new deals, administrators must be careful not to enact the new laws in the morning and ask people to obey them in the afternoon. So much unnecessary damage is caused by such lack of co-ordination. That is why reform is difficult and has often been accompanied by bloodshed. That is a tragedy. Policy decisions are usually based on realities, but sometimes they cause unpredictable results. Thought and care must be given to proposing policies.

In his book Smith sometimes expresses excessive criticism of merchants which readers in our time would consider exaggerated. But we should also be aware that merchants in Smith's time were not the kind we see now. Customs revenues were in the hands of certain corporations which used national tariffs as a means of making profits; the high costs of the Seven Years' War were partially financed by the East India Company, and business and politics were evilly interconnected. Wars in America were expensive and were fought mainly for the interests of commercial groups; Congressional representatives were nominated by negotiation; tax rates were set in conspiracy between merchants and decision-makers. This seriously damaged British laws and institutions at home. The various interest groups seldom care about the nation, as Smith so acutely shows in his book.

Naturally, policy-making is based on facts, but the implication behind policies is never impartial. Once time has passed and the environment has changed, one feels that the writer was exaggerating. If a scholar uncritically accepts what he reads, it will do more harm than good. All practical arguments are valid only for a certain time and place; they can be good newspaper articles but should not be taken as scientific truth. What science needs are general rules or laws that are valid for any time and place.

What Smith attacked most in British economic affairs was the East India Company (EIC), which was the most important economic corporation of that time, both in terms of its business volume and in terms of British economic strategy. EIC was built up by merchants during the time when the Mongolian dynasty in China was declining and the conflicts in India were heated. It is amazing that, within a few years, a particular group of (British) people occupied such an immense territory as China. They were more competent than Alexander the Great; even Anthony of Rome could point to no such achievement. Their success was so great that international observers watched their every activity. But in Smith's eyes, EIC was a strange combination: an economic organization which also played a significant role in politics. It did not rule the people nor improve their standard of living; rather, its policies were harmful to the people, and it made unreasonable profits through the monopoly granted to it by the King. This kind of behaviour is no different from national theft, but EIC was under state protection. A sage's insights are not valid if they are only temporary; only when they are long-lived can we see his real wisdom.

Some critics claim that Smith's book defended the profit-making class. They worry that if an economist is preoccupied with profit calculation, then his theory and doctrines will be profit-oriented; and that if the profit-oriented theory prevails, then the whole of society will be endangered. This is a very severe criticism. One has to understand that the object of science is to present what is true and what is not true. One must examine whether the reasoning is logical or not, rather than judge it by one's subjective preference. Moreover, Smith was analysing the methods of calculation and profit-making, not making profits for his own purpose. He exposed all kinds of possibilities so that people could learn from his book to prevent unnecessary pitfalls. The criticism is similar to reading a book on military tactics and holding the author responsible for invasions of other countries and the killing of people.

Smith proposed that the motivation for people to participate in a given group is not always goodwill. Any group must consist of four elements: food, wine, money, and sex. Few people's activities are intended for the good of others—people are self-interested—but there is an invisible hand that co-ordinates these self-interests into public welfare. Civilizations are made from self-interested behaviour. This theory was abhorrent to moralists, which is why Smith regretted his "invisible hand" theory, and claimed that his ideas had changed; he also intended to burn some of his lecture notes.

There are many different editions of *WN*. This translation is based on the edition annotated by Thorold Rogers and published by Oxford University Press (1880 second edition). Rogers himself was also an economist; he provided some valuable data on British wheat prices and his annotations and corrections are especially useful. I have taken some relevant notes and translated them in this Chinese edition; I have also taken notes from other editions and commented on them with my own observations. I hope these can be used for further discussions among my readers.

My translation of this book is different from my translation of T. H. Huxley (1891), *Evolution and Ethics* (Chinese edition 1898). In translating *WN*, I abridged the original text after I fully understood Smith's arguments. I added nothing to the text but some passages are omitted. In Chapter 11 of Book I ("Of the Rent of Land") there are some digressions on the fluctuation of silver prices over a period of four centuries; this passage is full of details, and so I provide only some of its main points. From Book IV Chapter 3 some details on the banks in Amsterdam have been omitted. From Book I London's wheat prices between 1202 and 1829 (completed by Rogers) have been deleted. I have added a chronicle table to compare major events in China and in the West, hoping that it will help readers to understand the historical background.

Economics is an important discipline which influences China's wealth or poverty. From a different perspective, economics also matters to the destiny of the Asian peoples. That is why when I felt that Smith's arguments were related to our current situation, or when his texts stimulated my sentiments, I have written down my comments as translator's notes. Sometimes they contain strong arguments, but I could not stop myself from writing these long and pointed notes.

The mechanisms of "natural selection" and "survival of the fittest" work twenty-four hours a day. The resources in this universe are finite. Those who are intelligent share a major part of these resources; the disfavoured and the weak have to survive with limited means. The affluence and poverty of a nation are determined by the same mechanism. One should not avoid talking about one's own defects; I do hope that Western science can be of help to the destiny of our unfortunate country.

Yen Fu

August 1902

1.4. Wu Rulun, 1902.
Preface to the First Chinese Edition of
⊤³ *The Wealth of Nations*

Translated by Cheng-chung Lai

Yen Fu has just translated an economics book by Adam Smith, with the Chinese title of *The Origins of Wealth*, and asked whether I can provide a preface. This book is widely known in Europe and America, but our country is still not aware of it. Yen Fu's translation is, therefore, indispensable.

Every country needs finances (money), and especially a country in crisis. The management of a country requires finances to facilitate administration. When a country is in danger, its financial situation is also in great deficit, and attempts to ensure the country's survival are often in vain. The question of finances is, therefore, particularly important when a country is in decline.

Traditional mandarins and intellectuals avoid talking about profits, money, and interest. They are also steeped in the doctrine "promote agriculture, oppress commerce"; the channels for creating more national wealth are thus often obstructed. Recently, the demand for finances has increased rapidly, but the wealth of our nation is scattered across the country without management or attention. If we disregard our own riches, then other countries will come to divide and share them as if they were entitled to them.

In fact, our country is now rejecting available national wealth, and not allocating resources to those who can use them appropriately. What is worse is that administrators are still focused on the old and limited channels to finance themselves. These channels are quickly exhausted and the whole nation becomes embarrassed by financial deficits. The situation now is that our country is not in our own hands, and our wealth is in the hands of foreign powers.

Although the danger and the crisis are so obvious, people are still not seeking alternative strategies to alter this unfavourable situation; they merely stand and look at each other without doing anything positive. Some have tried to change things but failed to propose a feasible strategy; some have tried hard with different methods but finally without significant result.

Looking back in Chinese economic history, the good administrators of wealth and finance were in fact rulers who were thrifty. Bad rulers deprived the people of wealth for their own purposes; this is what we called "narrowing down the sources of wealth". Thrift is a good strategy for times of peace, when it can finance the administration and wealth can be stored in warehouses. But this method is useless in times of crisis because there is nothing left to save. What is worse is that our production equipment is damaged, and so cannot be counted as assets. The vicious cycle repeats itself; the crisis grows deeper and deeper.

What can we do to change the situation? We can create wealth from our whole country with good management and not waste our resources in ignorance. This does not require particular talent; others have done it. What bars this possibility is people's mentality and customs. If rulers and administrators are still embarrassed to talk about profits and interest, and still fettered by the doctrine "promote agriculture, oppress commerce", they are unconsciously discarding the usable resources.

Under this constraint, how can we expect them to create wealth with good management? If one is ashamed of profits, then there is no way to develop knowledge of wealth management. If one is inclined to promote agriculture and oppress commerce, then the wealth to be managed will be meagre. The function of commerce is to circulate wealth; agriculture is but a means of creating wealth. Today people are closing the many channels of wealth creation and emphasizing only one source of wealth; they are indeed narrowing down the source. Unfortunately, our agricultural sector is now also in deficit.

In ancient China, there were many ways to create wealth. When wealth was abundant, commercial activities arose to circulate it. This is similar to taming a river (flood control): the water manager distributes water to different plants and fields, to adjust excesses and deficits, so that farmers need not try to meet their needs by themselves but can concentrate on production. Commerce has a similar function.

In ancient China, farmers could purchase fresh fish and meats, commodities circulated freely, and artisanal products were circulated. In this way, the wealth created from nature could be used and circulated, and thus commerce was encouraged. Every distribution route was open to merchants; there was no such absurd doctrine as "promote agriculture, oppress commerce".

This non-pro-agriculture policy created considerable national wealth, which was maintained until the time of Emperor Wu in the Han Dynasty (129–88 BC). Commercial activities declined because the stock of gold (money) was exhausted. China used gold as a means of exchange for two thousand years, but the exploitable gold mines are now exhausted. Our current sources of precious metals are insufficient. Our nation recently tried to reform, but a major problem are the financial deficits. Some people maintain that China is still the wealthiest nation in the world and that the problem of poverty is not our main worry.

Now is an appropriate time for Yen Fu's translation of Adam Smith's book on profits and wealth to appear. Some current opinion is critical of merchants' commercial behaviour and refers to the Chinese "oppress commerce" tradition. I do not agree with this tendency, and that is why I have put forward such a pro-commerce argument. If you are inclined to Western economic policies, then you can find their main arguments in Smith's book; if you are inclined to traditional Chinese wisdom, please remember what I have said in this preface, which I hope will be helpful to the circulation of human power and national wealth.

Wu Rulun

November 1902
(one year before his death)

Translator's comment: A major point in Wu's preface is that the traditional Chinese anti-commerce mentality was a major obstacle to creating national wealth, that this mentality had been absent in ancient China, and that it had appeared only since the Han Dynasty. He suggested that a balanced policy of agricultural and commercial growth was more appropriate. It is clear that he took in the free-trade message of Smith's book, and he argued that this would be a good prescription for China's disadvantaged economic situation. For us, his point seems elementary and shallowly argued, but it should be noted that he had his "enemy readers" in mind when he wrote. Both he and Yen Fu used a very elegant (but difficult) classical style of the Chinese language to argue current economic problems and policy—a useful style to induce those old closed-minded mandarins and intellectuals to read this book.

Part 2. Denmark

WN was translated into Danish by Frants Dræbye and published in 1779 (three years after the first English edition). The translation was initiated by Andreas Holt and Peter Anker, who were acquainted with Smith. Dræbye was a Dane who lived mainly in Norway, reflecting the fact that Norway was much more British-oriented than Denmark proper (Denmark and Norway were united until 1814, when Sweden took Norway away from the Danes; in 1905 Norway became an independent state). Norwegian merchants lived from exporting timber to Britain and tended on the whole to be adherents of a liberal economic policy, whereas the absolutist government in Copenhagen was more German-oriented and had economic views similar to those in contemporary Prussia.

The last twenty years of the eighteenth century in Denmark were dominated by a lively discussion of monetary policy and the institutional framework best suited to realize that policy. During the last decades of the century, the ideas of Smith did not play a major role, either for practical policy or in theoretical discussion. The main influence came from German writers, the most important being Johan Georg Büsch, the head of the chamber of commerce in Hamburg.

This Part contains three texts. The first consists of four letters by Smith concerning the Danish translation of WN (1779–80), written on 25–6 October 1780 and reproduced from *Correspondence of Adam Smith* (Oxford University Press, 1977, pp. 247–54). These letters reveal his deep concern about the reaction to his work abroad (as well as at home). He reacted passionately to both the Danish and French translations, as can be seen from his *Correspondence* ('Index", p. 464). By contrast, Smith did not comment in his *Correspondence* on the German translation which appeared in 1776 (the same year as the first English edition); and thus it seems that he was not aware of that publication during his lifetime.

Both Degen (1936) and Banke (1955) offer an interesting history of the translation and reception of *WN* in Denmark/Norway, and of the general economic background in these countries in the 1780s. The two articles are complementary. Degen's paper is more general, whereas Banke's analysis goes much deeper and acknowledges the greater influence of Smith's ideas.

Further Reading

Texts with a * are printed in this Part

*BANKE, NIELS (1955), "Adam Smith forbindelse med Norge og Danmark" (On Adam Smith's connections to Norway and Denmark), *Nationaløkonomisk Tidsskrift*, 93(3–4): 170–8.

BOSERUP, MOGENS (1980), "The International Transmission of Ideas: A Small-Country Study [Denmark]", *History of Political Economy*, 12(3): 420–33.

*DEGEN, HANS (1936): Om den Danske oversættelse af Adam Smith og samtidens bedømmelse af den (On the Danish translation of Adam Smith and contemporary opinion concerning it), *Nationaløkonomisk Tidsskrift*, 74(3): 223–32.

JOHANSEN, HANS (1966), "J. G. Büsch's Economic Theory and His Influence on the Danish Economic and Social Debate", *Scandinavian Economic Review*, 14(1): 18–38.

*SMITH, ADAM (1780): Letters 206–9 in *Correspondence of Adam Smith*, pp. 247–54, Oxford University Press, 1977.

2.1. Adam Smith, 1780.
Four Letters Concerning the First Danish Translation of *The Wealth of Nations*

no commentary

206. *To* [Thomas Cadell]

MS., Yale University Libr., unpubl.

Canongate, Edinburgh, 25 Oct. [1780][1]

Dear Sir

May I beg the favour of you, immediately after receiving this letter to send three copies of the second edition of My book concerning the Wealth of nations to Mr Peter Anker, Consul General of Denmark;[2] writing upon the blank leaf of one of them to Mr Anker from the Authour; of another, To Mr Holt[3] from the Authour, and of the third to Mr Dreby[4] from the Authour. Mr Dreby has lately translated me into Danish.[5] These copies must be handsomely bound and Guilded. I am afraid I am not only your best, but almost your only customer for this second Edition. Let me know, however, how this matter goes on.

So long ago as the year 1767, sometime in the month of march, a few days before I left London, I bought of you a copy of Andersons History of Commerce.[6] You happened not to have it in your own shop but you procured it for me from some of your Neighbours. In this copy I lately discovered an Imperfection of which John Balfour wrote to you sometime ago. If you could get this imperfection supplied, you would oblige me greatly. I ever am Dear Sir

Most faithfully and
affectionately yours
Adam Smith

207. *To* [William Strahan]

Canongate, Edinburgh, 26 Oct. 1780

Dear Sir:

I think it is predestined that I shall never write a letter to you; except to ask some favour of you, or to put you to some trouble. This letter is not to depart from the style of all the rest. I am a subscriber for Watts copying machine.[7] The price is six Guineas for the machine and five Shillings for the packing box; I should be glad too [if] he would send me a ream of the copying Paper, together with all the other specimens of Ink etc. which commonly accompany the Machine. For payment of this to Mr Woodmason, the seller, whose printed letter I have enclosed, you will herewith receive a bill of eight Guineas payable at sight. If after paying for all this there should be any remnant, there is a taylour in Craven Street, one Heddington, an acquaintance of James McPherson to whom I owe some shillings, I believe under ten, certainly under twenty, pay him what I owe. He is a very honest man and will ask no more than is due. Before I left London I had sent several times for his account, but he always put it off.

I had almost forgot I was the Author of the enquiry concerning the Wealth of Nations; but some time ago I received a letter from a friend in Denmark telling me that it had been translated into Danish by one Mr Dreby, Secretary to a new erected board of trade and Oeconomy in that Kingdom.[8] My correspondent, Mr Holt, who is an assessor of that Board, desires in the name of Mr Dreby, to know what alterations I propose to make in a second Edition. The shortest answer to this is to send them the second Edition. I propose, therefore, by this Post to desire Mr Cadell to send three copies of the second edition, handomely bound and gilt, to Mr Anker, Consul General of Denmark, who is an old acquaintance, one for himself, and the other two to be by him transmitted to Mr Holt, and Mr Dreby. At our final settlement I shall debit myself with these three Books. I suspect I am now almost your only customer for my own book. Let me know however how matters go in this respect.

After begging your pardon a thousand times for having so long neglected to write to you. I shall conclude with assuring you that notwithstanding this neglect, I have the highest respect, and esteem for you and for your whole family and that I am

Most Sincerely
and affectionately
ever yours
Adam Smith

208. *To* [Andreas Holt, Commissioner of the Danish Board of Trade and Economy]

[Edinburgh, 26 Oct. 1780]

Dear Sir

I am ashamed of having delayed so long to answer your very obliging letter;[9] but I am occupied four days in every Week at the Custom House; during which it is impossible to sit down seriously to any other business: during the other three days too, I am liable to be frequently interrupted by the extraordinary duties of my office, as well as by my own private affairs, and the common duties of society.

It gives me the greatest pleasure to hear that Mr Dreby has done me the distinguished honour of translating my Book into the Danish language.[10] I beg you will present to him my most sincere thanks and most respectful Compliments. I am much concerned that I cannot have the pleasure of reading it in his translation, as I am so unfortunate as not to understand the Danish language.

I Published more than two years ago a second edition of the inquiry concerning the Wealth of Nations, in which though I have made no material alteration, I have made a good number of corrections, none of which, however, affect even in the slightest degree, the general principles, or Plan of the System. I have by this Post directed Mr Cadell, to deliver two copies of this second edition, to your friend and pupil Mr Anker, of whom I have taken the liberty to ask the favour, of transmitting them by the first convenient opportunity to you. I hope you will be so good as to accept of one of them for yourself and present the other in my name to Mr Dreby.

I do not pretend that this second edition though a good deal more correct than the first, is entirely exempted from all errors. I have myself discovered several inaccurasies. The most considerable is in Vol. 2. page 482 where I say "In England for example, when by the land-tax, every other sort of revenue was supposed to be assessed at four shillings in the pound, it was very popular to lay a real tax of five shillings in the pound upon the salaries of offices which exceeded a hundred pounds a year, those of the Judges and a few others less obnoxious to envy excepted."[11] The tax upon such salaries amounts, not to five shillings only, but to five and six pence in the pound; and the salaries of Judges are not exempted from it. The only salaries exempted are the pensions of the younger branches of the Royal family, and the pay of the Officers of the army and Navy. This blunder which so far as I know is the grossest in the whole Book, and which arose from trusting too much to memory, does not in the least affect the reasoning, or conclusion which it was brought to support.

I have not thought it proper to make any direct answer to any of my adversaries. In the second edition I flattered myself that I had obviated all the objections of Governor Pownal.[12] I find however, he is by no means satisfied, and as Authors are not much disposed to alter the opinions they have once published, I am not much surprized at it.

The anonymous author of a pamphlet concerning national defense, who I have been told is a Gentleman of the name of Douglas, has Written against Me. When he Wrote his book, he had not read mine to the end. He fancies that because I insist that a Militia is in all cases inferior to a well regulated and well disciplined standing Army, that I disapprove of Militias altogether. With regard to that subject, he and I happened to be precisly of the same opinion. This Gentleman, if I am rightly informed of his name, is a man of parts and one of my acquaintance, so that I was a little surprized at his attack upon Me, and still more at the mode of it.[13]

A very diligent, laborious, honest Man of the name of Anderson, has published a large quarto volume concerning improvements; in this volume he has done me the honour to employ a very long chapter in answering my objections to the bounty upon the exportation of Corn.[14] In volume second page 101 of the first edition, I happened to say that the nature of things had stamped a real value upon Corn which no human institution can alter. The expression was certainly too strong, and had escaped me in the heat of Writing. I ought to have said that the nature of things had stamped upon corn a real value which could not be altered merely by altering its Money price. This was all that the argument required, and all that I really meant. Mr Anderson takes advantage of this hasty expression, and triumphs very much by showing that in several other parts of my Work I had acknowledged that whatever lowered the real price of manufactur'd produce, rais'd the price of rude produce, and consequently of corn. In the second edition I have corrected this careless expression, which I apprehend takes away the foundation of the whole argument of Mr Anderson.[15]

It is not worth while to take notice even to you of the innumerable squibs thrown out upon me in the newspapers. I have however, upon the whole been much less abused than I had reason to expect; so that in this respect I think myself rather lucky than otherwise. A single, and as, I thought a very harmless Sheet of paper, which I happened to Write concerning the death of our late friend Mr Hume,[16] brought upon me ten times more abuse than the very violent attack I had made upon the whole commercial system of Great Britain. So much for what relates to my Book.

I was much intertained with the account which you was so good as [to] send me of your travels into Iceland,[17] and of the different situation you have been in since I had the pleasure of seeing you in France,[18] and was Very happy to find in the end that you had obtained so comfortable and honourable an establishment at Copenhagen. The revolution in the administration of your Government, which you mention, I always believed to have been conducted with great prudence and moderation, and to have been indispensibly necessary for the preservation of the State.[19] It gives me great pleasure to hear the agreeable accounts which you give me of the young Prince and of the very proper manner in which he is educated. Since I had the pleasure of seeing you, my own life has been extremely uniform.[20] Upon my return to Britain I retired to a small Town in Scotland the place of my nativity, where I continued to live for six years in great tranquillity, and almost in complete retirement. During this time I amused myself principally with writing my Enquiry concerning the Wealth of Nations, in studying Botany (in which however I made no great progress) as well as some other sciences to which I had never given much attention before. In the Spring of 1773 a proposal, which many of my friends thought very advantageous was made to me to go abroad a second time.[21] The discussion of this proposal obliged me to go to London, where the Duke of Buccleugh was so good as to disuade [me] from accepting it. For four years after this London was my principal residence, where I finished and published my Book. I had returned to my old retirement at Kirkaldy and was employing myself in writing another Work concerning the imitative arts,[22] when by the interest of the Duke of Buccleugh, I was appointed to my present Office; which though it requires a good deal of attendance is both easy and honourable, and for my Way of living sufficiently beneficial. Upon my appointment I proposed to surrender the annuity which had been settled upon me by the Tutors of the Duke of Buccleugh, before I went abroad with him, and which had been renewed by his Grace after he became of age, as a thing for which I had no farther occasion. But his Grace sent me word by his Cashier, to whom I had offered to deliver up his bond, that though I had considered what was fit for my own honour, I had not consider'd what was fit for his; and that he never would suffer it to be suspected that he had procured an office for his friend, in order to relieve himself from the burden of such an annuity. My present situation is therefore fully as affluent as I could wish it to be. The only thing I regret in it is the interruptions to my literary pursuits, which the duties of my office necessarily occasion. Several Works which I had projected are likely to go on much more slowly than they otherwise would have done. Wishing you every sort of happiness and prosperity, I have the honour to be with the highest respect and esteem

Dear Sir your most affectionate
humble Servant

209. *To* [Peter Anker, Consul General of Denmark in Great Britain]

[Edinburgh, 26 Oct. 1780]

Dear Sir,

It gave me very great pleasure to find that I had not been altogether forgotten, either by you, or by your valuable friend Mr Holt. I can plead no other excuse for having delayed so very long to answer your very obliging letter,[23] except the great number of occupations in which I am necessarily involved by the duties of my Office and by my own private affairs. I did not chuse to answer your letter till I had answer'd Mr Holts,[24] which required more time than I have commonly to spare. I have at last taken the liberty to inclose to you my answer to his letter which I must beg the favour of you to transmitte to him.

I have likewise taken the liberty to desire Mr Cadell to deliver to you, three copies of the second edition of my Book; I hope you will be so good as [to] accept of one of them as a memorandum of old friendship and transmitte the other two to Mr Holt, the one as a memorandum of the same kind to him, the other as a present to Mr Dreby who has done me the honour to translate my Book into your language.

It gives me great pleasure to hear from you that the arm'd Neutrality of the northern powers, does not mean to be hostile to Great Britain.[25] Notwithstanding, however, the very high respect which I have for your authority, I must acknowledge that I dread a great deal from it, and hope very little. But whatever alterations may happen in the dispositions of our respective Nations towards one another, I trust no alterations will ever happen in those of our private friendship. I have the honour to be with the highest respect and esteem

Dear Sir, Your Most affectionate

humble Servant

P.S. I am not sure if my address to Mr Holt at Copenhagen is sufficiently distinct. After sealing the letter you will be so good as to supply what is defective.

Copies Letters to Messrs Holt and Anker October 26 1780.[26]

NOTES

1. The year "1760" at the end of the letter is an error, for it obviously belongs with the Letters 208 and 209, dated 26 Oct. 1780 and addressed to Holt and Anker.

2. Karsten and Peter Anker (1744–1832), sons of a Norwegian timber merchant, travelled to Britain in 1760, and were in Glasgow in 1762 when they met Adam Smith. They were in his company again in Toulouse in 1764 when he was writing *WN*.

3. Andreas Holt (1729–84), tutor to the Ankers, then Danish civil servant, head of the Norwegian secretariat of the Economic and Trade Department, and finally a State Councillor.

4. Frants Dræbye (1740–1814), tutor to the sons of a Norwegain merchant, James Collett, visited England with them 1773–6; trans. *WN* into Danish when he was head of the Norwegian Secretariat of the Economic and Trade Department in succession to Holt. The Ankers and Holt probably persuaded him to do the translating.

5. *Undersøgelse om National-Volstands Natur og Aarsag of Doctor Adam Smith . . .* Af det Engelske oversat og med nogle anmærkninger oplyst af F. Dræbye (Copenhagen, 1779–80). To the second volume was added Gov. Pownall's letter of 1776.

6. See Letter 102 addressed to Cadell, dated 25 Mar. 1767.

7. One of the remarkable inventions of James Watt (1736–1819), a device as universally employed as his more familiar mechanical productions. Patented 14 Feb. 1780, the duplicator employed a specially prepared ink impressed on a damp sheet of paper to produce a facsimile. Smith had known Watt since 1757, when the latter was appointed mathematical instrument-maker to Glasgow University. It was in his workshop there that Watt repaired the Newcomen steam engine in 1764, leading to his own discoveries in that field of technology.

8. See Letter 206 to Cadell, dated 25 Oct. 1780; also Letter 208 to Holt and Letter 209 to Anker, both dated 26 Oct. 1780.

9. Not traced.

10. See Letter 206, no. 5.

11. *WN* V.ii.i.7 (conclusion).

12. See Letter 174 from Pownall, dated 15 Sept. 1776 (Appendix A), and Smith's reply, Letter 182, dated 19 Jan. 1777.

13. *A Letter from a Gentleman in Edinburgh to his Grace the Duke of Buccleugh on National Defence, with some Remarks on Dr Smith's Chapter on that Subject in his Book, entitled "An Enquiry into the Nature and Causes of the Wealth of Nations"* (London, 1778). The initials "M. T." appear at the end of the preface; see *WN* V.i.a. 23, 27.

14. James Anderson, *Observations on the Means of Exciting a Spirit of National Industry* (London, 1777); *WN* IV.v. 4–25, also V.ii.k. 13.

15. See *WN* IV.v.a.23. Ed. 2 reads "The nature of things has stamped upon corn a real value which cannot be altered by merely altering its money price". Pownall in his *Letter* notices a similarity between Smith's arguments about the corn bounty and those of Necker in *Sur la législation et le commerce des grains* (1775); see appendix A, pp. 361–6.

16. Letter 178 dated 9 Nov. 1776, addressed to William Strahan.

17. Holt was overlandskommissær there.

18. They met at Toulouse in 1764.

19. A coup d'état in 1772 resulted in the exile of Queen Caroline Mathilde; the execution of her lover, Struensee, a German physician who had become Prime Minister after dominating King Christian VII from 1768; and the restoration of Danish leadership.

20. This para. presents a brief autobiography of the years 1766–80. The account of how Smith became a Commissioner of Customs is to be compared with his letters of Dec. 1777–Feb. 1778.

21. As travelling tutor to the Duke of Hamilton.

22. *EPS*, "Of the Nature of that Imitation which takes place in what are called the Imitative Arts".

23. Not traced; possibly these letters gave news of Dræbye's trans. of *WN*; see Letter 206 addressed to Cadell, dated 25 Oct. 1780.

24. Letter 208, dated 26 Oct. 1780.

25. On 9 July 1780, Denmark and Russia signed a treaty declaring "armed neutrality" in the face of the British Navy's enforcement of a policy of searching neutral vessels for arms and supplies for France and the former American colonies. The treaty was joined by Sweden and Prussia but proved of little value. The principles were reasserted, however, in 1797, in another treaty between Denmark, Norway, and Sweden, and this led to the battle of Copenhagen, 1801.

26. Date added in a later hand.

2.2. Hans Degen, 1936.
On the Danish Translation of Adam Smith and Contemporary Opinion Concerning It

Translated by Henrietta M. Larson (1938)

When the father of political economy in the year 1776 published his famous work, *An Inquiry into the Nature and Causes of the Wealth of Nations*, there had not yet appeared any Danish work that deserves to be mentioned in the history of economic thought as a link in the development which economic theory had gone through in the later centuries.

The reason for this lack of works, considering the new ideas and thinking of the period, must rather be sought chiefly in the then existing political, social, and economic organization in Denmark than in a lack of interest in political economy and the problems considered by economists. In the period after Holberg's death there was no lack, everything considered, of interest in political economy; on the contrary, it can be said that the time was characterized by a most vital interest in questions of an economic nature, which, for example, is illustrated in the first volume of *Denmark's and Norway's Economic Magazine*, in which that time is characterized as "this economic age," or, as it says in the preface to the eighth volume of the same work, "never was the world more economic minded." One hardly goes too far when one suggests that interest in economics was the style and that the words "economy" and "economic" were almost slogans of the day. But if it were the style to be interested in economic matters, the style was in this case not passing but peculiarly enduring. As early as 1782 the times are characterized in the monthly magazine *Danish Museum* as especially "enamoured of" economic and political speculations and considerations; and, even as late as 1812–13, there was so much

47

interest in economic thought that the administration of the government, that is the *Rentekammerets* and *General-Landoeconomi-* and *Commerce-Collegiets*, followed Professor Christian Olufsens's lectures on the "Foundations of Practical Political Economy."

When Adam Smith's book was published in its Danish translation in Copenhagen in the years 1779–80—that is scarcely four years after its publication in the home land of the author, one might be inclined to consider the existing interests in economic thought—as is indicated above—as the direct reason for the book's early translation and not only as one favourable factor in its appearance.

If one is, these many years later, to test whether this was a cause or only a contemporary situation, in the matter of the translation of Adam Smith's book, it will pay to look into the life and work of the translator and the circumstances, that he happened to be close at hand in those years before he undertook to give his contemporary readers his translation.

The man who came to translate Adam Smith's book, Frants Dræbye, was born in Copenhagen July 16, 1740, the son of whiskey distiller Frantsen. He was sent to school by his parents and was in 1761 sent up for examination from Copenhagen's school and five years later to take the examination in theology.

A short time after he had become a candidate, he hired out to Christiania's merchant James Collett as tutor for his sons. Dræbye's acquaintance with the great Norwegian merchant's house was surely not without meaning for his later work as translator of Adam Smith. Dræbye, who had grown up as a student in Copenhagen, had without doubt felt the difference, which there must have been, of coming from Denmark, with its strong associations with German thought and spirit and everything that was German, to Norway—and especially to a large Norwegian mercantile house—with its connections with England. This became of much greater importance as it fell to Dræbye's lot to take a trip with James Collett's sons through several of Europe's most important countries, a trip which brought them to England in the year 1776 when Adam Smith's book was published.

Here Dræbye, presumably with the Norwegian merchant's sons as his means of contact, had entry into English mercantile circles and by that means made considerable acquaintance with English conditions. What can be more natural to conclude than that Adam Smith's then recently published book was an important subject of conversation and that the importance which had been ascribed to the book was so great that Dræbye had got a desire to give to the Danish and Norwegian readers an acquaintance with such a significant and much discussed work.

When Frants Dræbye at the end of 1776 had returned to Denmark and had been appointed to be chief of the Norwegian secretariat of the Board of Economics and Trade,[1] he began with the translation. How far Dræbye had conferred with the publisher cannot be proved, since neither letter nor con-tract[2] can be found concerning the translation and the conditions under which Dræbye should work, but there is much reason to think that Dræbye first had to obtain, through friends and acquaintances, a certain number of subscribers, which probably also explains why a considerable number of subscribers were Norwegians.

There does not seem to have been issued any real public invitation to subscribe; at least in going through *Adresse-Contoirs Efterretninger* one finds for the first time on Monday, August 9 (No. 130) and Wednesday, August 11 (No. 132) the following advertisement: "The remarkable work, of the famous Dr. Adam Smith of the University of Glasgow, called Inquiries into the Nature and Cause of the Wealth of Nations, which Mr. Secretary Frants Dræbye translates into Danish, is under press, and the first part will be out late in September; if there is someone who has still neglected to subscribe, please inform Gyldendal in Silk Street No. 66 during the present month."

The book whose exact title reads: "Inquiries into the Nature and Cause of National Wealth by Dr. Adam Smith, member of the Royal Philosophical Society in London and formerly public teacher in moral philosophy at the University of Glasgow. Translated from the English with some points explained by F. Dræbye," was in its first part to be obtained in the trade from October 4, 1779, for on Monday, October 4 (No. 162), Wednesday, October 6 (No. 164) and Friday, October 15 (No. 169) is found in *Adresse-Contoirs Erterretninger* the following announcement by Gyldendal's: ". . . the first part subscribers can receive on print paper for 7 marks and on writing paper for 9 marks, but other buyers on print paper for 9 marks and writing paper for 10 marks at book dealer Gyldendal, Silk Street No. 66. The second volume will be ready in the winter."

Whatever the reason may have been, the promise that the second volume should be ready in the course of the winter was not kept, for not until the following summer does one find in the *Adresse-Contoirs Erterretninger* for Mon-day, June 12 (No. 96), Wednesday, June 21 (No. 102) and Friday, June 30 (No. 107), 1780, the following: "The second volume of Inquiries into the Nature and Cause of the Wealth of Nations . . . by F. Dræbye, with the addition of Governor Pawnall's letter to the author in which some of the arguments set forth in this work are considered, is now off the press . . . and on print paper costs [subscribers?] 1 *riksdaler* and 3 marks and on writing paper 2 *riksdalers*, but for other buyers the price is one mark more at book dealer Gyldendal in Silk Street No. 66."

Adam Smith seems not to have had until later any knowledge about the translation or publication of the book. It was in his time customary when the author of a work was approached for a commission to translate his work to announce the translation as authorized, and, since that little word is lacking on the title page of the book, Adam Smith's permission could scarcely have been secured.

After the success which the book met very soon after its publication in England—the issue, as known, in nine parts in the years 1776–1779—one might have expected that the book should also in Denmark have attracted attention and have been the subject of enthusiastic discussion. That was, however, not the case; the only place where one finds the book mentioned soon after publication is—excepting Gyldendal's own announcement in *Adresse-Contoirs Erterretninger*—in *Det almindelige danske Bibliotek*, 10th number for 1779 and 6th number for 1760, where the book is briefly mentioned in the notices of forthcoming publications with statement of its size and price.

Not until much later—in the year 1782—is there mention of the book. Announcements are found only in two monthly publications, namely, in *Denmarks litterariske Progresser* (1782, second volume, pages 172–175. Published in Odense), and in *Kiøbenhavnske nye Efterretninger for laerde Sager* (October 25, 1782, No. 43, pages 683–687. Published in Copenhagen).

[Here follow four pages of quotes from these publications. These have to do with the translation but particularly point out some of the matters discussed in the volume.]

As is seen from the above announcements they contain only a short summary of Smith's thoughts and ideas without any careful consideration or evaluation. But they turn rather to Dræbye, his language and his translation, with criticism which later is said to have come to Adam Smith's ear and caused him considerable concern.

That the book, after its publication, did not arouse any particular notice, can be explained by several concurrent circumstances. The conditions here at home were still hardly ripe for the book and for the time's revolutionary thinking; the industrial and commercial conditions—indeed the economic life as a whole—was still of such a nature that there was no particular desire for new points of view; everything went along somewhat peacefully under the king's paternalistic and sympathetic care so that the book did not here, as in England, make itself felt as "a word in the right time."

It has also been of importance that people here at home were much more in sympathy with the German spirit and thought than with the English. And also the developments of the immediate future may have weakened interest in the book.

Without exaggeration it can essentially be said that a quarter of a century was to pass from the time of the publication of the book in Denmark before Danish political economy fully made Adam Smith's theories and points of view its own. It took so long a time because the economic conditions as a whole in the years from 1780–1800 did not make desirable or necessary the changing of their concepts. That glorious commercial period had to pass before it was understood that we had altogether too little help in our own natural resources and that a different course was, therefore, necessary. Only when one had come so far could the new thinking find a nourishing soil so that it could develop strength with which to push aside the old ideas.

Notes

1. He [Dræbye] was appointed *Kammerraad* in 1781, *Kommitteret* in 1785. On account of illness was released from 1781 until about 1785. Became *Justitsraad* in 1797, Cabinet Minister in 1804. Member of the Royal Factory-direction in the period 1783–1789. Resigned in 1804. Died January 16, 1814, in Sorö.
2. Gyldendal's Archives are in the New Royal Collection.

[*Editor's note*: The English translation of this article is located at the Kress Library of Harvard University [Pam. Degen, Hans 1936]. It was translated by Henrietta M. Larson, professor at Harvard Business School, in April 1938. The typescript consists of seven double-spaced pages; the translator has omitted all the footnotes, and pp. 227–31 with the comment "Here follow four pages of quotes from those publications. These have to do with the translation but particularly point out some of the matters discussed in the volume." Degen provides a comment on these four pages: "As is seen from the above announcements they contain only a short summary of Smith's thoughts and ideas without any careful consideration or evaluation". This seems to justify the translator's omission of these four pages. It is reasonable to assume that the translation was encouraged by Professor Homer Vanderblue, who established the Vanderblue Memorial Collection of Smithiana in the Kress Library of Harvard Business School.]

2.3. Niels Banke, 1955
On Adam Smith's Connections to Norway and Denmark

Translated by Hans Johansen

I

In his large book *Socialøkonomik*[1] the Norwegian economist Aschehoug says that in 1779 *The Wealth of Nations* had already been translated into *our* language on the initiative of Norwegian merchants. He means of course the translation into Danish by Dræbye of Adam Smith's book. For Danes who want to stress that this is a Norwegian expression for events which took place in Denmark–Norway before 1814, the following account may be useful. The result is that what Aschehoug says is very close to the truth.

Hans Degen stresses in his article "On the Danish translation of Adam Smith and contemporary opinion concerning it"[2] that Dræbye was attached to the Christiania (Oslo) merchant James Collett. The importance of the Norwegians has also been emphasized by professor Axel Nielsen in some comments he gave to the Glasgow professor W. R. Scott in connection with two letters from Adam Smith to two Norwegians, Peter Anker and Andreas Holt, about the Danish translation of *The Wealth of Nations*.[3] These letters, which will be referred to later, and Axel Nielsen's comments have given rise to this investigation into Adam Smith's relations with Norwegian merchant families and Denmark.

II

An important commodity for the big Norwegian merchant houses in the eighteenth century was timber, of which the majority of the export was sailed to England. Because of the considerable business connections which in this way were created between England and Norway there was also an English influence on Norwegian culture and habits. This was the case with regard to the way the rich families educated their children. At that time young English and Scots noblemen were sent by their parents on a European journey lasting several years instead of going to university. Adam Smith explains this habit as a result of the decay of the universities.[4] Adam Smith had himself been elected as a teacher for one of the most distinguished young noblemen in Scotland, the duke of Buccleugh, on a journey which lasted from January 1764 to November 1766.[5] The journey gave Adam Smith a higher salary than as a university professor and secured him a life-long pension. Many things indicate that friendly relations developed between Adam Smith and his high-born student and were to last for life. In spite of this Smith in *The Wealth of Nations* without reservation writes that young men are sent on these journeys too early in their lives. They get a superficial knowledge, become conceited and debauched. According to Smith this is a bad education for young people, and the blame falls upon the universities.[6]

Some years before Adam Smith started on his journey, a Norwegian merchant with numerous interests, Erik Anker, sent his two sons Peter and Karsten on a journey abroad for several years in company with the Norwegian-born teacher and university student Andreas Holt. When well-to-do Norwegians in this respect followed English habits a contributing factor was the resentment in Norway of the university and university life in Copenhagen and the struggle to found a Norwegian university, which was strong by the end of the eighteenth century.

Andreas Holt and the two young Anker sons visited the largest and most spectacular cities in England and Scotland, and then continued to France. In 1762 they arrived in Glasgow, where much was made of them. They received the freedom of the city.[7] In Glasgow the brothers met with Adam Smith. In the diary and travel book which was kept during the journey Adam Smith has written:[8]

I shall always be happy to hear of the welfare & prosperity of three Gentlemen in whose conversation I have had so much pleasure, as in that of the two Messrs. Anchor & of their worthy Tutor Mr. Holt.

> 28th of May 1762.
> Adam Smith
> Prof. of Moral Philosophy
> in the University of Glasgow

In September of the same year Holt and the two Anker brothers arrived in London. They met there with four cousins, Bernt, Peder, Iver, and Jess Anker. Peter and Karsten undoubtedly told of their Scottish adventures, which meant that two more people who were later to become leading Norwegian personalities, Bernt and Peder Anker, from their youth had a vivid impression of Adam Smith. In the last decade of the century Bernt Anker was probably the richest merchant in Norway and a dominant figure in the cultural and social life of Christiania. He died in 1805. His brother Peder became the father-in-law of count Herman Wedel-Jarlsberg, a leading figure in Norway in the period when Norway changed from the union with Denmark to that with Sweden. Peder Anker was one of the leaders at the Eidsvoll Convention, which adopted the free constitution in 1814, and later became prime minister. Peter and Karsten, too, were delegates at Eidsvoll, where the latter, as a personal friend of the Danish prince Kristian Frederik, who was designated king of an independent Norway, played an important role.

Peter and Karsten Anker's juvenile journey continued to Paris and later to Toulouse. In this town they met again with Adam Smith and his student, the Duke of Buccleugh. In the diary there are the following compliments from the duke:[9]

Having had the pleasure of meeting Messieurs Anchers & Mr. Holt at Toulouse. It is with the greatest satisfaction that I member myself amongst their acquaintance.

Buccleugh
Toulouse 16th March 1764

These general greetings have been mentioned only because of their date.

At the same time Andreas Holt and Adam Smith must have met in Toulouse. Smith refers in his letter to Holt concerning the Danish translation to the time they spent together in France. Adam Smith and Buccleugh were in Toulouse for one-and-a-half years from February 1764. Holt and the Anker brothers left for Germany in 1764.

Smith's and Buccleugh's first months in Toulouse were rather boring owing, among other things, to language difficulties. It was then that Smith started on his *Wealth of Nations* in order to kill the time.[10] Meeting the Norwegians was undoubtedly, under these circumstances, a special event, and one can guess that Smith told Andreas Holt about his plans for the book.

III

Dræbye was, as mentioned by Degen, on a journey with two young Norwegians, brothers Peter and John Collett, about ten years later. This journey took place from 1773 to 1776, and their passage from the Continent to England was in the very year when *The Wealth of Nations* was published. Peter and John Collett also kept a travel diary, but they could scarcely have met with Adam Smith.[11] They did, however, undoubtedly visit Peter Anker, who was a relative and at that time Danish–Norwegian consul in Hull.

After returning to Copenhagen in 1776 Dræbye was appointed head of the Norwegian secretariat in the Royal College of Commerce (Board of Trade), where he succeeded Andreas Holt, who was promoted to another job in the central administration. Karsten Anker was at that time also working in the College of Commerce, and it is very likely that these two Norwegians, who both knew Adam Smith, urged Dræbye to start translating *The Wealth of Nations*.[12] Andreas Holt was probably the more important, since it was Holt and Karsten's brother Peter, who from 1777 was Danish consul-general in London, who wrote to Smith about the translation.

The letter to Peter Anker dates from October 1780 and is relatively short. Adam Smith excused his delay before replying, saying that he thought he would wait until he could send a reply to Holt at the same time. He enclosed this other letter and asked Anker to forward it to Holt. Adam Smith also said that he had asked his publisher to mail three copies of the second edition of *The Wealth of Nations* to Peter Anker and that two of these should be forwarded to Holt—one as a present to Dræbye, who had done Smith "the honour" of translating the book into Danish. The letter ends with a remark about the armed neutrality. Smith was happy to know that Anker did not find the armed neutrality hostile to Great Britain, but admitted that he feared that bad things would arise from it and had only little hope for good things.

The letter to Holt is a long and cordial one. It is a reply to another long letter from Holt. In that one Holt had asked what changes Adam Smith planned in the next edition of *The Wealth of Nations*. It was, thus, not known in Denmark that it had already been published in 1778.[13] It is quite clear from the first paragraphs in Smith's reply to Holt that it was only from Holt's previous letter that Adam Smith had got the news about Dræbye's translation. Smith gave details of the second edition of *The Wealth of Nations*, in which he had corrected a large number of errors, without, however, to the slightest extent changing the plan or system of the book. Even so the book was not faultless. Smith drew attention to the worst error he himself had discovered, a misstatement of the size—5sh. instead of 5sh. and 6d per pound—and of the exceptions to the English taxation of civil servants' salaries.[14]

Smith further reported in the letter that he had written no direct reply to those who had criticized him after publication. Concerning Pownall, whose letter to Adam Smith was reprinted at the end of the Danish edition of the book, Smith wrote that in the second edition he had taken due regard of all Pownall's objections, but without Pownall being satisfied. An anonymous critic, whom Smith thought he knew, had surprised him—not least because of the form used. This criticism deals only with Smith's position towards the defence question. Smith thought that the anonymous critic had misunderstood Smith's position towards a militia. The critic assumed that Smith was against a militia because in *The Wealth of Nations* he gave reasons why a standing army is more efficient.[15] Smith mentioned a third critic, Anderson, with great respect in connection with remarks on a sentence in Smith's book about bounties on exports of grain. These remarks also resulted in a correction in the new edition.[16]

Smith wrote that he did not pay any attention to the many satirical remarks in the newspapers and added that the book had given rise to less criticism than he had expected. A short letter[17] which he had written on the occasion of Hume's death had, on the other hand, occasioned ten times more anger than his own violent attack against the economic system of Great Britain.

Smith then thanked Holt for the report he had given about his travels in Iceland. (Holt had for a period been a civil servant in this remote part of the Danish kingdom.) Smith also refered to Holt's remarks about the Danish *coup d'état* in 1772 and expressed the belief that it was carried out with great skill and sense and was necessary for the preservation of the state. Smith was also happy with the account Holt gave of the young prince and his education.

Smith ended the letter with a report about his own life since returning from the journey with Buccleugh. In the following six years he had lived a quiet life in his native town, where he entertained himself by writing *The Wealth of Nations* and by studying botanicals and other sciences to which he had earlier paid little attention. With regard to botanicals he noted that he had made little progress. A suggestion about travelling abroad again as a teacher had brought him to London, but the journey had come to nothing, among other reasons because the Duke of Buccleugh had advised against it. Smith had remained in London for four years, where he completed *The Wealth of Nations*. He had then returned to his native town of Kirkcaldy, where he had started writing a treatise about the various arts.[18] Shortly after he had been appointed commissioner of customs in Edinburgh after being proposed by Buccleugh. Smith wrote of this position that it was easy and a great honour, but that it took much of his time, so that he had less time for writing than previously. But the position gave him good economic conditions, especially since the Duke continued paying the pension Smith had received since the return from France, in spite of the fact that Smith had suggested that this should no longer be the case.

This letter demonstrates that the relations between Smith and the Danish-

Norwegian civil servant Andreas Holt were more than just an ordinary travel acquaintance. The letter also confirms Adam Smith's wide-ranging interests.

IV

Since the intermediaries of the Danish edition of *The Wealth of Nations* were already interested in preparing a new edition in 1780, the first edition was probably a bigger success than suggested by Degen in the above-mentioned article. Danish–Norwegian connections with liberal ideas were presumably also more important for developments in the two countries than Degen assumed. His opinion seems to be that changes in a liberal direction did not take place until after 1800.

The spread of Dræbye's translation both in Denmark and Norway must have been a contribution to the propagation of those liberal thoughts, which can already be traced in the beginning of the 1780s in the dual monarchy. An example is the reports from the prefect of Akershus diocese Jørgen Erik Skeel, who in September 1784 wrote to the Exchequer that "it might be much desired that commerce, handicrafts and trade in general were less restricted by acts and other rights than they presently are"; and in November of the same year, "It is in accordance with the best political principles that everyone in the State should enjoy the liberties which he without harming the whole of the nation could be given and that this liberty should be reduced as little as possible."[19]

A few years later, in 1787, the so-called great finance commission was set up. Among the deliberations of the commission was the question of "whether a freer commerce than that practised under the present system might be advantageous to the King's realm". This task must be seen in the context of the fact that it was in these years that Johan Bülow, the learned teacher of the crown prince, taught his student that free trade should be enhanced. Furthermore, it was probably not unimportant that civil servants (Karsten Anker, Holt, and Dræbye) who were familiar with Adam Smith and his ideas were working in the economic colleges. As early as 1788 came the first result of the commission's work, which was a liberalization of the grain trade. It was the same commission which prepared the liberal customs act of 1797.[20] The basic principles in this act were written by the Minister of Finance, Ernst Schimmelmann, under the title "Remarks from the College of Commerce to a possible future change in the present factory system". These remarks were thus written in the college, where several civil servants had special contacts with Adam Smith. The remarks adhere in principle to free competition but only through a gradual dissolution of the prohibition system. This is also the procedure recommended by Adam Smith.[21] There is much similarity between Smith's and the college's motives for the moderate procedure in so far as the existing manufacturing industry is concerned. The Danish motives also contain, however, an element of an infant-industry argument, since it is stated that the superiority of the older and richer industrial nations may justify a certain protection.

V

The independent Norwegian state started its legislation at Eidsvoll in 1814 by including in the new constitution a liberal paragraph (101): "New and lasting reductions of the freedom of trade should not be given to anyone in the future". Jacob Aall has described the debate about this paragraph in the following way:[22]

The civil servants tried to denounce all privileges which hampered the freest development and functioning of all trades and found only in this freedom a security for public well-being. Especially in the beginning quick steps were taken in this sudden transition from all sorts of restraints and restrictions to a complete equality, and a great confusion might have taken place in existing relations had the steady and intelligent members of the constitutional committee not prepared a suitable middle way between old aristocratic and new democratic ideas.

Aall himself was undoubtedly an opponent of the civil servants, whose liberal thoughts had been worked out over a generation, but Aall was also under the influence of the liberal ideas of Adam Smith. In spite of the fact that he was a privileged ironworks owner, as a member of the new Norwegian parliament he was the driving force behind a series of acts which from 1816 dissolved existing exclusive rights.

Aall was a man of wide reading and had certainly studied *The Wealth of Nations*. He was probably himself the owner of a copy of Danish translation. The copy of the book in Deichman's Library in Oslo was at any rate donated to the library by a grandson of Jacob Aall.

VI

The Danish translation of Adam Smith's famous book on economics was published very early in Norway and Denmark. The book as a whole has never been translated into Swedish. It was thanks to the initiative of Danish-Norwegian civil servants that this translation was arranged. They had obtained their English contacts through their connections to Norwegian merchant families. Liberal ideas had a significant influence on legislation relatively early, in the dual monarchy, and after 1814 in an independent Norway. Liberalization took place through a gradual dissolution of the mercantile system. This legislative drive happened so early, at least as far as urban trades were concerned, that it cannot have been caused by economic pressures. All important factories and other large-scale trades existed thanks to privileges and monopolies, and their owners thought in general that the mercantile system was the basis for their activities. It was liberal ideas which started this transition in economic legislation, and the diffusion of these ideas in Norway and Denmark was linked to the direct contact with Adam Smith.

NOTES

1. See vol. 1, 1920, p. 87.
2. *Nationaløkonomisk Tidsskrift*, 1936, p. 223.
3. W. R. Scott, *Adam Smith as Student and Professor*, Glasgow, 1937, p. 280.
4. Cannan's edition of *The Wealth of Nations*, London, 1950, vol. 2, p. 261 (Book V, ch. I, pt. III, art. II).
5. Rae, *Life of Adam Smith*, London, 1895.
6. *The Wealth of Nations*, loc. cit.
7. Information from P. B. Anker, Oslo, who is a descendant of Karsten Anker. P. B. Anker has entrusted the family archives to H. N. Anker, who has informed me that among the family papers there is a wrapper in which the document from Glasgow was once kept. The document itself has been lost.
8. The diary is among the family papers in H. N. Anker's possession. He has given me a transcript but noticed that the date is written, not by Adam Smith, but by the same hand as that which wrote the list of contents of the diary. Adam Smith's words in the diary have previously been quoted by Yngvar Nielsen in "General-Major Peter Anker, Guvernør i Trankebar" (*Historisk Tidsskrift*, 1871, p. 273). This article tells the exciting history of Peter Anker's later life as governor of the Danish colony Trankebar in India.
9. Information from H. N. Anker. Yngvar Nielsen writes in the article mentioned in note 8 after the Smith quotation: "Compared to the name of Adam Smith that of the Duke of Buccleugh nearly fades away, as do those of several learned and other eminent men, who have written their names in this book, and who once were known in many circles, but now are totally forgotten." Yngvar Nielsen can scarcely have been aware of the relations between Adam Smith and the Duke.
10. Rae, *Adam Smith*, p. 178.
11. This diary or travel book is mentioned in Alf Collett, *En gammel Christiania-Slægt*, Christiania, 1883, p. 179. The volumes are owned by Dr Ada Ploak (née Collett), London, but that part which concerns England has been lost. Yngvar Nielsen has, according to one of his notes, seen the notices from the journey in England. Dr Polak has informed me that Dræbye is not mentioned in the diary.

12. Professor Axel Nielsen has told Scott that he thinks it was Holt or Karsten Anker who recommended that Dræbye translate *The Wealth of Nations*. See note 1, p. 280 in Scott, *Adam Smith as Student and Professor*.

13. Rae, *Adam Smith*, p. 358, where Smith's letter to the publisher about the three copies mentioned above is referred to.

14. The error was corrected in the third edition. See Cannan's edition of *The Wealth of Nations*, vol. 2, p. 351.

15. Smith was one of the first members of the Poker Club in Edinburgh, founded in 1762. This club worked for a militia in Scotland. It is consequently understandable that Scots nationalist defence supporters might feel disappointed by the treatment of the question in *The Wealth of Nations*, but in this as in other fields Smith's research results were not influenced by his personal life.

16. Cannan's edition of *The Wealth of Nations*, vol. 2, p. 17, n. 1.

17. A letter which Adam Smith wrote for Hume's autobiography. See Niels Banke, "Ved Adam Smiths grav", *Nationaløkonomisk Tidsskrift*, 1954, p. 7. The religious community had been offended because of his fine compliments to the "free-thinker" Hume.

18. In Adam Smith's posthumous *Essays on Philosophical Subjects*, London, 1795 is a treatise on the various arts.

19. Quoted after Edv. Holm, *Danmarks og Norges Historie 1720–1814*, vol. 6, notes, pp. 12 and 117.

20. See *Industriens historie i Danmark*, ed. Axel Nielsen, vol. 2, 1730–1820 by J. O. Bro Jørgensen, p. 146ff.

21. See especially Cannan's edition of *The Wealth of Nations*, vol. 1, p. 433 (Book IV, ch. II).

22. Jacob Aall, *Erindringer som bidrag til Norges historie fra 1800–15*, Christiania, 1859, p. 431.

Part 3. France

This Part begins with my translation of the first French review of *WN*, published in February 1777. The review contains three short paragraphs of comments and the entire "Introduction and Plan of the Work" translated into French.

The second text contains five letters from Smith to the translator (l'Abbé Blavet) and his publisher in London (Thomas Cadell) regarding the French translation of *WN*. His letter to Blavet shows Smith's deep concern about the French translation (which reminds us of his contacts with the physiocrats during his younger days) and his good command of the French language. I have translated the letter into English and presented it alongside the original French version. Of the letters to Cadell, only the paragraphs relating to the French translation of *WN* are included.

The third text is by Murray (1905), who offers a useful history of the first French translations of *WN*. It gives some detailed information about the translators and publishers of *WN* from the 1770s to the 1800s, and compares the The Hague and Blavet translations.

The final text is an informative and balanced, in-depth analysis of the relationship between Smith and Say. It is taken from the classic work on the history of economic thought by Gide and Rist (1967, this section was written by Rist). It is an essential reference which should be read in conjunction with another paper, by the modern historian of economic thought Evelyn Forget (1993). Forget devotes three full pages (pp. 123–6) to Say's varied career (one-quarter of the whole paper) and then discusses three issues: "Say on Smith: Method", "Theory of Value", and "Art of Administration". In terms of the relationship between Smith and Say, I feel there are some unresolved questions to be investigated.

Related texts not collected here include the long "review article" by Germain Garnier (Marquis Garnier, 1754–1821) which appeared as "Préface du traducteur" to the second edition of his translation of *WN*, published in Paris "chez Mme veuve Agasse, Imprimeur-Librairie" in 1822 (first edition, 1802). This preface contains three long sections (vol. 1, pp. i–xci); however, a shortened English translation, omitting the first section, appeared in an 1827 edition of *WN* published in London by T. Nelson & Sons. It is a good source document on the reception of *WN* in France from the viewpoint of economic theories, since Garnier compared Smith's doctrines with those of the French economists.

This second, 1822 edition contains six volumes, of which the first four are the translation proper and the last two are Garnier's "Notes du traducteur" (72 long translator's notes, 583 + 437 pages). The two volumes of translator's notes by Garnier are a great aid to understanding the reception of Smith's doctrines in France, going beyond mere policy problems such as "free trade: pro or con". Garnier went into great detail on many issues raised by Smith in *WN*, and it is obvious that these notes were written by a critical admirer of *WN*.

Garnier was a jurist (*magistrat*), nominated Préfet de Seine-et-Oise (1799), comte et sénateur d'Empire (1804), Président du Sénat, and marquis (1814); he also was a member of the Conseil privé and a membre de l'Institut (Leduc 1976: 801). It is rare in French intellectual history for such an important figure to translate a British academic book with such devotion.

Equally interesting, and in a similar vein, is a book by Louis Say (1774–1840), *Études sur la Richesse des nations, et réfutation des principales erreurs en économie politique* (Studies on the wealth of nations, and refutation of the main errors in political economy, Paris, 1836). Louis Say was J.-B. Say's young brother, and in this 156-page book he intended to show that "although Adam Smith contributed much to the advancement of the science of the wealth of nations, the incorrect theories and nasty terminology that Adam Smith introduced have generated many difficulties. I do not doubt the true principles of this science, as have been indicated by J.-B. Say, but what irritates people is that Say did not try to replace his theories with those of Adam Smith, which have been followed blindly by most modern authors" (p. iv). Together with Garnier's two volumes of notes, this work provides a very interesting and rich source of information to evaluate the reception of Smith's theories in France. It also re-examines the deeper intellectual relationship between Smith and J.-B. Say. Can we conjecture that Louis Say's book is an "unspoken and unspeakable" part of J.-B. Say's economic thinking? In other words, I am proposing two topics for further research: "Louis Say's objections to Adam Smith" and "German Garnier's critical notes to *The Wealth of Nations*".

Diatkine (1993) offers a concrete example to show that not only was the reception of *WN* affected by the problems of language, but that the different modes of thinking (between the Scots and the physiocrats) and technical difficulties in transmitting (Smith's central) economic ideas acted as barriers. This text is an instructive case study.

Sismondi's comments on *WN* can be found in Sismondi (1991). The relationships between Smith and Turgot are well exposed in Groenewegen (1969) and Lundberg (1964). Carpenter (1995) is a very detailed study of the French versions of *WN*; he "shows the movement of the French translations from marginality in 1778 to canonicity in 1802. It documents that the diffusion of the work of Adam Smith in the French language is closely tied to the cultural politics of the time". An English original typescript is available from him at Widener Library, Harvard University.

It is clear from all of this that a fuller picture on the interactions between Smith and France is needed.

Further Reading

Texts with a * mark are printed in this Part

CARPENTER, KENNETH (1995) *"Recherches sur la nature et les causes de la richesse de nation* d'Adam Smith et politique culturelle en France", *Economies et Sociétés*, Série P.E. No. 24, 10/1995, pp. 5–30.

CHEVALIER, MICHEL (1874), "Etude sur Adam Smith et l'origine de la science économique", *Journal des économistes*, 33–4: 8–33 (Discours prononcé à l'ouverture du cours d'Economie politique du Collège de France, le 9 décembre 1873).

DELATOUR, ALBERT (1886), *Adam Smith: sa vie, ses travaux, ses doctrines*, Paris: Librairie Guillaumin.

DIATKINE, D. (1993), "A French Reading of the *Wealth of Nations* in 1790", in H. Mizuta and C. Sugiyama (eds.), *Adam Smith: International Perspectives*, pp. 213–23, London: Macmillan.

FORGET, EVELYN (1993), "J.-B. Say and Adam Smith: An Essay in the Transmission of Ideas", *Canadian Journal of Economics*, 26(1): 121–33.

GARNIER, M. GERMAIN (1822), "A short view of the doctrine of Smith, compared with that of the French economist"; originally published as "Préface du traducteur" in his 1822 translation of *WN* (91 pages). It was adapted and translated into English with the above title and included in an 1827 Edinburgh University Press edition of *WN* (pp. xvii–xxx). The same version was republished by T. Nelson & Sons, in London, Edinburgh, and New York (1864).

*GIDE, CHARLES and RIST, CHARLES (1967), "The Influence of Smith's Thought and Its Diffusion: J. B. Say", *A History of Economic Doctrines: From the Time of the Physiocrats to the Present Day*, transl. R. Richards, 2nd edn., pp. 118–33, London: Harrap.

GROENEWEGEN, P. D. (1969), "Turgot and Adam Smith", *Scottish Journal of Political Economy*, 16(3): 271–87.

**Journal des sçavants*, Feb. 1777, pp. 81–4 [first French review of *WN*].

LEDUC, GASTON (1976), "Adam Smith et la pensée française", *Revue d'économie politique*, 86(5): 795–803.

LIST, FRIEDRICH (1916), "The System of Values of Exchange (continued)—Jean-Baptiste Say and His School", *The National System of Political Economy*, transl. Sampson Lloyd, ch. 32, pp. 282–9, London: Longmans, Green & Co.

LUNDBERG, I. G. (1964), *Turgot's Unknown Translator: The* Réflexions *and Adam Smith*, The Hague: Martinus Nijhoff.

LUTFALLA, M. (1976), "Sur une réédition abrégée de la Richesse des nations", *Revue d'économie politique*, 86(5): 804–5.

*MURRAY, DAVID (1905), "French Translations of *The Wealth of Nations*", Glasgow: James MacLehose and Sons for Glasgow University [pamphlet of 15 pages].

SALLERON, L. (1973): *La Richesse des Nations: analyse critique*, Paris: Hatier.

SAY, LÉON et al. (1876), "Le centenaire du livre d'Adam Smith", *Journal des économistes*, 127: 110–21.

SAY, LOUIS (1836), *Etudes sur la Richesse des nations, et réfutation des principales erreurs en économie politique* (Studies on the wealth of nations, and refutation of the main errors in political economy), Paris.

SISMONDI, SIMONE DE (1991): "Adam Smith's System: Division of the Rest of this Work", *New Principles of Political Economy: Of Wealth in Its Relations to Population*, transl. and annotated by Richard Hyse, ch. 7, New Jersey: Transaction Publishers.

*SMITH, ADAM (1782): Letters 218, 239, 240, 242, and 244 in *Correspondence of Adam Smith*, Oxford University Press, 1977.

SPIEGEL, HENRY (1992), "The Details of Smith's System and Its Reorganization by Say", *The Growth of Economic Thought*, 3rd edn., ch. 11, Duke University Press.

STUDNITZ, ARTHUR DE (1876), "Pèlerinage à la tombe d'Adam Smith", *Journal des économistes*, 125: 258–64.

3.1. 1777.

The First French Review of
The Wealth of Nations

An inquiry into the nature and causes of the wealth of nations. Recherches sur la nature & les causes de la richess des Nations, par Adam Smith, ancien Professeur de Philosophie à Glasgow. Londres, 1776; 2 vol. in-4°.

In this work one recognizes the superior genius and talent of the author of *The Theory of Moral Sentiments,* reprinted not long ago in its fourth edition in England. The most important economic questions are treated neatly in this work with order and profundity in an intelligible manner. The author has chosen the subjects in a novel way, justified them with observations, and then demonstrated them with a clever style, so that one can offer nothing but admiration, because this is extremely rare.

Some of our men of letters who have read it have come to the conclusion that it is not a book that can be translated into our language. They point out, among other reasons, that no one would be willing to bear the expense of publishing because of the uncertain return, and a bookseller least of all. They are bound to admit, however, that the work is full of suggestions and of advice that is useful as well as curious, and might prove of benefit to statesmen.

In order to provide a general idea, we translate the Introduction of this work, which sets out the plan.

[Here nine paragraphs of the "Introduction and Plan of the Work" (before Book I) are translated into French.]

[*Editor's note*: The earliest known French book review of WN was published in the February 1777 issue of *Le Journal des sçavants*, pp. 81–4. The style is exactly the same as the review in the *Annual Register* (London, 1776), pp. 241–3), although the short comments are different. The Widener Library of Harvard University has microfilms of *Le Journal des sçavants* from 1665 to 1790 (Film S 1633). I know of the existence of this review from C. Gide and C. Rist, *A History of Economic Doctrines: From the Time of the Physiocrats to the Present Day*, transl. R. Richards, 2nd edn., p. 121. London: George G. Harrap 1967. They quote the second paragraph of this three-paragraph review, which is reproduced here. I translate the first and third paragraphs to provide the full text.]

3.2. Adam Smith, 1782.
Five Letters Concerning the French
Translation of *The Wealth of Nations*

218. *To* Abbé Blavet

Edinburgh, 23 July 1782

Monsieur, mon respectable ami, Mr. Lumsden,[1] m'a fait l'honneur de me remettre votre lettre avec votre excellente traduction de mon ouvrage[2] dans le dernier séjour que j'ai fait à Londres, où j'ai été si occupé de différantes affaires, que je n'ai pas eu le tems ni le loisir de vous remercier de la grande faveur, ainsi que de l'honneur que vous m'avez fait. Je suis charmé de cette traduction et vous m'avez rendu le plus grand service qu'on puisse rendre à un auteur, en faisant connaître mon livre à la nation de l'Europe dont je considère le plus le gout et le jugement. J'étais fort content de votre traduction de mon premier ouvrage; mais je le suis encore plus de la manière dont vous avez rendu ce dernier. Je puis vous dire, sans flatterie, que par-tout où j'ai jeté les yeus dessus, (car comme il n'y a que peu de jours que je suis parti de Londres, je n'ai pas encore eu le tems de la lire en entier) je l'ai trouvée, à tous égards, parfaitement égale à l'original.

Quelques jours après avoir quitté Londres, j'ai reçu une lettre d'un gentil-homme qui est à Bordeaux. Il s'appelle le comte de Nort,[3] et il est colonel d'infanterie au service de France. Il me mande qu'il a traduit mon livre en français et qu'il se propose de venir à Ecosse pour soumettre sa traduction a mon jugement avant de la publier. Je lui écrirai par le prochain courier que je suis si satisfait de la votre, et que je vous ai personnellement tant d'obligation, que je ne puis encourager ni en favoriser aucune autre.

To Abbé Blavet

Edinburgh, 23 July 1782

Sir, my respectable friend, Mr Lumsden, honoured me by sending your letter and your excellent translation of my work during my previous sojourn in London. I was occupied by different affairs there, so that I had no time and leisure to thank you for this grand favour, and the honour that you have done me. I am delighted by this translation and you have done me the greatest service that one can do to an author, to make my book known in the European country that I consider to have the best taste and judgement. I was very pleased by your translation of my first work [*The Theory of Moral Sentiments*, French translation by Blavet, 1774]; and I am even more pleased by the way in which you have done my latest work. I can tell you, without flattery, that wherever I have cast my eye (because I only left London a few days ago, I have still not had the time to read it entirely), I found your translation, in all aspects, perfectly equal to the original.

A few days after leaving London, I received a letter from a gentleman who lives in Bordeaux. His name is le comte de Nort, and he is a colonel in the French infantry. He asked me if he can translate my work into French, and he proposes to come to Scotland to submit his translation for my judgement before publication. I will write to him by the next post that I am so satisfied with your translation, and that I am personally so obliged to you, that I cannot encourage or favour another translation.[4]

239. *To* [Thomas Cadell]

Custom-house, Edinburgh, 19 June 1784

Dear Sir

I received your very obliging letter in due course, and the Edition of my book now goes on in a manner that is most agreeable to me; for which I consider myself as much beholden to you.[5]

I understand that the Abbé Morellet has translated my Book into french and has published it in Holland in four or six octavo Volumes with large notes.[6] I should be much obliged to you if you could procure me a copy of this translation and send it to me by the first convenient opportunity. . . .

Dear Sir
most faithfully
and affectionately
every yours
Adam Smith

240. *To* [Thomas Cadell]

Custom-house, Edinburgh, 10 Aug. 1784

Dear Sir

. . . I received the leaf that was wanting in Chesterfields miscellanies: But you say nothing to me about the french translation by the Abbé Morellet which I am very anxious to see. I have another french translation by the Abbé Blavet. Remember me to all friends and believe me to be

My Dear Sir
Most faithfully
yours
Adam Smith

242. *To* [Thomas Cadell]

Custom-house, Edinburgh, 18 Nov. 1784

Dear Sir

I received this moment your favour of the 12 instt. I am much obliged to you for your attention in procuring me the Volumes of the Philosophical transactions which I wanted;[7] But you say nothing to me of the Abbé Morellet's translation of my Book, which I am extremely desirous of seeing.[8] I am sorry to give you so much trouble, but I beg you would endeavour to procure me a copy of it for Love or Money. The Abbé himselfe, I understand, is now or was lately in London with Lord Shelburne.[9] . . .

Dear Sir, Most affectionately, Yours
Adam Smith

244. *To* [Thomas Cadell][10]

Custom-house, Edinburgh, 21 Apr. 1785

Dear Sir

. . . I was misinformed with regard to the Abbé Morellet having translated my book. . . .

My Dear Sir
your most affectionate
humble Servant
Adam Smith

NOTES

1. ?Andrew Lumsden (1720–1801), private secretary to Prince Charles Edward 1745; in exile in France and Rome till 1773; pardoned, 1778.
2. Blavet's translation of *WN* was first sent in weekly instalments to the *Journal de l'agriculture, du commerce, des arts et des finances* (Jan. 1779–Dec. 1780). It was then printed as a book, both at Yverdon and Paris, in 1781. The Abbé Morellet, who had an unpublished translation on his hands, said "poor Smith was traduced [by Blavet] rather than translated". See David Murray, *French Translations of the Wealth of Nations* (Glasgow, 1905), 4–5.
3. Not traced.
4. Editor's translation.
5. Not traced but presumably dealing with *WN* ed. 3; see Letter 237, n. 1.
6. Morellet did translate *WN* but did not publish his work (*Mémoires*, 1823, 243). A French trans. of *WN* had appeared in Holland: *Recherches sur la nature et les causes de la richesse des nations* . . . traduit de l'Anglois de M. Adam Smith, par M***. [4 t.] (The Hague, 1778–9).

author

3.3. David Murray, 1905
French Translations of *The Wealth of Nations*

B12
B31 (A. Smith) (France)

The first edition of *An Inquiry into the Nature and Causes of the Wealth of Nations* was printed in the end of the year 1775, and was published at London in the beginning of 1776, in 2 vols. 4to. It was very favourably reviewed in the *Journal des Sçavans* of February, 1777 (p. 81 of the 4to, p. 239 of the 12mo edition), but the reviewer remarked that no author or publisher was prepared to take the risk of publishing a French translation.

The Abbé Morellet, writing to Lord Shelburne from Paris on 12th March, 1776, says: "I have got the loan of the first volume of the new book of M. Smith, in which I have found some excellent things. The developments are somewhat drawn out and the 'Scottish subtilty' is present in all its luxuriance. This possibly may not be pleasing to you, but the work has given me great pleasure, as I delight in such speculations" (*Lettres de l'Abbé Morellet à Lord Shelburne*, p. 105: Paris, 1898, 8vo). In his *Mémoires* the Abbé states that he spent the autumn of the year 1776 at Brienne, in Champagne, and occupied himself very assiduously in translating *The Wealth of Nations*: but an ex-Benedictine, the Abbé Blavet, the author of a bad translation of the *Theory of Moral Sentiments*, took up Adam Smith's new treatise and sent it in weekly instalments to the *Journal of Commerce*. "This," says Morellet, "was an excellent thing for the journal, as it filled its columns, but poor Smith was traduced rather than translated, according to the Italian proverb *tradattore traditore*. Blavet's version, which was dispersed through the columns of the journal, was soon issued in a collected form by a bookseller, and proved an obstacle to the publication of mine. I offered it first for a hundred louis, and then for nothing, but the competition caused its rejection. Long after I asked the Archbishop of Sens, during his ministry, for a hundred louis, and said that I would take the risk of publication, but he declined, as the booksellers had formerly done. It would have been a hundred louis well employed. My translation was carefully made. Everything of an abstract character in Smith's theory becomes unintelligible in Blavet's translation, but in mine may be read with profit" (*Mémoires de l'Abbé Morellet*, p. 243: Paris, 1823, 8vo).

The reprint of Blavet's version to which Morellet refers appeared at Yverdon in 1781 in 6 volumes 12mo, and at Paris in the same year in 3 volumes 12mo, and again at London and Paris in 1788 in 2 volumes 8vo, and revised and corrected, with Blavet's name as translator, at Paris An, ix, (1800–01) in 4 volumes 8vo.

In the meantime another translation, of no great merit, was made by Jeane Antoine Roucher, the poet, author of *Les Saisons*, and was published at Paris in 1790 in 4 volumes 8vo; again at Neufchatel in 1792 in 5 volumes 8vo, and lastly at Paris An. iii. (1795) in 5 volumes 8vo. According to Blavet, Roucher was more concerned with the language than the sense. He says that he did not understand English, and relied upon his version, although he pretended that he was not aware of any French translation of the work.

A third and better translation by Count Germain Garnier appeared at Paris An. x. (1802) in 5 volumes 8vo, with a portrait of Adam Smith. Other editions were issued in 1809 and 1822, the former in 3 the latter in 6 volumes 8vo, one being a volume of notes. This edition was revised by Jerome Adolphe Blanqui, and was republished at Paris in 1843 in 2 volumes 8vo as volumes 5 and 6 of Guillaume's *Collection des Économistes*.

As the Abbé Morellet lived until 1819, and depended for his livelihood, in his later years, on translations for the booksellers, it seems strange that he was unable to dispose of his MS. of *The Wealth of Nations* when other two translations found a market, notwithstanding that of Blavet.

In his edition of Paris, 1800–01, the Abbé Blavet, or Citizen Blavet as he then styles himself, gives some information regarding his translation. He made it, he says, entirely for his own use, and with no great exactness. He had no intention of publishing it until his friend M. Ameilhon happened to complain of a scarcity of interesting articles for his *Journal de l'Agriculture, du Commerce, des Arts et des Finances*,[1] which had just come under the control of the mercantilists. It struck him that he might offer it to him which he did, with the explanation that it was far from perfect. It was accepted, and appeared in the issues of the *Journal* between January, 1779, and December, 1780. He did not anticipate that it would go further, but scarcely had the last part appeared when it was reprinted and published at Yverdon in 1781, with more faults than in the serial publication. The edition of 1788 likewise appeared without his knowledge or consent, and was still more marred by errors than that of Yverdon. Blavet had stipulated with Ameilhon that his name was not to appear, but seeing the popularity the work had secured he sent a letter to the *Journal de Paris* of 5th December, 1788, claiming the authorship. This letter brought him into communication with M. Guyot, of Neufchatel, with whom he had hitherto been unacquainted. Guyot, who was a friend of Smith and of Dugald Stewart, said that although complaints had been made regarding the translation, the faults were of a kind that could easily be corrected, and he offered his assistance in doing this. He said that when the edition of 1788 appeared both he and Stewart believed that it was by the Abbé Morellet.

Blavet followed Guyot's advice, revised his translation, and published it with his name at Paris in 1800. In the British Museum there is a copy of the edition of 1788, with numerous MS. corrections, said to be by Blavet, most of which have been given effect to in the edition of 1800.

Adam Smith had a copy of Blavet's edition of 1788, and another of that of 1800. The latter bears the inscription, "À M. Smith de la part de son tres humble serviteur, l'Abbé Blavet." Although Blavet did not acknowledge the translation until 1788, it seems to have been known that it was by him, for he prints a letter from Smith to himself, dated Edinburgh, 23rd July, 1782, in which Smith says he had had a letter from the Comte de Nort, a colonel of infantry in the French Army, proposing a new translation, but he had written to him that it was not required. He adds that he did not propose to encourage or favour any other than that of Blavet.

While all of these translations are well known, and have been the subject of considerable discussion, there was a fourth and earlier one which seems to have been entirely overlooked. The title page of the first volume reads thus: Recherches | *Sur* | La Nature | Et Les Causes | *De Là* | Richesse | *Des* | Nations. | Tome Premier. | Traduit de l'Anglois de M. Adam Smith, par M. . . . | A La Haye | MDCCLXXVIII.

The book is in four volumes 12mo. Volumes I. and II. bear date 1778, volumes III. and IV. 1779.

Blavet's translation, as we have seen, appeared in the columns of the *Journal de l'Agriculture* between January, 1779, and December, 1780, so that the Hague translation was thus a year earlier in date, and was evidently by a different hand, as may be seen by comparing one or two passages.

The Hague | Blavet

I. INTRODUCTION

La travail annuel de la Société est le fonds qui lui procure originairement toutes les nécessités & les commodités de la vie qu'elle consomme annuellement, & qui consiste toujours ou dans le produit immédiat de ce travail, ou dans ce qu'elle achete des autres nations avec ce produit.

Ainsi, selon que ce produit ou ce qui est acheté avec ce produit, a plus ou moins de proportion avec le nombre des consommateurs, la Nation sera plus ou moins abondamment pourvue des nécessités ou commodités dont elle a besoin.

I. INTRODUCTION

Le travail annuel d'une nation est la source d'où elle tire toutes les choses nécessaires & commodes qu'elle consomme annuellement, & qui consistent toujours ou dans le produit immédiat de ce travail, ou dans ce qu'elle achett des autres nations avec ce produit.

Ainsi, selon qu'il y aura plus ou moins de proportion entre le nombre de ses consommateurs & ce produit ou ce qu'elle achette avec ce produit, elle sera mieux ou plus mal pourvu par rapport aux besoins & aux commodités de la vie.

[In the revised edition of 1800 the concluding words run thus: "pourvu des choses nécessaires et commodes dont elle a besoin." This alteration is not in the British Museum copy of 1788.]

BOOK I. c 1.

Le travail paroît tirer sa principale force; le talent, l'adresse, l'art qui l'applique ou dirige, paroissent tenir leurs plus grand succès de sa distribution.

BOOK I. c. 1.

La division du travail est ce qui semble avoir contribué d'avantage à perfectionner les facultés qui le produisent, & a donner l'addresse, la dextérité & le discernement avec lesquels on l'applique & on le dirige.

[The revised edition of 1800, after "produisent," reads "et de la dextérité, de l'habileté et du jugement." This alteration partly appears in the British Museum copy of 1788.]

BOOK I. c. XI

La rente, considérée comme le prix du loyer de la terre, est naturellement la plus forte que le Colon puisse payer au propriétaire relativement à l'état actuel de la terre.

BOOK I. c. XI

La rente considerée comme le prix payé pour l'usage de la terre, est naturellement le taux le plus haut que le tenancier puisse en donner dans les circonstances actuelles de la terre.

[The revised edition of 1800 for the last four words reads, "on se trouve la terre." The passage is unaltered in the British Museum copy of the 1788 edition.]

There is no copy of this early translation in the British Museum, or, so far as I can ascertain from catalogues, in any of the large libraries in the country. The collection of works by and relating to Adam Smith in the British Museum is very inadequate, and that in the library of the University of Glasgow—Smith's own university—is still more so.

Perhaps. I may add, as supplementary to Mr. Bonar's *Catalogue of the Library of Adam Smith*, that I have the following books bearing his bookplate:

(1) Cumberland (Richard).
    De legibus naturae.   Lubecae, 1694, 8vo.

(2) A volume of Tracts by Josiah Tucker.
    There is a list prefixed in Smith's handwriting.
    They are as follows:

    (a) Reflections on the expendiency of a law for the Naturalization of Foreign Protestants.
        Part i.   London, 1751, 8vo.

    (b) The same. Part ii.   *Ib.*, 1752, 8vo.

    (c) A Letter to a Friend concerning Naturalizations. Second edition.
                                        Ib., 1753, 8vo.

    (d) A second Letter to a Friend concerning Naturalizations. *Ib.*, 1753, 8vo.

    (e) An impartial Inquiry into the benefits and damages arising to the Nation from the present very great use of *Low-priced* Spirituous Liquors.   *Ib.*, 1751, 8vo.

    (f) Reflections on the expediency of opening the Trade to Turkey.
                                        Ib., 1755, 8vo.

    (g) Instructions for Travellers.   Dublin, 1758, 8vo.

    (h) Two Dissertations on certain Passages of Holy Scripture.
                                     London, 1749, 8vo.

        In 1756 Tucker's *Essay on the Advantages and Disadvantages which respectively attend France and Great Britain with regard to Trade* was reprinted at Glasgow. There can be little doubt that this was upon the suggestion of Smith.

(3) Virgilii Opera.   Glasgow, 1778, folio, 2 vols.
    A large paper copy is full polished calf; original binding. His name appears amongst those "of the Persons by whose encouragement this Edition has been printed."

NOTE

1. This is a third series of the *Journal de Commerce* of Camus and the Abbé Roubaud. Bruxelles, 1759–62, 24 vol. 12mo. It was discontinued for a short time and reappeared again at Paris in July, 1765, under the title *Journal d'Agriculture, du Commerce et des Finances*, and Dupont de Nemours was associated with the other two as principal editor. This series ran until December, 1774, in 114 monthly parts, making 48 vols. 12mo. The *Journal* had been the battle-ground of the mercantilists and the physiocrats. In 1767, the former having got the upper hand, dismissed Dupont de Nemours, who with his party found an organ in the *Ephémérides du Citoyen*, which was then edited by the Abbé Baudeau, who retired in favour of Dupont de Nemours in May, 1768. It stopped in March, 1772, but reappeared again in December, 1774, and ran until June, 1776. A copy for the years 1765–67 was in Adam Smith's library.

The *Journal d'Agriculture* was discontinued until January, 1778, when it appeared under the title in the text, with Ameilhon as editor. It ran until December, 1783, in 72 monthly parts, forming 24 vols. 12mo. It was then absorbed by the *Affiches, Annonces et Avis divers*, which in 1784 adopted the sub-title, *ou Journal général de France*, and became in 1785 *Journal général de France*. From 1787 to 1790 a Supplement devoted to agriculture was issued.

3.4. Charles Gide and Charles Rist, 1967
The Influence of Smith's Thought and Its Diffusion: J. B. Say

The eighteenth century was essentially a century of levelling down. In Smith's conception of the economic world we have an excellent example of this. Its chief charm lies in the simplicity of its outlines, and this doubtless accountd for his influence among his contemporaries. The system of natural liberty towards which both their political and philosophical aspirations seemed to point were here deduced from, and supported by, evidence taken direct from a study of human nature—evidence, moreover, that seemed to tally so well with known facts that doubt was out of the question. Smith's work still retains its irresistible charm. Even if his ideas are some day shown to be untenable—a contingency we cannot well imagine—his book will remain as a permanent monument of one of the most important epochs in economic thought. It must still be considered the most successful attempt made at embracing within a single purview the infinite diversity of the economic world.

But its simplicity also constituted its weakness. To attain this simplicity more than one important fact that refused to fit in with the system had to remain in the background. The evidence employed was also frequently incomplete. None of the special themes—price, wages, profits, and rent, the theory of international trade or of capital—which occupy the greater portion of the work, but has been in some way corrected, disputed, or replaced. But the structure loses stability if some of the corner-stones are removed. And new points of view have appeared of which Smith did not take sufficient account. Instead of the pleasant impression of simplicity and security which a perusal of Smith's work gave to the economists of the early nineteenth century, there has been gradually substituted by his successors a conviction of the growing complexity of economic phenomena.

To pass a criticism on the labours of Adam Smith would be to review the economic doctrines of the nineteenth century. That is the best eulogy one can bestow upon his work. The economic ideas of a whole century were, so to speak, in solution in his writings. Friends and foes have alike taken him as their starting-point. The former have developed, extended, and corrected his work. The latter have subjected his principal theories to harsh criticism at every point. All with tacit accord admit that political economy commenced with him. As Garnier, his French translator, put it, "he wrought a complete revolution in the science."[2] To-day, even although the *Wealth of Nations* may no longer appear to us as a truly scientific treatise on political economy, certain of its fundamental ideas remain incontestable. The theory of money, the importance of division of labour, the fundamental character of spontaneous economic institutions, the constant operation of personal interest in economic life, liberty as the basis of rational political economy—all these appear to us as definite acquisitions to the science.

The imperfections of the work will be naturally demonstrated in the chapters which follow. In order to complete our exposition of Smith's doctrines it only remains to show how they were diffused.

The rapid spread of his ideas throughout Europe and their incontestable supremacy remains one of the most curious phenomena in the history of ideas. Smith persuaded his own generation and governed the next.[3] History affords us some clue. To attribute it solely to the influence of his book is sheer exaggeration.A great deal must be set to the credit of circumstances more or less fortuitous.

M. Mantoux remarks with much justice that it was the American War rather than Smith's writings which demonstrated the decay of the ancient political economy and compassed its ruin. The War of Independence proved two things: (1) The danger lurking in a colonial system which could goad the most prosperous colonies to revolt; (2) the uselessness of a protective tariff, for on the very morrow of the war English trade with the American colonies was more flourishing than ever before. "The loss of the American colonies to England was really a gain to her." So wrote Say in 1803, and he adds: "This is a fact that I have nowhere seen disputed."[4] To the American War other causes must be added: (1) The urgent need for markets felt by English merchants at the close of the Napoleonic Wars; they were already abundantly supplied with excellent machinery. (2) Coupled with this was a growing belief that a high price of corn as the result of agricultural protection increased the cost of hand labour. These two reasons were enough to create a desire for a general lowering of the customs duties.

Subsequent events have justified Smith's attitude on the question of foreign trade. In the matter of domestic trade he has been less fortunate.

The French Revolution, which owed its economic measures to the Physiocrats, gave a powerful impulse to the principle of liberty. The influence of the movement was potent enough on the Continent. Even in England, where this influence was least felt, everybody was in favour of *laissez-faire*. Pitt became anxious to free Ireland from its antiquated system of prohibitions, and he succeeded in doing this by his Act of Union in 1800. The regulations laid down by the Elizabethan Statute of Apprentices, with its limitation of the hours of work and the fixing of wages by justices of the peace, became more and more irksome as industry developed. Every historian of the Industrial Revolution has described the struggle between workers and masters and shown how the former clung in despair to the old legislative measures as their only safeguard against a too rapid change, while the latter refused to be constrained either in the choice of workmen or the methods of their work.[5] They wished to pay only the wages that suited them and to use their machines as long as possible. These repeated attacks rendered the old Statute of Apprentices useless, and Parliament abolished its regulations one after another, so that by 1814 all traces of it were for ever effaced from the Statute Book.

But Smith did not foresee these things. He did not write with a view to pleasing either merchants or manufacturers. On the contrary, he was never weary of denouncing their monopolistic tendencies. But by the force of circumstances manufacturers and merchants became his best allies. His book supplied them with arguments, and it was his authority that they always invoked.

His authority never ceased growing. As soon as the *Wealth of Nations* appeared, men like Hume, and Gibbon, the historian, expressed to Smith or to his friends their admiration of the new work. In the following year the Prime Minister, Lord North, borrowed from him the idea of levying two new taxes—the tax on malt and the tax on inhabited houses. Smith was yet to make an even more illustrious convert in the person of Pitt. Pitt was a student when the *Wealth of Nations* appeared, but he always declared himself a disciple of Smith, and as soon as he became a Minister he strove to realize his ideas. It was he who signed the first Free Trade treaty with France—the Treaty of Eden, 1786.[6] When Smith came to London in 1787 Pitt met him more than once and consulted him on financial matters. The story is told that after one of these conversations Smith exclaimed: "What an extraordinary person Pitt is! He understands my ideas better than myself."

While Smith made converts of the most prominent men of his time, his book gradually reached the public. Four editions in addition to the first appeared during the author's lifetime.[7] The third, in 1784, presents important differences in the way of additions and corrections as compared with the first. From the date of his death in 1790 to the end of the century three other editions were published.[8]

Similar success attended the appearance of the work on the Continent. In France he was already known through his *Theory of Moral Sentiments*. The first mention of the *Wealth of Nations* in France appears in the *Journal des Savants* in the month of February 1777. Here, after a brief description of the merits of the work, the critic gives expression to the following curious opinion:

Some of our men of letters who have read it have come to the conclusion that it is not a book that can be translated into our language. They point out, among other reasons, that no one would be willing to bear the expense of publishing because of the uncertain return, and a bookseller least of all. They are bound to admit, however, that the work is full of suggestions and of advice that is useful as well as curious, and might prove of benefit to statesmen.

In reality, despite the opinion of those men of letters, several translations of the work did appear in France, as well as elsewhere in Europe. In little more than twenty years, between 1779 and 1802, four translations had appeared. This in itself affords sufficient proof of the interest which the book had aroused.[9]

Few works have enjoyed such complete and universal success. But despite admiration the ideas did not spread very rapidly. Faults of composition have been burdened with the responsibility for this, and it is a reproach that has clung to the *Wealth of Nations* from the first. Its organic unity is very pronounced, but Smith does not seem to have taken the trouble to give it even the semblance of outward unity. To discover its unity requires a real effort of thought. Smith whimsically regarded it as a mere discourse, and the reading occasionally gives the impression of conversation. The general formulae which summarize or recapitulate his ideas are indifferently found either in the middle or at the end of a chapter, just as they arose. They represent the conclusions from what preceded as they flashed across his mind. On the other hand, a consideration of such a question as money is scattered throughout the whole work, being discussed on no less than ten different occasions. As early as April 1, 1776, Hume had expressed to Smith some doubts as to the popularity of the book, seeing that its reading demanded considerable attention. Sartorius in 1794 attributed to this difficulty the slow progress made by Smith's ideas in Germany. Germain Garnier, the French translator, gave an outline of the book in order to assist his readers. It was generally agreed that the work was a striking one, but badly composed and difficult to penetrate owing to the confused and equivocal character of some of the paragraphs. When Say referred to it as "a chaotic collection of just ideas thrown indiscriminately among a number of positive truths,"[10] he expressed the opinion of all who had read it.

But a complete triumph, so far as the Continent at least was concerned, had to be the work of an interpreter. Such an interpreter must fuse all these ideas into a coherent body of doctrines, leaving useless digressions aside.[11] This was the task that fell into the hands of J. B. Say. Among his merits (and it is not the only one) is that of popularizing the ideas of the great Scots economist on the Continent, and of giving to the ideas a somewhat classical appearance. The task of discrediting the first French school of economists and of facilitating the expansion of English political economy fell, curiously enough, to the hands of a Frenchman.

J. B. Say was twenty-three years of age in 1789.[12] At that time he was Clavières's secretary. Clavières became Minister of Finance in 1792, but at this period he was manager of an assurance company, and was already a disciple of Smith. Say came across some stray pages of the *Wealth of Nations*, and sent for a copy of the book.[13] The impression it made upon him was profound. "When we read this work," he writes, "we feel that previous to Smith there was no such thing as political economy." Fourteen years afterwards, in 1803, appeared *Le Traité d'économie politique*. The book met with immediate success, and a second edition would have appeared had not the First Consul interdicted it. Say had refused to support the Consul's financial recommendations, and the writer, in addition to having his book proscribed, found himself banished from the Tribunate. Say waited until 1814 before republishing it. New editions rapidly followed, in 1817, 1819, and 1826. The treatise was translated into several languages. Say's authority gradually extended itself; his reputation became European; and by these means the ideas of Adam Smith, clarified and logically arranged in the form of general principles from which conclusions could be easily deduced, gradually captivated the more enlightened section of public opinion.

It would, however, be unjust to regard Say as a mere popularizer of Smith's ideas. With praiseworthy modesty, he has never attempted to conceal all that he owed to the master. The master's name is mentioned in almost every line, but he never remains content with a mere repetition of his ideas. These are carefully reconsidered and reviewed with discrimination. He develops some of them and emphasizes others. Amid the devious paths pursued by Smith, the French economist chooses that which most directly leads to the desired end. This path is so clearly outlined for his successors that "wayfaring men, though fools, could not err therein." In a sense he may be said to have filtered the ideas of the master, or to have toned his doctrines with the proper tints. He thus imparted to French political economy its distinctive character as distinguished from English political economy, to which at about the same time Malthus and Ricardo were to give an entirely new orientation. What interests us more than his borrowing is the personal share which he has in the work, an estimate of which we must now attempt.

(1) In the first place, Say succeeded in overthrowing the work of the Physiocrats.

The work of demolition was not altogether useless. In France there were many who still clung to the "sect." Even Germain Garnier, Smith's translator, considered the arguments of the Physiocrats theoretically irrefutable. The superiority of the Scots economist was entirely in the realm of practice.[14] "We may," says he, "reject the *Economistes'* theory [meaning the Physiocrats'] because it is less useful, although it is not altogether erroneous." Smith himself, as we know, was never quite rid of this idea, for he recognized a special productiveness of land as a result of the co-operation of nature, and doctors, judges, advocates, and artists were regarded as unproductive. But Say's admission was the last straw. Not in agriculture alone, but everywhere, "nature is forced to work along with man,"[15] and by the funds of nature was to be understood in future all the help that a nation draws directly from nature, be it the force of wind or rush of water.[16] As to the doctors, lawyers, etc., how are we to prove that they take no part in production? Garnier had already protested against their exclusion. Such services must no doubt be classed as immaterial products, but products none the less, seeing that they possess exchange value and are the outcome[17] of the co-operation of capital and industry. In other respects also—e.g., in the pleasure and utility which they yield—services are not very unlike commodities. Say's doctrine meets with some opposition on this point, for the English economists were unwilling to consider a simple service as wealth because of its unendurable character, and the consequent fact that it could not be considered as adding to the aggregate amount of capital. But he soon wins over the majority of writers.[18] Finally Say, like Condillac, discovered a decisive argument against Physiocracy in the fact that the production of material objects does not imply their creation. Man never can create, but must be content with mere transformation of matter. Production is merely a creation of utilities, a furthering of that capacity of responding to our needs and of satisfying our wants which is possessed by commodities; and all work is productive which achieves this result, whether it be industry, commerce, or agriculture.[19] The Physiocratic distinction falls to the ground, and Say refutes what Smith, owing to his intimacy with his adversaries, had failed to disprove.

(2) On another point Say carries forward Smith's ideas, although at the same

time superseding them. He subjects the whole conception of political economy and the role of the economist to a most thorough examination.

We have already noticed that the conception of the "natural order" underwent considerable modification during the period which intervened between the writings of the Physiocrats and the appearance of the *Wealth of Nations*. The Physiocrats regarded the "order" as one that was to be realized, and the science of political economy as essentially normative. For Smith it was a self-realizing order. This spontaneity of the economic world is analogous to the vitality of the human body, and is capable of triumphing over the artificial barriers which Governments may erect against its progress. Practical political economy is based upon a knowledge of the economic constitution of society, and its sole aim is to give advice to statesmen. According to Say, this definition concedes too much to practice. Political economy, as he thinks, is just the science of this "spontaneous economic constitution," or, as he puts it in 1814, it is a study of the laws which govern wealth.[20] It is, as the title of his book suggests, simply an exposition of the production, distribution, and consumption of wealth. It must be distinguished from politics, with which it has been too frequently confused, and also from statistics, which is a simple description of particular facts and not a science of co-ordinate principles at all.

Political economy in the hands of J. B. Say became a purely theoretical and descriptive science. The role of the economist, like that of the savant, is not to give advice, but simply to observe, to analyse, and to describe. "He must be content to remain an impartial spectator," he writes to Malthus in 1820. "What we owe to the public is to tell them how and why such-and-such a fact is the consequence of another. Whether the conclusion be welcomed or rejected, it is enough that the economist should have demonstrated its cause; but he must give no advice."[21]

In this way Say broke with the long tradition which, stretching from the days of the Canonists and the Cameralists to those of the Mercantilists and the Physiocrats, had treated political economy as a practical art and a guide for statesmen and administrators. Smith had already tried to approach economic phenomena as a scientist, but there was always something of the reformer in his attitude. Say's only desire was to be a mere student; the healing art had no attraction for him, and so he inaugurates the true scientific method. He, moreover, instituted a comparison between this science and physics rather than between it and natural history, and in this respect also he differed from Smith, for whom the social body was essentially a living thing. Without actually employing the term "social physics", he continually suggests it by his repeated comparison with Newtonian physics. The principles of the science, like the laws of physics, are not the work of men. They are derived from the very nature of things. They are not established; they are discovered. They govern even legislators and princes, and one never violates them with impunity.[22] Like the laws of gravity, they are not confined within the frontiers of any one country, and the limits of State administration, which are all-important for the student of politics, are mere accidents for the economist.[23] Political economy is accordingly based on the model of an exact science, with laws that are universal. Like physics, it is not so much concerned with the accumulation of particular facts as with the formulation of a few general principles from which a chain of consequences of greater or smaller length may be drawn according to circumstances.

A delight in uniformity,[24] love of universality, and contempt for isolated facts, these are the marks of the savant. But the same qualities in men of less breadth of view may easily become deformed and result in faults of indifference or of dogmatism, or even contempt for all facts. And are not these very faults produced by the stress which he lays upon these principles? Was not political economy placed in a vulnerable position for the attacks of Sismondi, of List, of the Historical school, and of the Christian Socialists by this very work of Say? In his radical separation of politics and economics, in avoiding the "practical" leanings of Adam Smith, he has succeeded in giving the science a greater degree of harmony. But it also acquired a certain frigidity which his less gifted successors have mistaken for banality or crudity. Rightly or wrongly, the responsibility is ascribed to Say.

(3) We have just seen the influence which the progress of the physical sciences had upon Say's conception of political economy; but he was also much influenced by the progress of industry. Between 1776, the date of the appearance of the *Wealth of Nations*, and the year 1803, when Say's treatise appeared, the Industrial Revolution had taken place. This is a fact of considerable importance for the history of economic ideas.

When Say visited England a little before 1789 he found machine production already in full swing there. In France at the same date manufactures were only just beginning. They increased rapidly under the Empire, and the progress after 1815 became enormous. Chaptal in his work *De l'Industrie française* reckons that in 1819 there were 220 factories in existence, with 922,200 spindles consuming 13 million kilograms of raw cotton. This, however, only represented a fifth of the English production, which twenty year later was quadrupled. Other industries were developing in a similar way. Everybody was convinced that the future must be along those lines—an indefinite future, it is true, but it was to be one of wealth, work, and well-being. The rising generation was intoxicated at the prospect. The most eloquent exposition of this debauchery will be found in Saint-Simonism.

Say did not escape the infection. While Smith gives agriculture the premier place, Say accords the laurels to manufactures. For many years industrial problems had been predominant in political economy, and the first official course of lectures given by Say himself at the Conservatoire des Arts et Métiers was entitled "A Course of Lectures on Industrial Economy."

In that hierarchy of activities which Smith had drawn up according to the varying degree of utility each possessed for the nation Smith had placed agriculture first. Say preserved the order, but placed alongside of agriculture "all capital employed in utilizing any of the productive forces of nature. An ingenious machine may produce more than the equivalent of the interest on the capital it has cost to produce, and society enjoys the benefit in lower prices."[25] This sentence is not found in the edition of 1803, and appears only in the second edition. Say in the meantime had been managing his factory at Auchy-les-Hesdins, and he had profited by his experience. This question of machinery, which was merely touched on by Smith in a short passage, finds a larger place in every successive edition of Say's work. The general adoption of machinery by manufacturers both in England and France frequently incited the workers to riot. Say does not fail to demonstrate its advantages. At first he admits that the Government might mitigate the resulting evils by confining the employment of machinery at the outset to certain districts where labour is scarce or is employed in other branches of production.[26] But by the beginning of the fifth edition he changed his advice and declared that such intervention involved interference with the inventor's property,[27] admitting only that the Government might set up works of public utility in order to employ those men who are thrown out of employment on account of the introduction of machinery.

The influence of these same circumstances must be accounted responsible for the stress which is laid by Say upon the role of an individual whom Smith had not even defined, though Cantillon had already emphasized that role, and who is henceforth to remain an important personage in the economic world, namely, the *entrepreneur*.[28] At the beginning of the nineteenth century the principal agent of economic progress was the industrious, active, well-informed individual, either an ingenious inventor, a progressive agriculturist, or an experienced business man. This type became quite common in every country where mechanical production and increasing markets became the rule. It is he rather than the capitalist properly so called, the landed proprietor, or the workman, who is "almost always passive," who directs production and superintends the distribution of wealth. "The power of industrial *entrepreneurs* exercises a most notable influence upon the distribution of wealth," says Say. "In the same kind of industry one *entrepreneur* who is judicious, active, methodical, and willing makes his fortune, while another who is devoid of these qualities or who meets with very different circumstances would be ruined."[29] Is it not the master spinner of Auchy-les-Hesdins who is speaking here? We are easily convinced of this if we compare the edition of 1803 with that of 1814, and we can trace the gradual growth and development of this conception with every successive edition of the work.

Say's classic exposition of the mechanism of distribution is based upon this very admirable conception, which is altogether superior to that of Smith or the Physiocrats. The *entrepreneur* serves as the pivot of the whole system. The following may be regarded as an outline of his treatment.

Men, capital, and labour furnish what Say refers to as productive services. These services, when brought to market, are given in exchange for wages, interest, or rent. It is the *entrepreneur*, whether merchant, manufacturer, or agriculturist, who requires them, and it is he who combines them with a view to satisfying the demand of consumers. "The *entrepreneurs*, accordingly, are mere intermediaries who set up a claim for those productive services which are necessary to satisfy the demand for certain products." Accordingly there arises a demand for productive services, and the demand is "one of the factors determining the value of those services."

On the other hand, the agents of production, both men and things, whether land, capital, or industrial employees, offer their services in greater or less quantities according to various motives, and thus constitute another factor which determines the value of these same services.[30]

In this fashion the law of demand and supply determines the price of services, the average rate of interest, and rent. Thanks to the *entrepreneur*, the value produced is again distributed among these "various productive services," and the various services allotted according to need among the industries. This theory of distribution is in complete accordance with the theory of exchange and production.

Say's very simple scheme of distribution constitutes a real progress. In the first place, it is much more exact than the Physiocrats', who conceived of exchange as taking place between classes only, and not between individuals. It also enables us to distinguish the remuneration of the capitalist from the earnings of the *entrepreneur*, which were confounded by Adam Smith. The Scots economist assumed that the *entrepreneur* was very frequently a capitalist, and confused the two functions, designating his total remuneration by the single word "profit," without every distinguishing between net interest of capital and profit properly so called. This regrettable confusion was followed by other English authors, and remained in English economic theory for a long time. Finally, Say's theory has another advantage. It gave to his French successors a clear scheme of distribution which was wanting in Smith's work, just at the time when Ricardo was attempting to overcome the omission by outlining a new theory of distribution. According to Ricardo, rent, by its very nature and the laws which give rise to it, is opposed to other revenues, and the rate of wages and of profits must be regarded as direct opposites, so that the one can only increase if the other diminishes—an attactive but erroneous theory, and one which led to endless discussion among English economists, with the result that they abandoned it altogether. Say, by showing this dependence, which becomes quite clear if we regard wages and profits from the point of view of demand for commodities, and by his demonstration that rent is determined by the same general causes—*viz.*, demand and supply—as determine the exchange value of other productive services, saved political economy in France from a similar disaster. It was he, also, who furnished Walras with the first outlines of his attractive conception of prices and economic equilibrium. This explains why he never attached to the theory of rent the supreme importance given to it by English economists. In this respect he has been followed by the majority of French economists. On the other hand, and for a similar reason, he never went to the opposite extreme of denying the existence of rent altogether by regarding it merely as the revenue yielded by capital sunk in land. In this way he avoided the error which Carey and Bastiat attempted to defend at a later period.[31]

(4) So far it is Say's brilliant power of logical reasoning that we have admired. But has he contributed anything which is entirely new to the science?

His theory of markets was for a long time considered first-class work. "Products are given in exchange for products." It is a happy phrase, but it is not in truth very profound. It simply gives expression to an idea that was quite familiar to the Physiocrats and to Smith, namely, that money is but an intermediary which is acquired only to be passed on and exchanged for another product. "Once the exchange has been effected it is immediately discovered that products pay for products."[32] Thus goods constitute a demand for other goods, and the interest of a country that produces much is that other countries should produce at least as much. Say thought that the outcome of this would be the advent of the true brotherhood of man. "The theory of markets will change the whole policy of the world," said he.[33] He thought that the greater part of the doctrine of Free Trade could be based upon this principle. But to expect so much from such a vague, self-evident formula was to hope for the impossible.

Still more interesting is the way in which he applied this "theory of markets" to a study of over-production crises, and the light which that sheds upon the nature of Say's thought. Garnier had already pointed out that a general congestion of markets was possible. As crises multiplied this fear began to agitate the minds of a number of thinkers. "Nothing can be more illogical," writes Say. "The total supply of products and the total demand for them must of necessity be equal, for the total demand is nothing but the whole mass of commodities which have been produced: a general congestion would consequently be an absurdity."[34] It would simply mean a general increase of wealth, and "wealth is none too plentiful among nations, any more than it is among individuals."[35] We may have an inefficient application of the means of production, resulting in the over-production of some one commodity or other—i.e., we may have partial over-production.[36] Say wishes to emphasize the fact that we need never fear general over-production, but that we may have too much of some one product or other. He frequently gave expression to this idea in the form of paradoxes. We might almost be led to believe that he denies the existence of crises altogether in the second edition of his work.[37] In reality he was very anxious to admit their existence, but he wished to avoid everything that might prove unfavourable to an extension of industry.[38]

He thought that crises were essentially transient, and declared that individual liberty would be quite enough to prevent them. He was extremely anxious to get rid of the vague terrors which had haunted those people who feared that they would not be able to consume all this wealth, of a Malthus who thought the existence of the idle rich afforded a kind of safety-valve which prevented over-production,[39] of a Sismondi who prayed for a slackening of the pace of industrial progress and a checking of inventions. Such thoughts arouse his indignation, especially, as he remarks, when it is remembered that even among the most flourishing nations "seven-eighths of the population are without a great number of products which would be regarded as absolute necessities, not by a wealthy family, but even by one of moderate means."[40] The inconvenience—and he is never tired of repreating it—is not the result of over-production, but is the effect of producing what is not exactly wanted.[41] Produce, produce all that you can, and in the natural course of events a lowering of prices will benefit even those who at first suffered from the extension of industry.

In this once-famous controversy between Say, Malthus, Sismondi, and Ricardo (the last sided with Say) we must not expect to find a clear exposition of the causes of crises. Indeed, that is nowhere to be found. All we have here is the expression of a sentiment which is at bottom perfectly just, but one which Say wrongly attempted to state in a scientific formula.

J. B. Say plays a by no means negligible part in the history of doctrines. Foreign economists have not always recognized him. Dühring, who is usually perspicacious, is very unjust to him when he speaks of "the labour of dilution" to which Say devoted his energies.[42] His want of insight frequently caused him to glide over problems instead of attempting to fathom them, and his treatment of political economy occasionally appears very superficial. Certain difficulties are veiled with pure verbiage—a characteristic in which he is very frequently imitated by Bastiat. Despite Say's greater lucidity, it is doubtful whether Smith's obscurity of style is not, after all, more stimulating for the mind. Notwithstanding all this, he was faithful in his transmission of the ideas of the great Scots economist into French. Happily his knowledge of Turgot and Condillac enabled him to rectify some of the more contestable opinions of his master, and in this way he avoided many of the errors of his succcessors. He has left his mark upon French political economy, and had the English economists adopted his conception of the *entrepreneur* earlier, instead of waiting until the appearance of Jevons, they would have spared the science many useless discussions provoked by the work of a thinker who was certainly more profound but much less judicious than Say, namely, David Ricardo.[43]

NOTES

1. This system is expounded in Book V, Chapter ii, Part II.
2. In the preface to his translation, 1821 ed., p. lxix.
3. Rae, *Life of Smith*, p. 103. The author of this famous phrase is not known.
4. J. B. Say, *Traité*, 1st ed., p. 240.
5. Mantoux, *La Révolution industrielle*, p. 83. M. Halévy gives expression to a similar idea in his *La Jeunesse de Bentham*, p. 193 (Paris, 1901).
6. So called in honour of the leading English representative, Lord Eden.
7. In 1778, 1784, 1786, 1789.
8. In 1791, 1793, 1796.
9. Professor Kraus, writing in 1796, declared that no book published since the days of the New Testament would effect so many welcome changes when it became thoroughly known (J. Rae, p. 360). By the beginning of the nineteenth century its influence had become predominant. All the Prussian statesmen who aided Stein in the preparation and execution of those important reforms that gave birth to modern Prussia were thoroughly versed in Smith's doctrines, and the Prussian tariff of 1821 is the first European tariff in which they are deliberately applied. (*Cf.* Roscher, *Geschichte der Nationalökonomik in Deutschland*).
10. In his introduction to the *Traité*, 1st ed. (The phrase was deleted in the 6th ed.)
11. J. B. Say, *Traité*, 1st ed., introduction, p. xxxiii.
12. He was born at Lyons on January 5, 1767. After a visit to England he entered the employment of an assurance company, and took part as a volunteer in the campaign of 1792. From 1794 to 1800 he edited a review entitled *Décade philosophique, littéraire et politique, par une société de républicains*. He was nominated a member of the Tribunate in 1799. After the publication of his *Traité* the First Consul, having failed to obtain a promise that the financial proposals outlined in the first edition

would be eliminated in the second, dismissed him from the Tribunate, offering him the post of director of the *Droits réunis* as compensation. Say, who disapproved of the new regime, refused, and set up a cotton factory at Auchy-les-Hesdins, in the Pas-de-Calais. He realized his capital in 1813, returned to Paris, and in 1814 published a second edition of his treatise. In 1816 he delivered a course of lectures on political economy at the Athénée, probably the first course given in France. These lectures were published in 1817 in his *Catéchisme d'économie politique*. In 1819 the Restoration Government appointed him to give a course on "Industrial Economy" (the term "Political Economy" was too terrible). In 1831 he was made Professor of Political Economy in the Collège de France. He died in 1832. His *Cours complet d'économie politique* was published, in six volumes, in 1828–29.

13. *Cf* a letter to Louis Say in 1827 (*Œuvres diverses*, p. 545.

14. Garnier's translation of Adam Smith, 1802, Vol. V, p. 283.

15. *Traité*, 1st ed., p. 39.

16. *Ibid.*, p. 21. Later on he employs the more comprehensive term "natural agents."

17. *Ibid.*, Book I, chapters xlii and xliii. By "industry" Say understands every kind of labour. *Cf.* 6th ed., pp. 70 *et seq.*

18. Malthus still appeared hostile to the doctrine of immaterial products, but Lauderdale, Tooke, McCulloch, and Senior accepted it, and it seemed definitely fixed when Stuart Mill confined the word "product" to material products only. For Tooke's view see his letter to J. B. Say in the *Œuores diverses* of the latter.

19. *Traité*, Book I, chapter ii. Is it not strange that Say should have failed to apply this idea to commerce? He regards the latter as productive because it creates exchangeable values. Nevertheless he criticizes Condillac for having said that mere exchange of goods increases wealth because it increases the utility of objects. This is because Say is perpetually mixing up utility and exchange value, a confusion that leads him into many serious mistakes.

20. *Traité*, 6th ed., p. 6. The word "laws" does not appear in the first edition. Say merely speaks of general principles. It is found for the first time in the edition of 1814: "General facts or, if one wishes to call principles by that name, general laws" (p, xxix).

21. Correspondence with Malthus, in *Œuvres diverses*, p. 466.

22. *Traité*, Introd., 1st ed., p. ix; 6th ed., p. 13.

23. *Ibid.*, 1st ed., Book I, p. 404.

24. There is no need for exaggeration, and no need to regard Say as indifferent to suffering and misery. He declares that "for many homes both in town and country life is one long privation," and that thrift in general "implies, not the curtailment of useless commodities, such as expediency and humanity would welcome, but a diminution of the real needs of life, which is a standing condemnation of the economic system of many Governments." (*Traité*, 1st ed., Vol. I. pp. 97–98; 6th ed., p. 116.)

25. *Traité*, 6th ed., p. 403.

26. *Traité*, 1st ed., Vol. I, p. 48.

27. *Ibid.*, 5th ed., Vol. I, p. 67.
28. The *entrepreneur* in fact has an important place in Cantillon's admirable *Essai sur la nature de commerce*, written in the middle of the eighteenth century.
29. Critical examination of McCulloch's treatise (1825), in *Œuvres diverses*, pp. 274–275.
30. *Traité*, 6th ed., p. 349.
31. "Rent," he says, "doubtless is partly interest on capital buried in the soil, for there are few properties which do not owe something to improvements made in them. But their total value is seldom due to this alone. It might be if the land were fertile but lacked the necessary facilities for cultivation. But this is never the case in civilized countries." (Critical examination of McCulloch's treatise (1825), in *Œuvres diverses*, p. 277).
32. *Traité*, 1st ed., p. 154.
33. "The theory of heat and of weight and the study of the inclined plane have placed the whole of nature at the disposal of mankind. In the same way the theory of exchange and of markets will change the whole policy of the world." (*Ibid.*, 6th ed., p. 51.)
34. *Traité*, 1st ed., Vol. II, p. 175.
35. *Ibid.*, p. 179.
36. *Ibid.*, p. 178.
37. "One kind of product would seldom be more plentiful than another and goods would seldom be too many if every one were given complete freedom." Too much stress has possibly been laid on the phrase "Certain products are superabundant just because others are wanting," and it has been taken as implying that even partial over-production is an impossibility. A note inserted on the next page helps to clear up the matter and to prevent misunderstanding. "The argument of the chapter," says he, "is not that partial over-production is impossible, but merely that the production of one thing creates the demand for another." He certainly seems unfaithful to his own position in the letters he wrote to Malthus, in which he tries to defend his own point of view by saying that "production implies producing goods that are demanded," and that consequently if there is any excessive production it is not the fault of production as such and cannot be regarded as *over-production*. In greater conformity with his own views and much nearer the truth is his reply to an article by Sismondi published in 1824 in the *Revue encyclopédique* under the title *Sur la Balance des Consommations avec les Productions* (*Œuvres diverses*, p. 250). His statements vary from one edition to another, and anything more unstable than Say's views on this question would be difficult to imagine. The formula "Products exchange for products" is so general that it includes everything, but means nothing at all; for what is money, after all, if it is not a product?
38. Letters to Malthus (*Œuvres diverses*, p. 466).
39. Malthus, *Principles of Political Economy*, Book II, chapter i, sec. ix.
40. *Sur la Balance des Consommations avec les Productions*, p. 252.
41. *Ibid.*, p. 251.
42. Dühring, *Kritische Geschichte der Nationalökonomie und des Socialismus*, 2nd ed., 1875,

p. 165. For the other side of the question one may profitably peruse the interesting study of Say contributed by M. Allix to the *Revue d'économie politique*, 1910 (pp. 303–341), and the *Revue d'Histoire des Doctrines*, 1911 (p. 321).

43. Stanley Jevons (*Theory of Political Economy*, 1888) has recognized in words too rarely quoted, but clearly confirmed by the modern development of economics, the superiority of the French economists over Ricardo. "The true doctrine may be more or less clearly traced through the writings of a succession of great French economists, from Condillac, Baudeau, and Le Trosne, through J.B. Say, Destutt de Tracy, Storch, and others, down to Bastiat and Courcelle-Seneuil. The conclusion to which I am ever more clearly coming is that the only hope of attaining a true system of economics is to fling aside, once and for ever, the mazy and preposterous assumptions of the Ricardian School." (Preface, p. xlix.)

Part 4. Germany

The literature on the translation and reception of *WN* in Germany is abundant. The references listed below reflect only part of the work of historians of German economic thought. As in the case of Japan, it would take an entire book to collect all the pertinent material as well as a comprehensive introduction, to give a full picture of German reactions to *WN*. But the problem is translating these rich texts into English. This needs to be done by experts who are familiar with the literature and modern German economic thought. This note represents an appeal for someone to undertake that task.

Three texts are assembled in this Part. Hasek (1925) is a "classic" which provides a general history and analyses the impacts of *WN*. His chapter 4, not reprinted here, analyses how statesmen used Smith's doctrines in social reforms and deserves reading. Palyi (1928: 210, n. 65) criticized this book as being "in the main confined to the time about 1810, without trying to exhaust even that limited period. It deals only with part of the works of Garve, Satorius, Kraus and Lueder, disregarding all other publications, even previous to 1810. Its merit lies in the analysis of Smith's influence on the Stein-Hardenberg reform work, elaborating the work done by historians like E. Meier (1881) and M. Lehmann (1902–5)". In retrospect, to be fair, Hasek is still a good general and comprehensive account of the introduction of *WN* in Germany, and it serves very well as introductory reading.

List (1841) is a good example of the rejection of Smith's doctrines. In under five pages, List explicitly attacked Smith's source of ideas and his "fundamental errors". He even stated that "[Smith's] system regards everything from the shopkeeper's point of view" (List, 1841: 279). He strongly emphasized the positive role of state power and the importance of "nationality". From today's point of view, List's opinions are not fair to Smith and lack a sympathetic understanding. Moreover, he failed to justify his accusations sufficiently. He made a similar attack on J.-B. Say in chapter 32 of his book.

Among other things, Tribe (1988) clearly analysed why for almost twenty years after *WN* was published it received little attention, and why then, just at the turn of the century, a phase of "Smithianism" began. He puts this question in a socioeconomic context to illustrate the reasons why Steuart's *Inquiry* (1763) was much better received, why *WN* was neglected for two decades after its German translation, and how it came gradually to be accepted. The references included are rich and up-to-date.

The following texts are not included in this chapter but deserve attention. Waszek (1993) is a highly readable, concise introduction to the issue. Winkel (1986) provides a modern account of the translation and reception of *WN* in Germany. Basically, Winkel discusses the responses to *WN* during the period 1776–1820, and his paper can be read as a new supplement to Hasek (1925).

Erämetsä (1961) is an unusual text in the literature on Smith, in the sense that the author presents a survey of how *WN* has influenced the growth of German economic vocabulary in different fields of economic activity. This is also by a wide margin the first attempt to undertake a linguistic investigation into the interaction of the terminology of political economy in different languages in the late eighteenth century—an important but neglected topic. Although this text *per se* is more interesting for German readers (in the sense that they can trace how German economic terminology was affected by *WN*), it will tell historians of economic thought in Japan, Russia, and elsewhere how Germans translated *WN* when their language had no sufficient vocabulary or similar patterns of thought.

Among the untranslated texts, Roscher (1867), Treue (1951), and Thal and Lehmann (1976) are particularly relevant. Roscher (1867) is comparable in approach to Hasek (1925); Thal and Lehmann (1976) and Treue (1951) are basically descriptive but contain some useful perspectives. To German readers, I recommend the less accessible but detailed analysis by a major figure of the German historical school (Roscher, 1867). Matsukawa (1968: 290–1) cites many German references on the introduction of Smith into Germany during three periods: 1776–93, 1794–1806, and 1807–30.

Further Reading

Texts with a * are printed in this Part

BORCKE-STARGORDT, GRAF HENNING VON (1958), "Aus der Vorgeschichte zu den preussischen Agrarreformen: Christian Jakob Kraus Gedächtnis", *Jahrbuch der Albert-Universität zu Königsberg*, 8: 122–42 [an article dedicated to the memory of a German follower of Adam Smith, Christian Jakob Kraus, 1753–1807].

BOTHA, D. J. J. (1976), "Adam Smith: A Homage from Germany", *South African Journal of Economics*, 44(4): 412–16.

CARPENTER, KENNETH (1977), *Dialogue in Political Economy: Translations from and into German in the 18th Century*, Baker Library, Harvard Business School.

ERÄMETSÄ, ERIK (1961), "Adam Smith als Mittler Englisch-Deutscher Spracheinflüsse" (Adam Smith as mediator of English-German literary influences: evidence from *The Wealth of Nations*), *Annales Academie Scientiarium Fennicae*, Series B, 125(1) [heavily condensed into English by the author, available from the editor].

FRAUL, HUGO (1928), *Das Eindringen der Smithschen Nationökonomie in Deutschland und ihre Weiterbildung bis zu Herman*, Inaugural Dissertation, Hall-Saal.

GOTTFRIED, PAUL (1977), "Adam Smith and German Social Thought", *Modern Age*, 21(2): 146–52.

*HASEK, C. W. (1925), "The Introduction of Adam Smith's Doctrines", *The Introduction of Adam Smith's Doctrines into Germany*, ch. 3, pp. 61–94, Columbia University Studies in History, Economics and Public Law 261.

KRAUSE, WERNER *et al.* (1977), "Die Aufnahme der politischen Ökonomie von Adam Smith (Ausgang des 18. Jh.)", *Grundlinien des ökonomischen Denkens in Deutschland, von den Anfängen bis zur Mitte des 19. Jahrhunderts*, pp. 312–28, Berlin: Akademie-Verlag.

*LIST, FRIEDRICH (1841), "The System of Values of Exchange (Falsely Termed by the School, the 'Industrial' System)—Adam Smith", *The National System of Political Economy*, transl. Sampson Lloyd, ch. 31, pp. 277–81, London: Longmans, Green & Co, 1916.

MATSUKAWA, SHICHIRO (1968), "The Introduction of Adam Smith into Germany", *Keizai Kenkiu*, 19(4): 289–96 (in Japanese).

PALYI, MELCHIOR (1928), "The Introduction of Adam Smith on the Continent", in J. M. Clark *et al.* (eds.), *Adam Smith, 1776–1926*, pp. 190–233, University of Chicago Press; repr. New York: Augustus Kelley, 1966.

RECKTENWALD, HORST (1976), "Der schottische Nationalökonome und Moralphilosoph und die Deutschen", *Adam Smith, sein Leben und sein Werk*, pp. 277–87, Munich: C. H. Becksche.

ROSCHER, WILHELM (1867), "Über die Ein- und Durchführung des Adam Smith'schen Systems in Deutschland", *Berichte über die Verhandlungen der Königlich-Sächsischen Gesellschaft der Wissenschaften zu Leipzig*, pp. 1–74, Leipzig: S. Hirzel.

THAL, PETER and LEHMANN, HERMANN (1976), "Die Smith-Rezeption in Deutschland am Ende des 18. und in der erstern Hälfte des 19. Jahrhunderts", in Peter Thal *et al.*, *Adam Smith gestern und heute*, pp. 79–95, Berlin: Akademi-Verlag.

TREUE, K. (1951), "Adam Smith in Deutschland: Zum Problem des 'Politischen Professors' zwinschen 1776 und 1810", in W. Conze (ed.), *Deutschland und Europa*, pp. 101–33, Düsseldorf: Droste Verlag.

*TRIBE, K. (1988), "The 'Smith reception' and the Function of Translation", *Governing Economy: The Reformation of German Economic Discourse 1750–1840*, ch. 7, Cambridge University Press.

WASZEK, NOBERT (1993), "Adam Smith in Germany, 1776–1832", in H. Mizuta and C. Sugiyama (eds.), *Adam Smith: International Perspectives*, pp. 163–80, London: Macmillan.

WINKEL, HARALD (1977), *Die Deutsche Nationalökonomie im 19 Jahrhundert*, Darmstadt: Wissenschaftliche Buchgesellschaft.

—— (1986), "Adam Smith und die deutsche Nationalökonomie 1776–1820: zur Rezeption der englischen Klassik", *Schriften des Vereins für Socialpolitik*, 115(5): 81–109. Translated by Barbara Lasoff as "The reception of the work of Adam Smith in Germany", available from the editor.

NA
excerpt

4.1 C. W. Hasek, 1925.
The Introduction of Adam Smith's Doctrines

I. The University of Göttingen

Within the confines of the straggling kingdom of Prussia, which in the eighteenth century extended from the Meuse to the Memel throughout northern Germany, lay the small electorate of Braunschweig-Lüneberg, or Hanover, the continental possession of the English Georges. This small state, which in 1795 had an area about equal to the states of Massachusetts and Connecticut and a population of almost one million,[1] lay between the Weser and the Elbe for a distance of about one hundred twenty-five miles from their mouths in a position which cut the Prussian monarchy into two unequal parts. To the west of it lay the small Westphalian and Rhine provinces of Prussia, comparatively prosperous and advanced in their economic organization; to the east lay the larger provinces of central and eastern Prussia, with their more primitive and more unified feudal organization. Thus Hanover, with its control over the commercial ports of Hamburg, Bremen and Lübeck, at the same time a state of the Holy Roman Empire and in the possession of an independent power, was in a peculiarly strategic position in respect not only to the political, but also to the cultural interests of Prussia.

Here was established in 1737 the University of Göttingen, which in the second half of the century became one of the three most influential universities in Germany, the other two being the universities of Halle and Leipzig.[2] Its peculiar significance was due to a combination of circumstances. It shared with the universities of Erlangen (founded 1743) and Münster (founded 1780) the distinction of being one of the youngest of the German universities, and therefore shared with them the privilege of being the least trammeled by tradition. Furthermore, it was established in the territory of the English king and at a time when English influence was being increasingly felt in Germany. That influence, which was one of the main motive forces back of the Sturm und Drang movement in German literature, and which furnished a decisive stimulus to philosophy in Kant's thought, thereby overthrowing the old Wolfian philosophy, was the prime cause for the development of the study of the science of state in the University of Göttingen. Through the untiring efforts of its first rector, Gerlach von Münchhausen (the hostility of the German princes prevented the calling of men from other universities), the department of political science and history was especially developed,[3] and came to possess a series of noted teachers, Gatterer, Achenwall, Spittler, Heeren, Schlözer, Feder in philosophy, and Pütter, "the Blackstone of the Empire".[4] The courses, as here given, while marked largely by the prevailing features of Cameralism, were also characterized by a spirit far more liberal than that which featured the usual instruction in Cameralistics.[5] English students attended in numbers, and added to the English influence.[6] Here, too, came the young nobility of Germany, and added to that spirit of worldiness and culture, quite different in its way from the pietism which characterized many of the German universities.[7] Among these students were Hardenberg (1766) and Stein (1773), and also those men who afterwards became the chief early expositors of Smith's doctrines in Germany—Sartorius, Lueder, Kraus, Hufeland.

The University of Göttingen, like the other universities of Germany, made its influence felt in two ways, (1) by contributing its quota to the number of active statesmen in the German states, and (2) through those of its students who entered the teaching profession and brought their influence to bear either through their writings or through their pupils. The universities of Germany at that time as at present, stood in close contact with the German governments; for university graduates in the social sciences, no less than in the physical sciences, were frequently called to service in the bureaucracy. The close relationship between Hanover and Prussia, the character of the training in the University of Göttingen, and the liberal policy of the Prussian kings in inviting into their service men of outstanding ability, thus made possible the state activity of Hardenberg and Stein.

II. Early Translations and Reviews

The first translation[8] of Adam Smith's *Inquiry into the Nature and Causes of the Wealth of Nations*, which was published in the spring of 1776, was made by J. F.

Schiller, a German who lived in London.[9] The first review of the translation, which appeared in the *Göttingische gelehrte Anzeigen* for March 10, 1777, by J. G. H. Feder,[10] professor of philosophy at the University of Göttingen, was very favorable.[11] In the words of the reviewer: "It is a classic; very estimable both for its thorough, not too limited, often far-sighted political philosophy, and for the numerous, frequently discursive historical notes," but the exposition suffers from too much repetition.[12] Smith's opposition to Steuart and his favorable attitude towards the Physiocrats are both noted.[13] The review takes up each book chapter by chapter with occasional comments. The argument for *laissez faire* evidently impressed the reviewer, but he is not disposed to yield the point without question, for he says:

The inferior goods and deceptions which result from too great competition, since customers can be obtained only through low prices and easy credit; the ruin of many who under such freedom choose attractive but unprofitable trades; and the result that many an able man, especially if he is likewise honest, is forced under through excessive competition, appear to be evils that outweigh any gains of such complete freedom.[14]

The reviewer also objects to Smith's use of the terms productive and unproductive, as well as to his attacks on a policy of regulated consumption.[15] The review is remarkable for its knowledge of and sympathetic attitude towards Smith's work as well as for the doubts it cherishes as to the universal applicability of its principles; for the reviewer declares "many of his propositions dare not be incorporated in the universal principles of state, but are valid only at a certain stage of industry, wealth and enlightenment."[16] The review, coming from the University of Göttingen, reflects a keen interest in and knowledge of English affairs together with the prevailing Cameralistic attitude of mind.

Two other reviews appeared about the same time, one in Nicolai's *Allgemeine deutsche Bibliothek* for 1777 and 1779, and the other in the *Ephemerides der Menschheit* of Isaak Iselin for 1777. Both are by men of the Physiocratic persuasion, who find Smith's views more or less in accordance with their own. Thus the writer in Nicolai's *Bibliothek* finds that, although Smith nowhere employs the language of the Economistes (Physiocrats), he is in full accordance with their views in his main thesis that the rise or fall of land rents is a certain indication of increasing or decreasing well-being.[17] Iselin also in his lengthy review by the skillful use of extracts from Smith's work conveys the impression that Physiocratic doctrines have received further corroboration.[18]

Until 1794, a period of nearly twenty years after these first discussions, the work of Adam Smith received scant attention in Germany. While Frederick II was living, Cameralism held undisputed sway in Prussia, and the economic changes which began with the outbreak of the French Revolution had still not gained sufficient momentum to awake the economic theorists from their dogmatic slumber. During this period, accordingly, the references to Smith's work by both Cameralists and Physiocrats are inconsequential and betray no real understanding of his position.[19] In 1793 a second review appeared in the *Göttingische gelehrte Anzeigen*, this time by George Sartorius,[20] dealing with the additions to the third edition of Smith's work.[21] In reply to the publishing company's complaint of the small sales of the translation, although such sales had slightly increased, the reviewer remarked: "Smith will not remain long on the shelves, for reason will assert itself in the end."[22] The reason for the lack of interest was to be found in the difficulty of the work.

A work that requires so much effort and thought will at first find little sale. The faith in old principles, which are to be found in so many compendia, is so mild and sweet, and thinking and comprehending a new, darkly worded doctrine requires so much time and effort, that a book of Cameralistic theory can be thrown together in less time than it takes to gain a comprehension of Smith.[23]

In 1794 appeared the second German translation of Smith's *Wealth of Nations*, this time by Christian Garve.[24] In the same year there appeared in the *Göttingische gelehrte Anzeigen* a review of the new translation, in which, in addition to favorable comment on the felicity of the translation,[25] the reviewer made the following significant comments:

Smith's principles must be more widely disseminated, and if they are false, they must be thoroughly refuted; this has as yet not occurred, and has not even been attempted here. Even if one does find his book cited here and there, it really seems that aside from the easy chapters, he had nothing to say and his book had never been read. He has yet had no influence whatever on the change of economic doctrine in our country; he has indeed been cited and praised, but the compendia continue as before; others are preferred, for they can be understood with greater ease.[26]

And yet in 1796 the translation received a second impression; a second edition was issued in 1799, and a third in 1810.[27]

III. Christian Garve

Christian Garve,[28] although not a member of the Göttingen University group, must be considered as among the important contributors to the spread of Smith's views. Himself a popularizer of philosophic doctrines, he was early attracted by the Scotch writers and became one of their foremost exponents in Germany.[29] Long before making his translation of Smith's work he had translated A. Ferguson's *Essay on the History of Civil Society* (1772), Burke's *On the Origin of our Ideas of the Sublime and Beautiful* (1772), and J. MacFarlan's *Inquiries Concerning the Poor* (1785), as well as works from the French, Greek and Latin. His first acquaintance with Smith was through Schiller's translation and the poverty of that rendering stimulated him to produce a better.[30] The translation was accordingly undertaken in 1791, and by December he had completed the first half of the first volume.[31] But it was primarily Smith's views which influenced him in the undertaking. As he states in the introduction to his translation: "It (Smith's work) attracted me as only few books have in the course of my studies through the number of new views which it gave me not only concerning the actual object of his investigations, but concerning all related material from the philosophy of civil and social life." The translation thus begun in 1791 was completed with the help of Ober-Post-Commissär Dörrien in Leipzig, who apparently translated a considerable portion of the latter part of the work,[32] and was ready for publication in 1794. It was Garve's intention to add to his translation in the form of appendices, (1) a summary of those ideas and principles of Smith which he considered new and real contributions to the sum of human knowledge, and (2) a further analysis of some of Smith's main theorems, a plan which was never carried out. The translation appeared with rather infrequent but extensive explanatory notes.

The principles which would have governed such an analysis are, however, to be found in Garve's miscellaneous essays. Among these essays are two which lie within the field of economics.[33] The first of these—On the Character of the Peasants and their Relation to the Gentry and to the Government—is a series of three lectures delivered before the Silesian Economic Society in 1786; the second—Contributions towards an Investigation of the Decline of Small Towns, the Causes, and the Means of Prevention—first appeared in the *Schlesische Provincialblätter*. It would be difficult to find in these essays any trace of Smithian influence. Garve was primarily a popular philosopher, critic, commentator and translator. His interests were chiefly in the field of philosophy and letters, and his interest in Smith is to be attributed first of all to his veneration for the Scotch school of philosophers. The translation of Smith's work was a task of Garve's leisure hours, to be undertaken when the important writing of the day was done, and incidentally to furnish the means of travel.[34] In his ideas on economic matters Garve must be considered an enlightened, rather liberal follower of the economic views prevalent in the days of Frederick II. His veneration for the views of this monarch, to which his lengthy work on the life and manners of Frederick II bears witness,[35] is shown in the following passage from the first of the above essays:

It is really fortunate for an author in the Prussian states that in respect to many points in state economy he is able, in any general investigation of what should be done, to agree with those rules which form the basis of the actions, or at least of the views, of his prince.[36]

In his proposals for reform of agricultural conditions he appeals to the good will of the gentry. The improvement of the landed class through better education and the attention of this class to the cultivation of its lands personally rather than through managers, will make unnecessary any sudden reforms which jeopardize property rights. The peasants on the whole are to be looked upon as the poor, even as children, and sudden reforms are to be avoided.[37] Garve was, furthermore, historically minded and inclined to stress the genetic viewpoint in economic matters. The rise and fall of the smaller cities of Germany are to be determined by an historical study of the changes in the institutions of that land.[38] Generalizations in the form of principles are avoided. The particular rather than the general is the subject of concern, especially in practical matters. Such were the views of Garve and on the basis of such views would have rested his criticism of Smith. Garve's great service to the change of viewpoint in economics in Germany was his preparation of an acceptable German version of Smith's work.

IV. Georg Sartorius

The first writer in Germany to give expression to Smithian influence in an original production was Georg Sartorius,[39] in a small volume entitled "Summary of State Economy, based on Adam Smith's Principles, for Use with Academic Lectures", which appeared in 1796.[40] As a pupil and friend of Feder, the professor of philosophy, who is credited with the first reviews of Smith's work in the *Göttingische gelehrte Anzeigen*,[41] Sartorius probably obtained from him his first stimulus to study Smith.[42] Although primarily a teacher of history, Sartorius began in 1792 to give a course in the principles of political economy according to Smith and stated in 1796 that he had been entirely successful in presenting Smith's ideas to students.[43] He was firmly convinced that Smith's analysis was true, and felt the need of furthering the dissemination of the truth in Germany by preparing this summary.[44] At a time when the old order was rapidly changing he felt that such a book was peculiarly needed,[45] and that, too, in spite of Garve's excellent translation and his promise of further analysis of Smith's work.[46]

The *Handbuch*, as thus prepared, presumably the outgrowth of repeated presentation of Smith's theories to students, is based entirely on Smith's work. It is divided into two parts, of which the first, the Elements of National Prosperity,[47] has two divisions, which present summaries of the first and second books of the original. The second part, State Economy,[48] likewise has two divisions which summarize books four and five of the *Wealth of Nations*. Thus for the first time in German economic literature appears the distinction between the principles of economics and economic policy. Such a distinction with its emphasis on policy is entirely explainable from Cameralistic practice and was followed by the later adherents of Smithian thought in Germany. But even in this first summary with its tone of enthusiasm and admiration for Smith's work, Sartorius is not disposed to overlook details. "In details Smith has made mistakes; many historical data referring to the continent are of course false; even some conclusions of his theory seem to lack solidarity, and have been changed."[49] But in spite of these objections and the different historical illustrations which appear in the text, the book remains largely an extract from the larger work of Smith.

A decade later the second contribution of Sartorius to economic literature appeared in two volumes, (1) Concerning the Elements of National Wealth and State Economy according to Adam Smith, (2) Essays on National Wealth and State Economy.[50] In the decade which had elapsed since the Handbuch of 1796 Sartorius had had time to develop the doubts which had found some expression even in the earlier work.[51] Rather than develop his objections in a new work, which would be only a restatement of Smith's ideas in another form, Sartorius chose to state his objections in a separate work, leaving the summary of Smith as before. The first of these two volumes which appeared in 1806 is accordingly a somewhat lengthier summary of Smith's work, which follows the original even more closely than the *Handbuch* of 1796.[52] The second volume, which was to have been the first of a series, presents the independent thought of Sartorius on Smithian economics.

This second volume contains four essays which deal respectively with Smith's labor theory of value, with saving in its relation to the increase of national wealth, with the differences obtaining between national wealth and private riches, and with the problem of the relation of the government of a state to private enterprise. The first three essays owe their inception apparently to the work of the Earl of Lauderdale which appeared in January 1804,[53] for they discuss the same topics to which he devotes the first, second and fourth chapters of his work. After the manner of Sartorius, summaries of these chapters of Lauderdale's work are given, followed by comment or criticism.

Smith's theory of value is found to be "partly indefinite, partly incomplete".[54] The first source of value of a thing is its use,[55] but value is also determined by the cost of production, and the rate of exchange with other things. Exchange value is, however, rather a resultant of the operation of the two other determinants, than of equal significance with them. Price, no less than value, is subject to the same complex interplay of forces,[56] hence money cannot serve as an unchanging measure of value. Labor, likewise, since it is subject to the same value determinants as all other things, for its value is determined by its serviceability, its cost of production, and its exchange value, can no more serve as an unchanging measure of value than money or corn. Thus Sartorius finds the labor theory of value "a strange and deceptive conclusion".[57]

In his second essay, however, on parsimony as a means of increasing the national wealth, he turns to the defense of Smith against Lauderdale. To the latter's objection that not parsimony but the productivity of land, labor and capital is the source of increasing national wealth, he opposes Smith's view that only the frugality of the individual can make such productivity possible.[58]

In the third essay Sartorius presents Lauderdale's views on the differences between public wealth and individual riches. The analysis turns on the application of the paradox of value to definitions of wealth. But Sartorius is here interested in the problem of the relation of prices, both nominal and real, to the increase or decrease of the national wealth. The causes of the rise of nominal prices are not those which affect the increase of national wealth; they are the forces which determine merely the redistribution of that wealth. The rise of the real prices of goods, however, may be the effect of the increase of national wealth, or the cause of such increase.[59]

The fourth essay, on the cooperation of the government of a state in the advancement of the national wealth, betrays a more independent analysis. Sartorius takes as his starting point Smith's proposition that each individual, by seeking to further his own interests, furthers the interests of all. This proposition he shows is subject to many exceptions. The large capitalist may crush the small, and exploit the public.[60] Entirely free disposal of the lands in the hand of the individual is a doubtful policy, for land cannot be increased at will.[61] In free trade one nation may crush another.[62] The evils that attend competition are pointed out.[63] Since the proposition advanced by Smith is thus of doubtful value, it is the duty of the government to take measures to offset the disadvantageous results which may arise.[64] Were the world all one state in an advanced stage of civilization, Smith's theory might be applicable, but with so many states, as in Europe, each seeking to maintain its national existence, the employment of tariffs, drawbacks, free ports, etc., becomes necessary.[65] The intervention of the state, often on an extensive scale, is thus frequently advisable. But Sartorius seeks the middle ground, and is not disposed to go to the opposite extreme from Smith.

Consequently a conditionally assumed freedom of acquisition and employment of property seems by all means the most commendable, wherever private property and inheritance exist. And so cooperation on the part of the government in advancing the national wealth, aside from protection against foreign enemies, the administration of justice at home, and the development of certain institutions, is also to be recommended, provided it remains within proper bounds. These bounds in part vary according to conditions and circumstances, but can in part be determined on general principles.[66]

Thus the objections which Sartorius raises to Smith's principles, in so far as they are his own, and not the result of the criticisms of Lauderdale, may be attributed to the continental location of their author. In the midst of European states, where the Mercantile system still largely held sway, and where its application appeared necessary to secure their economic existence, the principles of free trade developed by Smith could only seem unduly theoretical. Thus Sartorius seeks a compromise between the two systems of economic thought. Only in this one respect can his criticisms be considered as contributing anything positive to his Smithian inheritance. His remaining objections, largely conditioned by the thought of Lauderdale, were negative in character and led to no independent development of theory by their author.

V. August Ferdinand Lueder

The second work embodying Smithian views to appear in Germany was that entitled "Concerning National Industry and State Economy",[67] by August Ferdinand Lueder.[68] Lueder's work was primarily in the field of statistics, particularly geographical statistics, and in this connection he was editor of a sort of compendia, the first of which, entitled *Historical Portfolio* (*Historische Portefeuille*), appeared in 1787–1788, and the second, *Repository for History, Statistics and Policy* (*Repositorium für Geschichte, Staatskunde und Politik*), in the years 1802–1805. Apparently the review of foreign literature, which he was accustomed to make in connection with these compendia, brought him to the study of Smith's work.[69] A fourth work, *National Industry and its Effects, an Outline for Lectures*,[70] which appeared in 1808, was little more than a revamping of the earlier work. But in 1812 and 1817 appeared two remarkable productions, *Criticism of Statistics and State Policy*, and *Critical History of Statistics*,[71] in which an earnest attempt is made to show the futility of statistical analysis of a nation's activities.

The first and most extensive of Lueder's works, *On National Industry and State Economy*, is in part a mere paraphrase of the *Wealth of Nations*, but also in part a much more extensive formulation of a system of economics. In the introduction Lueder pays his respects to the memory of Smith and points out the apparently slight influence his work has had in Germany in spite of an excellent translation.[72] The difficulties in Smith's work, which possibly had prevented the diffusion of his ideas, are then indicated—the difficulties of the language, the lack of clarity and of sufficient explanation, the incompleteness of the analysis, and finally the extensive digressions, which break the force of the exposition. In the work which follows, the first book treats of the division of labour, the second of capital, and the third of nature. In that part of these books which follows Smith, Lueder's additions are chiefly in the form of illustrations drawn from his extensive reading in geography and statistics. The third book is entirely his own. Here are shown with an abundance of illustration the effects of natural conditions on the accumulation of capital, and on the development of markets, both domestic and foreign; e.g., no European state possesses so many good rivers as Prussia,[73] the imperfection of the Danube for shipping.[74]

In the remaining three books Lueder passes beyond Smith to a discussion of the aim of the state and state economy in the fourth book; in the fifth and sixth books he discusses the ways in which security, which alone it is the function of the state to provide, is prevented or destroyed by the acts of rulers, representative or non-representative assemblies, or the citizens themselves. Lueder was an ardent adherent of the idea of freedom, not only in the field of economic activity, but in all phases of social life, for he had been strongly influenced by the revolution in France, as well as by Smith. In the introduction to his *Critical History of Statistics*, he exclaims: "I hazarded everything for freedom, truth and justice; for freedom of industry as well as of opinions, of hand as of spirit, of person as well as of property."[75] It is the purpose of the state, accordingly, to furnish protection alone.[76] In keeping with this idea of freedom Lueder offers in the fourth book an extensive discussion of the evils of slavery. Thus this work, imbued with the Smithian spirit of economic liberty, passes beyond the limits of a treatise on economics to a discussion of the state and the ways and means of attaining individual freedom within it.

In these two extensive volumes it can hardly be said that Lueder has developed any objections to the work of Smith or made any advances upon it. As he states in his introduction, his aim is to correct and coordinate Smith's principles—presumably with the principles of political science which he develops in the second volume.[77] Only the first two books of Smith's work are used by Lueder. These, as well as the third book, contain a mass of new illustrations, largely from economic geography, but the Smithian theory is continued intact. Of the many citations of other authors, the great majority refer to geographic works or travels; only two economists are mentioned, Büsch and Steuart, and then only for illustration of special points. It was Lueder's object to unite a theoretical interpretation of man's industrial activity to an analysis of his other social relations, and for this purpose he drew upon Smith, without any modifications of the theoretical principles, unless extensive use of geographical and historical illustrations be considered such.

The influence of Smithian thought is likewise to be seen in Lueder's rejection of statistics along with state policy as it was practiced during the time of Cameralistic thought. As a consistent follower of Smith, Lueder felt that the principle of statistical investigation into the affairs of a nation had to be rejected, for it was inconsistent with that principle of individual freedom which lay at the bottom of Smith's thought. With the rejection of Cameralistic policy, there followed the rejection of Cameralistic methods. Lueder's position may be most clearly stated in his own words:

Statistics is not what it should be; it creates anything but knowledge of the state — it does not indicate at all what is healthy, what is diseased in the state: and it never will nor can indicate this. Policy, however, which should teach us how the commonweal is to be maintained and increased, how the diseased is to be cured; which bears the same relation to statistics as medicine to physiology; which is drawn alike from experience and reason, is still full of ridiculous things, full of contradictions and theories, which mock sound common sense and the most common daily experiences.[78]

Lueder's despair upon realization that adherence to the principle of the greatest freedom of the individual in the state made a large portion of his lifework vain, is vividly shown in the following:

On the strongest pillars and the firmest foundation the structure of statistics and policy seemed to me to rest. I had devoted the happiest hours of my life and the greatest part of my time to statistics and policy; . . . everything in me could not but revolt at the convictions which pressed upon me. But the current of the times flowed too swiftly. Ideas, which had entered my very marrow, had to be reviewed and exchanged for others; one prejudice after another had to be recognized as prejudice; more and more indefensible appeared one rotten prop after another, one rent and tear after the other; finally, to my no small terror, the whole structure of statistics collapsed and with it policy, which can accomplish nothing without statistics. As my insight grew and my viewpoint cleared, the fruits of statistics and policy appeared more and more frightful; all those hindrances which both threw in the path of industry, whereby not only welfare but culture and humanity were hindered; all those hindrances to the natural course of things; all those sacrifices brought to an unknown idol, called the welfare of the state or the commonweal, and brought with ridicule of all principles of philosophy, religion and sound common sense, at the cost of morality and virtue.[79]

Nowhere clearer than in these rhetorical periods of Lueder can we see the chaos which the swift march of events in the years following 1791 brought to those minds which were schooled in an older philosophy and could only with difficulty make any change. With the collapse of a lifework the bitterness of tone can be pardoned, while the confusion of the times concealed the illogicalness of his position.

The writings of Lueder betray an extensive reading and knowledge of literature, and like Sartorius, a keen understanding of English conditions. With his special knowledge of history and statistics he enriched his Smithian inheritance with many significant illustrations. Strongly influenced by the ideas of the French Revolution, as well as by Smith, he was an ardent disciple of the latter. But his style was strongly rhetorical and exaggerated, and his writings sketchy and more than tinged with pessimism. He was a man unable to adapt his views to a period of rapid change and his writings remain one of the most interesting phenomena of these troubled times.

VI. Christian Jacob Kraus

The third, and as a representative of Smithian economics in many respects the most important economist of this period, is Christian Jacob Kraus,[80] for it was through his influence upon his pupils, von Schön, the von Schrötters and von Auerswald, rather than through his writings that at least one of the important reforms of Stein's second ministry, the abolition of serfdom, was accomplished.[81]

While still a student at the University of Königsberg in 1776 Kraus turned to the study of English, and in a remarkably short time, by committing to memory Bailey's dictionary, had learned the language.[82] Shortly after this he began the translation of Young's *Political Arithmetick* and after great difficulties completed and published it in 1777.[83] The difficulties in translating this work, which made him feel that, although he had translated, he had not understood it, led to an extensive study of economic works and gradually aroused his interest in the field.[84] That Kraus should visit the University of Göttingen rather than any of the other German universities in 1779, may have been due to his admiration for the English people and the greater familiarity with English affairs there than elsewhere in Germany, but at any rate he came away from Göttingen with his interests in statistics and state economy deepened and strengthened.[85] During his first years as professor at the University of Königsberg he included in the subjects upon which he lectured not only state economy, the Greek classics, history, mathematics, and practical philosophy, but also Shakespeare's plays.[86] As the years passed, however, his interests became increasingly concentrated in economics and in 1794 his lectures were devoted entirely to finance, policy, trade, industry and agriculture.

It was during these years that Kraus became acquainted with the *Wealth of Nations* and began to introduce it gradually into his lectures on economic subjects. In a letter to a friend Jan. 1797 apropos of Sartorius' *Handbuch* of 1796, a copy of which he had just received,[87] he states that for six years previous he had presented in his lectures "the only true, great, beautiful, just and beneficial system."[88] In a letter to a friend, Oct. 1795, he says:

Adam Smith's work on national wealth is my main source. This work is certainly one of the most important and beneficial that have ever been written; and I shall not leave you in peace, in case you are not acquainted with it, until you study it in the new version of Garve. For us Prussians of today a deeper study of state economy is more necessary than ever, if only to be able to judge correctly the projects, which books are discussing for the good of our National Wealth and our national income.[89]

A year later in a letter to a friend his praise of Smith's work is even more unbounded:

For truly Scheffner is right in saying that the world has seen no more important book than that of Adam Smith; certainly since the times of the New Testament no writing has had more beneficial results than this will have, when it has become better known and has penetrated further into the minds of all who have to do with matters of state economy.[90]

Although he published little, it is this enthusiastic admiration for Smith's work, which rather increased than lessened with the years, which he instilled at first quietly and then more openly into his pupils, some of whom were destined to occupy positions of importance during the years of Prussian reform.[91] It was this admiration, too, which led to his criticisms of the Frederician economic system and to suggestions for reform which left their impress upon his students.

For a German professor Kraus published remarkably little.[92] An excessive fear of the reading public,[93] uncertainty as to the correctness of his own position, and the wideness of his interests, which led to many plans never completed, prevented the appearance until after his death of any works of significance. His early articles devoted to philosophical subjects were followed by such articles as *Ueber den Frachthandel* (1786) and *Ueber das Seesalzmonopol* (1786). After his death there were published by his friends *State Economy* in five volumes and *Miscellaneous Writings* in eight volumes.[94] Although he published little, he was a most influential teacher. His lectures were crowded and he was considered the most important teacher in the university with the exception of Kant.[95]

The most significant of Kraus' works and that also which shows his conception of economic science most clearly is the five-volume work entitled *State Economy*. The first four volumes of this work are little more than a free paraphrase of the *Wealth of Nations*. The order of analysis is even maintained, e.g., the history of the precious metals is inserted in the theory of rent.[96] Smith's words are used, e.g., the work of musicians and actors is called frivol (frivolous).[97] But illustrations from the history of Prussia are substituted for British illustrations and a much more minute classification is employed, which frequently runs to subheadings a, aa, aaa, etc. Smith's lengthy discussion of colonial trade is repeated, although it was in little keeping with Prussian conditions;[98] on the other hand the agricultural conditions of Prussia receive the limited treatment characteristic of Smith's analysis. This part of the work is thus a slightly modified presentation of the *Wealth of Nations*.[99]

The fifth volume, however, contains Kraus' original contributions to the needs of his time and of the Prussian state, in the form of an applied state economics. In sharp contrast with the preceding volumes the practical needs of Prussia, as viewed by the author in the years preceding 1807, are analyzed and remedies are suggested. This part of the work is a series of sketches, often in problem form, as prepared for the lecture room rather than for final publication. Entirely in accordance with Smith's viewpoint is the assumption of individual freedom of initiative, which is the basis of all Kraus' reasoning. It is assumed that men want to improve their lot.[100] If they do not, it is because either they cannot, or dare not, or lack the necessary knowledge, or sufficient incentive, or customary skill.[101] If laws are passed requiring certain actions or forbidding others, the question is with Kraus: why do men not do or cease doing this of their own accord? What will they do to evade the law and will they succeed?[102] In accordance with these questions Kraus analyzes the Prussian economic polity systematically from the points of view of production, manufacture and trade. In every case the evils of the current system of restraint are pointed out and greater gain is proved under a system of free enterprise. The evils of the feudal agrarian system are shown, and the necessity of provision for the division and alienation of the land is emphasized.[103] The economic waste of serfdom is shown and its removal proved necessary.[104] The evils of the land-credit institutions are investigated.[105] In the case of certain goods the reasonableness of moderate protective duties is recognized.[106] Finally the guilds are censured, and their elimination is recommended, but only with their approval and with indemnification of their vested rights.[107] This part of the work is thus the formulation of a new state policy of individual freedom, which shall take the place of the existing policy of restraint. In so far as it is policy, it continues the Cameralistic tradition of state intervention, but in so far as it is based on Smithian principles it is a new type of policy.

Of the eight volumes of miscellaneous essays the first two only are devoted to subjects of economic significance. Here are found eleven essays, written during a period of twenty-one years (1786–1807), and dealing entirely with matters of practical significance to the administration of East Prussia. Throughout these essays, written in the spirit of an advisory economist, runs the principle of greater freedom of private initiative. Again and again it is proven that the removal of restrictions will result in greater gain to the individual and the state. The practical nature of these essays precludes any discussion of their theoretical basis, which may correctly be assumed to be the principles of Smith's economics. These essays, however, are followed by a series of notes on economic matters,[108] which show that Kraus was not blind to some of the implications of Smith's principles.

The paradox of value had occurred to Kraus, also, and he questions just what Smith meant by the term value.

When Smith posits the national income as the value of the annual product of the soil and labour, the question arises, (1) if the product increases, will it also be greater in total value, or may it not decrease in value by that very growth in size? (2) May not its total value increase, when its volume decreases by reason of some accident, e.g., national calamity? Is not the quantity of products more important for a nation than their value? The question is, what does Smith mean by value? What does he mean by product of the soil and labour?[109]

The real exchange value of any product is defined as follows: "The original real exchange value of any ware is the cost of producing it and bringing it to market."[110] But the forces affecting market prices are various.

The market price, in so far as it is determined by the relation of demand to supply, is influenced not merely by the quantity really desired or offered, but also by that which is known or assumed will be paid or offered. Moreover, fear, hope and almost all passions influence the prices which are given or received.[111]

Smith's measure of value is not questioned by Kraus. "The unit or measure of exchange value, which Smith discovered, is as important for state economy as the unit discovered by Galileo in physics for velocity."[112] What is the true theory of the circulation of money in a country?

Smith in his discussion of banks sets down the principle that only a definite amount of gold and silver money can circulate in a given state of the national economy. But can not a new quantity of gold and silver introduced into the land increase the number of purchases and loans? As for example, the gold which flowed from America to Spain and Portugal, to France from the pillaging of conquered lands, to Rome from the victorious wars of the ancient Romans or from the superstitutions of the Papists.[113]

From the above quotations it is evident that Kraus is not disposed to accept entirely without reservations the principles of Smith. These objections and comments, however, found as scattered notes by their editor, were never incorporated in any systematic work of theory, nor are they all consistent with each other or indicative of a unified viewpoint other than that of Smith. With all his keenness of argument, Kraus accepted the economics of Smith with less questioning than Sartorius, or even Lueder. His mind was set on the practical problems of his day, as is shown by his independent essays, and these problems he attempted to solve from the viewpoint of Smithian free trade. And, indeed, his life-long associations in the University of Königsberg and with the citizens of a port, the very prosperity of which depended upon freer trade, could only lead to the almost unquestioning acceptance of such a viewpoint. Of the early German economists, he alone was in a situation similar to that of Smith in Glasgow, and of these economists, he accepts with the fewest reservations the ideas of Smith.

Such were the views of a man who was to a large extent responsible for the economic changes which took place in Prussia after 1807, in so far as they can be ascribed to Smithian influence. It is fitting to close this brief account of the man and his works with the eager defense and high praise of no less a personage than vom Stein, as given in Varnhagen von Ense's *Memoirs*:

He [Stein] then came to the subject of the merits of professor Kraus, who had died in Königsberg. He gave me his writings, recommended them highly and angrily defended him against recent attacks. In Berlin at that time Heinrich von Kleist was editor of a paper, in which Adam Müller greatly minimized the worth of Kraus, and declared him a mere repeater of Adam Smith, whose principles were no longer to be considered valid, since they favored industrial activity to the disadvantage of the nobility. Stein, however, said of Kraus: "The man has done more than these gentlemen will ever destroy. The whole province has gained in light and culture through him, his views forced their way into all parts of life, into the government and legislation. If he has set up no brilliant new ideas, he has at least been no glory-seeking sophist; to have presented the plain truth clearly and purely and correctly expressed, and to have communicated it to thousands of auditors successfully, is a greater service than to arouse attention through chatter and paradoxes . . . Kraus was no follower, Kraus had an unassuming but genial personality, which laid strong hold on its environment, he had flashes of new insight, of great applications, and often astonished us by his unexpected conclusions. . . . Read his writings, everything there is clear and simple, and at present you need nothing more."[114]

Thus in the field of economic thought it can be said that by the year 1808 Smithian principles were fairly launched in Germany. The process had been a slow one, for it continued well over a quarter of a century from the first notice of Smith's book, and well over a decade from the time of active propaganda in its favor. The contemporaries and successors of Sartorius, Lueder, Kraus—such men as Hufeland, Soden, Lotz, Krug and Jakob—accepted the Smithian tradition only with important modifications. During the years 1805–1808 the works of these men and of many others were appearing, testifying to the intense interest in economic affairs that the rapid changes in the political and economic life of Germany were causing. At no time before had so many books on economics appeared in so short a time. But during this time the Smithian principles were making themselves felt in another direction, in the activities of such statesmen as Stein, Hardenberg and von Schön, and to them we shall now turn.

Notes

1. Ford, G.S., *Hanover and Prussia 1795–1803* (New York, 1903), p. 32.
2. Paulsen, F., *Geschichte des gelehrten Unterrichts* (Berlin and Leipzig, 1921), vol. ii, p. 11.
3. *Ibid.*, pp. 11–12.
4. Seeley, J. R., *The Life and Times of Stein*, vol. i, p. 32.
5. *Cf.* Pütter, J. S., *Versuch einer akademischen Gelehrtengeschichte von der Georg-Augustus Universität zu Göttingen* (Göttingen, 1765), section 5, pp. 4–5: "If it has been in keeping with the spirit of the sciences to oppose a philosophical taste which has obviously gone too far with arbitrary concepts, hypotheses and conclusions and finally become involved in the empty husks of method (in which connection we have in mind the new educational philosophy of Wolff), and on the contrary to combine scholarship, literature, philology, criticism, history, experience, use of sources, and mathematics with a sound philosophy, and thus make the higher sciences (upper faculties) sound and useful, perhaps Göttingen may claim some share in this. Secondly, in so far as it has been possible to lead directly to the practical in all parts of the sciences, this has always been a striking characteristic of this university. Thirdly, if it were possible to banish all pedantry from learning, Göttingen must be praised for contributing its share to this."
6. *Cf.* Roscher, W., *Geschichte der National-Oekonomik* (München, 1874), p. 598: "That the *Göttingische gelehrten Anzeigen* took notice so quickly of Smith's work, is due to the following circumstances: the great significance of the University of Göttingen at that time in history and the sciences of state (Gatterer, Schlözer, Pütter, Feder, Meiners, etc.); the political connection between Brunswick and Great Britain, which brought such numbers of English students to Göttingen, that a man like Lichtenberg could announce courses for them alone."
7. Paulsen, F., *op. cit.*, p. 11.

8. *Untersuchung der Natur und Ursachen von Nationalreichthümern von Adam Smith. Weidemanns Erben und Reich*, Leipzig Bd. i, 1776, Bd. ii, 1778. *Non vidimus*.

9. *Göttingische gelehrte Anzeigen* for Aug. 22, 1778, p. 544.

10. *Allgemeine deutsche Biographie*, vol. 6, p. 596.

11. Feder upon comparison of the translation with the original found it good. "Of this important work (for such it is, even though much is open to objection, especially in the latter part) the first volume, to which our present review is devoted, has been published by Weidemanns Erben and Reich in translation, and indeed in a right good one." *Göttingische gelehrte Anzeigen*, March 10, 1777, p. 240. Not so the second reviewer, G. Sartorius: "Schiller has not always translated correctly, as the writer of this review has discovered from comparison; but the original is extremely difficult, and the language, by reason of the technical and juridical expressions, difficult and obscure even to a native Englishman." *Göttingische gelehrte Anzeigen*, Oct. 19, 1793, p. 1661. If the translation of the title is characteristic of the whole, the translation is poor.

12. *Göttingische gelehrte Anzeigen*, March 10, 1777, p. 234.

13. *Ibid.*, p. 234: "The author on various main points holds views quite different from those of Stewart, and rejects his principles at times with strong expressions, but without mention of his name. He is less removed from the system of the French school."

14. *Ibid.*, p. 237.

15. "The author appears to limit this idea [of productive] somewhat too narrowly, when he counts the occupations of the learned, and consequently that part of the national wealth devoted to their maintenance among the non-productive." *Ibid.*, p. 238. "He finds it quite vain and impertinent when kings and their ministers watch the economy of private persons, and seek to limit their expenditures by sumptuary laws and embargoes on foreign goods (a judgment, whose very expression betrays too much heat)." *Ibid.*, p. 239.

16. *Op. cit., Zugabe* of April 5, 1777, p. 219.

17. *Allgemeine deutsche Bibliothek*, 1777, vol. 31, pp. 588: "All [the books of Smith's work] however show that, in the words of our author, every improvement in the circumstances of society leads either directly or indirectly to the rise of real rent, and to the increase of the real means of the landowners to purchase the labour or the product of the labour of others; and that every decline in the condition of society lessens the rent of land. We have accordingly a sure indicator of the increasing or decreasing social well-being, the rising or the falling of the rent of land." Again, *op. cit.*, vol. 38, p. 300: "The Economistes and he are fundamentally of the same mind, and, with the exception of the theory of taxes, he makes no statements which they do not accept. Blessed be the Briton, who thinks so justly and wisely!".

18. Isaak Iselin, *Ephemerides der Menschheit*, vol. 2, 1777, pp. 170–206 (*non vidimus*); Roscher, W., *op. cit.*, pp. 9–11.

19. Roscher, W., "*Die Ein- und Durchführung des Adam Smith'schen Systems in Deutsch-*

land," in *Berichte über die Verhandlungen der königlich sächsischen Gesellschaft der Wissenschaften zu Leipzig*, vol. 19, 1867, pp. 1–74. In this report Roscher treats the subject of the introduction of Smith's doctrines into Germany somewhat more extensively than is the case in his *Geschichte der National-Oekonomik*. He cites, pp. 17–21, the names and views of some sixteen Cameralists and Physiocrats, who refer to Smith's work, but betray little or no understanding of its contents.

20. *Allgemeine deutsche Biographie*, vol. 30, p. 391.
21. *Göttingische gelehrte Anzeigen* of October 19, 1793, pp. 1661–1662. Feder's review had appeared in three parts, *ibid.*, March 10, 1777, April 5, 1777, August 22, 1778.
22 *Op. cit.*, p. 1662.
23. *Ibid.*, p. 1661. This review by Sartorius, as well as the one which follows, is inconsequential in comparison with Feder's judicial review, for the former makes no attempt to estimate the value of Smith's work or compare it with others. Feder is content to shake hands with Smith, but Sartorius falls upon his neck.
24. *Untersuchung über die Natur und Ursachen des Nationalreichtums von Adam Smith. Aus dem Engl. der vierten Ausgabe neu übersetzt*. Vol. i, 1794, xx + 476pp. in 8.
25. "As to the intrinsic merit of the translation, one need only open the book and compare in order to be convinced upon the first glance that this more recent work in respect to correctness, clarity, fidelity and diction is to be preferred." *Op. cit.*, Nov. 29, 1794, p. 1901.
26. *Ibid.*
27. Roscher, W., *op. cit.*, p. 21.
28. The life of Christian Garve is singularly devoid of incident. He was born in Breslau, Silesia in 1742, and died there in 1798 in his fifty-sixth year. His academic training he received partly at the University of Frankfurt an der Oder, partly at the University of Halle, therefore entirely within the Prussian kingdom. He was for four years, 1768–1772, *ausserordentlicher Professor der Philosophie* at the University of Leipzig, but retired to Breslau on account of ill health. In Breslau his time was devoted to writing and to his friends. The most memorable event in his career is his acquaintance with Frederick II, of which he gives a lengthy account in his writings. *Allgemeine deutsche Biographie*, vol. 8, pp. 385–392.
29. *Ibid.*, p. 385.
30. In a letter to his friend Weisse in March 1791, he says: "Smith's book on national wealth I consider one of the classic works of recent times. The German translation is so wretched, that it is hardly intelligible, let alone readable. It would be worth while to translate it again. And yet work on a book already old and known is neither so pleasant nor so profitable as on a new one of equal worth. Korn [the publisher] to be sure wanted to take over the new translation of Smith, but I still have considerable doubt, to say nothing of the extent and size of the work." Garve, C., *Briefe an Weisse* (Breslau, 1796), vol. 2, p. 12. In another letter to the same friend on Aug. 26, 1791, he writes: "Korn is willing to risk a new translation of Smith on National Wealth. I, too, am rather inclined to undertake it, as I esteem the book highly." *Ibid.*, p. 32.

It is impossible to determine to what extent the following portion of a letter from Friedrich von Gentz to his friend Garve was instrumental in turning the latter to the thought of translating Smith. Gentz was an ardent admirer and great friend of Garve and the passage quoted was written Dec. 5, 1790, not long before Garve took up the idea of making a new translation. "I recently finished two extensive, but not new readings. First, I have studied Smith on National Wealth for the third time with the greatest attention, and made an analysis of it to the extent of forty sheets. I recall that I have talked with you about this book occasionally, yet only incidentally; but it seems to me you have never expressed the unrestrained praise, which I have always felt it deserves. In my opinion it is in the first place by far the most perfect work that has ever been written in any language on this subject, and I cannot refrain from saying that Stewart, Forbonnais, Melon, Büsch, etc., and all others that have heretofore reached my hands, remain far behind Smith. Aside from this specific merit, however, I consider it in general, in respect to method and literary art as one of the most complete and perfect books, that exist in any science. Such clarity combined with such penetration, such a cool, calm investigation together with such ardent zeal for the welfare of mankind, such an unbroken orderliness even to the smallest parts and details of such an admirable system, and such unity throughout the whole is really found in extremely few philosophical investigations. In respect to style I confess that I consider Smith the most perfect English prose writer; neither Hume nor Ferguson, who may most readily be compared with him, and who may excell him in single qualities, in keenness, in force, in variety, do I find, when considered from all sides, so correct and faultless. Of German writers there is only one, in whose literary art I find any similarity, and indeed in many points, and he is Garve." Wittichen, F. K., *Briefe von und an Friedrich von Gentz* (Berlin, 1909), vol. i, pp. 181–182.

31. For an account of this and of his trouble with the publishers of the first translation, *vide* Garve, C., *Briefe an Weisse*, vol. 2, pp. 36–38.

32. Roscher, W., *op. cit.*, p. 21.

33. Garve, C., *Vermischte Aufsätze* (Breslau, 1796), "*Ueber den Charakter der Bauern und ihr Verhältniss gegen die Gutscherrn und gegen die Regierung,*" pp. 2–228; "*Bruchstücke zu der Untersuchung über den Verfall der kleinen Städte, dessen Ursachen, und die Mittel ihm abzuhelfen,*" pp. 373–444.

34. Garve, C., *Briefe an Weisse*, vol. 2, p. 37.

35. Garve, C., *Fragmente zur Schilderung des Geistes, des Characters, und der Regierung Friedricks des Zweiten, Gesammelte Werke* (Breslau, 1801), vol. 10, 11.

36. Garve, C., *Vermischte Aufsätze*, p. 196.

37. *Cf.* Garve, C., *Ueber den Charakter der Bauern etc., passim.*

38. *Cf.* Garve, C., *Bruchstücke etc., passim.*

39. Georg Sartorius was born in Cassel in 1765, and died in Göttingen in 1828 in his sixty-third year. He was distinctly a product of the University of Göttingen, and his life activity was largely confined to that university. He studied at Göttingen 1783–1788, occupied various positions in the library 1786–1794, and became *Privat Dozent*

1792, *ausserordentlicher Professor* 1797, *ordentlicher Professor* 1802. He was very productive; especially in the field of history, his best known and greatest work being *die Geschichte des hanseatischen Bundes*, 1802–1808. *Allgemeine deutsche Biographie*, vol. 30, pp. 390–394.

40. Handbuch der Staatswirschaft, zum Gebrauche bey akademischen Vorlesungen, nach Adam Smith's Grundsätzen ausgearbeitet, von Georg Sartorius. Berlin 1796, xxxxix + 234pp.

41. *Allgemeine deutsche Biographie*, vol. 6, p. 596.

42. The reviews of Smith's work, which appeared in the *Göttingische gelehrte Anzeigen* in 1793–1794, are the work of Sartorius. *Allgemeine deutsche Biographie*, vol. 30, p. 391.

43. "The author of the following summary has lectured for five years on the principles given here, and he is able to say that he has also been so fortunate as to make them comprehensible to beginners." *Preface to Handbuch*, p. 44. Kraus in a letter to a friend, Jan., 1797, is inclined to question the priority of Sartorius in presenting Smith's principles: "And so, dearest friend, I too can rejoice that in all Germany such a learned course of so-called Cameral sciences has never been taught as here for some time past; and it is ludicrous to see a man living in a great pile of books, swelling with pride—on the favourite principle 'There is nothing that we don't know'—and saying that he was the first to give academic lectures on Smith in Germany, when I, right in the midst of threatening storms, have for six years past and recently entirely without subterfuge not only presented the only true, great, beautiful, just and beneficial system, but have been able to inspire with it some fine fellows, as for instance a von Schön, whom our Minister von Schrötter has permitted to travel, and my favorite, Dohna Wundlacken." Voigt, J., *Das Leben des Professor Christian Jakob Kraus* (Königsberg, 1819), p. 388.

44. "The author is convinced that Smith has discovered the truth and he considers it his duty to contribute his share towards its dissemination." *Preface to Handbuch*, p. 4.

45. "The time which we have chosen to further the introduction of this theory, which we considered our duty, since we are convinced of its truth, seems excellently fitted for this. A greater effort has risen among us, as is said, to test the fundamental principles of science." *Ibid.*, pp. 42–43.

46. "However, to judge from many expressions of his [Garve], that undertaking will probably contain not a refutation, but a clarification of the system; this promised presentation will also have another purpose than this summary." *Ibid.*, p. 47.

47. "Concerning the sources from which the wants of a nation are satisfied, or the elements of national prosperity."

48. "Concerning state economy, or the rules which the government of a state must follow in order to enable the citizens to secure a satisfactory income, and to procure the same for the public expenditures of the state."

49. *Ibid.*, pp. 46–47.

50. *Von den Elementen des National-Reichthums, und von der Staatswirtschaft, nach Adam Smith. Zum Gebrauche bey akademischen Vorlesungen und beym Privat-Studio*

ausgearbeitet von Georg Sartorius, Hofrath und Professor zu Göttingen. Göttingen 1806, xxviii + 268pp. *Adhandlungen, die Elemente des Nationalreichthums und die Staatswirtschaft betreffend.* Th. I. Göttingen 1806. viii + 519 pp.

51. "Furthermore, he is convinced that Smith's views on the effects of trade and his examination of the Mercantile system are excellently done. But if he holds other opinions in regard to Smith's views on the value of things, and its unchanging measure, on the unconditional application of the principle of free disposal of industry and capital, on the harmony of individual and social interests, on productive and unproductive labour, on taxes, and on certain other points, this does not prevent him from recognizing the undying services of this excellent man to science; such difference of opinion did not require the development of an entirely new work, which in many respects would have contained Smith's ideas only in other forms or in other words." *"Preface, Von den Elementen"* etc., pp. 15–16.

52. *Ibid.,* p. 51.

53. Lauderdale, Earl of, *An Inquiry into the Nature and Origin of Public Wealth, and into the Means and Causes of its Increase* (Edinburgh, 1804).

54. *Op. cit.,* p. 1.

55. "The value of a thing is first estimated according to the use which can be made of it, the need which it satisfies, the pleasure which it affords." *Ibid.,* p. 2.

56. "Price is subject to the same numerous relations as the exchange value of a thing." *Ibid.,* p. 15.

57. *Ibid.,* p. 24.

58. *Ibid.,* p. 88 *et seq.*

59. *Ibid.,* p. 178 *et seq.*

60. *Ibid.,* p. 216.

61. *Ibid.,* p. 217.

62. *Ibid.,* p. 248 *et seq.*

63. *Ibid.,* p. 223.

64. *Ibid.,* p. 211.

65. *Ibid.,* p. 271 *et seq.*

66. *Ibid.,* p. 518–519.

67. *Ueber Nationalindustrie und Staatswirtschaft. Nach Adam Smith bearbeitet von August Ferdinand Lueder.* Berlin 1800–1802. Vol. i, 1800, xxxii + 462 pp. ; vol. ii, 1802, viii + 623 pp.

68. Lueder was born in Bielefeld in 1760 and died in Jena in 1819 in his fifty-ninth year. He also was a product of the University of Göttingen, and then became professor of history at the Carolinum in Brunswick in 1786, court councillor in 1797, professor of philosophy at the University of Göttingen 1810–1814, honorary professor at the University of Jena 1817. *Allgemeine deutsche Biographie,* vol. 19, pp. 377–378.

69. *Allgemeine deutsche Biographie,* vol. 19, p. 377.

70. *Die Nationalindustrie und ihre Wirkungen, ein Grundriss zu Vorlesungen,* 1808.

71. *Kritik der Statistik und Politik nebst einer Begründung der politischen Philosophie vom*

Professor Lueder in Göttingen (Göttingen, 1812), xii + 531 pp. *Kritische Geschichte der Statistik, von August Ferdinand Lueder* (Göttingen, 1817), xvi + 855 pp.

72. "The attempt [to portray the conditions which determine the wealth of nations] was successful to an extent which could be expected only from one of the greatest minds, but the effects of this attempt both in Germany and abroad remained as insignificant as the attempt itself was great, bold and happy. Smith's work attained canonical standing in the foremost of all legislative assemblies; it was translated into several languages; we are able to point to two translations, one partly from the hand of Garve, whose name makes any adjective superfluous; one impression after the other has been made of both the original and the translation and yet it is only with the greatest difficulty that any trace is to be discovered, not only in the writings of our country, but also of the other civilized European nations, of the spirit which lives in Smith's immortal works." *Preface*, vol. i, p. 12.

73. *Op. cit.*, p. 435.

74. *Ibid.*, p. 439 *et seq.*

75. *Preface, Critical History of Statistics*, p. 8.

76. "The state should afford security only; security can, however, be injured or entirely destroyed by the rulers themselves. This led to the theory of the forms of government, or to the investigation of the question: what is to be hoped and feared of every constitution and to what extent; and then to the advances and ennoblement of rulers, just as the people advances and improves. This security can also be injured by the citizens, and thus the fifth book on forms of government was followed by the sixth on laws and rights." *Preface, Ueber Nationalindustrie etc.*, p. 3.

77. "I have followed the path of my predecessor; subjected each of his assertions to a new examination; filled in the lacunae which I found; corrected errors, brought closer together and connected the parts of the whole. I have completely done over several parts, and, I may add, several of the most important parts, and also added the third book, which is lacking in Smith's work. I would have done over the whole work, had I known how to develop a better system." *Ibid.*, vol. i, p. xv.

78. *Kritik der Statistik und Politik*, p. 421.

79. *Preface, Kritik der Statistik und Politik*, pp. 6–8.

80. Kraus was born in Osterode in 1753, and died in Königsberg in 1807 in his fifty-fourth year. He attended the University of Königsberg for a lengthy period (1770–1779), and then became a tutor, and in this occupation spent a year at the University of Göttingen where he heard Heyne, Feder and Schlözer. While a student at the University of Königsberg he had attended Kant's lectures, later had attracted his attention and finally the two men had become warm friends, although they differed greatly in their views. In 1780 he took his doctor's degree at the University of Halle and was then called to the University of Königsberg as professor of practical philosophy and Cameralia, a position which he occupied until his death. *Allgemeine deutsche Biographie*, vol. 17, pp. 66–68.

81. "On Aug. 17 both the Immediate Commission and the Minister of the Province [von Schrötter] laid before the king projects for the restoration of the land. Both

proceeded essentially from the same economic principles, which had been taught for many years at the University of Königsberg by Professor Kraus and had entered into the convictions of his numerous auditors. Kraus followed the theories of Adam Smith; he had many connections with business men, landowners, merchants, had a keen penetrating judgment, and a gift of clear presentation; the place of his activity, a commercial city, which carried on a lively trade with England; the midpoint of the province of Prussia, where most of the officials received their education, favored the entrance of his principles. The most active member of the Immediate Commission, von Schön, the Minister von Schrötter, and the provincial president von Auerswald, were his pupils." Pertz, G. H., *Das Leben des Ministers Freiherrn vom Stein* (Berlin, 1850), vol. ii, p. 13.

82. Voigt, J., *Das Leben des Professor C. J. Kraus* (Königsberg, 1819), p. 44.

83. *Ibid.*, p. 57.

84. "He himself told one of his later friends that the fact that he had really understood little of Young's Arithmetick and had therefore studied with great effort the most important works on finance and several things on state economy in order to return to the translation with new views, had first aroused his interest in the study of state economy." *Ibid.*, p. 306.

85. "From Schlözer he brought to the academic field a predilection for statistics and state economy; of these the former became a part of his first lectures." *Ibid.*, p. 306.

86. *Ibid.*, p. 97.

87. "War Councillor Scheffner sent me during the Christmas vacation Sartorius' summary of Smith, which he had expressly ordered for himself. I worried my way through perhaps a hundred pages, then brought out my summary and believed I could say to myself like the painter: 'Anche io son pittore.'" *Ibid.*, p. 386.

88. *Vide* note 43.

89. *Ibid.*, p. 358.

90. *Ibid.*, p. 373.

91. *Vide* note 43.

92. It is a source of wonder to Roscher. *Die Ein- und Durchführung des Adam Smith'schen Systems in Deutschland*, p. 29.

93. Kraus, C. J., *Die Staatswirtschaft*, pp. v–viii; also *Hamanns Schriften* (Berlin, 1823), pt. v, p. 191.

94. *Die Staatswirtschaft von Christian Jacob Kraus. Nach dessen Tode herausgegeben von Hans von Auerswald* (Königsberg, 1808–1811), 5 vols. *Vermischte Schriften über staatswirtschaftliche, philosophische und andere wissenschaftliche Gegenstände von Christian Jacob Kraus. Nach dessen Tode herausgegeben von Hans von Auerswald* (Königsberg, 1808–1819), 8 vols.

95. Roscher, W., *op. cit.*, p. 29.

96. *Die Staatswirtschaft*, vol. ii, p. 200 *et seq.*

97. *Ibid.*, vol. i, p. 22.

98. *Ibid.*, vol. iv, p. 154 *et seq.*

99. Roscher, W., *op cit.*, pp. 30–31.

100. "The desire and effort of each individual to improve his lot is the basis of all state economy, like the force of gravity in the universe." *Ibid.*, vol. v, p. 3.

101. *Ibid.*, p. 4.

102. As an illustration of economic method I cannot refrain from quoting at length: "Whenever it is a question of a law or an arrangement, by which men are to be brought either to do something which they previously did not do, or not to do something which they previously did, then, in the second case, the first question is why did people not cease of their own accord? Then we can discover, if we put ourselves in their position, which of the four causes previously given is operative. Then follows the second question: What will men attempt to do in order to evade the law which conflicts with their interests? Then the third question: How far will that which they undertake in order to evade the law succeed? In the case of these second and third questions many striking views will be gained, which would otherwise have quite escaped us, as soon as we put ourselves entirely in the position of these men and make their situation our own. What has here been said of ceasing to do is of even greater validity when it is a question of doing; that is, when men are to be brought (enticed or forced) by laws or arrangements to do something which they previously did not want to do." *Ibid.*, pp. 5–6.

103. *Ibid.*, p. 43 *et seq.*

104. *Ibid.*, p. 45 *et seq.*

105. *Ibid.*, p. 91 *et seq.*

106. *Ibid.*, p. 239.

107. *Ibid.*, p. 198 *et seq.*

108. *Staatswirtschaftliche Bemerkungen, op. cit.*, vol. ii, pp. 85–138.

109. *Ibid.*, p. 125.

110. *Ibid.*, pp. 133–134.

111. *Ibid.*, pp. 118–119.

112. *Ibid.*, p. 102.

113. *Ibid.*, pp. 100–101.

114. Varnhagen von Ense, K. A., *Denkwürdigkeiten des eignen Lebens* (Leipzig, 1871), pt. iii, pp. 176–177.

NA excerpt

4.2. Friedrich List, 1916.
The System of Values of Exchange (Falsely Termed by the School, the "Industrial" System)—Adam Smith

Adam Smith's doctrine is in respect to national and international conditions, merely a continuation of the physiocratic system. Like the latter, it ignores the very nature of nationalities, seeks almost entirely to exclude politics and the power of the State, presupposes the existence of a state of perpetual peace and of universal union, underrates the value of a national manufacturing power, and the means of obtaining it, and demands absolute freedom of trade.

Adam Smith fell into these fundamental errors in exactly the same way as the physiocrats had done before him, namely, by regarding absolute freedom in international trade as an axiom assent to which is demanded by common sense, and by not investigating to the bottom how far history supports this idea.

Dugald Stewart (Adam Smith's able biographer) informs us that Smith, at a date twenty-one years before his work was published in 1776 (viz. in 1755), claimed priority in conceiving the idea of universal freedom of trade, at a literary party at which he was present, in the following words:

Man is usually made use of by statesmen and makers of projects, as the material for a sort of political handiwork. The project makers, in their operations on human affairs, disturb Nature, whereas people ought simply to leave her to herself to act freely, in order that she may accomplish her objects. In order to raise a State from the lowest depth of barbarism to the highest degree of wealth, all that is requisite is peace, moderate taxation, and good administration of justice; everything else will follow of its own accord in the natural course of things. All governments which act in a contrary spirit to this natural course, which seek to divert capital into other channels, or to restrict the progress of the community in its spontaneous course, act contrary to nature, and, in order to maintain their position, become oppressive and tyrannical.

Adam Smith set out from this fundamental idea, and to prove it and to illustrate it was the sole object of all his later works. He was confirmed in this idea by Quesnay, Turgot, and the other coryphæi of the physiocratic school, whose acquaintance he had made in a visit to France in the year 1765.

Smith evidently considered the idea of freedom of trade as an intellectual discovery which would constitute the foundation of his literary fame. How natural, therefore, it was that he should endeavour in his work to put aside and to refute everything that stood in the way of that idea; that he should consider himself as the professed advocate of absolute freedom of trade, and that he thought and wrote in that spirit.

How could it be expected, that with such preconceived opinions, Smith should judge of men and of things, of history and statistics, of political measures and of their authors, in any other light than as they confirmed or contradicted his fundamental principle?

In the passage above quoted from Dugald Stewart, Adam Smith's whole system is comprised as in a nutshell. The power of the State can and ought to do nothing, except to allow justice to be administered, to impose as little taxation as possible. Statesmen who attempt to found a manufacturing power, to promote navigation, to extend foreign trade, to protect it by naval power, and to found or to acquire colonies, are in his opinion project makers who only hinder the progress of the community. For him no *nation* exists, but merely a community, i.e. a number of individuals dwelling together. These individuals know best for themselves what branches of occupation are most to their advantage, and they can best select for themselves the means which promote their prosperity.

This entire nullification of nationality and of State power, this exaltation of individualism to the position of author of all effective power, could be made plausible only by making the main object of investigation to be not the power which effects, but the thing effected, namely, material wealth, or rather the value in exchange which the thing effected possesses. Materialism must come to the aid of individualism, in order to conceal what an enormous amount of power accrues to individuals from nationality, from national unity, and from the national confederation of the productive powers. A bare theory of values must be made to pass current as national economy, because individuals alone produce values, and the State, incapable of creating values, must limit its operations to calling into activity, protecting, and promoting the productive powers of individuals. In this combination, the quintessence of political economy may be stated as follows, viz.: Wealth consists in the possession of objects of exchangeable value; objects of exchangeable value are produced by the labour of individuals in combination with the powers of nature and with capital. By the division of labour, the productiveness of the labour is increased; capital is accumulated by savings, by production exceeding consumption. The greater the total amount of capital, so much the greater is the division of labour, and hence the capacity to produce. Private interest is the most effectual stimulus to labour and to economy. Therefore the highest wisdom of statecraft consists in placing no obstacle in the way of private industry, and in caring only for the good administration of justice. And hence also it is folly to induce the subjects of a State, by means of State legislative measures, to produce for themselves anything which they can buy cheaper from abroad. A system so consistent as this is, which sets forth the elements of wealth, which so clearly explains the process of its production, and apparently so completely exposes the errors of the previous schools, could not fail, in default of any other, to meet with acceptance. The mistake has been simply, that this system at bottom is nothing else than a system of the *private economy of all the individual persons in a country, or of the individuals of the whole human race, as that economy would develop and shape itself, under a state of things in which there were no distinct nations, nationalities, or national interests—no distinctive political constitutions or degrees of civilisation—no wars or national animosities*; that it is nothing more than a theory of values; a mere shopkeeper's or individual merchant's theory—not a scientific doctrine, showing how the productive powers of an entire nation can be called into existence, increased, maintained, and pre-served—for the special benefit of its civilisation, welfare, might, continuance, and independence.

This system regards everything from the shopkeeper's point of view. The value of anything is wealth, according to it, so its sole object is to gain values. The establishment of powers of production, it leaves to chance, to nature, or to the providence of God (whichever you please), only the State must have nothing at all to do with it, nor must politics venture to meddle with the business of accumulating exchangeable values. It is resolved to buy wherever it can find the cheapest articles—that the home manufactories are ruined by their importation, matters not to it. If foreign nations give a bounty on the export of their manufactured goods, so much the better; it can buy them so much the cheaper. In its view no class is productive save those who actually produce things valuable in exchange. It well recognises how the division of labour promotes the success of a business in detail, but it has no perception of the effect of the division of labour as affecting a whole nation. It knows that only by individual economy can it increase its capital, and that only in proportion to the increase in its capital can it extend its individual trades; but it sets no value on the increase of the productive power, which results from the establishment of native manufactories, or on the foreign trade and national power which arise out of that increase. What may become of the entire nation in the future, is to it a matter of perfect indifference, so long as private individuals can gain wealth. It takes notice merely of the rent yielded by land, but pays no regard to the value of landed property; it does not perceive that the greatest part of the wealth of a nation consists in the value of its land and its fixed property. For the influence of foreign trade on the value and price of landed property, and for the fluctuations and calamities thence arising, it cares not a straw. In short, this system is the strictest and most consistent "mercantile system," and it is incomprehensible how that term could have been applied to the system of Colbert, the main tendency of which is towards an "industrial system"—i.e. a system which has solely in view the founding of a national industry—a national commerce—without regarding the temporary gains or losses of values in exchange.

Notwithstanding, we would by no means deny the great merits of Adam Smith. He was the first who successfully applied the analytical method to political economy. By means of that method and an unusual degree of sagacity, he threw light on the most important branches of the science, which were previously almost wholly obscure. Before Adam Smith only a practice existed; his works rendered it possible to constitute a science of political economy, and he has contributed a greater amount of materials for that object than all his predecessors or successors.

But that very peculiarity of his mind by which, in analysing the various constituent parts of political economy, he rendered such important service, was the cause why he did not take a comprehensive view of the community in its entirety; that he was unable to combine individual interests in one harmonious whole; that he would not consider the nation in preference to mere individuals; that out of mere anxiety for the freedom of action of the individual producers, he lost sight of the interests of the entire nation. He who so clearly perceived the benefits of the division of labour in a single manufactory, did not perceive that the same principle is applicable with equal force to entire provinces and nations.

With this opinion, that which Dugal Stewart says of him exactly agrees. Smith could judge individual traits of character with extraordinary acuteness; but if an opinion was needed as to the entire character of a man or of a book, one could not be sufficiently astonished at the narrowness and obliquity of his views. Nay, he was incapable of forming a correct estimate of the character of those with whom he had lived for many years in the most intimate friendship.

"The portrait," says his biographer, "was ever full of life and expression, and had a strong resemblance to the original if one compared it with the original from a certain point of view; but it never gave a true and perfect representation according to all its dimensions and circumstances."

4.3 Keith Tribe, 1988.
The "Smith Reception" and the Function of Translation

Die Statswirthschaftslehre—franz. economie politique, Science de commerce et de finance; eng. political economy; ital. economia civile—hat die Gründung, Vermehrung und Verwaltung des *Nationalreichthums*—wealth of nations—zum Gegenstande.[1]

The sequence in which Physiocratic work appeared in translation was an important element in the German process of reception, but we should be wary of concluding that a work was culturally accessible simply because a translation of it existed. While it is evident that the publication of a text in translation made it available to a new readership, we need to consider carefully the selectivity with which such translated texts—more or less equally available to the reading public—were read. Here we will focus our attention on the interesting fact that, until the final decade of the eighteenth century, Sir James Steuart's *Inquiry* was better known, and more frequently cited than Smith's *Wealth of Nations*. Both works were translated into German very soon after their publication in Britain, yet it is well known that Smith's book was widely ignored. Steuart's text, on the other hand, is frequently encountered in cited literature and course announcements until the 1790s. This provides a ready example with which to investigate the function of translation in the propagation of new concepts and approaches in economics.

Such factors will be taken into account in this chapter, modifying the approach adopted with respect to Physiocracy, where a controversial foreign doctrine quickly found native protagonists who constructed their own variant of it. The process of reception did not depend on the actual availability of the Physiocratic literature, whether in the original French or in German translation.

When we turn to Smith's *Wealth of Nations* a different problem is encountered: for almost twenty years little interest was shown, and then, just at the turn of the century, a phase of "Smithianism" began. This is true of the reception of both the original English edition and of the original Schiller translation of 1776–9. Despite the rapidity with which a translation of Books 1 to 3 appeared, it was not until the publication of the Garve–Dörrien translation in 1794 that more general notice was taken. Both the "failure" of the first publication and the "success" of the second have to be explained in a manner which eschews any resort to our modern evaluation of the text's importance.

Various explanations have been advanced for the initial lack of interest in the *Wealth of Nations*, chief among them being the poor quality of the Schiller translation. The first of the two volumes, published in Leipzig in 1776, contained Books 1 and 2—that is, those books which have always been regarded as the theoretical core of the work. Many commentators suggest that the delay in acknowledging Smith's ascendancy is attributable to the poor quality of the Schiller translation, pointing for support to the rapid acceptance of the Garve and Dörrien translation on its appearance in the mid-1790s. But a brief comparison of the two translations disposes of this argument, for it is difficult to see how the detected variations can be viewed as anything more than stylistic difference. In any case, Garve himself disposed of this argument in his foreword, where he states that it was the style of the first translation that disturbed him, and not an obviously poor or inaccurate translation. Having read the text in Schiller's translation, he did not discover anything that had been hidden from him when he turned to the original English edition.[2]

It must also be recognized that many academics, especially in northern Germany, were quite capable of reading English. Indeed, it could be suggested that German translations of English scholarly works were not primarily destined for the "professional reader", but for a more diffuse audience of students and interested professionals.[3] In addition to this, one has to be careful about using publication histories as evidence of diffusion. The fact that Hume's *Political Discourses* appeared in translation in 1754, and then again in 1766, might lead us to conclude that the work was popular. In fact, the reverse was the case: the 1766 edition is identical to the 1754 printing, apart from the addition of a later flyleaf. A desperate bookseller was trying to shift his stock, not responding to demand.[4]

Another factor which must be taken into consideration is that, from the German point of view, Smith's *Wealth of Nations* was just one of several foreign economic treatises to appear in the latter part of the eighteenth century. It has already been noted that Forbonnais had a great influence on Sonnenfels, and that Cameralistic literature regularly cited the texts of Verri, Genovesi, and

Steuart. Today all these writers are regarded as "pre-Smithian", but such a judgement assumes the success of a reception process which we have to account for here. In order to explain how the *Wealth of Nations* came to be regarded as a touchstone of "modern economic thought", we need to look at other contemporary texts without those modern prejudices which, in part at least, derive from the very tradition Smith helped to found. Accordingly, this chapter will not confine itself to the diffusion of *Wealth of Nations* alone, but will start by outlining the literature of translation among which it first appeared.

Approximately twice as many translations from the French language as from the English were published in the later eighteenth century, and Italian texts were quite poorly represented—in part, at least, because of the difficulties in finding Italian translators.[5] Alongside the general impact of literature related to the Physiocratic reception, it was France rather than Britain that was regarded as the dominant foreign cultural influence; and, as the library built up at Lautern shows, it was far more usual to find original works in French than in English in collections of this period. One of the most successful translations of this time was that of Forbonnais's *Élémens du commerce*, which first appeared in German as *Der vernünftige Kaufmann* in 1755, and was intended to be the first in a series of translations of English and other writings on trade. It was subsequently reprinted and published in a second edition in 1767, the same year in which a translation of Forbonnais's *Principes et observations oeconomiques* appeared.[6] While the two editions of *Der vernünftige Kaufmann* contain the same number of pages and are superficially identical apart from the front matter, a closer comparison of the texts shows that the later one is indeed a reset version, and is not composed of sheets from the original printing. Unlike the translation of Hume's *Political Discourses*, it is safe to assume in this case that republication was a sign of success in the contemporary book trade, rather than of failure.[7]

The writings of Verri and Genovesi were also well received in Germany, with the former benefiting from two separate translations of his *Meditazioni sulla economia politica*, a treatise which emphasizes the interdependence of needs, trade, and welfare within an open economy.[8] The first translation was made from the French edition of 1773 rather than from the original Italian; and Schmid, who had used Verri together with Iselin's *Versuche über die Gesezgebung* for his lectures on state economy at Lautern, published the second in 1785, adding an essay of his own on projects.[9]

Schmid prefaced the textbook produced from these lectures with some recommendations for private reading: Genovesi's *Grundsätze der bürgerlichen Oekonomie*, Stewart's (sic) *Staats-wirthschaft*, and Montesquieu's *Von den*

Gesezen.[10] This was in 1780, by which time Sonnenfels' textbook had been completed and Smith's *Wealth of Nations* was also available in translation. Why, then, did Schmid make such an apparently perverse selection?

An examination of Genovesi provides some clue to its suitability for the kind of course Schmid was teaching. *Lezioni* begins with a chapter on "political bodies" which uses the same mechanical analogy as Iselin's *Versuche*. The economic activities of members of this body are distinguished as either productive or non-productive, and the relation of economy to polity is stated in familiar terms: "Each body is a large family, which can only be maintained through labour."[11] The main themes of *Lezioni* are population, commerce, money, and credit—there is not very much on policy, nor is there any detailed treatment of agriculture and manufactures. Nevertheless, it was easy to incorporate Genovesi into Cameralistic teaching, as Pfeiffer's extensive use—not to say plagiarism—of *Lezioni* in his *Grundriß der wahren und falschen Staatskunst* shows. Roscher goes so far as to suggest that Pfeiffer copied almost all of his book from Justi and Genovesi; but, rather than condemning Pfeiffer, we should note that such a charge, advanced by the leading historian of German economics, is really an indication of the ease with which such texts as Genovesi's could be assimilated into Cameralistic discourse.[12]

The most widely cited British text of the 1780s and early 1790s was two translations of Steuart's *Inquiry into the Principles of Political Oeconomy*, and Schmid's reference to it in the context of Verri, Genovesi, and Montesquieu is not untypical. The two German versions appeared at roughly the same time, a result of resentment on the part of the Tübingen publisher, Cotta, when he discovered that a translation of the *Inquiry* was being prepared for publication by the Hamburg Typographic Society. Cotta had published a translation of Steuart's "Dissertation upon the Doctrine and Principles of Money, Applied to the German Coin" in 1761, believing that this text was a preamble to the *Inquiry* and that he therefore had a form of copyright to continuations of Steuart's treatise. It would appear that Steuart had supplied Cotta's translator, Schott, with a copy of the *Inquiry* as soon as it was published in 1767,[13] and thus while the publisher's claim to priority was unfounded, it does seem that Steuart himself wanted the translation of his work to be undertaken by the Tübingen publisher. A translation was rapidly commissioned and Book 1, consisting of just over 200 pages, was published in the same year as the more substantial first section of the Hamburg translation.[14]

The speed with which Cotta's edition was prepared was partly due to the fact that the Tübingen translator, C. F. Schott, simply copied and incorporated large tracts of the Hamburg edition in his text—but it is not true, as some have contended, that after thirty pages of Schott's version the two editions are identical. After close examination, Ken Carpenter has confirmed that long passages certainly were lifted out of the Hamburg text in the preparation of Cotta's edition, but there are substantial deviations; added to which, Schott does try to make his translation text more purely German in its language than the Hamburg version.[15] It would appear that Cotta's edition sold quite well, with reprints being made in a somewhat haphazard sequence as stocks ran down of the earlier volumes.[16]

While this provides some insight into the business of translation in later eighteenth-century Germany, it is more important to note that Steuart actually drafted Books 1 and 2 of the *Inquiry* during a period of residence in Tübingen, and that the text bears more than a passing resemblance to contemporary Cameralistic literature. Exiled for his complicity in the Jacobite Rising of 1745, he spent several years in France before moving to Tübingen in June 1757. Here he continued the work that he had begun in 1755 on the manuscript which was later to become the *Inquiry*.[17] One year was spent in Tübingen, and then, after some time in Venice, Steuart returned in October 1760 for another period of residence, which came to an end with his departure for Holland and eventual return to Scotland in June 1761.

Little is known of Steuart's activities and contacts during his stay in southern Germany: what we know of Tübingen in this period, however, gives us grounds for supposing that Steuart could well have enjoyed direct contact with important political and legal scholars,[18] although, as earlier chapters have shown, it was only after this period that a Cameralistic orthodoxy began to gain ground in German universities. However much significance is given to Steuart's period of residence in Tübingen, it can be maintained that the *Inquiry* bears a close resemblance to contemporary French and German literature than it does to English texts of the same period.

The first book deals with population and agriculture, and opens with the familiar notion of the economy modelled on the household and directed by the head, "who is both lord and steward of the family".[19] The ruler is ascribed the same kind of powers and interests as we have seen elaborated in Justi's *Staatswirthschaft*: as the guardian of the country's welfare, he not only has to oversee the achievement of happiness on the part of his subjects, but he also has to adjust the relationships between his subjects "so as to make their several interests lead them to supply one another with their reciprocal wants . . . It is the business of a statesman to judge of the expediency of different schemes of oeconomy, and by degrees to model the minds of his subjects so as to induce them, from the allurement of private interest, to concur in the execution of his plan."[20] Steuart does not treat this population of subjects as a static entity; he introduces a dynamic element by linking population to agriculture or, more broadly, to subsistence. The size of the population is strictly regulated by the supply of food; but it should not be concluded from this that luxury is necessarily prejudicial to agriculture and the "multiplication" of the population. "While no-one can dispute that agriculture is the foundation of multiplication, and the most essential requisite for the prosperity of a state",[21] it does not follow that everyone should be employed in agriculture. The promotion of agriculture beyond the immediate demand for agricultural produce— the course of action to be followed by a wise statesman—creates a need for non-agricultural classes who can produce an equivalent acceptable to agriculturalists. Reciprocal wants must be created by the statesman "in order to bind the society together". As this process continues, luxury and money appear, creating more reciprocities and promoting population; while this certainly requires a proper proportion between the forms of labour employed in each class, it does not mean that there should be a priority of the one over the other: "let it therefore never be said, that there are too many manufactures employed in a country; it is the same as if it were said, there are too few idle persons, too few beggars, and too many husbandmen".[22]

The proportional distribution of the population affects geography as well as occupations—Steuart devotes Chapter 9 of Book 1 to the principles regulating the distribution of inhabitants between towns, villages, and hamlets, and there is a later chapter on the need for accurate records of births, deaths, and marriages. "Proportion" and "equilibrium" are the guiding principles for Steuart's statesman, extending to a consideration of the potentially harmful effects of the introduction of machinery.[23]

Book 2 extends this analysis to trade and industry,[24] with commerce being described as "abbreviating" the process of barter on the part of producers: "Instead of a pin-maker exchanging his pins with fifty different persons, for whose labour he has occasion, he sells all to the merchant for money or for credit; and, as occasion offers, he purchases all his wants, either directly from those who supply them, or from other merchants who deal with manufacturers in the same way his merchant dealt with him."[25] This idea directly precedes Steuart's consideration of price and profit, which is developed out of the process of exchange, therefore, and not, like Smith's, from both production and exchange. Thus, Steuart's account of price and profit does not involve a problem of value and its relation to the labour employed; at the theoretical level, we have here perhaps one of the most fundamental divergences between Steuart and the later development of classical political economy, which was to treat the problem of value as central to economic analysis. At the same time, this focus on exchange renders Steuart more assimilable by a Cameralistic tradition that was also uninterested in labour value as a prime economic category. And a concentration upon exchange and reciprocity is likewise closely related to Steuart's conception of the role of a statesman as preserving a balance without "great vibrations" or "harmful revolutions". Steuart does not deny that the principle of self-interest guides the efforts of an active population; he lays emphasis instead on the potential instability which can arise from the unfettered pursuance of such private interest, and on the need for the statesman to embody a public interest that is not the automatic outcome of individual activity.

Books 1 and 2 are followed by three further books: "Of Money and Coin"; "Of Credits and Debts"; and "Of Taxes". The main principles of Steuart's economics, therefore, are contained and elaborated upon in the two books that he drafted in Tübingen, and these are organized according to principles with which English commentators have grappled ever since. He does not treat the economic subject merely as a resource at the disposal of a ruler, as is implicitly the case in much Cameralistic writing; Steuart's population is a mass directed by conflicting interests which might or might not be beneficial to the interest of the whole. As Sen has rightly observed, Steuart is obsessed by the idea that the economy has a constant tendency to go wrong, and it is the task of the statesman to anticipate and correct instabilities. However, this does not give rise to what Sen dubs "the economics of control",[26] an economy based upon compulsion. The tasks that Steuart assigns to his statesman are precisely those with which *Polizei* was designed to deal— and, as we have seen, this does not so much involve "compulsion" as the anticipation and removal of potential mischief. Thus, in restoring a balance, Steuart's statesman was to "endeavour to load the lighter scale, and never, but in cases of the greatest necessity, have recourse to the expedient of taking any thing from the heavier".[27]

From this summary of the main arguments of Books 1 and 2 of the *Inquiry* we can perhaps begin to understand its attraction for a readership brought up on a diet of Justi, Darjes, and Schreber. Smith, on the other hand, studiously ignored Steuart's work, even though it was a treatise of similar scope to *Wealth of Nations* and it was available and was being reviewed in the period when Smith was completing his text. Clearly, Smith intended his work to be in part a rebuttal of the positive aspects of *Inquiry*, and he determined to emphasize the novelty of his principles by discouraging overt comparison with those expounded by his Jacobite predecessor. At home, Smith was largely successful: after 1776, *Wealth of Nations* enjoyed the reputation of being the most comprehensive and systematic of the treatises on the principles of economic legislation. In Germany, however, it was Steuart who, during the 1770s and 1780s, was regarded as the foremost Scottish writer on economic legislation. In part, at least, this was owing to the ease with which *Inquiry* could be assimilated into the Cameralistic tradition; but it was also due to the comparative lack of appeal of Smith's "system of natural liberty". Before we consider the reaction to the initial publication of *Wealth of Nations* in 1776, it is as well to recall those features of the work that are relevant to the eighteenth-century context.

Wealth of Nations presents a model of the progress of commercial society founded upon the positive effects of the pursuit of self-interest on the part of its citizens. Unlike Steuart, who feared that the unhindered exercise of individual interests would cause conflict and disequilibrium, Smith argued that the operation of an "invisible hand" would ensure the conversion of individual interests and actions into a totality beneficial to all—the growth and progress of society. The actual mechanism by which this would occur is not elaborated upon in *Wealth of Nations*, and it is sometimes assumed that the idea of the "invisible hand" simply represents the assertion of a deeper level of harmony in society beneath the play of self-interest. If that were so, then Smith could easily adopt the same position as Steuart and, while allowing for self-interest as a basic dynamic force in society and economy, could posit the necessary supervision of a statesman periodically to restore order. Smith does have an elaborated theory of social order, however, which had been outlined several years earlier in *The Theory of Moral Sentiments*.[28]

Taking as his point of departure conceptions of human action drawn from Hume, Hutcheson, and Shaftesbury which emphasize the human instincts of self-preservation and propagation, Smith inflects these instincts with a social dimension in the absence of which they can have no force. Individual instincts and passions remain the dynamic element in society, but at the same time they become a fundamental constituent of social integration. This leads to the Smithian concept of "sympathy", in which the exercise of human passions necessarily implicates a notion of an "impartial spectator" through which the achievement prospects of individual desires are assessed. The individual is rendered sociable by the operation of this principle of "sympathy", whereby each individual is judged by spectators and in turn judges them; and, by extension, when considering an action, the individual also considers the response he would make to such an action if he were in another's shoes. The individual interests of the human agent can only be realized with the passive or active assistance of others, who in turn are willed human subjects. This creates a system of reciprocities in which each judges his own actions in terms imputed to others—and thus arises the basic structure of social order essential to Smith's "natural system of liberty".[29]

The interactions within this social order also give rise to a social stimulation of wants and needs:

For to what purpose is all the toil and bustle of this world? what is the end of avarice and ambition, of the pursuit of wealth, of power, of pre-eminence? Is it to supply the necessities of nature? The wages of the meanest labourer can supply them. We see that they afford him food and clothing, the comfort of a house, and of a family. If we examined his oeconomy with rigour, we should find that he spends a great part of them upon conveniences, which may be regarded as superfluities, and that, upon extraordinary occasions, he can give something even to vanity and distinction.[30]

Ambition, vanity, and the desire for approbation spur on the rich as well as the poor; for a corollary to the doctrine of "sympathy" is that each seeks approval and praise from others—"the distinction of ranks, and the order of society" is founded upon this disposition.[31] The social needs thus stimulated necessarily exceed the immediate prospects of their fulfilment—for as soon as one need is sated, it is automatically displaced by another. The needs created by commercial society, therefore, are, in principle, insatiable—necessarily so if the society is to be wealthy, and, equally necessarily, this requires the existence of social and economic inequality, for emulation and envy both presuppose and generate inequality. Smith argues, however, that such a condition is the motive force of commercial society, not a sign of its decline (as was argued by Ferguson); and that a form of justice is created whereby the wealth generated by this "system of needs" supports even the poorest at a level superior to that of non-commercial societies.[32]

This is the rational core to the account of wealth and progress that Smith presents in *Wealth of Nations*. The function of liberty is to allow this system of self-regulation to operate properly; in broad terms, limitations on an individuals' ability to pursue his own interest will slow the overall accumulation of wealth and, by extension, the welfare of all. As Forbes pointed out many years ago, Smith's "progress" was part of the natural order;[33] interference with the mechanisms that create progress was equivalent to interference with the natural order. And, most probably with Steuart in mind, Smith asserted that: "The sovereign is completely discharged from a duty, in the attempting to perform which he must always be exposed to innumerable delusions, and for the proper performance of which no human wisdom or knowledge could ever be sufficient; the duty of superintending the industry of private people, and of directing it towards the employments most suitable to the interest of society."[34] Instead, the sovereign or statesman was to secure the society against foreign invasion; to protect members of the society from injustice and oppression; and to maintain those public institutions which it was not in the interest of any one individual or group of citizens to maintain, and which were of benefit to the whole of society.

While this is only a sketch of the principles underlying *Wealth of Nations*, it is nevertheless apparent that a substantial distance separates a Smith from a Justi or a von Pfeiffer. No Cameralistic writers developed the implications of their propositions into a systematic treatment of social and economic order that was separate from the treatises that they composed for largely practical ends. But, as the preceding chapters have demonstrated, it is possible to reconstruct a specific conception of the social and economic order that was constitutive of Cameralistic writing without doing violence to the sense of the discursive regularities which emerge from a survey of relevant texts. We will never encounter an open confrontation with the Smithian "system of natural liberty" that has just been outlined above—as we shall see, the process by which *Wealth of Nations* became a canonical text, drawing approbation and criticism in equal measure, did not lead to a sophisticated understanding of the principles advanced within it. Indeed, we have had to provide a brief account of our modern understanding of Smith's writing *precisely because* the history of its reception represents such a sorry story of distortion and over-simplification, but one which is the consequence of that very process of canonization that began in the early nineteenth century. Since this is the object of our current interest, it is not appropriate here either to judge or to condemn the way in which eighteenth-century readers approached Smith; but it is important to reconstruct this approach to the *Wealth of Nations* so that we can understand the contemporary characteristics of its reception.

This is all the more necessary since the literature that follows the course of the "Smith reception" fails to establish why German readers should have turned to Smith rather than to Steuart, for example. In the first essay dedicated to this theme, Roscher suggests that for the years 1776–94 there was no real comprehension of Smith's ideas; reference to the *Wealth of Nations* was made in such a way that it was obvious that no great significance was being attached to the work.[35] In our examination of this "negative" phase of its reception, we shall address our attention to the reviews that Smith received, before considering his penetration of the textbook literature.

Feder published the first review of the *Wealth of Nations* in the Göttingen *Anzeigen* in March 1777; his review was of the English edition, but some comparison was made with Schiller's translation of Books 1 to 3 which had recently appeared. Feder begins by noting that Smith was known as the author of *The Theory of Moral Sentiments*, which he (Feder) had also reviewed in the *Anzeigen*; but he does not detect any particular relationship between the two works. Instead, the comments that he made while presenting a summary of the main points of *Wealth of Nations* were to establish the terms in which Smith was to be discussed for the next two decades: it was rather repetitious, although the investigation was a complex one and required occasional summaries; the theses were distinct from those of Steuart, whose work was not mentioned by Smith; and if Smith was to be associated with any current school it was with that of the Physiocrats.[36] Soon afterwards, another reviewer, commenting on the German translation of 1776, took a similar line,[37] and a further review of the same translation made explicit use of Physiocratic terminology when summarizing the principles put forward by Smith, although it was noted that such terminology was not used in the *Wealth of Nations*.[38] Some two years later, a review of the second volume of Schiller's translation mentioned that Smith's conception of annual product differed from the Physiocrats', but that the critique of Physiocracy to be found in Book 4 was founded upon "mere logomachy" and that Smith on the whole agreed with the Physiocrats.[39]

In 1792, a third German volume was published which contained the additions and revisions from the third English edition of 1784—evidently this was to revive interest in the work, for, as the publisher complained in the preface:

While this work is of undoubted importance, the sales with which the translation has met in Germany have been for so many years so moderate that we have, especially since the death of the translator [Schiller], long been dubious of whether the publication of the additons and revisions would pay the effort of translation and the cost of printing. However, since the demand has perceptibly improved in the last few years we no longer have any objection . . . [40]

In a review of this additional volume, Sartorius assured the publisher that "reason would in the end prevail"; although, as we have already seen, it took the appearance of a new translation to mark the beginning of a more positive appreciation of *Wealth of Nations*.[41]

The new translation by Garve and Dörrien was duly reviewed in the *Anzeigen* of 1794, where it was noted that: "if here and there one finds note of his book [i.e. Smith's] it is as if . . . he has never been read, as if he had never spoken. He has still had absolutely no influence on the alteration of the doctrine of state economy in our Fatherland . . .".[42] This was to change in the years that followed, and it was Sartorius in fact who produced the first "Smithian" textbook to accompany his lectures in Göttingen. Here in 234 pages, we find a précis of the theses advanced in *Wealth of Nations*, although the later sections show some sign of accommodation between Smith and the more traditional German treatment of *Staatswirthschaft*.[43] This textbook marked the beginning of a more positive reception of *Wealth of Nations*, an account of which forms an integral part of the next chapter. What of the previous treatment of Smith, however, which, as Sartorius noted, was as if no one had ever read a line of *Wealth of Nations*?

We can begin by noting that, with one or two exceptions, references to the

Wealth of Nations in Cameralistic literature date from the later 1780s—confirming the point made by the publisher of the third volume in 1792 (that there had been a recent increase of interest), and underscoring the fact that, for some ten years after its appearance in translation, the work was all but ignored by those professionally concerned with the issues that it addressed. Moreover, those references that we do find before the mid-1780s are not especially significant—in the preface to Büsch's treatise on the circulation of money the name of Smith follows that of Steuart, but no influence of any consequence can be detected.[44]

In 1782, von Pfeiffer proposed to do the interested reader "a service in daring to shed a little more light upon this rather lengthy and occasionally obscure presentation". [45] In the context of a general review of prominent eighteenth-century writers on economic affairs, von Pfeiffer devotes some 150 pages to an exposition of *Wealth of Nations*. Much of this consists of a summary of the text without further comment; but occasionally von Pfeiffer remarks on the familiarity of Smith's propositions, or, when for example discussing the chapter on the accumulation of capital from Book 2, he asserts that Justi and Genovesi have made similar points. In general, von Pfeiffer treats Smith's *Wealth of Nations* as if it were simply a foreign variant of Cameralism, concluding that:

What then is the result of the investigation of Herr Dr. Smith's work, which indeed holds much that is good, true, and humane? It is a refined Physiocratic system which, because it has come from overseas, is not understood by many, and draped with new clothes, seems to be more acceptable than that which has been written on this subject by our dear fellow countrymen. The only point at which the author differs from the orthodox Physiocrats is that he allows a tax on luxury goods, while however subjecting it to unmistakable difficulties; and that he lays upon everything the duty of contributing proportionally to the expenses of the state, without providing usable rules concerning its purpose.[46]

In a later work, von Pfeiffer lifted whole sections and phrases out of *Wealth of Nations* without substantially altering the Cameralistic theses he was proposing.[47]

In the same year Sonnenfels added a reference to the *Wealth of Nations* in his discussion of manufacture in the fifth edition of the second volume of *Grundsätze*, noting the benefits to the manufacturer of the division of labour and the savings made by the use of machinery. These are certainly advantageous in terms of the number of workers employed and in terms of time; but Sonnenfels immediately qualifies this statement by affirming that any such innovation must not contradict the main end—the increase of employment.[48] It need hardly be said that Smith's notion of the division of labour plays a far greater role than that of a simple rationalization of production: on the one hand, it is the means to the extension of the market, and on the other, it represents the principal way in which a society expands its economic potential in manufactures. Neither of these ideas is taken up by Sonnenfels.

The context in which Smith's name does occur is well illustrated by the use made of his conception of the division of labour by Walther, Professor of Oeconomic Sciences at Gießen from 1790. In the fourth part of his *System*, Walther states that his general principles of state economy had been developed with the help of Genovesi, Schmid, Sartorius, Steuart, Verri—and Smith, referring to the first translation and not to the more recent one by Garve.[49] As this list of names demonstrates, the facility with which Cameralistic writers could borrow ideas from the *Wealth of Nations* testifies more to the flexibility of the discourse within which they worked than to its systematic nature. Niemann, whose invocation of a Smithian conception of national wealth is cited at the beginning of this chapter, refers to both Smith and von Pfeiffer when he states that the enrichment of nations and (indirectly) of the public finances is the object of state economy; and while Smith has a clear influence on the preliminary definitions, this is followed by an exposition of the conventional Cameralistic categories, beginning with population.[50] Likewise, Jung refers the reader to Smith merely as a useful source on *Gewerbepolizei*;[51] and the name of Smith is invoked in the surveys of Eggers and Gosch, teachers at Copenhagen and Kiel respectively.[52]

Without doubt, one could find some more explicit, as well as implicit, references to the *Wealth of Nations*, but it would be difficult to escape the conclusion which follows from these instances—that where Smith was noted, the specific arguments that he advanced were ignored in favour of his overall treatment as a Physiocrat, or they were simply submerged in a generally eclectic approach to "state economy". There is one example from the 1790s of what might, at first sight, appear to be an enthusiastic and positive response to Smith's writing—that of C. J. Kraus, a colleague of Kant's at Königsberg, and a teacher of leading members of the Prussian reform movement whose lectures on state economy were made compulsory for all candidates applying to the East Prussian Finance Department.

Kraus died in 1808 and his friend, von Auerswald, edited a collection of his papers into a five-volume text which he entitled *Staatswirthschaft*. It was primarily this text which prompted Adam Müller to dub Kraus a "disciple" of Adam Smith, considering Kraus's work to be no more than a lengthy reworking of *Wealth of Nations* with a few additions on Prussian economic conditions.[53] His friends did not deny this, and Roscher also drew attention to it in his history of German economics.[54] *Staatswirthschaft* was, in fact, the substance of lectures delivered by Kraus in the 1790s, and, since the presence of *Wealth of Nations* is so marked, it has generally been accepted that these lectures did involve a systematic presentation of Smith's doctrines which predated the work of Sartorius at Göttingen.

However, a study of the notebooks written up by von Schön from the lectures that he attended between 1788 and 1795 moderates this view. During the Winter Semester 1788–9, for example, Kraus lectured on "Encyclopedia of the Sciences", using as his main texts the *Wealth of Nations* and Büsch's treatise on the circulation of money. Little of Smith can be found in the lecture notes, however, and since these confirm that Kraus's method was simply to dictate his material, this cannot be ascribed to poor understanding on the part of the student. In 1791–2, a further course on *Staatswissenschaft* was delivered, but Smith is to be found here along with Arthur Young, Steuart, Sonnenfels, Justi, Büsch, Forbonnais, and even Gasser and Dithmar. Moreover, Kraus obviously preferred to cite others at length rather than to provide his own summary, let alone to make any comments. Kühn, whose study of Kraus has generally been overlooked, presents a summary of von Schön's notebooks and arrives at the following conclusion:

Kraus . . . was not capable of expressing a single thought without immediate recourse to an authority. Above all it is hard for him to recognise the correct judgement among many opinions, and he is then content to present them at as great a length as possible. It is improbable that he did this with the idea that his listeners should be able to immediately detect the correct opinion, for one does not gain the impression that he was sure of his material. . . . We arrive in this way at the remarkable result that a scholar of reputation was not only incapable of intellectual production or even the outlining of ideas, but that he had exceptional difficulty in detecting something certain and correct in the range of opinions and counteropinions before him.[55]

On the basis of the evidence advanced by Kühn, this is a balanced and fair judgement. Quite clearly, it is all too easy to overestimate Smith's influence during the closing decade of the eighteenth century; having shown that up to this time textual references (with the exception of von Pfeiffer's treatment) were sparse and misleading, it is very tempting to seize upon a figure like Kraus who, at first glance, seems to have been preaching *Smithianismus* in the lecture halls of a famous university.

None the less, from the 1790s it is possible to detect a shift within the discourses of economy and polity. Using the propagation of Smith's new doctrines as an indicator of the pace and extent of these changes may be unreliable, but this does not mean that the *Wealth of Nations* was irrelevant to this process. It would be more accurate to regard the rate of acceptance of some of Smith's views as evidence of transformations motivated elsewhere and which carried along with them a new conception of the possibilities of economic order. We have arrived at the threshold of the reformation of German economic discourse which was to bring about the construction of *Nationalökonomie*.

NOTES

1. A. Niemann, *Grundsätze der Statswirthschaft*, i (Altona, 1790), §, p. 1.
2. "Vorrede des Uebersetzers", in A. Smith, *Untersuchung über die Natur und die Ursachen des Nationalreichthums*, i (Breslau, 1794), pp. iv–v. Garve declared himself to be impressed by the easy style of the English original, but he was critical of its lack of conciseness, a criticism that was to become frequent in later years. The Garve and Dörrien edition appeared in four volumes between 1794 and 1796.
3. In Göttingen University Library it is customary to find copies of Italian, French, and English texts in the original, but translations of these works were seldom purchased in the eighteenth century.
4. D. Hume, *Vermischte Schriften über die Handlung, die Manufacturen und die andern Quellen des Reichthums und der Macht eines Staats* (Hamburg, 1754; 2nd edn. Leipzig, 1766).
5. K. Carpenter, *Dialogue in Political Economy* (Kress Library Publication, 23; Harvard Business School, Boston, 1977), 52, 11.
6. F. V. de Forbonnais, *Der vernünftige Kaufmann* (Hamburg 1755, 1767; translation of *Élémens du commerce* (Leyden, 1754)); *Sätze und Beobachtungen aus der Oekonomie*, 2 vols. (Vienna, 1767). This latter text contains a systematic critique of Physiocratic doctrine, and thus represents perhaps the first detailed treatment of Physiocracy to appear in German.
7. Carpenter, *Dialogue*, pp. 78–9; samples of the two editions are reprinted on pp. 80–1.
8. Published in Leghorn in 1771. Translated as *Betrachtungen über die Staatswirthschaft* (Dresden, 1774)—this also includes the detailed introduction of the 1773 Lausanne edition. A second edition of this translation was published in The Hague in 1777; see F. Venturi, "Pietro Verri in Germany and Russia", in his *Italy and the Enlightenment* (Longman, London, 1972), 170.
9. P. Verri, *Betrachtungen über die Staatswirthschaft* (Mannheim, 1785); translated from the Italian by Schmid. Cf. Carpenter, *Dialogue*, p. 58.
10. Schmid, *Lehre*, i. 4.
11. A. Genovesi, *Grundsätze der bürgerlichen Oekonomie*, 2 vols. (Leipzig, 1776); i. 193. Further: "The first law of oeconomy is this: *in a cultivated nation nothing may exist which is not subordinated to trade*" (i. 217). *Lezioni di commercio ossia de economia civile* was first published in 1765, and the German translation is apparently from the third edition of 1769.
12. A detailed examination of Pfeiffer's use of Genovesi has been made by M. D. Damianoff, *Die volkswirthschaftlichen Anschauungen Johannes-Friedrich von Pfeiffers*,

Diss. (Erlangen, 1908), 65ff. See also W. Roscher, *Geschichte der National-Oekonomik in Deutschland* (R. Oldenbourg, Munich, 1874), 556.

13. "Vorbericht des Verlegers" to J. Stewart, *Untersuchung der Grund-Säze von der Staats-Wirthschaft als ein Versuch über die Wissenschaft von der Innerlichen Politik bei freien Nationen*, i (Tübingen, 1769). The fact that most references to Steuart in the later eighteenth century misspelled his name in the manner of the Cotta edition is a possible indication of its greater influence than the Hamburg edition.

14. J. Steuart, *Untersuchung der Grundsätze der Staats-Wirthschaft, oder Versuch über die Wissenschaft der innerlichen Politik in freyen Staaten*, 2 vols. (Hamburg, 1769–70). The volumes were each of about 600 pages, and an announcement of the forthcoming translation, with a summary of its contents, was published in May 1768 ("Entwurf des Steuartischen Werkes von der Staatswirthschaft", *Hannoverisches Magazin*, 39 (13 May, 1768), cols. 609–24). The beginning of the first volume contains a list of subscribers which is principally composed of the names of state officials and councillors; of the professors noted, Schreber in Leipzig took 6 copies, and the secretary of the Leipzig Economic Society, 2. Other academic subscribers were Suckow and Baldinger in Jena.

15. Carpenter, *Dialogue*, p. 84.

16. M. Humpert, *Bibliographie der Kameralwissenschaften* (Kurt Schroeder Verlag, Cologne, 1937), gives the dates for the Tübingen edition as 1769–72, while the principal general bibliographic guide for the eighteenth century, Heinsius's *Bücher Lexikon*, 3, gives 1769–79. In Göttingen University Library, the copy of Cotta's edition bears publication dates of between 1769 and 1787 (4/2). The dates given by Humpert have proved to be the correct ones. It appears that Cotta printed more copies of the later volumes than of the first, reprinting the first three volumes in 1779 and then single parts in the 1780s. Comparison of the various copies shows that those bearing a later date are genuine new editions. I would like to thank Dr Marie-Luise Spieckermann of the Englisches Seminar, University of Münster, for resolving these confusions.

17. General Sir James Steuart, "Anecdotes of the Life of Sir James Steuart, Baronet", in *The Works, Political, Metaphisical, and Chronological, of the late Sir James Steuart of Coltness*, vi (London, 1805), 371.

18. In 1757, F. W. Tafinger, a professor in the Law Faculty, began a course of lectures on *Polizeiwissenschaft* "nach Justi" which he was to hold regularly for the next twenty years; he had previously published *Institutiones jurisprudentiae cameralis* (Tübingen, 1754, 1775). From 1753–61, von Lohenschiold, a professor in the Philosophy Faculty, taught *Statistik* according to Achenwall's *Staatsverfassung der europäischen Reiche*. During the winter of 1757–8, G. D. Daniel, Professor of Law, held mixed lectures on politics, oeconomy, diplomacy, numismatics, and heraldry; while Schott, a professor of philosophy, taught a course on trade in the Summer Semester of 1758. See K. W. C. Schüz, "Ueber das Collegium illustre zu Tübingen, oder den staatswissenschaftlichen Unterricht in Württemberg besonders im sechzehnten und siebzehnten Jahrhundert", *Zeitschrift für die gesammte Staatswissenschaft*, 6 (1850), 256.

19. Sir James Steuart, *Works*, 6 vols. (London, 1805), i. *An Inquiry into the Principles of Political Oeconomy*, 2.

20. Steuart, *Inquiry*, pp. 3, 4. A later reviewer seized on precisely this principle in criticizing Steuart: "In the first Book, on population, agriculture and trades, the author often expresses himself in a way conducive to misunderstanding and giving rise to an improper judgement of the theses which he advances. When Steuart has depicted the consequences of certain significant relationships among the members of a state, he often adds: the statesman (or ruler) must thus do this or that to prevent the occurrence of specific incongruities. If for example agriculture has too many hands, so men should be displaced from this class into another. Here every reader raises the question, how is the ruler to go about this? Whoever takes all this literally would be considerably misled. Steuart's statesman is an idea: his place is indeed frequently taken by the nature of things. The reader must often translate the principles attributed to the idealistic states-man into another language, and make out of them laws according to which the changes occurring in the civil world are not arbitrarily brought about, but rather arise of themselves." Anon., Review of Steuart, *Works*, in *Göttingische gelehrte Anzeigen*, 8 and 9, (13 Jan. 1806), 77–8.

21. Steuart, *Inquiry*, p. 32.

22. Ibid., p. 40.

23. Ibid., Book 1, ch. 9, p. 161: "In treating every question of political oeconomy, I constantly suppose a statesman at the head of government, systematically con-ducting every part of it, so as to prevent the vicissitudes of manners, and innova-tions, by their natural and immediate effects or consequences, from hurting any interest within the commonwealth.'

24. "INDUSTRY *is the application to ingenious labour in a free man, in order to procure, by the means of trade, an equivalent, fit for the supplying every want*" (Steuart, *Inquiry*, p. 223).

25. Ibid., p. 241. Here we can see that Steuart, like Smith, invokes the example of pin manufacture when discussing the advantages of the division of labour, but Steuart applies the idea to the sphere of exchange, not of production.

26. S. R. Sen, *The Economics of Sir James Steuart* (G. Bell, London, 1957), ch. 9.

27. Steuart, *Inquiry*, p. 308.

28. Published in London in 1759; translated as *Theorie der moralischen Empfindungen* (Brunswick, 1770). It is worth noting that records of Smith's library indicate that he owned very few works in German. Bonar estimates the proportions as: one third in English, one third in French, one quarter in Latin—and three German works, all presentation copies. See J. Bonar (ed.), *A Catalogue of the Library of Adam Smith* (Macmillan, London, 1894), p. xxix.

29. See D. D. Raphael, "The Impartial Spectator", in A. S. Skinner and T. Wilson (eds.), *Essays on Adam Smith* (Oxford University Press, London, 1975), 87–94; and H. Medick, *Naturzusland und Naturgeschichte der bürgerlichen Gesellschaft* (Vandenhoeck und Ruprecht, Göttingen, 1973), 216.

30. A. Smith, *The Theory of Moral Sentiments* (Oxford University Press, London, 1976), 50.

31. Ibid., p. 52.

32. This is elaborated in I. Hont, "The 'Rich Country—Poor Country' Debate in Scottish Classical Political Economy", in I. Hont and M. Ignatieff (eds.), *Wealth and Virtue* (Cambridge University Press, Cambridge, 1983).

33. D. Forbes, "'Scientific' Whiggism. Adam Smith and John Millar", *Cambridge Journal*, 7 (1954), 645.

34. A. Smith, *An Inquiry into the Nature and Causes of the Wealth of Nations* (Oxford University Press, London, 1976), 687.

35. W. Roscher, "Die Ein- und Durchführung des Adam Smith'schen Systems in Deutschland", *Berichte über die Verhandlungen der königlich-sächsischen Gesellschaft der Wissenschaften zu Leipzig*, 19 (1867), 17; pp. 18–21 presents a brief review of some of these writings. Similar points were also made in the relevant section of his *Geschichte*, ch. 25. Comparable in approach, while adding a socio-economic history of eighteenth-century Prussia, is C. W. Hasek, *The Introduction of Adam Smith's Doctrines into Germany* (Faculty of Political Science, Columbia University, New York, 1925), 63ff. See also J. Grünfeld, *Die leitenden sozial- und wirtschaftsphilosophischen Ideen in der deutschen Nationalökonomie und die Ueberwindung des Smithianismus bis auf Mohl und Hermann*, Diss. (Tübingen, 1913); M. Palyi, "The Introduction of Adam Smith on the Continent", in *Adam Smith 1776–1926* (Augustus M. Kelley, New York, 1966), 180–233 (orig. 1928); H. Graul, *Das Eindringen der Smithschen Nationalökonomie in Deutschland und ihre Weiterbildung bis zu Hermann*, Diss. (Halle, 1928); A. Nahrgang, *Die Aufnahme der wirtschaftspolitischen Ideen von Adam Smith in Deutschland zu Beginn des* XIX. Jahrhunderts, Diss. (Frankfurt-on-Main, 1933); W. Treue, "Adam Smith in Deutschland. Zum Problem des 'Politischen Professors' zwischen 1776 und 1810", in W. Conze (ed.), *Deutschland und Europa. Festschrift für Hans Rothfels* (Droste Verlag, Düsseldorf, 1951), 101–33

36. J. G. H. Feder, Review of *Wealth of Nations* in *Göttingsche Anzeigen von gelehrten Sachen*, 1/30 (10 Mar. 1777), 234–5.

37. Anon., Review of *Untersuchung der Natur und Ursachen von Nationalreichthümern*, i, in *Ephemeriden der Menschheit*, 5 (1777), 61–101.

38. "Px", Review of *Untersuchung der Natur und Ursachen von Nationalreichthümern*, i, in *Allgemeine Deutsche Bibliothek*, 31/2 (1777), 588.

39. "Kr.", Review of *Untersuchung der Natur und Ursachen von Nationalreichthümern*, ii, in *Allgemeine Deutsche Bibliothek*, 38/1 (1779), 300.

40. A. Smith, *Untersuchung der Natur und Ursachen von Nationalreichthümern*, iii (Leipzig, 1792), pt. 1, "Vorbericht der Verlags-Handlung".

41. G. Sartorius, Review of *Untersuchung der Natur und Ursachen von Nationalreichthümern*, iii, pt. 1, in *Göttingsche Anzeigen von gelehrten Sachen*, 3/166 (19 Oct. 1793), 1662.

42. Anon., Review of *Untersuchung über die Natur und die Ursachen des Nationalreichtums*, in *Göttingsche Anzeigen von gelehrten Sachen*, 3/190 (29 Nov. 1794), 1903–4.

43. G. Sartorius, *Handbuch der Staatswirthschaft zum Gebrauche bey akademischen Vorlesungen, nach Adam Smith's Grundsätzen ausgearbeitet* (Berlin, 1796).

44. J. G. Büsch, "Abhandlung von dem Geldumlauf in anhaltender Rücksicht auf die Staatswirthschaft und Handlung", in his *Schriften über Staatswirthschaft und Handlung*, i (Hamburg, 1780), n.p. On p. 379 there is a reference to the last chapter of *Wealth of Nations*. Büsch later admitted that he was barely acquainted with the work at this time.

45. J. E. von Pfeiffer, *Berichtigungen berühmter Staats- Finanz- Policci- Cameral- Commerz- und ökonomischer Schriften dieses Jahrhunderts*, iii (Frankfurt-on-Main, 1782), 3.

46. Ibid., pp. 150–1.

47. J. E. von Pfeiffer, *Grundsätze und Regeln der Staatswirthschaft*, ed. J. N. Moser (Mainz, 1787), 15.

48. J. von Sonnenfels, *Grundsätze der Polizey, Handlung und Finanz* (Vienna, 1787), ii. 219–21.

49. F. L. Walther, *Versuch eines Systems der Cameral-Wissenschaften*, iv (Gießen, 1798), 29.

50. Niemann, *Grundsätze*, i. 3.

51. J. H. Jung, *Lehrbuch der Staats—Polizey—Wissenschaft* (Leipzig, 1788), p. xlviii.

52. C. U. D. Eggers, *Ueber dänische Staatskunde und dänische politische Schriften* (Copenhagen, 1786), 37; J. L. Gosch, *Entwurf eines Plans zu einem vollständigen System der sämtlichen einem Staatswirthe nothwendigen Wissenschaften* (Copenhagen, 1787), 4–5.

53. See A. Müller, "Ueber Christian Jakob Kraus", *Berliner Abendblätter* no. 11 (2. October 1810) pp. 43–4; no. 48 (24. November 1810) pp. 187–9. F. Milkowski, *Christian Jakob Kraus. Lehrer der Staatswirthschaft in der Übergangszeit in Preußen vom 18. zum 19. Jahrhundert*, privately printed (Potsdam, 1968), 3.

54. Roscher, *Geschichte*, pp. 29ff.

55. E. Kühn, *Der Staatswirtschaftslehrer Christian Jakob Kraus und seine Beziehungen zu Adam Smith*, Diss. (Bern, 1902), 95–6.

Part 5. Italy

The study of the history of economic thought was and is very active in Italy. The literature on Smith and on *WN* is so abundant that the references listed below are only some of those in my file. They are useful not only for their analyses but also as a way of tracing the rich related literature cited.

What is inconvenient, however, is that there are few texts in English. I select only two Italian texts, translated and included in this chapter. Gioli (1972) treats an interesting question: the extent to which people knew about Smith and *WN* during the eighteenth century. This is an interesting point because in 1790 Smith was presented as "a great philosopher and first-class politician" in Naples. In time, Smith's name and work became better known. Meanwhile, Italian economic structure and policies were also changing; people who read *WN* brought to it their own perspectives and interpreted it in many different ways. This text has been heavily condensed by the author from a long Italian paper for this volume; since this necessarily lends it a tendency towards concise and sweeping remarks, interested readers should refer to the original text.

There was an Italian *Methodenstreit* during the 1870s, in which two schools of economists fought each other harshly, one attacking Smithian doctrines and the other defending him. The Association for the Progress of Economic Studies consisted of Germanophile economists, including Lampertico, Cusumano, Cossa, and Luzzatti. This group adopted the methods of analysis of the German historical school and emphasized the importance of historical experience; they despised the British preference for deductive analysis based on the axiomatic style of analysis. Another group, which united the free-traders Martello, Ciccone, and others, centred around the Adam Smith Society founded by Francesco Ferrara in order to defend the orthodoxy of British economic studies.

The paper by Luzzatti (1876) was a speech given at the Accademia dei Lincei in 1876 on the occasion of the first centenary of *WN*. Luzzatti was one of the main exponents of the Italian historical school; in his speech he proposed the thesis that Smith's economic thought was steeped in pragmatism, and that it was the fault of the Smithians that it had acquired a dogmatic image in the recent past. He then gave various interpretations of Smith's doctrines.

Of course, the opponents fought back. One of Ferrara's best students, Martello (1877), took issue with Luzzatti's interpretation. Unfortunately, I could not find his text to have it translated. The paper by Ricca-Salerno (1876) sees this debate from a methodological point of view; his opinion was that to speak of a link between the two schools was to exaggerate and that one should acknowledge the coexistence of Cartesian speculation and historicist observation. It is interesting to see this side-effect of the reception of *WN* in Italy, and its conflict with the Germanophile historical school. Ricca-Salerno also discussed the methodological aspect of *WN*, centred on the inductive and deductive perspectives. Although the method of discussion is not new to us, his arguments and criticisms still deserve our attention.

To voracious readers, I recommend the references listed below. Although not reprinted here, Gioli (1993) is highly recommended for the issues that it raises and for its well-structured arguments and evidence. It provides some complementary analysis and references to Gioli's 1972 and 1991 papers.

Further Reading

Texts with a * are printed in this Part

BIANCHINI, MARCO (1989), "Some Fundamental Aspects of Italian Eighteenth-Century Economic Thought", in Donald Walker (ed.), *Perspectives on the History of Economic Thought*, vol. 1, pp. 53–67. London: Edward Elgar.

EINAUDI, LUIGI (1953) "Adamo Smith", in his *Saggi bibliografici e storici intorno alle dottrine economiche*, pp. 69–101, Roma: Edizioni di Storia e Letteratura.

*GIOLI, GABRIELLA (1972), "Gli albori dello smithianesimo in Italia" (The knowledge of Adam Smith's *Wealth of Nations* in Italy in the eighteenth century), *Rivista di Politica Economica*, 62: 917–62.

—— (1991), "Adam Smith e la *Ricchezza della nazioni* nelle riviste economiche italiane (1890–1940)", *Studi & informazioni*, 2/91: 59–80.

—— (1993): "The Diffusion of the Economic Thought of Adam Smith in Italy, 1776–1876", in H. Mizuta and C. Sugiyama (eds.), *Adam Smith: International Perspectives*, pp. 225–49, London: Macmillan.

*LUZZATTI, LUIGI (1876), "Il centenario della publicazione dell'opera di A. Smith" (The centenary of the publication of Adam Smith's work), *Scienza e patria: studi e discorsi*, pp. 3–22, Florence: Editore Quattrini, 1916.

OKUTA, K. (1991): "*The Wealth of Nations* and the Enlightenment in Naples", *Mita Gakai Zasshi*, 83(4): 88–109 (in Japanese).

PAROLINI, M. L. (1980), "La risonanza del pensiero smithiano in Italia fra il 1776 e il 1860", in Viveza *et al.* (1980), pp. 143–240.

RICCA-SALERNO, GIUSEPPE (1876), "L'economia politica di Adamo Smith" (The political economy of Adam Smith), *Archivio Giuridico*, 17: 301–20 [translated by Silvia Klemm, available from the editor].

SARTORI, P. O. (1980), "Echi della cultura italiana nel pensiero di Adam Smith", in Viveza *et al.* (1980), pp. 82–142.

VENTURI, FRANCO (1983), "Scottish Echoes in Eighteenth-Century Italy", in I. Hont and M. Ignatieff (eds.), *Value and Virtue: The Shaping of Political Economy in the Scottish Enlightenment*, ch. 13, pp. 357–60, Cambridge University Press.

VERCILLO, OSLAVIA (1963), "Della conoscenza di Adamo Smith in Italia nel siecolo XVIII", *Economia e Storia*, 10: 413–24.

VIVEZA *et al.* (1980), *Aspetti della formazione culturale di Adam Smith: la prima diffusione del suo pensiero nella dottrina italiana*, Verona: Stamperia Zendrini.

5.1. Gabriella Gioli, 1972.

The Knowledge of Adam Smith's *Wealth of Nations* in Italy in the Eighteenth Century

Shortened and translated by the author

Foreword

This essay was written a long time ago: in 1972. Since then, the branch of research regarding the spread, or rather the "acclimatization", of economic ideas within a certain nation, and even more so in the international context, has made significant progress. While working on in-depth research into quantitative methodologies, scholars have also examined the evidence available on the cultural, social, and political features of the countries receiving these doctrines, so as to ascertain the impact of the introduction of an economic philosophy on any single context iin terms of its own cultural identity.

In the case of Italy, we can see that it is not only Smith who has been made the object of this type of research, but also another economist, perhaps closer to our way of thinking: J. Maynard Keynes. In this regard, it is of interest to consult *Keynes in Italia* (*Annali dell'economia italiana*, Roma, IPSOA, 1984). But the author who continues fundamentally to grab the attention of scholars and others because of the basic originality of his philosophy is Adam Smith.

Over the years, the phenomenon of this basic difference in his thinking has taken on certain distinctive characteristics: as soon as research into these questions has gone so deep that it appears to be near the point of exhaustion, it has immediately been taken up in another country, and always with renewed energy. All this is amply demonstrated in a recently published book to which I collaborate: *Adam Smith: International Perpectives*, edited by Mizuta and

Sugiyama, Macmillan, 1993. This is also, of course, one of the themes emphasized in the present publication, to which I have had the honour of making this
contribution.

This version of my essay originally published under the title "Gli albori dello
Smithianesimo in Italia" (The Dawn of the Philosophy of Smith in Italy, *Rivista
di Politica Economica*, 7 (1972): 917–62) introduces no substantial modifications.
Any changes made consist mainly of the omission of those parts which have no
direct bearing on the main theme of the spread of Smith's economic thought in
Italy. In terms of the original text, therefore, these marginal changes have
mainly consisted of a change in the numbering of the notes, and of their length
and importance. For quotations from *The Wealth of Nations*, we have referred to
the latest English edition (Oxford, Clarendon Press, 1976), already mentioned in
the notes to the main text.

It is only recently that the problem of research into the international diffusion of
economic thought has been given a certain importance in the field of historiography: it could be said that these studies have only just been born. We actually
know very little of Smith's "fortunes" in various countries.[1] It might therefore
be interesting, from a certain point of view, to inquire into *when* Smith became
known in Italy, which *channels* served this purpose, and *how* his thoughts were
interpreted in that country. This kind of research is in practice almost endless
and so the concrete results can be nothing more than provisional. However, it
would appear from our research that Adam Smith was known in Italy relatively
early on, although his economic doctrine spread rather slowly.[2]

With the exception of two economists, Giambattista Vasco and Francesco
Mengotti, the most appreciated aspect of Smith's thought was almost entirely
political: it was a message of political economy which introduced and spread
his ideas throughout Italy. For example, in the introduction to the first Italian
translation of *The Wealth of Nations* (Naples, 1790), Smith is presented as "a
great philosopher and first-class politician".[3]

However, we can find references to this work from 1777 on. In that year, the
Diario economico di agricoltura, manifattura e commercio mentions it as a "great
work" and expounds upon all its five volumes.[4]

The author of the *Diario* article considers the importance of Smith to lie
mainly in his statement that "a correct cultivation of the land; an active and
enlightened industry; [and] the constant and wisely distributed labour of the
members of the political body" are the factors which determine the wealth of a
nation and that it is incorrect to suppose that this wealth consists principally of
an abundant quantity of gold.

Regarding Book I, it is necessary to emphasize the wide scope of the description of the division of labour and its effects; it is also important to stress the interpretation given by the *Diario* author of Smith's distinction between "value in use" and "value in exchange". The difference is "more of a subtlety than an essential element, since it is its usefulness or either real or imagined merit which renders one object the price of another". Both have a "meaning, which extends into the domain of the other, since there is no use without exchange, and no exchange without use". The author also emphasizes the various characteristics of a "commercial and agricultural system".

It would appear that the weightiest factor to be taken into account when judging the author of the *Diario* article is that he appears to have a sound knowledge of *The Wealth of Nations*, without however appreciating its theoretical content. He does not seem to understand fully the theory of value, of accumulation, or of growth.

Another periodical, *Giornale enciclopedico*, seems more informed about Smith's works. In June 1777, it published the *Letter from Mr Adam Smith to Mr Strahan regarding Mr David Hume;*[5] in November 1781, it mentioned the French translation of Yverdun.[6] *The Wealth of Nations* is a work which should, according to the author of this article, be read—rather, studied—by all "political economists"; he takes advantage of the opportunity to mention that Smith had also "written and published another work, no less appreciated, under the title of *The Theory of Moral Sentiments.*" As we can see, the works mentioned so far are mere bibliographical indications.

We should however pay greater attention to Galeani Napione's work of 1781, entitled *Elogio di G. Botero.*[7] Sharing an approach common to many Italian economists before the middle of the nineteenth century, Napione considers G. Botero a precursor of many political and economic theories which were to be elaborated only considerably later. In his re-evaluation of Botero's thought, Napione feels it necessary to have recourse to the authority of Smith, especially regarding the importance of scholarship in the formation of thinkers, and in defining the qualities required of colonies in order to be able to be of service to their mother country.

These are however chance references, with no great theoretical significance. We may say the same about Napione's correct interpretation of Smith in respect of the English economist's criticisms of the errors of the "physiocrats". Napione is mainly interested in the relationship between agriculture and industry, in order to be able to maintain that both are necessary for the development of any economic system. However, in considering Napione's work, we certainly cannot take this as a thorough interpretation of Smith: his references to the latter's work are of interest mainly from the point of view of a wider bibliographical knowledge. The "deeper

Smith", as Napione calls him, is for him not too different from "Locke, Hume, Genovesi, Condillac".

Except for Napione, it would appear that Smith's ideas did not reach Italy until 1790. This is the date that marks the starting-point for more careful readings of his *Wealth of Nations*.

Angiolini, in his letter entitled *Di alcuni uomini illustri della Scozia* (On certain illustrious gentlemen of Scotland),[8] considers Smith "a great author on research into the nature and basis of the wealth of nations, one of the greatest men of profound genius to whom Great Britain has given birth . . . ". Because he holds this opinion, Angiolini later finds frequent occasion to refer to Smith in his letters. For example, when speaking of economic freedom, he affirms that "Adam Smith, a great partisan of the freedom of industry, has already sustained, in an ingenious work published at least forty years ago, that the laws prohibiting the export of wool implied the permission of monopoly granted to the owners of this wool, and kept its [the wool's] price below its natural value".[9]

These laws implicitly accredited a monopoly to the "wool-makers". The latter, as Smith states, had been able to obtain from the government the prohibition of the exportation of nationally produced wool, the abolition of duties regarding the import of foreign wool, and the obligation for Irish wool-producers to export their wool solely to England. The consequence of all this was that it had been possible, because of the greater competition in the home market, to keep the price of wool below its natural level.[10]

But Angiolini's thought does not go as far as this in his analysis of Smith's thinking: his only-partial knowledge of the latter's analysis leads him to criticize it, denying that in Great Britain a situation could exist permitting a monopoly in favour of the wool manufacturers. Angiolini concludes: "I have the feeling that in public economics it is best not to adopt maximum or minimum levels, it is best to follow the middle way".[11] As Angiolini sees it in his conclusions, theoretical thought is always subject to an analysis in the light of reality. It is from this viewpoint that most of the Italian political economists of the eighteenth century, particularly in Tuscany, approached the new economic theories.

Again in 1790, Turin's *Biblioteca ottremontana* shows interest in Smith's work, and speaks of him as a well-known author. In the same year, this authority mentions Roucher's French translation of the fourth edition of *The Wealth of Nations*, announcing the forthcoming publication of the third and last volume in 1791.[12]

At last, in 1790, the first Italian translation of *The Wealth of Nations* was published in Naples. In the preface by the Italian translator, we read: "The greatest English text in our possession is the Inquiry into the nature and causes of the Wealth of Nations, which I have faithfully translated into the Italian speech from the latest English edition. This is the famous work by Mr Smith, who was a Professor at the University of Glasgow, a great philosopher and first-class politician, with whom I have begun a correspondence . . . ".[13]

So it was only fourteen years after the first English edition that Italy had its translation; the importance of this event is diminished neither by its imperfections nor by certain erroneous pieces of information inserted by the translator.[14] It is possible to uphold the theory that the Italian translation of *The Wealth of Nations* was the result of wide knowledge of the original and the French editions of this work. This may be so. It must be stated, however, that it would appear from the research carried out in the course of the present work that not only at the time but also later, editions other than the Italian continued to be referred to. Adam Smith was officially introduced to Italy, in his translator's words, as a "great philosopher and first-rate politician". This is a description which may be considered to reassume the opinion of the majority of those who had come to know Smith's work without the assistance of an Italian translation.

There is, however, an author to whom we must acknowledge greater independence of thought and theoretical importance: Giambattista Vasco, who may be rightly considered the most important economist of the Piedmont region in the eighteenth century. His *Saggio politico della carta-moneta*, according to Prato's reconstruction,[15] would appear to date from 1790. This tract refers more specifically to Smith's work and particularly stresses monetary problems, which are most rigorously addressed. The printing of paper money, the amount in circulation, and what proportion of paper money to the total value of monies in circulation is to be considered desirable—these are the principal points on which Vasco refers to the opinion of the "celebrated" Smith.

Vasco does not appear to be altogether in agreement on the advantages of paper money. Perhaps fearing that a policy favouring an increase in the printing of paper money might be implemented in Piedmont, he wishes to highlight the difficulties which could arise from this decision. It is thus in the light of these eventual difficulties that he refers to Smith. As Vasco states, Smith, while favouring rather than otherwise the circulation of paper money, believes that industry and commerce, if "carried on the wings of paper money, will never be as safe as when they journey upon the solid ground of gold and silver. Beyond the perils to which they are exposed by the inexperience of those who guide the coach of paper money, there are many more from which all human knowledge and prudence could not preserve them."

We believe, however, that this quotation should be considered within the framework of Smith's wider thoughts on this subject. The crucial point is that he wishes to emphasize the great importance of banking operations, since they—through the use of bank-notes instead of gold and silver—enable "passive funds" to be converted into productive capital.[17]

In another of his writings, Vasco demonstrates his profound knowledge of *The Wealth of Nations*: this is the essay published in 1793 under the title *Delle Università delle arti e mestieri*.[18] This study consists of a critique of all corporative regulations and the demonstration of the advantage to the entire economic system of a policy of commercial freedom.

It seems to Vasco out-dated at that point still to be discussing the artisan's guilds, especially after the statements made by Turgot and Smith. The reason for this could be that the effort to concretize the theoretical principles proposed by these "philosophers" had had an opposite result to that which had been foreseen. Once it has been established that the wealth of every nation consists of "the value of the annual production of its land and industry", the author is interested only in creating the conditions in which capital and work can be employed to give "maximum profits". In the use of productive factors, it is only possible to reach a situation of maximum profitability through the abolition of the obligation to belong to the guilds and the acceptance of the principle of "general freedom in the exercise of all the arts".[19] Vasco then continues to speak of the effects of the legal fixing of the price of certain commodities, especially of bread, stating that this can never attain the purpose of the State, which is to reduce a certain category's profits in the public interest.

Another point made earlier by Smith and referred to by Vasco concerns taxation. In this regard, he criticizes "the pretty theories of those economists in favour of land tax";[20] these taxes must be levied both on the net product of the land and on the products of industry. In his opinion, this choice depends on the agricultural or industrial nature of the nation. On the methods by which to proceed regarding these levies, he agrees with the four maxims established by Smith.

Another opinion on certain features of taxation is expressed by Paolo Vergani, the Inspector General of Papal Finances, in reference to a statement by the "profound English writer, Adam Smith". Vergani, as an admirer of the English financial system, which he considered "strongly protectionist", advocated its adoption by the Papal State.[21]

The picture which we have been drawing of the introduction of Smith's work into Italy can be completed by an examination of the results of the competitions held in this period by the Academies of the various Italian States on the problem of economic freedom.

Between 1779 and 1797 at least five Academies held competitions on questions which, explicitly or implicitly, required a solution to the much-debated problem of whether to concede a form of controlled freedom of trade, or rather a general opening of both home and foreign markets. Any consideration regarding the knowledge of Smith's works as we see it through the documents pertaining to the competitions held by the Academies would appear, however, less easy to generalize than might be expected. The aspect of his work which appears to have been most widely accepted is his message in favour of freedom of exchange. Perhaps this was inevitable taking into account the title of the "questions" requiring an answer.[22]

At this point in our research, we may proffer two observations: the first is that *The Wealth of Nations* was at that time usually only known in fragmentary form. The writers we have mentioned lacked the ability to capture the sense of the overall content of this work, the problem of the accumulation of capital and the growth of the entire economic system. The second observation lies in the fact that Smith is generally referred to and specifically linked to a problem of economic policy, which tends to emphasize the advantages, and in some cases the disadvantages, of the realization of a system of free trade.

It is for this reason especially that the competition held by the Florentine Accademia dei Georgofili in 1791 acquires greater interest. This competition was the occasion for the emergence of Francesco Mengotti, a writer who may be considered the main exponent of Smith's thought, at least in its aspects relating to economic freedom.[23]

We must immediately state that Mengotti's entire analysis stands upon two basic tenets: the importance and universal validity of the principle of economic freedom as a criterion for the organization of any economic system; and a concept of progress in which an economic system develops through an evolutionary process, in *stages*, requiring, at any given moment in the economic history of a nation, that agriculture be given paramount importance.[24] Only by constantly bearing in mind these two objectives will it be possible to increase national wealth. To Mengotti, therefore, the error committed by those who would like to effect this increase in wealth by favouring the manufacturing industry through any form of constraint on "raw goods" is self-evident, even if all this should then be translated into measures having a depressive effect on the economy.

In this essay, we find an attempt to forge ahead of residual ideas regarding mercantile theories and physiocratic theory itself, by means of a first opening towards Smith's new theories on the policy of free trade. All this does not develop in a coherent and convincing manner, because the author still retains traces of various kinds of thought from which he is unable to free himself. At the same time, an opening to new economic thinking, even where his references are clearly stated, does not permeate the entire work, which suffers from the superimposition of various, and not infrequently contradictory, theories. In the final analysis, in this case also, the message contained in Smith's work which Mengotti most strongly embraces can be reduced to the ideology of free trade. Strictly speaking, as we can see, the basis of Mengotti's writing remains founded on political economy. However, these considerations must not allow us to underestimate the importance of his work, which played a fundamental role in the diffusion of Smith's ideas in Italy, if only of his ideas regarding the natural order of things.

In conclusion, we wish to observe that the importance of Mengotti's work lies in its attempt to leave behind mercantile and physiocratic doctrine, opening out towards the political and economic thinking of Adam Smith. Although this attempt is carried forward amid many theoretical uncertainties, and even though Mengotti has reference to a vast assortment of "sources" in his thinking, it remains true that he remains an extremely interesting witness to the necessity of accepting the new English theories in this field. For a long time, the theory of economic freedom in Italy would coincide with the ideas of *Colbertism*, in a book quoted and consulted by all those interested in the questions of economics and the development of Italian economic thought.

It is important to underline the fact that, apart from Mengotti, many other authors in the period from 1790 to 1794 demonstrated their knowledge of Smith's work, and not only at a superficial level.[25] A characteristic common to all of these authors is that the most well known and well assimilated of Smith's theories remains that regarding economic freedom. Both for those who approve his theories and for those opposed to them, the point of reference continues to be the principle of the necessity of accepting natural order. A solitary voice against this "reading" of Smith's theories is raised by Giambattista Vasco, who while engaged in reflections on monetary theory, appears to move along lines of theoretical reasoning clearly influenced by Smith.

In all other cases, sometimes even in Mengotti's work, Smith's theoretical independence is not fully appreciated. His theories are almost always confused with those of the exponents of physiocratic and mercantile doctrine, or the Italian economists of the eighteenth century. On the other hand, the authors allow that Smith holds a pre-eminent role, and recognize him as a "great thinker". Within this somewhat uniform landscape containing hardly any economists of real importance, it must be said that while Mengotti may not be the only one to assimilate some aspects of Smith's economic thought, he remains the one who probably contributed most to the diffusion of this thought. We must not forget his contribution even while—through a critical study of Mengotti's work—noting the incompleteness of his ideas and his difficulties in distinguishing correctly mercantile and physiocratic theories from those of the dawning English philosophy of the politics of free trade.

Thus, we may state that it is not possible to study Italian economic thinking in the eighteenth century (with a few well-known exceptions) through a search for precise steps in theoretical reasoning. This form of Italian economic thinking was born in a context of juridical, political, and—in the widest sense—social reflection which was not uncommonly centred upon the many-sided question of "public well-being". This latter perspective must be abandoned. The problematics approached in this study were of a quite different nature, and for this reason the conclusions we have reached must be seen in their necessarily wider, more generalized context. We can reform them thus:

First, we have found yet another confirmation of the fact that Italian economic thinking towards the end of the eighteenth century was actually mainly a reflection upon the best economic policy to be followed in order to aid the development of an economy still conceived as a system owing much to agriculture.

Second, this economic theory seen from the outside appears exceedingly eclectic. References to the economists of the past are often a source of confusion. Our main impression is that mercantilism remained a strongly rooted doctrine, undermined only by the political, economic, and physiocratic doctrine of Smith, which is all too often however interpreted univocally.

Third, the ideas of Smith as a theoretician of political economy reached Italy relatively early. This event took place extensively in the last decade of the century in many of the Italian States. But Smith was still seen in the light of the eighteenth century.

There is no trace of his theoretical model in any of the Italian economists of the time, just as, in our opinion, it was still not to be found in the decades immediately following.

NOTES

1. M. Palyi, "The Introduction of Adam Smith on the Continent", in *Adam Smith, 1776–1926*, ch. 7, p. 180, New York, Kelley, 1966. While not comprehensive, this is worth consulting.
2. For the period from 1776 to 1800, this essay has laid emphasis on all the Tracts and Compendia of political economy noted by L. Cossa; great attention has also been paid to the principal points of Luigi Einaudi's research regarding Smith's early impact on the Italian situation. Next, because of the importance at the time of the Academies of the various Italian States, the material still available regarding the competitions which these Academies had promulgated regarding the question of free trade has been studied in depth. L. Cossa, "Saggio di bibliografia dei trattati de

compendi di economia politica scriiti da italiani" ("Bibliobraphical essays on the tracts and compendiums on political economy written by Italians"), *Giornale degli economisti* (The economists' journal), supplement, September 1891, 2: 1–16, reprinted in *Saggi bibliografici di economia politica* (Bibliographical essays on political economy), Bologna, Forni, 1963; L. Einaudi, *Dei libri italiani posseduti da Adamo Smith, di due lettere non ricordate e della sua prima fortuna in Italia, I, Adam Smith* (On the Italian books in the possession of Adam Smith, on two forgotten letters and on his early fortunes in Italy), in *Saggi bibliografici e storici intorno alle dottrine economiche* (Bibliographical and historical essays on economic doctrines), Roma, Edizioni di storia e letteratura, 1953. Our research is confined to the two competitions held by the Academies in the period 1779–1800, quoted by A. Balletti in *L'economia politica nelle Accademie e ne' congressi degli scienziati (1750–1850)* (Political economy in the Academies and scientific conventions), Modena, 1891; repr. Bologna, Forni, 1966.

3. A. Smith, *Ricerche sulla natura, e le cagioni della ricchezza delle nazioni del signor Smith* (An Inquiry into the Nature and Causes of the Wealth of Nations), 5 vols., Napoli, Policarpo Merande, 1790. It is worth recalling that the first French translation of *The Wealth of Nations*, by the Abbé Blavet, appeared between January 1779 and December 1780 in the *Journal de l'agriculture, des arts et du commerce* (The Journal of agriculture, art, and commerce). The other French translations which preceded the Italian were Yverdon, in 6 volumes, 1781 and Paris, 2 volumes, 1788. Both of these, since they were also by the Abbé Blavet, may be considered actual reprints of the first version. Finally, in 1790, the edition edited by the poet Roucher was published (Paris, 4 volumes). According to Einaudi, this latter was based on Blavet's translation. L. Einaudi, "Dei libri italiani", p. 77. For the record, we can mention that the first German translation (J. F. Schiller, Leipzig) appeared between 1776 (vol. 1) and 1778 (vol. 2); and the first Spanish translation in 1794 (J. A. Ortiz).

4. See the *Diario economico di agricoltura, manifattura e commercio* (Journal of agriculture, manufacturing, and commerce), 3 (18 Jan. 1777): 17, Rome, Casaletti. On this subject, see also O. Vercillo, "Della conoscenza di Adamo Smith in Italia nel sec. XVIII" (On the knowledge of Adam Smith's works in Italy in the 18th century), *Economia e storia*, 3(1963): 413.

5. *Giornale Enciclopedico* (The Encyclopaedic journal), 6 (June 1777): 39–43, Vicenza.

6. *Giornale Enciclopedico* (The Encyclopaedic journal), 11 (Nov. 1781).

7. G. F. Galeani-Napione, "Elogio di Giovanni Botero, abate di S. Michele della chiusa" (In praise of Giovanni Botero, Abbot of S. Michele della chiusa), in *Piemontesi illustri*, vol. 1, Turin, Briolo, 1781–87.

8. L. Angiolini, *Lettere sopra l'Inghilterra, Scozia e Olanda* (Letters on England, Scotland and Holland), 5 vols., vol. 2, letter 18, pp. 355–8, Florence, Allegrini, 1790.

9. L. Angiolini, *Lettere . . . Delle manifatture di Leeds* (On the industries of Leeds), vol. 2, letter 6, p. 117. We are, however, of the opinion that Angiolini's reference to Smith's work is incorrect. Perhaps he is mistaking Adam Smith for John Smith, the author of *Chronicum rusticum-commerciale*, or *Memoirs of Wool*, London, 1747, quoted by A. Smith, *Ricerche sopra la natura e le cause della ricchezza delle nazioni*, Book I, ch. 11,

p. 215 and Book IV, ch. 8, p. 593, Turin, UTET, 1965, or A. Smith, *An Inquiry into the Nature and Causes of the Wealth of Nations*, ed. R. H. Campbell, A. S. Skinner, and W. B. Todd, Vol. 1, Book I, ch. 11, p. 248 and Vol. 2, Book IV, ch. 8, p. 653, Oxford, Clarendon Press, 1976.

10. A. Smith, *Ricerche*, Book IV, ch. 8, p. 585; A. Smith, *An Inquiry*, Book IV, ch. 8, p. 643.

11. L. Angiolini, *Lettere*, vol. 2, letter 6, pp. 108–9.

12. "This volume ends with an anlysis of the most famous work by Mr Smith, entitled *"Recherches sur la nature, et les causes de la richesse des nations"*. The editors state that this work is one of those which the English Nation may well be proud of . . . ". *Biblioteca oltremontana*, vol. 2, pp. 10, 179, 239, Turin, Reale Stamperia, 1790.

13. A. Smith, *Ricerche*, "Il traduttore italiano a chi leggerà" (The Italian translator to all those who read), p. ii.

14. On this point, and especially on the edition from which the Italian translation was made, see L. Einaudi, "Dei libri italiani", pp. 82 ff.

15. G. B. Vasco, "Saggio politico della carta-moneta" (A political essay on paper-money), in G. Prato, *La Teoria e la pratica della carta moneta prima degli assegnati rivoluzionari. Un trattato inedito di Giovan Battista Vasco* (The theory and practice of paper money before the time of the *assignats révolutionnaires*. An unpublished tract by Giovan Battista Vasco), *Journals of the Royal Academy of Science of Turin*, 65 (ser. 2): 4, n. 3, Turin, 1916.

On G. B. Vasco, see F. Venturi, *Illuministi italiani* (Italian illuminists), Vol. 3: *Riformatori lombardi piemontesi e toscani. G. B. Vasco* (Lombard, Piedmontese and Tuscan Reformers. G. B. Vasco), pp. 757–99, Milan and Naples, Ricciardi, 1958; O. Nuccio, *Appendice a G. B. Vasco "Scrittori classici italiani di economia politica"* (An appendix to G. B. Vasco's "Classic Italian Writers on political economy"), P. Custodi, vol. 35, 1803–1816, modern section; anastatic reprint, Rome, Bizzarri, 1967.

16. G. B. Vasco, "Saggio politico", p. 2.

17. See A. Smith, *Ricerche*, Book II, ch. 2, pp. 289–90; A. Smith, *An Inquiry*, pp. 320–1.

18. G. B. Vasco, *Delle Università delle arti e mestieri—Dissertazione* (On the Universities of the arts and crafts—A Dissertation), Milan, 1793; repr. in *Scrittori classici*, vol. 33, modern section, pp. 185–293.

19. Ibid. p. 244.

20. Ibid. p. 284.

21. P. Vergani, *Dell'importanza e dei pregi del nuovo sistema di finanze dello stato pontificio* (On the importance and merits of the new financial methods of the Papal State), Rome, 1794. Further information on Smith is given by the *Nuovo dizionario istorico* (New historical dictionary), Bassano, 1796, and by the Abbé Paolo Balsamo in 1799. P. Balsamo, *Sulle manifatture, Memoria IV, La mancanza dei corpi privilegiati dei differenti artefici, e dei coattivi regolamenti dei loro lavori non influisce punto nel miserabile stato delle manifatture della Sicilia* (On the manufacturing industry, memoir IV: The lack of privileged bodies for all crafts, and of obligatory regulations regarding their activities has no influence whatsoever on the miserable state of the manufacturing industry in Sicily), 19 Jan 1799, pp. 48–54 in *Memorie inedite di*

pubblica economia ed agricoltura (Unpublished Memoirs regarding the public economy and agriculture), 2 vols., Palermo, Muratori, 1845.

22. The competition held by the Virgilian Academy in Mantua in 1779 was the occasion for the publication of several memoirs: G. Scottoni, *Dissertazione sopra il quesito se in uno stato di terreno fertile* . . . (Dissertation on the question of whether in a fertile State the extraction of raw materials should take precedence over manufacturing), in *Scrittori classici italiani*, P. Custodi, vol. 31, modern section, pp. 287–320; and G. B. d'Arco, *Riposta al quesito: se in uno stato di terreno fertile* . . . (An answer to the question of whether in a fertile . . .), ibid. pp. 191–243.

On the occasion of the competition held by the Academy of Verona in 1780, G. Grecis published his work *Sulo spaccio delle sete veronesi* (On the Verona silk trade), Verona, Ramanzini, 1797. G. B. Vasco participated in the competition held by the Academy of Science of Turin in 1788 with his *Riposta al quesito: quali siano i mezzi di provvedereal sostentamento degli operai* . . . (Answer to the question of Ways of providing for the workers engaged in the twisting of silk in the mills . . .) in *Scrittori classici italiani*, P. Custodi, vol. 35, modern section, pp. 5–102. None of the papers submitted was awarded a prize. Some were later published, including G. d'Arco, *Dell'influenza dello spirito del commercio sull'economia interna de' popoli e sulla prosperità degli stati* (On the influence of the spirit of commerce on the internal economies of various peoples and the prosperity of nations), in *Scrittori classici italiani*, vol. 31, modern section, pp. 107–164.

Lastly, the Academy of Agriculture, Arts and Commerce of Verona issued, on 30 March 1789, a question relating to the retaining or otherwise of protective measures for certain activities.

23. The competition was held by the Accademia dei Georgofili in Florence and illustrated by a document dated 9 February 1791. The winning essay was F. Mengotti, *Ragionamento del signor Francesco Mengotti dell'Accademia di Padova, presentato alla Reale società economica fiorentina pel concorso al problema del 1791 e da essa premiato nella sessione del dì 13 giugno 1792* (The reasoning of Messer Francesco Mengotti of the Academy of Padua, presented in 1791 to the Royal Economic Society of Florence for the competition regarding this problem, the said Academy awarding it the prize on 13 June 1792), Florence, Pagani, 1792. Further editions were printed under the title of *Il Colbertismo* (The Colbertism), as can be seen in *Scrittori classici italiani*, P. Custodi, vol. 36, modern section, pp. 253–419, Milan, De Stefanis, 1804, reprinted Rome, Bizzarri, 1967. It is this latter edition to which we refer.

Regarding F. Mengotti, see M. Berengo, *La società veneta alla fine del settecento. Ricerche storiche* (Society in Venice at the end of the 1700s. Historical research), pp. 184–5, Florence, Sansoni, 1956; L. Iraci Fedeli, *Letture di economisti italiani dei secoli XVIII e XIX: Francesco Mengotti e il "colbertismo"* (Italian economists of the eighteenth and nineteenth centuries: Francesco Mengotti and "The Colbertism"), *Annali Istituto Feltrinelli*, pp. 560–76, Milan, Feltrinelli, 1959; F. Luzzatto, *Melchiorre Gioia e F. Mengotti, con documenti inediti* (Melchiorre Gioia and F. Mengotti, with unpublished documents), *Bollettino storico piacentino* (The Piacenza historical bulletin), Jan.–Mar. 1931, pp. 181–96; O. Nuccio, *Appendice*, in *Scritori classici italiani*, P. Custodi, vol. 36, II–XLV.

24. It would appear that on this question Mengotti agrees with Smith's statement in Book III, chs. 1 and 3, particularly regarding the "natural course of events". A. Smith, *Ricerche*, p. 347; A. Smith, *An Inquiry*, p. 374.

25. In regard to the way in which Smith's work slowly penetrated Italian circles, we may note that it was studied mainly from the French translation, although also known in the original. The States in which he would appear to have been best known were the Piedmont (which at that time was part of the State of Savoy) and the area under the dominion of Venice.

5.2. Luigi Luzzatti, 1876.
The Centenary of the Publication of Adam Smith's Work

Translated by Silvia Klemm

The societies of political economy of London, Paris, and Brussels have recently celebrated the centenary of the publication of the work by Adam Smith, recalling the attention of thinkers to meditate on the immortal volume. In the Middle Ages, the ideas of Aristotle were known through the commentary of Averroës, and when the scholars could read in the original manuscript the high philosophies of the Stagirite, a beam of new light penetrated into their intellects, which were obscured by the empty and arid entelechies, and the living word of the master freed them from the slavery of the commentators.

It is legitimate to hope for a similar effect today, when the thinking of the economists goes back, full of thanks, to Adam Smith, who, in his two works entitled *The Theory of Moral Sentiments* and *The Wealth of Nations* has plucked the flower of Scottish genius; a genius that adapts the production of resources to the cult of moral and religious ideas, causing the realities of life to prosper through the enlightenment of ideals. Scotland has solved some very severe problems of political economy with the levity of its innate traits. Multiple issuing banks, which around the end of 1600 issued banknotes payable on sight to the bearer, were finding a healthy restraint in the hidden power of integrity which corrects the excessiveness of individual interests. I do not deny the reciprocal action that morality has on the diffusion of credit and the diffusion of credit on morality; but there is no doubt that Scottish banks owe their flourishing greatly to the purifying action of that religious reform which with John Knox had renewed morality. This foreword stands to show that by transplanting the structures of Scottish banks into another country, reproducing only the economic characteristics without the aid of *the moral agent*, one would not obtain the identical results which have brought about this system in Scotland.

Adam Smith, trained to this austere and elevated order of civil virtues and economic experiences, became a distinguished philosopher, the prince of modern economists. Economic science was, before him, a heap of actions; he blew into it life-giving genius, and the deeds transformed themselves into poems. The creators of sciences all resemble Homer; they weave rhapsodies together, and they create immortal karmas. But the status of the great social volumes, even if they shine with admirable clarity, equals that of the Bible. Different interpretations generate sects. Each portrays God and science according to its individual soul. Isn't the Gospel clear in its moral aim? And yet, it is in its name, which opens the Gates of Heaven to all, that believers banish one another from Heaven.

Adam Smith launches; he does not close the opus of science. He adds to and does not terminate the path of economic truth. He stands out for his impartiality of judgement, for the modest temperance of his experimental method, for that sound good sense that shies from excesses; and he reduces the flights of abstract theory with historical and statistical observations. In philosophy, in history and economy, Scottish writers from Reid to Macaulay excel thanks to balanced ideas and axioms which keep exact count of all the elements out of which the life of all individuals and nations are made. Adam Smith has taken care to integrate the study of economic problems with the moral, political, and social elements; he recognizes that this powerful unity of life is not explainable by one theory only or by the supremacy of one element over other elements; and if at times he states a general, abstract principle, based only on its economic reasons of benefit, when he applies it to the institutions, he mitigates, modifies, and sometimes he even contradicts. It is the consciousness of reality that rules over the mind of the philosopher. I have prepared, my distinguished colleagues, a report of patient research on the method used by Smith, on the quality and the nature of his studies in relation to the time in which he lived and in relation to the present. It would not be possible for me to give you a complete report in the short time assigned to an academic lecture; but it will be helpful to select some typical examples of distinctive efficiency which refer to issues struggled with nowadays, with great passion, even in our country. I am making an allusion to credit, to international exchange, to the State's stock exchange, to the nature of taxes.

The laws that rule the circulation of banknotes and the events that have to hold them are magnificently exposed in volume two of the work by Smith. He had, as mentioned above, the unusual fortune of being able to deduce and determine the disciplines of credit through the image of domestic instances. Usually, the great economic institutions precede the doctrines of economists, and the Scottish statesman reasons around the more correct forms of credit, creating the anatomy and the physiology of those banking organisms that were flourishing in his homeland. There is an exact relationship between the forms, the symbols of credit, and social customs. In primitive, unadvanced, distrustful societies, credit takes place under the form of pawning; the creditor will not rely on any other form of personal guarantee. Later on we pass to mortgage, which makes it possible for the debtor to rely on the practice of security; finally, institutions of commercial credit gradually developed and took form; bills of exchange, cheques, and banknotes, which spiritualize credit, became widespread, thereby creating a type of society which is civically and morally very advanced. Smith with effective severity makes mention here and there of all these *profound forces of credit*; he clearly distinguishes, with a technical examination which one seeks in vain in the writers who preceded him, two degrees or *stages in the distribution of banknotes*: the circulation can be restricted among traders or extend itself between traders and consumers. The major or minor expansion is linked, according to him, to the devision of the banknotes. Notes which are not divided into low denominations keep the circulation amongst the merchants; when the denomination decreases, it spreads the circulation among the most humble layers of society. After a rigorous and comparative examination of the merits and defects of the two systems, he decides for that which prohibits low denomination notes and he expresses a desire for the law to intervene so as to regulate this issue. But the formidable objection which retracts qualities and means from the same principles of absolute and relative freedom which he has established interferes in this matter, and he proposes a series of doubts to his own fine conscience as an economist. He asks himself whether it is right to prohibit anyone from accepting a banker's note of any denomination in payment when he spontaneously wishes to do so; or whether it is right to prevent a banker from circulating any kind of notes when his neighbours agree to receive them. Wouldn't such restrictions constitute an offence to that natural freedom which the law has the duty to protect rather then violate? There is no doubt, he answers, that to a certain point, regulations of such kind can be considered to be an offence to natural freedom, but the practice of the natural freedom of some individuals could compromise the general security of society, and has to be restricted and regulated by laws in any kind of possible government—in the most liberal kind as in the most dictatorial one. The enforced ordinance of building dividing walls to prevent the spread of fire is also a violation of the natural freedom and precisely one of the same kind as the regulations which we are suggesting for banking commerce. Smith verbalized these illustrious thoughts for the sake of clarity and civic prudence, at a time when studies on the banknote—that very efficient tool of prosperity or ruin, depending on the way it is handled—were scarce and inconclusive; but his sound good sense looked clear-sightedly to the future and pointed to the necessity of a law to regulate the denomination of the notes, in the name of global security. His limpid, temperate, refreshing, and essentially practical ideas are more relevant than the absolutist theories of those economists who affirm that each man is born with the natural right to issue banknotes payable to the bearer at sight, and that there isn't any possibility of danger or redundancy in the emissions because freedom corrects all exuberance and saves the market from excessive or unreliable currency through the brake applied by the rate of exchange. If the sweet master could rise again, he most certainly would not find in all these ideas the wholesome effect of his immortal lessons.

His motto in regard to emissions resembles that of ancient wisdom: *Nullum numen abest si sit prudentia* (no god possesses such temperance). "One has to agree," he says, "that commerce and industry can rise higher with the aid of paper money: nonetheless, suspended, I dare say, on Icarus wings, they are not so secure on their path as if they lay on the firm ground of gold and silver." All the most deep and recent studies on credit, the great inquisitions undertaken by the most civilized and advanced nations, such as England and France, come to identical conclusions as Smith. One only has to look at the two most recent English volumes by Bagehot and by Bonamy-Price on the theory of the metallic supply in issuing banks, where the dispute is being picked up again between those who grant with Icarus wings and those who, even if freed in the air thanks to credit, do not remove themselves too much from the firm ground of gold and silver. The function of credit is to increase the exchange profit of money and represents, in various phases of its exercise, a great economy in its means of payment. England has come to the apogee and there is no other nation that has succeeded in arranging in such perfect manner the banking mechanisms and the tools of currency exchange. From the Bank of England to the Clearing House there is a series of intermediate institutions which replace the stock share of credit for that of money in a variety of ways, and Bagehot discloses them with magnificent evidence. The machine has been refined from year to year, and it has now arrived at a point where it compresses the maximum degree of strength. No one holds money idle anymore; it regenerates itself continuously within the vortex of circulation. From the Bank of England to the last provincial banker, everyone, at any moment, is debtor of a sum of money far larger than that which they possess, or than that which exists in the country.

It is the credit machine with its delicate organs which guarantees regeneration. If it were to stop for one instant only, if the magistery of exchange, of cheques, of clearings were to break down, there would be general bankruptcy. Please note that this perfection of circulation is based upon a universally accepted hypothesis, namely that there is a vast supply of funds in the form of metals capable of making up for monetary deficiencies of credit. If this hypothesis, if this universal trust falls short, the machine of credit loses its vitality. Dead funds, buried in the issuing banks, represent the hearth of the cauldron, which emits light, heat, and circulation. Those writers of economy who have not given any importance to the accumulation of the supply of metals, and who rise in the manner of Icarus wings so as to lose sight of the earth, have not meditated over Adam Smith. The supply of metals is one of the greater resources, because it facilitates and determines that credit arrangement which is among the principal sources of national prosperity. The more credit unfolds and advances, the more the supply of metal, which constitutes the common denominator of all valuables, becomes indispensable and precious. The issuing banks resemble those splendid Venetian palaces, which last through centuries in their superlative massive structure because they rest on indestructible precious woods.

From the economic considerations on movement, Smith goes on to the political ones, and he expresses the same note of prudence in issuing and the same advantage in maintaining the metal supplies in abundance. The economic and the political considerations indicate a common aim. "During an ill-fated war," he observes, "in which the enemy makes himself head of the capital and of the treasure that assures the credit of the banknotes, the affliction would be greater in a country where the majority of the circulation is of paper, than in one where it is made up of gold and silver. The habitual tool of commerce [which in Smith's hypothesis would be of paper] having lost its value, could not be exchanged anymore other than with barter or credit. All taxes would be usually paid with money, and the Prince would not have the means to either keep his troops nor to stock his warehouses and the country would find itself in worse conditions than if the greater part of the circulation had been of gold and silver. A Prince eager to preserve his Estates at all times in such conditions as to be able to defend them has to keep on guard not only against the tendency towards the multiplication of banknotes by the banks that generate them, but he also has to prevent the danger of excessive emission that aims at accomplishing, with paper only, the majority of the monetary movement of the country." It is a splendid maxim which integrates, with political reasoning, the economic necessity for a law which would regulate and restrict emissions. Smith's apprehension is not futile; if, as an example, the *Commune* of Paris had taken possession of the metal supply of the Bank of France, the movement of the social body would have been annihilated by paralysis; Jourde, the ephemeral minister of finances of the *Commune*, who had for certain not read Smith, became conscious of this vast misfortune when he contributed to saving the metal supplies of the Bank of France. In the field of credit, one cannot call upon the authority of the master in favour of liberty even when rejecting every idea of monopoly.

Smith's concepts in regard to the freedom of international exchange are no less temperate and full of caution. Today the cause of free exchange has been won, and the controversy is still alive as to the ways in which it is applied. There are those who want to apply it in full, without any tempering of time or social condition; on the other side are those who suggest the reform of free exchange with all the tempering required by the existing facts and by the errors of past systems, which create important knots which cannot be cut with a sword, but need to be untangled with the perseverance of time. Smith, if I am not mistaken, takes the side of the latter category of thinkers. He explains the reasons for free exchange with great pictures of deep insight, new at the time, common today. Nevertheless it seems to him that there are two occasions on which it would be better to establish some tax increase on foreign industry in order to "encourage" the national industry. The first situation is one in which "a particular type of industry is necessary to the defence of the country". For example, the defence of Great Britain depends primarily on the number of its warships and navy men. In this case Oliver Cromwell's Navigation Act, which bestows on English warships and navy men the monopoly of navigation, "by means of absolute prohibitions in some cases and heavy taxes on foreign navigation in other circumstances", is beneficial and useful.

Smith hereby analyses and summarizes with great diligence the dispositions of this rigid act, which had had a preceding example in the navigation arrangements of the Republic of Venice, and he lingers with singular force on the implications of the prohibition on importing by sea, from the places of production, merchandise of great volume if by means other than English ships. Holland, renewed by the freedom of consciousness and from misfortune, hinted at becoming the great warehouse centre of Europe; and Cromwell, according to the cruel practice of the time, aimed, with this disposition which Smith approved of, to weaken its power. Those regulations which established that salty fish of any kind and whale fats not prepared on board English ships had to pay double taxes were inspired by the same sentiments of envy towards Holland. England had succeeded in ruling on the seas and over the great caches and Holland was defeated also in this formidable and uncivilized ruling of the maritime monopoly. This is where the economic conscience of Smith becomes disturbed and filled with shame; but after some apprehension and fluctuation he takes pride in the sentiment of a holy national egoism and exclaims: "Even if the act of navigation was inspired by feelings of jealousy and animosity, that national hate aimed towards something wise, namely the weakening of the Dutch navy, the only rival power capable of threatening England." There is no doubt that the Navigation Act restricts the freedom of navigation and commerce and increases the price of maritime services as well as that of fish, which is one of the principal aliments of the people; but, according to Smith, "the security of a State is" of greater importance than that of its resources and the act of navigation is, perhaps, the wisest of all the regulations that govern English commerce.

In the volume in which he reasons on colonial politics and intuitively senses the liberal constitutions of the future given by England to its principal colonies, he is dominated by the proud idea of the maritime supremacy of his homeland and he observes yet again that "the maritime opulence of Great Britain has vastly increased since the establishment of the Navigation Act". We should remember that England was in truth hesitant to erase every trace of the Navigation Act from its maritime legislation up to 1854, even though today England congratulates itself, and with reason, on its full autonomy. It seems useful to bear in mind that in 1854 it was the ruler of the seas and could rely in total safety on its autonomy, causing the other maritime nations to follow its example. The great transformation of the sail boat in wood to the steam boat in iron assured to England, for natural reasons, a type of supremacy, and the Navigation Act had become a harmful device.

From this situation Smith goes on to another one in which an exception to the principle of free exchange seems justifiable. According to him, it would be appropriate to put "a tax on foreign industry to encourage the national industry when the product of the latter is burdened by some internal tax". Under such circumstances it seems reasonable to him to establish a similar tax on the same kind of product that comes from foreign factories. The word used by Smith in this case is incorrect; it isn't a matter of "encouraging", but of "compensating" the national industry. Some suggest *compensating* all the increases in taxes which burden the national merchandise not specifically through taxes on foreign goods, but through a general rule on tariffs. Smith does not find this demand unjust; but he rejects it on the grounds of the difficulty of the exact calculation. It is easy to determine the relationship of the tax to the special impost, but it would be extremely difficult to determine precisely how the increase of production caused by the taxes would relate to the imposts established on foreign merchandise. Such sagacious norms and careful calculations rule to this day the treaties of commerce of the most civilized nations.

Yet if there are two cases in which it can be useful to impose taxes on the foreign industry to encourage or compensate the national one, there are another two in which it can be appropriate to consider what to do each time the situation occurs; they are, according to Smith, the two dubious and debatable cases of free exchange. When a foreign nation closes its market with heavy taxes or prohibitions it could even be useful to use the method of retaliation. This seems to him a correct policy, when there is the probability that it would accelerate the revocation of such heavy taxes or prohibitions. The advantage of reacquiring a great foreign market will greatly compensate the inconvenience of paying for a while a higher price for foreign merchandise. All depends on the efficiency of the retaliations. But this question "does not belong", according to Smith, "to science, but to the art of governing, the ability of that deceitful and astute being that is called a statesman", who has to take notice of the circumstances. How much concern, oh gentlemen, there is in this advice! Retaliation is harmful because it increases the price of the merchandise wanted by the national consumers, but it can be a necessary ill if it succeeds in opening a foreign market. It would not be useless if this passage fell under the eyes of those ingenuous statesmen, if they can call themselves so, who go around blasting to the four winds that they are ready to grant to foreign industries every kind of concession, even if they deny these concessions at home, that they would open the doors wide to foreign products even if the foreigner jealously keeps these products from the people in his homeland.

The second dubious situation arises when, after an extended period of prohibitions or protection, the industries have expanded to such a point as to employ a great number of workers. "In this case," observes Smith, "a just sentiment of humanity could require that the freedom of commerce be restored gradually, slowly, with great circumspection and reticence. If all heavy taxes or prohibitions were to be suddenly abolished then the market could be showered by foreign merchandise and thousands and thousands of national citizens could find themselves without their usual occupation and without any means of survival." It is true that the entrepreneur of a large industry who has to close his factory because of the sudden diminution of taxes can put his capital to better uses; and yet, observes Smith, with the perspicacity of a statesman, the fixed capital, for example that which is immovable property, the building and machines, would suffer great losses. "A just consideration for the interests of this entrepreneur would require that such changes would never take place abruptly, but would take place slowly and in succession, and only after they have been announced well in advance." His words, so moderate and wise, make for a strange comparison with the following opinion of some very orthodox disciples of Smith: Let us abolish every kind of protective and maintenance tax, either the industries can prosper naturally and will not suffer losses, or they cannot do so, and their misfortune will be beneficial to the consumer. The more the industry suffers, the happier the consumer! Formulas of this kind reveal a great theoretical intrepidity, but also great inexperience in human things, and they certainly do not stem from Smith's branches.

Our author encourages England onto the path of freedom of exchange applied to manufacturing: it is already superior to other nations in the industries of wool, leather, and ceramics—perhaps even in the industry of silk materials. It cannot but gain from spreading such doctrines around the world. Owner of its own internal market for the output of these industries, England will by the reciprocation of mild taxes also gain possession of the foreign markets. These observations by Smith are prophecies. The mechanism applied to industries and the abundance of coal together with incomparable technical abilities have given England manufacturing sovereignty over other nations, and the abolition of taxes has, as Smith had predicted, momentarily impoverished only the industry of silk at Coventry and Spitalfields. England has followed the advice of its eminent economist: it lingered before abolishing the Navigation Act; it realized freedom of exchange for wheat, which it did not produce in sufficient amounts for its own sustenance, as well as for manufacturing products sent to every corner of the earth, which seems too narrow for the colossal production of its factories. In regard to negotiation strategies, England's statesmen possess an ability that Smith did not reject. Even recently, Cartwright, a very influential deputy, asked the government in the House of Commons to modify the system of English taxes on foreign wines, so essential to Italian oenology. The Chancellor of the Exchequer answered that the moment was not appropriate as the relaxation of the wine toll greatly mattered to Spain, Portugal, and Italy, and one had to consider how to make it work once those states were asked to reduce their taxes. He is applying Smith's theory, which can be explained in the following way, to wine: let the English drinkers patiently wait for foreign wine; they will savour it once it has become inexpensive, once, having negotiated new treaties with foreign powers, we are able to apply tax reductions on the manufacturing ouput of Yorkshire and Lancashire. In the meantime, let them enjoy our national beer!

Somewhere else in his great work, Smith considers fiscal taxes with that same investigative care applied to economic structure. Even though the author advises gradually taking away the purpose of protection from imposts, he does not want to abolish customs, and he attributes to it conspicuous entries for the State Treasury. One should read his thoughts on customs with great care. The economist Ricardo was a stockbroker; Smith practised the role of customs officer for many years; he speaks of all the events surrounding smuggling and of the ways to trace it with the refinement of experience. I am sorry that the brevity of time does not allow me to elaborate on a few fundamental ideas. He foresees and determines the importance of free storage and storehouses, he demonstrates the convenience of having merchants storing their goods in a public storehouse and only pay taxes when the merchandise passes to internal consumption, "If the merchandise gets re-exported, no tax would have to be paid." Yet Smith wanted wholesale and retail dealers who used this formula to be subject to the visit and the inspection of customs officials and to be liable to account, with regular documents, for the payment of taxes even for the quantity of merchandise stored in their own goods sheds or shops. Storehouses which were subject, according to English custom, to registrations and inspections would not be the only ones, as one had to continue to keep track of the goods so that no frauds against the state were committed. In this instance, the claw of the customs official takes away some degree of economic freedom! Nowadays we look at the system of free points in which all registration is eliminated with praise and we are not completely in accordance with Smith's rigid thoughts regarding the administration of customs.

We have recollected Smith's thoughts on international exchange, even though it is evident that today the path from protection to free exchange has to be faster and more straightforward.

If I may, I would now like to approach a more difficult and bitter query by examining the opinions of the author on the state's conduct. Those who attribute to Smith the conception of a state indifferent to human misfortune, a lazy contemplator of all infirmities, concerned only with protecting society against violence and invasion, with ruling justly and demanding taxes, are incorrect. Smith admits to a third state duty, namely the one of "creating and keeping public works and establishments out of which a great society can gain tremendous benefits; these works are of a kind that cannot be undertaken or preserved by this or the other individual, because *for them*, the profit would never compensate the expense. The fulfilment of such a state duty requires costs, the extent of which varies according to the different degrees of advancement of that society." Such foundations and institutions refer clearly to the resources needed to facilitate the national trades and cultivations. Smith's teachings on education do not seem to me to conform with today's pedagogical progress; but it isn't in this light that I'd like to consider them. I am anxious for you to notice the method, the spirit with which he debates the problem of the state's actions.

He asks himself whether the state should concern itself with the education of the people, and if so, in what measure. It all depends on the condition of society; there is nothing absolute in this argument. In certain circumstances the conditions are such that they exempt the government from direct intervention; in other situations "it is necessary for the government to take action to prevent the nation's body from deteriorating and decaying". And here he conveys an important observation. The division of labour, whose economic efficiency is one of Smith's rights to glory, immobilizes and sterilizes, according to him, the mind of man when he is kept under a sole occupation. Proudhon has, with his habitual glare of words, repeated the same idea, noting that the division of labour progresses and industry advances at the cost of the labourer's soul. This is why, explains Smith, it is necessary for the state in a society which has progressed in commerce and industry to give the most diligent care to the education of the people. *"The state should*, before the poor start to work, require them to study and it should institute the obligation to acquire the most essential parts of education *for the majority of the population*, forcing every man to take an exam or a test so as to obtain mastery in a corporation or the licence to exercise a trade in a village or annexed city." Those who have not studied would, according to Smith's conception, not be allowed to work. He imposes the obligation of instruction not only on children, on persons under age, but also on those who are of age, speaking in general terms *of the population's body*. It seems to me that the master is hereby exceeding himself in rigour and that he fails to give the state the means to impose the obligation of instruction on those of age and to implement the cruel sanction of work prohibition. But the healthy, vital part of this proposition which refers to the instruction of children and women has been put into practice in England (and later in the other more civilized countries) with laws on major and minor factories, on mines and on youth farm-labourers. The Factory Acts, which offer this type of legislation, link schooling to the prohibition on working under a certain age; they regulate the working hours of children, forcing the heads of factories and the owners not to employ them unless they have fulfilled the scholastic obligations prescribed by the law. From the education of the mind the author goes on to the education of the soul; he reminds us that the Greek and Roman Republics "gave the population the means to practise military and gymnastic exercise; by encouraging such exercise, imposing on the nation the necessity of learning these skills, they were cultivating the martial dispositions of the citizen. The security of a society depends on the warlike character of the population. With the advancing of civilization and industry, if the government does not take responsibility to keep this martial spirit alive, the habit of military exercise will decline and with it the national character". An apostle of peace and freedom of exchange, he does not forget the defence of the country.

There is a wonderful passage exuberant with social charity on the utility that the state would derive from educating the multitudes. He does not only concern himself with the common people but also believes the state must make universally available the study of science and philosophy to the middle classes, so as to correct the narrow-minded and superstitious sides of the population; and he does not leave out the need for the state to provide public entertainment to alleviate the melancholies and austerities in the souls of his fellow countrymen, rendered too painful by a relentless and dark religious doctrine such as the one of predestination of some Protestant denominations. To Adam Smith, the actions of the state do not appear to be, as they do to some rigid economists, a kind of insurance policy to which everyone pays a quota in proportion to the assets to be safeguarded by social preservation. The great principle of solidarity peeks out from the mind of the illustrious scholar. To give an example: reasoning on the means of communication, he defends the (at that time established) concept of road tolls, which corresponded to the construction and maintenance costs of the streets, then redeemed in large proportions in England as well. And even if the carriage of the rich ruins the roads far less than the heavy wagons of the farmers, he recommends the tax for the latter to be more moderate. He desires "for the vanity and indolence of the rich to contribute to the comfort of the poor very simply by decreasing the price of transportation of heavy merchandise". Talking about imposts, on one occasion he expresses the following assessment, which would later become the hammer of his future orthodox commentators: "it isn't unreasonable for the rich to contribute to the state expenses not just in proportion to their income, but somewhat beyond this proportion." Garnier, one of his loyal disciples and commentators, goes so far as to express regret that the master did not elaborate to further explain the sense of his words; words which may not answer the difficult and still unresolved problem for science of proportional and progressive taxes, but which seem in our opinion quite clear. They hint to the link which binds, within the association of humanity, ignorance to knowledge, poverty to affluence. The modern state has, in the name of this link of solidarity, grave and multiple duties also towards those with no property, who pay no taxes. The state is a bonding of justice and progress, of defence and charity: it is the great solidarity of the rich and the poor, the educated and the ignorant. Those with no property also benefit from the services of the state (charity, hygiene, instruction, means of communication, and so on) and are equal in front of the spirit of their country as they are in the face of God.

It is through these facts, which I have precisely quoted from the volume and which I researched with long studies and great passion, that the genius of Adam Smith comes out in all its admirable equanimity of doctrines. Like all great scholars, he does not belong to a sect, a school; he is fair and unselfish in researches such as the one for truth. He does not crystallize science in entelechies and apocalyptic, absolute categories but brings its formulas to life, adapting them with the method of observing social conditions. He does not belong to the rank of extreme thinkers, who see an offence to freedom in every action of the state; the state is for him not only a medium of justice, but also of progress, and it integrates with its actions the deficient activity of its citizen, with the aim of promoting those great institutions which individuals would not be able either to found or to keep. The character, the number, the modalities of such institutions cannot be determined beforehand; it is the examination of the facts, the historical sense which defines and classifies them. Every century, every nation has its own particular vocation. When Adam Smith was writing his immortal volume, the mechanics applied to industries had not yet brought about those immense plants, which have created so many new and formidable hygienic, moral, and economic problems for the state. But there is no doubt that he would not have wanted the state to wait for a solution as an impassive spectator.

As we have said, when speaking of education in industrial countries, he calls upon the great tutelage of public authority, because the division of labour darkens and diminishes the intellectual abilities of the workers. And he had not yet seen the more rational and extreme applications of the division of labour in a factory activated by steam. He had not yet seen the child or the woman absorbed for the whole day in following the strikes of the shuttle of several mechanical looms, exhausted by the routine of that untamable iron giant!

There is no doubt that the principal and most brilliant glory of Adam Smith is the theory of economic freedom, opposed, in a manner of good-natured challenge, to an artificial world of illegitimate state intrusions, of privileges and monopolies. Freedom meant truth, the knowledge within the ideal and the practical order. While Smith was preparing the code of economic freedom for the people of the Earth, Watt was discovering steam and by applying it to the working place he was creating the industrial machine. It was an admirable conciliation of economic and physical discoveries which were helping each other reciprocally. Without industrial freedom, the industrial mechanics would not have had the opportunity to evolve and prosper; without industrial mechanics, the applications of economic freedom could not have centuplicated the potency of production. And while economic science and mechanics were preparing those magnificent triumphs in which our century takes great pride, the common people of all of Europe were raising their heads against centuries-long oppressions, asking for a place in the sun of political liberty, sharpening their desires for moral and economic well-being, preparing millions of consumers for the giant plants animated by economic freedom and steam.

Following the glorious traditions of the master, economic science can sense new truths, it can correct its formulas, it can complete them with the observations of the facts which are developing in the world. Economic science, like all other social sciences, is nowadays exposed to an immense and minute process of revision and correction. Having discovered the most prime and fundamental truths, all disciplines now unfold unto themselves and study the fractions and limits which the abstract and idealistic principles suffer in their applications. The most important living Belgian freelancer, Emilio di Laveleye, said, at the banquet of Economists in London, that economic freedom applied to the production of wealth had triumphed all over, and had already consumed itself in our modern society: *consummatum est*. But, as Laveleye observes, there is the second part of science, the one of the *redistribution of wealth*, which today demands a deep inquisition and which concerns itself with the economic progress of the working classes. The negative and destructive part of the economic reforms is done, but the work of positive and constructive reforms, in which social, political, and religious institutions and the state have to play a role, still remains to be started. Smith's genius, in regard to this task, ahead of his times, has provided us with matter since the end of the last century; it is from him that the *sociological* work of the modern legislator, to be distinguished from *socialism*, takes shape and quality. The main traits of this social legislation are essentially Smithian and seem to us to be the following: very strong aspiration to better the conditions of the working classes; constant care to reconcile among themselves the various social elements of which life is made; exact investigation of the harms which one wants to eliminate and of the benefits which one wants to promote; well-considered state action, neither excessive nor weak, but exactly proportional to the degree of efficiency which the straightforward observation of things suggests in order to integrate with its action the deficient industriousness and ineptitude of the individual forces.

Economic science will in such a way neither exhaust itself nor consume itself; there is still an immense task assigned to it; it has to investigate which is, within the dense and dark entanglement of human interests, the impartial, predominant component which belongs to freedom and which is the minor, changeable one which belongs to authority—the two alternating forces which dispute over the governing of society. Kant, in his *Critique of Pure Reason*, observes that the dove flying up in the sky would want to complain about the resistance of the air, ignoring that she owes to that very resistance the fact that she can hold herself up high with her wings. This similitude can represent that perpetual and necessary friction between freedom and authority, with which economic science has toiled until today, and with which it will continue to toil in the future. *Hoc opus, hic labor* (that is the task; that is the labour); in this lies its nobility and its glory.

Part 6. Japan

Adam Smith studies in Japan have been very active since the first Japanese translation of *WN* in 1870. There are fourteen different versions of *WN* in Japan: some are partially translated, others are translated from different English editions, and others still are re-translations of previous, less satisfactory editions. One might ask why the Japanese are so concerned with Smith.

There is an Adam Smith Society in Japan (established in 1949) which had held 112 meetings by December 1983. Some representative papers read at the meetings were published in two books, *The Taste of Adam Smith* (vol. 1, 1965; vol. 2, 1984, Tokyo University Press). Smith scholars are well respected; the late President of Tokyo University, Professor Kazuo Okochi, who also translated *WN* (in 1968 and 1976), is a good example.

As in the case of Italy, Japanese scholars have published their Smith studies mainly in their own language. Hiroshi Mizuta's studies on Smith's library are the well-known exception. The abundance of studies on virtually all of the works and all aspects of Smith (including biography, theories, and policies) by Japanese Marxist and non-Marxist scholars makes the selection difficult. Under the constraints of few available English texts and limited space in this volume, I chose two basic texts translated from Japanese on the translation and reception of *WN* during the past century, plus one invited paper on the reception of Smith by non-Marxist economists.

The first, by the famous Professor Okochi, is a descriptive but informative piece on the history of Japanese translation of *WN*. The main body of Okochi's text gives a detailed history of the fourteen Japanese editions of *WN*, their translators, their styles, their reception, and variations in their contents. More importantly, it recounts the motives for translation under different economic conditions and currents of economic thought.

Another descriptive text is by Sugihara (1980). It was chosen for the general picture it gives of the introduction of, and research on, Smith in Japan. Unlike

Okochi's paper on the translation of *WN*, Sugihara offers a chronological account of the reception of *WN* during the past century.

It is common knowledge that in Japan there was and is a strong Marxist tradition in economics in general and the history of economic analysis in particular. It can safely be said that most Japanese specialists in Smith studies are Marxians or Marxist sympathizers, and the literature is also abundant. The paper by Wakatabe and Ikeo (1995) focuses on a different topic: the reception of Smith by non-Marxist economists. Their analysis covers the period from the 1930s to the 1980s and centres on the following major figures: Tokuzo Fukuda, Takeyasu Kimura, Ichiro Nakayama, Yasaburo Sakamoto, and the famous general equilibrium theorist Takashi Negishi.

Japanese studies on Adam Smith are so numerous that it is very difficult to select important and representative ones. Below are some of those in my hands. More comprehensive work in Japanese on the reception of *WN* in Japan is still needed, but this is no easy task. A century of history of the reception of Smith in Japan requires a whole volume to analyse.

Further Reading

Texts with a * are printed in this Part

"Adam Smith Commemoration Issue" (January 1924), *Keizai Ronso* (The Economic Journal), 18(2), published by Kyoto Imperial University Economic Society [contains fourteen articles on Smith, and previously published literature (foreign and Japanese) about Smith (in Japanese)].

Adam Smith Society (1965, 1984), *The Taste of Adam Smith*, 2 vols., University of Tokyo Press (in Japanese).

*IKEO, AIKO and MASAZUMI WAKATABE (1995), "Adam Smith in Japan: reconsidered from a non-Marxian perspective".

MATSUKAWA, SHICHIRO (1971), "The Introduction of Adam Smith into Our Country [Japan]: An Evidence", *Tosho*, 267: 56–63 (in Japanese).

*OKOCHI, KAZUO (1976), "A Short History of Japanese Translations of *The Wealth of Nations*", appendix to the 1976 translation under his supervision, vol. 3, pp. 453–69, Tokyo: Chuo-kononsha.

*SUGIHARA, SHIRO (1980), "Adam Smith in Japan", *Documents of Modern Japanese Economic Thought*, pp. 745, Tokyo: Nihon Keizai Hyoronsha.

SUGIYAMA, C. and MIZUTA, H. (eds.) (1988), *Enlightenment and Beyond: Political Economy Comes to Japan*, University of Tokyo Press.

SUGIYAMA, C. *et al.* (1993), "Adam Smith in Japan", in H. Mizuta and C. Sugiyama (eds.), *Adam Smith: International Perspectives*, pp. 293–313, London: Macmillan.

6.1. Kazuo Okochi 1976.
A Short History of Japanese Translations of *The Wealth of Nations*

Translated by Tatsuya Sakamoto

1

Dr Hyoe Ohuchi, having completed his painstakingly complete version of *WN* for the former Iwanami Bunko [Iwanami Library] edition, wrote in deep-felt realization, "Smith should be mortal, but he is someone who dies hard." Although I have no idea about whether *WN* "should be mortal" the fact that its marvellous novelty is still kept alive for all the shortcomings and logical inconsistencies does suggest that Smith is something who dies hard. Naturally the novelty of *WN* can be observed in different meanings and with changing emphases through different historical periods. Nevertheless *WN* is not merely a classic work written by Adam Smith, the founder of political economy. Through two hundred years of history since its publication, *WN* has been constantly provocative and has never failed to direct readers' attention to the fundamental mechanism underlying the superficial forms of economic life. Its attraction is so powerful that it seems as if it was born out of an immortal spirit.

Smith's chief work, *Kokufuron* [*Wealth* of Nations]—formerly translated as *Fukokuron* [*Wealthy* Nations] and in many current versions as *Shokokumin no Tomi* [Wealth of *Nations*]—has been through a number of Japanese versions by a variety of people during the hundred years of modern Japan since the beginning of the Meiji era [1868]. This has been the case through the Meiji, Taisho, and Showa eras and both before and after the Second World War. It may safely be said that the total number of complete, selected, and abridged versions of *WN* is well over ten. Of course, the social background to each Japanese translation is different from age to age. It was translated at one time in conjunction with a practical need for free-trade policy and at another from a purely scholarly point of view. Especially after the First World War, great importance was attached to *WN* as a source of social and economic ideas; furthermore it was evaluated in connection with socialist thought, and it was from this particular viewpoint that Japanese translation was attempted. It is not that the one and the same *WN* was translated in various ways according to different social backgrounds and social needs, but it may be that the attempt to read *WN* from those points of view naturally led people to recast their Japanese versions.

It is more than natural for the late-modernized Japanese capitalist economy to import and translate *WN* as a classic text of political economy produced by an advanced industrial nation. However, in Japan's case, Smith has been unfailingly studied and his *WN* has been constantly translated not only in the cradle years of the modern economy, but also during all those years of the ensuing transformation and military expansion, the Taisho Democracy from the First World War to the late Taisho era, and the violent oppression of freedom of thought—and yet more, during the years of the new constitution and the freedom of thought and movement. Surely it must be said that the Japanese passion and affection for Smith has become deeply and strongly rooted in their minds. Nothing has changed yet in this particular respect.

2

Although the translation history of *WN* in Japan can be traced back to the year Meiji 3 [1870], that was chiefly a summary account and an abridged version of Smith's argument concerning the division of labour. It was probably Eisaku Ishikawa who first started a complete translation of *WN*. An English booklet used as a textbook for the naval academy in Numazu was translated as *Seisan Michi Annai* [A Guide to Production] in May of the year Meiji 3 by Tokujiro Obata, and the chapter named "Division of Toil" (meaning division of labour) is the very first selection from *WN* in Japanese. However, it is probably safe to say that it was by Eisaku Ishikawa that a complete version of the *WN* was first attempted. Ishikawa's version began as a serial in the *Tokyo Keizaigaku Koshukai Kogiroku* [Transactions of the Tokyo Lectures on Political Economy], the first volume of which was published in April of the year Meiji 15 [1882], as *Fukokuron*; the original title "*Wealth of Nations*" [cited in Japanese characters] written by Mr Adam Smith of England; supervised by Shaku Sinpachi of Japan; translated by Ishikawa Eisaku of Japan. The *Kogiroku*, which were put out monthly by the *Tokyo Keizaigaku Koshukai* under the leadership of Ukichi (Uken) Taguchi, distributed among its members classic foreign texts translated mainly by the members themselves. The Transactions continued until volume 21 published in December of the year Meiji 16 [1883] and, in the fashion of correspondence course, seem to have gained some popularity. Ishikawa, a member of the editorial committee of the Lectures, was in charge of the laborious work of translating *WN—Fukokuron* in Ishikawa's rendering—but what was published in the *Kogiroku* from his translation was merely a slight portion of Book 1 (to the end of Book 1 Chapter 7, "Of the Natural and the Market Price of Commodities"). When Ishikawa's continued effort to translate had moved on from Book 1 to Book 4, Chapter 7, he contracted tuberculosis (possibly owing to the painstaking translation) and died with his version unfinished. Seisaku Saga took over the rest of the *Fukokuron*. Ishikawa's version had appeared (with some interruptions in the *Kogiroku* from volume 1 to the final volume 21 (volumes 1–6, 8, 10, 13, 15, 21) and was followed later by the publication of *Fukokuron* in twelve separate volumes. In June of the year Meiji 17 [1884] volumes 1–4 were published in one combined volume as *Fukokuron, the First Volume, written by Mr Adam Smith of England; supervised by Shaku Sinpachi of Japan; translated by Eisaku Ishikawa of Japan*, and in May of Meiji 18 [1885] volumes 5–8 appeared as *Fukokuron, the Second Volume, written by Mr Adam Smith of England; translated by Eisaku Ishikawa of Japan*. Volumes 9–12 were published in April of Meiji 21 [1888] as *Fukokuron, the Third Volume, written by Mr Adam Smith of England; translated separately by Eisaku Ishikawa and Seisaku Saga of Japan*. The first combined volume was 754 pages of A5 text, the second 787 pages, and the third 970 pages; all three were published by Keizai Zasshi-sha [the Economic Magazine Publishing Company] and printed by Shuei-sha. These three volumes were the first complete version of *WN* in Japan, and in April of the year Meiji 25 [1892] a two-volume reprinted edition was published.

Incidentally, prior to this, during the years Meiji 18–19 [1885–6], his translation of Book 4 of *WN* made Ishikawa realize its importance, so that apart from the complete set, he published Book 4 separately, in two volumes with the addition of an introduction by Ukichi Taguchi and entitled *Fukokuron Yoran* [A Manual of Fukokuron]. What his intentions were in this publication is described in clear terms in the "Translator's Preface".

accordingly Book 4 constitutes a detailed refutation of the errors of the commercial system by application of the principles and laws explicated in the several preceding Books and clarifies the truth that a vital means to advance the wealth of society is not a policy of intervention and protection but free trade. It is indeed the kernel of the entire work. Having arrived at this Book in my translating work, I was convinced that while one is unable to become familiar with the general outline of *WN* unless one has read through the whole five Books and has gained a deep appreciation of them, no other Book indeed is more profitable to the age than this Book and, even without reading the whole work, by the most careful examination of this chapter one comes to the knowledge of the faults of protectionist policy and can adequately realize the great benefit accruing to a free-trading society. Since it might happen that people find it somewhat inconvenient to read through such a voluminous work, the selective publication of this particular Book should do a great deal of good to the public by making it much easier to consult.

This comment speaks thoroughly of the social background of the first complete Japanese version of *WN*.

3

About twenty years after, *Fukokuron* translated by Seiki Mikami was to appear, but in the meantime Japanese militaristic expansion was getting under way through the Sino-Japanese War [1894–5] and the Russo-Japanese War [1904–5], in response to which a drastic change of domestic industry and external economic relations was taking place. Since under these circumstances an argument for free trade as presented in the early years of Meiji could no longer prove effective, and since instead of Smith, the Continental, particularly German Historical School-type of arguments for protection, regulated domestic economy, and ideological statism were gaining influence over public opinion, the way in which Smith was evaluated naturally became somewhat cool and detached. The economic climate of Japan which had promoted the complete translation of Adam Smith in the early Meiji underwent a great change during these decades. As clearly observed in the cases of the Keio Gijuku and the Imperial University of Tokyo, Smith's *WN* was used instead as an academic text at universities.

Adam Smith; Fukokuron translated by Seiki Mikami was published in July of the year Meiji 43 [1910] together with an introduction by Shigenobu Okuma's. At 367 A5 pages, it was based upon Professor Ashley's abridged text, *Selected Chapters and Passages from WN* (1895), which means that it was a selective, not summarized, version made up of only the theoretical parts of the books of *WN*. Since Ashley's edition was widely used in universities at the time, it is no wonder that Seiki Mikami's version was published. However, in general, it was presumably academic rather than policy-making interest which produced such a version as this.

Here a quotation from Shigenobu Okuma's "Introduction" added to this version should give a clue to a Japanese statesman's view of Smith in those days:

It should be superfluous for me to explain that Adam Smith established the foundation of political economy by abstracting from contemporary economic thought and, as the master of political economy, exercised an enduring as well as a predominant influence over European and American societies from the late eighteenth to the nineteenth centuries. Since then, the progress of time and a change in social conditions have naturally given rise to a change of doctrines. Hence the rise of the national and historical economic thought which developed in Germany in opposition to the doctrinal nature of Adam Smith and whose lineage appears to be in total contradiction. Nevertheless, when examined in detail, as well-informed people no doubt agree, the system of political economy in Germany is not a little indebted, with varying levels of accuracy, to Adam Smith in its origin. In Japan too, as anyone should know, the doctrinal nature of Adam Smith has made an effective contribution to the development of economic thought since the Restoration [1868]. Obviously, the social condition today is not entirely identical with the age of Adam Smith. Economic doctrines also are not entirely free from changes. Although the doctrine of individualist *laissez-faire* cannot be dogmatized, there is no room for doubting that *WN*, still a glorious classic in the world of political economy, provides healthy inspiration and valuable suggestions and enlightens readers considerably.

Here one can observe a change of attitude to Adam Smith and to the "great benefit" of "free trade".

4

Around fifteen years later, the year Taisho 12 [1923] was the bicentenary of the birth of Adam Smith. Let alone in Britain, in Japan the Keio Gijuku, the Imperial University of Tokyo, the Imperial University of Kyoto, and the Higher Commercial School of Tokyo (Hitotsubashi University) held their respective memorial conferences, public lectures on the doctrines of Adam Smith, and exhibitions of Smith's works—and every event turned out to be a success. Prior to this, in the year Taisho 3 [1914], the *Fukokuron* (No. 98, Akagi Library) translated by Sakuro Nagao was published and arguably received a wide circulation, but this was an abridged version. In terms of a complete version of *WN*, the *Fukokuron: A Complete Translation* (three volumes, years Taisho 10–12 [1921–3]) translated by Kenji Takeuchi was ready for the bicentenary, and *Adam Smith: Kokufuron* translated by Kanju Kiga was published as part of the Classics of Political Economy series in the year Taisho 15 [1926]. To our regret, only the first volume [out of the projected two] of Kanju Kiga's stylistically fine version was published and the translator died without publishing the second. While there was a partly translated *Fukokuron* by Bunzo Kaminaga in the year Taisho 14 [1925], Kenji Takeuchi's version was the only complete one after Eisaku Ishikawa's version. Successive translations of Smith's main work during the late Taisho years were possibly due to the bicentenary of Smith in Taisho 12, but that was not the only reason. On the contrary, the bicentenary itself and such ostentatious events as were carried out, nowhere else but here in Japan, with the full commitment of the academic world, may be accounted for by an enormous change of circumstances in the world after the First World War, the coming of a post-war recession within Japan combined with a standstill in the imperialistic expansion of the "Great Japanese Empire", an alternative outlook of individual liberty and social welfare seemingly representing a new age, and still more, an upsurge of labour questions and the socialist movement in Japan and a flood of Marxist thought and socialist literature flowing from abroad. Presumably these circumstances and the rapidly changing situation necessarily directed people's attention once again to *WN*. In this case, people characteristically tried to pick out chiefly the progressive element and social concern from Smith's scientific inquiry.

It should be noted that the *Fukokuron* translated by Kenji Takeuchi was based upon the second Cannan edition published in 1920 (first edition 1904), which means that it was based upon Smith's original fifth edition. The translator completed his version with Cannan's permission, but with the omission of all of Cannan's own headnotes (subtitles) and numerous footnotes, incorporating merely Cannan's relatively lengthy introduction. He entitled the three-volume work *Fukokuron* because, as he mentions in the first edition Introduction, "I simply follow the way in which this work has been generally entitled in Japan. There are some who call it *Shokokumin no Tomi* or *Kokufuron*. Later, in July of Taisho 14 [1925], Dr Takeuchi published from the same publisher, Yuhikaku, the first volume of "the revised and enlarged reprinted edition" ("revised edition" hereafter) under the new title *Kokufuron: A Complete Translation* with the recovery of the headlines and the abridged footnotes from the Cannan edition. It included Cannan's Introduction and the original first and second Books. Immediately after 10 August of the year Taisho 12 [1923], when the third volume of Takeuchi's older edition was published, the fire caused by the Great Kanto Earthquake destroyed the matrix and this, by coincidence, gave him an opportunity to revise the older edition in its entirety, the outcome of which was published as the first volume of the revised *Kokufuron* in the year Taisho 14 [1925]. However, since a rapid change of the conditions in the printing business subsequent to the Great Kanto Earthquake made it practically impossible to publish the second volume of this extremely magnificent and expensive edition, it was decided to publish a new, inexpensive three-volume edition from Kaizo-sha—the Kaizo Library—a volume at a time after the year Showa 6 [1931]. The revised first volume cost as much as 10 yen, whereas the Kaizo Library edition was merely 80 sen [0.8 yen]. Concerning this, Dr Takeuchi, the translator, writes as follows in his explanatory notes:

the first edition (in three volumes) was a hobby in my life as a businessman. It was full of dissatisfactions. Fortunately a total destruction of the matrix caused by that Great Earthquake gave me a good chance to revise my version. In July of the year Taisho 14 [1925] the first volume of the completely revised edition was published. My two-year stay in France, a flood at YEN-PON [the one-yen library], and the resultant sudden fall in the standard price of books has made it difficult till now to publish an expensive edition in the former style. I was fortunate this time to have Yuhikaku's ready agreement to publish a cheap edition which I here publicize as a new edition (for the Kaizo Library) with a lot of revisions.

Therefore the revised edition of *WN* published in the year Taisho 14 by the publisher Yuhikaku finished with the first volume, the second and subsequent volumes to be continued but never actually published, and the inexpensive Kaizo Library edition in three volumes was out in the world several years after.

The year after Taisho 14 [1925], when Takeuchi's revised first volume was published, the above-mentioned first volume of *Kokufuron* translated by Kanju Kiga was published by Iwanami Publishing Company. It was a bulky 810 A5 pages with the addition of "The explanatory notes for *WN*" and "The life of Adam Smith", both written by Seiichiro Takahashi. This version was only the first volume [out of the projected two] and as such, in the year Showa 2 [1927], it was put into the Iwanami Library with the omission of Dr Takahashi's essays. Later, in the years Showa 3–4 [1928–9], the complete version of *Kokufuron* translated by Suekichi Aono, based upon the original ninth edition, was published in two volumes. Both volumes are included among "The Complete Works of the *Great Thoughts of the World*" (published by Shunju-sha, vols. 11–12). This version was published against the background of the rising popularity of cheap complete series at that time and presumably received considerable circulation. The version, incidentally, was due to be published in a four-volume set in the Shunju Library in the year Showa 8 [1933] and mirrors the wide circulation of the Takeuchi version of *Kokufuron* in the Kaizo Library. Whatever the reason, the spread of cheap editions shows that such an academic magnum opus as *WN* was eventually putting down roots among the wider reading public. While the extent to which Adam Smith's economic thought was understood is to be questioned, it is none the less obvious that *WN* ceased to be the interest exclusively of a narrow circle of academic scholars. Notably it is certainly the case that there was a rising general interest in the name of Smith as well as that of Marx and in *WN* as well as the *Capital* in the sense that Marx and the *Capital* powerfully attracted people's interest and that Marxism began to exercise an overwhelming influence over the intellectual world of Japan under the prolonged recession and the economic crisis, global and financial, from the end of Taisho to the early Showa.

Thus, the *Kokufuron* translated by Kenji Takeuchi was published in a Kaizo Library edition—the first and second volumes in the year Showa 6 [1931] and the third volume in the year Showa 8 [1933]—and it is likely that *WN* had finally grasped a wide and stable part of the reading public. Later, in the year Showa 15 [1940], the first volume of the *Kokufuron* translated by Hyoe Ohuchi was published as part of the Iwanami Library by Iwanami Publishing Company. Since then till post-war today, *WN*, centring around this version with a change of title, has made a lasting and widespread contribution to the world of reading. This version was based upon the Cannan edition—the fifth edition of *WN* (the last during Smith's lifetime)—and accordingly included the translation of all of Cannan's footnotes, headnotes (headlines), introduction, index, and so on, from which it follows that, since the Cannan edition is itself difficult to obtain today, it is an infinitely serviceable version for readers in this respect.

5

As the foregoing accounts show, Hyoe Ohuchi's version, published in September of the year Showa 15 [1940] in the Iwanami Library edition, was based upon the Cannan edition and entitled *Kokufuron*. Concerning this point, the translator notes as follows in the "Translator's Introduction": "Although the title of the work should correctly be called *An Inquiry into the Nature and Causes of the Wealth of Nations*, I followed the abridged title *Kokufuron* in view of its fairly wide circulation in our academic world. Other abridged titles such as *Fukokuron* or *Shokokumin no Tomi* are also in use, but they do not seem significantly better than *Kokufuron*." Hyoe Ohuchi's version of *WN* was to be a five-volume set in the Iwanami Library and the second volume was published in the year Showa 16, the third in the year Showa 17, the fourth in the year Showa 18, and the fifth was published in the year Showa 19, consisting of the chapter on "The National Debt" (Book 5, Chapter 3 of *WN*) and the index, with the addition of the translator's lengthy "Explanatory Notes". To many readers, the completion of the Ohuchi version was undeniably a great delight which was enhanced by the excellence of its literary style despite the degraded paper quality, which suggested, in the final phase of the Pacific War, the increasingly worsened situation during the war. Presumably the translator, working under the war-time condition of limited freedom of the press, devoted his whole energy to translating *WN*. Since then, for a long period of time before and after the war, Ohuchi's Iwanami Library edition of *The Wealth of Nations* in five volumes has proved to be an enormous success thanks to an extensive reading public.

Incidentally, as late as the year Showa 34 [1959] Ohuchi's revised version was published as the same Iwanami Library edition (in five volumes) to be completed in the year Showa 41 [1966] with a change of title to *Shokokumin no Tomi* and by the joint translation of Hyoe Ohuchi and Sichiro Matsukawa. In the "Translator's Preface", one of the translators, Dr Hyoe Ohuchi, writes of the following circumstances:

The first volume of the older Iwanami Library edition of *WN* was published in September 1940 (the year Showa 15) and its final, fifth volume was published in November 1944. Although there was no assurance of the edition being particularly more distinguished than the other versions, it has gained a considerable number of readers over the last fifteen years. This is due to social recognition of the importance of Smith as a result of the study of economics growing rapidly popular in the post-war years, and partly to the fact that the edition was in the Iwanami Library. In the mean time, with its matrix getting worn out, my rendering outdated, and the use of syllabary old style, I had found it my duty to revise the edition. This was also a great wish on the part of Iwanami Publishing Company. However, since I was pretty busy, I recommended, for the translator to be commissioned to do the work, a friend of mine, Shichiro Matsukawa, to Iwanami Publishing Company. He was kind enough to agree on the condition that it be a joint work with myself and executed the painstaking translation. For all our agreement that I would further improve his version, reading through it made me realize that there was no room left for that. Therefore this version is his own work in its entirety. But, in the light of the foregoing circumstance and of the publisher's request, I decided to have my name included as a joint translator.

This clarifies the process by which the Ohuchi version developed into the Ohuchi–Matsukawa joint version, and a further account is given with reference to its relationship to the Cannan edition and its title.

The older version was based upon the Cannan edition but with the omission of Professor Cannan's "Introduction", "Editor's Introduction" and part of the footnotes. However, since all of these now have, in my view, a classic importance and provide readers with substantial reference to the variant readings of the original editions, the origin of the work, and the context of the author's thought, etc., they are incorporated into the present version. The abridged title given in the older version, *Kokufuron*, has been changed to *Shokokumin no Tomi* this time. It was decided after some discussion with the publisher to follow the latter title on the assumption that it has now a wider currency in Japan's scholarly world.

It is possible to see through the above comment on revised translation the process of joint translation, the motives for revision, and the reason for the change of title. Later, in the year Showa 44 [1969], the Ohuchi–Matsukawa joint version was reissued in a two-volume "deluxe hard-cover edition" to the delight of readers. In this deluxe edition further, more elaborate improvement and polishing was undertaken. It suggests that the pains to be taken in translating work are truly endless.

6

Such were the realization and the transformation of the Hyoe Ohuchi version of *Kokufuron* and of the Ohuchi–Matsukawa joint version of *Shokokumin no Tomi*. From this single subject we know the degree to which Japanese people have respected Adam Smith's economic writing and their inexhaustible affection for it as a true classic. The same thing can be imagined in further generalization by the fact that since the beginning of Meiji one and the same *WN* by Smith has repeatedly been rendered by the hands of different translators. It may arguably be called a unique phenomenon, no equivalent of which is observable in other countries.

On the other hand, Kenji Takeuchi's version of *WN* was later taken over by Keiyu-sha and still later by Tokyo University Press (3 vols., the year Showa 44 [1969]) to preserve the idiosyncrasy of his style of translation. There are very few as pertinacious in authenticity of rendering as him. To trace further back, in the post-war year Showa 24 [1949], the first volume of Tsuneo Hori's version of *WN* was published by Shunju-sha. This version translates as far as Book 1 Chapter 10 of *WN* for the first volume but following volumes have not been published. It is based upon the fifth edition but does not incorporate Cannan's headnotes (headlines) and footnotes. Its defining characteristic is found in the translator's own substantial notes to each chapter provided jointly with Professor Yasujiro Daido. While it is regrettabe that this version ended with the other volumes unpublished, its editorial policy is similar to ours in not depending upon Cannan's notes and in providing instead translator's notes from a standpoint of the history of economic doctrines.

Down to the year Showa 40 [1965], Professor Hiroshi Mizuta's laborious two-volume set ("The Great Thinkers of the World" vols. 14–15) was published by Kawade Publishing Company based upon the first edition (1776) of *WN*. It is unique in being based upon the first edition whereas other versions are all based upon the Cannan edition of the [original] fifth edition. It is not only extremely serviceable for comparing the variant readings between the first edition (1776) and the fifth edition (1789, the last during the author's lifetime), but also, with the addition of the translator's own explanatory notes upon the variant readings of each edition, greatly profitable to professional Smith scholars as well as to general readers.

In the year Showa 43 [1968] also, *WN* was published as one of "The Great Thinkers of the World" (vol. 31, ed. Kazuo Okochi, Chuo Koron-sha). This is based upon the Cannan edition but not a complete version. It selectively translates in one volume merely what are considered to be the most important parts; for the rest, several translators cooperated in making an abridged version to be inserted into the text to make good the defects of the selected version. Cannan's headnotes (subtitles and footnotes) were not followed and were replaced by the translators' own "subtitles". Additionally provided are translator's notes, as in the Tsuneo Hori version, many illustrations, and an index of the translators' own making. The opening substantial essay "Adam Smith and *WN*" (written by Kazuo Okochi) is of use to readers who want to understand the intellectual-historical significance and background of *WN*.

Appendix: Translator's Introduction to the 1976 Japanese Edition, by Kazuo Okochi

The circumstances which have finally led to the present Japanese version of *WN* must be traced back to the version of *WN* published for the first time as one of *The Great Books of the World* of Chuo Koron-sha (Showa 43 [1968]). *WN* in *The Great Books of the World* provided a complete translation of only some parts and gave abridged accounts for the rest. However, among those who joined in the translation (Yoshiro Tamanoi, Kyoji Tazoe, and Akio Okochi and myself) it was considered that, in order to correctly understand Smith, it would be necessary sooner or later to thoroughly translate these abridged parts also and to achieve a complete version of *WN*, and that although the abridged parts had so far been read relatively little by the general public, those parts were of rather greater significance for the grasp of Smith's economics, or preferably "political economy", from the perspective of practical issues as they really were.

Thus, while the project to produce a complete version of *WN* was under way among the related people early on, the translating work tended to be stagnant, pressurized by the consciousness of translating the "classic". It was also necessary to discover in Smith's text the relationships in which a seemingly indifferent passage had a serious meaning or in which an intimate and concealed connection existed between an author to whom Smith made merely a passing allusion and Smith's own thought, as was possibly the case in common with contemporary authors. Also required was to translate *WN* with a full knowledge of the problems of eighteenth-century economic history and particularly the problems revealed in the contrast between England and Scotland, as well as to identify the relationships with Smith's predecessors who had profound influence upon his economic thought and social thought. There are a considerable number of facts of which eighteenth-century British readers would have necessarily shared a common knowledge, but about which modern Japanese readers do not have the slightest clue. With all these considerations in mind, the idea of translating *WN* was extremely oppressive, but the fact that the bicentenary of the publication of *WN* was approaching whipped us up. We found it right to give our present version a sense of anniversary and, encouraged by this idea, we prosecuted the work vigorously but desperately.

As discussed among ourselves ever since we started the new translation of *WN*, it had to be decided whether it was right or wrong to base it upon the Cannan edition, which was then [and is now] widely used in Japan. The Cannan edition was originally based upon the fifth edition of *WN* (published in 1789), the last edition during Smith's lifetime. Even if its use was proper, Cannan's headnotes (subtitles), placed against almost every single paragraph and assuming the style of a continued account when followed independently, are likely to prevent one from grasping the textual meanings of *WN*. We found it necessary, therefore, to supply "subtitles", independently of Cannan's, which cover several paragraphs and represent what is being aimed at in Smith's accounts; and this policy is implemented in our version. Furthermore, as a number of "footnotes" in the Cannan edition are more concerned with technical investigation into the differences between editions of *WN*: wordings, expressions, etc. of each edition of *WN*, and sometimes about bibliographical curiosities, we found it still more important to supply our own translators' notes, upon the basis of the achievements of economics after Smith, and to insert notes at proper places in more generalized terms upon the problems of more fundamental importance to readers determined to read through *WN*, such as subjects of social and economic history or problems related to the history of economic thought. Consequently, with the total omission of Smith's "index", which was added by Smith himself to the end of editions after the third—though it is unlikely to have been composed by Smith himself—and of a vast amount of Cannan's footnotes and headnotes, we alternatively placed at proper junctures subtitles, translator's notes, and an index, which we made as useful as possible, in the translators' judgement, for understanding *WN*. Needless to say, Cannan's footnotes are extremely erudite, and from them, we happily acknowledge, the translator's notes of this edition derived enormous conveniences. Incidentally, in this new version, along with the translator's notes, a number of inserted notes are supplied in the text in order to complement those points which are not immediately clear in the translation.

The title of the present version has been given as *Kokufuron*. It is correctly *An Inquiry into the Nature and Causes of the Wealth of Nations*, and this original title was not changed between the first and the fifth editions. As titles of the Japanese version, there have been *Fukokuron*, *Kokufuron*, and *Shokokumin no Tomi* and in this version, *Kokufuron* is adopted. In Japan since the beginning of Meiji, there have been truly countless versions of Smith's chief work. In early years *Fukokuron*, and later on *Kokufuron*, were generally used, and after the Second World War, *Shokokumin no Tomi* began to be used (for this point, see "A Short History" above). It goes without saying that the present new version has benefited from the past versions of the Japanese translation, and we would like to acknowledge the infinite suggestions which we reaped particularly from Kenji Takeuchi's version of the *Kokufuron* and Hyoe Ohuchi's and Shichiro Matsusukawa's version of the *Shokokmin no Tomi*. The present new version has been made possible by the painstaking achievements of these predecessors. Notably, the present new version owes a great deal to the above two versions in the sense that these were based upon the Cannan edition, which is an annotated version of the fifth edition. However the present version is different from them in that, though similarly based upon the fifth edition of *WN*, we have supplied our own headnotes (subtitles), footnotes, and index in place of Cannan's.

[*Editor's note*: This text originally appeared as the appendix to the 1976 Japanese translation of *WN*, authored by Kazuo Okochi, late professor of economics at Tokyo University. The translator is Tatsuya Sakamoto of Keio University. Brackets in text are supplied by the translator, but parentheses are in the original. To provide complementary information, parts of Okochi's "translator's introduction" is also translated as the appendix to this English text.]

6.2. Shiro Sugihara, 1982.
Adam Smith in Japan

Abridged by Cheng-chung Lai and translated by Aiko Ikeo

It is evident that a copy of the original *Wealth of Nations* arrived in Japan for the first time between 1863 and 1868. It is recorded that two copies of *The Theory of Moral Sentiments,* one in English and another in French, were obtained by Japanese libraries before 1887. The fact that several versions of Japanese translations of Smith's works have been published since then tells us that Adam Smith has been popular among the Japanese for a little more than a hundred years. Six complete Japanese versions of *The Wealth of Nations* have become available, one before 1900, three in the first half of the twentieth century, two in the last half. It may be unique, in comparison with other countries, that three of them, by K. Takeuchi, by H. Ouchi and S. Matsukawa, and by H. Mizuta, are still widely read in Japan. Yet there is only one Japanese edition of *The Theory of Moral Sentiments,* which was translated by T. Yonebayashi.

Why has Adam Smith been so popular in Japan for such a long time? How was Smith read by the Japanese? These questions interest not only Smith specialists but also those who study the development of social sciences in Japan and/or the modernization of Japan's society. Let us discuss how Smith was read as a social scientist and thinker in Japan from a historical viewpoint. We will also review the historical study of Smith and classical economists.

We will examine the period before the end of the Pacific War in 1945 and that after 1945. There was a conspicuous trend for studying Smith in relation to Marx because Marxism has had a big influence on Japanese social scientists and social thinkers since around 1910, and even more so after the post-war period. Therefore, the historical development of Japanese social and economic thought cannot be told without referring to Marxism. It might be useful to consider how Smith was read by Marx to summarize Japanese interest in Smith. Sections 1 and 3 handle Smith in pre-war and in post-war Japan, respectively. Section 2 [omitted in this translation] considers Marx on Smith.

1. Adam Smith in Pre-War Japan

1. Yukichi Fukuzawa was one of the men who was responsible for making Adam Smith known to the Japanese in the 1870s. The following are passages from his writings. In his *Encouragement for Learning* (1874), "Adam Smith was the first to discuss economic laws and has changed the way of business completely." In his *Outline of Civilization* (1875), "As Adam Smith discussed economic laws, the wisest man would examine the causes of wealth in general and guide the people to this learning." In his *On the Private Economy* (1877), "The concept of the division of labour . . . has been included in introductory courses to political economy since an English economist named Adam Smith invented and discussed it." Fukuzawa not only referred to Smith in his writings but also taught his students at Keio University and the general reader of his publications the importance of economic life—the laws of which were explained by Smith—and therefore the importance of economic science, a social science which analyses the economy. Thus he contributed to enhancing Japanese people's interest in Smith as the father of the economic discipline.

Political economy was included in the curriculum of elementary and junior high school and earnestly taught in private as well as national and public schools. Many Keio graduates became teachers of political economy in such schools. Political economy was an important subject in special private schools, such as Senshu School and Tokyo Senmon Gakko (Waseda), which were established in the 1880s and later became universities. It was always lectured on in certain private law schools, too. It can be said that by around 1890 Adam Smith became well known in Japan as the father of political economy and the author of *The Wealth of Nations*.

It is certain that Smith's economic doctrine got spread partly by the complete Japanese version of *The Wealth of Nations* which was published in 1888 by E. Ishikawa and S. Saga, who were on the staff of an economic magazine organized by U. Taguchi. However, what was more important was the publication of various introductory books on political economy, especially M. G. Fawcett's *Political Economy for Beginners* (5th edn., 1880; 8th edn., 1896). Fawcett's book was the most widely read among this kind of books for beginners. It was reprinted in Japan, translated into Japanese, and explained in economic books originally written in Japanese. The book and related ones were used as textbooks and served as sources of standard economic knowledge in Japan. The following four points were important from her explanation of Smith's political economy. (1) Smith in his *Wealth of Nations* criticized Mann's *British Treasure in Foreign Trade* and revealed the fallacy of mercantilism. "[He] for the first time in England elucidated the genuine nature of money and made it clear that the exports and imports of a nation should be equilibrated by the abolition of the restricted tariffs." (2) Smith listed three merits resulting from the division of labour and clarified how they increased productivity. (3) Smith enumerated five possible causes of the wage differentials among various occupations. (4) Smith established four principles that should minimize the burden of taxpayers and maximize the state revenue.

It is true that the Japanese of the nineteenth century got a narrower understanding of Smith by mainly reading Fawcett. They did not systematically understand the above four points in the edifice of Smith's economic thought. Their understanding of Smith was so fragmented and pragmatic that they picked up each point individually, connected it directly to a current topic, and used it in policy-making. Yet Smith was well known not only among the intelligentsia and economic scholars but also by the general public. It may be said that Smith was regarded not just as a great economist of the past, but also to some degree as a living guide for people who were striving to create a new society. For example, they maintained that the freedom of business should be protected from state interventionism, that labour earnings should be equalized unless there is any definite reason for the wage differentials, and that arbitrary or inefficient taxation should not be allowed for states. They were confident that a society based on the division of labour and exchange can increase labour productivity. Looking at the nationwide social conditions of the time, the movement for freedom and democracy and the petition for the establishment of the national diet were the cores of the political campaign. The situation was backed up both by the steady economic development and by the learning of political economy by the people, including students in Tokyo and the general public in rural districts. This means that Japan's society was becoming mature enough to sympathize with Smith's thought and doctrine, I think. However, as Japanese capitalism was being shaped under the constitution granted by the Japanese Emperor, the Japanese chose to introduce social sciences from the German-speaking world rather than from the English-speaking world. Political economy degenerated into just a branch of *Staatswissenshaft* (German political science) rather than coming from the core of social sciences. At any rate, Japanese academicians gradually embarked on elaborated studies of economics around 1910, although they seem to have studied economics for its own sake. In the early twentieth century, economic magazines were divided into three kinds: academic journals of economics, business magazines for those who were launching into business, and labour magazines handling social and labour problems. All-round magazines such as U. Taguchi's *Tokyo Economic Magazine* (1879–), S. Tokutomi's *People's Magazine* (1887–), and T. Amano's *Japan Financial Magazine* (1889–) had lost their own distinctive role although they had played some part in focusing on economic problems.

2. Masayoshi Mikami translated William J. Ashley's abridged version of *The Wealth of Nations* (1895) into Japanese and published it in 1910. In the Introduction Shigenobu Okuma said, "Adam Smith's ideas contributed to the development of economic thought in Japan, too. . . . The current social conditions in Japan are not the same as in the time of Smith . . . so individual *laissez-faireism* is not necessarily regarded as a golden rule. However, *The Wealth of Nations* is as before shining classic literature in political economy." Tokyo Senmon Gakko, a private college school established by Okuma, was eager to introduce English social sciences, whereas the Imperial University of Tokyo was inclined to do German political science.

In their organ *Mita Gakkai Zasshi* Keio University had a memorial issue to Smith published in April 1911. It was the first special issue dedicated to an economist in Japanese journals and carried articles on Smith's economics, ethics, and politics. This implies that the writers tried to discuss Smith's edifice as a whole and the academicians embarked on serious studies on Smith. Special studies of Smith were made by K. Kiga, S. Takahashi, and S. Koizumi of Keio University, I. Nitobe of the Imperial University of Tokyo, T. Fukuda of Tokyo University of Commerce, and H. Kawakami of Kyoto Imperial University. The Japanese celebrated the bicentenary of Adam Smith's birth in 1923. They held lecture meetings and exhibitions in commemoration around 6 June, Smith's birthday, in Tokyo and Kyoto. Plenty of people got together for the events. The main academic journals in Japan published special issues on Smith one after another and enhanced the study of Smith to fever pitch.

The following two were the important background elements. In the first place, the Imperial University of Tokyo and Kyoto Imperial University finally established their departments of economics in 1919. In the second, the first complete Japanese version of Karl Marx's *Capital* and the second one of Smith's *Wealth of Nations* were published around 1920. These books helped raise the status of economic science in Japan and made the general public interested in economics. The new University Ordinance aimed to reshuffle higher education in Japan. It stated that in 1920 the two college schools of commerce were to be promoted to universities of commerce, and that Waseda and Keio were to be reorganized into universities with several departments. It also stated that the departments of economics should become independent of the departments of jurisprudence at the two imperial universities. This means that economics was liberated from German-style political science. The period after the First World War was accompanied by the rapid progress of Japanese capitalism and the aggravation of social conditions, so it needed social sciences, especially economics, which could handle the new social and economic problems. It was Marxism which was expected by some of the Japanese intelligentsia to meet the needs of the time and which played a part in enlightening the people about the importance of economic science which clarified the substructure of society. . . .

Hajime Kawakami reported the serious social problems in his *Tale of Poverty* (1917), initiated the journal entitled *Study of Social Problems*, and engaged in the study and dissemination of Marxism. He not only welcomed the publication of the Japanese translation of *Capital* but also recommended that Kenji Takeuchi translate *The Wealth of Nations* into Japanese. When Takeuchi was studying under Iwasaburo Takano in the Ohara Institute for Social Research and reading F. Engel's *The Condition of the Working Class in England*, he was advised by Kawakami to begin with Adam Smith and study British economists for a decade before reading Marxist literature. Thus the second complete Japanese translation of *The Wealth of Nations* was undertaken and later accomplished.

Some articles in the memorial issues on Smith referred to Marx. S. Kawatsu wrote, "it was reasonable from the situation of his day that Smith did not consider so-called capitalist–labourer relations. He tried to explain price by labour value. Yet he never expected that his ideas would become the basis for Karl Marx's socialism." K. Kiga argued differently and wrote, "Smith was always fair in making judgements from a broader viewpoint of social benefit. His impartial attitude is a good beacon for the narrow-minded contemporary thinkers who have been making a deep study of one thing." Kiga seemed to criticize Hajime Kawakami because Kawakami in his *The Modern History of Economic Thought* (1919) positioned Smith as the origin of Marx's thought. K. Tajima, who was hostile to Marx, thought that there were two currents of thought on value, subjectivism and objectivism, and regarded Smith as an example of the latter. Tajima said, "David Ricardo was the leading objectivist after Smith. However, socialists such as Lassalle and Marx engaged in a narrow and extreme speech campaign on the ground of their erroneous economic doctrines. Some factions of socialists often take Smith and Ricardo's doctrines as golden rules and decorate their own bigoted ideas with these doctrines. We really resent these socialists and feel a thousand pities for Mr Smith and others." On the other hand, C. Maide, K. Minabe, and H. Kawakami and Y. Taniguchi in their articles on Smith discussed Smith's labour theory of value in relation to Marx and anticipated the path of the historical development of economic doctrines on the basis of the comparison. This indicates that the special issues carried contradictory articles on Smith and Marx.

The later Smith scholars mainly picked up Smith's theory of value and distribution with reference to Marx's theory of value and surplus value. S. Kuruma, K. Mori, and K. Hatano published articles on Smith in this line while Marx's *The History of Economic Doctrines* was translated into Japanese by the staff of Ohara Institute for Social Research. C. Maide covered the studies on Smith along this line including the latest achievements in his *Outline of the History of Economic Thought*, vol. 1 (1937). Maide, whose 1923 article was the best written on Smith of the time, exposed Smith's entire economic doctrine in detail in more than a hundred pages of his mature 1937 book. He believed as much as in his youth that the labour theory of value was the core of Smith's economics.

3. The year 1940 was the one-hundred-and-fiftieth anniversary of Smith's death. Although Europeans seemed to be unable to do anything special for Smith owing to the Second World War, in Japan some universities held memorial lecture meetings, and a few newspapers and magazines had special issues on Smith. The mood in Japan had changed from the so-called Taisho Democratic Movement (1912–25), when the bicentenary of Smith's birth was celebrated cheerfully, to the tension in the final moments before the Pacific War (1941–5) in co-operation with other members of the Axis (i.e. Germany and Italy). So, the events for Smith were much more modest than in 1923. Scholars were forced to refrain from referring to Marx and the related literature in their publications.

A third vogue for Smith was witnessed in the plight during several years following 1940. A series of outstanding works on Smith were published. For example, the third complete Japanese version of *The Wealth of Nations*, in five volumes, was published between September 1940 and January 1945. The following four were the best works on Smith during the period: (1) Y. Daido's *The Economics of Smith in the Making* (November 1940); (2) Z. Takashima's *The Fundamental Problems in Econo-Sociology: Smith and List as Econo-Sociologists* (March 1941); (3) K. Okochi's *Smith and List: Economic Ethics and Economic Theory* (June 1943); (4) S. Shirasugi's series of papers on Smith during 1940 and 1943.

In Daido (1940), Smith's formation of economic thought during a period of seventeen years was examined from his *Lectures in Edinburgh* (1749) to his *Lectures in Glasgow* (1762–63) to his *Early Drafts* of *The Wealth of Nations* (1763), to his *Wealth of Nations* (1776). Daido elaborated Smith's inner history of economic study in relation to Smith's system of moral philosophy. Takashima

(1941) tried ambitiously to create econo-sociology, a third science which could unite the rational, objective understanding in modern economics and the intuitive, subjective understanding in political economy. He hoped to find a clue in the shift from Smith's human [or individual] productivity to List's national productivity. He inquired into how Smith had united the three worlds, moral, legal and economic (part 2, "Adam Smith on the problems of the civil society"). Okochi (1943) tried to clarify the following points from the viewpoint of the history of economic thought. Smith told us that the problem of economic ethics could not be solved without referring to the development of productivity. Both Smith and List in fact tried to create theories for the establishment and development of the national economy as a unit and focused on the problems of the domestic market, although their economics appeared contradictory. Shirasugi (1940–3) traced the foundation of individual economic ethics back to Smith and discussed the concepts of justice, patriotism, and love of mankind in Smith's *Moral Sentiments*. He concluded that they needed to go beyond Smith, but not to refuse Smith, in order to prevent the predominant public opinion from degenerating into a cry for totalitarianism in the critical situation of war.

It can be said that they had three messages in common, although each author had his own interest in his work. In the first place, they stood against the powerful tendency in the academic world of compiling traditional social sciences into a German-type unified political science which was based on the totalitarian stand-point, and insisted on returning to Adam Smith. In the second, they believed that they must consider, not just the economics of Smith, but Smith's edifice of thought, including his view of the society and mankind, and thus delve deeply into Smith, and that then they should be able to reach a full mastery of Smith. In the third place, their strong concern about the critical situation of the time was seen in their pure, academic studies. We need to read this between the lines in Daido (1940); however, the other three were worried about the future of Japan, which was in haste to place itself on a wartime footing without solving the structural conflict inherent in Japanese capitalism. They strongly resisted the inclination of the academic world, which was making a kind of partisan criticism against Western-born individualism and liberalism, and excluding them from Japan. They were courageous enough to choose Smith against the fashion of German and Japanese nationalistic economics in a tense situation. That is why they were able to produce prominent works on Smith and navigated the varied studies of the history of economic thought after the war.

[Here the translator omits from line 9 of page 19 to line 6 of page 20 and the whole of Section 2.]

3. Adam Smith after the War

1. The decade after the end of the War, 1945–55, witnessed a striking development of Smith studies in Japan. It also saw the vigorous study of the history of economic thought in general as well as economics and every other social science.

The following three conditions were found in the background to these superior Smith studies. In the first place, as outlined in Section 1, Smith studies in Japan had already reached a high level before the War. They were not interrupted during the war as were other social sciences under the so-called thought control by the special police. Rather they achieved new heights and provided the favourable conditions for the post-war study of Smith. In the second place, thanks to the three major democratic reforms in post-war Japan—i.e. the land reform of making owner farmers, the division of big financial cliques, and the organization of labour unions—the Japanese faced realistically the theoretical and practical problems which Smith had confronted in Britain in the last half of the eighteenth century. They approached Smith from both theoretical and practical viewpoints in a synthesized manner. In the third place, the study of Marx was resumed in the post-war period and enthusiastically developed to the core in sympathizing with Smith's problems and in studying Smith in terms of the future. These Marxist studies in fact boosted the study of Smith in Japan.

The Society of Adam Smith (1949–) and the Society for the History of Economic Thought (1950–) gave members significant opportunities to promote the study of Smith and exchange ideas. The members published their works one after another from 1952 until 1955: T. Fujizuka's *Adam Smithian Revolution* (1952), N. Kobayashi's *Mercantilism and Political Economy* (1952), Y. Uchida's *The Birth of Political Economy* (1953), H. Mizuta's *Introduction to Adam Smith* (1954), H. Asobe's *Classical Economists and Marx* (1955).

Section 2 below surveys Smith studies during the first decade after the war. Section 3 shows that the period after around 1955 saw not only studies in the previous line but also studies following a new line, which became more conspicuous after 1970.

2. S. Koshimura's *The Economics of Smith* (1946) and Y. Daido's *Smith Connection* (1947) included their papers published during the war and before; therefore they were not post-war works. It can be said, on the other hand, that K. Tanaka's *Smith and Marx* (1948) was newly written with the approach of the post-war period, as was reflected in the title. The comparison between Smith

and Marx was first taken up by S. Koshimura in his "Smith and Marx on wages" (1947) and Z. Takashima in his "Smith, List, and Marx" (1947). Tanaka (1948) made a laborious comparative study of Smith's and Marx's edifices of thought including economics.

Tanaka (1948) was soon reviewed by Y. Uchida and H. Mizuta. Uchida disagreed with Tanaka on the predominance of natural sciences over social sciences and pointed out some problems with Tanaka's documentation. However, Uchida praised Tanaka and said, "It is absolutely right to consider the two economists with reference to the edifice of their thought, namely, historical materialism and the philosophy of natural rights, and to extract the common elements and the limits of classical economics as the science of history. His acute approach has given Japanese historians of economic thought a direction for the study of Smith following his work." Uchida followed Tanaka and regarded the publication of *The Wealth of Nations* as the signal event of the establishment of economics which could serve as the basic science to help them recognize social systems in history. Mizuta also had the fundamental motif of "Smith and Marx". He studied Smith in the modern history of ideas after Hobbes in Britain. He devoted himself to investigating Smith's library collection and to writing the biography of Smith.

T. Fujizuka and H. Asobe also had the motif of Smith and Marx, although they were more interested in the history of economic thought than in the theoretical aspect. It may be said that N. Kobayashi, who compared Smith with List and Smith with Stuart, had the same motif, because Kobayashi used the legacy of Marx, who was the critical successor of Smith, when he needed a theoretical benchmark in discussing Smith in a historical perspective and comparing Smith with Marx.

Y. Uchida's *The Birth of Economics* (1953) was the most influential masterpiece on Smith in Japan, which portrayed Smith in a most comprehensive manner. Uchida in the introduction "The contemporary task and benchmark of classical studies" declared,

Among Western social sciences, British classical economists, who represented British social and historical sciences, were the first to scientifically delve down into the basic economic processes with the historical sense of social systems. . . . In this respect, British classical economics was not only the classics of economics but also, more importantly, the classics of the science of social systems or history. It should be studied as such. . . . I regarded Marxist economics as the fundamental theory of historical recognition, so the correspondence should be always considered.

Uchida (1953) aimed at opening a third path incorporating the legacy of the two traditional but conflicting approaches to Smith in Japan, one from the viewpoint of the history of value and surplus value theory and another from the history of British civil society in the making.

Uchida (1953) in the first part of two entitled "The birth of economics" examined the sources of Smith's economics, which was suggested by the subtitle "*The Wealth of Nations* as a criticism of the old imperialism". Uchida tried to show what current problems Smith tried to handle in *The Wealth of Nations* and how Smith designed his theoretical framework. Thus Uchida followed the second of the two traditional approaches (the historical approach to civil society) and reorganized it so as to relate it to the economic analysis in *The Wealth of Nations*. Uchida's novel and bold messages created a sensation. For example, Uchida maintained that Smith stood for bourgeois radicalism as he criticized both the Tory principle of authority and the Whiggish principle of utility. Uchida compared Smith's criticism with J. J. Rousseau's French criticism of mercantilism. Uchida asserted that Smith organized *The Wealth of Nations* beginning with the division of labour and ending with the role of states in the scientific, ascending method à la Marx, and that therefore Smith's approach to the analysis of the current topics in Part 4 should be understood as the core of his unified system.

Uchida (1953) in the second part of this essay, "The analysis of the system of *The Wealth of Nations*", followed the first of the two traditional approaches, the one from the viewpoint of the history of value and surplus value theory. Uchida explicated Smith's critical succession of F. Quesnay's reproduction theory and analysed the characteristics of Smith's theory. Thus Uchida tried to expand the study of Smith by incorporating the theory of accumulation. Uchida showed how Quesnay's category of pure product was overcome by Smith's theory of productive labour, which became the classical theory of accumulation.

Among the numerous reviews of Uchida (1953), N. Kobayashi and H. Mizuta's seem to have been the most important ones. Kobayashi disagreed on two points with Uchida although he paid his respects to Uchida's immeasurable passion for the objects, novel motif, and persuasive style. First, Kobayashi did not relate Smith to bourgeois radicalism. Kobayashi said,

I think that the contemporary relevance of Smith's economic system should be considered more cautiously not only in the sense that Smith turned the direct target of radicalism away by replacing political radicalism with economic reforms, but also in the sense that Smith's ideas were actuality used as the weapon for the conclusion of the commercial treaty by the British government.

Second, Kobayashi was dissatisfied with Uchida for his lack of any argument about Smith on money and said, "British mercantilism should be examined as deliberately as Quesnay as the source of Smith's economic theories."

Mizuta praised Uchida (1953) and said, "it is a supreme work on Smith in various points." Mizuta referred to Kobayashi's review and took up the above two points. In terms of the first, Mizuta did not judge Smith to be as radical from Smith's writings as did Uchida. Yet Mizuta halted there and said,

When we push on in Uchida's line, the relationship between Tucker and Smith receives too much emphasis. I presume further that the differences between mercantilism and classical economics will become blurred, and the historical role of bourgeois radicalism will vanish in that line.

On the second point, Mizuta had something to add to Kobayashi:

Kobayashi may be right because I was not so much impressed by Uchida's argument in the last part as by that in the introduction and in the first part. . . . At any rate, what is most questionable is Uchida's method in which he indicates the limits of Smith with reference to Marx while he is forming an intrinsic and positive estimate of Smith.

[The translator omits the last three lines on page 38.]

3. At the end of his review of Uchida (1953) Noboru Kobayashi stated,

It seems that the topic of the relationship of Smith to his forerunners is out there in the vast field to be explored. It can be said that the first materials of older editions provide us with a fertile plain to be cultivated.

Kobayashi later examined numerous writers such as Stuart, Tucker, Temple, Ostwald, Young, and the anonymous author of *Some considerations on rates of interest, especially rates of public bonds*. Kobayashi in his *An Early History of Economics* (1964) wrapped up a particular series of his studies and discussed Smith in the history, or historical reconstruction, of economic thought.

H. Mizuta continued to make a patient and laborious study to complete the catalogue of Smith's library, on the one hand, and published his "Adam Smith's library" (1970) and his *Adam Smith's Library: A Supplement to Bonar's Catalogue with a Checklist of the Whole Library* (in English, 1967). On the other hand, Mizuta further elaborated the biography of Smith and published his *A Study on Adam Smith* (1968), including as the main part "The Life of Adam Smith". Mizuta's third interest was in the so-called Scottish Historical School, which was advocated by Pascal, revived by Meek and Macfie, and promoted in Japan by Mizuta himself. Mizuta's papers in this line were also included in Mizuta (1968) and set the new trend of Scottish Historical School in the study of Smith in Japan.

Y. Uchida was active and undertook a more comprehensive study of Smith than his *The Birth of Economics* (1953). He edited two books, *A Study on Classical*

Economics (vol. 1, 1957) and *The Foundations of the History of Economic Thought* (1964) as volume 1 of *Handbooks on the History of Economic Thought*. He authored two books, *Lectures on the History of Economic Thought* (1961) and *Capitalistic Thought in Japan* (1966). He co-authored a book entitled *The History of Economic Thought* (1970). Uchida became more interested in the history of ideas than in the history of economic doctrines.

T. Hatori and R. Tomizuka followed Uchida and developed the historical study of classical economics. Hatori and Tomizuka published *Classical Economists on Capital Accumulation* (1963) and *The Theory of Accumulation* (1965), respectively. There was some controversy on the interpretation of Smith starting with Kobayashi and Mizuta's reviews on Uchida (1953), igniting Uchida vs. Kobayashi, involving Kobayashi and Hatori, and pulling in Kobayashi vs. K. Tazoe on Stuart.

There were two other new tendencies in the study of Smith apart from interest in the Scottish Historical School—on Smith's *Moral Sentiments* and on Smith on states or government policy. The first Japanese translation of *Moral Sentiments* was published by Tomio Yonebayashi in 1948 and 1949, and a facsimile edition of the original was made by the Society for the History of Economic Thought in Japan. Serious study of *Moral Sentiment* was started by M. Takagi, J. Okada, and A. Hoshino after 1955, and boosted by the papers which H. Mizuta and M. Nozawa presented at the annual meetings of the Society for the History of Economic Thought in Japan. It was to be promoted further by the publication of the new edition (1970) of Yonebayashi's translation and Mizuta's new translation of *Moral Sentiments*, which is forthcoming.

The study of Smith on government policy was effectively launched by H. Saito's "Smith and Marx on public finance and states" (1956) and piloted by R. Yamazaki and S. Wada. Scholars tried to expand Marxist economics into a system which included public finance and government policy according to Marx's plan of criticism of political economy and to respond to the current topic of so-called state-oligopolistic capitalism. This tendency is important because it reflects the approach of the younger generation. Wada in his "The agenda in the study of economic thought" (1963) proposed that this approach (or Marxist attitude) should be followed in the historical study of economic thought in general. S. Miyazaki was introducing the new European trend of reconsidering the long-lived prejudice in economic history and the history of economic thought that all the classicals were for *laissez-faire* and that the nineteenth century was the era of free trade. Miyazaki accepted the approach positively and presented an unconventional interpretation of Smith.

Finally, S. Wada's two articles "Two images of Smith" (1971) and "Stuart on government policy and Smith" (1972) are worth summarizing. Wada (1971) compared Uchida's image of Smith with that of Skinner, a leading British specialist on Smith. First, Wada claimed that both scholars tried to comprehend Smith's edifice as the grand system of social sciences in order to find a clue to the unified social science which contemporary historians of economic thought are groping after. They both mainly studied social thought or social philosophy rather than economic theory. Second, Wada discussed their differences in the following way. Uchida emphasized Smith's natural freedom and made it contrast Stuart's interventionism, whereas Skinner found the source of historical materialism (the Scottish Historical School) in Stuart and Smith. Historical materialism states that the way of politics changes in correspondence with the stages of economic development in each region. Wada attributed the difference in the image of Smith to the difference in the historical development of their countries. The Japanese image of Smith was useful in criticizing Japanese capitalism, which had been super-modernized before its civil society had matured, whereas Britain had the national problems of the gradual decay of its capitalism and its reforms in the process of gradual modernization over many years.

Wada (1972) compared Stuart and Smith on government policy, examined Uchida and Skinner's views, and reached the following conclusion:

Seeing the new system developing, Stuart explicitly took a conservative position, and tried to keep the balance and harmony between the old and the new system by the role of skilful hand as statesman. Smith regarded the merits of the new system as the ideals and tried to prove that a new balance and development can be accomplished by the invisible hand. He recognized that the actual imbalance should be cured by the states. Controversy between Smith and Stuart always repeats itself in somewhat different ways in the history of economic thought. A Smithian and a Stuartian doctrine always confront each other . . . in the actual mechanism of capitalism. This means that the actual mechanism of capitalism has the double-sided conflict which generates this confrontation. We should pay reasonable attention to how each doctrine grasps the two aspects of the conflict rather than idealize Smith and oppose him to Stuart if we try to understand the historical motion of capitalism through the study of the history of economic thought.

It can be said that this conclusion will cause a sensation in the controversy between Uchida and Kobayashi or the controversy on Smith. It seems that the study of Smith in Japan is rising thanks to Wada's works and to the others, following the new trend, by the younger generation.

[*Editor's note*: The original text is quite long (38 pages), I have omitted Section 2 (Marx on Adam Smith) and all notes. These notes contain numerous references of interest to Japanese readers. For consistency, the translator has also omitted certain sentences, as noted in the English text.]

6.3. Aiko Ikeo and Masazumi Wakatabe, previously unpublished (1995).
Adam Smith in Japan: Reconsidered from a Non-Marxian Perspective

1. Introduction

This essay discusses from a non-Marxian perspective how Japanese economists and historians of economic thought read Adam Smith's *Wealth of Nations* after 1920. After the reform of the educational system in 1919 and 1920, the number of economists was dramatically increased and they studied every kind of topic, for example, regional and urban problems as well as mercantilism, classical economics, the German historical school, Marxism, and neo-classical economics. It is hard to tell which school of political economy or economics was dominant in Japan in the 1920s and 1930s. In fact, there were a large number of economic studies in a variety of fields in comparison with the period prior to 1920. By contrast, it is clear that after the Second World War, Marxists were dominant in economic studies until the mid-1960s, and still are in the historical study of economic thought.

There are several survey articles on the study of Smith in Japan from the Marxian point of view. Sugihara (1972) and Okochi (1976) are good examples. Omori (1976) and, Sugiyama, Omori, and Takemoto (1993) also cover Marxist-oriented works on Smith, although the authors tried to be balanced and to include the works of non-Marxians. However, studies of Smith from non-Marxian points of view have not been given the attention they deserve. It is true that non-Marxian Japanese studies on Smith do not have any peculiar characteristics which can be used to differentiate them from ones made by those with other cultural backgrounds. Nevertheless, we should cover them to get an unbiased picture of the study of Smith in Japan. In fact, the number of such studies is substantial.

A number of non-Marxian economists or historians of economic thought have discussed Adam Smith in professional writings. They picked up Adam Smith's *Wealth of Nations* as a classic for occasional reference when they needed to deepen or organize their understanding of wealth, the working of the market mechanism, and the role of government. Scholars with new economic ideas, such as Keynesian macroeconomic analysis, shed new light on Smith's economics. Others with advanced analytical techniques formalized the economic growth which Adam Smith narrated in non-technical terms and they discussed the theoretical problems which neo-classical economists tend to overlook.

Section 2 of this essay shows how the Japanese non-Marxians organized their understanding of Smith's *Wealth of Nations* in the 1920s and the 1930s. Section 3 constructs the process of the arguing-out of Smith's concept of annual products to the modern concept of national income, and summarizes Smith studies under the influence of Keynesian macroeconomics. Section 4 reviews the new studies after 1977, the year when the Japanese edition of Samuel Hollander's *The Economics of Adam Smith* (1973) was published. Section 5 presents a few concluding remarks.

2. Smith from the Viewpoint of a General Equilibrium Theorist

Tokuzo Fukuda was the most important forerunner of economics in Japan, and introduced A. Marshall's neo-classical economics and then A. C. Pigou's welfare economics into Japan in the 1910s and the 1920s. He was trained by Lujo Brentano, a German historical economist, around 1900. Returning from Germany, he trained many leading Japanese economists in his seminars both in Keio-gijuku (Keio University after 1920) and the Tokyo University of Commerce (Hitotsubashi University after 1949). Fukuda delivered a lecture at the bicentenary celebration of the birth of Adam Smith and published his "Smith as a fighter for welfare philosophy" (1923) based on the speech. Fukuda concentrated his attention on Smith's discussion of military expenses. Fukuda argued for a militarily strong state, and maintained that the national security given by a government's defence policy was a part of human happiness.

Shinzo Koizumi, one of Fukuda's students who specialized in David Ricardo, published his *Adam Smith, Malthus and Ricardo* in 1934. He discussed what he regarded as the line of orthodox economics starting from Adam Smith. He called the economic ideas of mercantilism the pre-political economy, as did the Japanese economists of his day. His book included a good reading of the life and contribution of Adam Smith in Japanese.

Ichiro Nakayama was the scholar most responsible for the spread of general equilibrium theory—the idea of the interdependence of economic variables— in Japan. He was a student of Fukuda and also influenced by J. A. Schumpeter of the University of Bonn, who later compiled a history of economic analysis from the viewpoint of the general equilibrium theorist in his *The History of Economic Analysis* (1954). Nakayama published a kind of commentary entitled *Smith's Wealth of Nations* in 1936, which was requested by a publisher after the publication of his famous textbook *Pure Economics* (1933), which helped spread the idea of general equilibrium theory in Japan. Nakayama (1936) consists of three parts. Part one, the best, handles Smith on the division of labour, the theory of value and price, and the returns to the three factors of production— wage, profit, and rent. Part two examines Smith on capital or stock. Part three discusses Smith on the system of natural liberty, and the relationship between economic theory and government policy.

Nakayama characterized the economics of Smith in *The Wealth of Nations* as an equilibrium theory. He searched Smith's synthesis of economic theory, history, and government policy for the bones of equilibrium theory as if panning for gold ore. The chapter entitled "The division of labour and equilibrium" was the essence of the book. He paraphrased Smith's famous proposition that the division of labour was limited by the extent of the market, and said that the division of labour was restricted by the interdependence of markets. He naturally considered Smith's theory of value and price as an equilibrium theory. He not only said that the market price would converge to the natural price, but also asserted that the relation of demand and supply was so central in Smith because natural prices were determined by "the condition of the society". He thereby endeavoured to integrate the theory of price with that of distribution.

It can be said that Nakayama (1936) anticipated the later interpretations of Smith's economics from the equilibrium theorist perspective such as those of Schumpeter (1954) and Hollander (1973). Nakayama might be called a thoroughgoing general equilibrium theorist when he insisted that the most fundamental concept for Smith (i.e. the division of labour) was a good example of the interdependence of economic activities (i.e. the essence of general equilibrium theory). He appraised Smith's idea of the division of labour most, as did the economists of the day in their economics textbooks. He was deeply impressed by the example of a pin factory, which gave him an example of the interdependence of divided works in a factory in the case of pin-making.

Yasaburo Sakamoto of Kobe University of Commerce discussed Smith's theory of value and that of "natural price" by referring to the elements of neo-classical economics such as the marginal utility theory, which was then called the subjective theory of value. In particular, in his "A chapter in Smith's theory of value" (1935) he argued that Smith's "utility" meant the value in use and he found Smith's "merit" close enough to the current concept of utility.

3. The Study under the Influence of Keynesian Macroeconomics

From the 1930s on, the study of national income was conducted in earnest in order to measure economic welfare, the distribution of national income, and national strength as well as to calculate the financial power to run colonies and prepare for possible wars.[1] After the end of the Second World War in 1945, economists needed to know the current conditions of the Japanese economy, such as the inflation rates and the indicator of real economic activities, in making the plan for the recovery of their ruined economy. The economists discussed various definitions of wealth or income given by Adam Smith, A. Marshall, A. C. Pigou, and J. M. Keynes. They also started with Smith when they were creating the model of an economy which had a one-year cycle from production to distribution to consumption.

Yuzo Morita was a statistician. He had been lecturing on national income at the Tokyo University of Commerce and the Imperial University of Tokyo (the University of Tokyo after 1947) for twenty-three years when he published a textbook entitled *The Evaluation and Analysis of National Income* in 1949. Morita (1949: 10) argued that Smith's political economy contained not only the theory of individual exchange but also the theory of aggregate national income or the reproduction of "wealth". Morita argued as follows: the contemporary economists began to take a new look at Smith's aggregate analysis. They were organizing their macroeconomic knowledge of the whole process of a nation's economy. Yet, Morita (1949: 30–2) disagreed with Smith's distinction between productive and unproductive labour, when he stated that the service of civil servants and maids should be included in national income and national products because it contributed to the increase in economic welfare.

Taizo Takahashi of Hitotsubashi University argued in his *Economic Development and Employment* (1948) that T. R. Malthus and Keynes followed Smith's focus on annual products, which was called "wealth" by Smith, in the discussion of economic development and employment. Takeyasu Kimura of the

University of Tokyo, who was a welfare economist, developed a similar argument, as did Takahashi in his "Adam Smith and the analysis of national income" (1948). Kimura, in his "The Adam Smith tradition in the Cambridge school" (1949), placed Smith in the history of welfare economics, that is, in the line of J. Bentham, Marshall, Pigou, and A. Young. Kimura maintained that Smith's subjective concept of social benefit, people's happiness, or public good would correspond to what was called welfare by modern economists.

In 1953, Ichiro Nakayama was asked by a government agency which is now called the Economic Planning Agency to form a task-force to investigate the wealth of Japan of 1955. They spent five years and more than 100 million yen in compiling the first estimation of the national wealth of Japan, and the quality of the study was comparable with those of the then developed countries. Their survey entitled *The Structure of National Wealth of Japan* (1959) started with Smith's definitions of various stocks and then moved to the definitions of national income, national expenditure, national products, and national wealth mainly based on Pigouvian welfare economics. They clearly differentiated income in flow terms from wealth in stock terms. It is also noteworthy that the first inter-industry table of the Japanese economy (of 1951) became available in 1955.

There was, in fact, a fashion for treating Smith as a welfare economist. Fumito Fukushima's *The Development of Welfare Economics* (1983) reflected this trend and started with Jeremy Bentham and classical economists including Smith as the forerunners of welfare economics. This implies that these economists understood Smith's labour theory of value in terms of the purchasing power of a commodity over labour, not in terms of the amount of labour embodied in its production. This trend was also confirmed abroad in Mark Blaug's "Welfare indices in *The Wealth of Nations*" (1959). Blaug summarized the current situation and said, "[M]odern methods of making international comparisons of economic welfare per head are nothing but applications of Smithian welfare economics" (Blaug, 1959: 153).

It is also noteworthy that, after the Second World War, Keynesian macro-economics such as income analysis and effective demand, spread among non-Marxian economists, rapidly or gradually depending on their ages. Keynesian ideas attracted a few historians of economic thought, too.

Noboru Kobayashi was the first historian of economic thought who started to reorganize the understanding of classical economics and mercantilism using Keynesian ideas. He specialized in mercantilism, and made a comparative study between Adam Smith and James Steuart. He recognized the limitations of Adam Smith such as his ignoring the question of effective demand and therefore fiscal policy during economic depression. His study of Smith and mercantilism was written in a non-Marxian language from a historical perspective.

Ikuo Omori followed Kobayashi and published several articles on the comparison between James Steuart and Smith. He admitted that Smith made several mistakes in his works. Omori believed that he could reconstruct Smith's economics coherently by using modern economic ideas, such as the determination of prices by demand and supply, and the efficient allocation of resources. Omori in his "'Natural price' and 'effectual demand' in *The Wealth of Nations*" (1977) put a spotlight on Smith's effectual demand in contrast with that of J. Steuart. He also discussed Smith on the theory of value and price, the relationship between market prices and natural prices. He considered Smith's theory of natural price as a theory of resource allocation. Omori made a further study in this line in his "Adam Smith's theory of industrial structure and its application to the critical analysis of history" (1988). It is also noteworthy that Omori became a historian of economic thought in the feverish mood of the "Hollander Revolution", which will be discussed in the next section.

There were other studies of Smith made by non-Marxian economists before 1977. They focused on the concepts which could be easily connected with equilibrium theories rather than the labour theory of value or the concept of civil society. Susumu Irie discussed Smith's theory of natural and market prices in his series of papers starting with Irie (1952). Kan-ichi Minakata (1955, 1967) discussed capital accumulation and economic growth. Minakata (1962) chose the Marshallian perspective of supply and demand analysis to view the work of Adam Smith.

4. Smithian Studies from Theoretical Perspectives

The Japanese edition of Samuel Hollander's *The Economics of Adam Smith* (1973) was published in 1976. It was the first full-scale historical study of Smith from a non-Marxian perspective in Japan, although originally written by a non-Japanese. It lifted the "ban" on the publication of studies on Smith by Japanese non-Marxians. Studies of Smith from non-Marxian perspectives appeared one after another.

Junichi Okada, who specialized in the study of French economists including Jean-Baptiste Say and Leon Walras, took initiative for the Japanese translation of Hollander (1973), although the translator in charge was formally N. Kobayashi. Okada presented a comprehensive understanding of Adam Smith using a non-Marxian language in his compact *Adam Smith* (1977). This book was a good guide for those who did not want to get involved in the dispute on "civil society" in commencing study of Adam Smith's political economy. Okada, with reference to Smith's *The Theory of Moral Sentiments* and the famous *The*

Principles which lead and direct Philosophical Enquiries illustrated by the History of Astronomy, outlined the system of social science which Smith desired to construct.[2] Although a Smith specialist would say that there was nothing new about Smith in Okada (1977), the book did give its readers a good entry-point to Smith. Every generation of economists needs a good guide to Smith written in their own "language". What is also important is that Okada stressed the incompleteness of Smith's system.

It seems that Okada (1977) and a series of theoretical works on classical economics made by American and European economists such as Paul Samuelson stimulated Takashi Negishi, a theoretical economist, to embark on a serious study of early economists including Smith from a broad analytical point of view. It is also pointed out that Negishi studied classical economics when he was a student in the 1950s, as did many Japanese economics students. It was believed in Japan that it was not sufficient for students to study only textbooks in order to master economics and so they were obliged to read the classics of political economy in the first or second year. Usually these books were read in the classes designed for reading books on economics written in original (foreign) languages.

Negishi's publication on Adam Smith started with a critical assessment of Samuelson's formulation of Smith's theory of price in his "A mathematical model of Quesnay and Smith" (1980). Negishi's own summary of his articles on Smith can be seen in chapter three of his *History of Economic Theory* (1989). Negishi was dissatisfied with Samuelson's assumption of constant returns by his use of the linear-programming method. He constructed a model of a growing economy in the case of increasing returns prompted by the division of labour. He described the condition of demand deficiency in a market by introducing the so-called kinked demand curve in a figure where the price or cost of a good is measured vertically and the quantity horizontally. He naturally paid attention to Smith's case for international trade which would foster the division of labour. Thus Negishi showed by example that competition was compatible with increasing returns in Smith.

Negishi delved into the case of the coexistence of the higher wage and the higher rate of profit, another curious problem set off by Smith's writing on the division of labour and capital accumulation. By using a growth model, Negishi defended Smith from Ricardo's harsh criticism that Smith did not realize the fact of decreasing returns caused by the scarcity of land in farming. As Negishi (1988: 357) pointed out, for Smith, the natural wage (different from the subsistence wage) will be reduced, but the labour value of the real subsistence wage will be increased when the difficulty of providing food is increased. By contrast, Ricardo's natural wage is a constant real wage at the subsistence level.

He showed that in a growth model, "the natural rate of real wage is higher, when the rate of saving is higher, even if the difficulty of providing food remains unchanged". He also confirmed that in such a Smithian growth model, the role of demand should be taken into account in the formation of natural prices. Negishi (1994b) showed that an advance in the division of labour in the production of a commodity can reduce its natural price and increase the natural rate of wages and profit. He also demonstrated that Smith's numerical examples in the *Early Draft* of *The Wealth of Nations* can be generated from a balanced growth model.

Negishi has a strong analytical background like Samuelson, Don Patinkin, and Jürg Niehans, who have been supplying new insights in the study of classical economics. He had made important contributions in the fields of stability analysis, international trade, microfoundations of Keynesian macro-economics, and non-Walrasian economics. Negishi's reading of early economics shed new light on what has been neglected or overlooked by mainstream economists of the world.[3] In addition, his important papers are written in English and available for other economists in European and American libraries.[4] Therefore, it might be meaningless to regard his study on Smith as one made in Japan.

Young Masazumi Wakatabe and Hidetomi Tanaka were encouraged by Negishi's analytical works on early economics. Wakatabe's "Adam Smith on the division of labour" (1991) tried to extend Adam Smith's idea of the division of labour in a factory using the modern theory of internal organization. His "Adam Smith and entrepreneurship" (1992a) extracted what Smith regarded as the driving force in a capitalist economy by borrowing the modern Austrian concept of entrepreneurship. Wakatabe's "Adam Smith on joint-stock companies" (1992b) discussed the so-called principal–agent problem in Smith's work. Wakatabe believes that more comprehensive studies on Smith should be presented from a non-Marxian perspective than the ones made by Okada and has assigned this agenda to himself. Tanaka (1994) analysed Smith's vent for surplus with reference to a Harris–Todaro–Stiglitz-type model.

It is also noteworthy that Hirotaka Kato, a Japanese monetarist, is one of few economists who has advocated Smithian individualism directly to a Japanese audience. His *The Illusion of Keynesianism* (1986), stressed the fact that the Japanese live in a free economy which is based on private ownership and free economic activities, although admitting the presence of monopolistic agents such as big business and the government. He resorted to what he called Smith's fundamental vision that the pursuit of private interests by individuals would lead to the promotion of public interest and eventually result in the greatest value of the wealth in any nation.

5. A Few Concluding Remarks

Studies of Smith by Japanese non-Marxians have not attracted considerable attention so far, in contrast to those by Marxians. We can list three possible reasons for the relatively poor situation of the study of Smith by non-Marxians. The first two have formed a kind of vicious circle.

First of all, the number of studies of Smith by non-Marxians is so small compared with the enormous number by Marxians. In Japan, most historians of economic thought were not well trained in the use of neo-classical economic theories. On the other hand, those who had mastered neo-classical economics were least likely to major in the history of economic thought. This caused Hiroshi Mizuta (1992: 148) to say, "The community of the so-called modern economists or neo-classical economists hardly approves of historical studies, because modern economics does not require any historical sense by its nature".

Second, it is hard to find a continuity in the research on Smith by non-Marxian historians. Their studies are published only sporadically. This is in sharp contrast to the case of the Marxian tradition, which shows a striking continuity centred around the unique but ambiguous concept of "civil society" in Japan after the Second World War. Yet, Sugiyama, Omori and Takemoto (1993: 293) cynically defined civil society and said that it is "a civilized, unmilitaristic and secular or religion-free society with no remnants of feudalism in human and social relations".

Third, non-Marxians tend to focus on theoretical aspects of Smith's works such as the relationships between natural and market prices, the case of increasing returns and economic growth, capital accumulation, and the spread of the division of labour. On the other hand, the interest of the majority of Japanese Smith specialists has shifted to Smith as a social philosopher or his works prior to *The Wealth of Nations*, away from Smith as an economist. They share with European and American historians of social thought an interest in studies of the Scottish Enlightenment, such as I. Hont and A. Ignatieff's *Wealth and Virtue* (1983).

We can get something, say cultural differences in interpretation, from the international comparison of past studies on Smith in various countries which have diverse traditions, languages and cultures. However, it will be meaningless in the future to discuss the study of Smith made by the Japanese outside the context of the rest of the world. From now on, Japanese specialists in Smith also have to publish their articles in English, the language of communication of the majority of Smith scholars, if they are to be "real" specialists in Smith.

Notes

1. An argument similar to the one in this section can be found in chapter 12 of Ikeo (1994).
2. The Japanese version of *History of Astronomy* was produced by Chikakazu Tadagoshi in 1993.
3. Wakatabe commented on Negishi's formalization of classical economics, saying that Negishi is a master at formulating economic ideas and that his models are often difficult for others to use.
4. For this reason, we omit Negishi's "The role of demand in Adam Smith's theory of natural price" (1988) and "A Smithian growth model and Malthus's optimal propensity to save" (1993). Negishi (1988) was originally published in the *Seoul Journal of Economics* and was included in Negishi (1994a). Negishi (1993) was published in the very first issue of *The European Journal of the History of Economic Thought*, an international journal newly established for historians of economic thought in the world to go on the offensive.

References

BLAUG, MARK (1959), "Welfare Indices in *The Wealth of Nations*", *Southern Economic Journal*, 26: 150–3.

FUKUDA, TOKUZO (1923), "Adam Smith as a Fighter for Welfare Philosophy", *Shogaku Kenkyu* (Tokyo University of Commerce), 3(2): 389–424 (in Japanese).

FUKUSHIMA, FUHITO (1983), *The Development of Welfare Economics*, Tokyo: Shunjusha (in Japanese).

HOLLANDER, SAMUEL (1973), *The Economics of Adam Smith*, Toronto and Buffalo: University of Toronto Press.

HONT, ISTVAN and MICHAEL IGNATIEFF (eds) (1983), *Wealth and Virtue: The Shaping of Political Economy in the Scottish Enlightenment*, Cambridge: Cambridge University Press.

IKEO, AIKO (1994), *The Network of Economists in the 20th Century: Economic Studies As Viewed From Japan*, Tokyo: Yuhikaku (in Japanese).

IRIE, SUSUMU (1952–5), "On Adam Smith's Theory of Real Price", *Matsuyama Shodai Ronso*, 3(2–4), 4(1–2), 6(1) (in Japanese).

KIMURA, TAKEYASU (1949), "Adam Smith Tradition in the Cambridge School" *Issues in Economic Theory*, 21–106, Tokyo: Yuhikaku (in Japanese).

—— (1958), "Adam Smith and National Income Accounting", in K. Yanai *et al.* (eds.), *Studies in Classical Economics: Essays in Honour of the 60th Birthday of Tadao Yanaihara*, 64–89, Tokyo: Iwanami (in Japanese).

KOIZUMI, SHINZO (1934), "Adam Smith, Malthus and Ricardo", in *The Collected Works of Shinzo Koizumi*, vol. 5, Tokyo: Bungei-shunju, 1968 (in Japanese).

MINAKATA, KAN-ICHI (1955), "Adam Smith on Capital Accumulation: Part I. His Scheme of Reproduction", *Kokumin-Keizai Zasshi*, 92(1), 29–44 (in Japanese).

—— (1962), "A. Smith's Demand and Supply Theory", *Kokumin-Keizai Zasshi*, 106(3), 20–38 (in Japanese).

—— (1967), "The Employments of Capital in Smith's *Wealth of Nations*", *Keizai Kenkyu* (Kobe University), 14: 89–120 (in Japanese).

MIZUTA, HIROSHI (1992), "Around Adam Smith", *Meijo Shogaku* (Meijo University), 41 (supplement) (in Japanese).

MORITA, YUZO (1949), *The Evaluation and Analysis of National Income*, Tokyo: Toyo-keizai-Shimposha (in Japanese).

NAKAYAMA, ICHIRO (1933), "Pure Economics", Tokyo: Iwanami, in vol. 1 of *The Collected Works of Ichiro Nakayama*, Tokyo: Kodansha, 1972 (in Japanese).

—— (1936), "Smith's Wealth of Nations", Tokyo: Iwanami, in vol. 1 of *The Collected Works of Ichiro Nakayama*, Tokyo: Kodansha, 1972 (in Japanese).

NEGISHI, TAKASHI (1980), "Some Mathematical Models of Quesnay and Adam Smith", *Keizaigaku Ronshu* (University of Tokyo), 46(3): 16–24 (in Japanese).

—— (1988), "The Role of Demand in Adam Smith's Theory of Natural Price", *Seoul Journal of Economics*, 1(4): 357–65. Also in Negishi (1994a).

—— (1989), *History of Economic Theory*, Amsterdam: North-Holland.

—— (1993), "A Smithian Growth Model and Malthus's Optimal Propensity to Save", *The European Journal of the History of Economic Thought*, 1(1): 115–27.

—— (1994a), *The History of Economics*, vol. 2 of *The Collected Essays of Takashi Negishi*, Cheltenham: Edward Elgar.

—— (1994b), "Smith's Numerical Examples of Division of Labor", *Annals of the Society for the History of Economic Thought (in Japan)*, 32: 40–47.

OKADA, JUNICHI (1977), *Adam Smith*, Tokyo: Nihon-keizai-shimbunsha (in Japanese).

OKOCHI, KAZUO (1976), "A Short History of Japanese Translation of *The Wealth of Nations*", in the 1976 new translation under his supervision, vol. 3, pp. 453–69 (translated into English by Tatsuya Sakamoto, mimeo).

OMORI, IKUO (1976), "A Survey of the Studies on Smith in Japan", *Weekly Toyo Keizai: Special Issue in Commemoration of the Bicentennial of the Publication of The Wealth of Nations*, 134–40 (in Japanese).

—— (1977), "'Natural Price' and 'Effectual Demand' in *The Wealth of Nations*: Comparison with J. Steuart's Theory of 'Effectual Demand'", *Waseda Commercial Review*, 267/8: 3188 (in Japanese).

—— (1988), "Adam Smith's Theory of Industrial Structure and its Application to the Critical Analysis of History", in N. Kobayashi (ed.), *Thoughts of Economic Policy in the Capitalist World*, ch. 5, Kyoto: Showado (in Japanese).

Sakamoto, Yasaburo (1930), "Adam Smith on Value (1)", *Kokumin-Keizai Zasshi*, 48(2): 181–207 (in Japanese).

—— (1935), "A Chapter in Smith's Theory of Value: Relation between Utility, Merit, Scarcity and Value in Exchange", in *Essays in the Honour of the 30th Anniversary of the Establishment of Kobe College of Commerce*, pp. 29–68, Osaka: Hobunkan (in Japanese).

—— (1936), "On the Natural Price in Adam Smith's Lectures on Political Economy (1)", *Kokumin-Keizai Zasshi*, 60(4/5): 465–88 (in Japanese).

Samuelson, P. A. (1977), "A Modern Theorist's Vindication of Adam Smith", *American Economic Review*, 67(1): 42–9.

Schumpeter, J. A. (1954), *History of Economic Analysis*, New York: Oxford University Press.

Sugihara, Shiro (1972), "Adam Smith in Japan", in K. Okochi (ed.), *Studies on Wealth of Nations*, vol. 3, Tokyo: Chikuma-shobo (translated into English by Aiko Ikeo, mimeo)

Sugiyama, Chuhei, Ikuo Omori, and Hiroshi Takemoto (1993), "Adam Smith in Japan", in Hiroshi Mizuta and Chuhei Sugiyama (eds.), *Adam Smith: International Perspectives*, ch. 16, Basingstoke and London: Macmillan.

Tanaka, Hidetomi (1994), "Adam Smith's Vent for Surplus, Reconsidered", *Waseda Economic Studies*, 39: 22–49 (in Japanese).

Wakatabe, Masazumi (1991), "Adam Smith on the Division of Labour: Technology and Internal Organization", *Waseda Economic Studies*, 33: 97–109 (in Japanese).

—— (1992a), "Adam Smith and Entrepreneurship: On a Dynamism in the Economics of Adam Smith", *Waseda Journal of Political Science and Economics*, 307/308: 325–58 (in Japanese).

—— (1992b), "Adam Smith on Joint-Stock Companies: Division of Labour, Ownership and Entrepreneurship", *Waseda Journal of Political Science and Economics*, 312: 103–32 (in Japanese).

Part 7. Portugal

Research on the translation and reception of WN in Portugal is not fully developed, as shown by the (lack of) literature listed below. Cardoso (1990) is by far the most comprehensive piece of research. Cardoso analysed the background of Portuguese economics and currents of economic thought in the late eighteenth century; he also clearly contrasted the main proponents and adversaries of Smith's economic ideas.

Interestingly, the introduction of British-Smithian economic policy into Portugal was not without its costs:

During the Napoleonic era, external policy in Portugal was guided by a strong alliance with Britain . . . The alliance has ensured the survival of one of the older nation-states of Europe; but there was a price to be paid . . . The Anglo-Portuguese trade treaty of 1810 completely destroyed the old-style mercantilist relationship between Portugal and her most important colony. Brazil was also the axis of a new model of economic development based on "sane and liberal principles of political economy" that opened up Portuguese economy and put an end to exclusivity in colonial trade. (Cardoso 1990: 437)

To Portuguese readers I recommend the complete version of this paper, Cardoso (1988), which provides a brief history of the translation of WN into Portuguese (pp. 108–110).

Further Reading

Text with a * is printed in this Part

CARDOSO, J. (1988), 'A influência de Adam Smith no pensamento económico Português (1776–1811/12)', in J. Cardoso (ed.), *Contribuições para a história do pensamento económico em Portugal*, pp. 87–110, Lisboa: Publicações Dom Quixote.

Portugal

*Cardoso, J. (1990), 'Economic Thought in Late Eighteenth-Century Portugal: Physiocratic and Smithian Influences', *History of Political Economy*, 22(3): 429–41.

Das Neves, João César (1990), 'Memorial: duzentos anos da morte de Adam Smith (1723–1790)', *Economia*, 15(1): 159–66.

Neto, A. (1936), *Adam Smith: Fundador da Economia Politica*, pp. 26–35, Lisboa.

7.1. José Luís Cardoso, [1990].

Economic Thought in Late Eighteenth-Century Portugal: Physiocratic and Smithian Influences

B12   Portugal

I. Introduction

The international transmission and assimilation of economic doctrines and theories does not seem to be a problem that requires special attention today.[1] The phenomena of cultural interchange are a characteristic part of daily experience in both academic and professional life. However, we cannot take it for granted that these processes will take place, or that they are a natural result of cultural interchange, if one or both of the following constraints occur: (1) difficulties are inherent in the historical circumstances when interchange takes place; (2) disequilibrium exists between transmitting source and receiver country due to different levels of development of analytic economic thought.

The first type of constraint is related to the development of the media of transmission, such as speed of circulation of foreign books, general overall acquaintance with foreign languages, quantity and quality of translations, and facilities for private and institutional international contacts. It is also related to the level of scientific autonomy or academic recognition that economics may have reached. Finally, it is related to differences in economic development between the source country and the receiver country, which may be more or less apparent at different periods.

The second type of constraint can also be related to historical time, because each country goes through periods corresponding to different levels of theoretical creation. But basically the problem lies in the existence of long-lasting disequilibrium relationships between countries that have a tradition of innovation and creation in economic science and others that have no choice but to use a scientific discourse created abroad. One may be tempted to assume that in countries that have never been at the forefront of theoretical developments, the history of economic thought is reduced to a succession of foreign influences. But even if knowledge of and acquaintance with what is done "abroad" is a healthy sign of cosmopolitanism, it does not follow that the receiver country has to accept the greater part of those principles, theories, and recipes which only made sense in other historical circumstances. This means that the ease or difficulty with which economic theories and doctrines are accepted is always constrained by the particularities of economic reality, political institutions, and scientific environment in the receiver country. It is the way a country uses and adapts the influences received that makes the study of abstract economic knowledge worthwhile from a national point of view.

Late eighteenth-century Portugal offers an excellent case study where both constraints apply. The following presentation of some aspects of Portuguese economic literature of the years circa 1790–1810 not only covers a relatively unresearched field (even within Portugal) but may also illustrate the importance of studying processes of transmission and assimilation in the history of economic thought.

II. Physiocratic Influences

Portugal in the second half of the eighteenth century was deeply influenced by the rule of the Marquis de Pombal, chief minister of King José I from 1750 to 1777. From a sociological and political point of view, the reign of José I illustrates, thanks chiefly to the action of Pombal, what is usually called enlightened despotism. One can broadly describe the economic climate of the era by saying that under Pombal occurred the last and most important phase of Portuguese mercantilism. Inspired by the policies of Colbert, it was characterized chiefly by governmental support of the development of manufactures and by policies of exclusivity and monopoly in both production and commerce.

After the king's death in 1777 Pombal fell quickly into disgrace, and his former political victims regained their lost privileges and status. Pombal's mercantilist policies were also subjected to much criticism—criticism which in a sense was made possible by Pombal's own policies. The scholars who had benefited from new philosophical and scientific knowledge gained through the University of Coimbra, reformed by Pombal, were the ones who found and presented the strongest arguments against his political and economic ideas.

The Royal Academy of Sciences and Vandelli

The criticism of Pombal's policies had two main strands. One was that he had neglected agriculture, implementing an industry-led economic policy that had foundered due to stagnation in the agricultural sector. The other was that the pervading intervention of the state had hampered and constrained the actions of individual economic agents. These powerful criticisms made Portuguese authors receptive to arguments of the French physiocrats. This influence was felt from the beginning of the 1780s, and the Royal Academy of Sciences of Lisbon was the main centre of its diffusion. In 1789 the Academy began publishing a five-volume set of economic transactions (*Memórias económicas*, 1789–1815). Their main concern was to study the economic resources of the kingdom and of its colonies (which at the time included Brazil as the most important) and to propose technical and political projects and programs for improving their allocation. The authors gave special attention to the agricultural situation and to the reforms they felt were indispensable for its improvement. Among their major concerns were gradual solutions to ease the burden of the still-existent seigneurial structure of land use and property, the removal of barriers to the unification of the internal market, and the reform of the *ancien régime* tax system.

Although Portuguese historiography of economic thought, scarce as it is, takes it for granted that the *Memórias económicas* exemplify the influence and assimilation of physiocratic ideas, this claim must be qualified. The spread of physiocratic ideas outside France cannot be regarded as a simple diffusion of ideas and doctrines based on the overwhelming importance of land and agriculture. The confusion between agrarianism and physiocracy leads to a misunderstanding of the real significance of the work of Quesnay and his disciples, namely that its analytical features provided a new vision and understanding of the "economic process as a circuit flow that in each period returns upon itself" (Schumpeter 1954, 243). Writing a few years after the physiocrats' meteoric success, the Portuguese academicians were naturally receptive to arguments about the sterility of the nonagricultural sectors, and they were familiar with the concept of net product. They were also inclined to adopt the ideas that capital requirements could be regarded as different kinds of *avances* crucial to the creation of wealth and that some kind of *impôt unique* policy could reform the *ancien régime*'s multiple and unfair taxes. But despite their acceptance of some of the main tenets of physiocracy, they did not grasp the general framework of Quesnay's *Tableau économique*, which tied together and gave theoretical unity to these bits and pieces, presenting economic activities as flows of income between three different social classes.

Domingos Vandelli, an Italian who lived in Portugal from 1772 to 1810, was prominent among the authors who advocated economic reforms. He had been one of the main supporters of the reform of the University of Coimbra in accordance with the ideas of the Enlightenment, and he became the main activist in the economic efforts of the Royal Academy of Sciences of Lisbon. He wrote the only text in the *Memórias económicas* that attempted a systematic assimilation of physiocracy on the basis of underlying abstract principles. His presentation centered on two main ideas: that wealth originates not in commerce, but in production; and that a successful economy requires a market, free of external constraints, where value created in production may be realized. But the greater part of his writing was basically empirical, concerned as he was with the need for improved knowledge of natural resources and of the problems that prevented their full and effective use. Thus Vandelli joins a large group of minor (frequently anonymous) authors for whom the physiocratic approach was but an instrument and a pretext for criticizing prior mercantilist policy.

Physiocratic influences in the *Memórias económicas* are apparent only in the authors' advocacy of the principles of laissez faire and individual economic freedom. Their agrarianism was neither founded on nor supported by a theoretical argument and was basically the expression of their strong wish to change old-fashioned features of the *ancien régime* economy and society, for it was in agriculture that the anachronisms that hampered economic development were more visible. Their unconcern for industry was due more to their dissatisfaction with the policies of Pombal than to a theoretical disagreement about the source(s) of wealth.

Brito on Natural and Social Order

Although J. J. Rodrigues de Brito did not write for the Royal Academy of Sciences, his work is also important for the analysis of physiocratic influences in Portugal (Brito 1803–5). Brito claimed to be a disciple of Condillac, and his methodological approach seems to show acceptance of empirical methods that lead to the establishment of *évidences* and to the development of regulating principles of social order. But the main point is Brito's unquestioning assumption of the existence of a natural order and of a system of natural law which together give the rules that have to be implemented to obtain social harmony and durable social cohesion.

Brito believed that the sovereign's role is to clarify the natural law and implement, as a set of positive rules, the underlying laws of nature (the *évidences*). To make this possible, a guiding principle must be discovered; the system of natural law may then be divided into a set of subsystems, among which political economy has the major role. This means that the sovereign has as highest priority "the increasing of the wealth of the country as intensively as possible," and this makes political economy "the main lighthouse, the fixed star that should guide the law-giver to his sublime destination."[2]

As for the system of political economy itself, Brito divides it into different subsystems (agriculture, commerce, industry, and property) and considers that agriculture should be the main object of the sovereign's attention. Through this approach he arrived at the design of an economic development strategy based on agriculture and an explicit statement of a sympathetic attitude towards physiocratic doctrines. Brito also accepted the laissez-faire message of the French authors, supporting policies directed towards the dismantling of traditions that could hamper the full exercise of individual natural rights. His reasons for accepting physiocratic ideas were similar to those presented above for the *Memórias econômicas*, but the process through which assimilation took place was quite different.

Whereas Vandelli and the other royal academicians used an empirical and technical approach, giving strong emphasis to the decline of agriculture and to their intention of reversing it, Brito started from a philosophical and political basis. He justified his agrarianism by comparing the different "political values" of the various types of economic activity and concluding that economic development based on agriculture leads more easily to social harmony. His economic reasoning was underpinned by a theoretical and sociological analysis of *ancien régime* Portuguese society in which he attempted to show that well-functioning economic institutions are the main factor that ensures the establishment of a transcendent natural order. The enlightened sovereign should act so as to ensure that this harmony becomes real. These arguments reflect the French physiocratic doctrines of natural order and legal despotism.

If Brito adopted some physiocratic tenets, his acceptance of their ideas was by no means complete and unquestioning. His discussions of the problems of the origin of wealth or the determination of value reveal other influences—as will be shown in the next section of this article—that made him condemn "certain metaphysical principles, exaggerated expressions of dubious exactness, born from the enthusiasm and excessive zeal of their supporters." Nevertheless, though he was sometimes critical of the physiocrats, it is quite clear that he was attempting a rehabilitation of physiocratic discourse (at a time when its impact on European public opinion had dwindled to nothing) because it offered an approach well-adapted to a gradual and moderate change in society that would not shake the political foundations of the *ancien régime*.

III. The Influence of Smith

Like the physiocrats', Adam Smith's work only became influential in Portugal after a considerable lapse of time. The first Portuguese reference to Smith came fifteen years after the first edition of *The Wealth of Nations*, and there is no earlier indirect evidence of any acquaintance, however slight, with his work. In this first reference (Vilanova Portugal 1791) the author only refers to Smith in passing, to support the idea that the entail of property created difficulties for agricultural development. It should be noted that this reference to Smith is somewhat gratuitous, as there were physiocratic arguments that the author could have used to support a greater degree of freedom in the land market.

A few Portuguese texts written betwen 1792 and 1802 contain scattered references to *The Wealth of Nations* (*WN*), nearly always concerning the division of labor and freedom in production and trade. The increasing audience for laissez faire was a strong incentive for wider diffusion of the book. Thus Smith's ideas went hand in hand with other simultaneous influences towards a larger freedom of action for economic agents and criticism of the obstacles to efficient resource allocation (corporation laws, import prohibitions, excessively high duties, exclusive privileges, monopolies, bad communications, high local taxes, etc.). The continuity in the diffusion of physiocratic and Smithian influences on the Continent strengthened the ultimate dominance of Smith's theories: "The physiocrats helped to pave the road for the success of *The Wealth of Nations* while they lost the capacity to obstruct that success to any important degree. To some extent, at least, Adam Smith profited immensely by the general spread of their ideas, since what he offered was or worked itself out as the direct continuation and refinement of the physiocratic doctrine" (Palyi 1928, 199).

During this first period of assimilation of Smith's work (1792–1802) one Portuguese author, Rodrigo de Sousa Coutinho, Minister of the Realm from 1796 to 1803, adopted from Smith more than the simple message of laissez faire. Responsible for the Exchequer (1801–3), he dealt carefully with problems arising from the circulation of paper money—a practice begun in 1797 (against his advice) after an unsuccessful attempt to create internal public debt.[3] The sharp depreciation of paper money and the public's rapid loss of confidence in all financial operations of the court were justification enough to make Coutinho try to implement a coherent programme of financial restructuring. Among the main goals of this programme were the establishment of a Bank,[4] the gradual withdrawal of existing paper money, the operation of a carefully administered internal public loan, rigorous adherence to the rules and dates of loan repayments, reform of the tax system, reduction of superfluous public expenditure, and the rationalization of local and central financial institutions.

In his writings on some of these subjects Coutinho shows a knowledge of *WN*—in fact he strongly advises that it should be read—especially when he discusses the advantages and disadvantages of paper money. And on this topic he is sometimes more careful than Smith when he discusses the precautions concerning the control of the amount of circulating paper money and when he presents his recommendations about guarantees of convertibility.[5]

A new phase in the assimilation of Smith's works began in 1803. From that point *WN* was no longer merely mentioned or cited as an example of recommendations for financial or economic policies but was read and studied as a body of analytical ideas. Yet the Portuguese remained unimpressed by Smith's general theoretical system, being mainly interested in his theory of value and prices. Brito was the first author to discuss some of the more theoretical parts of *WN*. After presenting his own concept of "political value"—through which he was attempting to discover an objective criterion for choosing the system of legislation that should be supported and performed by the sovereign—Brito discussed the problem of value in economic terms. Essentially he believed that the major sources of the value of material goods are use, labor, and competition. Competition seemed to be "the ultimate and most powerful cause," because the evaluation that buyers and sellers make of the utility and need of a good is more important than the objective labor it contains or commands.

At this point Brito chose to devote a whole chapter of his book to refuting Smith, accusing him of considering labor as the only (or at least the main) source of value. In addition to the influence of the subjectivist tradition inherited from scholastic thought, and the influence of Condillac besides, Brito found his main inspiration for a critique of Smith in the French economist Canard. Following Canard—who had unsuccessfully attempted to use a mathematical approach—Brito arrived at the conclusions that the wishes, capacities, wills, and power of the diverse market participants determine the prices at which goods are bought and sold and that these prices are conceived as the real and ultimate expressions of value.

But when he attempted to find additional arguments for the idea that competition is the main explanatory cause of value, Brito contradicted his former explanation and came closer to the ideas of the author he was criticizing. He accepted Smith's distinction between natural and market price and, although he was unable to express it too clearly, he recognized that natural price is "the center of repose, the central price to which the prices of all commodities are continually gravitating" (Smith 1776, 1: vii: 15). Nevertheless he differed from Smith on the subject of equilibrium. For Smith it is the spontaneous and self-correcting market mechanism that ensures equilibrium, whereas for Brito it is the role of "wise government" that ensures there is no lasting disequilibrium between supply and demand: that is, the natural order requires the presence of an entity that prevents prices from being determined by "uncontrolled whims and opinions."

One year after the first two volumes of Brito's work appeared, José da Silva Lisboa published a book, a large part of which (roughly one-fourth) concerned Brito's criticism of Smith's theory of value (Lisboa 1804). In the following year Brito presented a rejoinder in the introduction to his third and last volume. Faithfulness to the Smithian inheritance was the main issue in this remarkable public controversy.

Besides restating the theses that labour is the source and measure of value and that in the long run, market and natural prices tend to the same equilibrium price, Lisboa attacked Brito's agrarianism, arguing that development of one economic sector can only take place with parallel development in other sectors. Lisboa believed that the prosperity of the realm depended on interaction among a great number of activities, and he thus accused Brito of following too closely the work of the physiocrats, which in his own opinion had been superseded by Smith's masterly book.

Brito labeled Smith a "plagiarist of the physiocrats" because Smith had kept secret the contacts he had in France with that school of thought. Brito also addressed the problem of value (and the role of competition in it) and devoted a large amount of space to justifying the importance he attached to agricultural development, as he regarded the other types of economic activity as "very weak sources of wealth, uncertain and not durable" and unable, by themselves, to ensure the harmony of the global social system.

This was essentially a debate between two authors who had different outlooks on the same external source they were trying to assimilate. Brito's approach seems to assimilate foreign influences without forgetting immediate economic and social aims and to take into account the need for adapting those influences to Portuguese conditions at the beginning of the nineteenth century. Lisboa, by contrast, specifically declared "the passion and devotion" that he felt towards Smith's book and seems to have been motivated by the purity of a self-contained doctrinaire vision that accepted no correction or adaptation. Lisboa also differed from his opponent in one important aspect that may have deeply affected his perspective: he was writing not in mainland Portugal, but in its chief colony, Brazil.

Lisboa's total acceptance of Smith's work was not confined to the chapter of his book in which he attacked Brito. In the remainder of the book he attempted a systematic presentation of some principles of *WN* and a comparison with the (to him) minor works of the physiocrats and James Steuart. The reason that he gave for his "passion" for Smith was Smith's clear-cut support of economic freedom and his total opposition to any type of restraint of individual action.

Praise for *WN* also appears again and again in a group of pamphlets Lisboa published in Rio de Janeiro from 1808 to 1810, amid a succession of events that were to condition the future development of the Portuguese economy and society. During the Napoleonic era, exernal policy in Portugal was guided by a strong alliance with Britain. When Portugal refused to accept the implications of the Continental Blockade and was invaded by the French at the end of 1807, the Portuguese court moved to Brazil. The final expulsion of the French, in 1811, was achieved only with the intervention of the British army under the command of Wellington. The alliance had ensured the survival of one of the older nation-states of Europe; but there was a price to be paid.

The opening up of the ports of Brazil to the ships of "friendly nations" (1808), the repeal of the prohibition against the establishment of manufactures in Brazil (also in 1808), and, above all, the Anglo-Portuguese trade treaty of 1810 completely destroyed old-style mercantilist relations between Portugal and her most important colony.[6] Brazil was not only the provisional location of the court, it was also the axis of a new model of economic development based on "sane and liberal principles of political economy" that opened up Portuguese economy and put an end to exclusivity in colonial trade.

Lisboa's pamphlets of 1808–10 were not mere praise of these new economic measures in the colony: they expressed the ideas of a Brazilian intelligentsia that was looking toward autonomous economic development. The pamphlets never mention political independence, and Lisboa seems to have accepted the political direction of the Portuguese court as giving coherence to antagonistic economic and social interests.[7] But there is absolutely no doubt that the end of the colonial pact had an important role in preparing Brazil for independence in 1822. The motives that made Lisboa such a wholehearted follower of Smith's doctrine of free trade thus become increasingly understandable: his role as a Brazilian author impelled him to it and justified the insistence with which he used Smith to explain the advantages of making Brazil part of the international division of labor.

Lisboa's eagerness for the dissemination of Smith's ideas influenced even his family circle; his son Bento da Silva Lisboa made the first Portuguese translation of *WN* (Smith 1811–12). In his short introduction,[8] the younger Lisboa explained the importance of the translation for understanding the profound changes that were taking place in Brazil. Here again, the acknowledged reason for the significance of *WN* was the doctrinal instrumentalization of the principles of laissez faire it contained, taking into account the liberalization of Brazil's economy.[9]

IV. Conclusion

Portuguese authors of 1790–1810 did not grasp—except episodically—the theoretical and analytical structures of mainstream European economic thought of the second half of the eighteenth century. Although statements about the importance of the study of political economy appear in their works, they do not seem to have clearly perceived the role of this new science in understanding and explaining economic reality. They saw political economy as an ancillary part of the "art of ruling." The ties that they created between political economy, the natural sciences, and the philosophy of natural law illustrate the difficulties of achieving scientific autonomy for a purely economic discourse. However, these ties also indicate very clearly the areas of intellectual knowledge from which political economy in Portugal would later spring.

Portuguese assimilation of the ideas of the physiocrats and Smith proceeded mainly in the realm of doctrine. The principles of laissez faire were used as an argument against the excessive role of the state in the economy and as a banner for a program of gradual reform of *ancien régime* institutions. These reforms were not meant to attack the political basis of Portugal's established system of enlightened despotism. The ideals of economic liberalism inspired changes but were primarily conceived as instruments to increase social cohesion.[10]

The doctrinaire nature of the assimilation inhibits a clear-cut distinction between the Portuguese authors and the sources that inspired them, insofar as the original message is filtered for nonscientific purposes. The Portuguese authors may have expressed a more or less explicit inclination towards the physiocrats or Smith, but they never acknowledged a general acceptance of the totality of the economic ideas that make those types of economic thought coherent and distinctive. Even on an issue that pervaded the whole literature of the period—antimercantilism—they did not always take a faithful stand (especially authors born outside Brazil who discuss the economic dependence between Portugal and her colonies). Thus they cannot be called disciples of these foreign masters; they were popularizers of a doctrinal message partially accepted as an instrument for desired reforms. This distinction deserves special emphasis, for it shows that the study of international flow of ideas in the history of economic thought belies the rigid time periodizations that—at least for the era under consideration—are assigned in textbooks.

Finally, taking these conclusions into account, we have to confront a problem that arises from looking at the international flow of ideas from the receiver country's point of view: the possibility of, or interest in, the construction of a national (Portuguese, in this case) history of economic thought. If such a history is seen merely as a chronological succession of transmission processes, this construction is doomed. To achieve a national history of economic thought, it is not enough to compile a detailed count of the number of quotations from foreign authors or assess how widely their books circulated, or the number and quality of translations, or the frequency of adaptation for internal textbooks (or any other indicators of transmission).[11] In the Portuguese case, where chauvinistic attempts to find forgotten authors who were the initial discoverers of some specific part of economic knowledge can only be viewed with amusement, such a history would be like a jigsaw puzzle that could not be finished because some of the pieces had been stolen. Boserup, speaking of Denmark, comes to doubt the possibility more generally: "Even in much larger countries with more scope for scientific self-sufficiency national histories of economic thought might be of dubious value, unless confined to short phases" (1980, 420). Nevertheless we can reject this rather pessimistic point of view if we stop looking at national histories of economic thought mainly as a process of transmission of theories and doctrines and instead concentrate our efforts on studying the concrete ways in which these theories and doctrines were assimilated.

NOTES

An earlier version of this article was presented at the History of Economic Thought Conference, Bristol, 1988. I would like to thank Professors D. P. O'Brien and Mark Blaug for their encouragement and the conference participants for their comments. I am also indebted to an anonymous referee and to José João Marques da Silva for their helpful suggestions and corrections improving the article's English style.

1. An overview of this problem was presented in the pioneer essays of Dorfman (1955), Hutchison (1955), and Spengler (1970), which I shall bear in mind in the few methodological remarks that follow. More recently the theme of the international flow of economic theories and doctrines was discussed within the research project "The institutionalization of political economy: its introduction and acceptance into European, North American and Japanese universities, circa 1750–1900" (which culminated at the Conference of San Miniato, Pisa, in April 1986), and also in Hutchison's (1988) work on the emergence of political economy in continental Europe. Both refer roughly to the same period I am studying, but neither considers the Portuguese experience.

2. Brito's analysis of the relation between natural law and political economy cannot be pursued here. Nevertheless it must be pointed out that such a relation is very important for a general understanding of Brito's thought in two aspects: (1) his

arguments for legal despotism, and (2) his difficulty in presenting an autonomous scientific discourse for political economy.

3. A short biography and some important financial writings of Coutinho are included in Funchal 1908.
4. The first Portuguese Bank was set up in 1821.
5. The same precautions and recommendations were at the time discussed in Spanish economic literature. See R. S. Smith 1957 and Marugan and Schwartz 1978.
6. After 1810, British goods were taxed in Brazil at a lower rate than Portuguese goods.
7. Lisboa's political conservatism is likewise indicated by the fact that he was the Portuguese translator of Burke's *Reflections on the revolution in France*: "Just as Burke's traditionalism became the doctrinal foundation on which many kinds of political theories opposed to French revolutionary system could be built up, so the liberalism of Smith supplied an arsenal of arguments against the Napoleonic system of Continental Blockade" (Palyi 1928, 181).
8. It is not a translation of the whole of *WN*: it omits Book 5 and all the digressions on the history of England. *WN* had already been translated into French (1779), German (1779), Italian (1779), Danish (1779–80), Spanish (1794), and Russian (1802–6).
9. The impact of this translation in mainland Portugal was practically nil.
10. The theme of social cohesion in British society has been discussed by Christie (1984). Despite a different type of political organization and economic development, the Portuguese experience shows some parallels in avoidance of political revolution.
11. This problem is accurately discussed for the Spanish case by Lluch (1980).

References

BOSERUP, MOGENS. 1980. The international transmission of ideas: a small-country case study. *HOPE* 12.3: 420–33.

BRITO, J. J. RODRIGUES. 1803–5. *Memórias políticas sobre as verdadeiras bases da grandeza das Nações*. 3 vols. Lisbon.

CHRISTIE, IAN R. 1984. *Stress and stability in late eighteenth-century Britain: reflections on the British avoidance of revolution*. Oxford.

DORFMAN, JOSEPH. 1955. The role of the German Historical School in American economic thought. *American Economic Review* 45.2: 17–28.

FUNCHAL, MARQUÊS DO. 1908. *O Conde de Linhares, Dom Rodrigo Domingos António de Sousa Coutinho*. Lisbon.

HUTCHISON, T. W. 1955. Insularity and cosmopolitanism in economic ideas. *American Economic Review* 45.2: 1–16.

—— 1988. *Before Adam Smith: the emergence of political economy, 1662–1776*. Oxford.

LISBOA, J. DA SILVA. 1804. *Princípios de economia política*. Lisbon.

LLUCH, ERNEST. 1980. Sobre la historia nacional del pensamiento economico. Introduction to Alvaro Florez Estrada, *Curso de economia política*. Reprinted. Madrid.

MARUGAN, F., and P. SCHWARTZ. 1978. El ensayo de José Alonzo Ortiz: monetarismo Smithiano en la España de los vales reales. In *Dinero y credito (siglos XVI a XIX)*, 393–435. Edited by Alonzo Ortazu. Madrid.

Memórias económicas da Academia Real das Ciências de Lisboa, para o adiantamento da agricultura, das artes e da indústria em Portugal e suas conquistas. 1789–1815. 5 vols. Lisbon.

PALYI, MELCHIOR. 1928. The introduction of Adam Smith on the Continent. In *Adam Smith 1776–1926: lectures to commemorate the sesquicentennial of the publication of the Wealth of Nations*, 180–233. Chicago.

SCHUMPETER, J. A. 1954. *History of economic analysis.* Oxford.

SMITH, ADAM. 1776. *An inquiry into the nature and causes of the wealth of nations.* Glasgow Edition. Oxford.

—— 1811–12. *Compêndio da obra da riqueza das nações.* 3 vols. Rio de Janeiro.

SMITH, R. S. 1957. The *Wealth of Nations* in Spain and Hispanic America, 1780–1830. *Journal of Political Economy* 65.2: 104–25. Reprinted in *Adam Smith: critical assessments*, 2: 58–80. Edited by J. C. Wood. Beckenham.

SPENGLER, JOSEPH J. 1970. Notes on the international transmission of economic ideas. *HOPE* 2.1: 133–51.

VILANOVA PORTUGAL, TOMÁS A. 1791. Qual foi a origem e quais os progressos da jurisprudência dos morgados em Portugal. In *Memórias de literatura portuguesa da Academia Real das Ciências de Lisboa* 3: 374–470. Lisbon.

Part 8. Russia

The literature on the translation and reception of *WN* in Russia is quite rich. The references listed below are representative enough to provide a general picture. The five texts selected here are at the same time too much and too little—too much in comparison with the space devoted here to other countries, too little to tell the whole complex story. Like Germany and Japan, the case of Russia deserves an entire book.

This Part starts with the relationship between Smith and his Russian followers. Alekseev (1937), which offers a general picture of the early connection between Smith and his Russian admirers, is perhaps the first attempt to analyse this history in English.

At the level of personal history, two interesting texts are recommended but not included in this chapter because of their limited relevance to the translation/reception of *WN* in Russia. Brown (1975), using Glasgow University archives and faculty minutes and various archives at Moscow University, provides a very informative story of the lives and activities of the two Russian students Desnitski and Tret'yakov. Brown (1975) is an expanded version of Brown (1974) which is included here; it is too long and too detailed for our purpose here. A similar account of the activities of these two Russian students at Glasgow is presented in Letiche and Dmytryshyn (1986), which provides a good supplement to Brown (1975). Readers interested further in the activities and influences of the two students should see Letiche (1964: 507–17 and 517–31). Anikin (1988, ch. 3) contains a photograph of Desnitski (p. 41) and some detailed information about these two early followers of Smith.

Taylor (1967) is in a more academic vein. He compares the texts of Smith's lectures with the texts of his Glasgow student Tret'yakov (published in Russia before 1776) to examine the degree of transmission and distortion of Smith's thought. Although somewhat technical, this is an interesting exercise in the examination of the transmission and reception of economic theories.

Brown (1974) analyses the relationship between Adam Smith's economic ideas and Desnitski's *Predstavlenie* ("'Proposals"), and how Desnitski's opinions on state finances were included in Catherine II's *Nakaz*. Readers familiar with *WN* will guess that the main ideas contained in Book V may have contributed something to the *Nakaz*, and Brown (1974) gives us a very satisfactory and highly readable analysis of this complex interaction.

McGrew (1976) offers a similar story via another personage: Heinrich Storch. Schumpeter explained the importance of Storch in his *History of Economic Analysis* (1954: 502–3) as follows:

H. F. von Storch (1766–1835) . . . though a German by race and training, is usually treated as Russian because of his career in the Russian service . . . his analysis may be best described by the term "critical Smithianism": his bases and conceptual apparatus are substantially Smithian but Storch disagreed with both Smith and Say on a number of important points. Particularly as regards income analysis . . . For the present, I want to make sure that the reader does not forget this man: though he does not rank high as a theorist, he is a significant figure.

McGrew's original text is quite long (41 pages), and only the pages directly related to our topic are selected: pp. 31–3, 35–8, 44–8, and 71. The Smith–Storch connection was more in economic thought than at a practical level. McGrew shows how Storch absorbed Smith's doctrines and spread them to Russian intellectuals; Storch's own critiques of some of Smith's theories are also analysed. This lengthy paper deserves to be read *in toto* by historians of Russian economic thought and development. The footnotes also contain rich references.

Two papers by Alexandrin can be considered together. His 1977 paper is well focused on the transmission and reception of *WN* in early Russia and perfectly fits our aim. In this overlooked paper, he proposes a framework to study the relationship of source–admirer–medium–transmitter–receptor and then lists policies suggested by Adam Smith (Table 1) and policy interests of Russia (Table 2) to investigate the effect of *WN*. I find the framework attractive, and the perspective is instructive. His 1993 text is structurally similar but provides much new and detailed evidence, and argues the topic better. These two texts are complementary, but limited by space his 1993 paper is not printed here.

Anikin (1976a) offers a profound analysis of Adam Smith's influence on the Russian intelligentsia (such as A. S. Pushkin) and activists (such as a major Decembrist, N. I. Turgenev). He also identifies Russian Smithianism and analyses the impact and criticism of Smith's economic ideas at different stages of Russian history, from Chernishevski, to the Populists and Lenin, up to the Soviet period. Unlike the papers above, which analyse a given period or a certain event, Anikin's paper provides a dynamic long-run analysis of the reception of Smith in Russia. His 1993 paper is also a good, concise summary of the translation and reception of *WN* in Russia.

Finally, a paper by Zlupko (1990) on Ukrainian Smithianism, although quite descriptive and lacking in concision, offers a less well-known aspect of the story: the reception of Smith in Ukraine and the economic ideas of some representative Smithianists.

Further Reading

Texts with a * are printed in this Part

*ALEKSEEV, M. (1937), "Adam Smith and His Russian Admirers of the Eighteenth Century", in R. W. Scott, *Adam Smith as Student and Professor*, app. 7, pp. 424–31, Glasgow University.

*ALEXANDRIN, GLEN (1977), "Reception of Adam Smith's *The Wealth of Nations* in Early Russia", *Social Science Forum*, 1(1): 1–13.

—— (1993), "Adam Smith and the Russian Connection" [draft, available from the editor].

ANIKIN, ANDREI (1976a), "Adam Smith i russkaja ekonomiceskaja mysl" [Adam Smith and Russian economic thought], *Voprosky Economiki* (Problems of Economics), 3: 112–22 [translated by Glen Alexandrin, available from the editor].

—— (1976b), "Adam Smith und die russische Wirtschaftstheorie des 18. und der ersten Hälfte des 19. Jahrhunderts", in Peter Thal *et al.*, *Adam Smith gestern und heute: 200 Jahre Reichtum der Nationen*, pp. 96–108, Berlin: Akademie-Verlag.

—— (1988), "The Russian Followers of Adam Smith", *Russian Thinkers*, ch. 3, Moscow: Progress Publishers.

—— (1993), "Adam Smith in Russia", in H. Mizuta and C. Sugiyama (eds.), *Adam Smith: International Perspectives*, pp. 251–60, London: Macmillan.

*BROWN, A. (1974), "S. E. Desnitski, Adam Smith, and the *Nakaz* of Catherine II", *Oxford Slavonic Papers*, 7(1): 42–59.

—— (1975), "Adam Smith's First Russian Followers", in A. S. Skinner and T. Wilson (eds.), *Essays On Adam Smith*, pp. 247–73, Oxford University Press.

CLENDENNING, P. H. (1972), "Eighteenth Century Russian Translations of Western Economic Works", *Journal of European Economic History*, 1: 745–53.

DMYTRYSHYN, Basil (1971), "Admiral Nikolai S. Mordvinov: Russia's Forgotten Liberal", *Russian Review*, 30(1): 54–63.

KOROPECKYJ, I. S. (1984), "Academic Economics in the Nineteenth-Century Ukraine", in I. S. Koropeckyj (ed.), *Selected Contributions of Ukraine Scholars to Economics*, pp. 163–221, Harvard University Press.

LETICHE, JOHN (ed. and Foreword) (1964), *A History of Russian Economic Thought: Ninth through Eighteenth Centuries*, Greenwood Press.

LETICHE, J. M. and DMYTRYSHYN, B. (1986), "The Adam Smith Russian Angle: Student

Years of Ivan A. Tretiakov and Simeon E. Desnitskii", *Rivista Internazionali di Scienze Economiche e Commerciali*, 33(1): 7–22.

MAVOR, JAMES (1914), *An Economic History of Russia*, New York: Dutton.

*McGREW, RODERICK (1976), "Dilemmas of Development: Baron Heinrich Friedrich Storch (1766–1835) on the Growth of Imperial Russia", *Jahrbücher für Geschichte Osteuropas*, 24(1): 31–71.

SACKE, GEORG (1938), "Die Moskauer Nachschrift der Vorlesungen von Adam Smith", *Zeitschrift für Nationalökonomie*, 9(3): 351–6.

*TAYLOR, N. W. (1967), "Adam Smith's First Russian Disciple", *Slavic and East European Review*, 45(105): 425–38.

ZLUPKO, S. (1990), "Adam Smith and the Development of Progressive Economic Science in the Ukraine", *Ekonomika Sovietskoi Ukrainy* (Economics of Soviet Ukraine) 12(341): 40–6 [in Russian, translated by Glen Alexandrin, available from the editor].

8.1. Michael P. Alekseev, 1937.

Adam Smith and His Russian Admirers of the Eighteenth Century

The once widely prevalent view advanced by Alexey Vesselovsky that the study of Adam Smith's teachings "had been delayed in Russia by a period of over 40 years"[1] may be regarded at present as having been finally renounced. Though the first Russian translation of the *Inquiry into the Nature and Causes of the Wealth of Nations*, made by N. Politkovsky,[2] was not published until 1802–1806 (in 4 parts) in Petersburg, a fairly large circle of Russian readers had been well acquainted with the ideas contained in this famous book for a long time past; moreover, the first signs of Russian "Smithianism" had even preceded by several years the publication of the English original of this work.

In the sixties of the eighteenth century the custom of sending young men abroad to get their university education became widely prevalent in Russia. At the time cases of Russians being sent to England or Scotland were not infrequent. For instance, in 1761 two Russian students, Simon Jefimovich Desnitsky and Ivan Andreevich Tretiakov, were sent to Glasgow University by order of the Curator of the Moscow University, Prince I. I. Shuvalov. Both of them, having taken their degree in philosophy and law at the Glasgow University, returned to Moscow and played a prominent part in the history of Russian legislative science.[3] Indeed, precisely these two people should be regarded as the first promoters of Adam Smith's teachings from the Russian University Chair. However, both these Russian students had enjoyed the benefit of Adam Smith's guidance but for a relatively short time, having arrived in Glasgow in 1761, while in January 1764 A. Smith left Glasgow on his way to France. And yet the lectures delivered by A. Smith and attended by them could not fail to leave an impression on them. The less gifted of the two students,

Tretiakov, returned to Moscow, having completed his course of studies at Glasgow University and taken his LL.D. degree on the presentation of his dissertation "Disputatio Juridica de in jus vocando" (Glasgow, 1767). The very next year he was appointed professor at the Moscow University where he began delivering his course of lectures. However, his pedagogical career was short-lived, lasting only to 1776. In the year 1779 he died at a relatively early age.[4] His literary works were likewise small in number; the only literary inheritance he left us consists of three inaugurals delivered by him on Speech Days of the Moscow University. One of these is of particular interest to us, for it is clearly based on the lectures read by Adam Smith. The inaugural in question was delivered by Tretiakov on the Speech Day of the Moscow University held on 30th June, 1772, and bore the following title: "Discussion on the Causes of Abundance and the Slowly Progressing Enrichment of States, Both Among Ancient and Modern Peoples".[5] It is of interest to note that *The Wealth of Nations* was first published four years later (1776) and yet in the above-mentioned speech Tretiakov had not merely laid down in brief the essential theses of Smith's treatise but in some cases had used the same illustrating examples as are given by Smith. Such were, for instance, the examples which served to confirm the theory of the division of labour.[6] This similarity should, of course, be attributed to the fact that Tretiakov had carefully followed the ideas advanced by Smith in the course of lecturing at Glasgow University and that his teacher had then been engaged in working out the separate parts of his future work. Indeed, Adam Smith is known to have expounded the essential theses of his economic teachings in his lectures on Jurisprudence read as early as in the fifties of the eighteenth century.[7] Unfortunately, Tretiakov has not left us any literary evidence of his sympathies with Adam Smith's ideas. In the year that *The Wealth of Nations* was first published Tretiakov resigned from his post at the Moscow University and never published anything during the last three years of his life, while all his papers have failed to reach us.

Tretiakov's friend and fellow student of the Glasgow University, S. J. Desnitsky, was a more important personality. The range of problems he was interested in was considerably wider; he took up the study of problems connected with the origin of statecraft, the history of the development of marriage and of family relations, of property and, lastly, the problem of capital punishment from the point of view of criminal law. "All these are not the problems whose scientific study is indissolubly connected with the name of Adam Smith", his biographer states. "In the choice of the subjects of his investigation Desnitsky was apparently entirely independent. But the lines along which he worked out these problems had been undoubtedly borrowed by him from Adam Smith."[8] And indeed, it can be shown that Desnitsky was extremely susceptible to the new ideas which had been revealed to him by Adam Smith's lectures. Desnitsky's works constantly reveal obvious traces of the influence of his Scottish professor. However, there is no reason to believe that these were merely clever interpretations of the ideas he had heard advanced in the lecture room of Glasgow University, as was the case with his friend and companion, Tretiakov. In Desnitsky we have a mature and original thinker whose literary talent and vast knowledge made him one of the most influential professors of the Moscow University in the late eighteenth century and provided him a Chair in the Russian Academy (1783).[9]

On his return to Russia in 1767, after he had taken his degree at the University of Glasgow, Desnitsky was appointed in 1768 to the Chair of Roman Law and Russian Jurisprudence at the Moscow University, a post which he held for twenty years. In 1787 he retired, and in 1789 he died, thus preceding Adam Smith by a year.

In one of his inaugurals, delivered on a Speech Day of the Moscow University, Desnitsky developed the idea that the power of some people over others was based on (1) their superiority in bodily qualities (such as corpulency, plumpness), (2) their superiority in mental qualities (cunning, shrewdness, sagacity), (3) their superiority in riches and the abundance of all things. "But what mostly endows a man with honour, dignity and superiority," states Desnitsky, "is his superior riches and abundance. This has been so extraordinarily well expounded by the judicious author of a new moral philosophy, Mr. Smith, that it no longer requires any description."[10] In yet another place Desnitsky mentions "Mr. Smith who has published his moral philosophy to the delight of the scientific world". Generally speaking, Desnitsky repeatedly quotes Smith in his literary works, always mentioning him with the greatest respect. Desnitsky's paper, published in Moscow in 1781, under the heading "Legal Discussion on the Possession of Property under Various Conditions of Community" seems to coincide more closely than any of his other works with the outlook of Adam Smith and to be imbued with a spirit of Anglophilia so characteristic of Desnitsky. His knowledge of Smith's ideas can also be seen from the critical notes supplemented to his Russian translations of the works of Blackstone (*Commentaries on British Laws*, 3 volumes, Moscow, 1780–82) and of Thomas Bowden (*A Guidebook on Husbandry*, Moscow, 1780). Many of Desnitsky's other works also contain lyrical passages imbued with the spirit of his Anglophil tendencies. (For quotations, see M. Sukhomlinov, *op. cit.*, pp. 5–6.) Desnitsky is known to have once said that "the heroes of classical antiquity seem pale and petty if compared with the genius of the men who have been bred by England." His preface to the Russian translation of Bowden's works is truly a laudable discourse, written in blank verse in praise of Britain "which is great in her undertakings, successful in her achievements, formidable in her battles, glorious in her victories . . . ".

During the same years that the two Russian pupils of Adam Smith were propagating their teacher's ideas from the Chair of the Moscow University there were yet other people in Russia who had developed independently an interest in his teachings. Many of them were able even then to become familiar with the famous treatise in the original. In 1774 N. S. Mordvinov (1754–1845), a future admiral of the Russian Fleet and one of the most prominent personalities among the Russian high officials of the time, was sent to England with the view of completing his education in marine sciences. He spent three years in England and in the course of that time seemed to have developed a profound admiration for Britain's literature, science and government institutions. To quote his biographer: "Adam Smith's treatise *The Wealth of Nations* was published while Mordvinov was in England, impressing him for life, so that even in his later views he generally appears to have been an ardent adherent of Smith's teachings."[11] This statement seems fully confirmed by facts; beginning with the seventies of the eighteenth century Mordvinov always continued an ardent admirer of Adam Smith, as well as a tireless promoter of his ideas in Russia. His infatuation with Smith's teachings never weakened as he grew more advanced in years, and even seemed to increase. In his letter addressed to J. Bentham's brother and dating from 1806, Mordvinov calls Smith "one of the greatest geniuses" among those "who have done most towards benefiting mankind" and ranks him together with Bacon and Newton.[12] The influence of the treatise *The Wealth of Nations* is clearly seen in many of the pages of Mordvinov's *Discussion on the Benefits which may follow from the Institution of Private Banks in Governments* (St. Petersburg, 1811). Smith's name is also frequently quoted in the numerous notes, considerations and suggestions which Mordvinov used to hand in to the Russian Government in the course of his long-lasting and incessant activity.[13]

Another Russian traveller, Princess E. R. Dashkova (1744–1810) visited England and Scotland a few years later than Count N. S. Mordvinov. Princess Dashkova stayed in Edinburgh from 1776 to 1779, hardly ever leaving the city, for her son was studying at the University there. Later she always spoke of that period as the merriest time of her life—she frequented there among people she liked, and often entertained at her place the best teachers of Edinburgh University. In her *Mémoires*, Princess Dashkova casually mentions that "l'immortel Robertson, Blair, *Smith* et Ferguson venaient dîner et passer journée chez moi deux fois par semaine".[14] Unfortunately, we lack any other information concerning these meetings. On the other hand, it is a well-known fact how keen an interest in Smith was felt by another family of Russian aristocrats, the

Princes Vorontsov, who were famous in the late eighteenth century for their Anglophil sympathies. The eldest of the brothers, Alexander Romanovich Vorontsov (1741–1805) developed a strong attachment to everything English in spite of his having stayed in England but for a short time. Later, when living at his country seat in Russia, Alexander Vorontsov never lost his interest in Britain, keeping in close touch with English literature through the agency of his brother, Simon Vorontsov (1744–1832), who for twenty consecutive years (1785–1806) held the post of Russian Ambassador in London and supplied his brother's excellent library with the most important literary works published in England and France. Late in 1786 Simon Vorontsov enclosed among the other books he was sending to his brother the recent edition of *The Wealth of Nations*, begging him to make note of all the chapters and passages which might contain ideas contrary to his own views. The letter which Alexander Romanovich wrote in answer to his brother's request has never reached us, but it is reasonable to assume that he, too, was greatly impressed by Adam Smith's work; at all events he is known to have sent several years later *The Wealth of Nations*—together with Condorcet's *Commentaries*—to Alexander Radistchev (1749–1802), a famous Russian publicist of the time, who was then in exile in Siberia.[15] With respect to Simon Romanovich Vorontsov it may be stated that his admiration of Adam Smith has been repeatedly proved. In his letters Simon Romanovich constantly mentioned Smith's "immortel ouvrage"; thus, in writing to Prince Chartoryisky, who was one of the high officials in the earlier years of Emperor Alexander the First's reign, Vorontsov said, "In the science of commerce Adam Smith has laid foundations which are as indisputable as those laid by Euclid in geometry";[16] while in a letter to Emperor Alexander (1801) Vortonsov calls Smith "l'auteur le plus classique qui ait jamais existé sur la commerce, les manufactures, les finances des états".[17] In the Scheme he drew up for the institution of a Diplomatic College which was to be under the auspices of the Russian Foreign Office (1802), Simon Romanovich wrote that in the seventh or the eighth year of studies "on leur ferait lire en original le traité d'Adam Smith sur la richesse des nations".[18] Having learnt from the newspaper that a new tariff was being worked out in St. Petersburg, Vorontsov suggested that the Emperor should order those engaged in the working out of the new law "to read and re-read A. Smith's book on the wealth of nations so as to know it by heart".[19] In one of his letters Simon Romanovich writes of "principes aussi sûrs que lumineux de l'immortel Adam Smith que le comte Roumanzew croit avoir été réfutés sans savoir et pouvoir nommer quand, par qui et comment".[20] Lastly, from his letter to Prince A. B. Kurakin—which bears no date but apparently refers to 1798—we learn of Simon Romanovich having personally known and met Adam Smith. "This view was held in the last years of his life by the world-famous Adam Smith, whom I used to know," says Vorontsov in some chance connection and then adds, "and the now famous Arthur Young is of the same opinion."[21]

Such were the Russian admirers of Smith in the eighteenth century. For many reasons the teachings of the great Scottish philosopher failed to become known to larger circles at the time; most of his admirers were people who knew English, who felt an interest in England's intellectual life or had visited the country. However, before long *The Wealth of Nations* found its way to the writing desk of every government official and spread a strong influence over the wider circles of readers. The new interest in political sciences and national economy which became particularly keen within the first two decades of the nineteenth century was to a great extent due to the spreading of Adam Smith's teachings. Following the publication of the Russian translation of *The Wealth of Nations* the number of Russian "Smithianists" showed a rapid increase. Smith's teachings were propagated both from University Chairs and by the press.

After the death of S. Desnitsky the popularization of Smith's ideas was taken up at the Moscow University by Christian Schlözer (1774–1831), who, having completed his education in Göttingen, returned to Russian in 1796 and was first appointed professor at Dorpat and later to the newly instituted chair of political economy at the Moscow University, a post which he held for twenty-five years (1801–1826). Christian Schlözer was also the author of *The Elementary Foundations of State Economy* (1805, 2nd Ed., 1821), a book which was simultaneously published in Russian (Moscow) and in French and German (Riga), and was completely imbued with Adam Smith's ideas.[22]

At the same period (from 1789 on) the post of teacher at the cadet corps (military training school) in Petersburg was held by another Russian of German extraction, Heinrich Storch (1766–1835), who was elected as a member of the Petersburg Academy of Sciences in 1796 and soon after appointed teacher of political economy to the Grand Dukes Nicholas (the future Emperor Nicholas I) and Michael. As a philosopher and economist Storch at once declared himself to be an ardent adherent of Adam Smith. The lectures he delivered to the Grand Dukes were the foundation of his comprehensive work *Cours d'économie politique ou exposition des principes qui déterminent la prospérité des nations* (1819).[23] The book served to popularize the teachings of Adam Smith and gave rise to some polemics between the writer and J. B. Say. The Russian translation of Storch's course could not be published at once for considerations of censorship, and therefore the work first appeared in French. However, extracts from Adam Smith's treatise, together with passages from the works of Ferguson and Bentham, were allowed to appear at the time in the official organ *The St. Petersburg Journal*, which was issued by the Foreign Office.

Another Petersburg periodical, *The Journal of Statistics* (1808, v. ii, part 2) was also allowed to publish the work of yet another Russian "Smithianist", G. Baludiansky, *On the Distribution and the Turnover of Wealth*, which actually repeated some of the ideas laid forth in *The Wealth of Nations*.[24] After the war of 1812 Adam Smith became extremely popular among the liberal youth of Russia who were organizing secret circles. In endowing the hero of his novel *Eugene Onegin* with a taste for economic problems and by making him read Adam Smith, Pushkin merely reproduced the actual feature of the time, the writer himself having had the same taste. In the Lyceum the great Russian poet studied political economy with Professor Kunitsin, who taught him the essential theses advanced by Adam Smith. The study of Smith's work greatly influenced the outlook of N. I. Turgenev and this influence made itself clearly felt in his book, *An Essay on the Theory of Taxes* (1818, 2nd Ed., 1819). Pushkin knew N. Turgenev personally, and, of course, must have read his book. The period from 1818 to 1825 being the time when Adam Smith's popularity in Russia was at its highest caused Puskin to make Eugene Onegin "a profound economist", arguing on the subject as to "why a state needs no gold when it has the natural product".[25] In another decade, at the time of governmental reaction, Adam Smith's popularity in Russia was considerably shaken. In one of his uncompleted stories (*Extracts from a Novel in Letters*, 1831) Pushkin jestingly mentions that in 1818 everyone in the Petersburg high society tried to look thoughtful and to discuss gravely Adam Smith—"at the time the severity of regulations and political economy were in vogue; we arrived at balls wearing our swords; we thought it unfit to dance and had no time to spare on ladies. . . . All this had changed. French quadrille has now taken the place of Adam Smith."

NOTES

1. A. Vesselovsky, *Western Influences in Modern Russian Literature*, Moscow, 1916, pp. 174–5. It is of interest to note that the same writer in mentioning in this book the name of an original Russian philosopher of the early eighteenth century, *i.e.* Ivan Pososhkov (1670–1726), and his peculiar views on a people's welfare and economic reforms, states that the work of the latter writer, *A Book on Scantiness and Wealth*, even at that early date "foretold the theories of Adam Smith" (*ibid.*, p. 44).

2. V. S. Sopikov, *An Essay on Russian Bibliography*, St. Petersburg, 1904, iii, N. 4511. The translator of this work received 5000 roubles from the Russian Government for its publication. See A. N. Pypin, "The Relations of Bentham with Russia", *Westnic Europy*, February, 1869.

3. Both matriculated under Anderson, Professor of Natural Philosophy, in 1761.

Desnitsky graduated M.A. in 1765 and LL.D. (by examination) in 1767. Tretiakov obtained the same degrees in the same years.

4. For references to I. A. Tretiakov see *Biographical Dictionary of Professors and Teachers at the Imp. Moscow University*, Moscow, 1855, ii, pp. 505–507.

5. See *Speeches Delivered at the Official Meetings of the Imperial Moscow University by the Russian Professors thereof, Containing Their Short Curricula Vitae*. Published by the Association of the Lovers of Russian Letters, Moscow, 1819.

6. For instance, Tretiakov writes: "If a watchmaker or the manufacturer of the most trifling article, such as a needle, were to produce by himself everything necessary for the completion of these objects or the like of them, he would hardly be able to manufacture one watch a year or one needle a day—*cf.* above, p. 328".

7. Zeyss, *Adam Smith und der Eigennutz*, 1889, S. 14–16. The student's notes on the "Lectures on Justice, Police, Revenue and Arms, delivered at the University of Glasgow by Adam Smith", published by Profesor Cannan (Oxford, 1896), give us a clear idea of the extensiveness of the course which was likewise attended by the above-mentioned Russian students. Unfortunately, their own notes on these lectures are not available and are supposed to have been destroyed with their other papers in the Moscow conflagration of 1812—*cf. Economic Journal*, September 1935, pp. 427–38.

8. N. M. Korkunov, *The History of the Philosophy of Law*, St. Petersburg, 1898, p. 295.

9. M. I. Sukhomlinov, *The History of the Russian Academy*, Issue V, St. Petersburg, 1880, pp. 3–8. See also *The Russian Biographical Dictionary*, St. Petersburg, 1905, pp. 331–5.

10. He was also indebted to the lectures of John Millar, Professor of Law—*cf. Observations concerning Distinction of Ranks in Society*, 1771.

11. V. S. Iconnikov, *Count N. S. Mordvinov*, St. Petersburg, 1873, pp. 4–5. See also A. M. Gnjevushev, "The Political and Economic Ideas of Count N. S. Mordvinov", *The University Review*, Kiev, 1907, N 2, pp. 6–7, 13, 19, 50–52.

12. *The Europe Herald* (Vestnik Evropy), February 1869, p. 816.

13. See *The Archives of the Counts Mordvinov*, published in ten volumes by V. A. Bilbasov.

14. Princesse Dashkova, *Mémoires*. Quotations have been taken from the best edition, reproducing the original manuscript (written in French)—*Archives des Princes Woronzow*, xxi (Moscow, 1881, p. 171).

15. V. N. Alexandrenko, *Russian Diplomatic Agents in London in the XVIII Century*, Warsaw 1897, i, pp. 387–388.

16. V. Alexandrenko, *op. cit.*, pp. 391–92.

17. *Archives de Pr. Woronzow*, x, p. 303. In another letter to the Emperor (dated 18th May, 1801), Vorontsov wrote: "Les gens instruits dans les matières de finances et de commerce, savaient depuis longtemps, mais Adam Smith l'a prouvé indisputablement dans son immortel ouvrage sur la richesse des nations que le commerce ne se fait qu'avec des capitaux, qu'il demande liberté et sûreté", etc. (*Arch.*, x, p. 360).

18. *Arch.*, xv, p. 438.

19. *Arch.*, x, p. 88.

20. *Arch.*, x, p. 179.

21. *Arch.*, xxx, p. 490.

22. *Biographical Dictionary of Professors and Teachers at the Moscow University*, Moscow, 1855, ii, p. 628.

23. In spite of the fact that many pages of Storch's course almost literally repeat certain passages of Adam Smith's treatise, the St. Petersburg economist should not be denied a certain originality in the working out of economical doctrines or in his independent criticism of some of the theses advanced by Smith, as, for instance, the definition of productive labour, the question of thriftiness, etc.

24. To establish the connection between this work and the theories of Adam Smith and of his school, see V. M. Stein, *The Development of Economic Thought*, Leningrad, 1924, i, p. 126.

25. N. L. Brodsky, *Commentary to Eugene Onegin*, Moscow, 1932, pp. 13–16.

8.2. Norman W. Taylor 1967.
Adam Smith's First Russian Disciple

If true delight you would afford him
You'd give him Adam Smith to read.
A deep economist, indeed,
He talked about the wealth of nations.
The State relied, his friends were told,
Upon its staples, not on gold—
This subject filled his conversations.[1]

So wrote Pushkin of the hero of his verse novel *Eugene Onegin*. But this was well on in the 19th century and the *Wealth of Nations* had been published in Russian in the years 1802 to 1806. Even before that many members of the Russian intelligentsia had read Adam Smith's work in the original English edition. All this is familiar; what is less well known, however, is that even before the *Wealth of Nations* was published at all, Adam Smith's ideas on economics were being propagated in Russian intellectual circles. The person responsible was one Ivan Andreyevich Tret'yakov, who, together with Semyon Yefimovich Desnitsky, had been sent by the curator of Moscow University to study in Glasgow, where they attended Smith's lectures. They arrived at Glasgow University in 1761 and returned six or seven years later to Russia, where both became professors at the Imperial Moscow University. Both of them had been much impressed by Smith's ideas, which they proceeded to transmit to their Russian audiences but, whereas Tret'yakov was very much interested in economic matters, Desnitsky gave his attention to questions of jurisprudence and philosophy and so passes from our consideration.

The surviving evidence of Tret'yakov's teaching on economics is meagre but compelling. It consists of the text of a public lecture delivered in 1772 at Moscow University and a few references in a lecture on the history of universities delivered in 1768. As a matter of interest, from the foundation of the university in 1755 until late in the 19th century every professor was required to deliver a two-hour public lecture six days a week.[2] What distinguishes the three Tret'yakov lectures whose texts survive[3] is that they were delivered on occasions of public celebration. They were therefore printed; a few copies escaped the burning of Moscow University during the Napoleonic occupation, in which most of Tret'yakov's papers may have been destroyed. The surviving discourse on economics was part of an address in honour of the tenth anniversary of Catherine the Great's accession to the throne.

Tret'yakov's teachings have been little discussed by scholars. He received a passing mention in the third edition of Luigi Cossa's successful *Guido allo Studio dell'Economia Politica* (1875). V. V. Svyatlovsky, in *Istoriya ekonomicheskikh idey v Rossii* (Moscow, 1923), noted that Tret'yakov embraced Smith's ideas but did not examine the question in detail. In 1954 I. S. Bak published an uncritical review of Tret'yakov's social and economic ideas, based on a reprint of the 1772 lecture in *Izbrannyye proizvedeniya russkikh mysliteley vtoroy poloviny XVIII-go veka*, Vol. 1 (Leningrad, 1952).[4]

Most interesting of all, not for its content but for its omissions, is a paper entitled "Adam Smith and his Russian Admirers of the Eighteenth Century", appended to W. R. Scott's *Adam Smith as Student and Professor* (Glasgow, 1937), in which Professor Michael P. Alekseyev of the University of Leningrad devotes a page or so to Tret'yakov. This mainly contains biographical information and makes only passing reference to the content of Tret'yakov's teaching. Alekseyev observes that "unfortunately Tret'yakov has not left us any literary evidence of his sympathies with Adam Smith's ideas". This is a rather curious remark. Surely, only the most pedantic interpretation of the term "literary" would eliminate the 1772 address from the definition; yet while it is clear that Alekseyev was familiar with this lecture, he chooses not to discuss its content. A possible reason will shortly suggest itself.

Tret'yakov is accorded four pages in a recently published history of Russian economic ideas.[5] The author is clearly I. S. Bak, since the discussion is largely a reproduction of his article referred to above. Bak asserts that in his political and economic views Tret'yakov had much in common with Adam Smith but that he did not simply repeat the latter's ideas. He makes other efforts to establish Tret'yakov's respectability from the Soviet standpoint. For example, he is anxious to refute a statement in one 19th-century reference work[6] to the effect that Tret'yakov was the son of a priest. He claims that he was in fact the son of an army officer.

If one reads Tret'yakov's 1772 lecture against the background of the *Wealth of Nations*, one is struck by numerous echoes of Smith's ideas. He embraces, for example, the fundamental anti-mercantilist proposition with which Smith begins his work—that the real wealth of nations stems from "the annual labour of every nation". He emphasises the division of labour as a prime source of economic growth. And his concept of capital as advances of subsistence and working materials is by Smith out of Quesnay. Smith is nowhere given credit for these and other ideas, but the reason for this may have been that Tret'yakov had thoroughly assimilated them into his own thinking. He uses Smith's famous diamonds-and-water metaphor and invokes the case of a pin factory to illustrate the advantages of division of labour. But neither of these examples was original to Smith;[7] in any case, since they are cited almost to the point of triteness in present-day textbooks, one can see that they would have caught the imagination of Smith's own students.

When, however, we read Tret'yakov's text together with the transcribed notes of Smith's Glasgow lectures, the resemblances become startling rather than merely striking. To demonstrate this, we print below, in the left-hand column, the full text of Tret'yakov's lecture (with the exception of the opening and closing eulogies to Catherine), and, in the right-hand column, parallel passages from Smith's *Lectures*.[8]

Tret'yakov's text	*Smith's Lectures*
To celebrate with due respect the anniversary of the accession to the throne of such a superior ruler [as Catherine] I have the honour to present to my audience, which joins in full admiration of her high-minded efforts, and also as a token of the close collaboration of this university with her, the following paper: "Of the causes of public opulence and of the slow enrichment of ancient and modern nations."	
The prosperity and wealth of nations are synonymous with cheapness and plenty, two factors closely associated with each other. Water is cheap because we have it in plenty, but in waterless regions or during marches we have to pay much for it; precious stones are expensive because they are scarce. In order to demonstrate the easiest method of achieving prosperity, let us first make clear what plenty means. First, however, I	Cheapness is in fact the same thing with plenty. It is only on account of the plenty of water that it is so cheap as to be got for the lifting; and on account of the scarcity of diamonds (for their real use seems not yet to be discovered) that they are so dear. To ascertain the most proper method of obtaining these conveniences it will be necessary to show first wherein opulence consists, and still previous to this we must consider what are the natural wants of

Tret'yakov's text	*Smith's Lectures*

must discuss man's basic needs which undergo development in the course of acquiring prosperity. There are different views on this matter; I will try now to substantiate my own [*sic*].

Nature provides in abundance everything that any living being needs, even if it is used without any further treatment. The main needs of every human being are: food, clothes, shelter. Most animals are already supplied with everything they need. Man, however, has special needs; there is hardly a thing which satisfies him in its natural state. Although the customs of primitive people show us that man's food needs no preparation, having learned the use of fire, man discovered that with it food might be made more palatable and digestible. Food, however, is not the only thing that may be improved. Man's organism is also affected by certain unfavourable features of the climate in which he lives, which during some seasons can be too difficult for him to endure. In countries where the temperature is consistently higher than that of the human body women smear themselves with special ointments to help them bear the heat and humidity. We can, however, make the following assertion— man's needs are not so numerous that he cannot satisfy them through his own labour. Every man can satisfy his own needs.

mankind which are to be supplied; and if we differ from common opinions, we shall at least give the reason for our non-conformity.

Nature produces for every animal everything that is sufficient to support it without having recourse to the improvement of the original production. Food, clothes and lodging are all the wants of any animal whatever, and most of the animal creation are sufficiently provided for by nature in all those wants to which their condition is liable. Such is the delicacy of man alone, that no object is produced to his liking. He finds that in everthing there is need of improvement. Though the practice of savages shows that his food needs no preparation, yet being acquainted with fire, he finds that it can be rendered more wholesome and easily digested, and thereby may preserve him from many diseases which are very violent among them. But it is not only his food that requires this improvement; his puny constitution is hurt also by the in-temperature of the air he breathes in, which, though not very capable of improvement, must be brought to a proper temperament for his body, and an artificial atmosphere prepared for this purpose. The human skin cannot endure the inclemencies of the weather, and even in those countries where the air is warmer than the natural warmth of the constitution, and where they have no need of clothes, it must be stained and painted to be able to endure the hardships of the sun and rain. In general, however, the necessities of man are not so great but that they can be supplied by the

Tret'yakov's text   *Smith's Lectures*

unassisted labour of the individual. All the above necessities everyone can provide for himself, such as animals and fruits for his food, and skins for his clothing.

While the delicate human body requires more care than that of an animal, man's delicate or much more sensitive mind requires even more consideration and therefore all the arts and sciences have been invented to satisfy it.

As the delicacy of a man's body requires much greater provision than that of any other animal, the same or rather the much greater delicacy of his mind requires a still greater provision to which all the different arts [are] subservient. (pp. 157–8)

And here, gentlemen, has been opened a vast realm of inventions born out of the power of man's mind. The human mind gave birth to enlightenment and to all which is now known under the names of Arts and Sciences.

All these creations of man's mind have gradually multiplied to such an extent that it is hardly possible to embrace all of them in a single mind. As a result, a need arose to make the division which we now observe among crafts and sciences.

The whole industry of human life is employed not in procuring the supply of our three humble necessities, food, clothes and lodging, but in procuring the conveniences of it according to the nicety and delicacy of our taste. To improve and multiply the materials, which are the principal objects of our necessities, gives occasion to all the variety of the arts. (p. 160)

The value of this division in crafts and sciences in promoting public opulence must not be minimised because it called forth the division in man's labour, and this division, as we know, helped to produce goods of greater quality, and also afforded better working conditions. In fact, if there had been no division of human labour, no workman could get rich by his own labour alone. He could scarcely even have earned his living. If a watchmaker, for instance, or a workman manufacturing such a simple thing as a pin, should make everything involved in the whole process of production, he would hardly be able to make a watch in

We shall next show how this division of labour occasions a multiplication of the product, or, which is the same thing, how opulence arises from it. In order to [do] this let us observe the effect of the division of labour in some manufactures. If all the parts of a pin were made by one man, if the same person dug the ore, [s]melted it, and split the wire, it would take him a whole year to make one pin, and this pin must therefore be sold at the expense of his maintenance for that time, which taking [it] at a moderate computation, would at least be six pounds for a pin. If the labour is so far divided that the wire is ready-made, he

Tret'yakov's text	*Smith's Lectures*

a year or a pin in a day; as it is, owing to the division of labour among various working hands a large quantity of similar objects is produced during one day and thus society acquires them more cheaply.

will not make above twenty per day, which allowing ten pence for wages, makes the pin a half-penny. The pin-maker therefore divides the labour among a great number of different persons; the cutting, pointing, heading, and gilding are all separate professions. Two or three are employed in making the head, one or two in putting it on, and so on, to the putting them in the paper, being in all eighteen. By this division every one can with great ease make 2000 a day. The same is the case in the linen and woollen manufactures . . .

When labour is thus divided, and so much done by one man in proportion, the surplus above their maintenance is considerable, which each man can exchange for a fourth of what he could have done if he had finished it alone. By this means the commodity becomes far cheaper, and the labour dearer. (pp. 163–5)

Having analysed the two chief causes of public opulence—namely, the division of labour and the emergence of crafts—I will now consider others.

Prosperity in England, Holland and in many other countries, gentlemen, clearly demonstrates that banks are very profitable for commerce. They greatly enrich every nation and have other beneficial results.

Many political writers have tried to refute the usefulness of banks by asserting that bank failures are very harmful because public opulence consists in the accumulation of silver and gold. The English people, however, do not think the bank failures are as harmful as many think them to be. It is true that many people can suffer losses thereby,

The ruin of a bank would not be so dangerous as is commonly imagined. Suppose all the money in Scotland was issued by one bank, and that it became bankrupt, a very few individuals would be ruined by it, but not many; because the quantity of cash or paper that people have in their hands bears no proportion to their wealth. Neither would the wealth of

Tret'yakov's text	*Smith's Lectures*
but these losses are not great since the amount of money in a country is small compared with the amount of wealth held in other forms; nor does the State itself undergo many losses from these bank failures because most of the State's treasury is not in gold and silver. Money is not an important part of the wealth of the nation. Therefore, the damage inflicted by a bank failure is not as frightful as many writers have depicted. There is one defence against the danger of bank failures; namely, the banks should not be allowed to be the property of one person. On the contrary, the multiplication of banking companies should be greatly encouraged. Where there are many banks there is competition. Because of this state of affairs in England banks often find their own notes being presented to them by other banks. Bank owners, however, should be very cautious and ready at any time to pay cash against the notes submitted to them. As for the erroneous notion that a nation's wealth consists in large amounts of gold and silver, this can be easily refuted by the following consideration.	the whole country be much hurt by it, because the hundredth part of the riches of a country does not consist in money. They only method to prevent the bad consequence arising from the ruin of banks, is to give monopolies to none, but to encourage the erection of as many as possible. When several are established in a country, a mutual jealousy prevails, they are continually making unexpected runs on one another. This puts them on their guard and obliges them to provide themselves against such demands. (p. 195)
Man's industriousness is the means by which both stock and money can be multiplied, although not always in equal proportions. Man is eager to apply his efforts to the cause which is the object of his wishes and whims; and this cause may increase as much as the man is able to apply his efforts to it. We always can have more bread and other such products than gold, silver, precious stones, and the like, because, with the application of some zeal, the former are easier to acquire than the latter. Almost every spot on earth	We may observe upon this that human industry always multiplies goods and money together, though not always in the same proportion. The labour of men will always be employed in producing whatever is the object of human desire, and things will increase in proportion as it is in the power of man to cultivate them. Corn and other commodities of that kind must always be produced in greater abundance than gold, precious stones, and the like, because they are more within the reach of human industry. Almost any part

Tret'yakov's text	*Smith's Lectures*

may be tilled in order to produce grain, flax, and the like, while gold is hidden in the bowels of the earth, and much time, labour and material things are required to get even a small amount of it.

Because of this, the quantity of money never reaches the amount of other goods produced. It follows that the value of money can become higher or lower according to how industrious people in the country are.

Money has great value in undeveloped nations. The reason for this is that they have no money of their own; their money is acquired by plundering because they do not understand how to create money in their own countries. If, however, the people are educated and acquainted with science the value of the money in the country drops. Then the people try to reach into the bowels of the earth and to mine ores, some of which are later changed into coins.

After the fall of the Roman Empire and until the acquisition of the West Indies, the value of money was very high and was steadily rising; later it dropped considerably.

The view that money alone is the source of the wealth of a nation has been subjected to much criticism in a number of countries and especially in England. I now want to present some of these criticisms.

The over-riding example of short-sighted behaviour arising from this fallacy is the prohibition against the export of money. Such a restriction is highly injurious to a country's interest because, in any country whatever, if money is not kept in circulation it must be regarded as

of the surface of the earth may, by proper culture, be made capable of producing corn, but gold is not to be found everywhere, and even where it is to be found, it lies concealed in the bowels of the earth, and to produce a small quantity of it, long time and much labour are requisite. For these reasons money never increases in proportion to the increase of goods, and consequently money will be sold at a cheaper rate in proportion as a country becomes opulent. (pp. 197–8)

In savage nations money gives a vast price, because savages have no money but [what] they acquire by plunder, for they have not that knowledge which is necessary for producing money in their own country. But when a nation arrives at a certain degree of improvement in the arts, its value diminishes; then they begin to search the mines and manufacture it themselves. From the fall of the Roman Empire to the discovery of the West Indies, the value of money was very high, and continually increasing. Since that latter period its value has decreased considerably. (p. 198)

In general, every prohibition [against export of coin] hurts the commerce of a country. Every unnecessary accumulation of money is a dead stock which might be employed in enriching the nation by foreign commerce. It likewise raises the price of goods and

Tret'yakov's text   *Smith's Lectures*

dead capital, or as a treasure buried in the ground.

Such a restriction was, for example, the main cause of poverty in Spain. When the Spaniards seized the Mexican gold mines the amount of monetary gold and silver they possessed rose substantially because they did not put any substantial amount of these precious metals to other uses. Meanwhile, foreign countries raised the prices of their goods which were scarce in Spain, and forced the Spaniards to pay twice as much. This was where the poverty started.

The poverty of a nation cannot originate from trade with foreign countries provided this trade be conducted with prudence and wisdom. Poverty springs from essentially different causes; mainly those that can impoverish a person. A man who spends more than he earns with his work will be impoverished; the same applies to a country if it spends more than it produces by its own labour inside its boundaries. Such a country would surely be reduced to a state of absolute poverty.

makes the country undersold at foreign markets.

It is to be observed that prohibiting the exportation of money is really one great cause of the poverty of Spain and Portugal. When they got possession of the mines of Mexico and Peru, they thought they could command all Europe by the continual supplies which they received from thence, if they could keep the money among them, and therefore they prohibited the exportation of it. But this had a quite contrary effect, for when money is, as it were, dammed up to an unnatural height, and there is more than the circulation requires, the consequences are very unfavourable to the country. Every commodity rises to an extravagant height. The Portuguese pay for English cloth, additional to the natural price of it, the expense and risk of carrying it there, for nobody ever saw a Spanish or Portuguese ship in a British harbour. (p. 202)

It is to be observed that the poverty of a nation can never proceed from foreign trade if carried on with wisdom and prudence. The poverty of a nation proceeds from much the same causes with those which render an individual poor. When a man consumes more than he gains by his industry, he must impoverish himself unless he has some other way of subsistence. In the same manner, if a nation consume more than it produces, poverty is inevitable; if its annual produce be ninety millions and its annual consumption an hundred, then it spends, eats, and drinks, tears, wears ten millions more than it produces, and its stock of opulence must gradually [go] to nothing. (p. 207)

Tret'yakov's text	*Smith's Lectures*
The factors that have prevented some societies from reaching the thriving conditions enjoyed by some countries have been either natural obstructions or political ones.	We come now to the next thing proposed, to examine the causes of the slow progress of opulence. When one considers the effects of the division of labour, what an immediate tendency it has to improve the arts, it appears somewhat surprising that every nation should continue so long in a poor and indigent state as we find it does. The causes of this may be considered under these two heads; first, natural impediments; and secondly, the oppression of civil government.
The concept of division of labour could not emerge in primitive societies. For a long period the amount of labour required for the production of various goods was such as to prevent people from reaching a very high level of living. Before division of labour could be introduced it was necessary to have a large amount of various articles in stock. Without certain necessary articles an artificer cannot set up a factory or a workshop; even a farmer, if he does not have a food supply for say a year, cannot start farming if he is not able to reap his harvest until summer is ended. For the same reason no artificer in an undeveloped country can drop the trade he is engaged in and try to make a living in another unless he has laid by a good supply of food for the future. In any case, it is well known how difficult it is to find a job that will give an added adequate income even in civilised countries. If it is so difficult to make a living in a civilised country, in a primitive society it would require much more effort because, with no stock laid by, people must spend their daily earnings to meet their daily requirements.	A rude and barbarous people are ignorant of the effects of the division of labour, and it is long before one person, by continually working at different things, can produce any more than is necessary for his daily subsistence. Before labour can be divided some accumulation of stock is necessary; a poor man with no stock can never begin a manufacture. Before a man can commence farming, he must at least have laid in a year's provision, because he does not receive the fruits of his labour till the end of the season. Agreeably to this, in a nation of hunters or shepherds no person can quit the common trade in which he is employed, and which affords him daily subsistence, till he have some stock to maintain him, and begin the new trade. Every one knows how difficult it is, even in a refined society, to raise one's self to moderate circumstances. It is still more difficult to raise one's self by those trades which require no art nor ingenuity. A porter or day-labourer must continue poor for ever. In the beginnings of society this is still more difficult. Bare subsistence is almost all that a savage can procure,

Tret'yakov's text	*Smith's Lectures*

This, then, is why uncivilised people have been at an economic disadvantage everywhere. In our enlightened times simple farmers in civilised countries have more profit and a better life than the peoples scattered over vast plains, wandering from place to place, lacking even a permanent home. If, however, these people acquire even a primitive tool, they can make progress and have more success.

and having no stock to begin upon, nothing to maintain him but what is produced by the exertion of his own strength, it is no wonder he continues long in an indigent state. The meanest labourer in a polished society has in many respects an advantage over a savage: he has more assistance in his labour; he has only one particular thing to do, which by assiduity, he attains a facility in performing; he has also machines and instruments which greatly assist him. An Indian has not so much as a pickaxe, a spade, or a shovel, nor anything else but his own labour. This is one great cause of the slow progress of opulence in every country; till some stock be produced there can be no division of labour, and before a division of labour takes place there can be very little accumulation of stock.

Another cause is the nature of government administration. In a primitive society the government has neither power nor authority to create well-being among its subjects, because it is not able to protect its people from invasions and looting by neighbouring peoples. Creation of the institutions necessary to protect against these dangers requires greater authority and long experience.

Under such circumstances, therefore, artificers and farmers, having inadequate protection, would become unable to produce significant amounts of output. A general feeling of depression and an aversion to labour would develop among the people. In place of industry comes idleness and there arises a large class of parasites who are a blight on society; first, they do not support their government

The other cause that was assigned was the nature of civil government. In the infancy of society, as has been often observed, government must be weak and feeble, and it is long before its authority can protect the industry of individuals from the rapacity of their neighbours. When people find themselves every moment in danger of being robbed of all they possess, they have no motive to be industrious. There could be little accumulation of stock, because the indolent, which would be the greatest number, would live upon the industrious, and spend whatever they produced. When the power of government becomes so great as to defend the produce of industry, another obstacle arises from a different quarter. Among neighbouring nations in a barbarous state there are

Tret'yakov's text	*Smith's Lectures*

and, second, what is still worse, they become a burden to it, consuming the scarce goods produced by the much smaller labouring part of the population.

When the government of a country finally became strong enough to maintain power over its subjects and an organised social system, it was still unable to defend its borders against the attacks of savage outsiders, who in those uncivilised times caused a dreadful destruction everywhere. The balance of power observed among all European nations at the present time was unknown in those days and, therefore, the invaders rampaged through other countries, subduing their peoples, ruining their lands and reducing them to complete destitution. The Arabs and other savage peoples moved in large hordes whose ferocity could not be withstood and so they entirely ruined many lands. We should briefly note, however, that in those times when government was still weak it was not only wars that caused much evil but also two other forms of God's punishment—hunger and pestilence.

perpetual wars, one continually invading and plundering the other, and though private property be secured from the violence of neighbours, it is in danger from hostile invasions. In this manner it is next to impossible that any accumulation of stock can be made. It is observable that among savage nations there are always more violent convulsions than among those farther advanced in refinement. Among the Tartars and Arabs, great bands of barbarians are always roaming from one place to another in quest of plunder, and they pillage ever country as they go along. Thus large tracts of country are often laid waste, and all the effects carried away. (pp. 222–4)

Another obstacle to a country's prosperity may be the conditions that affect people's motivations. Thus, among the Romans, the greater part of the population considered military pursuits as the most noble and important, giving all their devotion to them and looking with contempt on other occupations no less useful to their society.

This is why agriculture was neglected in the Roman Empire. Claudius and Caligula presented their warriors with plots of land for nearly nothing in the

In the latter times of the [Roman] Republic the Emperors tried several methods of promoting the cultivation of the country, but being ignorant that the real cause of their want was the immense quantity of corn daily imported from Egypt, and other parts of Africa, all their endeavours were ineffectual. Caligula and Claudius gave their soliders land for nothing, upon condition that they would cultivate it, but as the soldiers had no other motive, very inconsiderable improvements were made. (p. 229)

Tret'yakov's text	*Smith's Lectures*

hope that they would cultivate them. But, since a soldier, by virtue of his training, stands too far from this kind of thing, no noticeable success was achieved.

These are the factors that have impeded the rapid enrichment of nations. Different measures have been tried at different times to eliminate them. Placing her hopes on her wise ruler who on this very day ascended the throne, Russia is fortunate to enjoy all the opportunities that could be found for her enrichment and glorification.

Do these obvious similarities explain why Alekseyev abstained from discussing in detail the content of Tret'yakov's teaching on economics? He was familiar not only with the 1772 address but also with Cannan's edition of Smith's lectures.[9] While he discussed the ideas of Desnitsky, Mordvinov and other Russian disciples of Smith, he did not do so in the case of Tret'yakov, although he felt obliged to include him in the record. Was this from embarrassment or political discretion? Alekseyev was at pains to note that the other scholars he discussed frankly acknowledged their debts to Smith and on three occasions within three pages he compared Tret'yakov unfavourably with his fellow student, Desnitsky.

Be this as it may, it is clear that the recent attempt to elevate Tret'yakov's scholarly reputation is less than justified. Such a claim should rest on something more than the transmission of the master's ideas, unadorned and unacknowledged. Tret'yakov's sole merit is that he provides an independent check on the accuracy of that other student of Adam Smith whose notes were subsequently published by Edwin Cannan. Indeed, since Cannan drew the plausible conclusion that the anonymous student must have compiled his notes between 1760 and 1764,[10] it is possible that Tret'yakov and he were classmates.

By a stroke of irony Tret'yakov died in 1776.

NOTES

Assistance in translation by Mrs Natalie Iljinsky is gratefully acknowledged.

1. Babette Deutsch (tr.), *The Poems, Prose and Plays of Pushkin*, New York, 1936 (Random House Inc.).
2. Cyril Bryner, "Moscow University, 1755–1955" (*The Russian Review*, July 1955, p. 203).

3. "A Discourse on the Origin and Foundation of the Universities in Europe Sponsored by the Government," 1768; "A Discourse on the Development of Roman Law," 1769; "A Discourse on the Causes of Public Opulence and the Slow Enrichment of Ancient and Modern Nations," 1772.

4. "Obshchestvenno-ekonomicheskiye vozzreniya I. A. Tret'yakova" (*Voprosy istorii*, no. 9, Moscow, 1954, pp. 104–13).

5. *Istoriya russkoy ekonomicheskoy mysli*, ed. A. I. Pashkov, Moscow, 1955–8. An English version of this work, edited by John M. Letiche, was published under the title *A History of Russian Economic Thought, Ninth through Eighteenth Century*, Berkeley-Los Angeles, Calif., 1964.

6. S. P. Shevyrev (ed.), *Biograficheskiy slovar' professorov i prepodavateley Imperatorskoge Moskovskogo Universiteta za istekayushcheye stoletiye* . . . , 2 pts., Moscow, 1855.

7. As Cannan pointed out, the diamonds-and-water example dates from as early as Plato (*Euthydem*) and crops up frequently as, for example, in J. Law, *Money and Trade Considered* (1705) and Joseph Harris, *Essay on Money and Coins* (1757). Even the pin-factory example pre-dates Adam Smith. Two publications, with which he was probably familiar, contain similar descriptions—Chambers' *Cyclopaedia*, 1738, 1741; and the French *Encyclopédie* (1755).

8. Edwin Cannan (ed.), *Lectures on Justice, Police, Revenue and Arms, delivered in the University of Glasgow by Adam Smith and reported by a Student in 1763*, Oxford, 1896.

9. Scott, *op. cit.*, p. 425n.

10. *Lectures*, Introduction, p. xx

8.3. A. H. Brown 1974
S. E. Desnitsky, Adam Smith, and the
Nakaz of Catherine II

Semen Efimovich Desnitsky has strong claims to be regarded as one of the most outstandingly able Russian social and political thinkers of the second half of the eighteenth century. He was certainly one of the most influential figures in Moscow University circles from the late sixties to the middle eighties of the eighteenth century, and he is regarded both by pre-revolutionary and by Soviet legal historians as "the father of Russian jurisprudence".[1]

Desnitsky was also an important link between British and Russian social and legal thought at this time. As the translator of the first volume of Blackstone's *Commentaries* into Russian,[2] he helped to make the English jurist's ideas more widely known in Russia, but he played a role of even greater significance by introducing many of the ideas of Adam Smith and of other Scottish Enlightenment theorists (such as Millar, Robertson, and Kames) into Catherine II's Russia.[3] Though Desnitsky was not, of course, alone among educated Russians in his awareness of the work of Smith, Robertson, and other members of the "Scottish Historical School", he was the first Russian to take up a number of Smithian ideas. This he was in a peculiarly advantageous position to do since, along with a Russian colleague, Ivan Andreevich Tret'yakov (who, like Desnitsky, was appointed to a chair of law in Moscow in 1768), Desnitsky had been sent to Glasgow University in 1761 where he and Tret'yakov remained until 1767. During the first two and a half years of their studies in Glasgow, Adam Smith was still a professor there, and the Russian students attended his lectures and heard him expound many of the arguments which Smith himself did not commit to print until 1776 with the publication of *The Wealth of Nations*.[4] They also studied under the supervision of one of Smith's most brilliant pupils, John Millar, another pioneer in the social sciences, who held the chair of law in Glasgow from 1761 until his death in 1801.

The influence of Smith and Millar on Desnitsky's thought may be detected in virtually every published work of the Russian jurist. They were not, of course, the only influences on Desnitsky's intellectual development. Though Desnitsky was critical of Blackstone in certain respects, he also accepted a number of Blackstone's ideas, and the influence of Lomonosov may also be detected in his work. But the central features of Desnitsky's approach to the study of law and society—his comparative-historical method and the stadial theory of development which he employed—were direct fruits of his period of study in Scotland.

Desnitsky rejects the idea that "the various successes of the human race, its risings and falling" can be measured "on the basis of its imputed childhood, youth, maturity, and old age" and observes that "fortunately for our times, the newest and most assiduous explorers of human nature have discovered incomparably better means for studying nations in their various successes in accordance with the circumstances and conditions through which those peoples, starting from their primordial society with wild animals, rose to the highest degree of greatness and enlightenment".[5] Desnitsky goes on to outline "four such conditions of the human race" (conditions which, he suggests, were recognized also by ancient writers) of which the most primitive is "the *condition* of peoples living by *hunting* animals and feeding on the *spontaneous fruits* of the earth; the second is the *condition* of people living as shepherds, or the *pastoral*; the third is the *agricultural*; the fourth and last is the *commercial*".[6] These stages of development are precisely those which were recognized by Adam Smith and John Millar and employed by them as tools of analysis in their Glasgow lectures.[7] However, they figure, if anything, even more prominently in Desnitsky's public lectures, and in none more so than his *Yuridicheskoe rassuzhdenie o nachale i proiskhozhdenii supruzhestva u pervonachal'nykh narodov i o sovershenstve, k kakomu onoe privedennym byt'kazhetsya posledovavshimi narodami prosveshchenneishimi* (1775) (a work which owes a lot to Millar)[8] and his *Yuridicheskoe rassuzhdenie o raznykh ponyatiyakh, kakie imeyut narody o sobstvennosti imeniya v razlichnykh sostoyaniyakh obshchezhitel'stva* (1781) (an exceptionally systematic discussion of the four-stage theory of development).

In almost all of his works, Desnitsky emerges as a proponent of legal and political reform as well as a social theorist. The range of his writings includes, however, those in which he is mainly concerned with sociological analysis of a broad, generalizing type and others in which his main concern is with practical proposals for political reform. It is Desnitsky's most important work in the latter category, his *Predstavlenie o uchrezhdenii zakonodatel'noi, suditel'noi i nakazatel'noi vlasti v Rossiiskoi imperii*, with which I shall be concerned in this article, and I wish to pay particular attention to the last of four appendices which Desnitsky added to this work, that devoted to state finances.

Some attention must, first of all, however, be devoted to the *Predstavlenie* as a whole. Desnitsky wrote this remarkable work in response to the setting-up of Catherine II's Legislative Commission in 1767 and completed it early in 1768. Since it was addressed to Catherine herself, it was not published during Desnitsky's lifetime and, in fact, it remained unknown to scholars until 1905, the date of its first publication.[9] Yet the *Predstavlenie* has strong claims to be regarded as Desnitsky's most interesting single work and it is one which shows him to be an astute and independent political thinker. In it, Desnitsky elaborates a detailed plan of political reform for Russia, applying in an original way ideas about government which he had learned from observation, as well as from books and lectures, during the six years he spent in Britain. Though the British constitutional model was clearly one which Desnitsky found attractive, his proposals do not follow it in all respects but, on the contrary, are carefully adapted to Russian conditions.

Desnitsky not only discusses the setting-up of legislative, judicial, and executive authorities in the Russian empire, as the title of his work suggests, but he also introduces a fourth section to the main body of proposals entitled *grazhdanskaya vlast'*, in which he makes detailed proposals for the reform of local government, and he concludes his work with appendices on state inhabitants "of lower birth", on church government, on the Cossacks and nomadic peoples in the Russian empire, and on state financial policy and organization. In order to devote adequate space to a discussion of the last of these appendices, only brief notice can be taken of some of the most salient points in each of the four sections of the main body of Desnitsky's text.

In his first section on the legislative authority, Desnitsky proposes a radical reform of the senate whereby it would become an elected body composed of some six to eight hundred persons. It was to be composed not only of landowners in the various regions and provinces but of merchants and handicraftsmen, as well as ecclesiastics and scholars. Landowners were to be elected by their fellow landowners and the senators drawn from trade and commerce were to be elected by the merchants and craftsmen themselves, subject to a property qualification. Bishops with a diocese entrusted to them were to be allowed to become senators without election, whereas universities and other educational institutions, such as colleges of sciences and of arts, were to elect from their midst whomsoever they thought fit, "persons able to live on their own means, and who will make representations on their behalf".[10] Desnitsky finds it expedient to stress, however, that "in Russia . . . the monarchical condition and the unity of the fatherland" demand that this senate would have less independence than the parliaments of Britain and France and that its relationship to the monarch would be essentially an advisory one.[11]

In his proposals for the establishment of the judicial authority, Desnitsky suggests that there should be at least eight judicial circuits established in the Russian empire and centred upon such places as Riga, St. Petersburg, Tobol'sk, Novgorod, Moscow, and Kazan'. In each of these regions the judicial authority would be composed of twelve people comprising an advocate-general, four judges of criminal cases, and seven general judges of both civil and criminal affairs.[12] Desnitsky also advocates trial by jury. He expresses the hope that Russian monarchs might be "graciously inclined to legislate according to English example and to legalize the selection from among forty outsiders fifteen witnesses" who would be chosen from among the inhabitants of the town in which the court was sitting for the duration of the trial. Having heard the entire case, it would be the duty of these jurors to say under oath whether the accused was guilty or not and that having been done, it would be "the business of the judge to pronounce judgement in accordance with their vote or in accordance with the majority of their votes, and in order that this judgement should be executed".[13]

In fact there is rather more of a Scots example than of an "English example", to be detected in Desnitsky's proposals for a jury system. In England at that time twelve jurymen were chosen from a group of forty and they were required to reach a unanimous decision. (It was not until the passing of the Criminal Justice Act of 1967 that the possibility of a majority verdict was introduced into English law.) In Scotland, however, the number of jurors was fifteen (as in Desnitsky's proposal) and they were permitted to reach a majority verdict.

Adam Smith, in a course of lectures attended by Desnitsky in 1762–3, drew attention to this very point. Referring to the English jury system, he said: "The chief defect is that this jury must be unanimous in their opinion, unless they would choose to be greatly harassed and threatened with ignominy. And in this our Scots juries, though they do not appear to be so well contrived in other points, appear to be superior, as they are not required to be unanimous. It is very hard that they should thus be obliged to declare themselves of one opinion. The best men, and of the greatest integrity, may differ, and each think himself altogether certain that the matter is so; this must arise from the variety of human tempers, and the different lights in which men see things. . . ." Smith went on to emphasize that matters in Scotland were "on a very different footing. The number which is required to a jury is fifteen. Nor is unanimity required of these. It was some time ago, but has within the last 150 years gone into desuetude. . . .''[14]

British experience, and possibly the direct influence of Smith, has also some bearing on Desnitsky's emphasis on the importance of judges holding office for life, a point which is likewise stressed in Smith's lectures referred to above. The necessity of a judge remaining in office until his death arises, Desnitsky argues, from the need to safeguard him from threats to his independence and the necessity of enabling him "to judge everyone without exception". Desnitsky argues for the establishment of advocates in view of the fact that "in many states it has been found by experience that in the absence of argument in court there is no other means of achieving justice".[15] He supports the restoration of capital punishment for the crime of murder and does so by employing the specifically Smithian *terminology* (and, in an incomplete form, Smith's *concept*) of the "impartial spectator".[16]

So far as the executive power is concerned, Desnitsky suggests that this may be safely entrusted to governors in the provinces and in the best-known provincial towns only, so that one governor will not be dependent upon another but all will be directly responsible to the monarch. Such a decree he holds to be necessary in order to prevent great personages from overthrowing the governor because of the strictness which he would exercise in the fulfil-ment of his duties. Not only the governor, however, must be safeguarded from arbitrary interference. So must the people of the province be given protection against arbitrary action on the part of the governor himself. To ensure that he does not harm the innocent, he should be held answerable to the twelve judges in the chief provincial courts who "must at every trial publicly ask those present whether there are any complaints against the governor and whether anyone has suffered any harm from him".[17] Should a complaint or instance of injury turn up, the judges must report this to the senate, "where the governor will be subjected to a fine and punishment at the monarch's pleasure".[18]

The main duties of the governor would be to maintain peace and order within the area of his jurisdiction, to arrest criminals, and to keep those convicted in prison. For these purposes he would have under his control soldiers to assist him—one hundred infantrymen and twenty cavalrymen for the ordinary provincial governor and two thousand eight hundred in the capital cities. The governor is also entrusted with the duty of gathering such poll-taxes and duties from landed property owners within his province as will be decreed by the senate.[19]

In the fourth part of the main body of Desnitsky's proposals, that devoted to the civic authority, there is ample demonstration of Desnitsky's belief that the "commercial" stage of development is the highest stage to which society can advance and of his desire to further the interests of merchants and craftsmen and reduce the powers of the nobility. He stresses that civic power must be in the hands of those who live in the towns and, in particular, of the merchants and craftsmen. He proposes a civic authority of seventy-three people in the capital cities consisting of eighteen noblemen living in the city and fifty-five merchants.[20] For the principal provincial towns he proposes a smaller civic authority, but one in which merchants would also be in a clear majority.[21]

In the capital cities the civic authority of Desnitsky's design would be divided into six departments, each consisting of twelve people, while one member out of the seventy-three would be elected by his colleagues to be president of this local authority. Desnitsky's plan envisages a high degree of civic planning and supervision. The functions which he allots to the second department are of special interest as a clear instance of Desnitsky *rejecting* one of Adam Smith's major tenets. To the second department Desnitsky allocates the task of keeping an eye on "the cheapness of foodstuffs to be sold in the particualr city . . . that is, to observe a zealous supervision so that in all shops and in all markets the goods are sold at a known price and by weight and measure established by state decree. And in addition to that, the duty of the second department will be to stamp out profiteers and middlemen who, by increasing the price of things, cause the inhabitants unnecessary loss and make it difficult for them to maintain themselves."[22] While Adam Smith was well aware of the danger of traders acting in consort to raise prices, he believed that to provide other traders with access to the market would be a more effective means of keeping prices down than price regulation by any local or national authority.[23]

The duty of Desnitsky's first department is to conduct the affairs of the town in such a manner as their loan regulations will allow or the law of the senate require. The third department is charged with the supervision of the civic architecture, so that building will take place according to a plan prescribed by the senate and the town will not suffer from overcrowding or incongruities arising out of disorderly building or from buildings which are falling apart. The fourth department has the task of supervision of the repair of streets and canals, the removal of refuse, and the provision of street lighting. The task of the fifth is to collect duties from the inhabitants and traders in accordance with local needs while keeping within the limits laid down for the civic authority by the senate. The sixth department is charged with settling petty civil disputes where no criminal action is involved, such as the differences which will arise between cabmen, inn-keepers, and itinerant traders.[24]

The *Predstavlenie* as a whole contains many more acute observations and interesting proposals for reform than can be discussed within the scope of the present article. In summary, it is fair to say that its implementation would have set Russia far along the path towards constitutional monarchy. Desnitsky is an opponent of arbitrary power in all its forms, whether that of a provincial governor, of a landowner, or (though here he has to be more guarded) of an autocrat. Though it goes without saying that he cannot attack the absolute power of the monarch directly, Desnitsky's desire to create strong political institutions and his advocacy of a separation of the legislative, judicial, executive, and civic authorities, so that one would act as an overseer and check upon another, would lead not only to a curb upon the power of the nobility and (especially given the social composition proposed by Desnitsky for the legislature and the civic authorities) an increase in the power of commercial and professional interests. It would also have its effect upon the autocracy. The establishment of a representative assembly, of an independent judiciary, and of an executive authority subordinate to the law could scarcely, except in the very short term, be compatible with a continuation of the absolute power of the monarch. Given Desnitsky's close familiarity with, and admiration for, the British constitutional model, it is more than likely that he anticipated just such a gradual development towards constitutional monarchy.

It is highly probable that Catherine read the whole of Desnitsky's *Predstavlenie* and certain that she read at least part of it. It is an interesting but little-known fact that many points from Desnitsky's fourth appendix to his *Predstavlenie* (*O uzakonenii finanskom*) are incorporated by Catherine in the Second Supplement to her *Nakaz* which she completed on 8 April 1768. Since there are a number of clear traces of Adam Smith's influence on this fourth appendix of Desnitsky, it is evident that not only Desnitsky but (indirectly) Adam Smith exercised influence over Catherine's famous *Nakaz* which was published in Russian, French, German, and English eight years before the publication of *The Wealth of Nations* (in which Smith, *inter alia*, developed a number of the points that, via his Glasgow lectures, had appeared in the *Nakaz*). Some of Desnitsky's observations are taken over word for word by Catherine; others are somewhat altered; and some, of course, are ignored. But a sufficient number of entire sentences from the *Predstavlenie* are adopted by Catherine to put her debt to him beyond doubt.

In principle, Desnitsky's priority with regard to the material used in the *Nakaz* could be challenged. The main body of Desnitsky's *Predstavlenie* is dated 30 February 1768, an obvious mistake, though one which nevertheless suggests that the work was submitted for the attention of the monarch and her legislative commission at the end of February or beginning of March of that year. (Desnitsky, like Adam Smith, appears to have suffered from absent-mindedness.[25] Apart from this slip over dates, an example is also to be found in the letter which he wrote hurriedly on 31 December 1765, for submission to a

Glasgow University Faculty meeting the same day. At the end of the letter, written in English, he inserts the Russian word *goda* after the date.)

The circumstances of the discovery of the *Predstavlenie o uchrezhdenii zako-nodatel'noi, suditel'noi i nakazatel'noi vlasti v Rossiiskoi imperii* are described by Aleksandr Uspensky in his introduction to the publication in *Zapiski Impera-torskoi Akademii nauk.*[26] The main part of Desnitsky's work was contained in a notebook of Englsh paper, consisting of twenty-five unnumbered pages of small writing. Beside it in the archive in which it was discovered were four other notebooks (also of English paper) in which further (and even more detailed) advice to Catherine's legislative commission is to be found. There is no doubt that Uspensky was right in his judgement that both circumstantial evidence and the internal evidence of the texts indicate that these further proposals are also Desnitsky's work. Conceivably it could be argued that they were written later than the main part of the text and that Desnitsky incorpo-rated entire sentences from Catherine's Second Supplement to the *Nakaz* rather than the other way round. This, however, is an exceedingly unconvin-cing explanation of the correspondence between the texts. Desnitsky's writings invariably begin and end with the conventional, and virtually obligatory, tributes to the great wisdom and talents of the Empress, and the main text of his *Predstavlenie* is no exception to this general rule. It is unthinkable that in an appendix to that text, he could quote sentence after sentence from a newly-published work by Catherine without acknowledgement of, or tribute to, his source. For Catherine, on the other hand, nothing could have been simpler than the incorporation in her own work, without acknowledgement, of points made by a still obscure scholar, especially since she did not trouble to acknow-ledge many of her borrowings in the *Nazek* from the most illustrious European thinkers of her time.[27]

No fewer than twenty-six articles of the *Nakaz* (articles 575–600) bear a definite (and, in many cases, verbatim) relationship to Desnitsky's formulations. It is true that there are also some similarities between certain of Desnitsky's points and observations to be found in the *Encyclopédie*[28] and, to a lesser extent, in Bielfeld's *Institutions politiques.*[29] Though it is doubtful whether Desnitsky drew directly from either work, it is worthy of note that Catherine borrowed from Bielfeld and the *Encyclopédie* in other articles of Chapter 22 of her *Nakaz*. There is an important distinction, however, between general similarities of view and precise verbal links. The influence of Desnitsky on Chapter 22 is even clearer than that of the cameralists or encyclopaedists, as can be illustrated by a number of examples. Traces of Smith's influence on some of Desnitsky's views adopted by Catherine will also be noted.

Desnitsky observes that "finances may justly be divided into two main parts:

(1) the expenses of the state, (2) its revenues".[30] He recognizes four main expenses which, he states, it is necessary to formulate precisely before going on to consider taxation. The first of these concerns the personal needs of the sovereign: "The head of the society, that is the monarch, must have the resources and preserve the appearances appropriate to his illustrious office and in accordance with his supreme power. Decorum demands that affluence and magnificence should surround his throne; but it is befitting for him, as the source of prosperity of the society, to bestow awards, encouragement, and favours, from which virtue directly increases and zeal to serve the fatherland is multiplied."[31]

The second type of expenditure required, in Desnitsky's view, is that needed for guarding the internal order of the state, "consisting of supervision over the citizens and of the execution of judgement and punishment. For that purpose, it is necessary to maintain police, town governors, officials, their subordinates, and finally the courts and their buildings."[32]

Thirdly, Desnitsky takes account of various "undertakings conducive to the public benefit" which "especially in a state which has not yet been put in order, are divided into innumerable objects", among which he mentions "the building of towns and of roads, the making of canals, the cleaning of rivers, various institutions for the education and care of the people, and various establishments capable of bringing sciences and arts into a flourishing condition".[33]

But, finally, all this "would be without foundation", writes Desnitsky, "if the state did not possess defence from foreign attacks. From this it follows that it ought constantly to have various forces, both land and maritime, to build and maintain fortresses to preserve supplies of every kind of ammunition. From this results the fourth and most important kind of state expense."[34]

It is interesting to compare these views and priorities with those of Catherine the Great, on the one hand, and of Adam Smith, on the other. Catherine, in fact, follows Desnitsky on all four points, though whereas Desnitsky is tactful enough to give first place to the expenses required to maintain the appropriate affluence of the monarch (even though he states that his fourth point, the expense of defence of the state, is actually the most important), Catherine gives first place to defence (article 576 of the *Nakaz*) and, with reciprocal tact, accords fourth place to the personal needs of the sovereign (article 579). Her second and third points concerning internal order and public welfare (articles 577–8) follow Desnitsky both in their order and in substance. Very frequently, the correspondence between the texts is a verbatim one. Thus, on the personal needs of the sovereign (article 579 of the *Nakaz*), both Desnitsky and Catherine write: "Decorum demands that affluence and magnificence surround the throne", from which flows "awards, encouragement, and favours".[35] The correspondence between Catherine's and Desnitsky's third points is likewise, in places, word for word. Catherine's version of this type of public welfare expenditure which can be compared with Desnitsky's (above) reads in full: "Undertakings conducive to the public benefit. In this category is to be found the building of towns, the making of roads, the digging of canals, the cleaning of rivers, the establishment of schools and hospitals, and other innumerable objects, which the brevity of this work does not permit us to describe in detail."[36]

A comparison of these and other points from Desnitsky's financial appendix with the lectures of Adam Smith is, unfortunately, hampered by the fact that the student notes of Smith's lectures edited by Edwin Cannan (notes now thought to have been taken in the academic year 1763–4)[37] are highly abbreviated and by the further unfortunate fact that a significant part of the final economic section of the more recently discovered (and in general very much fuller) transcript of Smith's lectures on jurisprudence is missing.[38] In a lecture delivered on 30 March 1763, Smith promised to treat the study of opulence under five headings, of which the fourth was "Taxes or public revenue". The extant notes, however, break off with Smith still expounding the second of his five points, that devoted to money. Yet it seems quite likely that Desnitsky was in fact following Smith in his classification of the kinds of expenses which fall to the state (and that Smith touched upon the subject in his lectures), for the first chapter of Book V of *The Wealth of Nations* is divided into four parts which are (1) "Of the Expense of Defence"; (2) "Of the Expense of Justice"; (3) "Of the Expense of public Works and public Institutions"; and (4) "Of the Expense of supporting the Dignity of the Sovereign". Even should this be so, it must quickly be added that the comparison between Desnitsky's *Predstavlenie* and Catherine's *Nakaz*, on the one hand, and Smith's chapter 1 of Book V, on the other, cannot be taken very far, for this chapter by Smith contains some of the most brilliant sociological analysis to be found in any of his works, including an exceptionally interesting sociology of religion. This analysis has no counterpart in Catherine's works, nor in the *Predstavlenie*, though Desnitsky draws upon it (in its Glasgow lectures version) in some of his other writings.

Since the number of detailed suggestions from Desnitsky which Catherine adopts is too great for them to be discussed fully here, one or two further examples must suffice. In her discussion of the preliminary questions to be asked prior to the imposition of taxes, Catherine (articles 582–6) follows Desnitsky precisely. Her formulation reads:

1. On what objects ought taxes to be imposed?
2. How to make them least burdensome for the people?

3. How to diminish the expenses of collecting taxes?
4. How to prevent frauds in the revenue?
5. How is the revenue to be administered?[39]

Several of these points made by both Desnitsky and Catherine bear a marked resemblance to Adam Smith's "maxims with regard to taxes in general",[40] but the influence of Smith on Desnitsky, and hence on Catherine, becomes more clearly evident when we examine some of Desnitsky's and Catherine's remarks under the second of these headings.

In Catherine's version (article 590) we read: "But in order to make the imposts less sensitively felt by the subjects, it ought at the same time to be preserved as a general rule, that in all circumstances monopolies should be avoided, that is, a privilege should not be given to anyone, exclusive of all others, to trade in this or that commodity."[41]

Desnitsky, after making a strong attack on the practice of tax-farming, sums up his discussion of this point thus: ". . . in order, as far as possible, to make the imposts made upon the subjects not sensitively felt, it is necessary to preserve as general rules: (1) in all circumstances to avoid monopolies; (2) not to impose internal duties on any kind of goods; (3) when tax-farmers are to be found, to exercise extremely rigorous supervision over them".[42]

It is not only in Adam Smith's celebrated hostility to monopoly that Desnitsky has followed his Glasgow teacher. All three of Desnitsky's "general rules" were ones upon which Smith laid very great stress. On the first of the three points, the published notes of Smith's lectures taken by a student contemporary of Desnitsky are sufficiently eloquent: ". . . monopolies . . . destroy public opulence. . . . When only a certain person or persons have the liberty of importing a commodity, there is less of it imported than would otherwise be; the price of it is therefore higher, and fewer people supported by it. . . . In monopolies, such as the Hudson's Bay and East India companies, the people engaged in them make the price what they please . . . exclusive privileges of corporations have the same effect. The butchers and bakers raise the price of their goods as they please, because none but their own corporation is allowed to sell in the market, and therefore their meat must be taken, whether good or not."[43]

On the question of internal duties, Smith commented in his lectures: "In the method of levying our customs we have an advantage over the French. Our customs are all paid at once by the merchants, and goods, after their entry in the custom house books, may be carried by a permit through any part of the country without molestation and expense, except some trifles upon tolls, etc. In France a duty is paid at the end of almost every town they go into, equal if not greater, to what is paid by us at first: inland industry is embarrassed by theirs, and only foreign trade by ours."[44]

Smith follows these remarks immediately with some observations relevant to Desnitsky's suspicions of tax-farmers: "We have another advantage in levying our taxes by commission, while theirs (France's) are levied by farm, by which means not one half of what they raise goes into the hands of the government . . . the rest goes for defraying the expense of levying it, and for the profit of the farmer."[45] In *The Wealth of Nations*, Smith writes: "Even a bad sovereign feels more compassion for his people than ever can be expected from the farmers of his revenue. He knows that the permanent grandeur of his family depends upon the prosperity of his people, and he will never knowingly ruin that prosperity for the sake of any momentary interest of his own. It is otherwise with the farmers of his revenue, whose grandeur may frequently be the effect of the ruin, and not of the prosperity of his people."[46]

Catherine sometimes introduces significant variations into formulations which are basically Desnitsky's. Discussing (articles 593–4) taxes which produce little revenue, she goes on, interrogatively, to list a number of possible reasons for this state of affairs. Much of this section of chapter 22 (for instance, article 595: "Is it because money circulates less there than in other places?")[47] is taken verbatim from Desnitsky, and only at the end of the section is there any substantive variation. Articles 598–9 ask whether the deficiencies in certain places are because "the people there have few means of acquiring wealth; or does it proceed from laziness or from excessive oppression compared with others?"[48] Desnitsky (who makes it clearer than Catherine that when he is talking about arrears of taxation in certain places, he has in mind particular provinces of the *Russian empire*) makes no mention of laziness, but concludes by asking whether the deficiencies arise from the fact "that the people have few means of acquiring wealth or are more oppressed than others?"[49]

Even on paper Catherine shows somewhat less concern than Desnitsky with the protection of the interests of the poorer inhabitants of the Russian empire and with ensuring that taxation is strictly proportionate to wealth. Desnitsky, in the section of his *Predstavlenie* devoted to taxes on property, observes that such taxes can be divided into those imposed upon land and those imposed on buildings. He argues for a tax on land to be established on the basis of a reliable and precise calculation of its value, a course of action which, he suggests, would not increase the burdens upon the peasantry and upon agriculture, and he cites the example of England as sufficient demonstration of this. A tax on buildings in general would be even more useful, Desnitsky argues, in view of the fact that it is fixed "according to the amount of wealth of the citizen and the fact that the lower sort of people are free from these taxes".[50] In his discussion of the problem of how to make taxes least burdensome for the people, Desnitsky goes on to remark: "It is true that every citizen receives equal protection from the government, but great inequality is to be found in their condition with respect to property. Thus, prudence and justice demand that, if possible, taxes should be established in accordance with this inequality of condition, and, if one may so put it, they they be adjusted in geometrical progression."[51]

Catherine is less explicit than Desnitsky about the nature of property taxation and the principle of proportionality does not appear in the *Nakaz* in so precise a form as Desnitsky's *"po geometricheskoi progressii"*. The article of the *Nakaz* which is explicitly devoted to taxes on property and which may be compared with the passages from Desnitsky cited above reads: "Taxes which are considered the least burdensome are those which are paid voluntarily and without constraint, which affect all the state inhabitants in general, and which increase in relation to the degree of luxury of each (*po mere roskoshi usyakogo*)" (article 589).[52]

Desnitsky's advocacy of a tax upon buildings has no counterpart in the *Nakaz*, nor for that matter in the published version of Adam Smith's *Lectures*, though his remarks upon the land tax and upon egalitarian principles of taxation are fully in accord with Smith's views.[53] The specific advantages of land taxes mentioned by Smith are, firstly, that they are levied without any great expense, and, secondly, that they do not tend to raise the price of commodities, as the tax "is not paid in proportion to the corn and cattle, but in proportion to the rent".[54] In *The Wealth of Nations*, if not in the published *Lectures*, Smith lays considerable stress on the principle of proportionality. He summarizes "the four maxims with regard to taxes in general" as (1) equality; (2) certainty; (3) convenience of payment; and (4) economy in collection. Under the heading of equality, he argues: "The subjects of every state ought to contribute towards the support of the government, as nearly as possible, in proportion to their respective abilities; that is, in proportion to the revenue which they respectively enjoy under the protection of the state. The expense of government to the individuals of a great nation is like the expense of management to the joint tenants of a great estate, who are all obliged to contribute in proportion to their respective interests in the estate. In the observation or neglect of this maxim consists what is called the equality or inequality of taxation."[55]

Desnitsky's *Predstavlenie* is an altogether more concrete set of proposals for reform than Catherine's *Nakaz* and this is nowhere more evident than in a comparison of their observations on suitable objects of taxation. Though article 588 follows Desnitsky word for word on the five objects on which taxes are normally laid ((1) persons; (2) property; (3) domestic natural products used by the people; (4) goods exported and imported; and (5) deeds), Catherine elaborates less fully on each of these objects than does Desnitsky.[56] Thus, article 591, which is the only one which Catherine devotes to the third of the above-mentioned categories, is confined to some brief references to trifling imposts where the duty is not worth the expense of collecting it, and there is no mention of the salt and liquor duties which were an important part of the state revenues. (In 1767 the liquor tax produced 24.9 per cent and the salt tax 11.9 per cent of the state revenues.[57] Desnitsky is much more to the point. He rules out grain as an object of taxation under his third heading because it is a necessity of human life and should, therefore, be free from taxation. He holds that there thus remain three kinds of natural product liable to taxation: salt, liquor, and tobacco.[58]

He makes clear his opposition to the raising of revenue by means of the tax on salt, arguing that salt is necessary for food and so this is a compulsory tax, not a voluntary one (in the way in which taxes on less essential commodities could be held to be). At the same time it is a tax which bears especially heavily upon the poor, for salt is used in equal measure by "the nobility, merchants, the clergy, soldiers, petty officials and foreigners, as by the peasants". Liquor and tobacco, on the other hand, are in large part luxuries and so more appropriate objects of taxation than other things.[59]

In this case also Desnitsky's views, while they are not identical to those of Adam Smith, are on essentials in line with Smith's arguments. Smith argues that "taxes upon luxuries have no tendency to raise the price of any other commodities except that of the commodities taxed. Taxes upon necessaries, by raising the wages of labour, necessarily tend to raise the price of all manufactures, and consequently to diminish the extent of their sale and consumption."[60] Elsewhere he writes: "It must always be remembered . . . that it is the luxurious and not the necessary expense of the inferior ranks of people that ought ever to be taxed."[61] He notes that in Great Britain the principal taxes upon "the necessaries of life" are those upon salt, leather, soap, and candles and argues that such taxes "must increase somewhat the expense of the sober and industrious poor, and must consequently raise more or less the wages of their labour".[62] On the other land, "the different taxes which in Great Britain have in the course of the present century been imposed upon spiritous liquors, are not supposed to have had any effect upon the wages of labour". An additional tax of three shillings upon a barrel of strong beer had "not raised the wages of common labour in London".[63] In putting "spiritous liquors" in a different category from salt, Desnitsky is, however, anticipating these views of Smith's expressed in *The Wealth of Nations* and disagreeing with those which he heard Smith expound in his Glasgow lectures. In the *Lectures*, Smith argues that taxes "upon industry, upon leather, and upon shoes, which people grudge most, upon salt, beer, or whatever is the strong drink of the country" all tend to diminish a nation's opulence. "Man is an anxious animal," Smith observes in this context, "and must have his care swept off by something that can exhilarate the spirits. It is alleged that this tax upon beer is an artificial security against drunkenness, but if we attend to it, [we will find] that it by no means prevents it."[64]

The links between Adam Smith, Desnitsky, and Catherine II have been stressed in this work in view of the fact that they have up to now remained virtually unknown. A number of contemporary Russian writers[65] have contrasted Desnitsky's *Predstavlenie* with Catherine's *Nakaz* in general terms and have rightly pointed to the much greater radicalism of the former. They appear, however, to have overlooked the influence of Desnitsky upon a specific section of the *Nakaz*. In accepting some of the proposals of a young and (at the time) unknown Russian scholar, Catherine was almost certainly unaware that she was also partly following the advice of a European theorist who was to become as renowned as any of the French encyclopaedists and more famous than any of the German cameralists to whom she had consciously turned for instruction. If, however, Adam Smith's direct and lasting influence upon the thought of Desnitsky and his indirect influence over some of the formulations in chapter 22 of Catherine's *Nakaz* may be regarded as beyond doubt, this should in no way detract from the significance of Desnitsky himself.

In his financial proposals, more than in other sections of his *Predstavlenie*, Desnitsky transmits a number of Smith's ideas. But even here, as to a greater extent elsewhere, he develops many points independently. His *Predstavlenie* as a whole is a work remarkable for its coherence, for the understanding of the weaknesses of the Russian political and social structure which it displays, and for its radical reformism, albeit a radicalism tempered by prudential considerations of a kind which could scarcely be absent from a work addressed to the Empress in the prevailing conditions of autocracy. Most of Desnitsky's proposals proved to be far ahead of their time in so far as their institutional realization was concerned. Thus, to take as an example legal reform, the independent judicial system, equality before the law, and trial by jury which Desnitsky advocated in this work of 1768 were not officially proclaimed until 1864 and even then they were only very imperfectly realized in practice. Not surprisingly, such proposals as Catherine II accepted even in principle from Desnitsky were from his maxims concerning taxation and economic administration rather than from among the numerous suggestions in the *Predstavlenie* aimed at reducing the power of the nobility and, in the longer term, of the autocrat herself.

NOTES

1. See, for example, A. V. Evrov, "Istoriya metod nauki zakonovedeniya v XVIII vekie", *Zhurnal Ministerstva narodnogo prosveshcheniya*, 1835 no. 6, vyp. 2; *Biograficheskii slovar' professorov i prepodavatelei Imperatorskogo Moskovskogo universiteta*, i (M., 1855), 297; I.S. Bak, *Istoriya russkoi ekonomicheskoi mysli* (ed. A. I. Pashkov), i (M., 1955), especially 571; and S. A. Pokrovsky, *Politicheskie i pravovye vzglyady S. E. Desnitskogo* (M., 1955).

2. Only Volume 1 of Blackstone's *Commentaries on the Laws of England* was translated by Desnitsky. It appeared in three parts under the title *Istolkovaniya anglinskikh zakonov g. Blakstona* (Moscow University Press; I, 1780; II, 1781; III, 1782). The translation is of a very high quality, though occasionally it contains slight and apparently deliberate deviations from Blackstone's text. It also includes many annotations by Desnitsky, a number of which express his disagreement with particular views of Blackstone and some of which reflect the alternative views of Adam Smith and of John Millar.

3. See A. H. Brown, "Adam Smith's First Russian Followers" in: A. Skinner and T. Wilson (eds.) . . . *Adam Smith: Bicentenary Essays* (Oxford) 1995.

4. See the characteristically judicious essay of Academician M. P. Alekseev, "Adam Smith and his Russian Admirers of the Eighteenth Century", Appendix VII and W. R. Scott's *Adam Smith as Student and Professor* (Glasgow, 1937), 424–31. See also G. Sacke, "Die Moskauer Nachschrift der Vorlesungen von Adam Smith", *Zeitschrift für Nationalökonomie* (Vienna), Bd. ix (3), 351–6; and N. W. Taylor, "Adam Smith's First Russian Disciple" in *The Slavonic and East European Review*, xlv (1967), 425–38. Taylor's article is devoted to I. A. Tret'yakov, a scholar who, strictly speaking, should not be given precedence over Desnitsky as a transmitter of Adam Smith's ideas. While it should be emphasized that Desnitsky (unlike Tret'yakov) also did very much more than this, he did introduce many of Smith's ideas (sometimes in the form of verbatim renderings of passages in Smith's lectures) as early as 1768 in his *Slovo o pryamom i blizhaishem sposobe k naucheniyu yurisprudentsii*. The only work published as early as 1768 which bears Tret'yakov's name in the *Slovo o proisshestvii i uchrezhdenii universitetov v Europe na gosudarstvennykh izdiveniyakh*. But this work, as I pointed out in my article, "S. E. Desnitsky i I. A. Tret'yakov v Glazgovskom universitete (1761–1767)" (*Vestnik Moskovskogo universiteta: Istoriya*, 1967, no. 4, pp. 75–88) was in fact composed by Desnitsky.

5. S. E. Desnitsky, *Yuridicheskoe rassuzhdenie a raznykh ponyatiyakh, kakie imeyut narody a sobstvennosti imeniya v razlichnykh sostoyaniyakh obshchezhitel'stva* (Moscow University Press, 1781). It is reprinted in full in S. A. Pokrovsky (ed.), *Yuridicheskie proizvedeniya progressivnykh russkikh myslitelei: vtoraya polovina XVIII veka* (M., 1959), 242–58. The passage quoted above appears on p. 244.

6. Ibid

7. See Brown, op. cit. (n. 3), and R. L. Meek, "Smith, Turgot, and the 'Four Stages' Theory", *The History of Political Economy*, iii (1971), 9–27.

8. Cf. John Millar, *Observations Concerning the Distinction of Ranks in Society* (1771), especially the first two chapters. Desnitsky's explanation of the improvement of the position of women in society in terms of their increasing usefulness in the domestic economy takes up a major theme of Millar's. A great number of Desnitsky's particular examples and detailed citations may also be found in Millar. Desnitsky never refers to this book by Millar and the fact that it was not published until four years after his return to Russia may well mean that he never saw it. It is highly probable that it was the lectures of Millar which Desnitsky attended that were the major influence here rather than Millar's book, for Desnitsky was not slow to refer to books by other leading figures of the Scottish Enlightenment (such as Hume, Kames, and Robertson) and in particular to Smith's *Theory of Moral Sentiments*. We know from a letter in Glasgow University archives written by Desnitsky on 31 December 1765 that he had been attending Millar's classes ever since 1762 and other archival evidence in Glasgow shows that throughout 1766 and until his departure from Scotland in 1767 he continued to work more closely with Millar than with any other Glasgow professor.

9. Desnitsky's *Predstavlenie* was first published under the editorship of A. I. Uspensky in *Zapiski Imperatorskoi Akademii nauk*, vii, no. 4 (1905). It has been reprinted twice. The first occasion was in a collection of works by Desnitsky and others edited by I. Ya. Shchipanov, *Izbrannye proizvedeniya russkikh myslitelei vtoroi poloviny XVIII veka*, i (1952), 292–332; the second in Pokrovsky, op. cit. (n. 5), 101–42. The 1952 edition lacks Desnitsky's second appendix to his text (on church government), but the Pokrovsky reprint is complete. All subsequent citations of the *Predstavlenie* are from this latter collection.

10. *Predstavlenie*, 104.

11. Ibid. 105.

12. *Predstavlenie*, 107.

13. Ibid. 109.

14. The quotations are from a manuscript report of Smith's "Lectures on Jurisprudence", taken by a fellow student of Desnitsky in Glasgow in 1762–3 (Glasgow University Library: MS. Gen. 94, vol. 5, pp. 38 and 40). The manuscript is to be published by the Clarendon Press under the editorship of R. L. Meek, D. D. Raphael, and P. G. Stein. The same comparison between English and Scots law on juries is to be found in an abbreviated form in the set of student notes of Smith's lectures published under the editorship of Edwin Cannan. See Adam Smith, *Lectures on Justice, Police, Revenue and Arms* (Oxford, 1896), 52—3.

15. *Predstavlenie*, 110.

16. Ibid. 113. Cf. Adam Smith, *Theory of Moral Sentiments* (1759). See also D. D. Raphael, "The Impartial Spectator" (Dawes Hicks Lecture on Philosophy), *The Proceedings of the British Academy*, lviii (1972), 1–22.

17. *Predstavlenie*, 114.
18. Ibid.
19. Ibid.
20. *Predstavlenie*, 117.
21. Ibid. 119.
22. Ibid. 118.
23. Cf. Adam Smith, *The Wealth of Nations* (ed. E. Cannan), (University Paperback edition, 1961), i, especially 144 and 159.
24. *Predstavlenie*, 118.
25. As Ramsay of Ochertyre noted, Smith "sometimes offended serious people by laughing or smiling in the time of divine worship. They did not know that he was so much absorbed in thought, that he knew nothing of what was going on" (*Scotland and Scotsmen of the Eighteenth Century*, i (Edinburgh, 1888), 468). Some of Smith's other feats of absent-mindedness such as walking into a tan-pit while expatiating on the division of labour and, during a breakfast conversation, crumbling his bread into the tea-pot and pouring water on it, only to declare that "it was the worst tea he had ever met with", helped to earn him a reputation for eccentricity.
26. See n. 9.
27. The only puzzling aspect of this influence of Desnitsky upon Catherine is that it has gone almost completely unnoticed. For some time, indeed, I was under the impression that it had quite escaped the attention of other scholars in this field, for there is no mention of Desnitsky's influence on Catherine's *Nakaz* in the writings of the principal pre-revolutionary student of Desnitsky's works, N.M. Korkunov in his *Istoriya filosofii prava*, 5-e izd. (Spb., 1908), nor of Desnitsky's *Predstavlenie* in the most scholarly edition of the *Nakaz* (*Nakaz Imperatritsy Ekateriny II, dannyi kommissii o sochinenii proekta novago ulozheniya*, ed. N. D. Chechulin (Spb., 1907). Neither Uspensky nor the more recent editors of the *Predstavlenie*, I. Ya. Shchipanov (op. cit. (no. 9)) and A. A. Zheludkov in Pokrovsky, op. cit. (n. 5) have noted the links between the *Predstavlenie* and the *Nakaz*, and there is no mention of them in Pokrovsky's book, *Politicheskie i pravovye vzglyady S. E. Desnitskogo* (n. 1) or in a more scholarly work with the same title, P. S. Gratsiansky's unpublished Moscow University candidate's thesis of 1964. The same applies to other notable Soviet works which give a prominent place to Desnitsky, including M. T. Belyavsky's *M. V. Lomonosov i osnovanie Moskovskogo universiteta* (M., 1955, 234–51) and M. M. Shtrange, *Demokraticheskaya intelligentsiya Rossii v XVIII veke* (M., 1965, especially 193–200). Only recently, however, I have discovered valuable reinforcement of my strong conviction that a comparison of the fourth appendix to Desnitsky's *Predstavlenie* with Chapter 22 of the *Nakaz* points unmistakably to the influence of the former on the latter. It is to be found in the form of a four-page article by N. D. Chechulin published in 1913 in a *mélange* in honour of D. M. Korsakov (see N. D. Chechulin, "Predposlednee slovo ob istochnikakh "Nakaza"" in: *Sbornik statei v chest' Dmitriya Aleksandrovicha Korsakova* (Kazan', 1913), 22–5). Chechulin

points out that he had already completed work on his edition of Catherine's *Nakaz* which appeared in 1907 when Desnitsky's *Predstavlenie* was first published in 1905. Its publication threw light on one of the two substantial sections of the *Nakaz* whose sources had previously remained a mystery to him. Chechulin does not mention Adam Smith in his 1913 article, but he firmly holds that Desnitsky's work was the source for a large section of chapter 22 of the *Nakaz* and appositely suggests that Desnitsky's expositon probably reflected lectures he had heard rather than books which he had drawn upon.

28. See *Encylopédie*, viii (1765), 601–4, entry on "impôt".
29. Baron de Bielfeld, *Institutions politiques*, i (1760), especially 128 and 230.
30. *Predstavlenie*, 136.
31. Ibid. 137.
32. *Predstavlenie*, 137.
33. Ibid.
34. Ibid.
35. Desnitsky, ibid., and *Nakaz* (Chechulin ed. (n. 27), 153–4. In the passage within quotation marks there is, to be precise, a difference of one word. Desnitsky speaks of *ego prestol*, whereas Catherine naturally omits the word *ego*.
36. *Nakaz*, 153.
37. See R. L. Meek and A. S. Skinner, "The Development of Adam Smith's Ideas on the Division of Labour", *The Economic Journal*, lxxxiii (1973), 1096–7.
38. One of the editors of the forthcoming edition of the new set of Smith's lecture notes has written: "The new notes do not extend as far as the Cannan notes—they stop short in the middle of the economics section—but most of the material up to there is found in the new notes in greatly expanded form. My provisional hypothesis is that the new notes are a student's transcription of *shorthand* notes taken down by him in class during the 1762–3 session." (Meek, op. cit. (n. 7), 12).
39. *Nakaz*, 154.
40. *The Wealth of Nations* (n. 23), ii, 350–1.
41. *Nakaz*, 155.
42. *Predstavlenie*, 140.
43. Smith, *Lectures on Justice, Police, Revenue and Arms* (n. 14), 179–80.
44. Ibid. 244–5.
45. Ibid. 245. Desnitsky emerges as an equally strong opponent of tax-farming and of the privileges of the nobility in this sphere. "The Sovereign", he writes, "receives a known sum from the tax-farmer; but the tax-farmer for all his expenses in the course of the collection [of taxes] receives a large profit, sums which would remain with the people whenever a government gathered its revenues without a middleman. . . ." (*Predstavlenie*, 140).
46. *The Wealth of Nations* (n. 23), ii, 435–6.
47. *Nakaz*, 156.
48. Ibid.
49. *Predstavlenie*, 141.

50. *Predstavlenie*, 138.
51. Ibid., 140.
52. *Nakaz*, 155. Articles 631–2 (p. 162) may also be related to the principles enunciated by Desnitsky.
53. In *The Wealth of Nations* Smith discusses "Taxes upon the Rent of Houses" at some length (op. cit. (n. 23), ii, 366–73) and it is entirely possible that he also paid attention to this form of revenue from taxation in his Glasgow lectures, since (as has been mentioned) neither of the surviving sets of student notes of these lectures is a complete record of what Smith said.
54. Smith, *Lectures on Justice, Police, Revenue and Arms* (n. 14), 240–1. Smith also observes (p. 240): "In France . . . land, stock, and money are there all taxed in the same manner. Of these three only land is taxed in England, because to tax the other two has some appearance of despotism, and would greatly enrage a free people. Excepting the land tax, our taxes are generally upon commodities, and in these there is a much greater inequality than in the taxes on land possession."
55. *The Wealth of Nations* (n. 23), ii, 350.
56. Cf. *Nakaz*, 154–6 with *Predstavlenie*, 138–9.
57. S. M. Troitsky, "Finansovaya politika russkogo absolyutizma vo vtoroi polovine XVII i XVIII vv." in: N. M. Druzhinin (ed.), *Absolyutizm v Rossii* (M., 1964), 313. See also N. D. Chechulin, *Ocherki po istorii russkikh finansov v tsarstvovanie Ekateriny II* (Spb., 1906), especially 254–62.
58. *Predstavlenie*, 138–9.
59. Ibid. 139.
60. *The Wealth of Nations* (n. 23), ii, 402.
61. Ibid. 418.
62. Ibid. 403.
63. Ibid. 401.
64. *Lectures on Justice, Police, Revenue and Arms* (n. 14), 179. As if concerned to rebut his earlier view, Smith writes in *The Wealth of Nations*: "Under necessities . . . I comprehend, not only those things which nature, but those things which the established rules of decency have rendered necessary to the lowest rank of people. All other things I call luxuries; without meaning by this appellation, to throw the smallest degree of reproach upon the temperate use of them. Beer and ale, for example, in Great Britain, and wine, even in the wine countries, I call luxuries. A man of any rank may, without any reproach, abstain totally from tasting such liquors. Nature does not render them necessary for the support of life; and custom nowhere renders it indecent to live without them." (op. cit. (n. 23), ii, 400.)
65. See, for example, M. T. Belyavsky, *Krest'yanksii vopros v Rossii nakanune vossta-niya E. I. Pugacheva* (M., 1965), 171–2; and P. S. Gratsiansky, op. cit. (n. 27), especially p. 133.

8.4. Roderick E. McGrew, 1976.
Dilemmas of Development: Baron Heinrich Friedrich Storch (1766–1835) on the Growth of Imperial Russia

Abridged by Cheng-chung Lai

Between 1750 and 1850 the European world was changing from agrarian, hierarchic, and relatively stable social systems toward increasingly dynamic, pluralistic, urbanized, and industrialized forms.[1] These changes did not, however, occur evenly, and though most of Europe showed some modernizing trends, there were enormous differences in particular rates of growth, so much so that by the middle of the nineteenth century a significant cultural gap was opening between traditional, predominantly agricultural societies, and those whose more rapid evolution had already carried them into the industrial age. Among Europe's great powers at the mid-point of the nineteenth century, Imperial Russia was economically the poorest and culturally the least developed, a condition which affected her contemporary political situation adversely, and which contributed directly to the wrenching violence of the later passage into the twentieth century world.[2] Russia, however, had not always been so precariously placed. As late as 1800, though rather less developed than her competitors, the empire was clearly able to hold its own politically and militarily, and while problems undoubtedly existed, there was no hint of the crises which came fifty years later. The stark fact was that Russia's nineteenth century evolution as a modern society was sufficiently slow that, given more rapid growth in western Europe, the empire fell behind, leaving her at a disadvantage in international relations, and with vastly multiplied domestic problems which she lacked the means to solve. Russia's laggard performance ultimately affected both her own and the world's history, and as a consequence her potential for growth, the steps necessary to unlock it, and above all the attitudes toward development which dominated the critical early years of the nineteenth century have become historical issues of the first magnitude whose resolution has only begun.[3]

Obviously, any adequate treatment of these broad questions goes far beyond what can be accomplished in a single essay. It is, however, possible to see how growth, development, and change were understood, especially by the official world, and thus to gain some perspective on the climate of decision. Here the work of Heinrich Friedrich Storch is uniquely valuable. Storch was a talented and prolific writer whose career stretched from the last years of Catherine's reign through the turbulent first decade of Nicholas I. Taken together, his various writings form a comprehensive theory of development based on progressive economics, and include an extended review of Russia's achievements as well as recommendations for the empire's future growth. Nor was Storch's work obscure. He won, and still retains, a recognized place in the history of political economy, while in Russia his scholarly attainments and careful politics made him a fixture in court and academic circles. Given his place and standing, Storch's ideas help to clarify how development was thought about at the beginning of the nineteenth century, and give us further perspective on Russia's response to the challenge of economic growth.[4]

Although he spent his life in the Russian service while winning international recognition as an economic theorist, Heinrich Storch was neither Russian nor, originally, a political economist. Born near Riga on February 18, 1766 (O. S.), Storch was raised in a German environment, educated in Lutheran parochial schools, attended the University of Jena in 1784–1785, and subsequently transferred to Heidelberg in 1786 where he studied philosophy and jurisprudence.[5] His first book, published when he was in his early twenties, recorded his experiences and reflections during an extended tour of the Rhineland, southern Germany, and France. Written in an attractively unpretentious style, this journal reveals a sharp eye for social detail and a willingness to generalize on national character. The book was well received. A second and improved edition was published in 1790, and a Dutch translation appeared in Leyden in 1792.[6] The "Skizzen" brought Storch an offer from Heidelberg which he refused in favor of the Russian service. He had already won over Count N. P. Rumjancev, whom he met at Frankfurt am Main, and armed with Rumjancev's recommendation, he went to Petersburg in 1787 where he joined the Cadet Corps teaching staff and began to work on curricular questions. This produced his second publication, "Principes généraux de belles lettres à l'usage du Corps des Cadets" in 1789.[7]

. . . All Storch's works on Russia treat development, and from the beginning there are *laissez faire* overtones to his arguments. These become stronger between 1793 and 1803, suggesting that while he collated his data on the empire, he also read extensively in progressive economic theory with special emphasis on the English school and its interpreters.[8] Nor is this surprising. The new political economy had found its way to Russia at least a generation before Storch. Both Quesnay and Turgot were well known in the later eighteenth century, and in the early 1760's two Russian students, S. E. Desnickij and I. A. Tret'jakov, attended Adam Smith's lectures in Glasgow. Desnickij carried certain of the ideas he heard there back to Russia where they surfaced in the second supplement to Catherine's *Nakaz*.[9] Probably the first effort to develop a system of thought which included Adam Smith's ideas was the work of Christian von Schlözer, the son of the well-known historian, August Ludwig von Schlözer, who came to Russia after receiving his doctorate from Göttingen in 1796. Schlözer was both a cameralist and a follower of Adam Smith. He joined the Moscow University faculty in 1801, and four years later published a textbook on political economy. As it happened, Storch's first theoretical paper, which he presented to the Academy in 1806, was also an answer to Schlözer, and in fact included a savage attack on him for over-valuing the state's role in creating wealth.[10]

Schlözer's book, and Storch's response to it, marked the beginning of the high period of Adam Smith's influence in Russia. An inferior Russian translation of the *Wealth of Nations* was completed on commission by 1808, but this was undoubtedly less important than J. B. Say's influential treatise on political economy or Charles Garnier's excellent translation of the *Wealth of Nations* into French which was finished in 1802.[11] Whatever the source, during the next two decades Adam Smith's ideas achieved broad exposure and considerable popularity through essays in the publications of the Free Economic Society, in the "Mémoires" of the Imperial Academy of Sciences, in the "Statističeskij žurnal," and even in the prestigious "Vestnik Evropy." A whole generation of economic liberals appeared to expound what became a conventional wisdom based on Adam Smith, and though the post-Vienna reaction, particularly in the Petersburg University district, muted and temporarily scattered them, their ideas found resonance in the social and economic thinking of the Decembrists.[12]

Though Storch's interest in political economy matured after his arrival in Russia, he absorbed his theoretical ideas directly from Adam Smith or Smith's

European interpreters, not from Smith's Russian disciples, and he did so nearly a decade before the flowering of Smith's infuence in Russia. Storch's interest in Adam Smith can be traced in the "Historisch-statistisches Gemälde." The first two books, which were completed by October, 1796, and were published in 1797, stress Russia's rulers' creative roles in promoting progress and concentrate on demographic and cultural issues. There is little that could be interpreted as deriving from Adam Smith. In the next two books, however, Storch cited Smith on specific questions, while the work's focus shifted toward production, exchange, and economic values.[13] These volumes were completed in 1778 and published in 1799. This suggests the mid-1790's as the period when Storch was absorbing Smith's philosophy, and his source references support this conclusion. He cited the seventh English edition of the *Wealth of Nations*, a definitive edition published in London in 1793. No earlier version of Smith's masterpiece is cited, nor is there any reference to earlier translations.[14] Finally, the essay in which Storch announced himself as a formal theoretician and introduced a philosophy of culture based explicitly on Adam Smith was read before the Academy of Sciences on March 5/17, 1806. By that date we may account Storch a full-fledged disciple of the Scottish master.[15]

. . . As a philosopher, Heinrich Storch addressed universal questions, focussing on processes which transcended particular times or cultures, and seeking to formulate principles comparable to the laws governing the physical world. In this he was the objective scholar–scientist of the eighteenth century. He was also, however, a teacher, a man of affairs, and a political economist whose business was the economy's day-to-day functioning, who was responsible for connecting particular realities with theoretical postulates, and who spent a good portion of his adult life pointing out the paths Russia should take to young people who would have a voice in choosing the empire's direction. Because Storch was systematic as well as rational and enlightened, we will look first at the principles which framed his outlook and controlled the way he viewed policy questions. With the system in mind, Storch's view of Russia and his recommendations for development will be more meaningful. Finally, it should be noted at the outset that the ideas with which we work will be less notable for their originality than for their implications when applied to Russia. Storch synthesized rather than created. As a result, there is scarcely a major Enlightenment tradition which does not appear in his writings. Yet he was far more than an imitator, and his arguments deserve consideration as a whole since no one part, including what he took directly from Adam Smith, can adequately explain his intentions.

Heinrich Storch approached development through a general theory of cultural progress.[16] The argument leaned heavily on Adam Smith, but what Storch chose to emphasize was an historico-cultural interpretation which included and applied the familiar economic doctrines. This emphasis was entirely consistent with Storch's own development as a scholar. It was also necessary in order to apply Adam Smith's advanced economic concepts to a relatively undeveloped culture. Storch had already given economics a central historical role in his "Historisch-statistisches Gemälde" which contained as well the elements for a theory of civilization. That theory, however, was syncretic and unsystematic, embodying a loose agglomeration of causal principles which ranged from ethnic character through geography to historical accident.[17] What Adam Smith gave Storch was a generalizing principle, a law of gravitation for political economy, which applied at all time to all peoples, and which established the basis for a systematic philosophy of growth. It was that philosophy which formed the main argument of the *Cours d'économie politique*, and which provided the theoretical groundwork for his recommendations on Russia's modernization.[18]

Four basic ideas constituted the nucleus of Storch's system. There were: the principle of natural liberty; the division of labor; the psychology of self-interest; and an organic view of change. The first two came directly from Adam Smith, while the second pair, though consistent with Smith's doctrines, were in no sense uniquely his contribution. Not one of these ideas was exclusively economic in subject or application, though all were relevant to economics, but each did represent a policy determinant—either a condition to be realized or a limit on political action—and was, therefore, a component in framing legislation. Interestingly enough, Storch rejected Smith's labor theory of value, the natural penchant for exchange, and never used the invisible hand image. He put his heaviest stress on the principle of natural liberty, which he considered the most important single idea in modern political economy, and one whose realization was the necessary goal for any society dedicated to the expansion of wealth and the progress of civilization.[19]

The principle of natural liberty meant the recognition that man, freely pursuing his own interests, was the only true source of wealth.[20] Any restriction on economic freedom could only be valid if that restraint contributed to improving all individuals' search for wealth. This meant eliminating artificial barriers against free choice of occupation or possession of properties, but most of all it meant legal guarantees that the individual, regardless of class, could hold what he owned and enjoy what he had saved. This form of protection was the state's primary and unique contribution to development. Only law, as Storch pointed out, made it possible for men to work hard and save in the present to provide for future security, and he concluded: "If industriousness creates, it is the law which conserves; if in the first instance one owes everything to work, thereafter one is indebted for everything to the law."[21]

The motive force which made the principle of natural liberty so significant was the universal human trait of pursuing one's own interest. This trait rested on the psychological principle that all men desire to maximize pleasure and avoid pain.[22] Given the opportunity to improve the material circumstances in which he lives, man will spare no effort. Conversely, in circumstances which do not reward effort, self-interest will decree a minimum expenditure of energy in order to survive as comfortably as possible. Where effort is rewarded, however, and where there is freedom for men to choose, not only will industriousness become a first moral principle, but men will turn naturally to concentrating on what they do best, thereby dividing productive functions among them, and expanding the division of labor.[23] The division of labor, or functional specialization, restricts the productive role of any individual while vastly multiplying the services or products which a society may generate. But the progress of the division of labor depends on the degree of freedom which men have to choose their métiers. Thus the progress of the division of labor, to use Storch's terminology, reflects the extent to which the principle of natural liberty operates in society's institutions. Those societies with the fewest restraints on individual initiative and industry are also the societies where the division of labor is most advanced, and the accumulation of wealth is most rapid.[24]

While Storch recognized the importance of technologically advanced tools for multiplying productivity, he also affirmed the necessity for exchange to take place in order to realize the potential inherent in the division of labor. He identified communal self-sufficiency and the absence of trade with social primitivism, and he took exception to Smith's "natural disposition to exchange" as an explanation for commerce. Trade, in Storch's view, was firmly rooted in needs which could not be fulfilled in any other way. Obviously, as specialization progressed, the number of such needs would multiply and the level of commercial activity would increase.[25] Moreover, it was important to promote productive procedures which could enlarge or improve productivity, and Storch remarked rather pointedly that while not every nation was equally well placed to create technical innovations, they could at least not oppose innovative methods for reasons of habit or prejudice. There were limits, however, to what legitimately could be done to improve productive techniques, for both tools and trade had to be considered as part of the general process of cultural development.[26] This brings us to the organic aspect of Storch's theories which established limits on what a state or legislator could and could not do.

Storch considered political economy to be a science whose conclusions were as valid as any reached by natural science, and whose methods were as rigorous.[27] This meant that the political economist, like the physicist, botanist, or chemist, dealt with necessary relationships, both in terms of causation and chronology, while revealing principles which governed an ordered universe. In that universe, the order of being, of which social organizations were a part, obeyed immutable laws which included a natural succession of stages. Youth preceded age; spring came before fall; and development was always from the simple to the complex. "Nature," as Storch put it, "follows an invariable course in the development of every being, and one would seek in vain to interrupt that course and its proceedings."[28] What this meant in political economy was that each recognized form of socio-economic organization could emerge only when conditions were ripe for it to appear, and then only in its natural order. Thus it would be "impossible for a hunting society to embrace agricultural life without having passed through that of the shepherds, [and] and it is equally impossible that an agricultural people would become a manufacturing and commercial people before having given agriculture the fullest extension of which it is capable in that period of society."[29]

Storch explained the anatomy of these relationships at considerable length.[30] Though he used an organic metaphor to describe the hierarchy of forms, and the process of transformation from one level to another, he never invoked any "seed" or teleological principle, nor did he postulate any particular rate of change. Certainly Storch did not consider progressive change to be inevitable. On the contrary, nature's necessary hierarchy limited what it was possible to accomplish in much the way that gravitation puts limits on what a person can do physically. Beyond that, Storch was the voluntarist who insisted that "political economy considers man as a free being motivated by his own will," and who concluded that "man is himself the artificer of his wealth and civilization; it is he who makes them serve his needs and pleasures . . ."[31] In sum, human decisions determined whether societies, like individuals, would flourish or decline, while political economy provided the guide to sound principles and correct decisions. Even here, however, it was imperative to see men in their particular contexts. Storch's summary on this point could stand as a charge to social scientists of that day and this:

Political economy is founded on the study of man and men: it is necessary to understand human nature, the state, and the kind of societies existing in different times and
different places; it is necessary to consult historians and travellers; it is necessary to see
for oneself; not only to study laws and constitutions, but to know further how they are
executed; not only to pore over official tables, but to be familiar with the face of the

country, to enter into the bosom of families, to judge of ease and hardship, of enlightenment and prejudice, of the virtues and vices of the mass of the people, to verify insights with detailed observation, and to labor unceasingly to reconcile science with everyday inconstancy.[32]

. . . Heinrich Storch adds an important dimension to Russian official thought in the first half of the nineteenth century. Far from asserting traditional as opposed to modernizing values, or engaging in a romantic evaluation of Russia's real need for autocracy to express her historic personality, he argued the viability of the existing system as a modern, developing society. His political relativism, an inheritance from the pre-Revolutionary eighteenth century, permitted support for autocracy as the institutional form necessary to govern Russia. Modern economics, particularly Adam Smith's great treatise, offered the principles to guide an enlightened government toward a better future, while an evolutionary, essentially organic approach to change established the working limits on what a government should do. In the long term, Storch's relativism and his emphasis on an open society and capitalist values could legitimate a new Russian social order. In the short term, however, his arguments reflected and reinforced the cautious conservatism which charaterized later Alexandrine and Nicholaevan social and economic policies.

In the end, Heinrich Storch confronted the issues which made the nineteenth century while standing on the pre-industrial side of modernity's historical divide. And nineteenth century Russia continued to function according to eighteenth century perceptions and priorities, and in the light of pre-industrial achievements, until the nineteenth century was well past its middle point. Orthodoxy, autocracy, and nationality were critical elements in official Russia's view of itself, but so also was the conviction that the autocratic order was consistent with economic growth and modernization, and that nineteenth century Russia was and would remain competitive in the European world. Perhaps the ultimate conclusion to which this review of Heinrich Storch leads us is that Russia needed a shock comparable to the humiliating defeat Napoleon administered to Prussia, for it would appear that only such a trauma could have awakened her to the need for change, and forced her toward social policies consistent with the rapidly changing world in which she had to compete. On the other hand, the complacency, certainty, and optimism basic to Storch's theories help us better to understand how it was that imperial Russia could choose not to use the autocracy's powers actively to foster innovation in the critical years between Napoleon's defeat and the onset of the Crimean War, and by extension how Russia lost ground during the era of Europe's social and economic transformation.

NOTES

1. The orientation for this essay comes from the recent, and extensive, literature on modernization which treats development holistically while emphasizing industrial growth as a central feature in modernizing processes in the nineteenth century. See Marion J. Levy, Jr. *Modernization and the Structure of Societies. A Setting for International Affairs.* 2 vols. Princeton, N. J. 1966; S.N. Eisenstadt *Modernization. Protest and Change.* Englewood Cliffs, N. J. 1966; C. E. Black *The Dynamics of Modernization.* New York 1966. Black puts the concept in a broad historical and comparative framework. For a sampling of other approaches, see Myron Weiner (ed.) *Modernization. The Dynamics of Growth.* New York 1966. See also Alexander Gerschenkron *Economic Backwardness in Historical Perspective. A Book of Essays.* Cambridge, Mass. 1962, which has been particularly valuable for concepts of backwardness and development, and for their application to Russia. Two studies for judging the pace and character of change are Peter Laslett *The World We Have Lost.* New York 1965, and Phyllis Dean *The First Industrial Revolution.* Cambridge 1965. A very interesting recent essay on economic development from the Middle Ages at the end of the eighteenth century which stresses population factors and which treats the formation of economic infrastructures over a long period of development is Douglass C. North, Rogert Paul Thomas *The Rise of the Western World. A New Economic History.* Cambridge 1973.

2. See especially Gerschenkron *Economic Backwardness* pp. 28–30. C. E. Black *The Transformation of Russian Society. Aspects of Social Change since 1861.* Cambridge, Mass. 1960, organizes the essays in this collection on the assumption that significant modernizing development dated from serf emancipation, and that in the European context, Russia was clearly backward. Particularly if rates of industrial development are the standard for modernization, Russia was far behind in the second half of the nineteenth century. See W. O. Henderson *The Industrial Revolution on the Continent, Germany, France, Russia, 1800–1914.* London, Chicago 1961. Soviet interpretations follow portions of this pattern, though eschewing the modernization vocabulary and concentrating on socio-economic tendencies which created a "crisis in the feudal order" and generated serf reform as part of an emerging capitalist system. See P. A. Zajonckovskij *Otmena krepostnogo prava v Rossii.* Moskva 1960; 3rd ed. 1968. This has led to the further view that Russia's development between Reform and the outbreak of the First World War compares more closely with such nations as Italy than the "advanced" capitalist industrial societies. See, for example: *Rossija i Italija. Materialy IV Konferencii sovetskich i ital'janskich istorikov.* Rim 1969. *Russkij i ital'-janskij srednevekovyj gorod. Russko-ital'janskie ornošenija v 1900–1914 gg.* Red.koll.: A. A. Guber [et al.]. Moskva 1972.

3. Actual comparisons of the dynamics and pace of pre-Reform Russian growth with development in other European states have yet to be made. On the other hand, Russia's ability to compete with other European states at the end of the eighteenth century appears to be at least as clear as Russia's failure to industrialize rapidly in

the course of the nineteenth century. The problems involved are far too complex to be analyzed here. There are, however, guidelines. My own reading in European foreign office archives for the period 1790–1812 showed no perception of Russia as backward; on the contrary, European statesmen saw a great and powerful nation hampered by mismanagement, corruption, and eccentric leadership. For an overview of the archives covered, see R. E. McGrew. "A Note on Some European Foreign Office Archives and Russian Domestic History, 1790–1812," in: *Slavic Review* 23 (1964) pp. 531–536. See also R. E. McGrew "A Political Portrait of Paul I from the Austrian and English Diplomatic Archives," in: *Jahrbücher für Geschichte Osteuropas*. N. S. 18 (1970) pp. 503–529, and Idem "The Politics of Absolutism: Paul I and the Bank of Assistance for the Nobility," in: *Canadian-American Slavic Studies* 7 (1973) pp. 15–38. Cf. Marc Raeff "Russia's Perception of Her Relationship with the West," in: *Slavic Review* 23 (1964) pp. 13–19. Soviet scholars documenting Tarle's assertion that Russia under Catherine II was not backward, have assiduously argued the existence of comparable capitalist forms at the end of the eighteenth century. For an extreme and uncritical example, see K. E. Dzedzula *Rossija i Velikaja francuzskaja buržuaznaja revoljucija konca XVIII veka*. Kiev 1972, especially the introduction and first chapter, pp. 3–96. However comparable Russia may have been with pre-industrial capitalist Europe, Gerschenkron identifies significant missing elements in the Russian socioeconomic infrastructure for industrial growth. See Gerschenkron *Economic Backwardness* pp. 16–20. See also A. Gerschenkron "Problems and Patterns of Russian Economic Development," in: Black *Transformation* pp. 42–72. Walter Pintner *Russian Economic Policy under Nicholas I*. Ithaca, N. Y. 1967, offers an explanation for the general failure to correct these deficiencies and advance economic growth, while William L. Blackwell *The Beginnings of Russian Industrialization. 1800–1860*. Princeton, N. J. 1968, provides an excellent summary, useful demographic tables, and a comprehensive bibliography of relevant Soviet works. The focus on industrial development as the measure of modernization, while significant and central for the later nineteenth century, is problematical and possibly misleading for the early nineteenth century. For a perceptive essay on the differences between modernization and industrialization, a point particularly relevant for pre-Reform Russia, see E. A. Wrigley "The Process of Modernization and the Industrial Revolution in England," in: *The Journal of Interdisciplinary History* 3 (1972) No. 2, pp. 225–259.

4. There is no biography for Heinrich Storch, and relatively meager published biographical data. Career summaries appear in: *Russkij biografičeskij slovar̓*. 25 vols. Moskva, S.-Peterburg 1896–1918 (Reprint New York 1962), here vol. 23, pp. 428–432; *Ėnciklopedičeskij slovar̓*. Izdateli: F. A. Brokgauz, I. A. Efron. Vol. 78 (39A), S.-Peterburg 1903, pp. 919–920; and *Žurnal Ministerstva narodnago prosvěščenija* (1836) No. 10, pp. 44–56. The best brief statement on Storch's theoretical work is Hans Jürgen Serphim "Die Deutsch-russische Schule," in: *Jahrbücher für Nationalökonomie und Statistik* 122, 3. Folge 67 (1924) pp. 319–336. Seraphim corrects the more extended review of Storch's ideas in Wilhelm G. H. Roscher *Geschichte der National-Oekonomik in Deutschland*. München 1874, pp. 799–813. The most comprehensive Soviet review of

Storch's work is I. G. Bljumin *Očerki ėkonomičeskoj mysli v Rossii v pervoj polovine XIX veka*. Moskva 1940, pp. 173–194. Cf. F. M. Morozov "Russkaja ėkonomičeskaja mysl'v pervye desjatiletija XIX v.," in: A. I. Paskov (red.) *Istorija russkoj ėkonomičeskoj mysli*. Vol. 1, parts 1–2. Moskva 1955–1958, here part 2, pp. 5–202, especially pp. 111–116, for the current Soviet view. See also: Sir Robert Harry Inglish Palgrave *Dictionary of Political Economy*. 3 vols. London 1918, here vol. 3, p. 479; Jerome Adolphe Blanqui *History of Political Economy in Europe*. (Reprints of Economic Classics.) New York 1968, pp. 450, 486–488. See also Blackwell *Beginnings* pp. 123–128, who discusses Storch in connection with the emerging debate over development.

5. *Russkij biografičeskij slovař* vol. 23, p. 428.

6. See H. F. Storch *Skizzen, Szenen und Bemerkungen, auf einer Reise durch Frankreich gesammelt*. 2., verb. Aufl. Heidelberg 1790. I have yet to see the first (1787) edition to see how it has been "improved." The 1790 edition is in the British Museum. The Dutch translation is listed in the "Catalogue générale des livres imprimés de la Bibliothèque nationale." Vol. 178, Paris 1950, p. 1031.

7. *Russkij biografičeskij slovař* vol. 23, p. 428. If the "Principes généraux" were actually published, I have been unable to find it. Storch and F. Adelung later collaborated on another work surveying Russian literature: H. F. Storch, F. Adelung *Sistematičeskoe obozrenie literatury v Rossii v tečenie pjatiletija, s 1801 po 1896 god*. 2 vols. S.-Peterburg 1810–1811. A German edition appeared the following year at Petersburg and Leipzig.

8. Published sources do not reveal the extent of Storch's exposure to formal economic theory before 1790. His "Skizzen" is not concerned with political economy, nor, presumably, was the essay on *belles lettres*. The "Gemälde von St. Petersburg" (1794) shows a development orientation which combines a creative role for the monarch with the view that true growth—economic and cultural—must arise from the producing classes. See Storch *Picture of St Petersburgh* pp. 127–129; 133 ff.; 196–197; 249.

9. See A. H. Brown "S. E. Desnitsky, Adam Smith, and the Nakaz of Catherine," in: *Oxford Slavonic Papers*. N. S. 7 (1974) pp. 42–59; N. W. Taylor "Adam Smith's First Russian Disciple [I. A. Tret'jakov]," in: *The Slavonic and East European Review* 45 (1967) pp. 425–438. See also M. P. Alexeev "Adam Smith and his Russian Admirers of the Eighteenth Century," in: W. R. Scott *Adam Smith as Student and Professor*, Glasgow 1937, pp. 424–431; G. Sacke "Die Moskauer Nachschrift der Vorlesungen von Adam Smith," in: *Zeitschrift für National-Ökonomie* 9 (Wien 1938–1939) No. 3, pp. 351–356. For main currents of economic thought in eighteenth century Russia, see Morozov "Russkaja ėkonomičeskaja mysl'" pp. 22–23, 96–97, 99–100; and especially I. S. Bak "Načalo kritiki krepostnogo stroja," in: Paskov (red.) *Istorija russkoj ėkonomičeskoj mysli* vol. 1, part 1, pp. 519–587, here pp. 519–534, 558–570 [Tret'jakov], and 570–587 [Desnickij]. See also P. H. Chendenning "Eighteenth Century Russian Translations of Western Economic Works," in: *The Journal of European Economic History* 1 (1972) No. 3, pp. 745–753. In 1815, in addition to Adam Smith, Storch listed his sources as J. B. Say, Charles Garnier, Sismond di Sismondi, Turgot, Bentham-Dumont, Inverness, Stewart, and David Hume. H. F. Storch *Cours d'économie*

politique ou exposition des principes qui déterminent la prospérité des nations. Ouvrage qui a servi à l'instruction de Leurs Altesses Imperiales, les Grands-ducs Nicolas et Michel. 6 vols. St. Pétersbourg 1815, here vol. 1, pp. XXIII–XIV. Storch also knew and explained Quesnay's doctrines: ibid. vol. 1, pp. 123–135.

10. For a summary of Schlözer's ideas, see Roscher *Geschichte der National-Oekonomik* pp. 795–798. Cf. Morozov "Russkaja ékonomičeskaja mysl'" pp. 109–111. Soviet interpretations tend to pass over Schlözer as an early advocate of Adam Smith. In this, their views correspond closely with Storch's own. N. K. Karataev *Ėkonomičěskie nauki v Moskovskom Universitete (1755–1955)*. Moskva 1956, pp. 43–48, flatly denies that Schlözer taught Smith's doctrines and agrues that Schlözer was nothing but a "feudal cameralist." Schlözer's textbook was: *Anfangsgründe der Staatswirtschaft oder die Lehre vom National Reichthume*. Moskau 1805–1807. For Storch's critique, see H. F. Storch "Du principe constitutif de la science du gouvernement, presenté le 5 mars 1806" (in: *Mémoires de l'Académie Impériale des Sciences de St. Pétersbourg*. Séries 5, vol. 1 [1809], pp. 503–512).

11. Jean Baptiste Say *Traité d'économie politique: ou, simple exposition de la manière dont se forment, se distribuent, et se consomment les richesses.* 2 vols. Paris an XI–1803. The Russian translation of the "Wealth of Nations" was done by Nikolaj Politkovskij by order of the Ministry of Finances: *Ėnciklopedičeskij slovar. Izdateli: F. A. Brokgauz, I. A. Efron.* Vol. 60 (30 A), S.-Peterburg 1900, p. 541; Morozov "Russkaja ékonomičeskaja mysl'" pp. 96–97. The "Wealth of Nations" was first translated into French for "Journal de l'agriculture, du commerce, des finances, et des arts," 1779–1780. Other French translations appeared in 1781, 1788, 1790, and 1800. A French translation also appeared in Amsterdam in 1784. Charles Garnier's translation became available in 1802. J. F. Schiller's first German translation appeared in 1776 and 1778. It was unsatisfactory. The first sound German translation was done by Christian Garve in 1794. Further editions appeared in 1799 and 1810. See Roscher *Geschichte der National-Oekonomik* pp. 593–598. In sum, Smith was easily accessible to non-English readers in Russia, and the Russian translation is not necessary to explain the spread of his ideas.

12. On the spread of Adam Smith and the liberal economists, see Morozov "Russkaja ékonomičeskaja mysl'" pp. 96–111. For a broader view of liberalism's ideology, see Victor Leontovitsch *Geschichte des Liberalismus in Rußland*. Frankfurt am Main 1957. Part 1, pp. 1–35 covers our period. The Soviet approach always seeks to connect liberal thought with radical action, and to relate the Decembrists to a convergence of progressive ideas. Leontovitsch is a healthy corrective to this tendency. Among the "liberals," the most important were K. I. Arseněv, K. F. German (the statistician), M. A. Baluǵjanskij (Petersburg University Rector), and the well-known teacher, A. P. Kunicyn. For career profiles and biographical summaries, see: *Russkij biografičeskij slovar* vol. 2, pp. 317–321; vol. 5, pp. 51–54; vol. 2, pp. 451–455; vol. 9, pp. 551–552. K. I. Arseněv shifted his outlook from a liberal cosmopolitan view before 1825 to a national, patriotic approach. Compare his "Načertanie statistiki rossijskago gosudarstva" (S.-Peterburg 1818) with his "Statističeskie očerki Rossii" (S.-Peter-

burg 1848). All of these men had their primary impact as teachers and lecturers. Storch had no university forum, and identified closely with the established political leadership. There was no basis for giving his liberal economics a liberal political interpretation. See below.

13. In the "Historisch-statistisches Gemälde," Storch cited or quoted Alan Smith specifically on the economic importance of towns (book 3, p. 146); on labour and craft development (ibid. pp. 159–160); on economic dependence and the importance of manufacturing in wartime (ibid. pp. 368–371). In addition, without mentioning Smith, Storch laid down the principle of the division of labor as essential for economic fulfillment (ibid. p. 144); he argued that security of property was a first requisite to promote industry in both its meanings (ibid. p. 134); and he took a position on tariffs as a means for promoting industry that warns against the abuse of this powerful instrument, while concluding (ibid. p. 419) that free markets are best, and that the government is most effective in supporting economic growth when it levels obstacles to free development. Other instances could be cited as well.

14. There is no edition cited in the "Historisch-statistisches Gemälde." The citation is from the *Cours* (1815) vol. 1, p. 135, note 2. The comparison of page numbers bears out the conclusion that it was this edition Storch used in the earlier work. There is no evidence that Storch used the German translation, and the only French translation he mentions is Garnier's (1802).

15. See Storch "Du principe constitutif" pp. 512–513. It is here that Storch identifies the "principle of natural liberty" as the fundamental guide to political action relating to development, and he credits Adam Smith with isolating and explaining this law.

16. See especially: "Du principe constitutif"; "Développement"; *Cours* vol. 1, passim, which develops the definitions and development orientation for the remainder of the book, and vol. 5 which formulates a theory of civilization to encompass the economy of non-material values.

17. See: "Historisch-statistisches Gemälde," especially vol. 1 which surveys the peoples, resources, and history of Russia. The two factors which loom largest in this analysis are the people's industriousness and the rulers' wisdom. Consequently Storch stresses the size, composition, and cultural quality of the population and the efforts taken to increase and develop it. See: Tableau historique vol. 1, pp. 28–29; 31–35; 50–232 (a capsule history of Russia told through the histories of different peoples); pp. 239–244; pp. 253–368 (discussion of medicine, public health, and colonizing policies as a part of population growth); vol. 2, p. 54, stresses industriousness and energy as the key to a nation's success. "Historisch-statistisches Gemälde" vol. 5, p. 285 emphasizes the importance of enlightened governance, and pp. 285–296 discusses serfdom and how its effects may be ameliorated.

18. See *Cours* vol. 1, pp. 135–156 for Adam Smith's revolutionary impact on political economy. Storch quotes J. B. Say who compares Smith to Newton and who finds the same distance between Smith and the Economists that there was between Tycho Brahe and Newton. Storch further stressed that Smith's method was

inductive, building laws from observed facts rather than postulating *a priori* principles. Moreover, Smith opened the possibility of infinite development by making human labor the principal agent for creating wealth. *Cours* vol. 1, p. 138. This did not mean that Smith's work was definitive; Storch found much to criticize. See *Cours* vol. 1, pp. 140 ff. See also: "Du principe constitutif" pp. 512–515.

19. On value, see *Cours* vol. 1, pp. 56–58; 140–147; on exchange, pp. 75–81. In a note on p. 81 Storch rejects Adam Smith's penchant for trading in favor of reciprocal needs. On the "principle of natural liberty," see: "Du principe constitutif," especially pp. 512–513; see also: "Développement," passim.

20. Storch stressed the importance of shifting the focus of political economy from the state to society and the individual. *Cours* vol. 1, pp. II; 24–25, 187–189. Cf. Adam Smith *An Inquiry into the Nature and Causes of the Wealth of Nations*. 8th ed. 3 vols. London 1796; here vol. 3, book 4, chapter 9, pp. 42–43.

21. *Cours* vol. 5, p. 349. Security was the state's most important contribution for it permitted and protected individual action. "Du principe constitutif" pp. 503–506; 512; 560; *Cours* vol. 5, pp. 344–347. See also *Cours* vol. 1 (1823) pp. 6; 133–134; vol. 3, pp. 500–503. Smith credited David Hume with identifying security and liberty with the towns and their interests, and extending that principle to the country. Smith *Wealth of Nations* vol. 2, book 3, chapter 3, p. 119.

22. *Cours* vol. 1 (1823) pp. 41; 45; "Développement" part 2, p. 570.

23. This position is central to Storch's conviction that only men free to pursue their own interests can contribute to the accumulation of wealth and division of labor. This view is the crux of his opposition to slavery. See *Cours* vol. 4, pp. 269–274. See also: *Cours* vol. 1, p. 207 on necessity for free choice in division of labor; ibid. pp. 202–211 on division of labor generally; "Développement" part 1, pp. 516 ff.

24. Cultural stage affects division of labor and hence productivity. Storch held that agriculture is less amenable to division of labor than manufacturing since technological advances do not have the multiplying effect on agricultural productivity that they do in industry. Arkwright's spinning machine, for example, increased productivity in textiles twenty times, and this almost at once. No comparable advance can be seen in agriculture. Enlarged productivity meant greater wealth and a high level of cultural development, and these were necessary to more complex societies. Thus Russian grains were of similar quality and price to English grains, though English cultivation was more developed and more costly, but English manufactured goods were better and much cheaper because of high productivity owing basically to division of labor. See *Cours* vol. 1 pp. 209–214; 215–219 for market limits on division of labor; pp. 303–307 on need for capital to promote division of labor. The importance of free choice: *Cours* vol. 1, p. 207. See note 1: "It is one of the most deplorable consequences of servitude that it hinders the division of labor, and consequently the perfecting of industry and the accumulation of wealth." Thus Russia was underdeveloped compared, for example, with the early United States because lack of freedom in choice restricted the accumulation of capital through inhibiting the division of labor. See *Cours* vol. 1, pp. 317–322.

25. See note 48 on tools and technology; *Cours* vol. 1, pp. 280 ff. One measure of Russia's cultural backwardness was the inferiority of her technological development: *Cours* vol. 1, pp. 284–285. On trade, *Cours* vol. 1, pp. 75; 80–81; *Cours* vol. 1 (1823), pp. 67–68. *Cours* vol. 1, p. 206 for statement of connection among division of labor, exchange, and growth.

26. Storch noted that technological progress was connected with both the division of labor and the progress of enlightenment. Not only were Russian tools inferior, but Russian workers, from ignorance and prejudice, rejected improvements. "Though they work wonders with clumsy and primitive tools, the society would benefit more if the observer could admire the perfection and cheapness of products rather than simply the worker's dexterity and patience." *Cours* vol. 1, pp. 284–286.

27. See *Cours* vol. 1, pp. 35–36; *Cours* vol. 1 (1823) pp. 18; 33.

28. *Cours* vol. 5, p. 152.

29. *Cours* vol. 4, p. 248.

30. See: "Développement" part 1, passim, for an early statement. See *Cours* vol. 5, passim, and especially pp. 137–160. See also: *Cours* vol. 4, pp. 174–177; 180–181; 235–236; 248 ff.; *Cours* vol. 3 (1823), pp. 341–342.

31. *Cours* vol. 1, pp. 187; 24.

32. *Cours* vol. 1, pp. 41–42.

8.5. Glen Alexandrin, 1977
Reception of Adam Smith's
The Wealth of Nations in Early Russia

The ideas of Adam Smith came to be known widely to Russian intellectuals and policy makers by 1770. *The Wealth of Nations* itself was read there in English by 1780. The French editions from 1781–1802 and the Russian four volume translations, 1802–1806, widened the circle of Adam Smith's audience. His ideas were then more available as a weapon for the fight for economic freedom—a vital tool of combat against the burden of serfdom which was a concern to all.

Adam Smith's way of expressing economic ideas within the framework of the Enlightenment was warmly and enthusiastically received. His book was studied by government officials and by would-be revolutionaries. But his ideas in Russia were short-lived. It was only in the hands of the later nineteenth century academic economists that Adam Smith came into the mainstream of Russian economic thought. He is today a vital element for controversy in the Soviet textbooks on economic thought.

In 1937, Michael Alexeev, and in 1938, George Sacke, published evidence in English and in German of the presence of Russian students of Adam Smith in Glasgow in the early 1760's. Two students, Desnitsky and Tretyakov, were then identified by name. Particular importance was given to them more recently by Jacob Viner in 1965.

For Russians, N. M. Korkunov in his 1915 *History of Philosophy of Law*, had already discussed these students at length; the fact that they immersed themselves in the Glasgow atmosphere; the importance to them of the lectures of Adam Smith; the brilliance and oratorical gifts of Desnitsky, and dullness of Tretyakov, who was ill most of the time and died early; and their role as conveyors of Smith's lectures:

It does not follow, however, that the speeches of Desnitsky were a simple transliteration of what he had heard in the auditoria of Glasgow University. Adam Smith even then was concerned primarily with the questions of national economy. It is known that in the fifties, in his lectures on moral philosophy, which he divided into four parts: natural religion; ethics; natural law; and politics; Adam Smith had already developed the basic foundations of his economic teachings. Therefore if Desnitsky simply re-told in his own words the lectures of Adam Smith, one would find that the topic of the development of the wealth of nations would occupy the primary role. This in fact happened to the less gifted comrade of Desnitsky, Tretyakov. Thus in 1772—in fact four years before the publication of the *Wealth of Nations* of Adam Smith—he, Tretyakov, outlined some of these basic presuppositions regarding economics in "Discourse on the Causes of Wealth and the Slow Enrichment of States in the Ancient as Well as in the Recent Times." (Korkunov, 1915: 292)

In the past ten years, in part due to the impeding bicentennial of the *Wealth of Nations* which was celebrated in 1976, we have seen the swelling of Adam Smith studies, including those on Adam Smith's students in early Russia. It is well to note the important early contribution of Norman Taylor (1967) on Tretyakov, and also A. H. Brown's papers (1974, 1976). One of these refreshingly reviews Alexeev's work and the other explores the possibilities that Desnitsky was an effective transmitter of pre-*Wealth of Nations* ideas of Adam Smith.

Comparison of one country to another of the dissemination of Adam Smith's thought leads us to a seemingly surprising situation, and points to the uniqueness of the Russian students as ideas-monitoring apparatus. Whereas in most of the cases, the ideas and work of Adam Smith travelled as one would expect, by boat or coach, or *linearly*, that is, from London, to Paris, to Zurich, in the case of Russia, the trip was *curvilinear*—the space restricted and time reversed. Russians were in Glasgow. Go back in time: Russians were learning *Wealth of Nations* before it was written or published in London!

The situation, although striking, is surprising only in appearance, for two reasons. First, it is well known and often stated by students of intellectual history that the intellectuals at the time were eager correspondents, fond of gossip about all things, including new ideas, and that it did not take as much time as we would now imagine for mail to go through. They also visited each other. Secondly, under Peter the Great, the resources of the entire nation had been marshalled toward planned development of the military, in the area of crafts, academia, science, and even economics. In his *Project* of 1724 which established the Academy of Sciences, Peter declared:

And also economics shall be studied, which is meritorious and terribly useful because all the people can gain from its study and this results in benefits.

Elsewhere, says Ostoritianov, he sent provisions for the "inventing" of libraries, educating corps of translators and developing liaisons with scientific societies, including the Royal Society. (1958: 22, 56)

Peter was in a hurry to Westernize Russia and he had started the trend towards Western education by ordering fifty of the sons of his *boyars* to go to Europe to study. (Wolf, 1962: 352) At the same time, and for the next thirty years, Western scientists were successfully encouraged to journey to the new capital. The Academy of Sciences, for example, was quite solidly in German hands until the time of Lomonosov (c. 1760) whose struggles to establish the supremacy of the Russian language in teaching are well known.

Catherine the Great did not make any sharp breaks with Petrine "educational" policy. The routes of the itinerant scholars were well-trodden by the 1760's. Professors and students came and went. The apparatus for obtaining and disseminating information, exemplified by the Academy of Sciences, was designed, constructed and operational, although the number of people involved varied and decreased in Catherine's time.

The work of Adam Smith can be broadly defined as including not only published materials and lectures, but also the verbal dissemination of his ideas and the influence which these ideas may have had on people's thoughts and on their actions.

Thus, even before the appearance of the *Wealth of Nations* in London on the ninth of March, 1776, several Russians were in the position to learn about the economic views of Adam Smith: Desnitsky; Tretyakov; Countess Catherine Dashklov, *née* Vorontsov; her very young son Paul (1763–1807); Count Modvinov, who was also sent to London to "specialize"; and Count Vorontsov, who was the Russian ambassador to the Court of St. James.

We wish to investigate here the effects of these people on the lives of other people. The assessment of these effects can never be, and perhaps should never be, conclusive. The disciplines of psychology and of psycho-history are now investigating them, but only in part.

In order for us to attain even indicative or tentative conclusions on Adam Smith's reception in Russia, however, it is necessary to use precise terms, and we suggest these:

A Student —A Scholar of Adam Smith's works or a student at Glasgow, (e.g., Dashkov—son);

Admirer —A person familiar with Adam Smith, or his thought in general terms, (e.g., Dashkov—mother);

Transmitter—A student expounding publicly or semi-publicly Adam Smith's views, (e.g., Tretyakov, Desnitsky);

299

A Medium —A student or an admirer who is also an influential statesman, (e.g., Mordvinov);

A Receptor —An "enlightened" person, (e.g., Catherine the Great).

The fact that Tretyakov and Desnitsky were *transmitters* of Smith's thought has been established. The memoires of the Countess Dashkov which were written in French, appeared in Russian, English, French, again in English, and have been re-printed and well studied. She was an impressive woman, active in the scientific circles, and a member of the Philosophical Society of Philadelphia. She may be called an *admirer* of Adam Smith. Her son, a contemporary *student*, although aware of Adam Smith's thought "made little use of it, preferring to enjoy life in ways more orthodox for a rich young guards officer of the period. (Fitzlyon, 1958: 298)

Both Count Mordvinov and Count Vorontsov left voluminous memoirs. Vorontsov was clearly a *transmitter* as he sent volumes of Adam Smith in English to his brother in Russia. And, in the case of Mordvinov, it is clear that he also was an *admirer* (Alexeev, 1937: 816) and a *medium* of influence, in some ways more effective than Desnitsky.

According to this author's definition, an appropriate person for a *medium* of influence would be a person: (1) well versed in Smith; (2) sitting in the high councils of the empire; (3) writing rough drafts of the laws; and (4) of action and initiative. There is reason to believe that Count N. S. Mordvinov (1754–1845) was such a person.

Count Mordvinov, according to M. P. Alekseev (1937: 427), was indeed one of the *admirers* of Adam Smith. He worked to implement the ideas of Smith for the benefit of mankind and was in the position to do so as he was in the high councils of state for some forty years.

His life shows devotion to Catherine II, to ideas, and to an active adminis- tration of policy for the betterment of the people. He utilized the language of Jeremy Bentham and Adam Smith in order to give greater effectiveness and diction to his thoughts.

In the preface to Volume I of *The Mordvinov Archives*, N. A. Bilbasov, the editor, says that the family of Count Mordvinov was associated with the Navy and that they were "people of effort, people of action." (1901: vii)

N. S. Mordvinov, like his father and brothers, was sent abroad as a matter of course to complete his education. Mordvinov spent three years in London, at the time that the *Wealth of Nations* appeared. All his life, Mordvinov was considered to be a student of Smith and was interested in augmenting the nation's wealth and the revenue of the Russian treasury. The fact that he copied by hand, Catherine II's commentary on the financial project for increasing government revenue by eight million rubles, submitted by a Frenchman "Dubosque," has been quoted by Bilbasov (1901: xiii) as a measure of his interest in Catherine's reforms, of his loyalty to Catherine, and of his interest in economics.

Bentham considered N. S. Mordvinov's activities of state beneficial to the Russian Empire. Rileev, a contemporary man of letters wrote N. S. Mordvinov an ode entitled "Statesman." Derzavin, the poet laureate did the same, pointing out in it that N. S. Mordvinov had a preoccupation with increasing the total wealth of the people. Bilbasov says:

N. S. Mordvinov never identified national wealth with the interests of the treasury. He was the enemy of the state subsidy and of state monopolies which acted as a brake of the correct development of economic and social life. His economic and financial viewpoint was derived from the assumption that total welfare is based on individual welfare which is realized through personal initiative and free enterprise much better and more fully than through the medium of governmental intervention. This thought he expressed many times in the following clear formula: "The management of man and capital which are weapons of activity, must have full freedom. The measure of freedom is the measure of acquired wealth. Found national interest upon the private initiative. The latter is the living root of society. It is the source of wealth." (1901: xii)

The Count Mordvinov *Archives*, particularly Volume IV, contain a good deal of Smith-influenced material, including a direct quote from Smith on the management of state-created monopolies.

Thus we can see that the ideas of Adam Smith flowed freely and naturally, from the point of view of the establishment, into Russia. We feel that these ideas were welcomed and were easily accepted into the minds of receptive people. One of the explanations for this lies in the nature of the ideas.

The Enlightenment, which may have started slowly in the eighteenth century, had become a major intellectual force with deep roots in philosophy and in physics by the time Smith wrote his book. These ideas were expounded, accepted and, indeed, firmly believed in by many people in Europe and in Russia. A climate of opinion was created. One of its key concepts was natural law. And from belief in this, many things relating to the legislation, rights of people and the obligations of kings, were deduced. Adam Smith, then, epitomized the extension of the Enlightenment through his "discovery" of the laws for economics. If these laws were applied and if an enlightened man followed these laws, all would be well. From this it followed logically that economic independence was sensible and necessary.

It is this common element in the ideas of enlightenment that people admired and understood in Adam Smith for it was like re-reading Montesquieu or

Diderot, but in a more systematic form and well applicable to the more tangible, immediate and obvious world of economics. The very fact the *Wealth of Nations* matched the tenor of the times made its acceptance easier for the people whose minds were molded in the same way as that of Adam Smith.

The fact that the book was written in English, published in London, and written by a sensible, personable University of Glasgow professor—a friend of Hume—added legitimacy to the thoughts in the *Wealth of Nations*, a new life and independent collaboration of their truth.

At the time, England was, in Russian eyes, a symbol of superlative naval power, technology and engineering. Its nascent manufacturing was admired and, doubtless, watched with envy.

Like any other period in human affairs, the eighteenth century was a time of flux. Individuals, nations and ideas clashed. Progress towards freedom was an uneven and sometimes reversible process. In Russia the measure of progress and the necessity for serfdom and bondate were questioned; liberal laws were promulgated, restrictions were imposed, very often by the same individuals or groups of individuals. The ideas of the enlightenment, however including those of Smith, were available in Russia to various individuals for discussion, thought and, sometimes, entertainment. They were also known to the rulers of Russia, some of whom considered themselves to be among the "enlightened."

Previously we have shown that in Russia there were students, teachers, professors and statesmen familiar with the thoughts of Adam Smith. The question that arises is, how many? No definite answer is available at the moment but we would say "about a hundred."

We turn now to the ticklish question of the transmission and the influence of Adam Smith's *Wealth of Nations* or Adam Smith's other thoughts. As far as we know, for the period under consideration, two people have established that Desnitsky—as a *student* of Adam Smith—exerted a two-pronged influence. A. H. Brown (1974) has shown, by comparing Desnitsky's speeches and papers to the language of Catherine's *nakaz*, the specific, narrow, economic or fiscal application of Adam Smith to promulgated legislation. The Russian jurist Korkunov (1915: 292–3) shows that Desnitsky creatively applied the moral, political, philosophical and legal views of Adam Smith to help create the beginnings of the structure of the Russian law. Soviet historians feel equally strongly about this matter:

Desnitsky demanded equality of all the people . . . He spoke of the superiority of the English laws . . . with which he was well familiar as he studied in the university of Glasgow under the direction of the "father of classical political economy"—Adam Smith. (Academy of Sciences, 1967: Vol. 3)

In an attempt to assess the degree of Smith's influence, let us juxtapose one table, "Policies suggested by Adam Smith," with another table, "Policy interests in Russia." If the two tables coincide, in general, we can conclude that it would have been possible for Adam Smith's thought to exert an influence on Russian policy and that, in fact, it was an influence behind such relevant legislation.

In Table 1 are policy suggestions of Adam Smith. Parts of this table are based on Samuel Hollander's (1973) excellent study of the economics of Adam Smith, and are so identified. To his list, have been added several policy categories which we attribute to Adam Smith. These together, we feel, reflect those thoughts of Adam Smith that could have been appropriate policy needs of Russia at the time. Basically, if promulgated effectively, they would have contributed to the more efficient operation of his free enterprise system, and a more "rational" determination of economic situations.

Table 2 contains a variety of indices of the "Policy interests of Russia." An attempt is made to include in this catalogue only the "real," intended policies, policies that Russian administration wanted to see work. The source for this is a volume of documents (edited by S. S. Dmitriev and M. V. Nochkina) in the history of Russia and the USSR, 1682–1856. This was published in Moscow in 1953. This source may be limited in time and may have a tendency to exclude some of the liberal and progressive legislation in order to stress the grim and the oppressive side of the tzarist regimes. The source, however, although it does not contain all the laws known to Western historians, is still the most complete source of Russian laws of the period.

In selecting the items for inclusion in Table 2, an attempt has been made to

Table 1. Policies suggested by Adam Smith

Relinquish monopoly in colonial trade (and in general) (Hollander, 1973: 265).

Government interference, such as protection, on the grounds that this is good for defense (Hollander, 1973: 264).

Non-intervention with capital allocation (Hollander, 1873: 264).

Slackening of economic growth if growth leads to excessive specialization and dehumanizing effects upon the laborer (Hollander, 1973: 266).

Free trade.

In favor of agriculture (Hollander, 1973: 290).

In favor of foreign investment and capital flows (Hollander, 1973: 300).

Freeing of land.

Freeing of labor.

Enhancement of the bourgeoisie.

Enhancement of industry.

Table 2. Policy interests of Russia, as expressed in *Ukazes* (Edicts), *Nakazes* (Orders), *Gramotas* (Charters), Manifestos, and *Raspiskas* (Notes)

I: *Money and Banking*

Catherine II *Manifesto* established two banks to print money.	29 Dec., 1768 (II, 201–2)

II: *Freeing of Land*

Ukaze allowing merchants, citizens and state peasants to buy land for themselves but without serfs (N. S. Mordvinov's doing).	12 Dec., 1801 (II, 415)

"It is clear that the *ukaze* gave the possibility to representatives of the rising bourgeois elements to acquire land."

III: *Freeing of Labor*

Ukaze about free agricultural serfs (due to S. Rumantzev). Allowed landlords to free serfs if this be to their mutual satisfaction.	20 Feb, 1803 (II, 417–419)
Ukaze of Alexander I forbidding the advertising of sale of serfs in the newspapers.	28 May, 1801 (II, 415)

IV: *Enhancement of Industry*

Ukaze allowing merchants, citizens and state peasants to buy land for themselves but without serfs (N. S. Mordvinov's doing).	12 Dec., 1801 (II, 415)

"It is clear that the *ukaze* gave the possibility to representatives of the rising bourgeois elements to acquire land."

Manifesto declaring duties of serfs in factories.	21 May, 1779 (II, 238–240)

V: *Monopolizing of Land*

Charter of Nobility, granting rights to buy land only to "well-born persons."	21 Apr., 1785 (II, 240–250)

VI: *Enslaving of Labor*

Note given by Catherine II rewarding the participants of the court coup (against Peter II).	1762 (II, 189)

"Beginning then Catherine II started praticing widely the giving-way of peasants to nobility. In thirty-four years of her reign she gave away more than 800,000 peasants to nobility as their private property."

Ukaze regarding bondage of Ukrainian peasants.	3 May, 1783 (II, 258)

"This spread the Russian norm of serfdom to the Ukraine."

VII: *Expression of Reactionary Views*

Ukaze breaking relations with France (Louis XVI decapitated; Catherine II put the court into mourning for six weeks).	31 Jan., 1793 (II, 332)

Catherine said "L'égalité est un monstre, il veut être roi."

Ukaze forbidding printing presses; set up censorship.	16 Sep., 1796 (II, 335)
Alexander I's instructions to the director of Kazan University	17 Jan., 1820 (II, 525)

"Teaching will show that monarchial regime is the oldest and established by God."

"The teacher must spurn Machiavelli and Hobbes."

"The teacher will show that the law derives from Moses, David . . . but best of all in supreme lawgiver."

Source: Dmitriev and Nechkina (1953).

include those which would have supported Adam Smith's views as well as those which would have been opposed.

A study of the two tables demonstrates that no amount of "piety or wit" will make them appear the same. The categories and the concepts are different. Adam Smith wrote about the functioning or the improvement in the functioning of free, independent, established and *operable* economic units. Catherine, on the other hand, was concerned with building the political, social, and administrative basis of the infrastructure of her continent-sized kingdom. Although Catherine and her successor stated an intent to facilitate the creation of manufacturing and to aid the rise of the bourgeoisie, at the same time they continued enslaving their people and venting their reactionary views.

It may be interesting to note here that the language of the legislation is exceedingly rough and primitive. Although the literary language of the Enlightenment was beginning to be translated into Russian, one could hardly conceive of economics and economic policy in Russian. To fully discuss these subjects in Russian would have been almost impossible. There was at this time a "striking absence of both economic terms and business terminology" and only about "two dozen borrowed words which could be stretched to suit" economic concepts (Gerschenkron, 1970: 81).

Taking the legislation in Table 2 at its *face value*, it appears to reflect policy needs which were of a social and political nature, and very much in line with traditional Russian Imperial policy. The "Adam Smith element" in this kind of overall analysis, tends to become swamped by other considerations.

As previously shown, the thoughts of the "father of economics" were available to policymakers through the mechanisms of the *mediums*, the *transmitters* and the *receptors*. Adam Smith thus came to Russia early. The fact remains, however, that the soil of Russia was not ready for the acceptance of the views of Adam Smith in general terms. Credit none the less must be given to these early Russian friends of Smith who did see the general validity of his thought.

In our assessment of Table 2, the question can be raised to what extent the "Enlightenment" legislation was promulgated for effect and to what extent real reform was intended. This question can only be answered in part. Soviet historians, in particular, take a strong view regarding some of Catherine II's legislation. They begin with the quote attributed to Catherine II herself that she "robbed blind" Montesquieu of his ideas. They feel that the so-called "enlightenment legislation" was largely a piece of plagiarism intended, on one side, to appease the unsettled masses, and on the other side, as a hand-holding gesture with the leading thinkers of the West. Their conclusion is that all of the ". . . phraseology regarding the well-being of people . . ." and that all the ". . . promises Catherine made, she never dreamed to realize" (Beskrovni, 1963: 464–465).

Our specific conclusion may be restated: although some coincidence is indicated, consideration of the two tables above shows that the economic, social and the "humanitarian" objectives of Adam Smith and of the then Russian government were widely disparate on the whole. It is interesting to compare the conclusions reached through the methods employed in the present study with those of other students of this period. If other people's conclusions may be summarized, and this is a perilous business, we can say that Catherine II and her immediate successors were pre-occupied with the issue of serfdom and the maintaining of the autocratic feudal order. Indeed, there were at least 278 serf rebellions from 1776 to 1798 (Palmer, 1964: 140). Catherine, in particular, did not believe in the quality of "humanity" which was taken to be an objective reality by the true *receptors* (as were other concepts such as "natural law," "reason" and "perfectability"). For her they may have been objective reality. In addition, even if Catherine had been anxious to improve the conditions of the peasantry, *"she was unable to carry her designs into effect*, because the whole administrative machinery was in the hands of the class whose power over the peasantry it was necessary to curtail" (Mavor, 1965: 315).

Catherine depended on the nobility to command her military, expand her empire and manage her government. Her Charter of Nobility of 1785, rather than being a statement favoring the rights of man, actually created a new aristocracy to better govern or dominate the mass of people. She created an island of liberty to enslave the country. As R. R. Palmer says (1959: 403):

What this amounted to was an attempt, in an enormous agrarian empire that rested on unfree labour and on military force, to map out an area on personal *status*, liberty and security for those persons without whom the empire could not carry on.

In addition J. B. Wolf states (1962: 477–478):

... Catherine II gave Russia as enlightened a rule as the land was ready to accept ... she went through the motions of reforms in the western manner ...

In retrospect, much of the work of Catherine II seems to have been inspired by the traditions of Russia rather than by the *philosophes* of the Enlightenment ... Catherine was an enlightened despot in the manner that Peter I had been ... The *philosophes* who welcomed Catherine into their ranks because she distributed pensions and patronized the arts and sciences, seem also to have been blind to the fact that Catherine was a Russian despot rather than an enlightened one.

An inference from the above quotation is that Catherine II was a *receptor*, that she may have had enlightened thoughts but that she either was incapable of understanding them, or could not pay attention to them in her actions, or, most likely, that she saw their inapplicability to Russia only in future circumstances.

The second point which confirms our conclusion centres on the *bourgeoisie* or the rising capitalist element in Russia, for it was this element which indeed unfolded the banner of Adam Smith. In essence, W. L. Blackwell states (1974: xxv), there was neither a *bourgeoisie* nor industrial capitalism in Russia during Catherine's time. Thus, capitalism matured in the later nineteenth century, some fifty or more years after the period under consideration. The Soviet historians conclude that the Industrial Revolution *began* about 1830. A. Gerschenkron (1970) does not see any dynamism usually associated with capitalism until the liberation of the serfs.

Adam Smith, as one of the *philosophes*, assumed that with proper instruction a despot might rationalize society and give man a government that would end abuses, contribute to the dignity and rights of man and further the love of humankind.

Although the rulers in Russia might have agreed with the fundamental ideas of the Enlightenment and even with their application in the area of physical sciences, with a few exceptions they were blind to the possibility of their application to social and economic affairs.

To say that Adam Smith influenced economic policy one would have to argue that Catherine was truly an enlightened despot. There seems however to be much evidence to the contrary; that she employed the ideas of the *philosophes* in a cynical way to further her ends.

On the other hand, there is little doubt that the Russian contingent of *admirers*, *transmitters* and *students*, explicitly influenced progressive Russian thought for many decades until the Decembrists uprising in 1825, when a period of severe restriction of such thought followed. Many of the liberal reforms which were underway at that time were stopped. Many intellectuals were banished from the places where they could have put these thoughts into action.

In our opinion it was the immortal lines of Pushkin, in the 1830's, ("Instead he read the works of Adam Smith, who was a studious Economist"), which imprinted the name of Adam Smith and the word "economist" on the Russian language, making Smith a household word. Adam Smith's doctrine of free external trade and freedom in social and economic relations at home and abroad, never seems, however, to have been very influential in the Russian world of economic reality.

References

Academy of Sciences of the USSR. 1967. History of the USSR III. Moskow: Nauka.

ALEXEEV, M. P. 1937. "Adam Smith and his Russian Admirers in the Eighteenth Century." pp. 424–431 in W. R. Scott, Adam Smith as a Student and Professor. Glasgow: Jackson and Sons.

BESKROVNI, L. G. (ed.). 1963. Hrestomatia po istorii SSSR, XVIII V (Source Documents in the History of USSR, Eighteenth Century). Moskow.

BILBASOV, V. A. (ed.). 1901. Arhiv Grafov Mordvinovih (The Archives of Counts Mordvinov) I. St. Petersburg: I. N. Skorohodov.

BLACKWELL, W. L. (ed.). 1974. Russian Economic Development from Peter the Great to Stalin. New York: New Viewpoints.

BROWN, A. H. 1974. "S. E. Desnitsky, Adam Smith and the Nakaz of Catherine II." Oxford Slavonic Papers (New Series) VII: 42–59.

—— 1975. "Adam Smith's First Russian Followers." pp. 247–273 in A. S. Skinner and T. Wilson, Essays on Adam Smith, Oxford: Oxford University Press.

DMITRIEV, S. S. and NECHKINA, M. V. (eds.). 1953. Hrestomatia po istorii SSSR (A Source Book in the History of USSR, 1682–1856). Moscow.

FITZLYON, R. 1958. The Memoirs of Princess Dashkov, London: Calder.

GERSCHENKRON, A. 1970. Europe in the Russian Mirror. Harvard: University Press.

HOLLANDER, S. 1973. The Economics of Adam Smith. Toronto.

KORKUNOV, N. H. 1915. Istoria Filosofii Prava (The History of the Philosophy of Law.) St. Petersburg.

MAVOR, JAMES. 1965. An Economic History of Russia I. New York: Russel and Russel.

OSTOVITIANOV, K. V. (ed.). 1958. Istoria Academii Nauk SSSR (History of the Academy of Sciences of USSR) I. Moscow.

PALMER, R. R. 1959. The Age of Democratic Revolution (Challenge). Princeton.

—— 1964. The Age of Democratic Revolution (The Struggle). Princeton.

SACKE, GEORG. 1938. "Die Moskauer Nachschrift der Vorlesungen von Adam Smith." ("The Moscow Papers of Adam Smith.") Zeitschrift für Nationalökonomie IX: 331–356.

TAYLOR, NORMAN W. 1967. "Adam Smith's First Russian Disciple." The Slavonic and East European Review (July): 425–438.

VINER, JACOB. 1965. Guide to John Rae's Life of Adam Smith. New York: Kelly.

WOLF, J. B. 1962. The Emergence of European Civilization. New York: Harper.

Part 9. Spain

Spanish studies on the translation and reception of WN are worthy of notice, and the three texts printed here are highly informative. Smith (1957) is a classic work which provides detailed evidence of the translation history of WN in the Hispanic world. It also relates Smith's opinions on colonies to Spanish colonial activities. This paper focuses on the policy impact of WN; by contrast, his short 1967 paper deals, *inter alia*, with the translation problems (including the ignorance of the translator) and the condemnation of WN by the Spanish government. In another, related paper not included here, Smith (1968) provides some complementary information on this topic, especially in the first two sections.

The text by Perdices de Blas (1993) emphasizes the reception of WN by Spanish economists. He argues that Spanish economists did not delve deeply into Smith's work, and that Smith was not the most widely read or translated economist in Spain. Instead, Smith's ideas were picked up from reading other authors such as Say or Bastiat. Perdices de Blas concludes that Smith's influence in Spain was not significant: Spanish economists did not learn all their pro-freedom ideas from Smith. In fact, Say, Mirabeau, and Bastiat were more successful than Smith among Spanish economists.

Lasarte (1974) analyses both the translation and reception problems. Rodríguez Braun (1997) is a most recent related paper, easily accessible.

Further Reading

Texts with a * are included in this Part

LLUCH, ERNEST (1973), *El pensament econòmic a Catalunya, 1760–1840*, Barcelona.

LASARTE, JAVIER (1974), "Adam Smith ante la Inquisición y la Academia de la Historia", *Economía y Hacienda al final del Antiguo Régimen*, pp. 17–66, Madrid: Instituto de Estudios Fiscales.

Spain

*PERDICES DE BLAS, LUIS (1993), "*The Wealth of Nations* and Spanish economists (draft)".

RODRÍGUEZ BRAUN, CARLOS (1997), "Early Smithian economics in the Spanish empire: J. H. Vieytes and colonial policy", *European Journal of the History of Economic Thought*, 4(3): 444–54.

*SMITH, R. S. (1957), "The *Wealth of Nations* in Spain and Hispanic America, 1780–1830", *Journal of Political Economy*, 65(2): 104–25; repr. in John C. Wood (ed.) (1984), *Adam Smith: Critical Assessments*, no. 59, vol. 2: 58–80, London: Croom Helm.

*—— (1967), "The First Spanish Edition of *The Wealth of Nations*", *South African Journal of Economics*, 35: 265–8; repr. in John C. Wood (ed.) (1984), *Adam Smith: Critical Assessments*, no. 63, vol. 2: 121–4, London: Croom Helm.

—— (1968), "English Economic Thought in Spain, 1776–1848", *South Atlantic Quarterly*, 67(2): 306–37.

9.1. R. S. Smith, 1957

The Wealth of Nations in Spain and Hispanic America, 1780–1830

I

Eighteenth-century Spain, as Jean Sarrailh has so ably demonstrated,[1] was not wholly the benighted land that foreigners, and even more often Spaniards themselves, were wont to disparage. Enlightened statesmen, economists, scientists, professors, and even a few clergymen made up an elite who eagerly embraced new ideas and earnestly strove to apply rational methods to the solution of grave national problems. To men like Feijóo, Campomanes, and Jovellanos—to mention the most illustrious of a goodly host—reforms in agriculture, industry, education, and public administration seemed to offer the hope of rescuing Spain from its material and spiritual backwardness.

Mercantilist thought reached its zenith in 1724 with the publication of Gerónimo de Uztáriz's *Théorica y práctica de comercio y de marina.*[2] During the rest of the century few writers on economic questions failed to acknowledge the authority of Uztáriz, but the ideas of foreign economists made up a significant part of the migration of thought which nourished the Spanish Enlightenment. For those unable to read foreign languages, Spanish translations of Addison, Belloni, Biefeld, Condillac, Condorcet, Davenat, Filangieri, Galiani, Genovesi, Herbert, Hume, Necker, Quesnay, Smith, Turgot, and probably others were available before 1800.[3]

Despite the number and variety of foreign economic works chosen for translation, often the Spanish version appeared many years after the publication of the original. Thus Quesnay's *Maximes générals* did not have a Spanish translator until 1794, thirty-six years after the first French edition. By this time many Spaniards were familiar with Smith's criticism of physiocratic ideas and, of course, with his attack on the mercantile system. I have found no statistics of sales or library circulation to show how widely known in Spain was the *Wealth of Nations*; but the perusal of Spanish economic writings makes it possible to identify those who read Smith, quoted him, or developed ideas directly or indirectly inspired by the English classic. While the prompt translation of Say's *Traité*[4] undoubtedly served to widen the sphere of Smith's influence, the assertion that in Spain and Italy "Smith became popular in large part through the influence of Say and other French writers"[5] minimizes the accomplishments of eighteenth-century economists in both countries. Spaniards read the *Wealth of Nations*, in English or in French translations, prior to the publication of the Spanish version of Condorcet's synopsis in 1792 and Ortiz' translation in 1794. Even in the Spanish colonies the *Wealth of Nations* "was not long in becoming known . . . to the enlightened youth, who longed for the independence of these territories."[6]

Colmeiro, usually a reliable guide, appears to have erred in crediting Danvila y Villarrasa with use of Smith in the preparation of a text published in 1779.[7] Danvila cites Cantillon, Condillac, and "David Hum" (*sic*): but the date of publication, the failure to mention Smith, and the superficiality of Danvila's seven "lessons" in economics persuade me that he was unfamiliar with the *Wealth of Nations*.[8] In the 1780's Vicente Alcala Galiano, secretary of the Segovian Economic Society, lectured widely on economic questions: and, in discussing taxation, he reflected "much foreign influence, especially of Adam Smith."[9] In the schools sponsored by the Economic Society of Saragossa, Lorenzo Normante y Carcavilla taught courses in "civil economics and commerce," expounding principally the ideas of the French economist Jean François Melon. Although his defense of luxury and usury, his attack on sacerdotal celibacy, and other "audacious doctrines" provoked "no small scandal" in Spain, I lack direct evidence that Normante knew Smith's work.[10]

Valentin de Foronda, a member of the Basque Economic Society and a fellow of the Philosophical Society of Philadelphia, where he resided as Spanish consul-general, defended extremely liberal views on economic questions. Addressing an imaginary prince, he recommended the reading of the *Wealth of Nations* for a clear explanation of physiocracy. Although he referred to Quesnay as the "ingenious author of this system," Foronda condemned "the economists" for applying the "humiliating designation of sterile or unproductive class" to artisans, manufacturers, and merchants. He called himself "a copyist, a translator, a plagiarist"; he mentioned Smith several times: but he left largely unfulfilled his promise to disclose the "warehouses" from which he stocked his mind.[11]

Foronda denounced guild privileges, government subsidies to industry, and price-fixing; but it is his uncompromising defense of free trade that sets him apart from his Spanish contemporaries, most of whom espoused liberalism guardedly. Foronda challenged those who, accepting the principle of free trade, insisted on making an exception of trade in grain. This was as absurd as to argue that the earth, unlike the other planets, does not revolve around the sun. Tariffs and embargoes on grain imports raised prices to consumers; restrictions on exports discouraged growers and increased the threat of scarcity. Ruling out the possibility of monopoly, because grain dealers were numerous and scattered. Foronda maintained that competition would naturally set prices which would protect the public and reward the producers.

In breadth of vision, catholicity of interests, and respect of the scientific method, Gaspar Melchor Jovellanos had few peers among eighteenth-century economists and statesmen. Though Jovellanos' liberalism was not the product of a single influence, Smith impressed him profoundly. His unpublished papers include a thirteen-page "Extract from the Work of Mr. Smith" and a translation of parts of the *Wealth of Nations*.[12] Jovellanos' diary reveals that on May 23, 1796, his secretary, Acevedo Villarroel, "began to read Smith" to him; but for Jovellanos this was a third reading. He first read the "anonymous French translation" (perhaps the 1778–79 edition); then the original English; and in 1796 the "Roucher translation, made for Condorcet's notes."[13] Almost daily from May to November, he recorded "reading Smith," or simply "Smith," frequently noting that Villarroel was reading with him. In June he exclaimed, "What a remarkable picture he analyzes'; and in July he was moved to comment, "How well he proves the advantages of free trade with the colonies." He finished the final volume on November 9 and, apparently forgetting the previous entry, declared that he had now read the book four times.[14]

Long before he became familiar with Smith, Jovellanos had doubted the wisdom of restrictive commercial policies. In 1774, while sitting as a jduge in Seville, he was called upon to write an opinion concerning the embargo of olive-oil exports when the domestic price rose to a specified level. He took the position that no one could say what price would sufficiently encourage the producer without hurting the consumer. "We should like," he said, speaking for the court, "to restore completely the liberty which is the soul of commerce, which gives to exchangeable things that appraisal corresponding to their abundance or scarcity, and which fixes the natural justness of prices." Never a complete non-interventionist, Jovellanos foresaw circumstances under which exports might be curtailed in the public interest.[15] In 1784, writing a report for the Royal Board for Money and Commerce, he vigorously defended navigation acts.[16] England, he asserted, owed the "astonishing increase of its merchant marine . . . in great part" to the acts of 1652 (i.e., 1651) and 1660. Jovellanos, possibly referring to the *Wealth of Nations*, observed that the first law was directed against the Dutch; but he did not cite Smith's dictum that "national animosity at that particular time aimed at the very same object which the most deliberate wisdom would have recommended" (Book IV, chap. 2).

One of Jovellanos' most forceful essays (1785) was an attack upon guild privileges. In addition to abridging the individual's free choice of occupation, guilds restricted output, thwarted the introduction of new crafts, and impeded the technical progress which specialization and the division of labor made possible. Prophetically, he observed:

The greatness of nations will no longer rest, as in other times, on the splendor of its triumphs, in the martial spirit of its sons . . . Commerce, industry, and the wealth which springs from both, are, and probably will be for a long time to come, the only foundations of the preponderance of a nation; and it is necessary to make these the objects of our attentions or condemn ourselves to an eternal and shameful dependency, while our neighbors speed their prosperity upon our neglect.[17]

Jovellanos wrote boldly and extensively on other questions of economic policy, but his fame as an economist rests largely on his treatise on agrarian reform.[18] Sponsored by the Economic Society of Madrid, this celebrated report attacked the century-old privileges of the grazers' guild, which had impeded the enclosure of arable land, denounced (as had Count Campomanes thirty years earlier)[19] the perpetuation of large entailed estates, and advocated the expropriation of the inalienable real property of numerous religious foundations. Jovellanos cited Smith, as well as other foreign authors, in support of his analysis of the benefits of small-scale peasant proprietorship, improved farming practices, and free access to markets for agricultural products. Within two years of its publication, the report was denounced as "anticlerical"; and its illustrious author, who had advised the crown to strip the Inquisition of its power to censor books, was driven from his post as minister of justice.[20] Posthumously, Jovellanos' *Informe* was added to the Roman index of prohibited books.[21]

II

Carlos Martínez de Irujo helped to make Smith better known in Spain by publishing, in 1792, a partial translation of Condorcet's analysis of the *Wealth of Nations*.[22] The Inquisition had just placed the French translation of Smith's work on the Index of Prohibited Books;[23] but Martínez' *Compendio* was printed at the Royal Press, by government order, without benefit of inquisitorial review. The translator, a one-time official in the State Department, apparently had the support of the prime minister, Manuel de Godoy, whose relatively liberal ideas often thwarted the Inquisition.[24]

Martínez may not have been certain that his work would escape an unfavorable scrutiny. Hoping, perhaps, to confuse those who had condemned Smith, the translator of the *Compendio* always refers to the English economist as "the Author." The *Wealth of Nations*, he said, was "the best work on political economy which has been written until now." It was to be regretted, however, that the author made some "improper applications" of his theories. Such "levity" ought not to be an excuse for depriving Spaniards of the "treasures" found in the book. The *Compendio* effaced the blemishes of the original work but preserved "those principles which can be looked upon as the axes of political economy."

In his Preface, Martínez advised the reader that Smith's work was "authoritative, abstract and profound" but "almost useless for those who read it without [an understanding of] principles." Dealing with the "first elements of a science until now little known in Spain," the author employed a "special nomenclature, which it is necessary to understand." Indeed, a "knowledge of economics" was required "to comprehend the important results which the *Compendio* affords." The translator was inspired by love for his country; and, if Spain should apply Smith's "solid principles" to the furtherance of national prosperity, he would feel well rewarded.

The *Compendio* closely follows Condorcet's book-by-book analysis of the *Wealth of Nations*.[25] Martínez frequently paraphrased Condorcet's text, instead of making a literal translation; and he suppressed entire paragraphs. The most serious expurgation occurs in connection with Smith's article, "Of the Expense of the Institutions for the Instruction of People of All Ages" (Book V, chap. 1, Part III, Art. III). Condorcet's condensation reduced the article (twenty-six pages in the Cannan edition) by more than a half, but the Spanish translator retained only two paragraphs.[26] If Martínez had followed Condorcet, he would have reproduced a fair share of Smith's discussion of religious tolerance, sectarian differences, and clerical sinecures.

Using the "original English," Martínez added his own summary of Smith's digression on the Bank of Amsterdam. In a solitary footnote he took issue with the Smithian dictum that the individual is more competent than the state to select the most advantageous employment of capital. This may be so, Martínez observed, in an enlightened country; elsewhere "capitalists need the government, so to speak, to lead them by the hand so that they may put their funds in circulation and employ them gainfully."

The translator of the first Spanish version of the *Wealth of Nations* was José Alonso Ortiz, a lawyer attached to the royal councils and chancery in Valladolid and a professor of canon law and sacred theology. Godoy mentions Ortiz' translation as one of the works on political economy which he helped to get published,[27] and the evidence suggests that this is true.

On February 15, 1793, Ortiz appeared before the Inquisition, explaining that "some time ago" he translated the English text of the *Wealth of Nations*, "purging it of various impious proposals . . . and eliminating entirely an article . . . in which the author favours tolerance on points of religion, so that it stands cleansed of anything that could lead to error or relaxation in moral and religious matters."[28] The next day the Supreme Council of the Inquisition sent Ortiz' translation, together with a copy of the proscribed French translation, to its examiners (*calificadores*). Ortiz, meanwhile, asked the royal Council of Castile for permission to publish the work, pleading that the Inquisition had not banned the English *Wealth of Nations*, from which he made his translation, and asserting that he had deleted the passages which led to the prohibition of the French edition. He thought the Council should grant his request, since it had allowed Condorcet's *Compendio* to be published. The Council submitted Ortiz' work to the Royal Academy of History for censure.

On April 30 Ortiz declared that the three censors appointed by the Academy of History had approved his translation. He requested the Inquisition to concur in this decision or advise him what had to be changed. Not satisfied with the opinion of two censors that Ortiz' work avoided the errors of the French text, on May 29 the Inquisition named a new panel of examiners, including the friar who had condemned the French translation. In July, however, the latter had to be replaced by another clergyman. On September 27 the reviewers reported that they found one passage "a little dangerous." Smith said that the revenue derived from stock by one who lends it to another is called "interest or the use of money." Ortiz had paraphrased this as "interest or lawful usury." To meet the censors' criticism, he reworded the passage to read "usury or revenue from money"; and, further on, he changed Smith's phrase "interest of money" to "interest on money or usury understood in this sense." These minor textual changes, together with the expurgation discussed below, satisfied the Inquisition. The manuscript was returned to Ortiz on October 22, and the work was published, with government permission, in 1794.[29]

The 1794 edition was republished in 1933–34.[30] The editor, José M. Tallada, referred to his work as a "revision and adaptation to modern Spanish" of Ortiz' translation; in fact, he made little more than unimportant orthographical and grammatical changes. Neglecting to consult the English text Tallada perpetuated the errors, omissions, and distortions committed by Ortiz in 1794.

Finally, in 1956, Amando Lazaro Ros gave the Spanish-speaking world the first faithful and unabridged translation of the *Wealth of Nations*.[31] Ignoring completely the work of Ortiz, Ros translated directly from the Cannan edition, omitting Cannan's notes. In a brief prologue Ros observes that, even after two centuries, Spaniards and Spanish-Americans should find interesting what Smith had to say about the results of the discovery of America. Equally notable, Ros observes, is Smith's condemnation of the seizure of Gibraltar, which lost to England its "natural ally," Spain. Finally, the "clarity and historical insight" with which Smith analyzed the problems of the British Empire, when the American colonies were revolting, "today produces astonishment."

III

Ortiz dedicated his translation to Manuel de Godoy, who encouraged him because of his (Godoy's) desire to spread "throughout the nation the deepest understanding of civil economy." Spain, Ortiz correctly observed, had not been without able economists; but, generally, they failed to treat economics in a "scientific method" or to make it a "true science." Smith succeeded, to a greater extent than any of his predecessors, in constructing a "general system" and in "expounding economic ideas in an abstract manner." He discovered the "universal principle of wealth, which is the productive labor of man." The reader, Ortiz warned, would find Smith's ideas "profound" and "highly metaphysical," requiring "repeated reading to penetrate the spirit of his assertions."

Ortiz erroneously identified his work as a translation of the eighth (and latest) English edition—the edition published in London two years after the appearance of the Spanish version.[32] He was drafting the translation in 1792 and could not have used the seventh edition (1793). He may have had the sixth edition (1791) before him, but I think it more likely that he had the fifth edition (1789) and mistook "5th" for "8th." For the purposes of the following discussion I have compared Ortiz' translation with the well-known Cannan edition.

In the Preface, Ortiz announced the suppression of "some details, but very few, either because absolutely irrelevant to our country or hardly in keeping with the holy religion which we profess." The "essence of the work," he insisted, was "in no way adulterated" by the expurgation. He failed to reveal that he omitted all of Article III, Part III, chapter 1, Book V—the section which Martínez de Irujo reduced to two paragraphs. Furthermore, in Ortiz' translation the heading "Article III" was transposed to another place in the chapter, as though nothing had been deleted.

Smith's discussion of tithes and taxes (Book V, chap. 2, Part II, Art. I) also suffered serious expurgation in translation. "In the dominions of the king of Prussia," Smith related, "the revenue of the church is taxed much higher than that of lay proprietors." This sentence Ortiz retained, but he dropped the following sentences: "The revenue of the church is, the greater part of it, a burden upon the rent of land. It seldom happens that any part of it is applied towards the improvement of land; or is so employed as to contribute in any respect towards increasing the revenue of the great body of the people." Smith continued: "His Prussian majesty had probably, upon that account, thought it reasonable, that it should contribute a good deal more towards relieving the exigencies of the state. In some countries the lands of the church are exempted from all taxes. In others they are taxed more lightly than other lands." Ortiz revised these sentences, as follows: "His Prussian majesty concluded that these revenues [taxes on church property] should contribute more than any others to the exigencies of the state; but there are some countries in which the lands of the church are entirely exempted from every tax or lay contribution and others in which they are not entirely tax-free but are much less burdened than lay property."

In the same article Ortiz suppressed an entire paragraph, beginning with the sentence: "The tythe, as it is frequently a very unequal tax upon the rent, so it is always a great discouragement both to the improvements of the landlord and to the cultivation of the farmer." In a footnote the translator endeavored to explain the difference between inequality and justice in taxation. The tithe, as Smith observed, was "very unequal," but Ortiz regarded it as just. Furthermore, as "all the canonical authors" had pointed out, tithes had never been uniformly exacted at the rate of one-tenth of the produce or rent but were subject to downward adjustment in many cases.[33]

In Book V, chapter 1, Part III, Article II, Smith said: "The more they [the inferior ranks of people] are instructed, the less liable they are to the delusions of enthusiasm and superstition, which, among the ignorant nations, frequently occasion the most dreadful disorders." Smith concluded the paragraph with the observation that "in free countries, where the safety of government depends very much upon the favorable judgment which the people may form of its conduct, it must surely be of the highest importance that they should not be disposed to judge rashly or capriciously concerning it." In Ortiz' words, this sentence becomes: "All these advantages, and many others infallibly follow from the principles of good education." Such discrepancies are surely too great to excuse on the grounds of linguistic difficulty.

Elsewhere, Ortiz saw fit to add a sentence, apparently for the purpose of softening the bluntness of Smith's criticism. In the conclusion to chapter 11 of Book I, Smith noted that merchants and manufacturers generally had a better understanding of their own pecuniary interests than country gentlemen had of theirs. Consequently, landowners were often prevailed upon to accept policies beneficial to the mercantile classes "from a very simple but honest conviction" that the measures were in the interest of the public. Ortiz mutilated these sentences in such a way as to conceal the thought that the interests of merchants and landlords might conflict. Then, after reproducing faithfully the sentence in which Smith denounced "an order of men . . . who have generally an interest to deceive and even oppress the public," Ortiz manufactured the following conclusion: "We are speaking thus with respect to the tendency of the class in general, not with reference to those individuals who, loving the nation and mindful of the common welfare, administer their affairs to their own point and without injury to the public interest."

Understandably, Ortiz found it superfluous to reproduce verbatim the long discussion of the English malt tax (Book V, chap. 2, Part II, Art. IV): and he gave due notice that he had condensed the text and suppressed the statistics. Similarly, he paraphrased a large part of Book IV, chapter 8 ("Conclusion of the Mercantile System"), in which Smith explained in detail the rise and development of bounties and embargoes. It may not be true, as Ortiz insisted, that the illustrative material from English history would be "without the slightest use" to the Spanish student of economics; in any case, it is not a serious matter. By the same token, one need not be too critical of his manipulation of the tables at the end of Book I, chapter 11. Of the three columns of wheat prices for 1202–1601, Ortiz retained only the "average price of each year in money of the present time"; but he added his own dubious estimates of equivalent prices in Castilian vellon reals. He also computed a Spanish price series to match Smith's wheat prices at Windsor, 1595–1764; and he published a series of wheat and barley prices for Burgos, 1675–1792, purporting to show yearly averages of high and low prices in the Castilian market. Finally, he devoted two pages to reporting legal maximum prices for wheat and barley in Spain from 1350 to 1699.

Unlike the original, Ortiz' *Investigación* is heavily interlarded with footnotes, in which the translator compares Spanish conditions with Smith's description of England, raises questions concerning the author's historical accuracy, especially in connection with Spain, or challenges the correctness of Smith's views on economic policy. No fawning adulator of the Glasgow professor, Ortiz gives the lie to Spanish writers who have ridiculed their countrymen for blind acceptance of economic liberalism.[34]

Most offensive to Ortiz were Smith's strictures on the motives for founding colonies (Book IV, chap. 7). Parts of the text, he declared, might well have been omitted in translation, but he finally decided that it would be better to refute the charges than to suppress them. In discussing the Spanish conquests in America, Smith fell into the error of most foreigners, who wilfully overlooked the "just causes which motivated the Spanish establishments in the New World." The "incontestable facts of history" proved that Spain settled "deserted land and islands, or lands whose natives were neither familiar with a civilized state nor lived in a society, wherefore no one doubts that under the law of nations their occupation was just." While admitting that the discovery of gold mines was sometimes the deciding factor in the settlement of a particular region, Ortiz declared: "It is not absolutely certain that it happened this way generally, as the author [Smith] supposes, and as all those foreign writers suppose who lose no opportunity to besmirch our nation with the stigma of greed, solely because there may have been in Spain, as in all nations, some greedy individuals, whose vice our government always punished severely." To spread the "true religion," to gain markets for its industry, "at that time more flourishing in Spain than in other European countries," to bring savages the benefits of a civilized community—these were some of the fundamental reasons for Spain's overseas ventures, and they were not essentially different from the aims of other colonizing powers.

With respect to Spanish imports of American gold and silver, Ortiz knew of no way to improve upon the estimates which Smith derived from the works of Megens and Raynal (Book I, chap. 11). Indeed, he considered it unimportant as well as impractical to attempt the sort of statistical verification of imports of treasure which Profesor Hamilton brought to fruition nearly a century and a half later.[35]

What Smith had to say about paper money, Ortiz asserted, provided "as much as can be desired for complete instruction in the matter"; and he urged that the entire chapter (Book II, chap 2) "be meditated with much reflection." Spain's first experiment with paper money consisted of an issue of interest-bearing treasury certificates (*vales reals*) in 1780. After circulating at a discount for many months, the *vales* rose to parity with silver in 1785. Ortiz believed that the public's unfamiliarity with this type of money had contributed significantly to its depreciation. Eventually, the "good opinion with which the public was accepting this paper money" facilitated new issues. The government, Ortiz said, realized that the paper money stimulated the circulation of immobilized funds and kept within the country the interest payments which in the case of a foreign loan would have gone abroad. In any case, Spain in the 1780's "exiled the hoary misconception that only gold and silver can be useful instruments of commerce and the sole means of increasing national wealth."

Following Smith's "Disgression concerning banks of deposit, particularly concerning that of Amsterdam" (Book IV, chap. 3), Ortiz inserted a forty-page appendix on the Bank of San Carlos (later styled the Bank of Spain).[36] He thought the bank had been "scarcely scrupulous" in making loans against its own shares as collateral, and he expressed a mild criticism of the bank's role as a contractor for provisioning the armed forces. On the other hand, he noted with satisfaction that the bank had settled foreign balances by remitting specie, confident that "the country from which that precious metal is withdrawn need not remain less wealthy as, falsely, common prejudice is accustomed to imagine." Two years after the appearance of his translation of the *Wealth of Nations*, Ortiz published a substantial treatise on paper money and public credit.[37] Believing that "the subject in itself is not susceptible of much that is new," Ortiz disclaimed having made any contribution except that of making available to Spaniards the ideas of French and English economists. Besides Smith, the greatest authorities on paper money were Mortimer, Hume, Genovesi, and Dutot. All their teachings, Ortiz concluded, proved that "the only support and the true foundation on which rests the soundness and stability" of paper money "is the public credit."

In expounding the "interest of money" (Book I, chap. 9), Smith, Ortiz noted, had in mind "compensatory or mercantile interest" not "lucrative usury, generally known by the generic term usury, prohibited as illicit by all laws, which is to give something more than the principal at risk by reason of mere accommodation [*mutuo*]." It is doubtful that this clarified the matter for the readers of footnotes or that they were enlightened by the note (Book II, chap. 4) in which Ortiz made another attempt "to obviate the errors of the uninformed reader on the point of interest on money." The gist of his argument is that interest is permitted, up to the maximum legal rate, in ordinary mercantile and commercial transactions; but, when a loan is made "with no other reason than the benefit it bestows in ministering to the need of the borrower," the taking of interest is unlawful.

Ortiz devoted several notes to the exceptions which he presumed Smith had overlooked in propounding the principles of free trade (Book IV). He agreed that a "natural tendency" would be obstructed by protecting any industry in a country which, because of a high level of industrialization, had little to fear from foreign competition. But a generally backward economy, of which Spain seemed to be the prime example, could never advance without tariffs. Domestic manufacturers had to have the "privilege of an exclusive market, at least for a certain time and until national industry may place itself in a position to compete for the foreign." Free trade, in Ortiz' mind, was "advantageous when it does not serve as a positive obstacle to the improvement of the domestic industry in a backward country." It was necessary, Smith to the contrary notwithstanding, to limit Spanish exports of gold and silver; otherwise excessive quantities of the precious metals would be exchanged for foreign wares, "with recognizable harm to our factories, because these are not yet in a state to compete with the foreign factories."

With respect to the grain trade, Ortiz thought Spanish policy had been "much more lenient and prudent than that of England." A new departure from age-old Spanish legislation was the corn law of 1765, recommended by Count Campomanes, who had been greatly influenced by the Physiocrats. The act abolished legal price ceilings and removed most of the restrictions on the domestic grain trade. Exports of wheat were permitted as long as prices remained below 35 reals per fanega in Asturias, Galicia, Andalucia, Murcia, and Valencia, below 32 reals in the Cantabrian provinces, or below 22 reals in the border towns. Imported wheat had to be warehoused within six leagues of the port of entry, but it could be withdrawn for sale in interior markets when domestic prices were above the prices specified in the regulations governing exports. The corn laws of 1789 and 1790 restored many of the pre-1765 restrictions on the grain trade, but (Ortiz insisted) Spain had "adopted the maxim of free trade, if not in an absolute manner, at least in a way most compatible with the circumstances of the country." The "circumstances" included the machinations of greedy and unprincipled grain dealers who persistently conspired to raise prices.

Commending Smith's attack on privileged trading companies, Ortiz pointed out that Spanish policy had been "more prudent" than that of England, because Spain "never granted such companies sovereign power nor the right to have and maintain garrisons and fortifications." Furthermore, Spain had granted exclusive rights to trade only for a limited number of years. Ortiz noted the privileges possessed by the powerful Five Greater Guilds of Madrid but failed to make a vigorous attack, as others had done, on the Guilds' virtual monopoly of several branches of trade, industry, and government procurement.

Ortiz generally agreed with Smith on the harmful effects of craft guilds (Book I, chap. 10). A case could be made for guild regulations limited to the improvement of the workers' manual skills and to technical innovations in production. Inherently, however, guild objectives exhibited a "prejudicial tendency; and it will be a very rare case, if one is found, that keeps them within legal and just limits, according to the intentions of the government." In one matter Spain was ahead of England, Ortiz found, because it had never interfered with the migration of workers within the country. There were laws to control vagrancy and mendicancy but nothing comparable to English laws "to remove a man who has committed no misdemeanour from the parish where he chooses to reside," in "evident violation of natural liberty and justice."

Ortiz disagreed with Smith's explanation of the low pay for military service as compared with the wages of common laborers (Book I, chap. 10). It was not the prospect of honors and metals that caused young men to enlist but genuine hatred of the country's enemies, eagerness to defend its religion, and patriotism. Similarly, Smith's comparison of the worker's wages with the emoluments of curates was considered inapplicable to Spain, where some bishoprics were well endowed and others had meager means for supporting the parish priests. On the other hand, the constant concern of both church and state lest the number of Spanish clergy increase inordinately lent support to Smith's observation that the "hope of much more moderate benefices will draw a sufficient number of learned, decent, and respectable men into holy orders."[38]

The article, "Of the Expense of the Institutions for the Education of Youth" (Book V, chap. 1, Part III, Art. II), evoked thirteen long notes in Ortiz' translation. In one place Smith observed that, when the university professor was salaried and not dependent upon student fees, his interest was "set as directly opposite to his duty as it was possible to set it." Ortiz found this view "quite judicious, well-founded, and in keeping with experience." He saw no way to make the buying and selling of education competitive: "stimulus and advancement in the arts and sciences and costly education in these subjects are two entirely incompatible things." But Smith's charge that the professor tended "to consent that his neighbor may neglect his duty, provided he himself is allowed to neglect his own," struck Ortiz as "false" and "impudent." Similarly, he doubted that students had to choose a college or university "independent of the merit of reputation of the teachers"; he felt that "emulation" was strong enough to make the education afforded scholarship students as good as that provided those who paid full fees.[39] The translator vigorously objected to Smith's insistence that the "discipline of colleges and universities is in general contrived, not for the benefit of the students, but for the interest, or more properly speaking, for the ease of the masters." On the other hand, Ortiz regretfully corroborated Smith's reference to "some Spanish universities . . . in which the study of the Greek language has never yet made any part of that course" (theology). Only three universities, Ortiz said, had chairs of Greek and Hebrew.

Elsewhere, Smith made the caustic comment: "Were there no public institutions for education, a gentleman, after going through, with application and abilities, the most complete course of education which the circumstances of the times were supposed to afford, could not come into the world completely ignorant of every thing which is the common subject of conversation among gentlemen and men of the world." Baffled, apparently, by the abstruseness of the sentence, Ortiz rewrote it, as follows: "If these public institutions did not exist, men perhaps would receive a more useful and beneficial education." In any event, he regarded the statement as "puerile," equivalent to saying: "If there had been no masters who taught science, there would not have been masters who taught erroneous things; so, in order that there be no one who teaches errors, all the masters who teach science must be removed from the world." I doubt whether either Smith or Ortiz furnishes much help on means to rid educational systems of pedantry, sophistry, error, and nonsense.

Ortiz' footnotes on the second chapter of Book V are devoted to describing the Spanish tax system and to commenting on Smith's criticisms of fiscal policy. He agreed with Smith that it was improper to tax "revenue arising from stock," and he deplored inheritance taxes, which in certain parts of Spain and Portugal deprived close relatives of the major portion of even paltry estates. Wages were taxed in Spain, but Ortiz considered the Spanish practice "never . . . so burdensome as in other parts of Europe." On the other hand, sales taxes, both general and selective, had reached intolerable levels. For more than a century, as Ortiz pointed out, Spanish economists had deplored their depressing effect upon trade and the unfair burden on the poor. As a general rule, Ortiz asserted, "the principal defects which customarily underly taxes . . . are the inequality in their imposition and arbitrariness in their collection, which originate either in the very nature of the tax, concerning which our author [Smith] reasons skilfully, or in the extrinsic or accidental circumstances which by reason of the difficulty of reducing them to an exact calculation are, as it were, another [defective] characteristic." If called upon to improve the tax system, Ortiz would have favored the introduction of a single property tax (*contribución única*), a reform proposed by the Treasury in the first half of the eighteenth century.

Commenting on public debts (Book V, chap. 3), Ortiz spoke of the sinking fund as a necessary guaranty of the repayment of a loan as well as a bulwark of credit which would facilitate new borrowing in an emergency. He also considered it praiseworthy that the nation's paper money had been protected by a redemption fund for its eventual retirement from ciculation. Although he had misgivings about the accuracy of the available data, he thought the Spanish national debt was smaller in relation to national wealth than the public debts of England and France. This consideration seemed to Ortiz to be more to the point than Smith's reminder that part of Spain's public debt, contracted in the sixteenth century, had never been retired.

For the serious student of the *Wealth of Nations* the usefulness of Ortiz' translation was greatly enhanced by a sixty-page synopsis ("Indice General") of the five books.

After Ortiz, the most influential critic of the work of Smith was the Catalan jurist Ramón Lázaro de Dou y de Bassols. In a work on public law, composed during the closing years of the eighteenth century, he acknowledged the "profundity" of the *Wealth of Nations* as well as the superiority of Englishmen in "economic speculation," but he refused to accept Smith's views on commercial policy. Dou criticized his compatriots who, "in the spirit of novelty and scepticism," were "opposed to tariffs and taxes on the import and export of produce and manufactures, defending themselves with the authority of Smith, whom they represent as the Achilles of their opinion." England had never adopted free trade, and Dou believed that "the further a nation is from equaling or surpassing other nations in industries, the further it must be from adopting Smith's system."[40] Without examining the logic of the case for free trade, Dou eagerly espoused a vigorous program for the industrialization of Catalonia behind tariff walls.

After serving as president of the Cortes of Cádiz in 1810, Dou became chancellor of the University of Cervera.[41] Here he published, in 1817, a commentary on the *Wealth of Nations*, based on excerpts from the second edition of Ortiz' translation.[42] Calling Smith the "Neuton [*sic*] of political economy," Dou declared that the Scotsman's genius consisted in having discovered, as from a high watchtower, that Europeans, dazzled by the brilliance of the mercantile system, were straying very far from the paths they ought to follow." On the other hand, Dou thought, Smith had erred in not presenting "with as much extension and force as it seems they should be presented some important exceptions in the matter of the mercantile system." Dou set out to show how the wisdom of Smith would profit the reader, but he felt free to refute him at will, especially on points which "do not seem to me consistent with his own system."

Dou said he had heard many complain that they could not fathom some of Smith's ideas; and Dou admitted his "embarrassment" because he had had to read parts of the *Wealth of Nations* several times before understanding the "sublimity" of the doctrines. Furthermore, he thought that poor organization and Smith's failure to elaborate points which would be obscure to all except the most erudite helped to explain the "scarce fruit" which the *Wealth of Nations* had borne in Spain.

Criticizing Smith, Dou repeated much of his earlier defense of protectionism. Duties on imports, which incidentally constituted a good source of revenue, were essential for an industrially backward country: "Whatever may be said against tariffs . . . seems to me an illusion or economic madness." Uztariz proved to be a better guide to commercial policy than Smith. Furthermore, Dou thought Smith had "confessed" the "utility, or to put it better, the necessity of the mercantile system."

Dou also reached a conclusion "somewhat contrary to the disdain which some, with the title or the pretext of being disciples of Smith, have for the precious metals." The poverty of Spain and Portugal, in the midst of a plethora of gold and silver, had been exaggerated: what these two countries lacked was the necessary intelligence to use their money as a means of expanding agriculture and industry. Gold must be counted as a part of the wealth of nations, since its production demanded "an astonishing quantity of labor . . . permanent labor which does not perish with time or with fire."

Usury, Dou cautioned, was "a delicate matter . . . on which, because of the sole circumstance of religion, we should depart from Smith"; but Dou supposed that Smith's views, applying to purely mercantile transactions, supported his own position. Unfortunately, Ortiz had given Dou a garbled translation of the third chapter of Book V. Smith said: "To trade, was disgraceful to a gentleman; and to lend money at interest, which at that time was considered usury, and prohibited by law, would have been still more so." Ortiz' version reads: "To trade (he is speaking of olden times) was not well thought of for a gentleman: to lend money at interest, without taking into account the circumstances which can make this contract lawful, was then commonly regarded as usury, and consequently prohibited, as it now is, [and] which in reality is usury." In other words, Dou supposed that Smith recognized "lawful usury" as interest on loans qualifying under the Thomist doctrine of *lucrum cessans* and *damnum emergens*. He challenged the idea that the Catholic position was inimical to national prosperity. "Economics in all its parts and in a thousand ways, blended perfectly with religion, governs and must govern affairs so as to destroy usury."

Dou regarded the labor theory of value an "enlightening principle." So clearly had Smith shown that the quantity of labor determined the value of goods that it was "unnecessary to look for other sources of wealth than labor." But Dou objected that land and capital were not independent sources of value: they created wealth only "in proportion to the labor they contain." Dou disagreed with Smith and the "majority" of economists who regarded large entailed estates as inimical to agricultural progress and contrary to natural rights. He also doubted the wisdom of Jovellanos' views that the "interest of cultivators will never be more active than when they are proprietors."[43] Finding strong sanction for entail and primogeniture in civil, natural, and divine law, Dou proposed to remove the obstacles to better farming by the use of emphyteusis. In two pamphlets published in 1829 and 1831, apparently Dou's last work, he found support in the *Wealth of Nations* for his scheme to generalize the practice of long-term hereditary leases for small holdings.[44]

IV

Towards the end of the eighteenth century Ramón Campos, a physics professor and the author of works on logic, attempted to make the ideas of Smith better known through a text on "economics reduced to exact, clear and simple principles." Smith, he declared, "made himself immortal by the brilliance with which he presented the substance of Stewart's [*sic*] work." It was Campos' ambition to publicize the findings of both economists, so that the science, "so mysterious until now, may through my work become widely known, being universally accepted among the number of exact sciences." In eight chapters Campos covered concisely, but accurately, the Smithian theories of prices, wages, profit, capital, and taxation; and he devoted an appendix to public debts. It is not clear for whom the miniature volume was intended or how widely it was read.[45]

In the Preface to the 1821 edition of Say's *Tratado* the translator, Juan Sánchez Rivera, exclaimed: "How much honor befalls our nation and how much happiness we should promise ourselves, and even more our children, from a great number of laws and dispositions of the Spanish legislature of 1820, all founded on the brilliant ideas of Say, Smith, Ricardo, Steward [*sic*], Filangieri, Beccaria, and other celebrated writers, who have dedicated their talents to enlightening this essential part of human knowledge"! Foremost among the liberal deputies in the Cortes of 1820 was the economist, Alvaro Flórez Estrada. A member of the commerce committee, Flórez Estrada supported legislation to reduce tariffs and remove other restrictions on trade. "As far as I am concerned," he declared, "would to God that I could persuade Congress to abolish all tariffs from this day forward!" To prohibit imports was "contrary to all the principles of political economy." Equally bad were the exclusive privileges of the Philippines Company, and those who thought the example of the English East India Company proved the advantages of trading monopolies were mistaken: "There is no informed Englishman who has touched on that Company who does not consider it inimical to public happiness."[46] José Canga Argüelles, one of Flórez Estrada's colleagues in the Cortes of 1820, cited Smith in defense of the proposition that lower tariffs increase the revenue from customs duties.[47]

Both Canga Argüelles and Flórez Estrada were exiled to England upon the restoration of Fernando VIII's absolute rule in 1823. A former finance minister (1811), Canga Argüelles published in London a number of works on public finance, including a five-volume *Diccionario de hacienda*. A potpourri of economic, historical, and statistical information, the *Diccionario* cites Smith several times. It was the *Wealth of Nations* which explained the fallacy of the favourable-balance-of-trade argument, showed the beneficial effects of circulating capital in domestic trade, and revealed the "prodigious increase" in production made possible by the division of labor. Canga Argüelles quoted Smith—but not accurately—in an article which denounced the granting of exclusive privileges to foreign traders.[48]

Flórez Estrada's *Curso de economía política*, first published in 1828, has been described as the "first systematic treatise on economics written by a Spaniard." Although relying primarily on the *Wealth of Nations* and other English works, Flórez Estrada advanced the original doctrine that private ownership of land is the cause of the "laborer's failure to obtain the entire fruit of his labor," anticipating Mill and Henry George.[49] Neglecting Say, he asserted that no Spaniard had ever written a "complete treatise on political economy" or translated into Spanish a work which unfolded the "great discoveries" in the science during the preceding thirty years. Flórez Estrada's *Curso* attempted to inquire methodically into the means of increasing national wealth. He considered Smith the "true founder of the modern system of political economy" and held that the *Wealth of Nations* "ought to be placed among the works which have brought the most good to the human race." But Smith's masterpiece had its faults; it lacked clarity; it was not well organized; and its digressions, if not useless, were often unnecessary. Smith was mistaken, Flórez Estrada believed, in regarding agriculture as the most productive type of economic activity, and he erred in calling labor unproductive unless expended on an exchangeable commodity. But Smith's "capital error" was his insistence on the stable value of wheat and the natural adjustment of wages to the price level.[50]

In the *Elementos de economía política*, first published in 1829, the Marqués de Valle Santoro endeavored to synthesize the theories of Smith and Say, eliminating the "discussion and digression" found in the economists' works, "so that beginners may form forthwith a clear idea of the status of the science without being distracted by other purposes." Smith was often mistaken, but "no one can take away from him the glory of having been the founder of Political Economy." Unfortunately, the "error of Smith [*sic*] in believing and writing that the creators of immaterial goods were not producers of wealth did much harm during the past revolutions because, dividing men into useful or productive and sterile or unproductive classes, it was easy to inflame one against the others, considering them as just so many leeches who lived at the expense of their sweat and robbed them of their sustenance." Finally, the "celebrated Adam Smith" thoroughly discredited the tenets of mercantilism. What he failed to recognize was the dependence of commercial policy on a country's stage of economic development; only the most advanced nations could afford to adopt free trade.[51]

V

Liberal economics seeped into the Spanish colonies through several channels. The Ordinance of 1778, which introduced the policy of *comercio libre*, has sometimes been identified as a free-trade measure.[52] It was, of course, nothing of the sort; it merely opened to trade a number of Spanish and American ports which for two and a half centuries had been denied the right to engage in overseas commerce. Possibly, as González Alberdi suggests,[53] the *Wealth of Nations* encouraged some colonists to press for even greater freedom in their economic affairs—freedoms which proved inconsistent with Spain's concept of colonial dependence. Few, it would seem, were persuaded to accept all the principles in defense of which Smith and Say wrote so cogently.

In Buenos Aires, in the early years of the nineteenth century, Juan Hipólito Vieytes founded a weekly newspaper to disseminate useful information on agriculture, industry, and trade.[54] The pages of the *Semanario* constitute, according to Weinberg, the "most intensive and systematic exposition of political economy which had been achieved up to that time in the Rio de la Plata."[55] Actually, although Vieytes called Smith the "sublime economist," he gave his readers little more than extracts of some Smithian ideas found in Samuel Crumpe's essay on the means of providing employment for people."[56]

The ablest and most prolific writer on economic questions in Argentina was Manuel Belgrano. Educated in Spain, Belgrano learned of Smith through Martinez' *Compendio*; but, as Gondra points out, no Smithian influence marks the addresses on agriculture, industry, and commerce which Belgrano delivered before the Consulado of Buenos Aires in 1796–1802.[57] He showed his predilection for the Physiocrats in a book published in 1796.[58] In the first number of the *Correo de comercio*, founded by Belgrano in 1810, he discussed Smith and published a résumé of the first chapter of Book IV of the *Wealth of Nations*. In subsequent issues Belgrano attacked monopoly, championed laissez faire, and echoed many of the views of liberal economists. "Self-interest," he declared, "is the only motive force in the heart of man and, well managed, it can furnish infinite advantages." Elsewhere, he assured his readers that he would "never tire of repeating to you that competition is the judge which is able to regulate the true price of things." In an essay on commerce (1810) he enumerated "nine principles which the English, that is to say, the wisest people in matters of trade, propound in their books in order to judge the utility or the

disadvantage of commercial undertakings." Unfortunately for Belgrano's reputation as a student of English economics most of the "principles" may be
traced not to Smith but to seventeenth-century mercantilists.[59]

The *Wealth of Nations* was one of several European works which influenced
Chilean economic thought in the early years of the nineteenth century. Manuel
de Salas, Juan Egaña, and Camilo Henríquez, the founders of the Instituto
Nacional (1813), recommended the works of Genovesi, Say, and Smith for the
Institute's course in political economy.[60] Salas, the energetic syndic of the
Santiago Consulado, wrote voluminously on questions of agricultural and
commercial policy. He cited Hume; but, if he knew Smith's work, he never
found it worth mentioning. For Salas, the ideas of the Spanish reformers
Campillo and Ward seemed adaptable to Chilean conditions.[61] Egaña owned
copies of Say's *Tratado*; but the only writing in which he may have expressed an
opinion of Say (and Smith) has not survived.[62] Although Henríquez, the
founder of two periodicals, *La Aurora* (1812) and the *Mercurio de Chile* (1822)
learned English for the sake of reading the works of English economists, his
writings make no direct reference to Smith.[63]

An anonymous "Economist," writing to the editors of the Santiago *El
Telégrafo* (May 25, 1819), quoted Say and Smith in defense of the right to export
coin and specie freely. "The silver and gold . . . produced in Chile," he
asserted, "should be regarded in the same light as copper, wheat, wool, or
any other product." Export duties on precious metals should be so moderate
that it would not be worth the risk of confiscation to engate in contraband
trade. Adam Smith, he said, "explains this doctrine very well."[64]

José Joaquín Mora, a Spaniard who had lived several years in London, came
to Chile in the 1820's. After establishing the Liceo de Chile, which included
political economy in its curriculum, Mora launched *El Mercurio chileno* to
popularize his political and economic beliefs. In the issue of May 1, 1828, he
explained Smith's canons of taxation, supplementing them by four "precepts
no less just" which he took from Say. In an article on banks and money he
attacked the "principal dogma" of the mercantilists that "true wealth consists
only in the abundance of precious metals." He extolled agriculture and noted
that "Adam Smith, whose opinions can be contradicted and modified, but who
is rarely mistaken in matters of fact, calculates the value of the land rent as the
fourth part at least of the product of the labor employed in its cultivation."
This represented a better return than was possible from the use of labor in
manufacturing. Furthermore, as Smith pointed out, "the merchant and the
manufacturer . . . are citizens of no country" and, hence, less desirable than
agriculturists. In later articles Mora's paper referred to Smith as the "father of
political economy" and asserted that the Scottish economist had demonstrated

that the only way to eradicate smuggling was to lower tariffs. Smith, Mora wrote, first explained the advantages of the division of labor, but Say "expresses the same idea in a still more convincing manner." Quoting the "most respectable of the authorities in political economy who can be cited," Mora called attention to Smith's observation that complaints of the death of money are universal; like wine, money necessarily appears scarce to those who lack the wherewithal to buy it.[65]

Debates over economic measures in the early legislatures of Chile frequently elicited references to Smith, usually as one of several European economists whose views threw light on the matters under consideration.[66] There was, apparently, no continuing influence of this early acceptance of the doctrines of Smith and other classical economists. Chile, however, experienced a rebirth of academic and official interest in economic liberalism in the 1850's, when the government employed the French economist Jean Courcelle-Seneuil to serve as a professor of economics and an advisor on economic policy.[67]

The *Wealth of Nations* is included in a list of "recognized works of political economy" recommended for the library of the Consulado of Veracruz (1802), but it is not clear that the merchant guild ever acquired the books.[68] In the Mexican Congress of 1823 Manuel Ortiz de la Torre presented an unusually vigorous and enlightened discourse on commercial policy. Quoting the Spanish edition of the *Wealth of Nations*, as well as the works of a dozen other European economists, he argued that a new nation could best maintain its independence by trading with all countries on equal terms. After analyzing the harmful effects of a prohibitive tariff, Ortiz concluded that the level of important duties should be adjusted to accomplish two objectives: (1) produce needed revenue, taking into account the yield of other taxes, and (2) equalize the prices of imported and domestic goods. But protective duties should be reduced gradually over a period of years, during which the protected industries would either acquire sufficient skill to compete with foreign producers or give way to domestic industries which could survive without protection.[69] Ortiz had no influence on legislation and, apparently, little influence on the writings of other Mexican economists.[70]

In Guatemala the Economic Society inaugurated a course in political economy in 1812 and selected the outstanding intellectual, José Cecilio del Valle, to teach the subject. In a preliminary statement on the curriculum, Valle said that he accepted Smith's principles but considered the *Wealth of Nations* too difficult for an elementary course. Smith was the "man from whose mind the science [of economics] sprang already formed"; but much of his thought was too abstract for the beginner. Say, he felt, was "capable of greater perfection in style and thinking" than Smith.[71] In 1814 ·Father Francisco Garcia Pelaez prepared a syllabus of "Notes on Civil Economy Taken from Adam Smith" for the first course in political economy offered in the Guatemalan University of San Carlos. The surviving records indicate that after one or two meetings Father Garcia abandoned the course for lack of students.[72]

Francisco de Arango y Parreño, an official of the Havana city council, drew upon the "opinion of the profound and wise Smith" in preparing essays on agricultural improvement (1792 and 1808). Arango thought that Smith "had given the mortal blow to the mercantilist system," though other exceptions than navigation acts, which Smith had praised, should be admitted to the rule of laissez faire.[73] In 1818 the Economic Society of Havana founded a chair of political economy in the Seminario de San Carlos. Justo Velez, the first professor, used his own translation of Say's *Traité* as a text but lectured on both Smith and Say.[74]

VI

In Spain and Spanish America the main currents of economic thought were enriched by borrowing from streams that flowed, not always uninterrupted, across the boundaries of language and intolerance. If, perchance, the present essay has identified the principal channels through which the ideas of Adam Smith moved, many rivulets remain for others to explore. A search of unpublished lectures and university curriculums, for instance, might reveal a wider diffusion of *Wealth of Nations* than may be surmised from the published works of Foronda, Ortiz, Jovellanos, Dou, and Flórez Estrada. It is improbable, though, that Spain ever experienced an academic interest in Smith comparable to the movement which made the Scotsman so well known in German universities.[75] Works on political and legal questions, especially in the period which brought forth the first Latin-American constitutions, may yield further evidence of familiarity with, if not respect for, the tenets of classical economics.[76] Not only Smith but Say, Ricardo, Malthus, and other liberal economists had their translators and followers among Spanish-speaking people. If their number was not legion, nor their infuence far-reaching, explanations may be sought in the pages of social and political history, in the New World as in the Old.

NOTES

1. *L'ᵒᵒEspagne éclairée de la seconde moitié du xviiiᵉ siècle* (Paris, 1954).
2. Earl J. Hamilton, "The Mercantilism of Gerónimo de Uztáriz," in *Economics, Sociology and the Modern World* (Cambridge, Mass., 1935), pp. 111–29. The English

translation of Uztáriz (*Theory and Practice of Commerce and Maritime Affairs*, trans. John Kippax [London, 1751]) was, apparently, the only work of a Spanish economist found in Adam Smith's library (James Bonar, *A Catalogue of the Library of Adam Smith* [London, 1894], p. 116). Smith cited Uztáriz in the *Wealth of Nations*. Book V, chap. 2, Part II, Art. IV.

3. Joseph Addison, *Reflexiones sobre las ventajas que resultan del comercio al estado*, trans. Cristóbal Cladera (Madrid, 1785); Girolamo Belloni, *Disertución sobre la naturaleza y utilidades del comercio*, trans. José Labrada (Santiago, 1788): Jakob Friedrich Bielfeld, *Instituciones politicas: Obra en que se trata de los reynos de Portugal y España*, trans. Valentin de Foronda (Bordeaux, 1781), and *Instituciones politicas: Obra en que se trata de la sociedad civil, de las leyes, de la policia, de la real hacienda, del comercio y fuerzas de un estado*, trans. Domingo de la torre y Mollinedo (6 vols.: Madrid, 1761–1801); Étienne Bonot de Condillac, "Tratado sobre el comercio y el govierno, considerados con relación reciproca," in *Memorias instructivas y curiosas sobre agricultura, comercio, industria, economia, chymica, botánica, historia natural,* & (12 vols.: Madrid, 1778–91), III, 219–386, and IV, 3–116: Charles Davenant, "Del uso de la aritmética politica en el comercio y rentas," in Nicolás Arriquivar, *Recreación politica (*2 vols.: Vitoria, 1779), I, 1–24; Cayetano Filangieri, *Reflexiones sobre la libertad del comercio de frutos* (Madrid 1784) and *Ciencia de la legislación* (5 vols.: Madrid, 1787–89); Fernando Galiani, *Diálogos sobre el comercio de trigo* (Madrid, 1775); Antonio Genovesi, *Lecciones de comercio o bien de economía civil*, trans. Victorián de Villalva (3 vols.; Madrid, 1785–86); Claude Jacques Herbert, *Ensayo sobre la policia general de los granos, sobre sus precios y sobre los efectos de la agricultura*, trans. Tomás Anzano (Madrid, 1795); David Hume, *Discursos politicos* (Madrid, 1789); Jacques Necker, *Memoria reservada sobre el establecimiento de rentas provinciales*, trans. Domingo de la Torre y Mollinedo (Madrid, 1786), and "Sobre la legislación y comercio de granos," in *Memorias instructivas y curiosas . . .* , VIII, 3–237; François Quesnay, *Máximas générales del gobierno económico de un reino agricultor* (Madrid, 1794): A. R. J. Turgot, "Reflexiones sobre la formación y distribución de las riquezas," in *Memorias instructivas y curiosas . . .* , XII, 3–100. The translations of Condorcet and Smith are noted below.

4. Juan Bautista Say, *Tratado de economía política o exposicion simple del modo come se formen, distribuyen y consumen las riquezas* (3 vols.; Madrid, 1804). There were at least seven other editions of the *Tratado* (1807, 1814, 1816, 1817, 1821, 1836, 1838), three editions of the *Cartilla de economia politica* (1816, 1818, 1822), two editions of the *Catecismo de economía política* (1822, 1823), two editions of *Cartas a Mr. Malthus* (1820, 1827), and an *Epitome de los principios fundamentales de economía política* (1816).

5. Melchior Palyi, "The Introduction of Adam Smith on the Continent," in *Adam Smith, 1776–1926* (Chicago, 1928), p. 191.

6. Paulino González Alberdi, *Los Economistas Adam Smith y David Ricardo* (Buenos Aires, 1947), pp. 42–43.

7. Manuel Colmeiro, *Biblioteca de los economistas españoles de los siglos xvi, xvii y xviii* (Madrid, 1880), p. 78.

8. Bernando Joaquin Danvila y Villarrasa, *Lecciones de economia civil* (Madrid, 1779).

The book, written for use in the Royal Seminary for Nobles, was reprinted (Saragossa, 1800), with the author's last name changed to Villagrasa.

9. Jaime Carrera Pujal, *Historia de la economía española*, IV (Barcelona, 1945), 343. Carrera Pujal takes Alcalá Galiano to task for his "great attachment to direct taxes, when the idiosyncracy of the country required preferably indirect taxes, since the former were more easily mocked by false declarations than were the latter by fraud." In his early addresses, published in the *Actas y memorias de la Real Sociedad Economica de los Amigos del País de la Provincia de Segovia*, Vol. I (Segovia, 1785), Alcala Galiano showed no Smithian influence. I have not located the fourth volume of the *Actas*, containing the piece to which Carrera Pujal refers.

10. Sarrailh (*op. cit.*, pp. 274–77, 591–92) details the controversy between Normante and his clerical opponents. The "scandal" is referred to in Marcelino Menendez y Pelayo, *Historia de los heterodoxos españoles*, Vol. VI (Madrid, 1930 ed.), 272–73, and in Clemente Herranz y Lain, *Estudio critico sobre los economistas aragoneses* (Saragossa, 1885), pp. 58–60. Apparently, influential friends at court saved Normante from official censure. One of his attackers, Father Gerónimo José de Cabra, declared that Normante's errors included the assertion that the study of the causes of human happiness represented "the most sublime use of one's reason and intelligence"; the belief that "free trade in grain is useful in Spain"; the condemnation of "some laws and observances of ecclesiastical bodies and establishments" which checked the increase of population; the argument that "sales taxes are inimical to the development of industry"; the view that sumptuary laws are "contrary to the true spirit of economics"; and the insistence that restrictions on interest-bearing mercantile loans keep money out of circulation (*Pruebas del espíritu del Sr. Melon y de las proposiciones de economia civil y comercio* 2 parts: Madrid, 1787).

11. *Cartas sobre los asuntos mas exquisitos de la economia politica y sobre las leyes criminales* (2 vols.; Madrid, 1789–94). The letters were first published in the *Espiritu de los mejores diarios literarios que se publican en Europa* (Madrid), from November 10, 1788, to November 23, 1789. An earlier work, *Miscelánea o colección de varios discursos* (Madrid, 1787), contains speeches on agriculture, banking, and trade delivered before the Basque Economic Society.

12. Julio Somoza de Montsoriu, *Inventario de un jovellanista* (Madrid, 1901), pp. 81, 125.

13. *Obras de D. Gaspar Melchor Jovellanos: Diarios (Memorias intimas)*, 1790–1801 (Madrid, 1915), p. 304. On May 10, 1795, Jovellanos saw the "entire translations of Smith" at the home of Vicente Salamanca but failed to say whether it was the Spanish translation published in 1794. In November, 1795, he loaned the *Wealth of Nations* to his friend, José Pedrayes, a mathematician; the following May he referred to the "original English, which I gave to Pedrayes" (*ibid.*, pp. 222, 277, 304).

14. *Ibid.*, pp. 304–323. But "things repeated sevenfold will be pleasing" (*septis repetita placebunt*), Jovellanos concluded.

15. "Informe del Real Acuerdo de Sevilla al Consejo Real de Castilla sobre la extraccion de aceite a reinos extrangeros," in *Biblioteca de autores españoles* (Madrid, 1859), L. 1–6.

16. "Informe de la Junta de Comercio y Moneda sobre formento de la marina mercante," *ibid.*, pp. 20–28.

17. "Informe dado a la Junta General de Comercio y Moneda sobre el libre ejercicio de las artes," *ibid.*, pp. 33–45.

18. *Informe de la Sociedad Económica de esta Corte al Real y Supremo Consejo de Castilla en el expediente de ley agraria* (Madrid, 1795).

19. Conde de Campomanes, *Tradado de la regalia de amortización* (Madrid, 1765).

20. Edith F. Helman, "Some Consequences of the Publication of the *Informe de ley agraria* by Jovellanos," *Estudios hispánicos: Homenaje a Archer M. Huntington* (Wellesley, Mass., 1952), pp. 253–73.

21. The *Index librorum prohibitorum Sanctissimi Domini nostri Pii IX. Pont. Max. iussu editus* (Rome, 1877) continued the ban of the *Informe*, first decreed in 1825.

22. *Compendio de la obra inglesa intitulada Riqueza de las naciones, hecho por el marqués de Condorcet* (Madrid, 1792). There were two other editions: Madrid, 1803, and Palma, 1814.

23. León Carbonero y Sol, *Indice de los libros prohibidos por el Santo Officio de la Inquisición Española* (Madrid, 1873), p. 607. In a letter dated Munich, December 4, 1792, Sir John Macpherson wrote Edward Gibbon that the Spanish government had "permitted an extract of the Wealth of Nations to be published, though the original is condemned by the Inquisition." Macpherson, referring to sentences of the Inquisition "pasted upon the church doors," says that Smith's work was banned because of the "lowness of its style and the looseness of the morals which it inculcates" (*The Miscellaneous Works of Edward Gibbon Esq.* [London, 1814], II, 479). Fernando de los Rios believed that the proscription, far from hampering "its spread inside and outside of the universities," was "an incentive to its diffusion" (*Encyclopaedia of the Social Sciences* [New York, 1930], I, 296).

24. "Royal censors of the press," declared the "Prince of the Peace," "were ordered gradually to slacken the reins, and to allow great latitude to literature; always providing, that religion and the principles of monarchy were respected. The same indulgence was extended to foreign books and journals, so that they did not openly preach atheism or anarchy, and were calculated to promote the progress of science or of the art" (J. B. D'Esmenard [ed.], *Memoirs of Don Manuel de Godoy, Prince of the Peace* [2 vols.: London, 1836], II, 176).

25. "Recherches sur la nature et les causes de la richesse de nations," in *Bibliothéque de l'homme public*, III (Paris, 1790), 108–216, and IV (1790), 3–115. The article is not signed, but Condorcet, one of the founders of the *Bibliothéque*, was undoubtedly the author. Doctor Robinet (*Condorcet, sa vie, son œuvre, 1743–1794* [Paris, n.d.]. pp. 98–99) claims that Condorcet also wrote a volume of "notes on political economy" for the Roucher translation of the *Wealth of Nations* (*Recherches sur la nature et les causes de la richesse des nations, traduites de l'anglais de M. Smith, sur la quatriéme edition, par M. Roucher, et suivies d'un volume de notes par M. le marquis de Condorcet* [4 vols.; Paris, 1790–91]). There were several editions of the Roucher translation, but I have seen none which contains Condorcet's notes. A French review of the first

edition was printed in translation in the *Espiritu de os mejores diarios literarios*, X (1790), 282–85.

26. As follows: "The establishments concerned with the instruction of people of all ages are principally those which have for their object religious instruction. Those who give this instruction are maintained, as are teachers of any other kind, either by the voluntary contributions of their hearers or by funds to which they are entitled under the laws of the land; and they ordinarily manifest more zeal and industry when they live solely on the liberality and charity of their hearers.

"There is probably not a single Portestant church in which the zeal and industry of the clergy is as active and fervent as in the Roman Church. The clergy of its parishes obtain the greatest part of their support from alms and voluntary oblations of the people; and the parochial clergy, like those teachers whose compensation in part depends on a fixed fund and in part upon the contributions of their students, consequently depend for their well-being on their reputations and good conduct."

27. *Memoirs of Don Manuel de Godoy*, II, 169.

28. Archivo Histórico Nacional, Madrid, *Papeles de Inquisición, No.* 1327. Excerpts from this document were kindly furnished me by Don Miguel Bordonau y Más.

29. *Investigación de la naturaleza y causas de la riqueza de las naciones* (4 vols.; Valladolid, 1974). Ortiz, apparently, was responsible for the second "greatly corrected and improved" edition (4 vols.; Valladolid, 1805–6). Published in a smaller format (but with 15 per cent more pages), the second edition represents a comparatively minor revision of style and terminology. The most notable omission is the flowery dedication to Manuel de Godoy, who was no longer influential at court. Ortiz also dropped his own appendix (Book IV, chap. 3) on the Bank of Spain.

30. *Investigación e la naturaleza y causes de la riqueza de las naciones* (2 vols.; Barcelona, 1933–34). There were several printings, some in three volumes.

31. *Investigación de la naturaleza y causas de la riqueza de las naciones* (Madrid, 1956).

32. C. J. Bullock, *The Vanderblue Memorial Collection of Smithiana* (Boston, 1939), p. 4.

33. The further mutilation of the text in this section includes the suppression of such phrases as: "As through the greater part of Europe, the church"; "The parson of a parish"; and "The tythe in the greater part of those parishes."

34. Menéndez y Palayo was particularly harsh on eighteenth-century economists who found something of value in the work of Smith and the Physiocrats.Smith's so-called science of wealth, "developed in an incredulous and sensual century, came forth contaminated with a utilitarian and basely practical spirit, as though it aspired to be an independent science and not a branch and end of morality. In the Latin nations, furthermore, it was from the very beginning a powerful aid to revolution and a formidable battering ram against the property of the Church" (*Historia de los heterdoxos españoles*, VI, 22.)

35. Earl J. Hamilton, *American Treasure and the Price Revolution in Spain, 1501–1650* (Cambridge, Mass., 1934), pp. 11–45.

36. Earl J. Hamilton, "The Foundation of the Bank of Spain," *Journal of Political Economy*, LIII (1945), 97–114.
37. *Ensayo económico sobre el sistema de la moneda papel, y sobre el credito publico* (Madrid, 1796).
38. Ortiz practically rewrote Smith's paragraph on this point, cutting out altogether the phrases, "In England and in all Roman Catholic countries" and "The example of the churches of Scotland, of Geneva, and of several other protestant countries."
39. In the first edition Ortiz deleted without comment the paragraph in which Smith discussed the bad effects of assigning tutors to students, instead of allowing them to choose their tutors. The passage was restored in the second edition.
40. *Instituciones del derecho publico general de España* (9 vols.: Madrid, 1800–1803). V. 247.
41. Now Cerbère, France, but no longer a university town.
42. *La Riqueza de las naciones, nuevamente explicada con la doctrina de su mismo investigador* (2 vols.; Cervera, 1817). Dou refers to the 1805–6 edition of Ortiz' work as though it were the first translation of Smith.
43. *Informe*, p. 74.
44. *Conciliación económica y legal de pareceres opuestos en cuanto a laudemios y derechos enfiteéticos* (Cervera, 1829); *Pronta y fácil egucición del proyecto sobre laudemios, fundada principalmente en una autoridad del Dr. Adam Smith* (Cervera, 1831).
45. *La Economia reducida a principios exactos, claros y sencillos* (Madrid, 1797). Four years before the publication of Say's *Tratado*, Johann Herrenschwand's *Principios de economia politica*, translated by the probably pseudonymous Juan Smith (Madrid, 1800), gave Spaniards another smattering of Smithian economics.
46. *Diario de las sesiones de Cortes: Legislatura de 1820* (3 vols.; Madrid, 1870–73), Vols. II (1664) and III (1705, 1737–38, and 1877). The tariff acts of 1820 occasioned Jeremy Bentham's *Observations on the Restrictive and Prohibitory Commercial System: Especially with Reference to the Decree of the Spanish Cortes of July 1820* (London, 1821).
47. *Diario de las sesiones de cortes*, I, 110.
48. *Diccionario de hacienda para el uso de los encargados de la suprema dirección de ella* (5 vols.; London, 1826–27), I, 263; II, 146, 374; V, 97–98, 109. There was another edition of the *Diccionario*: Madrid, 1833–34 and 1840 (*Suplemento*). Earlier, Canga Argüelles published the *Elementos de la ciencia de hacienda* (London, 1826: Madrid, 1833).
49. G. Bernacer, "Alvaro Flórez Estrada, "*Encyclopaedia of the Social Sciences* (New York, 1931), VI, 285.
50. The second edition of the *Curso* was published in Paris (2 vols., 1831), as was the French translation (*Cours éclectique d'économie politique* [1833]). There were Spanish editions, published in Spain in 1833, 1835, 1840, 1848, and 1852. Blanqui considered Flórez' work "one of the most notable treatises which have been published since that of J. B. Say ... methodical like Say, social like Sismondi, algebraic like Ricardo, experimental like Adam Smith, it differs in many respects from all these great masters and shares in its good qualities without falling into all their defects" (Adolphe Blanqui, *Histoire de l'économie politique en Europe* [Paris, 1837], pp. 299–300).

51. Marqués de Valle Santoro, *Elementos de economía política con aplicación particular a España* (Madrid, 1829). There was a second edition (Madrid, 1833). Valle Santoro also wrote a *Memoria sobre la balanza del commercio y examen del estado actual de la riqueza en España* (Madrid, 1830).

52. *Regamento y aranceles reales para el comercio libre de España a Indias de 12 de octubre de 1778* (Madrid, n.d.).

53. See above, no. 6.

54. *Semanario de agricultura, industria y comercio: Reimpresión facsimile publicada por la Junta de Historia y Numismática* (5 vols.; Buenos Aires, 1928–37). The original paper commenced publication on September 1, 1802, and suspended on February 11, 1807.

55. Felix Weinberg, "Estudio preliminar," in *Antecedentes económicos de la Revolución de Mayo* (Buenos Aires, 1956), pp. 18–19.

56. Twelve issues of the *Semanario* (February–July, 1805), about forty pages in all, were devoted to extracting Crumpe's *An Essay on the Best Means of Providing Employment for the People* (London, 1793). This essay, awarded a prize by the Royal Irish Academy, appeared in a second edition (London, 1795) and was translated into French and German.

57. Luis Roque Gondra, *Las ideas económicas de Manuel Belgrano* (Buenos Aires, 1923), pp. 71–74.

58. The *Principios de la ciencia económico-política, traducidos del francés por D. Manuel Belgrano* (Buenos Aires, 1796) is based on and in part taken directly from the writings of Dupont de Nemours and Karl Friedrich of Baden.

59. Thus: "The importation of foreign goods of pure luxury in exchange for money, when money is not a product of the [importing country . . . is a real loss to the state" (Manuel Belgrano, *Escritos económicos* [Buenos Aires, 1954], p. 201). See also L. R. Gondra, "Argentina," in *El pensamiento económico latinoamericano* (Mexico, 1953), pp. 9–19.

60. Domingo Amunátegui Solar, *Los Primeros años del Instituto Nacional* (Santiago, 1889), pp. 160–61.

61. Miguel Cruchaga, *Estudio sobre la organización económica y la hacienda pública de Chile* (Madrid, 1929 ed.), I. 155.

62. "Tratado de economia politica: encargado a mi hijo don Joaquin." Another son, Mariano Egaña, was Chilean minister to Great Britain in the 1820's. While in Europe he collected a library of over four thousand volumes, one of the largest private collections in Latin America. Letters to his father indicate that he bought Smith's *Theory of Moral Sentiments* as well as the works of Malthus, Lauderdale, Hume, and Steuart (*Cartas de don Mariano Egaña a su padre, 1824–29* [Santiago, 1948], pp. 207–8).

63. Miguel Luis Amunátegui, *Camilo Henriquez* (Santiago, 1889), I, 59; II, 238.

64. Another Santiago paper, *La Clave* (November 2 and 12, 1827), published in article on tariffs copied from the Buenos Aires *La Crónica*, in which José Mora quoted the *Wealth of Nations* to show how duties tended to foster monopoly.

65. *El Mercurio chileno*, No. 2 (May, 1828), pp. 53–55; No. 4 (July, 1828), pp. 149–52; No. 5 (August, 1828), pp. 203–7; No. 6 (September, 1828), pp. 245–60.

66. *Sesiones de los cuer pos legislativos de la República de Chile, 1811–1845* (Santiago, 1889, VI, 134–6; VII, 196–98.

67. I owe practically all this material on Chile to the kindness of Robert M. Will, who put at my disposal many of the notes he made in preparation of a doctoral dissertation (Duke University, 1957) on the development of Chilean economic thought.

68. I. A. Leonard and R. S. Smith, "A Proposed Library for the Merchant Guild of Veracruz," *Hispanic American Historical Review*, XXIV (1944), 84–102.

69. *Discurso de un diputado sobre la introduccion de efectos extrangeros* (Mexico City, 1823), reproduced in *El Trimestre económico* (Mexico City, 1945), XII, 283–315. Ortiz, a deputy from Baja California and a signer of the constitution of 1824, also wrote a *Discurso sobre los medios de formentar la población riqueza e ilustración de los Estados-Unidos Mexicanos* (Mexico, ca. 1825).

70. Jesús Silva Herzog (*El Pensamiento económico en México* [Mexico City, 1947], pp, 34–39) discusses Tadeo Ortiz, who wrote a tract on economic liberalism in 1832; but Ortiz de la Torre escaped his attention.

71. José del Valle y Jorge del Valle Matheu, *Obras de José Cecilio del Valle* (Guatemala, 1829), II, 25, 55, 269–70.

72. Archivo General del Gobierno, Guatemala, Al. 3, leg. 1905, exp. 12,609: "Fundación de la primera cátedra de economía política." I owe this note to the kindness of Professor John Tate Lanning.

73. *De la factoria a la colonia: Cuadernos de cultura* (2d ser.,k No. 5 [La Habana, 1936]). See also H. E. Friedlaender, *Historia económica de Cuba* (La Habana, 1944), pp. 139–41.

74. Gerardo Portela, "Cuba," in *El Pensamiento económico latinoamericano*, pp. 125–27.

75. Carl William Hasek, *The Introduction of Adam Smith's Doctrines into Germany* (New York, 1925), pp. 60–94.

76. Antonio Nariño, one of the heroes of Colombian independence, mentioned the "famous Smith" and the *Wealth of Nations* in a speech to the electoral college in June, 1813 (Thomas Blossom, "Antonio Nariño, Precursor of Colombian Independence" [Ph.D. thesis, Duke University, 1956], p. 193).

9.2. R. S. Smith 1967
The First Spanish Edition of
The Wealth of Nations

Writing from Munich in December, 1792, Sir John Macpherson told Edward Gibbon that the Spanish government had "permitted an extract of Adam Smith's *Wealth of Nations* to be published, though the original is condemned by the Inquisition."[1] The "extract" was a 300-page book, published at the Royal Press "by superior order."[2] Labelled a "Compendium," the work was an expurgated translation of Condorcet's synopsis of the *Wealth of Nations*.[3] The translator, Carlos Martínez de Irujo, not only suppressed or garbled parts of Condorcet's work but failed to identify the original as the work of Smith.

It was not the English text but a French translation which the Inquisition banned on March 3, 1792. Macpherson thought it "curious" that the *Wealth of Nations* should be condemned for "the lowness of its style and the looseness of the morals which it inculcates." Actually, the censors objected that the book, "beneath a captious and obscure style, favours tolerance in religion and is conducive to naturalism."[4]

John Rae expressed surprise that within two years after banning the *Wealth of Nations* the Inquisition permitted the publication of a Spanish translation. Unaware that the proscription applied to the French edition, he surmised that a "change must have speedily come over the censorial mind."[5] In fact, the "censorial mind" was plural: the Royal Council of Castile, the Royal Academy of History, and the Inquisition all had a hand in deciding that the expurgated Spanish translation avoided the errors which won the French translation a place in the Index.[6]

Smith's first (and until 1956, *only*) Spanish translator was José Alonso Ortiz, a lawyer and professor of canon law and theology at the University of Valladolid.[7]

342

In 1792 Ortiz came to Madrid with a translation of the eighth (sic) edition of the *Wealth of Nations*. (Undoubtedly, he used the fifth edition; why he thought it was the eighth, I do not know). The translation, Ortiz affirmed, was purged of "various offensive propositions"; and he deleted an entire article (Book V, ch. 1, pt. iii, art. iii) in which "the author favours tolerance in religious matters, so that the translation contains nothing which could lead to error or laxity on religious or moral grounds." In February, 1793, he advised the President of the Supreme Council of the Inquisition that he had submitted his manuscript to the Council of Castile. Government approval of Martínez de Irujo's *Compendio* seemed to strengthen the argument that Spaniards should have an opportunity to read a direct (but censored) translation of "a work of such great value in economic matters." Ortiz appealed to the Inquisition to review his manuscript promptly and approve its publication.[8]

The Inquisition agreed to appoint two censors to compare Ortiz' work with the offensive French translation, but no appointment had been made when he renewed his petition in April. Meantime, the Council of Castile, accepting the advice of censors appointed by the Academy of History, had granted permission to publish the Ortiz translation.[9] To obviate all doubts Ortiz again requested the Inquisition's approval.

On May 2 the Inquisition commissioned Father Manuel de San Vicente and another priest of his choice to examine the French and Spanish translations. (Curiously, it was never suggested that Ortiz's translation be collated with the English text; the French version was repeatedly referred to as the "original".) Father San Vicente and Father Gabriel de Santa Ana reported on May 28 that the Ortiz translation of the work of Scith (sic) was indeed "purged of the causes for which the original work was prohibited." They noted specifically his "correction" of Smith's observation (Book I, ch. 4) that "the avarice and injustice of princes and sovereign states, abusing the confidence of their subjects, have by degrees diminished the real quantity of metal, which had been originally contained in their coins." According to the Spanish translator, "sometimes out of necessity, other times for lack of experience, neglect, or bad advice, and on other occasions for reasons of state not well understood, some princes and sovereign states have commonly decreased gradually the real quantity of metal which the coins used to contain." Similarly, the censors concluded that Ortiz had "revised" the chapter on prices (Book I, ch. 6) "in terms quite different from the original . . . correcting its doctrine so that in the translation there is no proposition against which can be levied the censure accorded at this point to the propositions in the original." Nevertheless, the Inquisition wanted Father Antonio de la Santisima Trinidad, who had censured the French translation, to review Ortiz' work; but this idea was abandoned because of Fray Antonio's absence from Madrid.

None of the deliberations of the Inquisition were communicated to Ortiz, who on July 31 complained bitterly that he was forced to remain in Madrid awaiting a decision which should be easy to reach since only "purely economic points" were involved. The Inquisition had already designated two new censors, Father Tomás Muñoz and Father Luis Garcia Benito, to review the manuscript. They agreed that the translation contained nothing objectionable except the expression "interest, or lawful usury" (*interes, o usura licita*). The word "lawful" was not only unnecessary but "a little dangerous, principally because no distinction is made between moderate and immoderate usury, between what is prohibited and what is permitted by civil law, between what is fixed and what is not regulated by public authority."

The Inquisition then asked Father San Vicente to comment on this point. He replied that Ortiz had correctly differentiated interest, wages, and rent, and that nothing remained to censure. The Inquisition, however, sided with Muñoz and Benito and required Ortiz to substitute "usury or yield on money" for Smith's "interest or the use of money" and to write "interest on money, or usury understood in this manner" for the original "interest of money". The manuscript was returned to Ortiz on October 22, 1793, and the following year his translation was published in Valloadolid.[10]

Although the Academy of History reviewed four manuscript volumes of Ortiz' work, the Inquisition's censors commented on the fact that they had seen only one volume, corresponding to not quite all of Smith's Book I. They supposed that the rest of the manuscript would be submitted for criticism, but there is no evidence that the Inquisition ever passed on the text of Books II–V. This anomaly, if it is anomalous, may be explained by the government's decision to expedite the publication of certain works without the clerical imprimatur. In his memoirs Manuel de Godoy boasts of his "great services" to literature, science, and the arts and mentions economics and political science as objects of his "preferential attentions". He then cites Smith's *Wealth of Nations* and Hume's *Political Discourses* among the many books which were published "at the expense of or with the aid of the government."[13] Ortiz' first edition (but not the second) contains a flowery dedication to the Prince of Peace, who encouraged him because of his (Godoy's) desire to spread "throughout the nation the deepest understanding of civil economy."

The second "corrected and improved" edition, like the first, falls short of representing the author's thoughts faithfully. In the preface Ortiz admits to the suppression of "some details, but very few, either because they are irrelevant to our nation or hardly in keeping with the holy religion we profess." The omissions, he asserted, did not "adulterate" the fundamentals of Smith's work: an impartial comparison with the original would convince the reader that the expurgation was inconsequential. Although he advised the censors of the omission of an entire article in Book I, he failed to mention this fact in the preface; and at no point in the text did he give notice of the deletions, revisions, free translation, and gratuitous additions to the original *Wealth of Nations*. The result, as Beltran observes, was a "mutilated" version of Smith's immortal work.[12]

Surprisingly, more than a century later, when José M Tallada undertook to edit a new Spanish edition of the *Wealth of Nations*, he used the Ortiz translation and made only unimportant orthographical and grammatical revisions.[13] At long last Amando Lázaro Ros gave the Spanish-speaking world a complete and accurate translation (Madrid, 1956), and Gabriel Franco and Manuel Sánchez Sato brought out a second unexpurgated Spanish version (Mexico, 1958). Both follow the Cannan edition, and Franco and Sánchez reproduce Cannan's notes.

Notes

1. *The Miscellaneous Works of Edward Gibbon, Esq.*, II (London, 1814), 479.
2. *Compendio de la obra inglesa intitulada Riqueza de las naciones* (Madrid, 1792 and 1803, and Palma de Mallorca, 1814).
3. First published as "Recherches sur la nature et les causes de la richesse des nations," *Bibliothèque de l'homme public*, III (Paris 1790), 108–216, and IV (1790), 3–115.
4. The handbill posted by the Inquisition in Seville (March 4, 1792) includes *Recherches sur la nature et les causes de la richesse des nations* (specifically, the London edition of 1788) in a long list of "Prohibited" works but not in the shorter list of titles "Prohibited even for those who have permission," i.e., to read prohibited texts. A copy of this handbill is found in the Servicio Histórico Militar, Madrid, *Colección documental del Fraile*, tomo 863, fol. 152.
5. *Life of Adam Smith* (London, 1895), pp. 360–361.
6. Where it remained, at least until 1842 (*Indice general de los libros prohibidos* [Madrid, 1844], p. 318).
7. Alonso Ortiz interest in English literature had already led him to translate poems of Ossian (*Obras de Ossian, poeta del siglo tercero en las montañas de Escocia*; Valladolid, 1788) and Alban Butler's *Lives of the Saints* (*Vida de los padres, mártires y otros principales santos:* 13 vols., Valladolid, 1789–91). Narciso Alonso Cortés identifies him as a "lawyer, from Granada" (*Diario Pinciano* [facsimile edition, Valladolid, 1933], p. v). That Alonso Ortiz was more interested in economics than in theology is suggested not only by his two editions of *Wealth of Nations* but by the intervening publication of a substantial treatise on money and credit. *Essayo económico sobre el sistema de la monedapapel y sobre el crédito público* (Madrid, 1796).

8. Unless otherwise noted, the source for the remainder of this paper is the manuscript "Expediente de calificaión de la obra de Adam Smith initulada Investigación de la naturaleza y causas de las riquezas de las naciones traducidas en castellano y expurgado por el Lic. *do* d.*n* José Alonso Ortiz" (Archivo Histórico Nacional, Madrid, *Inquisición*, egajo 4484, no. 13). I have to thank the Servicio Nacional de Microfilm for a filmcopy of this document.

9. Between 1746, when the Council of Castile first called on the Academy of History to review manuscripts submitted for publication, and 1792, the Acaemy examined 822 titles and rejected more than one-fourth (*Memorias de la Real Academia de la Historia*, I [Madrid, 1796], xcviii–c). There were three separate decisions on Ortiz' manuscript, but only two censors are named, Father José Banqueri and Don Casimiro Ortega (*Boletin de la Real Academia de la Historia*, XXXV [Madrid, 1899], 412–413).

10. *Investigación de la naturaleza y causas de la riqueza de las naciones, escrita en inglés por el Dr. Adam Smith, y traducida al castellano por o el Lic. D. Josef Alonso Ortiz, con varias notas y ilustraciones relativas a España* (4 vols., Valladolid, 1794). There was a second "corrected and improved" edition: 4 vols., Valladolid, 1805–1806.

11. *Principe de la Paz, Memorias*, I (*Biblioteca de autores españoles*, tomo 88; Madrid, 1956, pp. 197–297).

12. Lúcas Beltrán, *Historia de las doctrinas económicas* (Barcelona, 1961), p. 97. I have pinpointed some of Ortiz' mutilations in "The Wealth of Nations in Spain and Hispanic America." *Journal of Political Economy,* LXV (1957), 102–125.

13. *Investigación de la naturaleza y causas de la riqueza de las naciones* (3 vols., Barcelona, 1933–34, 1947).

9.3. Luis Perdices de Blas, 1993.
The Wealth of Nations and Spanish Economists (draft)

The Wealth of Nations is a work that one is amazed by. In the sharpness of its analysis and in its range it surpasses any other book on economics, nevertheless its pre-eminence is worrying. What have we been doing for the last 200 years? Certainly our analysis has become more sophisticated, but we do not show a more profound analytical understanding of the economic system and, in some aspects, our approach is not as good as Adam Smith's. And when we come to the insight into public policy, we find unknown propositions that Adam Smith proved so forcibly that they are almost self-evident. I do not really know why this is the case, but perhaps part of the answer lies in the fact that we do not read *The Wealth of Nations*.

R. S. Coase

R. S. Coase's opinion on Adam Smith's famous work brings together that of various economists of the past and the present. There are many who began their economic studies by reading *The Wealth of Nations* and found it fascinating, from D. Ricardo, T. R. Malthus, and J. B. Say to A. Marshall, including among others J. S. Mill and K. Marx. Spanish economists in the last two hundred years have appreciated the importance of A. Smith and some read *The Wealth of Nations*, but the question I raise in this work is whether Spaniards learnt economics by reading this work, and if so, whether they continued and developed Smith's thought either to perfect it or criticize it, as their foreign contemporaries did.

R. S. Smith in his classic 1957 article and once again in another, in 1968, was the first to give a broad list of the possible writers influenced by Smith's thought in Spain and Latin America, though he did not go deeply enough into the subject. In the last thirty-three years various studies have appeared on economic schools of thought in Spain and articles on the most outstanding economists, along with editions of their main works, which has meant that the influence of Smith in this country has been limited. In this sense and as will be seen later, Barrenechea argues that it is a mistake to consider Foronda as a follower of Smith. Two recent works, as yet unpublished, by Juan Hernández Andreu and Pedro Schwartz conclude that the economists most influenced by Smith are Gaspar Melchor de Jovellanos, Vicente Alcalá Galiano, and José Alonso de Ortiz. Nevertheless, as is mentioned in these two works and in the present one, the three above-mentioned economists showed the influence of other authors and even at times contradicted the Scotsman's conclusions. The argument I am defending maintains that Spanish economists did not delve deeply into Smith's work, and hence the aim of this work is to show how the Scotsman has not been the most widely read or translated economist in Spain. Not only that, they did not learn all their arguments in favour of economic freedom from Smith. They preferred to pick up the Smith's ideas from the reading of other authors such as Say or Bastiat. Many read different authors, among them Smith, and synthesized and modified the general principles when applying them to Spain. Thus it can be claimed that eclecticism is one of the characteristics of the writings of many of our economists.

First of all, I shall give a list of the authors who we know read or quoted *The Wealth of Nations* in their works. In the next four sections I will attempt to lay out the four reasons on which I base my contention that Smith's influence in Spain was not significant: in the second section I will deal with the Spanish translations of *The Wealth*, in the third I will show how Spaniards, and especially the enlightened ones, did not learn all their pro-freedom and other ideas from Smith. In the fourth I shall present an analysis of the eclecticism of Spanish economists and the fifth will show the preference of nineteenth-century liberal politicians for Bastiat's work.

1. Smith and Spanish Economists

The most important Spaniards who read or quoted *The Wealth of Nations* in their works, according to the studies dealing with the topic, are the following:[1]

Revdo Padre Juan Geddes, who translated some chapters of *The Wealth of Nations* around 1777 and suggested to Campomanes translating the whole of the work.

Agustín de la Cana and *Manuel Sixto Espinosa*, in a report presented to the

Sociedad Matritense on 13 December 1793, on three occasions quoted paragraphs from *The Wealth of Nations* directly translated from English.[2]

Carlos Martínez de Irujo (1763–1824), an official in the first State Secretariat and later Minister Plenipotentiary to the United States, translated the synthesis of *The Wealth of Nations* made by Condorcet because the French economist had eliminated the "unsuitable implications", though recording the basic principles of the Scotsman as far as the subject of economic growth was concerned. The translation has a preliminary study in which a brief synthesis of Smith's thought was given which, along with some translations direct from the English, leads one to the conclusion that Martínez de Irujo was highly familiar with the work (see Lluch and Argemí, 1987: 148–53).

José Alonso de Ortiz (1755–1815) published the first translation of *The Wealth of Nations* in Valladolid (1794). In the prologue he mentioned that Spaniards, unlike Smith, "did not try to reduce the subject matter to a scientific method, a general system". One of Ortiz's own works is the *Ensayo Económico sobre el sistema de la moneda-papel y sobre el crédito público* (Madrid, 1796), in which he applied Smith's monetary theory to the defence of a system of Royal Promissory Notes (*vales reales*) and the National Debt carried out in the reign of Carlos III and Carlos IV. In view of the article by Schwartz and Fernández Marugán (1978), I consider this to be the book of a Spanish economist where the influence of Smith is most marked.

Ramón Lázaro de Dou (1742–1832) published the *Riqueza de las naciones nuevamente explicada* (Cervera, 1817).

Melchor Gaspar de Jovellanos (1744–1811) read *The Wealth* at least three times as we know from his diaries and made a thirteen-page "Abstract of Mr Smith's work" and a translation of several parts of the same work (R. S. Smith, 1957: 1220–1).

Valentín de Foronda (1751–1821) is one of the economists who was traditionally said to have been influenced by Adam Smith, though, as we shall see later, Barrenechea had a different view.

Ramón Campos (*c.*1760–*c.*1809), a Physics teacher, considered Smith the Newton of economics and followed the pattern of *The Wealth of Nations* in some of his works. Among them special mention should be made of *La Economía reducida a principios exactos, claros y sencillos* (Madrid 1797) and *De la desigualdad personal en la sociedad civil* (Barcelona, 1799, 1838) (see Elorza, 1970: ch. 7; Schwartz, 1990).

Vicente Alcalá Galiano (1758–1810) in the fourth volume of the *Actas y Memorias de la Real Sociedad Económica de los Amigos del País de la Provincia de Segovia* published a work entitled "Sobre la necesidad y justicia de los tributos, fondos de donde deben sacarse y medios de recaudarlos" (On the need for and justice of taxes, from which funds they should be obtained and means of collecting them; written in 1788 and published five years later), in which he repeatedly showed his debt to A. Smith. Particularly from the taxation point of view he was very pro-Smith when he said: "In a nutshell, the simplicity of taxes, the uniformity of their rate and levying, the clarity and publicity of the laws which establish them, the freedom of domestic trade and, what is a consequence of this, the lower number of dependants, are the real means in which they are fair, in which they are not odious, and in which the Government is happily obeyed by its subjects" (Alcalá Galiano, 1793: 52–6). This led Elorza (1970: 178) to conclude that this work "constitutes the best summary, both of Alcalá Galiano's thoughts on finance and the presence of Adam Smith in our intellectual milieu at the end of the eighteenth century".

Martín Fernández de Navarrete (1765–1844) is another author who read Smith, as can be seen if one looks at his work entitled *Discurso sobre los progresos que puede adquirir la economía política con la aplicación de las ciencias exactas y naturales, y con las observaciones de las Sociedades Patrióticas, pronunciado en la Real Sociedad Matritense en Junta particular de 29 de enero de este año* (Madrid, 1791).

Alvaro Flórez de Estrada (1766–1853), in his *Curso de Economía Política*, recorded the ideas of Smith, Ricardo, and Say, though the organization of the book was inspired by James Mill and Say.

José Canga Argüelles (1770–1843) is another economist who several times quoted Smith in his work (R. S. Smith, 1957: 1243–4).

Fray Eudaldo Jaumeandreu (1774–1840), Professor of Economics in Barcelona at the beginning of the last century, in his *Rudimientos de Economía política* (1816) set forth the doctrines of Smith and Say, and tried to adapt Smith's thought to Spain as Say had done for France. In another work, *Curso elemental de Economía política con aplicación a la legislación económica de España* (1836), he was seen as a liberal except in foreign trade.

El Marqués de Valle Santoro (?–1840) also tried to give a synthesis of Smith and Say's work in his *Elementos de Economía Política*. In this manual he said that in Smith's case "no one could take away from him the glory of having been the founder of political economy".

Manuel Colmeiro (1818–94) in his *Principios de Economía Política* (Madrid, 1870) summarized Smith's doctrines and those of other authors of the classical school, among whom Ricardo is the most noteworthy (Beltrán, 1976: 106).

R. S. Smith (1957: 1246–53) quoted *other possible authors influenced by Smith in Latin America*, though in fact the influence is rather slight and superficial. These authors are: in Argentina, Juan Hipólito Vieytes and Manuel Belgrano (he was familiar with Smith's work though influenced by other authors); in Chile,

Manuel de Salas, Juan Egaña, and Camilo Henríquez recommended reading Smith, but their writings do not show Smith's imprint; also in Chile, José Joaquín Mora published the *Mercurio Chileno* in which Smith was quoted, but Say more so; in Mexico, Manuel Ortíz de la Torre; in Guatemala, José Cecilio del Valle and Francisco García Peláez; in Cuba, Francisco de Arango y Parreño and Justo Vélez. Other economists who have quoted Smith extensively in their work are Gonzalo de Luna, Ramón Canêdo, Juan López Pekalver and Casìmiro Orense (Lluch and Almenar 1992: 104–5).

If these are the authors regarded as having been most influenced by Smith, it has also been emphasized that other important authors showed no sign of Smith's influence, as was the case with Bernardo Joaquín Danvila y Villarrasa and Lozano Normante y Carcavilla. The importance of these two economists, as we shall see later, lies in the fact that they were the first to give economics classes in Spain, the former in Madrid and the latter in Zaragoza. The two were influenced by Cantillon's *Essai sur la nature du commerce en général*.

Below I will go on to set out the four arguments on which I base my opinion that Smith's influence in Spain was slight.

2. Spanish Translations of *The Wealth Of Nations*

In the eighteenth century works were translated dealing with agriculture and, more specifically, free trade in cereals in the years before and after the royal decree of 1765. Among other economists there were translations of Herbert (1755, 1765, and 1795), Nickolls (1755 and 1771), Mirabeau (1764), Galiani (1775), Necker (1783), and Genovesi (1785) (Reeder, 1973). In the nineteenth century, the most often translated works were those of Say, between the beginning of the century and 1830 (the *Tratado de economía política* of 1803 had eight editions between 1804 and 1838; the *Catecismo de economía política* six editions between 1816 and 1833; and other works were also translated from the French), and those of Bastiat, between 1840 and 1860 (between 1846 and 1859 six Spanish editions were published of the *Sofismas económicos*; between 1856 and 1870 three editions of the *Armonias Economicas*, and in 1880 two more editions were published; other works by the same author were published; see Cabrillo, 1978: 72ff.). As we shall see later, Say's *Treatise* was translated because it was one of the key books for disseminating political economy in Spain, and Bastiat because he was an author who explained clearly, albeit superficially, the arguments in favour of free trade.

From the eighteenth century to the present day, few translations have been made of *The Wealth of Nations* and only three editions of *The Theory of Moral*

Sentiments.[3] In view of the publication dates of the translations of *The Wealth of Nations*, we can state that this work was more widely read in Spain before Say's *Treatise* was published. That is to say it was mainly the last generation of Enlightened scholars who read Smith, rather than nineteenth-century liberals. The editions of *The Wealth of Nations* in Spain are the following:

1792. Carlos Martínez de Irujo made a partial translation of the summary that Condorcet had produced (Paris, 1790–92) under the title *Compendio de la obra inglesa intitulada Riqueza de las Naciones.* There were two more editions, one published in Madrid (1803) and the other in Palma (1814) (Reeder, 1973: 71). This translation was made despite the Inquisition's condemnation in 1791 of the 1788 French edition of *The Wealth.* In the same year as it was published, the *Gaceta de Madrid* of 4 September 1792 published a glowing review which stated, "[This work] is extremely useful for anyone in public life, and especially for spreading in private companies true principles which must guide their operations towards the general benefit of the Monarchy".[4]

1794. La Oficina de la Viuda e Hijos de Santander published that year in Valladolid the first translation from the original English (of the eighth edition), undertaken by José Alonso Ortíz.[5] The work was modified in several ways for it to pass both religious and civil censorship, in subjects related to education, tithes, usury, unfavourable references to Spain and the Catholic religion. This translation was also given a highly favourable review by the *Gaceta de Madrid* of 12 September 1794. Emphasis is given, as in the prologue to the translation, to the fact that the translated work deals with matters of political economy as if they were an "exact science, in which the principles and general rules are laid down which must guide the efforts of industry and commerce, so that private interests conspire by their very tendency to the public progress of society; an aspect which has not normally been considered by our writers on economics, since although several of them have made an effort to write accurately and successfully on some of these topics, they have done so in isolated writings and on purely practical points, limited to certain circumstances, periods, and places, depending on when they were writing, but without producing a scientific system of this popularized idea of Political Economy".[6] The second edition of this translation "much corrected and improved" seems also to have been done by Ortíz and was published in 1805–6 (Valladolid, Oficina de la Viuda e Hijos de Santander, 4 vols.).

1933–4. During the Second Republic the first two volumes of the José M. Tallada edition were published in Barcelona. That is, four of the five books which make up *The Wealth of Nations* appeared. The editor described his work as a "reproduction" of the Ortíz translation, but revised and adapted to modern Spanish. At the end of the Civil War the Bosch publishing house brought out three reprints of this edition in three volumes (the last one reproduces the fifth book of *The Wealth*): the first in 1947–9, the second in 1954, and the third in 1955–6. In 1983, Ediciones Orbis S.A. (Barcelona) brought out a new edition of this version. Tallada in the prologue made clear Smith's theoretical value but placed special emphasis on showing how despite the crisis of the 1930s and interventionist rumblings, "it is still about the essential ideas of Adam Smith that the bloodiest battles are waged nowadays". The writer of the prologue, even though admitting changes in the declaration of the liberal proposal, pointed out that this doctrine had not failed and should not be stored away in "museums". He criticized those who maintain that liberalism has failed, those who want greater intervention, and particularly those who defend the soviet experience; "And in view of such a failure [of liberalism], wishing to give a brisk leap in the slow evolution of human societies, they wish to convert the world into a guinea pig to experiment on imperfectly conceived institutions for which human society is not ready" (A. Smith, 1983: prologue, 29).

1956. Amando Lázaro Ros made the first reliable and complete translation (Madrid, Aguilar). He translated from the Cannan edition, but removed the latter's notes. It was reprinted in 1961. The revision of the translation and the prologue is by Germán Bernacer Torno. This economist emphasized Smith's importance but, unlike Tallada, did not show himself in favour of economic liberalism. He pointed out that "it was not even put into practice in Great Britain, and even less in continental Europe, because it was found that [Smith's doctrine] was a beautiful thought but not a realistic idea" (A. Smith, 1961: preface, p. x).

1958. The Fondo de Cultura Económica published the Gabriel Franco version in Mexico, along with a preliminary study by the same author. On this occasion the Cannan edition was also translated, but with the latter's notes. This edition was reprinted in 1979, 1981, 1982, 1984, and 1987.

1988. Oikos-Taus published in Barcelona in two volumes the translation by J. C. Collado Curiel and A. Mira-Perceval Pastor. This latter edition of Smith's work in Spain was based on that of R. H. Campbell and A. S. Skinner, which appeared to commemorate the bicentenary of the publication of *The Wealth of Nations.*[7]

To sum up, if we include Martínez de Irujo's translation and the different reprints of the same edition, between 1792 and 1988 Smith's work was published nineteen times. But, until 1956 there was no complete reliable translation of *The Wealth of Nations* in Spain. Prior to 1806 there were only two editions of *The Wealth* in Spanish and the synthesis published in 1792. From 1806 to 1933 no edition was published of Smith's masterpiece. This was due to the fact that Say and Bastiat were the authors most widely translated and read by nineteenth-century Spaniards: it appears that Smith was more widely read by the men of the Enlightenment than by the liberals of the nineteenth century.

3. Not All New Ideas on Freedom Were Learnt from Smith

We can establish approximately the birth of political economy between the year of the publication of Hume's *Essays* (1752) and that of the publication of Smith's *The Wealth of Nations* (1776). They were the years when it was discovered that in the economic world there exists a regularity and in which the works of Galiani, Steuart, Cantillon, Quesnay, Mirabeau, and Turgot, among others, were published. In Spain around this time, we had no economists of the stature of those mentioned above, but study of the new science was encouraged. It even became fashionable among the enlightened minority. Jovellanos, in the *Elogio de Carlos III*, which was more of a hymn of praise to political economy, argued that Spain owed to the reign of that monarch the introduction of the "spirit of enlightenment" and, especially, "the glory of converting its vassals completely to the study of the economy", the most important science among the "useful" ones. He added that "Spain reads its most famous writers, examines their principles, analyses their works; there is talk, argument, writings, and the nation begins to have economists" (Jovellanos, 1952–6: vol. 1, 511ff). A result of this publicity was the setting-up of various chairs of political economy in some non-university institutions such as those of Normante in Zaragoza.

This vogue for political economy gave rise to books on theoretical economy by European authors and books on applied economy by Spanish authors being read in Spain before the publication of Smith's work. Let us consider the eighteenth-century economists, who were the ones who most read Smith directly. Before the reading of the Scotsman's book advances had been made in many areas such as free domestic trade, free trade with the colonies, the importance of the institutional framework for economic growth, and the debate on tax reform. These ideas were taken from other Spanish economists and from European economists such as Child, Davenant, Mirabeau and Herbert, among others, most of them translated, as we have seen previously.

Freedom of Domestic Trade

In another work on the arguments proposed in favour of the freedom of domestic trade during the reign of Carlos III, I have shown that the debate on this topic in Spain is autonomous and parallel to the one taking place in other European countries (Perdices de Blas, 1988). This argument, which was of interest not only to economists but also to the general public and government, had as its leading figures, among others in Europe, Quesnay, Turgot,

Smith, Galiani, and Herbert. The debate in Spain did not begin in the eighteenth century. In the sixteenth and seventeenth centuries as in the eighteenth, a distinction could be drawn in Spain, as E. P. Thompson (1979) did for eighteenth-century England, between the defenders of "a moral economy of the poor" and a *"laissez-faire* model". Bearing in mind various nuances, these two schools of thought could be synthesized with the following words: the former considered the consumer and the latter the producer. The second school considered that if the producer was unhindered, (one hindrance were fixed prices), production would be encouraged and would give rise to an abundance of goods, benefiting the consumer.

Defenders of the former were Pedro de Valencia and Gregorio de Mayáns i Siscar, and defenders of the latter were Luis de Molina, Campomanes, Olavide, Jovellanos, Cabarrús, and Foronda. In Spain as the eighteenth century progressed, various authors pleaded for greater freedom of trade. Before 1765, particularly noteworthy were Uztáriz, Zabala y Auñón, Ward, Olavide, and particularly Campomanes in his famous *Respuesta fiscal sobre abolir la tasa y establecer el comercio de granos* (1764) and Cray Winkel. Ward (1982: 173) said that "freedom is the soul of trade and any type of monopoly its greatest opponent". Campomanes raised the following questions:

1. Whether the cereal tax is a means of "assuring that we have an abundance of cereals in times of shortage" and at a "reasonable" price; and if this is compatible with farmworkers' subsistence and the encouragement of agriculture.
2. Whether the cereal trade was the best system for restraining prices in times of shortage, and "whether there are insuperable disadvantages to this providence: or whether those that so far have been considered as such stem from the imposition of the tax, or are a consequence of it".
3. Whether it would be worthwhile to promote exports in times of plenty to prevent the ruin of the farmworker, who could have no other outlet for his surpluses, and in times of high prices to allow imports.

Campomanes' replies to these questions were that the fixed price is "insufficient" for the aim established, that the only way to promote abundance in the kingdom is by a free trade in cereals (and of all products in general), and that merchants in years of plenty should be allowed to "hoard" or to "remove" surpluses from the kingdom and in times of high prices to "sell at a higher price" and to "bring in" from outside whatever was "physically" in short supply.

Olavide maintained that "modern enlightenment" was in favour of freedom, and supported Campomanes' arguments:

- Freedom of trade is the best supply policy. "What legislation can claim that any product is cheap in a year when the crop was poor? The Law which tries by force to reduce the price to make it cheap for a day makes it expensive for a century". He also said that "self-interest, the sole motive for human operations, will make sure that everyone will continue to keep their shops supplied with what the public needs as long as they can make a profit from their labours and the freedom for all to take part will make sure that such a profit will never be excessive, with an equilibrium occurring between the freedom to sell as they wish and other sellers copying them".[8]

- Freedom of trade encourages agriculture. If freedom of trade benefits the consumer who obtains goods in abundance and cheaply, it also benefits the producer who gets a good price for his goods, which motivates the farmworker and encourages agriculture (Perdices de Blas, 1988: 56ff).

- Olavide proposed freedom of domestic trade for individuals to import grains in years of scarcity and to export in years of plenty. In this sense both Olavide and Campomanes are more radical than Jovellanos, as we shall see in section four.

Olavide, like other enlightened writers such as Campomanes, in the formulation and elaboration of their arguments, took their ideas from the Spanish economists quoted above, and they read foreign economists, mainly the French agricultural economists such as Mirabeau in *L'Ami des hommes* or the *Disertación sobre el cultivo de trigo*. In this book Mirabeau (1764: pp. lxiii–lxiv) concluded: "the ease and freedom with which [grain] gets on to the market gains the high price; this encourages the workforce and brings abundance, favours the population, and achieves the welfare of the inhabitants". He did not accept the physiocrats' arguments since in his writings none of their analytical tools appears. We can say without exaggeration that Mirabeau was the most influential author on eighteenth-century economists in Spain. *L'Ami des hommes* is his main book. Another author read by Olavide and Campomanes was Herbert and his *Ensayo sobre la política general del grano*, which, like Mirabeau's book *L'Ami*, was in both their libraries. Olavide, like Herbert, and therefore Campomanes, was in favour of free trade in grain because it encouraged agriculture by maintaining firm prices and achieved a plentiful supply of grains, as well as permitting exports when there was an abundance in the country and imports when it was expensive. Consequently, the approach of Spanish agricultural economists such as Campomanes and Olavide was similar to that of the French such as Herbert.

Freedom of Trade with the Colonies

Uztáriz, in his *Theorica*, put forward measures which would tend to establish freedom of trade with the colonies. Thus, he was against trade monopolies and showed the advantages of freedom when he analysed Dutch trade (Uztáriz, 1968). Campomanes in his *Reflexiones sobre el comercio español a Indias* (written in 1762 and unpublished until 1988) developed this approach more profoundly, and for this purpose used the work of the English mercantilists, particularly that of those who had come to be known as "liberal mercantilists". The aim of the *Reflexiones*, based upon several authors ranging from Child and Davenant to Law, Mirabeau, and Herbert, and including Uztáriz and Ulloa, is to spread news about the colonies and European trade and to draw up a new order for relationships between Spain and her colonies. A return to the free trade which existed before 1543 and which led to its "remarkable" growth was proposed. Firstly from the Seville monopoly and later transferred to Cadiz, as well as "the heavy duties imposed", came the decline in economic relations between Spain and her colonies. Chapters 15–17 dealt with the prosperity of the English colonies (this based on Child's work), and other European countries' trade. The English have taken advantage of their colonies owing to the settling of population there and to "giving navigation rights to the colonies to the whole nation". He criticized monopoly and trade restrictions, but never mentioned the colonies' independence (Rodríguez de Campomanes, 1988).

Other authors who had not read Smith agreed with this defence of freedom of trade with the colonies. This was so with Arriquíbar and Gándara. The latter, in his *Apuntes sobre el bien y el mal de España*, tried to show in detail the two main causes of Spanish economic backwardness, which he called *puertas abiertas, puertas cerradas* (open doors, closed doors). That is, doors open to the export of raw materials and the imports of manufactured goods and doors closed to trade with the colonies. The wealth of nations, according to Campomanes, Arriquíbar, and Gándara, is based on not alienating industry to foreigners. In other words, the state should have tried to obtain a favourable trade balance and for that purpose it ought to have promoted domestic industry and Spanish-managed trade. Nevertheless, without reading Smith, they defended free domestic trade, arguing for trade between Spain and her colonies and for the export of goods under certain conditions. To all this must be added their criticisms of monopolies, the abandoning of the idea of the importance to a nation of accumulating gold and silver (which was already present in many *arbitristas*—Spanish seventeenth-century economists), and their highlighting the drawbacks of certain types of intervention (Perdices de Blas, 1996).

The Institutional Framework and Economic Growth

The importance of the institutional framework for economic growth was not necessarily something that Spanish economists derived from Smith, as Barrenechea has shown in Foronda's case.

Foronda analysed society from a philosophical viewpoint based on a natural order, essentially physiocratic ideas. The second letter in his *Cartas sobre los asuntos más exquisitos de la Economía-Política y sobre las leyes criminales* (1789–94) showed that rights to property, freedom, and security are the three pillars on which economic and political life must rest in any civilized society and are the necessary conditions for economic growth. Almost certainly Foronda took these ideas from the physiocrat Mercier de la Rivière, who, in his *L'ordre naturel et essentiel des societés politiques*, held that "Property, Security, Freedom: this is the complete social order". Barrenechea (1985: 182) pointed out that this physiocratic influence "helps us to understand the link existing in Foronda between morality and economics, the need for a value system which would give coherence to the social world, the importance of upbringing, the idea that free competition is a natural institution, his enlightened optimism with regard to progress, as well as his criticisms of the institutions and economic thought of the *ancien regime*". Though Foronda claimed to be interested in the philosophical aspects of physiocracy, he did not set out its analytical framework or a large number of its economic policy proposals. Barrenechea (1985: 183) concluded that "The physiocratic background to Foronda's work also broadly determines the range of influences to which it laid itself open. But it is a wide range that covers anti-Aristotelian ideas stemming from Descartes, the liberal political movement which, flying in the face of its own intentions, was born with Hobbes and was developed by Locke, the philosophy of Condillac, the utilitarianism of Helvetius, etc. All of this made his writings less coherent. However, in our opinion, neither Rousseau nor Adam Smith, nor the revolutionary spirit of the former British colonies in America explain, as some authors have pointed out, Foronda's economic thought."

In another work on Foronda, Barrenechea (1984: 196) delved more deeply into this issue and came to the following conclusion:

Foronda's economic writings are an attack on all the institutions and social practices which prevent the best use of resources . . . Given this starting-point, it is therefore not strange that Foronda feels more attracted to a group of writers such as the physiocrats, which places special emphasis on the optimum use of resources and on reforming the institutional structures which restrain development, which fathered classical British economics and *The Wealth of Nations*. Although Foronda has been seen as a follower of

Smith, this idea seems a mistaken one to us. He only quoted him twice throughout the first two editions of *Political Economy* and it can be said that that was for fairly unimportant reasons; and, as far as the 1821 edition is concerned, although he was more frequently mentioned, it was never as a source of new ideas, but to support his primitive arguments regarding craft unions, Customs, self-interest freedom of contracting, etc. Though Foronda showed great respect for Smith, his harsh judgement on the Scotsman must not be overlooked.

In fact, Foronda expressed a harsh judgement on Smith when the latter defended navigation laws: "this same oracle of political economy is a writer of panegyrics of the greatest affront that has ever been made to global free trade in the country's navigation law".[9]

The Debate on Tax Reform

On issues relating to public finance advances had been made in Spain prior to receiving the influence of the classical English economists. Juan Hernández Andreu (1990) maintains that during the eighteenth century a financial and tax doctrine arose which sprang basically from the "original and modern tax experience of the Single Tax of the Marqués de Ensenada". He adds that indigenous economic thought on these questions was characterized by focusing attention on "empirical knowledge, fiscal experience, and by a practical and realistic view in dealing with financial topics".

The first to propose a single tax were Zabala, the Marqués de Santa Cruz, and the Marqués de la Ensenada. The latter's plan was to introduce a direct tax which would attempt to unify the tax system and did not correspond to theoretical concepts, but had been inspired in the Catalan poll tax. Campomanes and Floridablanca criticized this plan, and its followers understood the concept of a single tax in the sense of an administrative simplification. Thus, when Vicente Alcalá Galiano criticized the single tax he was registering Floridablanca's criticisms. From the starting-point of the conclusions of this debate, which took place during the eighteenth century in Spain, he supported his criticism by quoting the maxims on taxation of *The Wealth of Nations* (Hernández Andreu, 1978: 160–1; 1990). That is, before Alcalá Galiano read Smith the ground was already prepared. Consequently, Hernández Andreu concludes that "the financial thought prevalent among Spanish fiscalists of the period was innovatory and modern in nature, reacting to the tax and institutional maxims typical of liberal economics, and also to the Spanish institution of the Single Tax, which would not be put into practice in a stable form until the Mon-Santillan reform of 1845, when a century had gone by between the Single Tax being conceived and direct taxes being consolidated in Spain" (Hernández Andreu, 1990).

The conclusion we can reach from this section is that Spanish economists had advanced in their knowledge of economics before reading *The Wealth of Nations*. The ideas of free domestic trade and free trade with the colonies, the importance of the institutional framework, and tax reform preceded Smith. Jovellanos, to mention one of the most notable Spanish economists, learnt his ideas on freedom of trade in the social gatherings in Seville of his beloved and admired teacher Pablo de Olavide between 1767 and 1776. Also, he had learnt from Campomanes and some *arbitristas* the arguments in favour of freedom of trade with the colonies and criticisms of the identification of precious metals with wealth. In Olavide's social gatherings and in others, as well as in various Spanish and foreign works, Jovellanos learnt what were the obstacles to economic growth in agriculture. Spaniards had already highlighted the obstacles related to legislation (legal framework, tax, and structure of property for instance), those stemming from wrong opinions relating to types and system of cultivation, among others, and those springing from nature.[10] In Spanish and foreign economists they had read about the importance of economic institutions for economic growth, and the elimination of obstacles to self-interest. Later on, Jovellanos' readings of English writers, to which Polt (1976) refers, did not always give him new theories and doctrines.

4. The Eclecticism of Spanish Economists

As a result of Enlightenment publicity in favour of political economy the teaching of this subject began towards the end of the eighteenth century. From 1779 B. J. Danvila gave courses on political economy in the Seminario de Nobles de Madrid. This teacher did not read Smith but did read Cantillon, as was shown in his *Lecciones de Economía Civil o de el Comercio*, which were a plagiarism of the famous *Essai sur la Nature du commerce en général* by Cantillon (Estapé, 1971). 24 October 1784, was the date of the inauguration of the Chair of Civil Economics and Trade promoted by the Sociedad Económica of Zaragoza. In charge of it was the lawyer of the Royal Council and doctor in jurisprudence from the University of Zaragoza, Lorenzo Normante y Carcavilla. His teachings were given by means of a choice of the works of Spanish, French, Italian, and English economists. Nevertheless, the royal order creating the chair recommended the use of the *Lecciones de Economía Civil o de el Comercio* by Bernardo Danvila y Villarrasa. Normante himself, who was a popularizer rather than an economic theorist, published three books, among which the outstanding one was the *Espíritu del Señor Melon en su ensayo político sobre el comercio* (Zaragoza, 1796). As the title itself indicates, the professor was influenced by the work of the French economist Jean François Melon, who was another economist who plagiarized Cantillon's essay. In his *Proposiciones de Economía Civil y Comercio* (Zaragoza, 1785), Normante, basing his ideas on the above-mentioned authors and on Uztáriz, Ulloa, Ward, Campomanes, and Genovesi among others, followed the scheme of mercantilist writings; exhibiting distrust of freedom of foreign trade and presenting the typical populationist–agricultural–trade–currency–tax analysis of those writers.

In the Chair of Zaragoza between 1790 and 1800 the books in use were those by Genovesi and Danvila, and those given to students were by Uztáriz, Jovellanos, Arríquibar, and Argumosa among others. In 1804 one of the texts used was Condorcet's extract from *The Wealth*, but Fornies (1976: 118) concluded that "Economic science was studied without a defined trend; instead the axioms of the mercantilist, physiocrat, and free exchange schools were put forward, through Spanish works or translations, thus keeping in fashion the useful works of Bernard Ward, or Nicolás de Arríquibar, for example, while deliberating the excellences of A. Smith". Finally, we know that in 1807 the text in use was Say's *Treatise*.

From these early economics teachings we can draw conclusions which are subsequently valid for those which would be developed during the nineteenth century: (1) the economics taught was an eclectic economics which frequently did not depart from the old mercantilist scheme; (2) general principles were modified when applied to Spain, which meant that their proposals were not very different from those of Spanish liberal mercantilists; (3) the reading of Smith took place not directly but through Say's work.

The second conclusion is very important, since the enlightened Spaniards who most read Smith's work were also the first who were going to modify the general principles when they applied them to Spain. This was the case with the following economists:

Martínez de Irujo in the only note he wrote, introducing the translation of *El Compendio de la obra intitulada La Riqueza de las Naciones*, modified one of the basic points of Smith's system. Smith, in his famous paragraph where he dealt with the invisible hand, said that each individual "only seeks his own profit, and in this, as in other cases, he is guided by an invisible hand promoting an aim which was not part of his purpose". Lluch and Argemí (1987: 149) stated correctly that the translator changed *the invisible hand* into *the hand of the government*. Referring to Smith's paragraph, Martínez de Irujo commented: "This comment may be accurate in an enlightened country where private individuals are generally aware of the most advantageous way in which they can use their money; but there are others where capitalists need to be led by the hand by the government, so to speak, to put their funds to use, and to use them gainfully. The profit motive is a powerful stimulant, but it requires a certain knowledge to guide it. This is, in my opinion, the aim of the temporary rewards with which England favours certain sectors, which cease when the government sees that individuals must do in their own interest what they undertook through the stimulus of reward."

Ortíz is another Smith supporter who did not accept his free exchange ideas for backward countries and who even presented in a rudimentary form the "infant industry" argument. In Book IV of *The Wealth*, in the second part, when Smith criticized extraordinary restrictions on the introduction of foreign products, there appeared a note from Ortíz which said, "It must be borne in mind that all this free trade is advantageous when it is not used as a positive hindrance to progress in industry itself in a backward country, because in that case restrictions would be indispensable in trade in foreign goods within certain limits and for a certain period of time, and because manufacturing industry is a sector which must be given priority over the commercial sector, which in comparison has only a secondary influence on a nation's wealth". A few pages further on, he said that care must be taken over the importing of manufactured goods since our factories are not "competitive with foreign ones" (A. Smith, 1983: vol. 2, 263 and 280; see Schwartz, 1990).

Jovellanos, too, on certain occasions differed from the general principles. In one of his writings he suggested subsidies "to favour more particularly the exporting of Asturian coal through incentives and franchises" (Jovellanos, 1952–6: vol. 5, 229). In the *Informe sobre la ley agraria* he was in favour of restrictions in questions of foreign trade in cereals because Spain did not have surpluses in normal years. He proposed that cereals imports should only be allowed in very special circumstances and always under government control. With regard to exports, he maintained that "they could raise the normal cereals prices and in this sense favour agriculture, but also, taking out a part of the grain needed for home consumption could cause severe shortages, which naturally are very harmful to industry and the arts, and because of its inevitable repercussion on to agriculture" (Jovellanos, 1979: 266; see Schwartz, 1990). This last standpoint, as Polt maintains (1976: 53), was rectified by Jovellanos in his *Apuntes para una memoria económica* (Jovellanos, 1952–6: vol. , 50–3), in which he maintained that exports could not be accurately regulated and thus should not be regulated at all.

Vicente Alcalá Galiano, in his *Sobre economía política*, in 1793 pointed out that the customs as well as being a procedure for increasing state revenue, are also used as a means of indirectly promoting domestic industry. As Herr said, Alcalá Galiano as he approached closer to reality was still a mercantilist (see Elorza, 1970: 177; Herr, 1958: 46).

Jaumeandreu and *Dou* have been studied by Lluch (1973: chs. 9, 12, and 13) and he has shown us that in questions of foreign trade they were not liberals and proposed protectionist measures for domestic industry. Dou (1800–3: vol. 5, 247) went so far as to say that "the further a country is from equalling or leading others in industry, the further it must be from adopting Smith's system". In *La riqueza de las naciones, nuevamente explicada con la doctrina de su mismo investigador* he insisted on exceptions to free exchange. Jaumeandreu was a defender of intervention in matters of tariffs and trade, protectionist towards domestic industry, and a defender of industrial and agricultural development based on the setting-up of a home market. In short, he set out the ideology of Catalonian industrialists.

We can therefore observe that Smith's system had not taken root among Spaniards. Those whom we know had read *The Wealth of Nations* were also the first in placing restrictions on his doctrine when applied to Spain. Therefore, it seems that he only influenced Ortíz in questions of currency and the occasional fiscalists such as Vicente Alcalá Galiano.

The Royal Decree of 12 July 1807 included political economy as a subject in the curriculum of Spanish universities, though in the absolutist decade it was dropped owing to its being considered a dangerous subject. The problem which arose was that of finding suitable manuals. First of all, foreign texts were used. Between 1776 and 1806 Smith and Genovesi were recommended. But immediately Smith was to be substituted by Say, who was translated very early on, as we have seen above. As Cabrillo and Martín Rodríguez have concluded,[11] in the first half of the nineteenth century Say was the most widely read economist.

The reason for the success of Say's books was to be found in the fact that they were more suitable than *The Wealth of Nations* for teaching purposes (neither must it be forgotten that Spaniards translated from French more easily than from English). The French economist was clearer than the Scotsman and his text was more orderly and lighter. Dou admitted that he had to read *The Wealth of Nations* several times in order to understand and comprehend the "sublime nature" of his theories. Flórez Estrada (1980: 48 ff) regarded Smith as the founder of our discipline, but he was lacking in clarity and organization and made several useless digressions. Valle Santoro likewise considered the Scotsman as the most important economist, but several "arguments" and "digressions" would have to be removed from the work. R. S. Smith referred to José Cecilio del Valle, who taught economics courses in Guatemala and who thought *The Wealth of Nations* too abstract for beginners, whereas Say was "capable of greater perfection in style and thoughts" than Smith.[12] In short, as the Spanish editor of *The Wealth of Nations*, José María Tallada, said in 1933: "Our Latin spirit, fond of order and method, frequently gets lost among the digressions and examples which are so common in the book. Only after reading it and thinking about it can the main principle which informs the work and gives unity to the system be seen" (A. Smith, 1983: prologue, 21).

The first Spanish manuals recommended by the Dirección General de Estudios del Reino (Administration for Studies in the Kingdom) were: M. de Valle Santoro, *Elementos de Economía Política con aplicación particular a España* (Madrid, 1829); A. Flórez Estrada, *Curso de Economía Política* (London, 1828); and M. Torrente, *Revista General de la Economía Política* (Habana, 1835). The common characteristic of the three authors was their knowledge of Spanish economists of the past and of the classical English and French schools.

Let us analyse the case of the Marqués de Valle Santoro. His book was the first political economy manual written by a Spaniard, published in our country (1829), and officially studied in Spanish universities (though Flórez Estrada's *Curso de Economía Política* was published in London in 1828). The author stated in the introduction that his aim was to synthesize Smith and Says' theories in a clear form for didactic purposes, but in fact he moved away from these authors in the course of the book. Let us look at the organization of the book and at how he applied the general principles to the Spanish economy. My intention is to show that Spaniards learnt from this manual a type of economics which can best be described as eclectic.

Basing his ideas on the German economist K. H. Rau,[13] Valle Santoro divided his lessons broadly into two major parts, one theoretical and the other practical, devoted to the application of theoretical principles to the Spanish economy. This distinction is basic since Valle Santoro modified some of his theoretical principles when they applied to our country. In questioning Smith and Says' principles, his recommendations were more protectionist when referring to Spain. Whether or not the distinction is made between the theoretical and practical part of Rau, and without the need to read List, it must be pointed out that this modification of general principles when applied to Spain had been normal, as we have seen, even among eighteenth-century Spanish readers of Smith's work.

The organization of the eight treatises making up the theoretical part showed varying influences. The first treatise ("On the production of wealth"), the second ("On the distribution of wealth"), the third ("On the consumption of wealth"), and the fifth ("On the value of things and of the currency") broadly followed Say's *Tratado de economía política* (published in 1803 and translated into Spanish in 1804–7). It must be emphasized that this synthesis was not happily done when dealing with wealth distribution and consumption. The structure of Say's treatise was adopted by other authors such as Jaumeandreu in his *Rudimentos de Economía Política*, set out in the form of questions and answers, and consisting of five books: (1) "On production"; (2) "On currency"; (3) "On the value of things"; (4) "On income"; (5) "On consumption" (see Lluch, 1973: 305ff.). On the other hand, Jaumeandreu in the *Curso elemental de economía política con aplicación a la legislación económica de España* (Elementary course on political economy as applied to economic legislation in Spain, 1836) organized the subject matter in a similar manner to that of the *Curso de Economía Política* (Political economy course, 1825–35) by Alvarez Flórez Estrada (the latter had in turn copied from James Mill and Say the organization of his book). The two books had the same layout, production, distribution, value, and consumption (Lluch, 1973: 308ff).

Nevertheless, Valle Santoro in the following treatises deviated from Say. The structure of the sixth treatise ("On different causes influencing public wealth"), among other topics, examined population, the colonies, public expenditure, taxes, public debt, and luxury; the seventh ("On the influence of laws on agricultural wealth") and eighth ("On the influence of laws on commercial and industrial wealth") remind one of the traditional mercantilist population–tax–agriculture–industry–trade division.

Among the treatises which followed Say and those of a mercantilist nature, one is included (the fourth, entitled "On the right to property") in which the foundations were laid for the importance of respect for private property in a society's development and, by proposing the need for compensation, a limit was imposed on the few cases in which this right could be violated. This idea, as we have seen in Foronda's case, had been learnt by the Spaniards from the physiocrats.

It is in the mercantilist-type treatises where there is more ambiguity and eclecticism in the topics dealt with. In agriculture, industry, and domestic commerce he recommended those principles of political economy in favour of freedom. The government merely has to protect property, maintain the social order, provide communications, not reduce the value of the currency, not grant privileges, economize on expenditure, simplify public administration, and hardly anything else.

On the other hand, when Valle Santoro scrutinized the study of foreign trade he expressed his doubts about the principles recommended by the new science. He stressed that "The maxim that nobody gains in trade, rather the other loses, has been destroyed" and other criticisms of mercantilist fallacies, but he did not dare to propose free foreign trade, "Despite the opinion of the wise men [who were in fact none other than Smith and Say] who have defended it, either because the relative interests of different nations are opposed to this advantage, or because it has still not been clearly and convincingly demonstrated that the general principle can be applied without exception to all nations on earth".

Therefore, "at the moment it is not advisable to follow the restrictive system exclusively nor to abandon oneself in practice to the principles of modern statesmen" (Valle Santoro, 1989: 167–75). In the following paragraphs he gave a synthesis of his viewpoint:

But, nonetheless, it must be noted that the absolute wealth of the globe is not the same as the relative wealth of each nation, and the former can be increased more quickly than that of any given country and therefore the latter can be relatively lower than the others. For this reason the principles of the wise men may be true with regard to general wealth, while it may not be necessarily in the interests of every nation to adopt them. (p. 171)

That mutual freedom of trade may inexorably ruin the industry of the most backward one and therefore, only the most advanced can adopt it or those without industry, such as the colonies if at the same time they have virgin and extremely fertile territory. (p. 174)

The same doubts exist with regard to the colonies, coastal trade, or the promoting of new industry. In short, Valle Santoro's insistence that "theory is one thing, and practice another" meant that his book became eclectic.

The first edition of Alvaro Flórez de Estrada was published in London in 1828. As Almenar said in his first books the toolbox of this Spanish economist is the reworking of various previous instruments: "some come from late agricultural mercantilism and even from seventeenth-century Castilian anti-bullionist mercantilism, others are from more recent authors such as David Hume, Condillac, and Adam Smith" (Flórez Estrada, 1980: preliminary study, p. xlv). In the *Curso*, according to Flórez, he tried to provide a manual to give wide publicity in Spain and South America to "the great discoveries made in this science during the last thirty years". In view of the brief history of doctrines he offered in the "Preliminary speech" it can be concluded, and this has been confirmed by Almenar, that to produce this manual he made use of the following authors: J. R. McCulloch, James Mill, J. B. Say, Henry Storch, David Ricardo, J. C. L. Simonde de Sismondi, Destutt de Tracy, Jovellanos, and José Canga Argüelles.

Almenar stressed that the lengthy quotes made by Flórez from *The Wealth of Nations* are paragraphs included in the *Principles* of Ricardo or McCulloch (Flórez Estrada, 1980: preliminary study, p. lxiii). Smith's influence is indirect. The organization of the book is taken from James Mill (production, distribution, changes, and consumption), an organization in turn inspired by Say. The greatest influence is that of McCulloch, an author highly influenced by Smith. With regard to the application of the principles to Spain, he devoted several comments and a chapter (to tax and agricultural reform), but he never divided the book into theory and practice. He maintained his free trade radicalism, though he modified it somewhat towards the end of his life (ibid. p. xciv).

As a general conclusion it can be said that the possible influence of Smith on the authors mentioned in the second section of this article is lessened if their works are subjected to deeper analysis. The eclecticism of Spanish economists is reflected both in their reading and in the organization of their books and the habit of modifying general principles when applied to our country.

5. Liberal Politicians Prefer Bastiat

If liberal teachers preferred Say for his clarity and simplicity, more radical liberals preferred the books of Bastiat, among which the most outstanding was *Economic sophisms*. A proof of the importance of Bastiat's work in Spain is the numerous translations (see Cabrillo, 1978). The free trade–protectionist debate did not always run along academic lines and the use of Bastiat's book lowered the theoretical level of the debate. Smith was used as a symbol, but the book read was Bastiat's. Even on some occasions Jovellanos' testimony would be more quoted than Smith and Say (Velasco, 1990: 110). I am not going to get involved in the free trade–protectionist discussion during the nineteenth century, for which there is an extensive bibliography ranging from Pugés's (1931) classic book to Velasco's (1990) book, but I can point out the importance of Bastiat for these politicians and for that purpose analyse the thought of one of those considered as one of the ideologues of the economists' school favourable towards the free trade thesis: Luis María Pastor, a politician who was more rhetorical than theoretical.

Pastor (1804–72) was born in Barcelona and held very important public posts: he was a deputy for the moderates and director general of the National Debt in 1847, Finance Minister in 1853, senator for the Progressive Party in 1863 (he left the Moderates because of his disagreement with their economic programme, which was not as liberal as he would have liked), and adviser to Figuerola between 1868 and 1872 in matters relating to budgets, public debt, tariff reform, and the drawing-up of a new trade statute.

He proudly confessed that he had devoted the best years of his life to studying political economy and managed to build up a vast knowledge of English, French, American and Spanish economic literature.

In spite of the advantages, development, and spread of political economy in more advanced countries, Pastor stressed the existence in Spain of backwardness and even "prejudice" against such a commendable discipline. This backwardness led him to devote part of his life to the spreading of political economy through the societies in which he participated and through his writings.

He was a member and chairman of the meetings of the Sociedad Libre de Economía Política de Madrid (Free Political Economy Society of Madrid), founded in 1857 by Laureano Figuerola and other economists. In 1859 he took part in creating the Asociación para la Reforma de los Aranceles de Aduanas (The Association for the Reform of Customs Tariffs), of which he was president. The zeal he showed in propagating political economy and liberal principles in these institutions led him to be regarded as the "centre of the economist school" which gained power in 1868. We can say that Pastor was the main propagator of the school's liberal ideas and Figuerola the main executor. In fact, Figuerola was an author who in the classes he gave in Barcelona explained economics according to Bastiat's books instead of via the book *Curso de Economía Política* by the protectionist Eusebio María del Valle (Cabrillo, 1981: 51).

Pastor shared with members of the school of economists, with whom he had a close friendship (particularly with Figuerola, Sanromá and Gabriel Rodríguez), the fascination for political economy from which his defence of economic freedom stemmed. His books were school manuals, and some of them were even printed on the presses of the *Gaceta Economista*, considered the organ of opinion of the above-mentioned authors. I refer to the *Lecciones de Economía Política*.

A review of his main books shows the most weighty subjects were those related to credit, public debt, taxes, and economic freedom. In those an attempt was made both to highlight the favourable effects of economic freedom on economic growth and to stress the unfavourable effects of prohibitions and restrictions on entrepreneurial freedom, monopolies, privileges, tariff franchises, or controls on economic activity in general. Well known are the works devoted to subjects related to public debt and the tax system, such as *Filosofía del Crédito deducida de la historia de las naciones más importantes de Europa, con un apéndice en que se aplica la teoría al estado actual de España y al arreglo de su deuda* (1st edn. 1850, 2nd edn. with a prologue by J. M. Sanromá), *Historia de la Deuda pública española y proyecto de arreglo y unificación* (1863), and *La hacienda española en 1872* (1872). In *Libertad de bancos y colas del de España* he criticized the granting of a monopoly to the Bank of Spain in note issuing and maintained that theory and practice have proved the benefits of "the healthy doctrine of free banking". *La ciencia de la contribución* (1856) is a book of fiscal theory in which an attempt was made to formulate a general tax theory based on Bastiat.

Another important part of his work was devoted to the propagation of the principle of economic freedom. In this section are included all the articles he wrote in the press and some of the speeches read in the different institutions he belonged to; for example, *Las conferencias libre-cambistas, Discursos pronunciados en el Ateneo Científico y Literario de Madrid* (1863) and, along with Güell y Ferrer (leader of the protectionists), *Polémica sobre cuestiones económicas* (1869). The most outstanding book was the one entitled *Lecciones de economía política* (1868), which became a propagantist book for spreading free trade doctrines.

In the *Lecciones* he stated that the economists he admired most were Say and Flórez Estrada, and above all Bastiat: "If Smith created the science, if Say and Flórez Estrada reduced it to specific formulae, Bastiat raised it to the point where it found its relationship with philosophy, by giving it the generalized character it has recently acquired" (Pastor, 1868: 188). He stressed the role played by Smith in laying the foundations of our discipline and therefore the first nine chapters of the sixteen comprising the *Lecciones* synthesize Smith's thought. But this synthesis was based on Say and Flórez Estradas' work. It is not surprising because he stated that "Say and Flórez Estrada gave Smith's doctrine a more didactic and elevated character than its founder had given it" (Pastor, 1868: 184).

Nevertheless, in the *Lecciones* the most noticeable influence is that of Bastiat. He emphasized the topics dealt with by Bastiat, and furthermore from a philosophical rather than strictly economic viewpoint (not like Flórez Estrada, who when defending, for example, freedom of trade, used the classical English theory of international trade). He could not give higher praise to Bastiat's work than in the next paragraph: "Bastiat reduced Proudhon's sophisms to ashes, and his immortal works made available to everyone the mysterious laws guiding the destinies of mankind, and which only economic science has managed to understand and explain" (Pastor, 1868: 188).

Bastiat was an optimistic author who trusted in the natural order ("the laws of the social world," he said, "are harmonic and tend in all senses to the perfection of mankind"). Consequently, he did not agree with the pessimistic forecasts of Malthus and Ricardo, and regarded freedom and private property as the two pillars of society. These basic ideas of Bastiat and others are repeated in Pastor's *Lecciones*. In them his optimism was given full rein when he stressed that the real economy "tends to follow the impulses of human reason and to expand and restrain more and more men's relationships with each other, by providing them with the greatest possible amount of pleasure and welfare" (Pastor, 1868: 249). As a result of his Bastiat-inspired optimism, he criticized the Malthusian population theory and Ricardo's theory, and thus distanced himself from the two authors' pessimism. Against the two empirical statements of the population principle (the population increases in a geometrical progression and the means of subsistence in an arithmetical progression) he said that "the progress of civilization heralds an inverse progression in the two terms of the comparison" (Pastor, 1868: 168). That is due to the possibility of fertilizing the land, and the foresight and morality which is being disseminated throughout society. As for Ricardian theory, "it was not long before it succumbed to the result of the examination and study of the facts" (Pastor, 1868: 175).

Also, Pastor particularly stressed and began with the statement of the "fundamental principle of property" and in the long seventh chapter studied the three basic conditions for economic growth: freedom, security, and justice. He pointed out that "it is necessary for complete freedom to exist and no type of monopoly, since competition depends on the latter and from competition come all the advantages of perfection and cheapness" (Pastor, 1868: 78–9). At another time he said that "it is, thus, a constant rule that freedom is the fundamental basis of labour. In order for this to produce the greatest possible utility, it is an essential condition that it should encounter no shackles, obstacles, or restraints which could hinder the observing of the law of competition, which will take care to level out and regularize all the profits in a fair and accurate manner" (Pastor, 1868: 87). He always insisted on the advantages deriving for the consumer from the producer working within a competitive framework.

Another important section of the *Lecciones* is the one devoted to criticizing both the socialist school (chapter 15) and the protectionist one (chapter 16), following Bastiat very closely. He criticized List's protection of the infant industry argument:

No more accurate is the other assumption which consists in the supposed disadvantage of new industry in comparison with the old ones. Every old industry, merely by being old, suffers from defects which are shown up by constant progress in the elements of manufacturing, and the new industry always has in its favour the example of those that have gone before, the use of more improved tools . . . Furthermore, protection far from helping to encourage industry and correcting its faults, inevitably gives rise to the opposite effect; because it kills off the stimulus of competition, which is what produces improvements, as List himself recognizes.

He insisted that "nothing is so vague or so arbitrary as the national concern", where prohibitions are the greatest "threat to private property" and where protectionism "is aristocratic socialism, which is the worst of all socialisms and the worst of all aristocracies".[15]

To sum up, we may conclude that the *Lecciones*, in which an attempt was made to disseminate the most recent progress made in economics, in its approach, which lays special stress on a philosophical rather than an economic explanation, and its theories and the topics highlighted, followed the doctrines of the *Economic harmonies*, the *Economic Sophisms* and other essays by Bastiat rather than the work of Say or Smith. Pastor used as a starting-point the synthesis of Say and Flórez, but always followed Bastiat. The ideologue of the free trade school used Bastiat's arguments rather than Smith's.

6. Conclusions

In view of what has been stated in this article and the conclusions of the studies on Spanish economists consulted, it seems reasonable to maintain that the influence of *The Wealth of Nations* in Spain was not very great. Smith was to be a symbol for the free trade supporters and the father of economics for teachers, but in fact *The Wealth of Nations* was not very widely read and had few translations if we compare it with the works of Say and Bastiat. The last generation of eighteenth-century enlightenment thinkers, who were the ones who most read Smith, did not take from this author the arguments in favour of free domestic trade or free trade with the colonies, nor the idea of the importance of setting up sound economic institutions to achieve greater economic growth, nor the ideas set out in the debate on fiscal reform. There were many enlightenment and nineteenth-century economists, such as Valle Santoro, who deviated from Smith's proposals when they applied them to Spain. Smith's ideas in the nineteenth century were known not directly through reading *The Wealth of Nations*, but largely from the numerous translations of Say. It should also be added that the economics that Spaniards learnt in manuals written by their fellow-countrymen was an eclectic economics. The final conclusion is that liberal politicians, more rhetorical than theoretical, preferred Bastiat's arguments to Smith's in defending free trade and anti-interventionist arguments. To sum up, Mirabeau, Say, and Bastiat were more successful than Smith among Spanish economists.

NOTES

A version of this chapter was presented at the congress on "Adam Smith: Doctrina y Economía" organized by the Instituto Universitario de Economía de Mercado held in the Facultad de Ciencias Económicas y Empresariales de la Universidad Complutense de Madrid, 27–28 November 1990. I am grateful to Victoriano Martín, Enrique Fuentes Quintana, John Reeder, and Pedro Schwartz for the comments they have made on the draft of this work. The responsibility for errors and omissions is completely mine.

1. The most notable ones are Anes (1988), Beltrán (1976), Elorza (1970), Llombart (1992), Lluch and Argemí (1987), Lluch and Almenor (1992), Hernández Andreu (1990), Perdices de Blas and Fuentes Quintana (1996), Reeder (1978), Schwartz and Fernández Marugán (1978), Schwartz (1990), and R. S. Smith (1957, 1968).

2. On these two authors and Geddes see Schwartz (1990); Llombart (1992: 296–305).
3. The first one published by the Colegio de México in 1941, the summary published in México, F.C.E., 1978, first reprinting 1979, and the third published in Madrid, Alianza, 1997.
4. This summary is published in Lasarte (1976: 120).
5. Reeder (1973: 72). On the mishaps of this translation, Lasarte (1976) should be consulted, and on Ortíz's life and work, Schwartz and Fernández Marugán (1978), Schwartz (1990) and, of course, R. S. Smith (1957) and Elorza (1970).
6. The summary has been edited by Lasarte (1976: 121).
7. Two new Spanish editions of *The Wealth of Nations* are: Smith (1994) and Smith (1996).
8. This text and the previous one by Olavide are cited in Perdices de Blas (1988: 50–1).
9. Foronda (1821: vol. 1, 96). Even Barrenechea (1984: 286) concluded that political and anti-despotic liberalism was taken from the physiocrats (Grivel and Holbach). Barrenechea stressed Foronda's contradiction when, on the one hand, he recognized the existence of a natural order of a physiocratic type and, on the other, he was a utilitarian "who proposed the maximization of pleasure as a rule of human behaviour and, in dealing with the problem that the abuse of rights harms some individuals, forgot these negative elements and made the abuse of the right a prerogative granted by natural order and justice" (Barrenechea, 1984: 196–7).
10. See Argemí d'Abadal (1988), who compiled the texts of Spanish economists who stressed each above-mentioned obstacle.
11. See Cabrillo (1978: 72); Martín Rodríguez in the preliminary study to the book by the Marqués del Valle Santoro (1989); Perdices de Blas (1996).
12. *Obras* by José Cicilio del Valle, Guatemala, 1829, vol. 2; cited in R. S. Smith (1957: 1251).
13. Schumpeter (1971: 564) said that the *Lehrbuch der politischen ökonomie* (1826–37) by Rau (1792–1870) was a widely read textbook which divided the study of economics into theory, applied economics, and public finance. Moreover, it should be mentioned that in 1849 a translation was made of *La política comercial y el comercio internacional con relación a la industria y a la agricultura* (1844) by List (1769–1846) (see Cabrillo, 1978: 94).
14. The last four quotations are taken from Pastor (1868: 232–3, 244, 235, and 238, respectively).

References

ALCALÁ GALIANO, VICENTE (1793), "Sobre la necesidad y justicia de los tributos de donde deben sacarse y medios de recaudarlos", *Actas y Memorias de la Real Sociedad Económica de los Amigos del País de la Provincia de Segovia*, vol. 4, Segovia.
—— (1992) [1781–1788], *Sobre la economía política y los impuestos*, edited by J. M. Vallés, Academiade Artilleria, Segovia.
ALMENAR, SALVADOR and VELASCO, ROGELIO (1987), "Una etapa en la consolidación del

librecambio en España; el viaje de Richard Cobden por Andalucía 1846" in Gumersindo Ruiz (ed.), *Andalucía en el pensamiento económico*, Editorial Arguval, Málaga.

ANES ALVAREZ, RAFAEL (1988), "Economía y pensamiento económico en España", *Enciclopedia de Historia de España*, vol. 3: *Iglesia. Pensamiento. Cultura*, Alianza Editorial, Madrid.

ARGEMÍ D'ABADAL, LLUIS (compiler) (1988), *Agricultura e Ilustración*, Ministerio de Agricultura, Pesca y Alimentación, Madrid.

ARRIQUIBAR, NICOLÀS DE (1987) [1779], *Recreación política. Reflexiones sobre el Amigo de los Hombres en su tratado de población considerado con respecto a nuestros intereses*, preliminary study and edition by Jesús Astigarraga and José Manuel Barrenechea, Instituto Vasco de Estadística, Bilbao.

BARRENECHEA, JOSÉ MANUEL (1984), *Valentín de Foronda, reformador y economista ilustrado*, Diputación Provincial de Alava, Vitoria.

—— (1985), "Valentín de Foronda ante la fisiocracia", in Lluch and Argemi (1985).

BASTIAT, FREDERIC (1968), *Economic Harmonies*, Foundation for Economic Education, New York.

BELTRÁN, LUCAS (1976), *Historia de las doctrinas económicas*, Editorial Teide, Barcelona.

CABRILLO, FRANCISCO (1978) "Traducciones al español de libros de economía política (1800–1880)", *Moneda y crédito*, 147: 187–91.

—— (1981), "El programa de Economía Política de D. Laureano Figuerola", *Moneda y crédito*, 162: 49–59.

CANGA ARGÜELLES, J. (1968) [1826–7], *Diccionario de Hacienda Pública*, Instituto de Estudios Fiscales, Madrid.

COSTAS, ANTÓN (1988), *Apogeo del liberalismo en "La Gloriosa". La reforma económica en el Sexenio liberal (1868–1874)*, Siglo XXI, Madrid.

DÍEZ DEL CORRAL, LUIS (1973), *El liberalismo doctrinario*, 3rd edn., Instituto de Estudios Políticos, Madrid.

DOU, RAMÓN LÁZARO DE (1800–3), *Instituciones del derecho público general de España*, 9 vols., Madrid.

—— (1817), *La riqueza de las naciones, nuevamente explicada con la doctrina de su mismo investigador*, 2 vols., La Universidad, Cervera.

ELORZA, ANTONIO (1970), *La ideología liberal en la ilustración española*, Tecnos, Madrid.

ESTAPÉ, FABIÁN (1971), "Algunos comentarios a la publicación del *Ensayo sobre la naturaleza del comercio en general* de Cantillon", *Ensayo sobre historia del pensamiento económico*, Ariel, Barcelona.

—— (1990), *Introducción al pensamiento económico. Una perspectiva española*, Espasa Calpe, Madrid.

FLÓREZ ESTRADA, ALVARO (1980) [1828], *Curso de economía política*, 2 vols., edition and preliminary study by Salvador Almenar and introduction by Ernest Lluch, Instituto de Estudios Fiscales, Madrid.

FORNIES CASALS, JOSÉ FRANCISCO (1976), "La cátedra de economía civil y comercio de Zaragoza en el período de la ilustración (1784–1808)", *Información Comercial Española*, 512: 108–18.

FORONDA, VALENTÍN (1821), *Cartas sobre los asuntos más exquisitos de la economía política y sobre las leyes criminales*, 2 vols., Ramón Domingo, Pamplona.

GÁNDARA, MIGUEL ANTONIO DE LA (1988), *Apuntes sobre el bien y el mal de España*, edition and preliminary study by Jacinta Macías Delgado, Instituto de Estudios Fiscales, Madrid.

GARCÍA RUIZ, JOSÉ LUIS (1988), "Luis Maria Pasor: un economista en la España de Isabel II", Revista de Historia Económica, XIV(1): 205–7.

HERNÁNDEZ ANDREU, JUAN (1978), "La evolución histórica de la contribución directa en España desde 1700 a 1814", *Historia Económica de España*, CECA, Madrid.

—— (1990), "Problemas hacendísticos y pensamiento financiero en España a finales del siglo XVIII y principios del XIX", manuscript.

HERR, RICHARD (1958), *España y la revolución del siglo XVIII*, Aguilar, Madrid.

JOVELLANOS, GASPAR MELCHOR DE (1952–6), *Obras publicadas e inéditas*, 5 vols., edition by Cándido Nocedal and Miguel Artola, B.A.E. Madrid.

—— (1979) [1795], *Informe sobre la Ley Agraria*, edition by José Lage, Cátedra, Madrid.

LASARTE, JAVIER (1976), "Adam Smith ante la Inquisición y la Academia de la Historia", in *Economía y Hacienda al final del Antiguo Régimen. Dos Estudios*, Instituto de Estudios Fiscales-Ministerio de Hacienda, Madrid.

LLOMBART, VICENTE (1976), "A propósito de los intentos de reformas de la Hacienda castellana en el siglo XVIII: Campomanes frente al proyecto de única contribución", *Hacienda Pública Española*, 38: 123–32.

—— (1992), *Campomanes, economista y político de Carlos III*, Alianza, Madrid.

LLUCH, ERNEST (1973), *El pensament econòmic a Catalunya (1760–1840). Els orígens ideològics del proteccionisme i la presa de conciencia de la burguesía catalana*, Edicions 62 SA, Barcelona.

—— and ARGEMÍ, LLUIS (1985), *Agronomía y fisiocracia en España (1750–1820)*, Institución Alfonso El Magnánimo, Valencia.

—— —— (1987), "La difusión en España de los trabajos económicos de Condorcet y Lavoisier, dos científicos entre el enciclopedismo y la revolución", *Hacienda Pública Española*, 108–9.

—— and ALMENOR, SALVADOR (1992), "Diffusión e influencia de los economistas clássicos en España (1776–1868)", in José Luis Cardoso and Antonio Almondovar, *Actas do Encontro Ibérico sobre Historia do Pensamiento*, CIESP, Lisbon.

MARTÍN MARTÍN, VICTORIANO (1968), "La libertad de comercio bajo Carlos III: Cabarrús, Jovellanos y Foronda", *Información Comercial Española*, 663: 7–43.

MIRABEAU, VICTOR RIQUETI, MARQUÉS DE (1756–1758), *L'' Ami des Hommes, ou traité de la population*, 5 vols., Avignon.

—— (1764), *Disertación sobre el cultivo de trigos, que la Academia de Agricultura de la ciudad de Berna en Suiza premió en el año de 1760 en Francia por el marqués de Mirabeau y traducido al castellano por Don Serafín Trigueros*, Joaquín de Ibarra, Madrid.

NEGRO, DALMACIO (1988), *El liberalismo en España. Una antología*, Unión Editorial, Madrid.

NORMANTE Y CARCAVILLA, LORENZO (1984) [1784–6], *Discurso sobre la utilidad de los conocimientos Económico-Políticos y la necesidad de su estudio metódico, Proposiciones de Economía Civil y Comercio, Espíritu del Señor Melón en su Ensayo Político sobre el comercio*, edition under the aegis of Antonio Peiró Arroyo, Diputación General de Aragón, Zaragoza.

PASTOR, LUIS MARÍA (1868), *Lecciones de Economía Política*, Gaceta Economista, Madrid.

—— (1973) [1873], "La hacienda de España en 1872", *Revista de Economía Política*, 63: 197–300.

PERDICES DE BLAS, LUIS (1988), "La lucha por la libertad de comercio interior en el reinado de Carlos III", *Información Comercial Española*, 663: 48–58.

—— (1992), *Pablo de Olavide (1725–1803), el Ilustrado*, Universidad Complutense, Madrid.

—— (1996), *La economia politica de decadencia de Castilla en el siglo XVII. Investigatión de los arbitrstas sobre la naturaleza y causas de la riqueza de las naciones*, Síntesis, Madrid.

—— and FUENTES QUINTANA, ENRIQUE (1996), "Estudio prelminar" in Smith (1996).

POLT, J. H. E. (1976), "El pensamiento económico de Jovellanos, y sus fuentes inglesas", *Información Comercial Española*, 512: 23–56.

PUGÉS, MANUEL (1931), *Como triunfó el proteccionismo en España (la formación de la política arancelaria española)*, Editorial Juventud, Barcelona.

REEDER, JOHN P. (1973), "Bibliografía de traducciones, al castellano y catalán, durante el siglo XVIII de obras de pensamiento económico", *Moneda y crédito*, 126: 57–77.

—— (1978), "Economía e ilustración en España: traducciones y traductores 1717–1800", *Moneda y Crédito*, 147: 47–70.

RODRÍGUEZ DE CAMPOMANES, PEDRO (1764), *Respuesta fiscal sobre abolir la tasa y establecer el comercio de granos*, Madrid.

—— (1988) [1762], *Reflexiones sobre el comercio español a Indias*, edition and preliminary study by Vicente Llombart, Instituto de Estudios Fiscales, Madrid.

SAY, JEAN-BAPTISTE (1838) [1803], *Tratado de Economía Política o exposición simple de cómo se forman, se distribuyen y se consumen las riquezas*, 2 vols., Fuentenebro-A. Gómez, Madrid.

SCHUMPETER, JOSEPH A. (1971), *Historia del análisis económico*, Ariel, Barcelona.

SCHWARTZ GIRÓN, PEDRO (1970), "'De la libertad de comercio' por José Joaquín de Mora: Una defensa del libre-cambio a mediados del siglo XIX" *Anales de economia*, 5–8: 187–224.

—— (1990), "La recepción inicial de la 'Riqueza de las Naciones' en España", manuscript.

—— and FERNÁNDEZ MARUGÁN, FRANCISCO (1978), "El ensayo de José Alonso Ortíz, monetarismo smithiano en la España de los vales reales", in Alfonso Otazu (compiler) *Dinero y Crédito (siglos XVI a XIX)*, Editorial Moneda y Crédito, Madrid.

SMITH, A. (1958) [1776], *Investigación sobre la naturaleza y causas de la riqueza de las naciones*, edited by Gabriel Franco, F.C.E. Mexico.

—— (1961) [1776], *Indagación acerca de la naturaleza y causas de la riqueza de las naciones*, edited by A. Lazaro Ros, 2nd edn., Aguilar, Madrid.

—— (1983) [1776], *Investigación de la naturaleza y causas de la riqueza de las naciones*, edited by J. M. Tallada, Ediciones Orbis SA Barcelona.

SMITH, A. (1988) [1776], *Investigación sobre la naturaleza y causas de la riqueza de las naciones*, edited by J. C. Collado and Mira-Perceval, Oikos-taus, Barcelona.

—— (1994) [1776], *La riqueza de las naciones*, edited by C. Rodríguez Braun, Alianza, Madrid.

—— (1996) [1776], *Investigación de la naturaleza y causas de la riqueza de naciones*, edited by Enrique Fuentes Quintana and Luis Perdices de Blas, Junta de Castilla y León, Salamanca.

SMITH, ROBERT SIDNEY (1957), "La riqueza de las naciones en España e Hispano-américa 1780–1830", *Revista de Economía Política*, 8(3: 1215–53), published by *The Journal of Political Economy*, 65(2: 104–25); also published in *Hacienda Pública Española*, 23: 240–258.

—— (1968), "English Economic Thought in Spain 1776–1848", in C. W. Goodwin and I. B. Halley, *The Transfer of Ideas: Historical Essays*, Duke University Press, Durham.

THOMPSON, E. P. (1979), "La economía 'moral' de la multitud en la Inglaterra del siglo XVIII", *Tradición, revuelta y consciencia de clases. Estudios sobre la crisis de la sociedad preindustrial*, Critica, Barcelona.

UZTÁRIZ, GERÓNIMO (1968) [1724], *Theorica y Práctica de comercio y Marina*, facsimile edition with an introduction by Gabriel Franco, Aguilar, Madrid.

VALLE SANTORO, MARQUÉS DE (1989) [1829], *Elementos de economía política con aplicación particular a España*, preliminary study and edition by Manuel Martín Rodríguez, Instituto de Estudios Fiscales, Madrid.

VARELA, JAVIER (1988), *Jovellanos*, Alianza Universidad, Madrid.

VELASCO, ROGELIO (1990), *Pensamiento económico en Andalucía (1800–1850). Economía política, librecambio y proteccionismo*, Editorial Librería Agora, Málaga.

WARD, BERNARDO (1982) [1779], *Proyecto económico*, edition by Juan Luis Castellano, Instituto de Estudios Fiscales, Madrid.

ZAPATERO, JUAN CARLOS (1975), "El caso español en la "Riqueza de las Naciones"", *Revista Española de Economía*, 2: 205–12.

Part 10. Sweden

It is somewhat surprising to learn that Sweden, which awards the Nobel Prize in economics, does not yet have a complete translation of *WN*, although several partial translations were published in different forms as early as the late eighteenth century. Perhaps an explanation lies in the fact that, during the eighteenth century, there existed close ties between Britain and Sweden, and most intellectuals can read English-language works.

On the reception of *WN* in Sweden, we have only one text, written by Professor Vallinder of Lund University for this volume. Although there are some texts that touch indirectly on the impact of Smith in Sweden (listed below), Vallinder's text is directly suited to our purpose. His main focus is on the reception of *WN* during the past two centuries (1776–1990) by university professors in economics, history, philosophy, and law; politicians and practical economic policy problems are left aside here. The references cited are also informative for Swedish readers.

Further Reading

Text with a * is printed in this Part

Heckscher, Eli (1953), "A Survey of Economic Thought in Sweden, 1875–1950", *Scandinavian Economic History Review*, 1(2): 105–26.

Magnusson, Lars (1977), "Economic Thought and Group Interests: Adam Smith, Christopher Polhem, Lars Salvius and Classical Political Economy", *Scandinavian Journal of History*, 2: 243–64.

Påhlman, Axel (1933), "Adam Smith's *Wealth of Nations*", *Ekonomisk Tidskrift*, 35(5–6): 183–6.

Sandelin, Bo (ed.) (1991), *The History of Swedish Economic Thought*, London: Routledge.

Vallinder, T. (1987), "Adam Smiths genombrott i Sverige", *Economisk Debatt*, 3: 229–32.

*—— (1995), "University Professors and Amateur Writers: *The Wealth of Nations* in Sweden up to 1990" [prepared for this volume].

10.1. Torbjörn Vallinder, 1994.
University Professors and Amateur Writers:
The Wealth of Nations in Sweden up to 1990

Introduction

To give a comprehensive treatment of the influence of Adam Smith's major work *The Wealth of Nations* (hereinafter *WN*) in Sweden for 200 years would be an arduous task. Adam Smith, as is well-known, was not only an economist but a social scientist in the broadest sense. This fact is clearly demonstrated in *WN*, a scholarly work of economics, social history, sociology and philosophy—but at the same time also a political treatise. Thus, in Sweden as elsewhere, university professors from different areas as well as writers and politicians of different persuasions have been interested in *WN*. However, in this article I shall concentrate on university professors, primarily in departments of economics, history (including economic history), and philosophy, as well as in law faculties. Some amateur writers in the economic field are also included. Politicians, on the other hand, are excluded here.

There has, to my knowledge, up to now been no comparative study of the impact of *WN* in different countries. However, I would guess that the knowledge and influence of Smith's book spread comparatively early in Sweden. If so, there were three main causes behind this development. First, during the eighteenth century there existed close ties between Britain and Sweden, politically and culturally (see esp *Lindroth,* 1978: 42ff). Second, as an example of the first point, Smith's contributions to moral philosophy, starting with his book *The Theory of Moral Sentiments* (1759), were widely discussed by Swedish professors of philosophy during the later decades of the century, thus paving the way for *WN* (Segerstedt 1937). Third, Sweden was one of the first countries to institute chairs in economics.

Thus, in 1741 a professorship of *jurisprudentiae, oeconomiae et commerciorum* was established in the faculty of law of the university of Uppsala. This chair was the fourth one in Europe, the earlier three having been instituted in Germany. In 1750 a professorship of economics, botany, and natural history was established at the university of Lund (Liedman, 1989: esp. 36ff; cf. Goldsmith, 1885: 387).

However, the economic element in those posts did not become permanent. The chair in Uppsala fairly soon declined into a traditional legal one. In Lund the natural-science aspect got the upper hand and during the nineteenth century primarily one holder, Carl Adolph Agardh, carried out serious economic research, to be described below (L. Lönnroth, 1991: 18ff). A modern economic science did not emerge in Sweden until the turn of the twentieth century. We shall soon meet its founding fathers here. (A complete list of professors of economics in Sweden 1741–1989 is to be found in Engwall, 1992: 189ff).

Mention should, lastly, be made of a most remarkable writer in economic and political matters called Anders Chydenius, a minister in the Church of Sweden, active in Finland (which belonged to Sweden up to 1809), and a member of the Swedish parliament, the *Riksdag*, for three periods between 1765–1792. During the 1760s, thus before the publication of *WN*, he fought against mercantilist legislation and for liberal economic and political reforms, in the *Riksdag* and in different publications. Chydenius has rightly been described by an American scholar as a predecessor to Adam Smith (Uhr, 1963).

From the 1780s to the Turn of the Twentieth Century: A Mixed Company of Writers

The influence of *WN* reached the universities in Uppsala and Lund and other Swedish cultural centres in different ways. Fairly soon copies of the book were procured by libraries in Stockholm and, somewhat later, in the university towns.

Kungl. Biblioteket (The Royal Library–National Library of Sweden) has in its collections a copy of a French edition of *WN* printed in Yverdon in 1781. We cannot be sure that the book was the private property of the king (Gustavus III, who was murdered in 1792) but it must have been available in the corridors of power at the time. The Library also owns a copy of an English edition printed in London 1802. Those three volumes need not have been the private property of the king (Gustavus IV Adolphus, who was dethroned through a *coup d'état* in 1809) but they must have been available to him and his advisers.

The University Library of Uppsala also has several editions of *WN*. The oldest copy, printed in London in 1776, was procured before 1796. Another one, printed in London in 1778, became the property of the Library no later than 1830.

The University Library of Lund has some copies of *WN*, most of them procured fairly late. However, a French edition, printed in Paris in 1790–1, was bought in 1816.

Needless to say there were academic teachers who had private copies of *WN*. One of them was Gustaf Abraham Silverstolpe, a reader in political science and bookseller in Uppsala. According to an advertisement in a local newspaper in 1796, the book was for sale in his shop.

In 1800 Johan Holmbergsson, a reader in law in Uppsala, published a Swedish translation of a book by a German professor of philosophy, Georg Sartorius. In English the title of the book would run "Handbook of political economy according to the principles of Adam Smith". The book was not a German/Swedish translation of *WN*, but rather a paraphrase of it. During the academic year of 1800–1, when Holmbergsson was acting *juris, oeconomiae et commerciae* professor, he decided that the Swedish version should be included in the syllabus for law students (see Vallinder, 1987 for detailed references).

In 1810 Holmbergsson was appointed professor of law at the university of Lund. We do not know for sure whether he included Sartorius's book in the syllabus there too.

During the later years of the eighteenth century there were, outside academia proper, different types of writer interested in *WN*. An equal or even a superior, intellectually and socially, of the university professors was Nils von Rosenstein, nobleman, civil servant, philosopher, and permanent secretary of the Swedish Academy established in 1786 by Gustavus III. In 1789, the year of the outbreak of the French Revolution, von Rosenstein gave in the Royal Academy of Sciences a much-observed speech "On Enlightenment", which was printed a few years later. There he remarked: "The best book we have in public finance has been given to us by a *metaphysicus: Smith's enquiry into the Nature and Causes of the wealth of Nations*" (italics in the original text; Segerstedt 1937: 251, (n. 32).

Another important writer, at a somewhat lower intellectual level than von Rosenstein, was David von Schulzenheim, nobleman, physician, country squire, and politician. He was well read in the British economic literature and a great admirer of Adam Smith. His starting-point was Smith's theories of e.g. free trade and of labour value. In the middle of the 1790s von

Schulzenheim published an extensive work on Swedish public finance. In the name index of the work one entry reads: *"Smith,* formerly professor in Glasgow, the best teacher of *oeconomia publica."*

Von Schulzenheim also published shorter articles in the review *Läsning i blandade ämnen* ("Miscellaneous reading"), an organ of the opposition to the absolutist and obscurantist regime of Gustavus IV Adolphus. The editor of the review was count Georg Adlersparre, an army officer and a political writer who in 1809 was to become one of the prime-movers behind the dethronement of the king.

Adlersparre too was an admirer of Adam Smith. In 1799–1800 he published in the *Läsning* his own Swedish translations of several selections from *WN.* In some cases Adlersparre added footnotes, making it easier for the readers to apply Smith's ideas to Swedish conditions (Vallinder, 1987; Brougham, 1871: 162, *Appendix* 1).

Those translations, to the best of my knowledge, were the first ones of Adam Smith in Sweden. They were followed by translations of other parts of *WN,* published in 1800 and 1808. This time the translator was Erik Erland Bodell, an official of the Swedish Customs and thus, if you like, a colleague of Adam Smith (Vallinder, 1987; *see also Appendix* 1).

The *coup d'état* in 1809 put an end to royal absolutism in Sweden. A new constitution, characterized by the division of powers, was enacted and the freedom of the press, which had been in force from 1766 to 1772, was re-established. More liberal political and economic reforms were to follow during the nineteenth century. However, not until around 1920 did Sweden become a full-fledged democracy.

Thus, since 1809 research and debate have been free and unbound in Sweden, at the universities and elsewhere. Before 1889, when the first modern chair in economics was instituted, economic research was carried out by non-specialists, more or less qualified.

Carl Adolph Agardh, professor of botany and practical economy in Lund 1812–35, then a bishop in the Church of Sweden, was a productive polyhistoric scholar. In 1820–1 he attended the lectures of Jean-Baptiste Say in Paris. From around 1830 onwards Agardh published several books and articles in economics, theoretical as well as policy-oriented. In the main Agardh was a supporter of the classical political economists, but by no means an uncritical one. Thus, he raised several objections to Adam Smith's theories as presented in *WN.*

Generally Agardh took a somewhat more positive view of the activities of government than did Smith. In his criticism on this score, Agardh overlooked the fact that *WN* explicitly stressed the importance of political action in the fields of infrastructure and education (Smith, 1976: 723ff). Nevertheless Agardh went further than his Scottish master in this regard. Agardh also criticized Smith's theory of prices. He tried to distinguish between the price of a commodity (supply) and the value of it (demand): "We must derive the value of a commodity from its character of being a stimulant." Further Agardh took a more negative view of the division of labour than Smith (Wadensjö, 1990).

Erik Gustaf Geijer, professor in Uppsala 1817–46, was one of the leading historians in Sweden during the nineteenth century, maybe even the leading one. He was also politically active: at first in the conservative camp but in 1838 he 'defected' to the liberals. For some years he was a member of the *Riksdag*.

Geijer was deeply interested in intellectual, political, and economic developments in Britain, owing in particular to his stay there during 1809–10. During his conservative period he was distinctly critical of central tenets in *WN*. Thus, in a lecture in 1816 Geijer attacked egoism and materialism as exemplified, in his opinion, by Smith. He maintained that Smith's "comfortable" concept of liberty, in combination with economic utilitarianism, had contributed to the outbreak of the French Revolution in 1789. From his religious-romantic standpoint Geijer consequently looked to the Holy Alliance on the European Continent as something grand and promising.

During the second half of the 1830s Geijer changed his mind. He formulated what he called a "personality principle" (*personlighetsprincip*) for economic life. A good government, Geijer declared, is without any doubt a suitable means to promote happiness for the greatest number of people. He added, however, that the best means is to enable everybody to take care of his own affairs. Through the free development of the individual alone was the common good to be promoted. This statement he called "the eternal law of liberty". This is to say that the liberal Geijer had accepted central points in the message of Adam Smith—and that of Jeremy Bentham (Hessler, 1937: 199ff; 1947: 163ff).

During the nineteenth century there were also, after Holmbergsson, a few scholars in the law faculties interested in political economy. The most famous of them was Gustaf Knut Hamilton, who, after an academic career in Uppsala, was professor of administrative law and economics in Lund 1862–99. Especially in economic matters Hamilton was a pronounced liberal with Adam Smith and, even more, Frédéric Bastiat as his idols. In 1858 he published a thesis called *Om den politiska ekonomins utveckling och begrepp* ("On the development and concepts of political economy"). It was a fairly short and uncomplicated book in which Hamilton in his Overview summarized some central aspects of *WN* and other important works in the field.

In the main Hamilton, of course, took a positive attitude towards Smith. The section on *WN* opened like this: "On 5 June 1723 in Kirkcaldy the founder of the presently valid system of political economy was born: Adam Smith." Hamilton especially praised Smith's critical examination of mercantilism (*WN* Book IV). On the other hand he criticized Smith's theory of rent and his distinction between productive and unproductive labourers (*WN* Book I; Hamilton, 1858: 60ff). Three years later Hamilton published another thesis, *Om Penningar och Kredit* ("On money and credit"). Again *WN* was among his main references. However, this book was more technical and contained no explicit assessments of *WN* or Smith (Hamilton, 1861).

To conclude this section it should be noted that a Swedish translation of the chapters on the division of labour in *WN* was published in 1869 (see *Appendix* 1).

The Founding Fathers of Economic Science in Sweden: Davidson, Wicksell, Cassell and Heckscher

Around the turn of the twentieth century chairs of economics were instituted at the Swedish universities in Uppsala (1889), Lund (1901), Gothenburg (1903), and Stockholm (1904). In 1909 another chair was established in Stockholm, this time at the School of Economics.

The first holder of the chair in Uppsala was David Davidson. Nowadays he is primarily remembered for having started in 1899 the scholarly journal *Ekonomisk Tidskrift*, which he edited for almost forty years. (The review is still published, since 1976 under the title *The Scandinavian Journal of Economics*). Davidson's main field was monetary theory. He was further interested in the theory of public finance and capital. Davidson was well read in the classical political economists, particularly David Ricardo. "As a theorist Davidson appears a transitional figure endeavouring to bridge the gap between classical, especially Ricardian, economics and neoclassical economics in the realms of value and distribution theories" (Uhr, 1991: 46).

His doctoral thesis, published in Swedish in 1878 and dealing with the economic laws for capital formation, had *WN* as one of its main sources. On important points Davidson took a critical view of the book: Smith's doctrines were detrimental to economic science since some of his theories, e.g. of labour value and capital value, were wrong and his terminology was ambiguous and unclear (Davidson, 1878: esp. 17ff). In a book two years later on the theories of rent Davidson described and discussed Smith's contribution in that area. Here Davidson was less critical, stating that Smith's contribution was of great importance (Davidson, 1880: 25ff; see also Uhr, 1975: 48ff).

Knut Wicksell, professor at the University of Lund 1901–16, is today internationally the best known of the four "founding fathers". After his retirement he moved to Stockholm, where he had frequent contacts with younger economists, and to some extent also with his professorial colleagues Gustav Cassel (of the University) and Eli F. Heckscher (of the School of Economics). Cassel held his chair between 1904 and 1933. During his later years as a professor he was considered by many experts of the time, not least by himself, the leading economist in the world. Heckscher too was a brilliant scholar. He was a professor of economics from 1909 to 1929, when he accepted a chair of economic history. Thus, Heckscher was not only one of the founding fathers of economics but also the founding father of economic history in Sweden. From 1916 until 1926, when Wicksell died, he, Cassel, and Heckscher created around themselves in Stockholm an outstanding and exciting scholarly environment, unique in the history of Swedish economic science, maybe even in the history of Swedish learning (cf. Henriksson, 1991: 152ff).

As a matter of principle, none of the four founding fathers ever ran for political office. However, in contradistinction to Davidson, who was a conservative, the other three should be described as liberals in a broad, European sense. The most leftist of them was clearly Wicksell, a radical liberal with good personal contacts with the leaders of the Social Democratic Party. In a chronological sense Cassel should be labelled a liberal–conservative and Heckscher a conservative–liberal i.e. during his scholarly life Cassel grew more and more politically conservative whereas Heckscher moved in the opposite direction (see generally Carlson, 1988).

Wicksell is the only one in the quartet whose life and work has been described in a full-length biography (Gårdlund, 1958). Thus, it is possible to follow his scholarly development in detail. Wicksell started his career as a mathematician and natural scientist. Not until the middle of the 1880s, when he was almost 35, did he take up the study of economics. In doing so, he went abroad. In November 1885 he settled down in the reading-room of the British Museum in London to read the classical and neo-classical economists: "While struggling with the mathematics of Jevons and Walras, he also studied Adam Smith's *Wealth of Nations* and the economic works of John Stuart Mill" (Gårdlund, 1958: 105).

Thus, Wicksell came to know his classics very well and became and remained an admirer of Adam Smith. Around 1910 he also assisted his former student and successor as economics professor in Lund, Emil Sommarin, with the translation of *WN*, still the most complete we have in Sweden. In this connection he wrote to a friend in Uppsala, "It is almost unbelievable that we have been denied this masterpiece for 125 years and our economic policy is a result of the omission" (Gårdlund, 1958: 252).

J. A. Schumpeter, in his well-known standard work on the development of economics, wrote of the leading scholars of the period between 1870 and 1914, among them Wicksell, that they "visualized the economic process much as had J. S. Mill or even A. Smith . . . they saw the subject matter of economic analysis, the sum total of things that are to be explained, much as Smith or Mill had seen them . . ." (Schumpeter, 1954: 892). Against this background it is quite natural that Wicksell in his books on economic theory—e.g. about prices, interest rates, and public finance—now and then referred to Adam Smith. A single, fairly early example can be found in his still-famous work in the theory of public finance, *Finanztheoretische Untersuchungen* (published in German in 1896, but never translated into English). There Wicksell, just in passing, referred to Smith on the first page of the main text (Wicksell, 1896: 1; cf. Buchanan, 1967: 114ff).

Recurrent examples are to be found in Wicksell's most widespread book, *Lectures on Political Economy*, which was originally published in Swedish in 1901–6 and later translated into German, English, Spanish, and Italian. Part I, "The Theory of Value", in particular contains frequent references to *WN*. As an example—I did not write a typical example—I would like to quote a comparison which Wicksell made between Smith and Ricardo: "In his [Ricardo's] work, the structure of economic theory appears, for the first time, as a coherent, logical system. But his conclusions thereby frequently assume an abstract and even unreal character. In this respect, he compares unfavourably with Adam Smith" (Wicksell: 1934–5: vol. 1, 23).

After his appointment as professor in Lund, Wicksell soon decided to include *WN* in the syllabus for more advanced undergraduates. Thus, in the 1904 study handbook of the law faculty four classical political economists— Smith, Malthus, Ricardo, and John Stuart Mill—were included in the reading list for honours marks (*Studiehandbok*, 1904: 34; cf. Erik Lindahl in Wicksell, 1958: 25, n. 2). Wicksell also wrote many articles on economic and political matters in different newspapers and reviews. However, as far as I have been able to find out, none of those aricles was primarily devoted to *WN* (cf. Knudtzon, 1975; Jonung, 1992: 40).

Cassel has aptly been described as a popularizer and enigmatic Walrasian (*Magnusson,* 1991). Of the four founding fathers he was the least interested in the classical political economists—and also the least interested in acknowledging his intellectual debt to other scholars (cf. Schumpeter, 1954: 953; n. 1). Like Wicksell, Cassel started his career as a mathematician. Cassel too went abroad to study economics. In the late 1890s he spent a considerable period in Germany, where Gustav Schmoller and Adolf Wagner, of the German

Historical School, were among his teachers. In a letter to a colleague in Stockholm he gave an outline of a work in progress: "The first section will lay the very foundation for my methods in theoretical economics, will show how it is possible to handle this science as a quantitative problem. Here I shall be fairly strongly opposed to all preceding schools, the Smith–Ricardo–Marxian theory of value as well as the opposite theory of marginal utility" (Giöbel-Lilja, 1948: 144). Thus, fairly early in his career as an economist, Cassel repudiated central tenets in *WN*. Further, he very seldom, if ever, mentioned Adam Smith in his scholarly works.

As far as can be judged from the titles, the same seems to be the case with Cassel's numerous newspaper articles, primarily in the *Svenska Dagbladet*, which from about 1910 was the chief organ of the Conservative Party (Carlson and Jonung, 1989, Jonung, 1992: 40). In his voluminous memoirs (about 900 pages) entitled *I förnuftets tjänst* ("In the service of reason"), Cassel mentioned Smith only once, in a quotation from an article in a German newspaper on the occasion of Cassel's sixtieth birthday. The article stated, *inter alia*, that Cassel would in the future be mentioned in the same breath as Smith and Ricardo (Cassel, 1940–1: vol. 2, 136).

Heckscher may be described, scientifically and politically, as the most Smithian of the four founding fathers. In the field of theoretical economics Heckscher is world famous, especially outside Sweden, for a 1919 article in Swedish in the *Ekonomisk Tidskrift*, published in English thirty years later as "The effect of foreign trade on the distribution of income". The article laid the first cornerstone of what is commonly known as the Heckscher–Ohlin theory of international trade. The second cornerstone was laid by Bertil Ohlin in 1924 (Heckscher, 1991). However, in this case Heckscher's starting-point was Ricardo, not Adam Smith.

Among Swedish scholars—and also many foreign ones—Heckscher is nowadays primarily remembered for his excellent achievements in the field of economic history. Here Smith and *WN* were of great importance to Heckscher, in two ways. First, as a historian also Heckscher often stressed the usefulness of theory in scholarship. Here *WN* was his starting-point. In an essay on the origin of economic-historical research Heckscher strongly pointed to his Scottish master, writing that Smith, among the founders of economic science, was the one who more than the others entertained an interest in economic phenomena in earlier times: "What Adam Smith wanted to achieve above all through his great book was two different things, neither of which, *per se*, could be easily combined with a historical perspective—namely, partly to present a general, coherent doctrine, and partly to pave the way for a new economic policy through striking down the traditional order" (Heckscher, 1936: 10).

Second, in his empirical studies Heckscher liked to walk in the footsteps of Smith. This is especially striking in his book on Smith's favourite enemy, *Mercantilism*. In that book references to *WN* abound. *Mercantilism* is an internationally renowned standard work, published, *inter alia*, in two English editions. In the second edition Heckscher had the exquisitive pleasure of drawing the line, as he saw it, from mercantilism to his own favourite enemies, socialism and Keynesianism (Heckscher, 1955: vol. 2, 337 ff).

Heckscher's third field was contemporary economic and political questions. He was also very active here, and very much from a Smithian starting-point. His main forum was the *Dagens Nyheter*, during his time the chief organ of the Liberal Party (cf. *Eli F. Heckschers bibliografi*, 1950; Jonung, 1992; 40). Heckscher also published several policy-oriented pamphlets and books. The most important of these is *Gammal och ny ekonomisk liberalism* ("Old and new economic liberalism"). This small book (about 100 pages) can be described as Heckscher's economic-political credo. After a short definition of economic liberalism Heckscher rapidly went on to a quotation from *WN*, the famous passage in Book IV about an invisible hand (Smith, 1976: vol. 1, 456). Then Heckscher took off for an elegant overview of the merits of economic freedom, in the spirit of Adam Smith (Heckscher, 1921).

Outside the departments of economics and economic history there have been, during the last hundred years, a few university professors interested in *WN*. One example is Harald Hjärne, professor at the university of Uppsala, who was around the turn of the twentieth century the leading Swedish historian. For some periods he was a member of the *Riksdag*, at first as a liberal, then as a conservative. He was also the admired teacher of Heckscher, who started his career as a historian.

Hjärne was an immensely learned scholar with a wide range of interests. Two of his favourite topics were the British cabinet system and British imperialism. Needless to say, he knew *WN*; and he may be described as an admirer of Adam Smith (Heckscher, 1936: 174). However, to my knowledge, Hjärne hardly ever expanded on *WN*. The only item I have found in his works on this score is a newspaper article from 1903 where, in passing, he described British political economy as based on the doctrine of Adam Smith, itself an offspring of the Empire and its *optimistic reliance* (H. Hjärne 1940 p. 145).

In the 1930s two professors of philosophy, both in Lund, took up aspects of *WN*. In a short essay entitled "Adam Smith's fiction" Hans Larsson discussed the so-called Adam Smith problem. This problem refers to the alleged discrepancy between the basic perspectives expounded in *The Theory of Moral Sentiments* and *WN*, namely, with a clear oversimplification, sympathy and egoism respectively. Referring to Thomas Buckle, author of *History of Civilization in England*, and John Stuart Mill, Larsson contended that the problem is one of instructive refinement of two interrelated factors. Such a refinement has always been used as a methodological device, Larsson remarked; and this was what he meant by Smith's fiction (Larsson, 1935: 86ff).

At about the same time Gunnar Aspelin published an essay on the best-known and most debated theme in *WN*, the invisible hand. Like Larsson, Aspelin stressed the similarities between Smith's two most important books. Further he pointed to the affinity between Adam Smith's economic liberalism and Edmund Burke's conservatism. On the other hand, Aspelin also maintained that the doctrine about the invisible hand contains an element which can be developed into a radically democratic line of thought. The *polemics* of Adam Smith aim at the absolute state which seeks to direct the actions of its subjects in detail. His ideal, instead, is a democratic state where every citizen participates and the best institutions emerge as a result of free competition between different opinions, Aspelin concluded (Aspelin, 1933).

Among amateur writers of our own century I would like to mention just one, E. H. Thörnberg, in all conceivable respects a self-made man. Thörnberg was a self-taught journalist, a lecturer to temperance societies and other organizations, the author of books on political parties and other popular movements, and an amateur sociologist who in 1939 was awarded an honorary PhD degree at the University of Uppsala. Thörnberg, himself a radical liberal, was most interested in political ideologies, maybe especially liberalism, including, of course, that of Adam Smith, and he wrote about such themes in his books and articles.

In 1923, to celebrate Smith's 200th birthday, Thörnberg published an extensive, erudite newspaper article. Thörnberg started by pointing to the two main forces which shaped modern society, the steam engine and liberalism. Then he expanded on the crucial year of 1776, when several highly important documents were published: the Declaration of Independence, Jeremy Bentham's *Fragment on Government* and, of course, *WN*. At the end of the article Thörnberg summarized Adam Smith's importance thus:

Adam Smith spoke in the right way, in the right place, in the right time . . . He had an excellent knowledge of the existing circumstances. Intuitively he understood quite a lot of what was to come. And he was able to write about what he knew and saw, able, page after page, to reach his audience, generation after generation, and become part of their consciousness. (Thörnberg 1923)

To conclude this section it should, once more, be noted that the most complete translation of *WN* which we have was published in 1909–11 (*see Appendix* 1).

The Stockholm School of the 1930s: Ohlin, Myrdal, Lundberg *et al.*

The term "the Stockholm School" was coined in *The Economy Journal* in 1937 by Bertil Ohlin, who was the leading member of the "school". The title of his article was "Some notes on the Stockholm theory of savings and investment". According to Ohlin, the intellectual roots of the school were to be found in the writings of Knut Wicksell, especially *Geldzins und Güterpreise*, published in German in 1898 (English version 1936). Of more recent works Ohlin first mentioned one book by Gunnar Myrdal and one by Erik Lindahl, both published in Swedish. A revised version of Lindahl's book was later translated into English (*Lindahl*, 1939).

These writings were the theoretical background for the work done by four economists engaged by the ministerial commission on unemployment to write monographs on different aspects of anti-unemployment policy, Ohlin continued. Those four economists were Dag Hammarskjöld, Alf Johansson, Myrdal, and Ohlin himself:

The high degree of unanimity between the writers mentioned, and the fact that they were all influenced by the Wicksell–Myrdal–Lindahl writings and by Cassel with regard to the anti-classical approach to price and distribution theory, make it justifiable to talk about a Stockholm school of thought. (The only non-resident in Stockholm is Lindahl, who worked in Stockholm for many years.) (Ohlin, 1937: 57)

To those scholars Ohlin added one more: Erik Lundberg, who was just about to publish his doctoral thesis on the theory of economic expansion. Thus, to sum up, the Stockholm School included Ohlin, Myrdal, Lindahl, Hammarskjöld, Johansson, and Lundberg.

In some respects the members of the Stockholm School differed from their teachers, the founding fathers. Several of the members were very active in party politics. Ohlin was for more than thirty years a member of the *Riksdag* and for more than twenty years the leader of the Liberal Party. For a short period, 1944–45, he was also Minister of Commerce in the wartime National Coalition Government. Myrdal was for two different periods a member of the *Riksdag* for the Social Democratic Party. In 1945, succeeding Ohlin, he was appointed Minister of Commerce, retiring from that post in 1947. Hammarskjöld, although never an MP, was, before his election as Secretary-General of the United Nations in 1953, for two years a member of the Social Democratic Government. Lindahl,

Johansson, and Lundberg never sought political office. However, Johansson was a noted member of the Social Democratic party and Lundberg an outspoken liberal. Lindhal avoided making clear policy-oriented statements but should be described as a radical liberal or a cautious social democrat. In the following I shall concentrate on Ohlin, Myrdal, and Lundberg.

Bertil Ohlin at first studied in Lund, where Wicksell and Emil Sommarin, the translator of *WN*, were his teachers of economics. Then Ohlin moved up to the Stockholm School of Economics to attend Eli Heckscher's lectures and seminars. He also studied abroad, particularly at Harvard University, where, among other things, he took a course from Alleyn Young in the history of economic doctrines. In 1924, with Heckscher and Cassel among his teachers, Ohlin presented his doctoral thesis at the University of Stockholm, *Handelns teori* ("The theory of trade"). One year later, at the age of 26, Ohlin was appointed professor at the University of Copenhagen. There he remained until 1929, when he succeeded Heckscher as professor of economics at the Stockholm School of Economics.

Ohlin's main scholarly field was the theory of international trade. Through his doctoral thesis he laid the second cornerstone of the Heckscher–Ohlin theory in the area (see above). Here Ohlin's starting-point, just as Heckscher's five years earlier, was David Ricardo, not Adam Smith. In 1933, following up his thesis, Ohlin published the first edition of his famous work *Interregional and International Trade*. The book revolutionized the theory of trade by freeing it from the bonds of classical labour theory and marrying it to general price theory. It is still an internationally acknowledged standard work and it was Ohlin's basic contribution when, in 1977, he shared the Nobel Prize in economics with James Meade (Ohlin, 1978).

In the book Ohlin mentioned Adam Smith only once, and in passing at that, quoting Smith's statement "Man is of all sorts of luggage the most difficult to be transported" (Ohlin, 1967: 208; cf. Smith, 1976: 93). Likewise, in his other writings in theoretical economics Ohlin very seldom, if ever, mentioned Smith.

As a politician Ohlin wrote several pamphlets and books. He also gave numerous speeches, in the *Riksdag* and at public meetings, and he published about 2,000 newspaper articles, primarily in the *Stockholms–Tidningen*, one of the largest liberal dailies (Jonung, 1992: 40). Even on those occasions, as far as I have been able to find out, he very seldom referred to *WN* or Smith.

Let me give an example. In 1936, as the chairman of the Liberal Youth Organization in Sweden, Ohlin published his most important policy-oriented book, which for decades to come set the tone for the ideological development of the Liberal Party, *Fri eller dirigerad ekonomi* ("Free or centrally planned economy"). In the introduction he started by stating his basic economic and political goals, which included an expanded standard of living, especially for poor people, and safeguarding the rights of the citizen, particularly the freedom of speech. In the book Ohlin devoted one chapter to a critique of *laissez-faire* liberalism. He did not equate this liberal variant with the doctrine of Adam Smith, and rightly so (cf. e.g. O'Brien, 1979). Ohlin only mentioned Smith, just in passing, quoting his famous expression about the invisible hand, without any further comments (Ohlin, 1936: 40).

The fact that the liberal Ohlin very seldom referred to Smith, and for that matter to other liberal thinkers, can be explained in different ways. Maybe he was not particularly interested in the history of economic doctrines. Maybe he found Smith and other classical economists irrelevant for his times. Maybe he thought that, without outside help from them, he was fully capable of refuting the arguments of his political opponents; if so, his opinion was not unfounded.

Gunnar Myrdal was the favourite student of Gustav Cassel and in 1933 he succeeded his master as professor of economics at the University of Stockholm. In 1960 he accepted the chair of international economics there. In 1974 he shared the Nobel Prize in economics with Friedrich A. Hayek (Myrdal, 1975).

As a theoretical economist Myrdal started with contributions to price theory and monetary theory, e.g. *Monetary Equilibrium* (1939). There he did not mention Adam Smith or *WN*. From the beginning Myrdal also entertained a keen interest in the history of economic doctrines. In 1929 he published a book called *Vetenskap och politik i nationalekonomin*, issued in English in 1953 as *The Political Element in the Development of Economic Theory*. In that development, according to Myrdal, there have been three main foci:

the idea of Value; the idea of Freedom; and the idea of Social Economy or collective housekeeping (*Volkswirtschaft*). These three notions, variously combined, have given economic doctrines their political content. Naturally, the three main normative ideas cannot be kept separate and distinct; as a matter of fact they are closely related logically. Nevertheless, it will be found that this book deals with each of them in turn (Myrdal, 1953: p. xi).

Myrdal's basic tenet in *The Political Element* was that, in the works of the classical political economists, there are important strains of metaphysical ideas. Thus, Myrdal set out to unveil elements of natural-law reasoning in his predecessors of the eighteenth and nineteenth centuries. He found and documented very many examples in the classical texts, maybe even in places where there were none. Needless to say, references to Adam Smith abound in the book. Already in the early 1930s, when writing about contemporary social

problems in Sweden, Myrdal as an economist had developed in an institution-
alist and thus, if you like, a Smithian direction. This tendency became even
more marked when from 1938, commissioned by the Carnegie Corporation of
New York, he directed a study of racial problems in the United States. The
main result was the voluminous book (almost 1500 pages) *An American
Dilemma. The Negro Problem and Modern Democracy* (1944).

In that impressive work Myrdal applied a broad social-scientific, mainly
sociological approach. *WN* was mentioned only once and just in passing,
when Myrdal touched upon a book by William Graham Sumner. There Myrdal
referred to Smith's well-known dictum that trade barriers, though, of course,
irrational and cumbersome, will, in the broad overview, not amount to much,
as the smugglers will pierce them, acting as the agents of "the natural laws".
Thus, the "invisible hand" will inevitably guide human activity (Myrdal, 1944:
1055).

After giving up his political career in 1947, Myrdal was appointed Executive
Secretary of the United Nations Economic Commission for Europe. Ten years
later he left this post to direct a study of economic trends and policies in South
Asia for the Twentieth Century Fund. The main result was *Asian Drama. An
Inquiry into the Poverty of Nations* (three volumes, 1968). The subtitle is, of
course, a conscious—and self-conscious—allusion to *WN*. There is also a
certain similarity in the structure and general character of the two books.
Just as *WN*, *Asian Drama* is a work of economics, social history, and political
science—and at the same time a collection of policy recommendations. In the
preface Myrdal explicitly stressed Smith's influence on his book:

It is not altogether a pretentious metaphor when I describe my endeavor to apply an
institutional approach in this study as an attempt to analyze the development problems
of South Asia in the manner that Adam Smith studied England's development problems two hundred years ago. Smith, of course, never dealt with economic problems
as purely "economic", and the same can be said in general of the whole classical
school, including toward the end Karl Marx . . .

But Adam Smith's England contained only about 7 million people, while the present
study concerns a fourth of mankind; and the fact that there is a vast amount of
literature relating to various aspects of the South Asian situation proved to be a mixed
blessing (Myrdal, 1968: vol. I, p. x).

Asian Drama also contains a few direct references to *WN*. Thus, Myrdal points
out that Smith and the other classical political economists laid great stress on
such non-economic factors as rationality, enterprise, efficiency, mobility, skills,
education, and honest government, as preconditions of production (vol. III,
1905).

Thus, as a scholar Myrdal liked to walk in the footsteps of Adam Smith. However, in important respects his policy recommendations differed from those of his eighteenth-century predecessor, not only because Myrdal wrote 200 years after Smith but also because he was a socialist with clear sympathies for central planning (see e.g. Myrdal, 1960).

In 1937, after completing his doctoral thesis (mentioned earlier), Erik Lundberg entered the *Konjunkturinstitutet* (the National Institute of Economic Research, a government agency). There he remained until 1955, from 1946 as the director of the Institute. From 1946 he was also professor of economics in Stockholm, first at the University, later at the School of Economics. From 1968 to 1971 he was president of the International Economic Association.

In his earlier years Lundberg was a staunch Keynesian interventionist. He remained a Keynesian but, following at close distance the post-war economic policy of the Social Democratic Government, he developed in a more classical economic liberal direction. This change of mind became strikingly evident when, in 1953, Lundberg published a book called *Konjunkturer och ekonomisk politik* ("Business cycles and economic policy"). The book contained an incisive critical examination of the strongly interventionist economic policy of the government and caused a prolonged and heated debate among economists and politicians in Sweden. In the last chapter Lundberg presented his own views on the goals and means of economic policy, thus, as he himself remarked in the introduction, leaving the province of science. The book ended with a declaration which, as Lundberg explicitly stated, had a close relation to Adam Smith's view of man and society. These are some of the central sentences in that declaration:

The goal must be to find forms for our economic system which do not make us dependent on having just a few excellent persons, politicians, administrators and economic experts at the top and trust what they might possibly achieve at their best and under the best possible circumstances. It is a proof of greater wisdom and better understanding of human nature on the model of Adam Smith if, on the contrary, we try to find forms for our public life which reduce the possibilities for fallible people to cause trouble. The system should, in other words, have the characteristic that incompetent politicians, administrators, and economists, who will always exist, will have as small a chance as possible to do harm . . . . The decentralized market economy should also have the character of not giving much space for monopolistic power and administrative arbitrariness (Lundberg, 1953: 509f).

To that declaration Lundberg added a reference in a footnote to Smith's famous remark about the invisible hand (Smith, 1976: 456). Lundberg's declaration can reasonably be described as the most eleoquent Smithian credo ever formulated by a Swedish economist.

Contemporary Economists and Economic Historians in Sweden

During the post-war period the Stockholm school of Swedish economists has, by and large, faded away. It has not been succeeded by any new, specifically Swedish school. On the contrary, economic science in Sweden, as in other countries, has rather become more and more internationalized, i.e. Americanized (see e.g. Sandelin, 1991; L. Engwall 1992). During the most recent decades that Americanization, among other things, has implied a rising interest in the classical political economists from Adam Smith onwards. Thus, Smithian impulses have been brought about by three Nobel Laureates of the University of Chicago, F. A. Hayek, Milton Friedman, and Georg Stigler.

Of the older generation of contemporary Swedish economists I shall present three, Sven Rydenfelt, Erik Dahmén, and Hugo Hegeland, all of them of a liberal or liberal-conservative persuasion.

In 1976 Sven Rydenfelt, than a retiring associate professor at the University of Lund, published a book called *Det sjuka 70-talet. Om massarbetslöshetens återkomst och sysselsättningens fjärde dimension* ("The sick seventies. On the return of mass unemployment and the fourth dimension of employment"). The book bears the subtitle *Adam Smith Redivivus*. During the spring term of 1976 the author used the book as the basis for a post-graduate course at the Department of Economics in Lund.

In the book Rydenfelt first portrayed Smith as a staunchly oppositional political economist who started a general attack on government economic oppression, bureaucratic planning, corporate monopolies, and mercantilist obstacles to trade. Following Smith, Rydenfelt stressed that this mercantilist society favoured manufacturers and producers at the expense of workers and consumers.

Rydenfelt then drew a parallel between British society of the 1770s and "the new mercantilism" of the 1970s, e.g. in Britain and Sweden. Two hundred years ago Adam Smith defended the underdogs of his time, the workers, against the combined force of the politicians and the manufacturers. In our society, ruled by a combination of socialist parties and labour unions, Smith, if still alive, would have defended the present underdogs, the industrialists, Rydenfelt maintained. Again following Smith, Rydenfelt stressed that such combinations harm not only the oppressed group but also the oppressors themselves (Rydenfelt, 1976, esp. 19 ff).

In the book Rydenfelt also made some brief comparisons betwen liberal and socialist economic systems. He returned to that theme some years later in a new book with the expressive title *A Pattern for Failure Socialist Economics in Crisis*. Also here, when comparing agriculture in the Soviet Union, the United States, and Sweden, Rydenfelt quoted *WN*, to wit the sayings that a small proprietor is generally of all improvers the most industrious, the most intelligent, and the most successful and that the work done by slaves is in the end the dearest of any (Rydenfelt, 1983, 34, cf. Smith, 1976, 98 ff).

Erik Dahmén was professor of economics and economic and social history at the Stockholm School of Economics 1958–85. He was also for the thirty years up to 1981 an economic adviser to one of the leading Swedish commercial banks. One of his research areas is the role of industrialists and entrepreneurship. In an article in a *Festschrift* for a leading Swedish banker, Marcus Wallenberg, Dahmén briefly touched upon *WN*. He maintained that Adam Smith had a great deal to say about the role of merchants in a market economy. On the other hand, Dahmén continued, there is in *WN* very little about the creative role and its importance for the transformation of commercial and industrial life and of society as a whole (Dahmén 1974).

In 1994 a new Swedish translation of parts of *WN* was published. The volume is entitled *Den osynliga handen. Adam Smith i urval* ("The invisible hand. Selections from Adam Smith"); it also contains a section from *The Theory of Moral Sentiments* (*see Appendix* 1). Dahmén provided an introduction to the volume. He opened by saying that no other book has had such an importance for economic theory and practice during such a long time as *WN*. It could not be said, Dahmén went on, that the book was pathbreaking from a theoretical point of view. In this respect most of the statements had been made earlier.

However, first, no one had earlier presented such a broad perspective and well-integrated theoretical basis. Second, no one had earlier provided so many concrete examples from real life—facts that many knew but did not understand the economic meaning of. Third, the pedagogy of the book was excellent, with pertinent metaphors and also aphorisms. Thus, even somewhat circumstantial parts were made stimulating, Dahmén stressed. Taken together these characteristics made the critical analysis of the then-prevailing mercantilism easy to understand. The book disclosed the defects of a system which was not socialist in the sense of state ownership but which was characterized by isolationist nationalism and detailed state-run planning which in turn was detrimental to economic development during the eighteenth century, otherwise a promising period. Proceeding to our own century Dahmén remarked that we need not attach the label "the new mercantilism" to the decades after 1945 to see that we have more to learn from *WN* than our forefathers had in the late nineteenth century. Thus the book is still of topical interest (Dahmén, 1994).

Hugo Hegeland has been active at different Swedish universities, e.g. as professor of economics at the University of Umeå in the 1960s. From 1982 until 1994 he was a member of the *Riksdag* for the Conservative Party. In his doctoral thesis *The Quantity Theory of Money*, presented at the University of Gothenburg in 1951, Hegeland started with some chapters about the historical development of that theory. In discussing the views of the classical political economists he noted that Adam Smith, in *WN* and elsewhere, aired criticism of the theory. However, "Fundamentally Adam Smith agrees with the essence of the quantity theory: the main function of money is to circulate consumable goods" (Hegeland, 1951, 49).

Concerning Smith, Ricardo, and John Stuart Mill, Hegeland pointed out that the classics' discussion of the quantity theory is very indicative of the ambiguity of its real meaning. Smith views the theory as the theory of the determination of the value of money (*i.e.* coins); hence he discards it since his cost-of-production theory is thought of as having general applicability:

For he cannot connive at the assumption of a sudden increase (or decrease) in the quantity of money; instead, he immediately inquires as to the cause of this sudden change. And for him this change must be the effect of a change (absolute or relative) in the cost of production of money. One might perhaps say that Adam Smith thinks in economic terms and relations only; therefore the purely mathematical formulation of the quantity theory appears as an unmeaning statement to him (Hegeland, 1951: 72).

In other, more popular books, e.g. *Från knapphet till överflöd* ("From scarcity to abundance", 1967), Hegeland has returned to Adam Smith and *WN*. Hegeland has also published political pamphlets where he has used quotations from Smith, among others, to beat his political opponents.

In going over to the younger generations of economists and economic historians now active at Swedish universities, I shall, besides traditional printed matter, use data from an informal inquiry which I have made among nearly twenty of them (including three or four retired professors). A few of those scholars have published books or articles where Adam Smith and *WN* have been taken up fairly extensively.

Bo Gustafsson has been professor of economic history at the University of Uppsala since 1977. For a brief period around 1970 he was the leader of a small left communist splinter party. In the 1970s he published an elementary text-book about the development of economic science; part 1 runs from Aristotle to Adam Smith. In that book the chapter on Smith comprises about fifty pages. It consists of a clear, thorough, and objective survey of *WN*, without any political overtones.

Bo Sandelin is an associate professor of economics at the University of Gothenburg. In the early 1980s he published an essay in Swedish on Adam Smith's political economy and the economic science of our time. Sandelin opened with a personal confession, stating that he had only recently read the historical foundation of economics, *WN*. Thus he had earlier more or less accepted the traditional, vulgar stereotypes about the message of Adam Smith and other classical economists, incisively criticized by Lionel Robbins in a well-known standard work (Robbins 1952). Now, after his conversion, Sandelin gave a balanced presentation of that message and its importance for modern economics. Quoting extensively from *WN*, he stressed that Smith was by no means a supporter of *laissez-faire* policies in the strict sense and that, in class matters, Smith's sympathies were with the lower orders.

Sandelin also commented upon the general approach and style of *WN*. Modern economists primarily write for their colleagues whereas Smith wrote for a broader audience, not least the politicians. He avoided mathematization of economic reasoning, although tendencies in that direction were noticeable already in his time. Sandelin further stressed that Smith was an economic historian just as much as an economist. Quoting examples from the current Swedish debate on labour market policy Sandelin sarcastically remarked that "even respected economists *can* be bad social scientists". Smith was certainly not included in that category of course (Sandelin, 1981, 72).

Johan Lönnroth is an associate professor of economics at the Univesity of Gothenburg, presently (1994) on leave as a member of the *Riksdag* for the Left Party (formerly the Left Party of Communists); he is also vice-chairman of the party organization. In his writings he has shown a clear interest in the history of economic doctrines, thereby at times touching upon those of Adam Smith (cf. the Introduction above). In political debates Lönnroth now and then quotes Smith in order to beat his conservative opponents. Unavoidably most profes-sors of economics and economic history sometimes touch upon Adam Smith and *WN* during their lectures and seminars. Some of them do so more than others; let me give three examples.

In the Department of Economic History at the University of Lund, Associ-ate Professor Carl-Axel Olsson regularly teaches the history of economic doctrines. In such courses, needless to say, *WN* constitutes an important feature. For post-graduate students in the department parts of the book are included in the list of assigned readings.

Also outside historically oriented instruction, parts of *WN* may, of course, come up. Lars Söderström, who is a professor of economics at the University of Gothenburg and an expert in wage theory, often uses Adam Smith as his starting-point in class. More specifically, that usually means the famous tenth chapter in Book I of *WN* (Smith 1976, 116ff). Also when taking up welfare theory and institutional economics Söderström regularly refers to Smith.

Labour market theory and the history of economic doctrines are the two main areas of interest of Eskil Wadensjö, professor of labour market policy in the Institute for Social Research at the University of Stockholm. In the second area he has written about Carl Adolph Agardh's relationship, among other things, to Adam Smith (cf. the section about the period 1780–1900 above). When teaching labour market theory Wadensjö, like Söderström, often takes *WN* Book I Ch. X as his starting-point.

As an addendum I would like to mention that in the late 1980s, Hertha Hanson, associate professor of the history of ideas and sciences at the University of Lund, published an article in Swedish about "Visible and invisible in Adam Smith's *Wealth of Nations*". Her starting-point was the relationship between education and industrial society. Like Bo Sandelin, Hanson, to begin with, rejected the traditional, vulgar stereotypes about Adam Smith. The image of society presented in *WN* is full of economic, social, and cultural conflicts. In that society the state cannot restrict itself to a watchman role. On the contrary, the sovereign, according to Smith, also has positive duties to attend to, Hanson pointed out, referring to clear statements in *WN* (Smith, 1976, 687ff). Those duties include promoting public education for the lower orders: "The cure for the 'degeneracy' of the workers is for a long time to come, for Smith and for many others, education" (Hanson, 1988, 61).

The Early 1990s: A New Start for *WN* in Sweden?

During the first half of the 1990s there were in Sweden some signs of a mounting interest in Adam Smith. The most important one was the publication in 1994 of the earlier-mentioned book *Den osynliga handen*. This volume contains the second-most extensive translation of *WN* ever published in Sweden (cf. *Appendix* 1). As said earlier it starts with an introduction by Erik Dahmén.

Two more significant facts can be noted. In 1993 a political scientist in Uppsala, Nils Karlson, published a doctoral thesis called *The State of State*. That somewhat enigmatic title was made clear through the subtitle, *An Inquiry*

Concerning the Role of Invisible Hands in Politics and Civil Society. The invisible hand, according to Karlson, "is a metaphor for dynamic social processes which explain aggregate and ordered social patterns and outcomes as specific kinds of unintended consequences of human action". Following Robert Nozick, Karlson calls "the description and specification of a process that aggregates separate and incremental actions into a social macro-outcome an *invisible hand explanation*" (Karlson, 1993, 16, italics in the original; cf. *Nozick*, 1774, 18).

Karlson's basic aim is to investigate the role of invisible hands in politics and civil society:

How do invisible hands emerge? How do they work? How are they maintained? I shall also explore how the invisible hands in civil society are affected by political interventions. Furthermore, how do the repercussions of political intervention in civil society affect politics itself? Can they be used to explain the invisible hands within the state? And are there any specific invisible hands within the political process? (Karlson, 1993: 13).

Quite obviously Karlson has been strongly influenced by the terminology and, more important, the way of thinking of Adam Smith; references to *WN* are frequent in the thesis. However, inspiration has also come from the works of, among others, F. A. Hayek and James Buchanan.

There are also, although more in passing, some references to *WN* in another doctoral thesis in political science presented in Uppsala in 1993, by Emil Uddhammar. His book describes the more or less unopposed emergence of the big state in Sweden, a theme not unlike that of Nils Karlson. Uddhammar refers briefly to *WN* when discussing the role of the state, the information problem in a modern economy, and also the tax system (Uddhammar, 1993: 90ff, 101f).

Those two theses, especially Karlson's, can perhaps be seen as indicators of the closer contacts in recent years, in Sweden as elsewhere, between the political and economic sciences. Thus Karlson and Uddhammar contribute to bringing Adam Smith back into the area of Swedish political science (cf. the discussion of Gustaf Abraham Silverstolpe in the section about the period 1780–1900 above).

Conclusion

A recent biography of the author of *WN* opens like this:

Adam Smith is a past master for all manner of persons, for Conservatives and for Marxists, for liberals and for antiradicals, for economists, philosophers, and sociologists. Different groups admire different things in his work and one may sometimes doubt whether all the different things can be held together consistently. Still, each of them is persuasive enough to have made its mark as a truth of some profundity.' (Raphael, 1985: 1).

As can be learned from the foregoing pages, this statement is certainly also applicable in Sweden. There scholars and other writers, during many periods, of different persuasions and from several university departments have studied and written about *WN*, regularly though of course not exclusively with approbation.

H. T. Buckle once wrote about *WN* that "looking at its ultimate results, [it] is probably the most important book that has ever been written" (Buckle, 1865: vol. 1, 197). However, as all social scientists know, it is very difficult to gauge and compare the influence of different factors in political and economic life. Speaking of the influence of books and ideas, that task is extremely difficult. Nevertheless it could safely be said that in Sweden, as in many other European countries, Adam Smith's *WN* has for more than 200 years been a very influential book, directly and, more importantly, indirectly, e.g. through other writers.

Most of the actors described in this article have been academic teachers, not professional politicians, even if some of them have tried to combine the two roles. However, through their books and articles the university professors must have influenced not only their academic colleagues but also the politicians and the general public. Thus, the writings about *WN* mentioned here must, through the years, have had a clear influence on Swedish economic and political life.

References

Aspelin, G. (1933), "Den osynliga handen. Ett tankemotiv i Adam Smiths socialfilosofi", *Vetenskaps-societeten i Lund Årsbok* (Yearbook of the New Society of Letters at Lund), pp. 31–49.

Brougham, H. (1871), *The Life and Times of Henry Lord Brougham*, 3 vols., Edinburgh and London; Blackwood and Sons.

Buchanan, J. M. (1967), *Public Finance in Democratic Process. Fiscal Institutions and Individual Choice*, Chapel Hill: Univ. of North Carolina Press.

—— (1987), "The Constitution of Economic Policy", *Les Prix Nobel 1986*, Stockholm: Almqvist & Wiksell.

Buckle, H. T. (1865), *History of Civilization in England*, 5 vols., Leipzig: Brockhans.

Carlson, B. (1988), *Staten som monster, Gustav Cassels och Eli F. Heckschers syn på statens roll och tillväxt* (With a summary in English), Lund: Studentlitteratur.

Carlson, B. and Jonung, L. (1989), *Gustav Cassels artiklar i Svenska Dagbladet*, Lund: Ekonomisk-historiska institutionen.

CASSEL, G. (1940–1), *I förnuftets tjänst. En ekonomisk självbiografi*, 2 vols. Stockholm: Natur och Kultur.

DAHMÉN, E. (1974), "Nationalekonomerna och företagarverksamheten—en teorihistorisk skiss", *Från skilda fält. Uppsatser tillägnade Marcus Wallenberg*, Stockholm: Norstedts.

—— (1994), "Introduktion", A. Smith, *Den osynliga handen. Adam Smith i urval*, Stockholm: Ratio, pp. 9–12.

DAVIDSON, D. (1978), *Bidrag till läran om de ekonomiska lagarna för kapitalbildningen*. Uppsala: Lundequistska Bokhandeln.

—— (1880), *Bidrag till jordränteteorins historia*, Uppsala: Esaias Edquists Boktryckeri.

ENGWALL, L. (ed.) (1992) *Economics in Sweden. An Evaluation of Swedish Research in Economics*. London and New York: Routledge.

GÅRDLUND, T. (1958), *The Life of Knut Wicksell*, Stockholm: Almquist & Wiksell.

GIÖBEL-LILJA, I. (1948), *Gustav Cassel. En livsskildring*, Stockholm: Natur & Kultur.

GOLDSMITH, O. (1885), *The Works*, ed. by J. W. M. Gibbs, vol. 2; London: George Bell and Sons.

HAMILTON, G. K. (1858), *Om den politiska ekonomins utveckling och begrepp*, Uppsala: C. A. Leffler.

—— (1861), *Om Penningar och Kredit*, Uppsala: Edquist & Co.

HANSON, H. (1988), "Synligt och osynligt i Adam Smiths *Wealth of Nations*", *Insikt och handling, Hans Larsson Samfundets årsbok*, 16: 39–66.

HECKSCHER, E. F. (1921), *Gammal och ny ekonomisk liberalism*, Stockholm: Norstedts.

—— (1936), *Ekonomisk-historiska studier*, Stockholm: Bonniers.

—— (1955) *Mercantilism*, rev. edn., 2 vols., London: Allen & Unwin.

—— (1991), *Heckscher–Ohlin Trade Theory.* trans., ed., and introduced by Harry Flam and M. June Flanders, Cambridge, Mass.: MIT Press.

Eli F. Heckschers bibliografi 1897–1949 (1950), Stockholm: Ekonomisk-historiska institutet.

HEGELAND, H. (1951), *The Quantity Theory of Money. A Critical Study of its Historical Development and Interpretation and a Restatement*, Göteborg: Elanders Boktryckeri.

—— (1967), *Från knapphet till överflöd. En studie över knapphetsbegreppet i nationalekonomin*, Stockholm: Natur och Kultur.

HENRIKSSON, R. G. H. (1991), "Eli F. Heckscher: The Economic Historian as Economist", in B. Sandelin (ed.), *The History of Swedish Economic Thought*. London: and New York: Routledge, pp. 141–167.

HESSLER, C. A. (1937), *Geijer som politiker. Hans utveckling fram till 1830*. Stockholm: Gebers.

—— (1947), *Geijer som politiker II. Hans senare utveckling*. Stockholm: Gebers.

HJÄRNE, H. (1940), *Engelsk imperialism och parlamentarism*, Stockholm: Bonniers.

JONUNG, L. (ed.) (1991), *The Stockholm School of Economics Revisited*. Cambridge: Cambridge Univ. Press.

—— (ed.), (1992), *Swedish Economic Thought, Explorations and Advances*, London and New York: Routledge.

KARLSON, N. (1993), *The State of State. An Inquiry Concerning the Role of Invisible Hands in Politics and Civil Society*. Uppsala: Almqvist & Wiksell International.

KNUDTZON, E. J. (1976), *Knut Wicksells tryckta skrifter 1868–1950*. Lund: Gleerups.

LARSSON, H. (1935) *Minimum*, Stockholm: Bonniers.

LIEDMAN, S.-E. (1989), "Utilitarianism and the Economy", in T. Frångsmyr (ed.), *Science in Sweden. The Royal Swedish Academy of Sciences 1739–1989*. Canton M. f. Watson Publishing International, pp. 23–44.

LUNDBERG, E. (1953), *Konjunkturer och ekonomisk politik. Utveckling och debatt i Sverige sedan första världskriget*, Stockholm: Studieförbundet Näringsliv och Samhälle.

LÖNNROTH, J. (1991), "Before Economics", in B. Sandelin, (ed.), *The History of Swedish Economic Thought*, London and New York: Routledge, pp. 11–43.

MYRDAL, G. (1939), *Monetary Equilibrium*, London: Hodge.

—— (1944), *An American Dilemma. The Negro Problem and Modern Democracy*, New York: Harper.

—— (1953), *The Political Element in the Development of Economic Theory*, London: Routledge.

—— (1960), *Beyond the Welfare State. Economic Planning in the Welfare States and its International Implications*, London: Duckworth.

—— (1968), *Asian Drama. An Inquiry into the Poverty of Nation*, 3 vols., Harmondsworth: Penguin.

—— (1975), "Gunnar Myrdal", *Les Prix Nobel 1974*, Stockholm: Norstedts.

O'BRIEN, D. P. (1975), *The Classical Economists*, Oxford: Clarendon Press.

OHLIN, B. (1924), *Handelns teori*, Stockholm: Centraltryckeriet.

—— (1936), *Fri eller dirigerad ekonomi*. Uddevalla: Hallmans Bokhandel.

—— (1937), "Some Notes on the Stockholm Theory of Savings and Investment", *The Economic Journal* 47: 53–69, 221–40.

—— (1967), *Interregional and International Trade*, rev. edn., Cambridge Mass.: Harvard Univ. Press.

—— (1978), "Bertil Ohlin", *Les Prix Nobel 1977*, Stockholm: Almqvist & Wiksell International, pp. 325–31.

RAPHAEL, D. D. (1985), *Adam Smith*, Oxford: Oxford University Press.

ROBBINS, L. (1952), *The Theory of Economic Policy in English Classical Political Economy*, London: Macmillan.

RYDENFELT, S. (1976), *Det sjuka 70-talet. Om massarbetslöshetens återkomst och sysselsättningenbs fjärde dimenstion. Adam Smith Redivius 1776–1976*, Lund: Studentlitteratur.

—— (1984), *A Pattern for Failure. Socialist Economies in Crisis*, New York: Harcourt Brace.

SANDELIN, B. (1981), "Adam Smiths politiska ekonomi—och vår tids nationalekonomi", M. Lundahl, (ed.), *Ideologi, ekonomi och politik. Tankar i tiden*, Stockholm: Rabén & Sjögren, pp. 55–80.

—— (ed.) (1991), *The History of Swedish Economic Thought*, London and New York: Routledge.

SARTORIUS, G. (1796), *Handbuch der Staatswissenschaft zum Gebrauche bey akademischen Vorlesungen, nach Adam Smith's Grundsätzen ausgearbeitet*, Berlin: Bey Fredrich Unger.

SCHUMPETER, J. A. (1954), *History of Economic Analysis*, New York: Oxford Univ. Press.

SEGERSTEDT, T. T. (1937), *Moral senseskolan och dess inflytande på svensk filosofi*, Lund: Gleerups.

SMITH, A. (1909–11), *En undersökning av folkens välstånd, dess natur och orsaker*, 2 vols. Lund: Gleerups.

—— (1976), *An Inquiry into the Nature and Causes of the Wealth of Nations*, 2 vols. Indianapolis, Ind.: Liberty Classics.

—— (1994), *Den osynliga handen. Adam Smith i urval*. "Introduktion" by Erik Dahmén, Stockholm: Ratio.

Studiehandbok för de studerande inom Juridiska fakulteten vid Universitetet i Lund (1904), Lund: Berlingska Boktryckeriet.

THÖRNBERG, E. H. (1923), "Adam Smith. Ett tvåhundra–årsminne", *Svenska Dagbladet* 6 June.

UDDHAMMAR, E. (1993), *Partierna och den stora staten. En analys av statsteorier och svensk politik under 1900-talet*. English summary. Stockholm: City University Press.

UHR, C. G. (1963), *Anders Chydenius 1792-1803. A Finnish Predecessor to Adam Smith*, Åbo.

—— (1975), *Economic Doctrines of David Davidson*, Uppsala and Stockholm: Almqvist & Wiksell International.

—— (1991), "David Davidson: The Transition to Neoclassical Economics", B. Sandelin, ed., *The History of Swedish Economic Thought*, London and New York: Routledge, pp. 44–75.

VALLINDER, T. (1987), "Adam Smiths genombrott i Sverige", *Ekonomisk debatt*, 15 229–32.

WADENSJÖ, E. (1990), "Carl Adolph Agardh", in C. Jonung and A.-C. Ståhlberg, (eds), *Ekonomporträtt Svenska ekonomer under 300 år*, Stockholm: SNS, pp. 73–89.

WICKSELL, K. (1896), *Finanztheoretische Untersuchungen nebst Darstellung und Kritik des Steuerwesens Schwedens*, Jena: Gustav Fischer.

—— (1934–5), *Lectures on Political Economy*, 2 vols., London: Routledge.

—— (1936), *Interest and Prices. A Study of the Causes Regulating the Value of Money*, with an Introduction by Professor Bertil Ohlin, London: Macmillan.

—— (1958), *Selected Papers on Economic Theory*, ed. with an Introduction by Erik Lindahl, London: Allen & Unwin.

Appendix.

Translations of *The Wealth of Nations* in Eighteen Languages

This appendix offers convenient tables to check the different editions of *WN* in eighteen non-English languages. Brief explanations are provided in the "Remarks" column of each table. The numbering in these tables refers to the number of the translation and/or printing; for instance, "no. 5.3" means the third printing of the fifth translation. Where no title is given in the body of the table it is because multiple editions shared the same title(s); in these cases, the title(s) can be found at the foot of the table. Items marked with a dagger (†) are known to exist but are not in the holdings of the Vanderblue Collection of Smithiana.

These tables have been compiled primarily from the catalogue and holdings of the Vanderblue Memorial Collection of Smithiana, Kress Library (within the Baker Library, Harvard Business School). I have tried to request corrections from Smith experts and librarians in each language, but am alone responsible for all errors. Corrections and additions are requested for future revisions.

Table A1. Arabic version of *WN*

No.	Title	Translator	Year	Publisher	Vols.	Pages	Remarks
1	*Tharwat al-uman*	unknown	1959	Cairo: Daral-gahira li-tibà	1	95	Arabic translation of 12 selections from *WN* (Kutub siyasiyya, 92) (Kress: 1959 S Excerpts).

Table A2. Chinese versions

No.	Title	Translator	Year	Publisher	Vols.	Pages	Remarks
1	*Yuan Fu* (The origin of wealth)	Yen Fu (1853–1921)	1901–2	Shanghai: Nan-yang College	1 (8 pt.; 24cm)	582	Selected translation of the original text. He added 310 translator's notes (about 14% of the space in the Chinese version). Based on the Thorold Rogers (1869) Oxford edn. Still in print, owing more to the importance of the translator than the contents of *WN* he translated.
			1929–	Shanghai: Commercial Press	9/3/1/ etc.	978	
2.1	*Kuo Fu Lun*	Kuo Ta-li (1905–76); Wang Ya-nan (1901–69)	1931	Chung-hua Book Co.	2	1077	Translators were Marxists. Full translation, based on the 1880 Oxford University (Clarendon) Press edn. (see Zhu Shaowen (1993), "Adam Smith in China", in H. Mizuta and C. Sugiyama (eds.), *Adam Smith: International Perspectives*, p. 286, London: Macmillan). Kuo translated Bks. II–IV, Wang Bks. I and V.
2.2	See Remarks	Same as 2.1	1972–4	Beijing: The Commercial Press	2	382, 511	The Chinese title is exactly translated from the English title, rather than the previously shortened *Kuo Fu Lun*. Wang Ya-nan wrote a Preface in 1965 for this revised version explaining its modifications. 1997 marks the 8th printing of this version.
3	*Kuo Fu Lun*	Chou Hsien-wen (1907–89); Chang Han-yü (1913–)	1964	Bank of Taiwan	2	868	Based on the Cannan edn. Vol. I translated Cannan's annotations, together with some translator's notes. Full translation. Chou translated Bks I–III, Chang Bks IV–V. Reprinted at least eight times, still reprinting.

Table A3. Czech version

No.	Title	Translator	Year	Publisher	Vols.	Pages	Remarks
1	*Blahobyt národu, vybrané kapitoly*	Dr Josef Macek	1928	Prague: Vydal Jan Laichter	1	345	Translated from selected chapters of *WN*. Preložil ing. Antonín Patocka, preklad prehlédl a uvod napsal Dr Josef Macek. (Half-title: *Otázky a názory*, vydává Jan Laichter, kniha LVIII) (Kress: 1928 S Excerpts).

Table A4. Danish versions of *WN*

No.	Title	Translator	Year	Publisher	Vols.	Pages	Remarks
1	*Undersøgelse om National-Velstands Natur og Aarsag*	Frants Dræbye	1779 (v.1) 1780 (v.2)	Copenhagen: Trykt paa Gyldendals forlag	2 (8°)	575; 778	All five books were translated; appears to be a complete translation. The long letter from Governor Pownall to Adam Smith (25 Sept. 1776) is added as the Appendix (vol. 2, pp. 683 ff).
2	*En undersøgelse af Nationernes Velstand, dens Natur og Årsager*	Per Lyngsaae Olsen	1976	Copenhagen: Rhodos (Teorihistori Skrifter)	1	287	Based on the 1971 Everyman's Library Edition. With a preface by H.-J. Schanz (44 pp.). Kress has vol. 1. Translation was severely criticized because of poor quality and the vulgar Marxist nature of the preface. The publisher cancelled further publication.

Table A5. Dutch version

No.	Title	Translator	Year	Publisher	Vols.	Pages	Remarks
1	*Naspeuringen over de natuur en oorzaaken van den rijkdom der volkeren*	Dirk Hoola van Nooten	1796	Amsterdam: Wouter Brave	1	589	Only Bk. I, Chs. 1–10 were translated. Microfilm reproduction of original in the Koninklijke bibliotheke, The Hague (Kress Room: 1796 Film S).

Table A6. Finnish version

No.	Title	Translator	Year	Publisher	Vols.	Pages	Remarks
1	*Kansojen varallisuus, tutkimus sen olemuksesta ja tekijöistä*	Toivo T. Kaila	1933	Helsinki: Werner Söderström osakeyhtiö	1	601	Based on the Cannan edn. Bk. V was not translated. With a preface (Alkulause) by Suomentaja (pp. v–ix). Part of John Rae's *Life of Adam Smith* was translated as "Adam Smithin Elämä" (pp. xiii–l).

Table A7. French versions

No.	Translator	Year	Publisher	Vols.	Pages	Remarks
1.1	M***	1778 (v.1–2) 1779 (v.3–4)	The Hague, Holland	4	688, 387 485, 520	Murray (Ch. 3.3 above) proved that the Hague translation was thus a year earlier in date, and was evidently by a different hand [i.e. not Blavet]. See also Carpenter (1995) notes.
2.1	Anonymous (l'Abbé Blavet)	1779–80	Paris	3	612, 611, 884	Translation first published in *Journal de l'agriculture, du commerce, des arts et des finances*, Jan. 1779–Dec. 1780. "Blavet made it entirely for his own use, and with no great exactness" (Murray, Ch. 3.3 above). Microfilm of the University of Edinburgh Library copy (Kress Room: 1778 Film S).
2.2	Anonymous (Jean Louis Blavet)	1781	Yverdon, Switzerland	6	298, 366, 292, 239, 310, 368	Based on 2.1 but "with more faults". Translator's name was not printed on the title page. Identified from the *Catalogue général de la Bibliothèque nationale*. Blavet wanted to be anonymous because he was aware of the errors of translation.
2.3	l'Abbé Bl***	1781	Paris	3	612, 611, 884	Reprint of 2.2. Microfilm of the University of Edinburgh Library copy (Kress Room: 1781 Film S).
2.4	Anonymous (Blavet)	1786	London and Paris: chez Poinçot	6	298, 266 292, 239 310 368	Copies at Kress Library are in very good condition.
2.5	Anonymous (Blavet)	1788	London and Paris: P. J. Duplain	2	265, 496	Same as 2.2.

					Kress	
2.6	Anonymous (M.***)	1789	Amsterdam	4	688, 387 485, 520	This is an exact reprint of 1.1, but with a different title: *Recherches très-utiles sur les affaires présentes, et les causes de la Richesse des Nations, dédiées aux Etats-généraux.*
3.1†	Jeane Antoine Roucher (1745–94)	1790 (v.1–3) 1791 (v.4)	Paris: chez Buisson	4	570, 312, 602, 591	Based on the 5th English edn. Murray (Ch. 3.3 above) says that this is a translation "of no great merit".
3.2	J. A. Roucher	1791 (v.1–3) 1792 (v.4)	Avignon: J. J. Niel	4	540, 296 528, 519	Same as 3.1, with a new expository introduction by Fortia on WN.
3.3	J. A. Roucher	1792	Neufchatel: de l'imp. de L. Fauche-Borel, impri. du roi	5	384, 406, 400, 437 432	Reissue of 3.1.
3.4	J. A. Roucher	1794 (1795?)	Paris: chez Buisson	5	438, 494 624, 411, 370	"Reviewed and considerably corrected". Publication year is the "third year of the République".
4†	Prévost	1797	Bern	5		With a different title: *Recherches sur les richesses des nations.*
2.7	Blavet	1800 (v.1–2) 1801 (v.3–4)	Paris: Larren et cie.	4	500, 521 460, 436	Reissue of 2.1 with revision. This is the first time Blavet allowed his name to appear on the title page.
5.1	Germain Garnier (1754–1821)	1802	Paris: chez H. Agasse	5	368, 493, 564, 556, 588	New translation. Vol. 5 contains 42 notes and observations, with a portrait of Smith. Kress has two sets of this edn. Manuscript notes by Louis Say.
3.5	J. A. Roucher	1806	Paris: chez Arthus Bertrand	5	438, 494 624, 411, 370	Reissue of 3.4.
5.2†	Garnier	1809	Paris	3		

Table A7. (cont.)

No.	Translator	Year	Publisher	Vols.	Pages	Remarks
5.3	Garnier	1822	Paris: chez Mme. veuve Agasse	6	368, 493 564, 556 670, 572	Rev. edn. of 5.1, with two volumes of new notes and observations (vols. 5–6 contain 72 notes).
5.4	Garnier	1843	Paris: Guillaumin	2	520, 714	Entirely revised and corrected, and with a preface and biographical note by Jerome Adolphe Blanqui (membre de l'Institut). With the commentaries of Buchanan, Germain Garnier, MacCulloch, Malthus, J. Mill, Ricardo, Sismondi, and the unpublished notes of J.-B. Say, with historical background explanation by Blanqui. Printed as vols. 5–6 of *Collection des principaux économistes*.
5.5	Garnier	1859	Paris: Guillaumin	3	407, 468 367	Revised and corrected version of 5.4 by Joseph Garnier. Further notes by Bentham, Storch, Turgot, Dufrense Saint-Léon, and J.A. Blanqui were added.
5.6†	Garnier	1860	Paris: Guillaumin	3	?	New revised and expanded version, with explanatory notes by Joseph Garnier (1813–81, Blanqui's brother-in-law, no relation to Germain Garnier). J. Garnier was "Secrétaire perpétuel de la Société d'économie politique, Professeur à l'Ecole des ponts et chaussées, etc.". He wrote a new preface (4pp.).
5.7	Garnier	1880 (v.2) 1881 (v.1)	Paris: Guillaumin & Cie.	2	506, 661	5th exp. edn. with a preface and an analytical summary by Joseph Garnier (pp. xxiii–xl). Germain Garnier's long preface was deleted.

5.8	Garnier	1950	Paris: Alfred Costes	4(?)	394, ?, ?, ?	Kress has only vol. 1. This is based on 5.4. The Cannan (1904) English edn. preface, editor's introduction, notes, and marginal summaries are translated and added by F. Debyser.
5.9†	Garnier	1966	Osnbrück, Germany	?	?	Reissue of 5.4 (known from 5.10, p. 518).
5.10	Garnier	1991	Paris: Grenier-Flammarion	2	531, 637	Title: *La richesse des nations*. Based on 5.7 with a new introduction by Daniel Diatkine, but deleted copious notes and some informative pages contained in 5.4. G. Garnier's preface and Blanqui's notice in 5.7 are also deleted.
6	Paulette Taieb	1995	Paris: Presses universitaires de France	1	1512	*Enquête sur la nature et les causes de la richesse des nations*. Collection: Pratiques théoriques. Based on the 1776 1st ed.

There are also some partial translations:

1	Reverdil	1778	Lausanne: Chez la Société typo.	1	2 pl., viii, 170p.	Title: *Fragment sur les colonies en général, et sur celles des Anglois en particulier*. With translator's "Avertissement" (pp. i–viii). This is a translation of Bk IV, Ch.7 "Of colonies"; in Smith's text there are 3 parts in this chapter, this translator divided pt. III into 4 chs. (with his own chapter names), making his translation into 6 chs.
2	Anonymous	1888	Paris: Guillaumin et Cie.	1	264	Title: *Richesse des nations*.
3†	Courcelle Seneuil	1908	Paris: Alcan	1	?	Known from 5.10, p. 518.
4	Garnier	1950	Paris: Dalloz	1	297	Title: *Adam Smith: textes choisis (et préface)* by G. H. Bousquet. Based on 5.7.

Table A7. (cont.)

No.	Translator	Year	Publisher	Vols.	Pages	Remarks
5	Garnier	1976	Paris: Gallimard (Idées & Folio)	1	445	Title: *La richesse des nations*. Edited with a preface by Gérard Mairet.

Title: Recherches sur la nature et les causes de la richesse des nations. The exceptions are 2.6, 4, 5.10, and 6.

Note: French versions of *WN* are analysed in detail in Carpenter, Kenneth (1995), "*Recherches sur la nature et les causes de la richesse de nation d'Adam Smith et politique culturelle en France*", *Economies et Sociétés*, Série P.E. No. 24, 10/1995, pp. 5–30.

Table A8. German versions

No.	Title	Translator	Year	Publisher	Vols.	Pages	Remarks
1.1	1	Johan Friedrich Schiller	1776 (v.1) 1778 (v.2)	Leipzig: Weidmanns Erben und Reich	2	632, 740	According to Kayser's *Vollständiges bücherlexikon*, 1750–1832, the translators were Johan Friedrich Schiller and Chr. A. Wichmann
1.2	1	Johan Friedrich Schiller	1776 (v.1) 1778 (v.2) 1792 (v.3)	Leipzig: Wiedmannsche Buchhandlung	3	632, 740, 140	2nd issue of 1.1, with a "vol. 3" (140pp.) which is bound together with vol. 2, with the following statement: "Zusätze und verbesserungen zu der erstern ausgabe der Untersuchung der Natur und Ursachen von Nationalreichthuemern". Vol. 3 is a translation by C. A. Wichmann of Smith's addition and corrections to the 1st and 2nd edn. of *WN*.

2.1	2	Christian Garve and Dörrien	1794 (v. 1–2) 1795 (v. 3) 1796 (v. 4)	Breslau: W. G. Korn	4	464, 274, 451, 484	Aus dem englischen der 4. ausg. neu uebers. C. W. Hasek (see Ch. 4.1 above): "The translation thus begun in 1791 was completed with the help of Ober-Post-Commissär Dörrien in Leipzig, who apparently translated a considerable portion of the latter part of the work, and was ready for publication in 1794". Garve added two appendices: a summary of Smith's ideas and principles; a further analysis of Smith's main theorems. Rather infrequent but extensive explanatory notes.
2.2	2	Garve and Dörrien	1796 (v. 1–2) 1799 (v. 3–4)	Frankfurt and Leipzig	4	435, 260, 420, 460	Aus dem englischen der 4. ausg. neu uebers.
2.3	2	Garve and Dörrien	1799	Breslau und Leipzig: W.G. Korn	3	460, 702, 474	Zweyte, mit Stewarts Nachricht von dem Leben und den Schriften des Autors verm. Ausg.
3	2	George Sartorius	1806	Göttingen: J.F. Röwer	1	xxviii + 268	Partial translation (Kress: 1806 S Excerpts).
2.4	2	Garve and Dörrien	1810	Breslau und Leipzig: W.G. Korn	3	412, 631, 422	Aus dem englischen der 4. ausg. neu uebers. Dritte, mit Stewarts Nachricht von dem Leben und den Schriften des Autors vermehrte Unveraenderte ausg.
2.5†	2	Garve and Dörrien	1812	Berlin: G. Hayn	?	?	gek. Ausgabe mit Anm. von F. von Colin (known from 10, below, p. 838).
2.6	2	Garve and Dörrien	1814	Wien: B.P. Bauer	3	400, 616, 412	Reprint of 2.4.

Table A8. (cont.)

No.		Translator	Year	Publisher	Vols.	Pages	Remarks
4.1	3	Max Stirner	1846 (v. 1–2) 1847 (v. 3–4)	Leipzig: O. Wigand	4	374, 215, 367, 334	Added title page: *Die nationaloekonomen der Franzosen und Engländer*. Based on the 4th English edn. (1786).
5.1†	4	Dr C. W. Asher	1857	Hamburg:	?	?	Known from 10, p. 838.
5.2	4	Dr C. W. Asher	1861	Stuttgart: J. Engelhorn	2	488, 502	With a foreword by the translator, who was "Correspondirendem Mitgliede des Commission centrale de Statistique du Royaume Belge, des statistichen Gesellschaften zu London und Frankfurt a. M. und der Société d'économie charitable zu Paris".
6.1	5	F. Stöpel	1878	Berlin: Expedition des Merkur	4	354, 298, 247, 364	Bound in two volumes. Added title page: *Bibliothek der volkswirtschaftslehre und gesellschaftswissenschaft.*
7.1	6	Dr Wilhelm Loewenthal	1879	Berlin: E. Staude	2	512, 467	
7.2	6	Dr Wilhelm Loewenthal	1882	Berlin: E. Staude	2	512, 467	Reissue of 7.1.
6.2	5	F. Stöpel	1905–7	Berlin: R.L. Prager	4	354, 298, 247, 364	Reissue of 6.1. Bibliothek der volkswirtschaftslehre und gesellschaftswissenschaft, (III). Bound in 1 vol.
4.2	7	Max Stirner	1908	Jena: G. Fischer	3	350, 561, 367	Unter zugrundelegung der übersetzung Max Stirners, aus dem englischen original nach des ausg. letzter hand (4. aufl. 1786) ins deutsch übertragen von dr. Ernst Grünfeld und eingeleitet von prof. dr. Heinrich Waentig. *Sammlung sozialwissenschaftlicher Meister, XI.*

Table A9. Italian versions

No.	Title	Translator	Year	Publisher	Vols.	Pages	Remarks
1	*Ricerche sulla natura, e le cagioni della richezza delle nazioni*	Anonymous	1790 (v.2–4) 1791 (v.1,5)	Naples: Presso G.P. Merande	5	267, 267, 260, 299, 290	"Tr. per la prima volta in italiano dall'ultima ed. Inglese". The translator maintained that he knew Smith personally and had correspondence with him, but in fact this translation was based on Blavet's 1779–80 French edn. Kress has two identical sets of this edn. The first one (v.2–4, 1790; v.1,5, 1791) is in soft cover, a little damaged, and seems likely to have been the first Italian printing. The second set (v.1–4, 1790; v.5, 1791) is in hard cover and in excellent condition; it could be a much later reprinting to judge from paper quality and binding technique. The two sets are set in different typefaces.
2.1	*Ricerche sopra la natura, e le cause della richezza delle nazioni*	Anonymous	1851	Turin: Cugini Pomba e comp.	1	704	"Tr. eseguita sull'ultima ed. inglese del sig. MacCulloch, preceduta dalla vita dell'autore, del sig. V. Cousin". Cousin wrote a long introduction about Smith's life and work (pp. vii–lxviii); A. Blanqui's notes on Smith were translated from the French (pp. lxviii–lxxi); pp. lxxii–lxxiii explain the "present edition"; and G. Garnier's long preface on *WN* was also translated from the French (pp. lxxiii–lxxx) in an abridged form. The translation is clearly independent from 1.1.

4.3	8	Max Stirner	Leipzig: A. Kröner	1910	2	245, 324	Nach der Übers. von Max Stirner u, d, Ausg. von Cannan (1904), hrsg. von Heinrich Schmidt (Kröners volksausgabe).
4.4	7	Max Stirner	Jena: G. Fischer	1920	3	350, 561, 367	Reissue of 4.2.
4.5	7	Max Stirner	Jena: G. Fischer	1923	3	350, 561, 367	Reissue of 4.2.
4.6	8	Max Stirner	Leipzig: A. Kröner	1924	2	428, 570	Nach der Übers. von Stirner u, d, Ausg. von Cannan (1904), hrsg. von dr. Heinrich Schmidt.
4.7	7	Max Stirner	Leipzig: A. Kröner	1926	3	350, 561, 367	Reissue of 4.2.
8	6	Friedrich Bülow	Leipzig: A. Kröner	1933	1	xxxviii + 348	Printed in Gothic style.
9	9	Peter Thal	Berlin-Ost: Akademie-Verlag	1963	3	lxv + 341	Nur Bd. 1 erschienen (Kress has only vol. 1).
10	10	Horst Claus Recktenwald	München: C.H. Beck	1974	1	lxxix + 859	Another 4-vol. edn. (brosch.) by the same publisher. Also collected in the pocket series: dtv klassik 2208.

Titles:

(1) *Untersuchung der Natur und Ursachen von Nationalreichthümern.*
(2) *Untersuchung über die Natur und die Ursachen des Nationalreichthums.*
(3) *Untersuchungen über das Wesen und die Ursachen des Nationalreichtums.*
(4) *Ueber die Quellen des Volkswohlstandes.*
(5) *Untersuchung über das Wesen und die Ursachen des Volkswohlstandes.*
(6) *Natur und Ursachen des Volkswohlstandes.*
(7) *Eine Untersuchung über Natur und Wesen des Volkswohlstandes.*
(8) *Der Reichtum der Nationen.*
(9) *Eine Untersuchung über das Wesen und die Ursachen des Reichtums der Nationen.*
(10) *Der Wohlstand der Nationen: Eine Untersuchung seiner Natur und seiner Ursachen.*

Note: According to the Vanderblue Collection catalogue (pp. 32–7), partial translations were issued in the following years: 1806, 1913, 1920, 1924, 1933, 1946.

	Title	Translator/editor	Year	Publisher	Vol.	Pages	Notes
2.2	Same as 2.1	Anonymous	1927	Turin: Unione tip.-editrice torinese	1	803	Reissue of 2.1, with a preface by Achille Loria.
3	Ricerche sopra la natura e le cause della ricchezza delle nazioni	Alberto Campolongo	1945	Turin: Unione tip.-editrice torinese	1	885	With an introduction by Augusto Graziani (pp. ix–xxx). 2nd edn. 1950.
4†	Indagine sulla natura e le cause della ricchezza delle nazioni	F. Bartoli; C, Camporesi; S. Caruso	1973	Milan: ISEDI	1	1030	With an introduction by Maurice Dobb (pp. xiii–xxvi) and translator's note by Sergio Caruso (pp. xxvii–lxviii).
5†	La ricchezza delle nazioni	Anna e Tullio Bagiotti	1975	Turin: UTET	1	1264	With an introduction by Tullio Bagiotti (9–38) and a biographical note by A. Pellanda (39–60).
6	La ricchezza delle nazioni	Ada Bonfirraro	1976	Rome: Newton Compton	3	311, 416, 260	With critical essays by Lucio Colletti, Claudio Napoleoni, and Paolo Sylos Labini (pp. vii–xx). Cannan's "Editor's Introduction" was translated as the "Introduction" (5–37).

Note: Samuel August A. D. Tissot (1782), *Del pane e della economia e coltura de'grani* (Venice) is in the holdings of the Kress Library. To this translation from the French has been added 'Osservazioni sopra i pomi di terra, ossiano patate' (141–5). This is a translation of Bk I, Ch. II, pt. I of *WN* and is the first translation of Adam Smith into Italian.

Additional source: Da segnalare anche l'antologia della *Inquiry* . . . di A. Smith a cura di Piero Barucci, *Adam Smith e la nascita dell'economia politica*, p. 250. Milan: Mondadori, 1981.

Table A10. Japanese versions

No.	Title	Translator	Year	Publisher	Vols.	Pages	Remarks
1	Seisan Michi Annai (A Guide to Production)	Tokujiro Obata	1870	Tokyo: Shokodo	2	68, 40	Partially translated, and rewritten based on Smith's text. It is not clear on which edn. of WN it was based.
2.1	Fukokuron	Eisaku Ishikawa (Bk I–Bk IV, Ch.7); Seisaku Saga (Bk IV, Ch.8–Bk V)	1884 (v.1) 1885 (v.2) 1888 (v.3)	Tokyo: Keizai zasshi-sha	12 pts. then 3 v.	754, 787, 970	Full translation. Originally published in 12 pts. (1882–3), then combined into 3 vols. in 1884, 1885, 1888 respectively.
2.2	Fukokuron	Eisaku Ishikawa	1892	Tokyo: Keizai zasshi-sha	2	812, 968	Reissue of 2.1. A quite popular edn. Only Ishikawa was listed as the translator; Saga's name was omitted from the title page.
3	Fukokuron	Seiki Mikami	1910	Tokyo: Nisshindo	1	367	With an Introduction by Shigenobu Okuma. A translation of Ashley's selected chapters, 4th rev. edn. (Kress: [1914] S Excerpts).
4†	Fukokuron	Sakuro Nagao	1914	Tokyo: Akagi Library, No. 98	1	100	Based on the Ashley edn. Selective translation.
5.1	Fukokuron	Kenji Takeuchi	1921–3	Tokyo: Yuhikaku	3	517, 439, 379	Based on Cannan's 2nd edn. (1920).
5.2	Fukokuron	Kenji Takeuchi	1931 (v.1–2) 1933 (v.3)	Tokyo: Kaizosha	3	786, 602, 538	Completely revised edn., collected in "Kaizo Library".
5.3	Fukokuron	Kenji Takeuchi	1947–9	Tokyo: Kaizosha	6	267, 287, 204, 194, 169, 185	With a new translator's preface. In 1969 Tokyo University Press reissued a 3-vol. edn.

No.	Title	Translator	Year	Publisher	Vols	Pages	Notes
6†	*Fukokuron*	Bunzo Kaminaga	1925	Tokyo: Shincho sha	1	228	Partial translation. Edn. not identified.
7	*Kokufuron*	Kanju Kiga	1926	Tokyo: Iwanami shoten	1	810	Based on the 5th English edn. (1789) and the 1904 Cannan edn. Designed to be 2 vols. but the translator died after vol. 1 was published. Also reissued in Iwanami Bunko no. 16–20 (1927), 489pp.
8	*Kokufuron*	Suekichi Aono	1928 (v.1) 1929 (v.2)	Tokyo: Shunjusha	2	540, 528	Based on the 9th English edn. (1799) and Cannan's edn. Reissued in 1933 by the same publisher in 4 vols. (Shunju Library).
9	*Kokufuron*	Hyoe Ohuchi	1940 (v.1) 1941 (v.2) 1942 (v.3) 1943 (v.4) 1944 (v.5)	Tokyo: Iwanami Bunko	5	481, 260, 484, 465, 146	Based on the 1937 Cannan edn. (Smith's 5th edn.). With detailed Japanese text index.
10	*Kokufuron*	Tsuneo Hori	1949	Tokyo: Shunjusha	1	268	Based on the Cannan edn., designed to be published in 5 vols, but only vol. 1 has been published (up to Bk. I, Ch. 10). With translator's notes.
11	*Sumisu Kokufuron*	Hiroshi Mizuta	1965	Tokyo: Kawade-shobo-shinsha	2	467, 443	Based on the 1st edn. (1776). With translator's notes showing WN's later revisions and additions, and some informative tables and expository essays. 2nd printing 1972.
12	*Sho kokumino tomi*	Hyoe Ohuchi and Shichiro Matsukawa	1959–66	Tokyo: Iwanami Bunko	5	382, 500, 509, 404, 120	A revision of Ohuchi's 1940–4 translation. Edited with an introduction, notes, marginal summary, and an enlarged index of Cannan's 6th edn. (1950). Japanese index in vol. 5 (144pp.). Reissued in 1969 in 2 vols. (1402pp.) by the same publisher.

Table A10. (cont.)

No.	Translator	Year	Publisher	Vols.	Pages	Remarks
13	*Kokufuron*	Yoshiro Tamanoi; 1968 Kyoji Tazoe; Akio Okochi; ed. Kazuo Okochi		Tokyo: Chuo Koron sha	1	582	Based on Cannan's 1920 edn., but others were consulted. A truncated and, in part, summarized translation (about 50% of the full text), with translators' notes.
14	*Kokufuron*	As 13	1976	Tokyo: Chuo Koron sha	3	1665	Based on Smith's 5th edn. Completed version of 13, with detailed information on Smith's life and work and translators' notes, etc. At the end of vol. 3, "A Short History of Japanese Translations of *WN*" was prepared by Kazuo Okochi (who was the President of Tokyo University. See Ch. 6.1 above).

Note: In 1873 Tohru Hoshi and Takeshi Arishima translated "Stamp duty" (probably from Bk V, Ch. 2, pt. II "Of Taxes", 4th article) into Japanese as "Inshi-zei Ryaku-setsu" (A brief introduction to stamp tax), published by the Japanese Ministry of Finance (11pp., 25 cm, block printed on double leaves folded in the centre. Kress: 1873 S Excerpts).

Table A11. Korean versions

No.	Title	Translator	Year	Publisher	Vols.	Pages	Remarks
1	*Kukpuron*	Choi Ho-chin and Chung Hai-dong	1957	Seoul: Chunjosa	2	1394	Based on the 6th printing of the Cannan edn. (1950).
1.2	*Kukpuron*	Choi Ho-chin and Chung Hai-dong	1992	Seoul: Bomusa	2	1212	Based on the Cannan edn. (1976), reissue of 1.1
2	*Kukpuron*	Choe Im-hwan	1970	Seoul: Ulyu Munhwasa	2	1060	Same as 1.1.
3	*Kukpuron*	Yu In-ho	1977	Seoul: Tongso Munhwasa	2	1111	Same as 1.1.
4	*Kukpuron*	Kim Suk-hwan and Kim Il-gon	1986	Seoul: Yangdang	1	482	Selected translation.
5	*Kukpuron*	Kim Soo-haeng	1992	Seoul: Dong-a Chulpansa	2	947	Based on the Glasgow edn. (1976).

Note: assistance from Professor So Jinsu of Kangnam University in compiling this table is gratefully acknowleged.

Table A12. Polish versions

No.	Title	Translators	Year	Publisher	Vol.	Pages	Remarks
1	*Badania nad natura i przyczynami bogactwa narodów*	Oswald Einfeld and Stefan Wolff	1927	Warsaw: Naklad Gebethnera i Wolffa	1	274	Only Bk. I was translated, the 2nd vol. has not yet been published in 1935. Bibljoteka wyzszej szkoly handlowej.
2	*Badania nad natura i przyczynami bogactwa narodów*	J. Drewnowski and E. Lipinski (eds.). Bk. I translated by G. Wolff and O. Einfeld; Bks. II–III by Z. Sadowski; Bk. IV by A. Prejbisz; Bk. V by B. Jasinska; general revision by Cz. Zanmierowski.	1954	Warsaw: Panstwowe Wydawnictwo narsdów	2	541, 810	The first complete Polish translation. Half-title: Polska akademia nauk. Komitet nauk ekonomiznych. Biblioteka dziel ekonomii politycznej, angielska klasyczna.

Table A13. Portuguese versions

No.	Title	Translator	Year	Publisher	Vol.	Pages	Remarks
1	*Compêndio da Obra da Riqueza das Nações*	Bento da Silva Lisboa	1811 (v.1) 1812 (v.2)	Rio de Janeiro: Impressão Régia	3 in 1	204, 127, 187	Bk. V not translated. Bks I–IV half-translated. Kress: 1811–12 S Excerpts. Another excerpt published in 1936 with an introduction by António Lino Neto, Lisboa (85pp, Kress: 1936 S Excerpt).
2	*Inquérito sobre a natureza e as causas da Riqueza das Nações*	Teodora Cardoso and Luís Cristovão de Aguiar	1981	Lisbon: Fundaçáõ Calouste Gulbenkian	2	824, 815	Translated from the 6th English edn., London: Methuen, 1950.

Table A14. Romanian versions

No.	Title	Translator	Year	Publisher	Vols.	Pages	Remarks
1	*Avutia natiunilor o cercetare asupra naturii si cauzelor ei*	Alexandre Hallunga	1934–8	Bucharest: Editura Bucovina	5 pts in 4	468	Based on Cannan's 1904 edn. (World Classics). Film reproduction of original in the library of the Academiei Române (Negative, Kress Room Film S; another copy positive).
2	*Avutia natiunilor o cercetare asupra naturii si cauzelor ei*	Alexandre Hallunga	1962 (v.1) 1965 (v.2)	Bucharest: Editura Academiei Republicii populare Romîne, Institutul de Cercetäri Economice	2	343, 474	Based on Cannan's 1930 edn. "Adam Smith, classic al economiei politice burgheze" by N. N. Constantinescu (vol. 2, 405–71).

Table A15. Russian versions

No.	Title	Translator	Year	Publisher	Vols.	Pages	Remarks
1	Izsledovane svoistva i prichin bogatstva narodov	N. Politkoffski	1802 (v. 1) 1803 (v. 2) 1805 (v. 3) 1806 (v. 4)	St Petersburg: V. Tip Gos. meditsinskoi kollegii	4	577, 354, 644, 561	
2	Izsledovaniia o prirodie i prichinakh bogatstve narodov	Bibikov, Petr Alekseevich	1866	St Petersburg: V. Tip I.I. Glazunova	3	496, 612, 464	Contains an account of the life and works of Adam Smith by A. Blanqui, plus an introduction by Garnier (perhaps translated from the French).
3	Izsledovaniia o bogatstve narodov	Shchepkin, Mitrofan Pavlovich	1895	Moscow: Tip M.G. Volchaninova	1	288	Translated by M. Shchepkin. Ed. K. T. Soldatenkov. Biblioteka ekonomistov (Kress: 1895 S Excerpts). Perhaps based on the French version.
4	Issledovanie o bogatstve narodov	P. I. Liashchenko	1924	Petrograd: Izd. "Priboi"	1	218	Sokrashchennyi perevod pod redaktsiei i so vstupitel'noi stat'ei Prof. P.I. Liashchenko (Kress: 1924 S Excerpts).
5	Issledovanie o prirode i prichinakh bogatstva narodov		1931	Moscow: Gos. sotsial'no-ekonomicheskoe izd.	2	436, 552	At head of title: Institut K. Marksa i F. Engelisa. Adam Smit.
6†	Same as 5		1935	Moscow: Sotsekgiz	1	371	

Table A16. Spanish versions

No.	Title	Translator	Year	Publisher	Vols.	Pages	Remarks
1.1	*Compendio de la obra inglesa intitulada Riqueza de las Naciones*	Carlos Martínez de Irujo (Oficial de la Primera Secretaría de Estado)	1792	Madrid: En la Imprenta Real	1	302	According to Smith (1967): (1) This version was an expurgated translation of Condorcet's synopsis of *WN*, published in French *Bibliothèque de l'homme public*, III (108–216) and IV (3–115), published in Paris (1790). The translator "not only suppressed or garbled parts of Condorcet's work but failed to identify the original as the work of Smith". For a detailed account of Condorcet's synopsis, see Diatkine (1993). (2) The Spanish "Inquisition" banned the original (French) version of *WN* on March 3, 1792, but permitted an extract of *WN* to be published in Spanish in 1792 (Kress Library has this copy: 1792 S Excerpts). (3) On the title page it is stated "Hecho por el Marqués de Condorcet, y traducido al castellano con varias adiciones del original". The translator wrote a "Discurso preliminar" (pp. i–xi), and divided the translation into 5 "books".
1.2	Same as 1.1	Same as 1.1	1803	Same as 1.1	1	300	
1.3	Same as 1.1	Same as 1.1	1814	Palma: Imprenta de Miguel Domingo	1	264	

Table A16. (*cont.*)

No.	Title	Translator	Year	Publisher	Vols.	Pages	Remarks
2.1	*Investigación de la naturaleza y causas de la riqueza de las naciones*	José Alonso Ortiz	1794	Valladolid: Oficina de la Viuda e Hijos de Santander	4	464, 392, 328, 499	According to Smith (1967: 62–3), this translation was based on the 5th edn. (1789), but Ortiz thought it was the 8th edn. (1796). Some sections were omitted. With various notes and illustrations relative to Spain. With an "Indice general" in vol. 4 (pp. 431–99). This 60-page synopsis of the 5 Books is useful for serious students of *WN*. The translator was a lawyer attached to the royal councils and chancery in Valladolid and a professor of canon law and sacred theology.
2.2	Same as 2.1	Same as 2.1	1805–6	Same as 2.1	4	444, 523, 529, 456	2nd edn. of 2.1, with extensive correction and improvement (corregida y mejorada). Corrections and notes were added to vol. 1 (pp. 423–44, incorrectly paginated as 244), vol. 2 (509–23), vol. 3 (517–29), vol. 4 (341–71); "Indice general" (v.4: 373–456). This edn. was criticized by Beltran as "a 'mutilated' version of Smith's immortal work" (Smith 1967: 123).
2.3	Same as 2.1	Same as 2.1	1933–4	Barcelona: España Bancaria	3	339, 455, 262 + xlvi indice	Revision and adaption in modern form from the translation of José Alonso Ortíz (1794) by José M. Tallada, but he "made only unimportant orthographical and grammatical revisions" (Smith 1967: 123), and also prepared a prologue (Kress does not have vol. 3).

2.4	Same as 2.1	Same as 2.1	1947	Barcelona: Bosch	3	same as 2.3	A reissue of 2.3 (2nd printing). Vols.1–2 are undated, vol. 3 is dated 1947. The dates are now identified as: vol. 1, 1947–9; vol. 2, 1954; vol. 3, 1955–6 (see Ch. 9.3)
2.5	Same as 2.1	Same as 2.1	1983	Barcelona: Ediciones Orbis S.A.	3	same as 2.3	Reissue of 2.4.
3	Same as 2.1	Amando Lázaro Ros	1956	Madrid: Aguilar	1	847	Based on the Cannan edn. A first Spanish "complete and accurate translation", with a translator's "Prologo". Cannan's notes were all omitted.
4.1	Same as 2.1	Gabriel Franco and Manuel Sánchez Sarto	1958	Mexico: Fondo de Cultura Económica	1	917	Based on the Cannan edn., reproduced Cannan's notes. With an introduction by Max Lerner (Modern Library edn.). New translation with a preliminary study by the translator (pp. viii–xxxix). Reprinted 1979, 1981, 1982, 1984, 1987.
4.2	Indagación acerca de la naturaleza y causas de la Riqueza de las Naciones	Same as 3.1	1961	Same as 3.1	1	893	2nd edn. of 3.1, with a different title. Revised with a Prologue by Germán Bernacer Torno.
5	Riqueza de las Naciones	Anonymous (J. Ortíz)	1977	Mexico: Publicationes Cruz O., S.A.	2	455, 554	Appears to be a reprint of 2.4. Only Smith's text is printed, translator's name and introduction etc. are omitted.

Table A16. (cont.)

No.	Title	Translator	Year	Publisher	Vols.	Pages	Remarks
6	*Investigación sobre la naturaleza y causas de la Riqueza de las naciones*	J.C. Collado Curiel and A. Mira-Perceval Pastor	1988	Barcelona: Oikos-taus	2	584, 459	Based on the 1976 Oxford University Press edn.
7	*La naturaleza y causas de la Riqueza de las naciones*	Carlos Rodriguez Braun	1994	Madrid: Alianza Editiorial	1	808	Abridged version of *WN*, edited by the translator.

Additional sources: D. Diatkine (1993), "A French Reading of *The Wealth of Nations* in 1790'', in H. Mizuta and C. Sugiyama (eds.), *Adam Smith: International Perspectives*, pp. 213–223, London: Macmillan; Smith (1967) is reprinted as Ch. 9.2 here; R. S. Smith (1968), 'English Economic Thought in Spain, 1776–1848', *South Atlantic Quarterly*, 67(2): 306–37.

Table A17. Swedish versions

No.	Title	Translator	Year	Publisher	Vol.	Pages	Remarks
1	*Undersökning om kongl. stora sjö- och gränse-tullar, samt acciser och små-tullar, med flera consumtions-afgifter* (An inquiry into the duties on imported commodities as well as excises and inland duties)	Erik Erl. Bodell	1800	Stockholm: C. Deleen & J.G. Forsgren	1	93	A translation of Bk V, Ch. 2, art. 4. (Kress: 1800 S Excerpts). The translation starts from p. 869 ("Taxes upon . . .") in 1976 Oxford University Press edn. The Swedish title of the book is very complicated even to a Swede.
2	*Politisk undersökning om lagar, som hindra och tvinga införseln af sådana utländska varor, som kunna alstras eller tillverkas inom landet* (A political inquiry into laws preventing and directing the import of such foreign commodities as can be produced or made in the country).	Erik Erl. Bodell	1804	Gothenburg: S. Norberg	1	6 p.l. 51	The translator was a customs official. Translated from Bk IV (Kress: 1804 S Excerpts). The Swedish title is very complicated.

Table A7. (cont.)

No.	Title	Translator	Year	Publisher	Vol.	Pages	Remarks
3	Om arbetets delning (On the division of labour)	unknown	1869	Stockholm: O.L. Lamms förlag	1	19	In National-ekonomiskt bibliotek. Smith's text was printed together with texts by F. Bastiat and I. R. McCulloch.
4	En undersökning av folkens välstånd dess natur och orsaker (An inquiry into the wealth of nations: its nature and causes)	Emil Sommarin	1909 (v.1) 1911 (v.2)	Lund: C.W.K Gleerups förlag	2	191, 179	Översättning med uteslutning av vissa partier av d: r. Emil Sommarin (translation with the exclusion of some parts by Dr Emil Sommarin). Vol. 1 contains, with some exclusions, Bk. I; vol. 2 contains, with some exclusions, Bks. IV–V. Knut Wicksell assisted this translation around 1910. The translator was his former student and successor as professor of economics in Lund.
5	Den osynliga handen Adam Smith i urval (The invisible hand. Selections from Adam Smith)	Dagmar Lagerberg	1994	Stockholm: Ratio	1	307	With selections from Theory of Moral Sentiments (pp. 309–86: "Om moraliska känslor").

Notes: There is still no complete Swedish translation of *WN* today. Some partial Swedish translations of *WN* were published in different journals in 1780–1799 (see *The Vanderblue Memorial Collection of Smithiana*, 1939, pp. 32–5); a notable one is *Läsning i blandade ämnen* (Miscellaneous Reading), Kress has the 1799 volume. Information provided by Prof. Torbjörn Vallinder (Lund University) is gratefully acknowledged.

Table A18. Turkish version of *WN*

No.	Title	Translator	Year	Publisher	Vol.	Pages	Remarks
1	*Milletlerin Zenginligi*	Haldum Derin	1948 (v.1–2) 1955 (v.3–4)	Istanbul: Milli Egitim Basimevi	4	393, 340, 386, 415	Vols. 3–4 published in Ankara by Maarif Basimevi.

Index

Index